STRATEGIES

FOR

ARGUMENT

A Reader and Sourcebook

EDITED BY

SALLY DE WITT SPURGIN
Southern Methodist University

A BLAIR PRESS BOOK

PRENTICE HALL, ENGLEWOOD CLIFFS, NJ 07632

Library of Congress Cataloging-in-Publication Data

Strategies for argument: a reader and
sourcebook / [compiled by]
  Sally De Witt Spurgin.
      p.   cm.
  "A Blair Press book."
  Includes index.
  ISBN 0-13-853268-0.—ISBN 0-13-853276-1 (instructor's ed.)
  1. College readers. 2. English language—Rhetoric.
  3. Persuasion
  (Rhetoric)   I. Spurgin, Sally De Witt.
  PE1417.S8725 1992
  808' .0427—dc20   91–15193
                               CIP

Cover design: Bruce Kenselaar
Interior design: Sally Steele
Prepress buyer: Herb Klein
Manufacturing buyer: Patrice Fraccio
Cover art: Marcel Duchamp, *Tu m'*. 1918. Oil and
graphite on canvas, with brush, safety pins, nut
and bolt, $27\frac{1}{2}$" × 10 3/4." Yale University Art Gallery,
New Haven, Connecticut. Bequest of Katherine S.
Dreier.

Acknowledgments appear on pages 614–617, which
constitute a continuation of the copyright page.

Blair Press
Statler Building, Suite 1113
20 Park Plaza
Boston, MA 02116-4399

© 1992 by Prentice-Hall, Inc.
A Simon & Schuster Company
Englewood Cliffs, New Jersey 07632

Printed in the United States of America
10 9 8 7 6 5 4 3 2 1

ISBN 0-13-853268-0
    0-13-853276-1 (Instructor's Edition)

Prentice-Hall International (UK) Limited, *London*
Prentice-Hall of Australia Pty. Limited, *Sydney*
Prentice-Hall Canada Inc., *Toronto*
Prentice-Hall Hispanoamericana, S.A., *Mexico*
Prentice-Hall of India Private Limited, *New Delhi*
Prentice-Hall of Japan, Inc., *Tokyo*
Simon & Schuster Asia Pte. Ltd., *Singapore*
Editora Prentice-Hall do Brasil, Ltda., *Rio de Janeiro*

FOR MY HUSBAND, BOB SPURGIN,
AND MY MOTHER, HESTER DE WITT,
WITH LOVE AND THANKS

PREFACE

FOR

INSTRUCTORS

Strategies for Argument is a reader for writers. It is intended to make students think, to encourage them to talk, to give them interesting ideas and important issues to write about. At the same time, it aims to help students face the sometimes daunting task of writing sound and persuasive arguments. Of necessity, then, this book had to offer more than the typical collection of argumentative essays on subjects of topical interest.

To begin, the introductory chapter provides advice from experienced teachers of writing about strategies for reading critically and developing written arguments. Students then follow the process (and progress) of a student writer as she reads, analyzes, and evaluates arguments and then writes her own argument, drawing on the texts she read for support. Some of the student's notes, reading summaries, and comments from classmates are included, along with three drafts of her essay.

Similarly, in the first part of the book, "Strategies for Argument," each chapter's readings begin with selections focusing on a particular writing and reasoning strategy. These are written by several gifted writers and teachers, rather than by a single textbook author. You will find, for example, Irving Copi on logical reasoning (Chapter 3), Monroe Beardsley on emotional appeals (Chapter 4), William Zinsser on humor (Chapter 5) and Walker Gibson on style (Chapter 6). The second group of readings in each chapter *illustrates* the particular strategy, while at the same time focuses on a shared issue. For example, in Chapter 5, Judy Brady, Calvin Trillin, Bill Cosby, and (of all people) Katherine Anne Porter argue—with humor—about marriage. And the third group of readings in each chapter offers a wide array of "raw material"—statistical data, quotations, advertisements, charts, illustrations, flawed or unusual arguments—for students to discuss or to use as supporting data for their own arguments. Chapter 2, for example, provides statistics on college education; Chapter 5, editorial cartoons on controversial issues; Chapter 6, poems and reproductions of paintings.

In the second part of the book, "Pros, Cons, and Maybes," readings are grouped by subject matter, arguing varied and often opposing positions on issues of current or enduring interest. Rather than implying that issues must be drawn only in black and white, however, these readings show a range of viewpoints and perspectives. They offer, as well, a range of subjects, from everyday concerns such as recycling to thorny philosophical (and sometimes political) problems such as defining and limiting obscenity. These "Pros, Cons, and Maybes" may be taken up on their own or as additional examples of the writing and reasoning strategies in the previous part of the book.

The final part of the book, "Data and Debate," offers substantial material on two broad subjects—college sports and affirmative action—for analysis, comparison, and response. Enough material is provided, including objective reports and statistics as well as arguments, for students to write documented arguments without additional resources. Some of the readings are examples of writing in the professions: for example, a report from a professional accounting journal, an essay from a professional sociology journal, a historical summary of labor policies related to gender and race from the *Monthly Labor Review*.

So, while *Strategies for Argument* can be used as a traditional argument reader, it has the potential to be much more. It can serve as a rhetoric for instructors who use the first essays to teach each strategy and the subsequent essays to provide varied examples of it—and to stimulate discussion and generate topics for writing. The book also provides material that students can *use* as well as read and analyze: The third section of each "Strategies for Argument" chapter and all of "Data and Debate" provide raw material from which students can develop and support written arguments of their own.

The subjects taken up in *Strategies for Argument* range from advertisements to affirmative action to art. Most of the essays are examples of effective reasoning and writing; some are cautionary examples of fallacious reasoning and ineffective writing. Each reading in the book is preceded by a note of biographical information about the author, a description of the original rhetorical context of the argument, and a few words about the essay—often including some questions to consider while reading it. Each reading is followed by questions designed to elicit thoughtful response and reasoned consideration of the essay and the issues, particularly in light of the strategic concerns of the chapter.

This is a reader with reasoning and writing in mind. Students want and need to be able to read critically. They need to be able to synthesize what they have read, to think creatively beyond the limits of the texts. They also need the skills to develop sound written arguments. No textbook by itself can bring about these desired ends, but *Strategies for Argument* is intended to help both instructor and student make them possible.

Finally, to the people who made this book possible, my thanks. First, special thanks to a gifted editor and the publisher of Blair Press, Nancy Perry. In every sense of the phrase, Nancy Perry really did make this book possible. Its strengths are due in no small part to her keen eye and sharp pencil; its weaknesses, alas, are my own. And to Leslie Arndt, assistant editor at Blair Press, many thanks for her careful editing and timely suggestions, not to mention her long hours tracking down biographical data and obscure references. My grateful appreciation as well to the manuscript reviewers: Kathleen L. Carroll, University of Maryland; Mary Lou Henneman, Youngstown State University; Patricia G. Morgan, Louisiana State University; Charles Reinhart, Vincennes University; John H. Rogers, Vincennes University; Eileen M. Schwartz, Purdue University–Calument; and Randy Woodland, University of California–Los Angeles. Thanks are due also to Frances Bell, Steve Housewright, and the entire Humanities staff of the Dallas Public Library, who made the Writers' Study Room available to me and offered both help and encouragement along the way. I am grateful to friends and colleagues at Southern Methodist University for sharing ideas or their students' work with me: in particular, Dianne Hawkins of the School of Law and Carolyn Channell, Catherine Civello, M. L. Lawhon, and Nina Schwartz of the Department of English. Thanks also to Bronwen Jeffcock, an Englishwoman from whom Mary Poppins could take lessons, and to two small people, Alice Ann and Steve Spurgin, who cheerfully wrote and illustrated dozens of books while I worked on this one. And, last but most, to my husband, Bob, and my parents, Hester and Bill De Witt. When all else failed, as it regularly did, they were there. I thank them, with love.

Sally Spurgin

PREFACE

FOR

STUDENTS

This book is about argument: writing that looks for and offers reasons. Argument is not merely a thesis paragraph, three supporting paragraphs, and a conclusion; rather, argument is discovery, the search for truth, the passionate defense of strongly held convictions, the astute criticism of mistaken ideas.

Argument is everywhere, as the readings in this book will illustrate. You can find arguments in surprising places, from an article in a glossy fashion magazine to an ostensibly objective report in a scholarly journal. You will find them in forms far removed from "traditional" essays: advertisements, political cartoons, poems. You will find them written seriously, mysteriously, and even humorously. The term *argument* covers a wealth of writing. What, then, *isn't* an argument? A meditation, a recipe, a list of pool safety rules. The directions for operating a VCR. A claim without any reasons offered in support of it. But when you start looking for reasons, for explanations, you usually find (and often create) argument.

Reading is often part of the process of writing argument. You read to find evidence, examples, and arguments that may support or challenge your thinking. When you read an argument, you read to learn—to discover ideas you hadn't considered, to find instructive and often unexpected ways of looking at things or events. When the reasoning goes astray, or the arguer makes unwarranted assumptions about your knowledge and your preconceptions, you challenge the argument. You may finally reject it.

But challenging and rejecting come later. First, you should try to *understand* the writer's viewpoint and the argument's claims and evidence. Again, you read first to learn. Only then do you analyze the reasoning and ask the hard questions. If you reverse the process, you shut off your chance to learn and to gain understanding—of a writer's position, of an unfamiliar subject or an unusual stance. At its best, argument is not the defense of irrefutable theses; it is the search for truth.

That is why reading arguments becomes an integral part of nearly any writing course that emphasizes argumentation. Few writers have all the answers, or even very many: Arguments drawn exclusively from personal beliefs and experiences too often tend to express preconceptions and biases, defended with enthusiasm but without much reflection. So you read. Even when you understand an issue well, you still read to learn why others differ—and consider how to answer their objections.

The readings in *Strategies for Argument* include argumentative essays that can serve both as inspiration for argument and as models of effective writing. In developing your own written arguments, you may find it helpful to see how other writers—both professional and student—have succeeded. Additionally, some readings offer advice from professional writers and teachers on key argumentative strategies. But you need not be intimidated by either the models or the advice, or think that you must determine the one right position on any given issue. Indeed, you will read here some equally strong arguments that take widely different positions on controversial issues.

Strategies for Argument will show you more than models of effective argument. The book also includes some flawed arguments, for you can always learn from others' and your own mistakes. You will see, for example, how some writers have failed to reason well or to consider their audiences. Understanding their shortcomings can help you to spot such problems in your own reasoning and writing. Also, with the aim of expanding possibilities rather than exhausting them, this book includes a great deal of "raw" material for analysis and argument— statistics, surveys, advertisements, political cartoons, reproductions of paintings, poetry, research summaries, and more.

This is an argument reader: a reader not only *of* arguments but *for* argument. It provides a starting point. It is up to you to determine where it leads: I hope it will be to some fascinating insights and some timeless truths—with some fun and a few good challenges along the way.

Sally Spurgin

CONTENTS

CHAPTER 3   Supporting Claims with Logical Reasoning   123

CHAPTER 4   RECOGNIZING AND AVOIDING FALLACIES   190

CHAPTER 5   USING HUMOR IN ARGUMENT   248

CHAPTER 6   ARGUING WITH STYLE   281

CHAPTER 7   REASONING ABOUT THE AESTHETIC   320

PART TWO
PROS, CONS, AND MAYBES
367

CHAPTER 8   RECYCLING AND WASTE DISPOSAL   369

CHAPTER 9   THE COSTS OF AIDS   397

PART THREE

DATA AND DEBATE
497

APPENDIX
USING AND CITING SOURCES
599

1

READING AND
WRITING ARGUMENTS

This book is a reader for writers, and so we begin with some words of advice about reading *and* writing arguments. In the following pages, Vincent Ryan Ruggiero reminds you of important distinctions you must make as you read arguments. When you prepare to write arguments in response to what you have read, Sheridan Baker's discussion will be invaluable in helping you sharpen your thesis, or main point. A list of probing questions compiled by Tommy J. Boley points to possible areas of development for your essay. Donald M. Murray shows how revision, that task dreaded by so many novice writers, can be the most satisfying part of writing. And Nan Payne provides what may be the best kind of advice: a good example. In reading her notes and drafts for her student paper, "The Zoo Paradox," you can follow much of the process of writing an argument based on critical reading.

Many, perhaps most, writing ventures begin with *critical reading*. Critical reading describes the process of understanding, evaluating, and judging texts. It is the kind of reading you should bring to every essay in this book, every editorial in *Time* or the *Washington Post*, every cover story in *The Atlantic*. Critical reading means first comprehending, then questioning, analyzing, evaluating. Can you accurately summarize the arguments you read? Do the writers give plenty of evidence for their conclusions? Do they use fair examples? Do they avoid assuming what they ought to be proving? Can you follow their reasoning clearly?

Critical reading presents challenges. Argumentative writing based on critical reading demands even more. Not only must we read, comprehend, analyze, possibly compare, and certainly evaluate, we must also find the right words to express our conclusions and our reasons for those conclusions to an audience we may not know well, or at all. We must write, in words that will be persuasive, arguments that will be convincing. How writers manage to do all this successfully

1

may seem like a mysterious process. Nevertheless, reading the arguments of others and writing evaluations, comparisons, and refutations of them are precisely the tasks we face, both in college courses and in other contexts. The process can appear daunting, but, broken into manageable segments, writing an argument that draws upon readings need not be an overwhelming challenge.

What, then, are some "manageable segments" into which the task can be broken?

1. Make sure you understand the assignment—both what you must cover and what you need not or should not include. Are you to evaluate or answer an argument, or are you to use some of its evidence to support your own argument?

2. Think about the subject matter: What about it, if anything, do you already know? And if you do know something about the subject, what are your biases? (Recognizing these is difficult but essential if you are to write a well-reasoned argument.)

3. Read the assigned material carefully and critically. Be sure that you can summarize each argument accurately. Then evaluate it. Take no unsupported assertions on faith; watch for distortions (such as slanted language) and omissions. Particularly note any apparent contradictions or unanswered questions. These may point you to a controlling idea, or thesis, for your own argument.

4. If your own argument responds to or draws from more than one source, write careful notes to identify exact references for all the material you use. If you use several sources, writing summaries of each will help you keep them straight without constant rereading. If you are responding to a single essay, writing a summary is a good way to make sure you understand it thoroughly—and can help remind you that your own paper must be more than a summary. Your paper must present an argument: It must take a stand.

5. Think about your audience: Who will read the paper you write? Your instructor and fellow students? A wider audience on campus? Readers of a city newspaper? Is another, hypothetical audience identified in the assignment? Consider the needs and the probable biases of the audience designated: What do your anticipated readers know about the subject? What will they want to know? What likely biases will you need to overcome? Consider your audience as you go through every step of the writing process. Your argument will be all the stronger, and you will have a clearer sense of what you need to say and what you can or should omit.

6. Use whichever invention strategies work best for you— freewriting, brainstorming, making lists of observations, and so

on—to sharpen your focus on your subject. Tommy J. Boley's "A Heuristic for Persuasion," included in this chapter, offers one time-tested strategy: a list of pointed questions to ask about your subject. Asking some of those questions may help you find an "argumentative edge" and a tentative thesis for your paper. To help you remain open to discovery, you may elect to pose your tentative thesis as a question at this stage. A statement can be dogmatic; a question remains open to change.

7. Your argument will take preliminary shape as you think about the answers to your thesis question and consider how best to convey those answers to your intended audience. Depending on the assignment, offer reasons and examples drawn from one or more readings in this book, from library and other research, or from a combination of resources. Even anecdotes and illustrations drawn from your own experience may be appropriate. Sometimes your own experience will contradict your sources, and sometimes your sources will contradict each other. When that occurs, your argument must seek to resolve the contradictions.

8. As you work, add to and reassess your argument. A convincing and engaging argument is likely to go through several drafts. From start to finish, you must be willing to modify your position if the evidence does not support it. If possible, put each draft away for a day or two so that you can reread it with more objectivity. Ask classmates or friends to read it and tell you at what points they do not follow your reasoning or remain unconvinced. Don't look only for praise: Your toughest critic may be your truest friend.

However you generate and develop them, arguments do not occur in a vacuum. Each has a *rhetorical context:* a writer, an audience, and an occasion. It is the rhetorical context that shapes the argument. First, in the process of writing, each writer creates a *persona,* an image of the writer as perceived by the reader. A trustworthy and engaging persona is vital to effective argument. Second, each writer addresses an audience. The writer judges the audience's knowledge and biases, and this judgment affects all aspects of the argument, from the amount of evidence required to particular choices of examples and illustrations—even to choices of words. And third, the writer has a particular occasion for writing, whether it is a college class assignment, a letter of advice to a client, or a memo requesting action from a colleague. The occasion will affect the writer's tone, the complexity of the argument, and more. All the elements of the rhetorical context are interrelated.

It is challenging to keep all this in mind as you read and write, of course. But the essential points to remember are these: Read first receptively, and then critically. Write honestly, with your readers' needs clearly in mind. In so doing, you will find what you need to say, and how best to say it.

Reading Is Reasoning
VINCENT RYAN RUGGIERO

Vincent Ryan Ruggiero is professor emeritus at the State University of New York, Delhi College, and the author of many essays and textbooks about writing and reasoning, among them *The Moral Imperative* (1984) and *Beyond Feelings* (1989). The following selection is from Ruggiero's *The Art of Thinking: A Guide to Critical and Creative Thought,* 2nd ed. (1987). In this excerpt, Ruggiero reminds us of some important distinctions we must make if we are to read critically and well: We must judge arguments on their merits and not on their authors' reputations; we must determine what is arguable and what is only a matter of taste; we must be able to recognize irony; we must distinguish between what is argued and how well it is said. We must, in short, make many distinctions before we can even begin to draw conclusions. We must reason as we read.

Almost 400 years ago, Francis Bacon warned about the danger of 1 reading the wrong way. He advised people as they read not to dispute the author's view, nor to accept it uncritically, but to "weigh and consider" it. In the nineteenth century, British statesman Edmund Burke expressed the same view in more dramatic terms. "To read without reflection," he said, "is like eating without digesting."

The definition of reading these men had in mind is best explained 2 as follows:

> There is one key idea which contains, in itself, the very essence of effective reading, and on which the improvement of reading depends: *Reading is reasoning.* When you read properly, you are not merely assimilating. You are not automatically transferring into your head what your eyes pick up on the page. What you see on the page sets your mind at work, collating, criticizing, interpreting, questioning, comprehending, comparing. When this process goes on well, you read well. When it goes on ill, you read badly.[1]

Reading with the mind, and not just with the eyes, is not equally 3 intense during every reading occasion. A bus schedule or a menu, for example, can be read well with little or no reasoning. But even the smallest reading challenges involve considerably more reasoning than we realize at the time. Consider the following sentences:

---

[1] James Mursell, *Using Your Mind Effectively* (New York: McGraw-Hill, 1951), pp. vi–vii.

He who hesitates is lost. (Proverb)

We never step into the same river twice. (Heraclitus)

The girl who can't dance says the band can't play. (Yiddish proverb)

The first one, of course, is familiar enough that you may be 4
unaware you are reasoning when you read it. But consider the first
time you encountered it (probably as a small child). You undoubtedly
wondered, "Just who does 'he' refer to in this sentence? And what
does 'lost' mean here?" In time, when you considered and tested some
possible meanings, you reasoned out the meaning.

The other two sentences are even more challenging. The key to the 5
Heraclitus line is the relationship between *same* and *river*. Only when
you perceive that, and grasp the idea that the river is constantly
changing, can you be said to have read the line. And you can understand the Yiddish proverb only when you see that the message is not
just about girls and bands, but about anyone who can't do something
and resorts to face saving.

The kind of reading Bacon and Burke had in mind, and which 6
concerns us here, is not a passive process, but an active, dynamic one.
It consists of examining ideas and deciding what they mean and
whether they make sense, rather than merely receiving and accepting
them. Unfortunately, most of the reading done in grade school and
high school consists of getting the facts—and remembering them for
the examination. Not only do the teachers expect that—the textbooks
offer no real alternative to it. They are filled with facts to be accepted,
rather than ideas to weigh and consider. If your school experience has
been similar, you are bound to be a little uncomfortable with critical
reading. More specifically, you are apt to be confused by long or
complex passages, and nervous about reaching conclusions.

Such reactions are completely understandable. But it is important 7
to realize that any difficulty you experience . . . is a result of the
material's newness, not of your lack of capacity. Thinking, remember,
is largely a matter of acquiring the right skills and the habit of using
them.

One of the best ways to overcome confusion about ideas is to make 8
important distinctions—that is, to avoid lumping all considerations
together indiscriminately. Here are the distinctions that are most often
overlooked. Keep them in mind whenever you are reading (or listening):

Distinctions Between the Person and the Idea

Your reaction to a sentence beginning "Adolf Hitler said . . ." 9
would likely be very different from your reaction to one beginning

"Winston Churchill said . . ." In the first instance you might not even continue reading. At the very least you would read with great suspicion—you'd be ready to reject what was said.

There's nothing strange about that. You've learned things about 10 Hitler and Churchill, and it's difficult to set them aside. In one sense, you *shouldn't* set them aside. Yet in another sense, you *must* set them aside to be a good thinker. After all, even a lunatic can have a good idea, and even a genius will, on occasion, be wrong.

If you do not check your tendency to accept or reject ideas on the 11 basis of who expresses them, your analysis of everything you read and hear is certain to be distorted. You will judge arguments on whether the speaker is of your race, religion, or political affiliation, or whether you like her hair style. And so you might embrace nonsense and reject wisdom. Aristotle's contemporaries tell us he had very thin legs and small eyes, favored conspicuous dress and jewelry, and was fastidious in the way he combed his hair.[2] It's not hard to imagine some Athenian ignoramus muttering to his fellows the ancient Greek equivalent of "Don't pay any attention to what Aristotle says—he's a wimp."

To guard against confusing the person and the idea, be aware of 12 your reactions to people and try compensating for them. That is, listen very carefully to those you are inclined to dislike and very critically to those you are inclined to like. Judge the arguments as harshly as you wish, but only on their merits *as* arguments.

Distinctions Between Matters of Taste and Matters of Judgment

There are two broad types of opinion: taste and judgment. They 13 differ significantly. In matters of taste we may express our personal preferences without defending them. In matters of judgment, however, we have an obligation to provide evidence.

Many people confuse taste and judgment. They believe their right 14 to hold an opinion is a guarantee of the opinion's rightness. This confusion often causes people to offer inadequate support (or no support at all) for views that demand support. For example, they express judgments on such controversial issues as abortion, capital punishment, the teaching of evolution in the schools, mercy killing, hiring discrimination, and laws concerning rape as if they were matters of taste rather than matters of judgment.

Keep in mind that whenever someone presents an opinion about 15 the truth of an issue or the wisdom of an action—that is, whenever

---

[2] James Harvey Robinson, *The Mind in the Making* (New York: Harper and Brothers, 1921), p. 46.

someone presents a judgment—you not only have a right to judge his view by the evidence. You have an *obligation* to do so.

Distinctions Between Fact and Interpretation

A fact is something known with certainty, something either objec-   16
tively verified or demonstrable. An interpretation is an explanation of meaning or significance. In much writing, facts and interpretations are intertwined. It is not always obvious where one leaves off and the other begins. Here is an example of such intertwining:

The Writer's Interpretation (Note that merely calling interpretation fact does not make it so.) ⟨	People don't seem to care much about family life any more. A recent study has made that unfortunate fact very clear. The study, in which 1596 Americans were surveyed, was conducted for Psychology Today magazine in March 1982, by Potomac Associates.[3] It revealed that Americans are more concerned about the standard of living, personal health, economic stability, and employment than about family concerns. William Watts, president of Potomac Associates, commented as follows: "Traditionally, when asked to talk about their most important hopes and fears, Americans have ranked family concerns near the top of the list . . . Americans now talk less in interviews about the happiness and health of their families." The cause of
The Writer's Interpretation (Both the classification of the trend as a "moral decline" and the assertion about its cause are interpretive.) ⟨	this moral decline is without question the emphasis on the self that has dominated our culture for the past two decades.

Right brace spanning middle section: } Fact

The danger in failing to distinguish between fact and interpreta-   17
tion is that you will regard assumptions that ought to be questioned and contrasted with other views as unquestionable. If the habit of confusing the two is strong enough, it can paralyze your critical sense.

---

[3] "Family Life No Longer That Vital to America," *Oneonta Star*, 1 September 1981, p. 3.

Distinctions Between Literal and Ironic Statements

Not everything a writer says is intended literally. Sometimes a 18
writer makes his point by saying the exact opposite of what he means
—that is, by using irony or satire. Suppose, for example, you encountered this passage in your reading:

> The present administration is right in reducing the taxes of the
> wealthy more than those of the working classes. After all, wealthy
> people not only pay more into the treasury, but they also have a
> higher standard of living to maintain. If the cost of soybeans has
> risen, so also has the cost of caviar; if the subway fare has increased,
> so has the maintenance cost of a Rolls-Royce and a Lear jet. If the
> government listens to the minor grumbling and whining of the un-
> employed, it surely should be responsive to the plight of the affluent.

On the surface, this certainly looks like a plea on behalf of the rich. 19
But on closer inspection it will be seen as a *mockery* of that plea. The
clues are subtle, to be sure—the reference to the higher standard of
living, the comparison of travel by Rolls-Royce or jet with travel by
subway, the reference to the "plight" of the rich. Yet the clues are
undeniable.

Such tongue-in-cheek writing can be more biting and therefore 20
more effective than a direct attack. Yet you must be alert to the subtlety
and not misread it, or the message you receive will be very different
from the writer's intention.

Distinctions Between an Idea's Validity and the Quality of Its Expression

A thought's expression can deceive us about its validity. This is 21
why a mad leader like Hitler won a large popular following even
among intelligent and responsible people, and why Jim Jones' follow-
ers killed their children and committed suicide in Guyana. Impassioned, eloquent expression tends to excite a favorable response, just
as lifeless, inarticulate, error-filled expression prompts a negative response. Compare these two passages:

> A man's gotta love his Momma and Daddy more than he love a
> stranger. If he don't do right by his kin, he can't never be a righteous
> man.

> To achieve success in a competitive world, you must honor the first
> principle of success—treat well those people who can benefit you
> and ignore the others.

The first passage is less appealing than the second. And yet it 22
contains an idea most philosophers would enthusiastically endorse,

while the second contains an idea most find reprehensible. The careful thinker is able to appraise them correctly because she is aware that expression can deceive. Careful thinkers make a special effort to separate form from content before judging. (The careful writer strives for clarity and correctness of form for exactly the same reason.) Thus he is able to say "This idea is poorly expressed, but profound" and "This idea is well expressed, but shallow."

QUESTIONS AND IDEAS FOR DISCUSSION

1. Discuss the following statements from Ruggiero's selection with reference to (and specific examples from, if possible) your own experience as a reasoning reader:

> If you do not check your tendency to accept or reject ideas on the basis of who expresses them, your analysis of everything you read and hear is certain to be distorted. (paragraph 11)

> [L]isten very carefully to those [speakers and writers] you are inclined to dislike and very critically to those you are inclined to like. (12)

> If the habit of confusing [fact and interpretation] is strong enough, it can paralyze your critical sense. (17)

2. In paragraphs 13 and 14, Ruggiero mentions "matters of judgment" but does not define (beyond a list of examples) what kinds of subjects *are* matters for judgment. Discuss this question and establish some criteria.

3. As Ruggiero indicates, irony creates real problems—confusion at the least—if a reader fails to recognize it. Is it best, then, for writers to avoid irony lest they be misunderstood? Discuss.

4. It has often been said that *how* something is said and *what* is said—style and meaning—are inextricably connected. Yet Ruggiero declares, "Careful thinkers make a special effort to separate form from content before judging" (22). Can you resolve the paradox of these apparently conflicting statements? Explain.

The Argumentative Edge

SHERIDAN BAKER

Sheridan Baker is professor emeritus of English at the University of Michigan (Ann Arbor), the author of the *Harper Handbook of Literature* (1985), and a contributor of poems and articles to *New Yorker* and other magazines. In this excerpt from his college writing textbook, *The Complete Stylist*, 3rd ed. (1976), Baker offers some advice on developing interesting and supportable theses for the essays you write. In so doing, he offers as well a broad definition of argument: All prose with a thesis is argument. If we have a point, and support it, we have an argument. Consider, as you read, whether or not you agree with Baker.

You can usually blame a bad essay on a bad beginning. If your 1 essay falls apart, it probably has no primary idea to hold it together. "What's the big idea?" we used to ask. The phrase will serve as a reminder that you must find the "big idea" behind your several smaller thoughts and musings before you start to write. In the beginning was the *logos*, says the Bible—the idea, the plan, caught in a flash as if in a single word. Find your *logos*, and you are ready to round out your essay and set it spinning.

The big idea behind our ride in the speeding car[1] was that in 2 adolescence, especially, the group can have a very deadly influence on the individual. If you had not focused your big idea in a thesis, you might have begun by picking up thoughts at random, something like this:

> Everyone thinks he is a good driver. There are more accidents caused by young drivers than any other group. Driver education is a good beginning, but further practice is very necessary. People who object to driver education do not realize that modern society, with its suburban pattern of growth, is built around the automobile. The car becomes a way of life and a status symbol. When teen-agers go too fast they are probably only copying their own parents.

A little reconsideration, aimed at a good thesis-sentence, could 3 turn this into a reasonably good beginning:

> Modern society is built on the automobile. Children play with tiny cars; teen-agers long to take out the car alone. Soon they are testing their skills at higher and higher speeds, especially with a group of friends along. One final test at extreme speeds usually suffices. It is usually a sobering experience, if survived, and can open one's eyes to the deadly dynamics of the group.

---

[1] A previously mentioned idea for a paper topic. [Ed.]

Thus the central idea, or thesis, is your essay's life and spirit. If 4
your thesis is sufficiently firm and clear, it may tell you immediately
how to organize your supporting material and so obviate elaborate
planning. If you do not find a thesis, your essay will be a tour through
the miscellaneous. An essay replete with scaffolds and catwalks—"
We have just seen this; now let us turn to this"—is an essay in which
the inherent idea is weak or nonexistent. A purely expository and
descriptive essay, one simply about "Cats," for instance, will have to
rely on outer scaffolding alone (some orderly progression from Persia
to Siam) since it really has no idea at all. It is all subject, all cats, instead
of being based on an idea *about* cats.

The *about*-ness puts an argumentative edge on the subject. When 5
you have something to say *about* cats, you have found your underlying
idea. You have something to defend, something to fight about: not
just "Cats," but "The cat is really a person's best friend." Now the
hackles on all dog people are rising, and you have an argument on
your hands. You have something to prove. You have a thesis.

"What's the big idea, Mac?" Let the impudence in that time- 6
honored demand remind you that the most dynamic thesis is a kind of
affront to somebody. No one will be very much interested in listening
to you deplete the thesis "The dog is a person's best friend." Everyone
knows that already. Even the dog lovers will be uninterested, convinced they know better than you. But the cat . . .

So it is with any unpopular idea. The more unpopular the view- 7
point and the stronger the push against convention, the stronger the
thesis and the more energetic the essay. Compare the energy in "Democracy is good" with that in "Communism is good," for instance.
The first is filled with platitudes, the second with plutonium. By the
same token, if you can find the real energy in "Democracy is good," if
you can get down through the sand to where the roots and water are,
you will have a real essay, because the opposition against which you
generate your energy is the heaviest in the world: boredom. Probably
the most energetic thesis of all, the greatest inner organizer, is some
tired old truth that you cause to jet with new life, making the old
ground green again.

To find a thesis and to put it into one sentence is to narrow and 8
define your subject to a workable size. Under "Cats" you must deal
with all felinity from the jungle up, carefully partitioning the eons and
areas, the tigers and tabbies, the sizes and shapes. The minute you
proclaim the cat the friend of humanity, you have pared away whole
categories and chapters, and need only think up the arguments sufficient to overwhelm the opposition. So, put an argumentative edge on
your subject—and you will have found your thesis.

Simple exposition, to be sure, has its uses. You may want to tell 9 someone how to build a doghouse, how to can asparagus, how to follow the outlines of relativity, or even how to write an essay. Performing a few exercises in simple exposition will no doubt sharpen your insight into the problems of finding orderly sequences, of considering how best to lead your readers through the hoops, of writing clearly and accurately. It will also illustrate how much finer and surer an argument is.

You will see that picking an argument immediately simplifies the 10 problems so troublesome in straight exposition: the defining, the partitioning, the narrowing of the subject. Not that you must be constantly pugnacious or aggressive. I have overstated my point to make it stick. Actually, you can put an argumentative edge on the flattest of expository subjects. "How to build a doghouse" might become "Building a doghouse is a thorough introduction to the building trades, including architecture and mechanical engineering." "Canning asparagus" might become "An asparagus patch is a course in economics." "Relativity" might become "Relativity is not so inscrutable as many suppose." Literary subjects take an argumentative edge almost by nature. You simply assert what the essential point of a poem or play seems to be: "*Hamlet* is essentially about a world that has lost its values." You assume that your readers are in search of clarity, that you have a loyal opposition consisting of the interested but uninformed. You have given your subject its edge; you have limited and organized it at a single stroke. Pick an argument, then, and you will automatically be defining and narrowing your subject, and all the partitions you don't need will fold up. Instead of dealing with things, subjects, and pieces of subjects, you will be dealing with an idea and its consequences.

Come out with your subject pointed. Take a stand, make a judg- 11 ment of value. Be reasonable, but don't be timid. It is helpful to think of your thesis, your main idea, as a debating question—"Resolved: Welfare payments must go"—taking out the "Resolved" when you actually write the subject down. But your resolution will be even stronger, your essay clearer and tighter, if you can sharpen your thesis even further—"Resolved: Welfare payments must go because _____." Fill in that blank, and your worries are practically over. The main idea is to put your whole argument into one sentence.

Try, for instance: "Welfare payments must go because they are 12 making people irresponsible." I don't know at all if that is true, and neither will you until you write your way into it, considering probabilities and alternatives and objections, and especially the underlying assumptions. In fact, no one, no master sociologist or future historian, can tell absolutely if it is true, so multiplex are the causes in human affairs, so endless and tangled the consequences. The basic assumption—that irresponsibility is growing—may be entirely false. No one, I repeat, can tell absolutely. But by the same token, your guess may be as good as another's. At any rate, you are now ready to write. You have found your *logos*.

Now you can put your well-pointed thesis-sentence on a card on the wall in front of you to keep from drifting off target. But you will now want to dress it for the public, to burnish it and make it comely. Suppose you try:

> Welfare payments, perhaps more than anything else, are eroding personal initiative.

But is this fully true? Perhaps you had better try something like:

> Despite their immediate benefits, welfare payments may actually be eroding personal initiative and depriving society of needed workers.

This is really your thesis, and you can write that down on a scrap of paper too.

Notice how your assertion about welfare mellowed as you revised. And not because you have resorted to cheap tactics, though tactics may get you to the same place, but rather because you brought it under critical inspection, asking what is true in it: what can (and cannot) be assumed true, what can (and cannot) be proved true. And you have asked yourself where you stand.

You should, indeed, look for a thesis you believe in, something you can even get enthusiastic about. Arguing on both sides of a question, as debaters do, is no doubt good exercise, if one can stand it. It breaks up old ground and uncovers what you can and do believe, at least for the moment. But the argument without the belief will be hollow. You can hardly persuade anyone if you can't persuade yourself. So begin with what you believe, and explore its validities.

Conversely, you must test your belief with all the objections you can think of, just as you have already tested your first proposition about welfare payments. First, you have acknowledged the most evident objection—that the opposition's view must have some merit—by starting your final version with "Despite their immediate benefits. . . ." Second, you have gone a little deeper by seeing that in your bold previous version you had, with the words *are eroding*, begged the question of whether responsibility is in fact undergoing erosion; that is, you had silently assumed that responsibility *is* being eroded. This is one of the oldest fallacies and tricks of logic. To "beg the question," by error or intent, is to take for granted that which the opposition has not granted, to assume as already proved that which is yet to be proved. But you have saved yourself. You have changed *are eroding* to *may be eroding.* You have gone further in deleting the *perhaps more than anything else.* You have come closer to the truth.

You may wonder if it is not astoundingly presumptuous to go   17
around stating theses before you have studied your subject from all angles, made several house-to-house surveys, and read everything ever written. A natural uncertainty and feeling of ignorance, and a misunderstanding of what truth is, can well inhibit you from finding a thesis. But no one knows everything. No one would write anything if he waited until he did. To a great extent, the writing of a thing is the learning of it.

So, first, make a desperate thesis and get into the arena. This is   18
probably solution enough. If it becomes increasingly clear that your thesis is untrue, no matter how hard you push it, turn it around and use the other end. If your convictions have begun to falter with:

> Despite their immediate benefits, welfare payments undermine initiative . . . .

try it the other way around, with something like:

> Although welfare payments may offend the rugged individualist,
> they relieve much want and anxiety, and they enable many a father-
> less family to maintain its integrity.

You will now have a beautiful command of the major objections to your new position. And you will have learned something about human fallibility and the nature of truth.

Once you believe in your proposition, you will discover that prov-   19
ing it is really a venture in persuasion. *Rhetoric* is, in fact, the art of persuasion, of moving the reader to your belief. You have made a thesis, a hypothesis really—an opinion as to what the truth seems to be from where you stand, with the information you have. Belief has an unfolding energy. Write what you believe. You may be wrong, of course, but you will probably discover this as you probe for reasons, and can then reverse your thesis, pointed with your new conviction. The truth remains true, and you must at least glimpse it before you can begin to persuade others to see it. So follow your convictions, and think up reasons to convince your reader. Give him enough evidence to persuade him that what you say is probably true; find arguments that will stand up in the marketplace and survive the public haggle. You must find public reasons for your private convictions.

QUESTIONS AND IDEAS FOR DISCUSSION

1.   Baker declares that "you can usually blame a bad essay on a bad beginning" (paragraph 1). But just what constitutes a "bad beginning"? Write a "bad" introductory paragraph (to, let's say, an argument on air pollution) to share with the class. Discuss the common features you find in "bad beginnings." Does the term apply only to introductory paragraphs? Explain.

2. In your judgment, what are some other characteristics of a "bad essay"? Identify and create some examples of those characteristics. For instance, if the class or discussion group agrees that a bad essay often makes unsupported, sweeping generalizations, you might offer as an illustration: "Gun rights advocates are dangerous people, whether they wear camouflage and flak jackets or business suits," or "Nuclear energy offers the only hope our world has of surviving into the next century."

3. Are all "bad essays" intrinsically flawed, or might some be appropriate for one audience, in one context, and not another? Discuss.

4. "If you do not find a thesis, your essay will be a tour through the miscellaneous," Baker claims (4). He further claims that any essay with a thesis is an argument. Do you think such sweeping claims are fair? Discuss, offering specific examples if possible.

5. While Baker's excerpt makes helpful points, it offers little detail about specifically how to move from the "thoughts at random" illustrated in paragraph 2 to the focused thesis ending the sample introduction in paragraph 3. Discuss how *you* would go about determining the "about-ness" of a broad subject, such as all-terrain vehicles, keeping exotic birds as pets, or the math requirement at your college. Compare your strategies for invention of a thesis with those of your classmates. Then, write several possible thesis sentences for one of the broad subjects above, given a hypothetical audience of college students who may know little about all-terrain vehicles or exotic birds, but who are probably aware of the math requirement for a degree from your college. Compare theses with your classmates. Decide which ones have an "argumentative edge," and talk about the kinds of arguments you might develop to support those thesis concepts.

6. Baker argues that any essay written without conviction "will be hollow" (14). It will lack what Aristotle called *ethos*, the "ethical appeal." (An essay with a strong ethical appeal is believable, even if its claims are unusual or contrary to expectations.) How do you suppose words on a page can convey the ethical appeal of an absent, perhaps even unknown, writer? What specific features might contribute to an essay's ethical appeal? Give examples if possible.

7. In your judgment, does Baker's own essay avoid the various pitfalls he discusses? Give examples from the text to support your answer.

A Heuristic for Persuasion

TOMMY J. BOLEY

Tommy J. Boley teaches rhetoric at the University of Texas at El Paso. In this selection, he proposes a "heuristic," or "aid to discovery and learning," to help student writers develop persuasive arguments. This heuristic first appeared in 1979 in a journal for composition instructors, *College Composition and Communication,* but systematic lists of questions for the invention of arguments follow a long tradition going back to Aristotle. Aristotle proposed questions, or "topics," to help arguers narrow, define, and develop the issues about which they proposed to speak. Writers also can benefit from the same kinds of aids to invention.

You will notice that Boley's questions cover three aspects of argument: ethical argument, pathetic (that is, emotional) argument, and logical argument. According to Aristotle, the best arguments have ethical, emotional, and logical appeal. The writers of such arguments try to show themselves, through their words, to have "good sense," "goodwill," and "high moral character." After all, could we trust their arguments otherwise?

Heuristics such as this one may be used at many points in your prewriting and writing of arguments. Just after you have decided on or have been assigned a subject, read the questions to see what possibilities they suggest. As you work, read the list again to test your arguments, to see what else you need to add or develop further. A systematic heuristic such as this one is particularly valuable when you feel "stuck," at a dead end. After you have finished writing, read the questions once more. Have you done everything possible to reach your audience with a sound and persuasive argument?

Not all questions will apply to all writing contexts. And some of the terminology may be unfamiliar to you, notably in Part III. Footnotes will clarify these terms as you come to them. However, even if you skip questions involving such terms as *syllogism* or *enthymeme,* you will find many helpful suggestions and reminders as you work.

I. *Ethical argument:* attention to ethical appeals of good sense, good will, and high moral character; an attempt to establish character or authority
  A. Good Sense
    1. Shall I reveal that I have expert training, intelligence, expertise in the area of the subject matter I have chosen? Why, or why not?
    2. What expertise do I actually have?
    3. How much of my expertise shall I reveal? What is the limit to which I should go in revealing my intelligence?
    4. What will be the likely effects of my expertise on my audience?
  B. Goodwill
    1. Shall I reveal that I have the goodwill of my audience as a primary interest? Why, or why not?
    2. What feelings of goodwill do I actually have?

        3. How strong should my goodwill appeal be? What is the limit to which I should go in informing my audience of my feelings of goodwill?

        4. What will be the likely effects of showing a sense of goodwill toward my audience?

   C. High Moral Character

        1. Shall I reveal that I am a person with a strong sense of what is right and what is wrong in relation to the subject? Why, or why not?

        2. What moral feelings do I actually have in relation to this subject matter for the audience?

        3. How strongly should I reveal my trustworthiness? What is the limit to which I should go in informing the audience of my honesty?

        4. What will be the likely effects on the audience of my revealing a moral sense toward the subject?

II. *Pathetic argument:* attention to emotional appeals

   A. If I am going to use an emotional approach, which emotions will work best to persuade my audience to accept my beliefs?

        1. Shall I appeal to one or more of the basic senses of sight, smell, hearing, taste, or touch?

        2. Shall I appeal to one or more of the physical needs or desires for food, shelter, sex, protection, cleanliness?

        3. Shall I appeal to human emotions such as love, beauty, security, thrift, freedom, escape, patriotism, loyalty, hope, optimism?

        4. Shall I appeal to human emotions such as fear, loneliness, alienation, rejection, disappointment, disillusionment, pity?

   B. How many emotional appeals shall I include? What is the limit to which I should go in using an emotional argument with my audience?

   C. What will be the likely effects of my use of emotional arguments in this persuasive writing for this particular audience?

III. *Logical argument:* attention to appeals to inductive or deductive reason from probability; "seeming logic," as contrasted with "logic of certainty" in scientific argumentation (dialectic)[1]

   A. Induction: reasoning by the process of forming a generalization from particular examples[2]

        1. Use of factual examples

           a. What are the important facts, data, statistics, or expert testimonies of the past or the present which I may use as examples to support my generalization (my proposition)?

           b. How many of these examples do I need to use in order to sufficiently support the generalization?

---

[1] Dialectic: The art of arriving at the truth by disclosing and resolving contradictions in opposing positions. [Ed.]

[2] This is but one form that inductive reasoning can take. Broadly, inductive conclusions go *beyond* the premises (supporting statements), while deductive conclusions are drawn *out of* the premises. The distinction does not affect the usefulness of the questions in this section, however. [Ed.]

    c. Do the examples I am using represent a cross section of the population involved with my subject?

    d. What special considerations must I make of the different factors (such as age, economic level, academic achievement, etc.) which can directly affect my choice of examples for support of the generalization?

    e. Do the examples I have chosen strongly support the conclusion as one of probability?

    f. What must I do to be certain that my examples are accurate, that my sources are trustworthy?

    g. Have I included in the text the names and titles of those whom I am citing?

  2. Use of invented examples

    a. Shall I create a comparison or an analogy between some actual happening and the argument I am presenting? For my comparison/analogy, what shall I consult from the following?

      A historical document? A political document? A legal document? A newspaper? A magazine? A professional journal? Another source?

    b. Shall I create a comparison or an analogy between some persuasive or literary source and the argument I am presenting? For my comparison/analogy what shall I consult from the following?

      An editorial? An advertisement? A literary passage? A legend? A myth? A fable? A Biblical passage? Another source?

    c. Is the relationship clear between the examples I have created and the generalization? Do the comparisons/analogies strongly support the conclusion drawn?

B. Deduction: reasoning by the process of extracting a *probable* conclusion from given premises[3]

  1. Underlying assumptions (unstated premises): from examination of my proposition, what underlying assumptions appear to be in the background?

    a. Are there *universal truths* which I can expect my audience to acknowledge readily? (List these truths.)

      Examples: Following the summer rains in the American Southwest, the desert will bloom.

            Now that Spring is here, school vacation is not far away.

            Excessive amounts of sugar will prove fatal to a diabetic.

      Shall I state the universal truths behind my proposition? Or shall I omit these truths because my audience is already tuned into the premises?

---

[3] In formal logic, deductive conclusions to sound arguments are not merely probable, they are guaranteed. Boley here is concerned with informal reasoning along deductive lines. (Deduction, again, is the drawing out of conclusions implicit in premises.) [Ed.]

    b. Are there *probabilities* which are generally true that I can expect my audience to accept without contest? (List these probabilities.)

        Examples: Rich people drive expensive cars.

                Chrysanthemums in a bouquet will outlast roses.

                Dogs obey their masters.

        Shall I state the probabilities behind my proposition? Or shall I omit these probabilities as being obvious?

    c. Are there *maxims* (aphorisms, sayings), which are general statements concerning human action, that can bring positive response from my audience because of their familiarity with the sayings and their general acceptance?

        Examples: A little learning is a dangerous thing.

                Fish and guests smell after three days.

                Experience is the best teacher

        NOTE: One contemporary form of maxim is the slogan found in advertising, politics, religion, etc.[4]

            Examples: When you're out of Schlitz, you're out of beer.

                    All the way with LBJ.

                    Christians aren't perfect—just forgiven.

2. Factual evidence

    a. What important facts, data, statistics, or expert testimonies are available for support of the premises that lead to my proposition?

    b. How many of these pieces of evidence do I need for establishing the premises?

    c. Do the evidential examples I have chosen strongly support the premises of my deductive argument?

    d. What must I do to be certain that the evidence I am using is accurate and that my sources are reliable?

    e. Have I included in the text the names and titles of those whom I am citing?

3. Form of argument—syllogism[5] or enthymeme[6]:

After examining the subject of my proposition, its relationship to my audience, the nature of the underlying assumptions, and the available factual evidence, what form of deductive argument will I use—the complete syllogism or the enthymeme?

---

[4] James L. Kinneavy, John Q. Cope, and J. W. Campbell, *Aims and Audiences in Writing* (Dubuque, Iowa: Kendall/Hunt 1976), 17–19.

[5] Syllogism: A syllogism is a deductive argument reduced to its simplest expression. While there are several deductive forms, the classic example is "All men are mortal. Socrates is a man. Therefore, Socrates is mortal" (All *A* are *C*. *B* is *A*. Therefore *B* is *C*.) [Ed.]

[6] Enthymeme: An enthymeme is a syllogistic argument with, typically, one premise suppressed. Enthymemes usually deal in probabilities rather than certainties. A variation of the argument about Socrates' mortality might take this form in an enthymeme: "Because Socrates is an intelligent man, he is almost certainly aware of his own mortality." The suppressed premise, that all intelligent men are almost certainly aware of their own mortality, is obvious from the context and is unlikely to be challenged. Accordingly, the premise is left implicit. [Ed.]

    a. Is it neccesary for me to establish both a major[7] and a minor[8] premise with my audience in order to lay the foundation for my proposition? (Construct the syllogism and consider each part in relation to the audience.)

    b. Or are the premises evident and likely to be acceptable to my audience without receiving special treatment? (Extend the enthymeme into a syllogism in order to check the advisability of omitting one of the premises from the presentation.)

C. Induction and Deduction

    1. Will my argument necessarily involve both the inductive and deductive processes?

    2. If I use both logical approaches, what will be the dominant process in the presentation? For example, will the inductive process perhaps serve to establish one of the premises of the deductive syllogism by presenting specific examples that can lead to formulation of the premise?

QUESTIONS AND IDEAS FOR DISCUSSION

1. According to Boley (and long-standing rhetorical tradition) you must consider the "ethical" appeal of your argument as you plan, write, and revise it. But how can you convey—through words alone—the qualities he enumerates in Part I of the heuristic? Explain as fully as possible. If it strikes you as impossible or unnecessary to include these considerations in your own writing strategy, explain your objections to that part of the heuristic.

2. The second part of Boley's heuristic centers on the use of emotional appeals—a problematic element of argument. Can it ever be truly ethical to use emotional appeals in a calculated way, such as the heuristic proposes? Even in purely practical terms, aren't emotional appeals likely to backfire, to offend readers? Comment.

3. If you decide to use emotional appeals in a particular argument, the heuristic will remind you to consider your audience. Suppose you are writing a letter to the editor of your local newspaper in favor of maintaining women's rights to obtain a legal abortion. Your hope is to influence public opinion and action; your audience is the citizens of your community. Given that audience and that purpose, how would you answer the following questions from Boley's heuristic?

---

[7] The "major premise" of a deductive argument is the premise most often left unstated in an enthymeme, the premise broadest in scope ("All men are mortal"). [Ed.]

[8] The "minor premise" of a deductive argument is usually the heart of the argument, the point to be proven if the conclusion is to be granted. It is usually the premise narrower in scope. In an argument worth developing, it will not be as automatically acceptable as in our example, "Socrates is a man." [Ed.]

II.B. . . .What is the limit to which I should go in using an emotional argument with my audience?

II.C. What will be the likely effects of my use of emotional arguments in this persuasive writing for this particular audience?

4. One of the thorniest problems in writing arguments can be deciding how much to tell your readers and how much to assume they know (you don't want to bore or offend them by stating the obvious). If you plan to write an argument opposing the confirmation of a Supreme Court nominee, what kinds of general ideas and specific knowledge would you expect each of the following audiences to have about the candidate and the nomination process?

   a. The U.S. Senators from your state
   b. The readers of your college newspaper
   c. The readers of the *New York Times*
   d. The readers of *Newsweek* magazine

5. In Part III, the heuristic distinguishes "factual examples" from analogies. Analogies are called "invented examples." Why? To what extent do you need to consider your audience in choosing analogies for a written argument? Explain.

The Maker's Eye: Revising Your Own Manuscripts

DONALD M. MURRAY

Donald M. Murray won a Pulitzer Prize for editorial writing in 1954 and since has won acclaim as a poet, prose fiction author, and teacher of writing at the University of New Hampshire. Some of his more recent writing textbooks are *Writing for Your Readers* (1983), *Write to Learn*, 3rd ed. (1990), and *Read to Write*, 2nd ed. (1990). This essay was originally addressed to professional writers (in *The Writer* magazine in 1973), but its point is crucial for all writers: If you do not revise, you set yourself up for disappointment—even unnecessary failure. If you do revise, you improve your odds of creating a convincing and readable argument, one so finely crafted that it appears seamless.

When students complete a first draft, they consider the job of 1
writing done—and their teachers too often agree. When professional writers complete a first draft, they usually feel that they are at the start

of the writing process. When a draft is completed, the job of writing can begin. . . .

Writers must learn to be their own best enemy. They must accept 2 the criticism of others and be suspicious of it; they must accept the praise of others and be even more suspicious of it. Writers cannot depend on others. They must detach themselves from their own pages so that they can apply both their caring and their craft to their own work. . . .

The writer must learn to read critically but constructively, to cut 3 what is bad, to reveal what is good. Eleanor Estes, the children's book author, explains: "The writer must survey his work critically, coolly, as though he were a stranger to it. He must be willing to prune, expertly and hard-heartedly. At the end of each revision, a manuscript may look . . . worked over, torn apart, pinned together, added to, deleted from, words changed and words changed back. Yet the book must maintain its original freshness and spontaneity."

Most readers underestimate the amount of rewriting it usually 4 takes to produce spontaneous reading. This is a great disadvantage to the student writer, who sees only a finished product and never watches the craftsman who takes the necessary step back, studies the work carefully, returns to the task, steps back, returns, steps back, again and again. Anthony Burgess, one of the most prolific writers in the English-speaking world, admits, "I might revise a page twenty times." Roald Dahl, the popular children's writer, states, "By the time I'm nearing the end of a story, the first part will have been reread and altered and corrected at least 150 times. . . . Good writing is essentially rewriting. I am positive of this."

Rewriting isn't virtuous. It isn't something that ought to be done. 5 It is simply something that most writers find they have to do to discover what they have to say and how to say it. It is a condition of the writer's life.

There are, however, a few writers who do little formal rewriting, 6 primarily because they have the capacity and experience to create and review a large number of invisible drafts in their minds before they approach the page. And some writers slowly produce finished pages, performing all the tasks of revision simultaneously, page by page, rather than draft by draft. But it is still possible to see the sequence followed by most writers most of the time in reading their own work.

Most writers scan their drafts first, reading as quickly as possible 7 to catch the larger problems of subject and form, then move in closer and closer as they read and write, reread and rewrite.

The first thing writers look for in their drafts is *information*. They 8 know that a good piece of writing is built from specific, accurate, and interesting information. The writer must have an abundance of information from which to construct a readable piece of writing.

Next writers look for *meaning* in the information. The specifics 9
must build to a pattern of significance. Each piece of specific information must carry the reader toward meaning.

Writers reading their own drafts are aware of *audience*. They put 10
themselves in the reader's situation and make sure that they deliver
information which a reader wants to know or needs to know in a
manner which is easily digested. Writers try to be sure that they
anticipate and answer the questions a critical reader will ask when
reading the piece of writing.

Writers make sure that the *form* is appropriate to the subject and 11
the audience. Form, or genre, is the vehicle which carries meaning to
the reader, but form cannot be selected until the writer has adequate
information to discover its significance and an audience which needs
or wants that meaning.

Once writers are sure the form is appropriate, they must then look 12
at the *structure*, the order of what they have written. Good writing is
built on a solid framework of logic, argument, narrative, or motivation
which runs through the entire piece of writing and holds it together.
This is the time when many writers find it most effective to outline as a
way of visualizing the hidden spine by which the piece of writing is
supported.

The element on which writers may spend a majority of their time is 13
development. Each section of a piece of writing must be adequately
developed. It must give readers enough information so that they are
satisfied. How much information is enough? That's as difficult as
asking how much garlic belongs in a salad. It must be done to taste,
but most beginning writers underdevelop, underestimating the reader's hunger for information.

As writers solve developmental problems, they often have to 14
consider questions of *dimension*. There must be a pleasing and effective
proportion among all the parts of the piece of writing. There is a
continual process of subtracting and adding to keep the piece of
writing in balance.

Finally, writers have to listen to their own voices. *Voice* is the force 15
which drives a piece of writing forward. It is an expression of the
writer's authority and concern. It is what is between the words on the
page, what glues the piece of writing together. A good piece of writing
is always marked by a consistent, individual voice.

As writers read and reread, write and rewrite, they move closer 16
and closer to the page until they are doing line-by-line editing. Writers
read their own pages with infinite care. Each sentence, each line, each
clause, each phrase, each word, each mark of punctuation, each section of white space between the type has to contribute to the clarification of meaning.

Slowly the writer moves from word to word, looking through 17 language to see the subject. As a word is changed, cut, or added, as a construction is rearranged, all the words used before that moment and all those that follow that moment must be considered and reconsidered.

Writers often read aloud at this stage of the editing process, muttering or whispering to themselves, calling on the ear's experience with language. Does this sound right—or that? Writers edit, shifting back and forth from eye to page to ear to page. I find I must do this careful editing in short runs, no more than fifteen or twenty minutes at a stretch, or I become too kind with myself. I begin to see what I hope is on the page, not what actually is on the page. 18

This sounds tedious if you haven't done it, but actually it is fun. Making something right is immensely satisfying, for writers begin to learn what they are writing about by writing. Language leads them to meaning, and there is the joy of discovery, of understanding, of making meaning clear as the writer employs the technical skills of language. 19

Words have double meanings, even triple and quadruple meanings. Each word has its own potential for connotation and denotation. And when writers rub one word against the other, they are often rewarded with a sudden insight, an unexpected clarification. 20

The maker's eye moves back and forth from word to phrase to sentence to paragraph to sentence to phrase to word. The maker's eye sees the need for variety and balance, for a firmer structure, for a more appropriate form. It peers into the interior of the paragraph, looking for coherence, unity, and emphasis, which make meaning clear. 21

I learned something about this process when my first bifocals were prescribed. I had ordered a larger section of the reading portion of the glass because of my work, but even so, I could not contain my eyes within this new limit of vision. And I still find myself taking off my glasses and bending my nose towards the page, for my eyes unconsciously flick back and forth across the page, back to another page, forward to still another, as I try to see each evolving line in relation to every other line. 22

When does this process end? Most writers agree with the great Russian writer Tolstoy, who said, "I scarcely ever reread my published writings; if by chance I come across a page, it always strikes me: all this must be rewritten; this is how I should have written it." 23

The maker's eye is never satisfied, for each word has the potential to ignite new meaning. This article has been twice written all the way through the writing process, and it was published four years ago. Now it is to be republished in a book. The editors made a few small suggestions, and then I read it with my maker's eye. Now it has been re-edited, re-revised, re-read, re-re-edited, for each piece of writing to the writer is full of potential and alternatives. 24

A piece of writing is never finished. It is delivered to a deadline, 25
torn out of the typewriter on demand, sent off with a sense of accomplishment and shame and pride and frustration. If only there were a
couple more days, time for just another run at it, perhaps then . . .

QUESTIONS AND IDEAS FOR DISCUSSION

1.   Murray wrote this essay for an audience of professional (and
would-be professional) writers. You, as a college student, were not
part of his original audience, a fact that may explain why Murray felt
free to begin the essay with a sweeping assertion about you: Students
write single drafts of their essays. Discuss this claim; if possible, refute
it! Do student writers who write single drafts *always* set themselves up
for failure, or at least disappointment? What about the students who
get their highest marks on the papers they write in the least time, in a
single draft? Analyze the extent to which revising improves or fails to
improve your own writing. If revising does not seem to improve your
writing, what would you respond to Murray's claims?

2.   Would the orderly revising process Murray encourages work for
you? Explain why or why not. What approaches, if any, might work
better for a college writer (as opposed to the professional writers
Murray addresses)?

3.   Tommy J. Boley's heuristic indicates (Part I) that the audience's
perception of the writer is important to persuasion. As Murray's audience here, what is your sense of Murray in this essay? Do you accept
him as an expert worth heeding? Do you find him appealing and
believable? Describe Murray's persona in this essay. (The persona is
the image of the writer conveyed to the reader through the writing.)
Can you trust a man, offering you advice, who suggests that revising
is fun (paragraph 19)?

4.   Developing a fitting conclusion to an argument can challenge even
a professional writer. How effective do you find Murray's conclusion
to this essay? Why? What do you believe a conclusion should accomplish?

The Zoo Paradox

(Student Essay-in-Progress)

NAN PAYNE

The process of reading and writing arguments is as individual as it is challenging. In this selection, you can see how one student, Nan Payne, met those challenges. You will read Payne's original assignment, some of her writing-journal notes, her summaries of readings, comments by her instructor and other students, different versions of her thesis, and three drafts of her essay. In Chapter 13 of this book, you will also find one of the professional articles that Payne read and drew upon to support her argument: "Against Zoos" by Dale Jamieson (page 477). You can judge how well Payne understood and used this article to support her own argument on the morality of zoos.

Essay Assignment

Assignment: To consider an environmental issue, research its causes, influences, possible developments, and solutions. To find source material that offers evidence and arguments concerning the issue. To focus on a fairly narrow aspect of that issue. To then develop an original argument that sheds new light for your readers (the members of this class)—and, perhaps, for you—on the issue. This argument should cite authorities as well as your own convictions; it is to be a documented essay.

Reminder: Keep notes of your ideas and questions in your journal—and remember to bring the journal with you to class meetings.

Ideas: waste disposal
　　　　recycling
　　　　overpopulation
　　　　water pollution
　　　　air pollution
　　　　extinction of species
　　　　wasteful use of resources

Student's Writing Journal Entry

Either recycling or maybe extinction of species.
But so much has been said about recycling. We all
know we should do it; none of us does much.

Extinction. How do we preserve endangered species from extinction? How many species have become extinct in this century? Gee, what else is there to say--this all seems pretty cut and dried....
What about Darwin and the survival of the fittest-- maybe it's supposed to be? But humans have messed up that equation, I guess. I don't know. Maybe I should get into clean water stuff. There might be something interesting about chemical experiments to clean dirty water. But no arg. edge to that that I can see. I like animals--all those trips to the zoo as a kid! Get back to the extinction: What about that? What about zoos, maybe? They offer a last refuge for lots of species. No arg. edge, there, either. Everybody likes zoos. Maybe I'll look up "zoos" and see if anything leaps out at me.

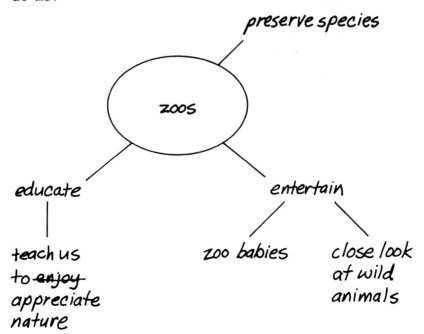

Note: Got to remember to keep this related to
"environmental issue" as stated in assignment. If
I talk about the entertainment value of zoos, I may
be getting off the track.

Student's Journal Notes During Writing Group Discussion

Janice: Believes that zoos are immoral--caging up
   animals. Better off in wild or at least large
   animal preserves.

Walt: Thinks that maybe I could do something about
   the way zoos are changing--making habitats more
   like the wild. Moving away from concrete and
   steel cages.

Hassan: Says Janice is being extreme. Zoos do lots
   of breeding--surely animals won't breed well in
   poor environments. Find out about preserving
   endangered species through zoo breeding?

Journal Entry

It has never occurred to me before that anyone
might disapprove of zoos. Here's an angle with an
argumentative edge!! Are zoos immoral? That's a
big value statement--no way to manage in 5-7 pp.
Got to find an angle I can cover. Make a list of
things zoos do that are good; things that might
be bad.

ZOO'S ACCOMPLISHMENTS	DRAWBACKS
interest in animals' welfare	living conditions not ideal in most zoos (I'd guess)
research	no zoo can reproduce the wild really
breeding programs	
education	the more natural the habitat, the less well visitors can observe the animals
entertainment	

Instructor's Comment in Journal

And on what criteria do they fit on one list and not the other?

Journal Entry

SOURCES FOUND:

In Readers' Guide:

The Futurist, Jan-Feb. 1988: 44-45   "Noah's
    Archive" A footnote mentions additional source:
    Karlyn Barker, "There's More to the Zoo than the
    Cuddly Panda," The Washington Post, Aug. 19,
    1987.

The Animals' Agenda, March 1988: 14-54   Merritt
    Clifton, "Chucking Zoo Animals Overboard"

The Animals' Agenda, Sept.-Oct. 1988: 33, abt.
    beating of elephant at San Diego Zoo

The Animals' Agenda, Dec. 1988: 28, abt. "coverup"
    at San Diego Zoo

Found at Mom and Dad's over spring break:

Leon Harris, "New Life at the American Zoo," Town &
    Country, March 1989: 161-67.

In Card Catalog, nothing useful under "Zoos," but
    under "Animal Welfare":

In Defence of Animals, ed. Peter Singer (New York:
    Basil Blackwell, 1985).

    "Against Zoos," by Dale Jamieson, 108-17.

    A footnote refers to: Paul and Anne Ehrlich,

    Extinction

Journal Entry

Preliminary thesis:

While zoos cannot be just like animals' natural
habitats, they do important services toward
preserving species and educating the public.

Support:

Discuss breeding programs (most animals come from
other zoos, not from the wild); educational
programs

Instructor's Comment in Journal

*Do zoos' educational services actually result in
making zoo visitors more concerned about animal
welfare, more environmentally aware? Does anyone
offer evidence for these widely made claims? Your
concession ("zoos cannot duplicate the wild") is a
good idea — shows you are reasonable and have*

considered other viewpoints. Think about rephrasing the main clause ("they do important services. . ."). It's sort of fuzzy. Is your thinking about this issue still "fuzzy"? What makes your thesis special; where's its argumentative edge?

Also, remember the assignment: Keep focused on ecological aspect. If you talk about education, you need to do so in this context.

Journal Entry

SUMMARIES AND NOTES ON READINGS

Leon Harris, "New Life at the American Zoo." Town & Country Mar. 1989: 161-68.

Odd place to find a good zoo argument--"society" magazine. Good specific examples of different zoos. "Pro" zoo.

Says a lot about how "in" it is now to be on a zoo's board of directors (appeals to audience of readers of this magazine). Tells about how zoos work constantly to improve their functions: (1) using "natural" habitats; (2) focusing on taking good care of more limited numbers of species; (3) concentrating on most endangered species; (4) no longer taking most animals from the wild (instead, buying from other zoos--some good statistics here). Describes in some detail six outstanding zoos; gives short descriptions of nine other good zoos. Talks about how Zoo Atlanta has improved from being one of the worst to a very good one.

Does describe one really bad zoo: Franklin Park
in Boston.

A solid and persuasive defense of zoos. Use.

Karlyn Barker, "There's More to the Zoo than the
Cuddly Panda." The Washington Post 19 Aug. 1987:
C1-2.

A short article with some good info. about
responsible breeding. The Post should be a solid,
reasonably unbiased source with reliable statistics
and examples.

All about the National Zoo (part of
Smithsonian). Lots of data about logistics of
feeding so many animals, etc. Some good specific
information about responsible breeding programs and
cooperation between zoos ("Animal Exchange") in
obtaining needed species and selling surplus.

Use this?

"Noah's Archive" (unsigned). The Futurist
Jan.-Feb. 1988: 44-45.

Short. Discusses some specific zoo efforts to
save endangered species. Further references at end
of article. The Futurist looks like it has an
ecological, save-the-planet slant on most
subjects. Too optimistic?

"Zoos may increasingly serve as 'Noah's
Archives'--preservers of the world's species"
(44). Examples given are at Center for
Reproduction of Endangered Species at the San Diego

Zoo (black-footed ferret, Asian elephant, etc.) and National Zoo (red panda, Sumatran tiger, etc.). Methods used include artificial insemination, embryo transfer, hormonal fertility tests. These zoos use "natural" habitats to prepare animals for return to wild when there are enough of them.

Use some of this data for support.

Merritt Clifton, "Chucking Zoo Animals Overboard: How and Why Noah Culls the Ark." The Animals' Agenda Mar. 1988: 14+.

This publication evidently directed to animal rights advocates and their bias on issues concerning animals. No pretense at taking a "middle" position.

Long essay. Surprisingly (given the magazine it's in) not totally opposed to zoos, but thesis is that they "breed and cull excessively" (14). Lots of evidence here, but also some unsupported claims. (For example, a dealer asserts that "[o]nly 20 percent of all zoos have appropriate facilities" [19], but gives no clue who has come up with that statistic, or how.)

Zoos really are needed to save species, but they're doing some inhumane things with the non-endangered species. Many zoos breed lots of babies because the public loves to see them. But the "extra" babies are either euthanized or sold to organizations that often don't treat them well, including many circuses and research labs.

Discusses in detail what happens to "zoo-surplus primates" (22+). Birth control is one possible solution, but it limits gene pool and keeps animals from learning "reproductive behavior" (54) and so can cause problems. Concludes that zoos will have to continue to cull (increasingly meaning "kill"), however distasteful the practice.

How to deal with this material?? Can't ignore it.

Megan Murphy-Hamilton, "America's Worst" (Sidebar to Clifton's essay) 21.

Very brief. Some useful statistics (only 9.4% of animal exhibitors in U.S. in 1986 were accredited). Briefly describes Prospect Park Zoo in Brooklyn, one of the worst. Also discusses the Atlanta zoo's turnaround.

Dale Jamieson, "Against Zoos. " In Peter Singer (ed.), In Defence of Animals (New York: Basil Blackwell, 1985) 108-17.

This book is a collection of essays that seem to be written for a very educated audience. The essays are complex and mostly written by university researchers. The slant is strongly pro-animal preservation.

The Jamieson essay is long, but very clearly organized and VERY persuasive. Gives brief history of zoos, four arguments for zoos (refuting each in turn), and two arguments against zoos. This one

almost makes me change my mind--in fact, I feel
much more undecided than I was about zoos.

Zoos were begun by the Romans, who kept them
mostly to have animals for the games. There are
moral reasons why zoos should not exist (109-10).
Today, zoos are defended on four major grounds:
"amusement, education, opportunities for scientific
research, and help in preserving species" (110).
None of these bears scrutiny, and it is impossible
to achieve all of them together (116). Further,
captivity not only deprives animals of liberty, but
also endangers their health. Last, and most
important, "[z]oos teach us a false sense of our
place in the natural order" (117). They make us
think that animals exist only for our benefit.

Journal Entry

--Visiting zoos a favorite childhood experience
    Get readers' interest--all are former children!
--Educational role of zoos--for children AND adults
    Important to make people care about animals
    How can you really care about an animal you've
    seen only in a book?
--Preserve species--This is what we want to educate
    people to support
    Details of specific projects, specific zoos (Use
    Harris, Barker, Futurist article for evidence)

"Zero" Draft[1]

When I was a kid, my dad would take me to the zoo if I remembered to make my bed every morning for two weeks straight. It was one of the greatest experiences of my childhood. The animals from my picture books--right there before me! I'm sure my love of animals comes from those hours at the zoo. (Certainly my love of lemonade and cotton candy does!)

I'm sure I was just typical of kids all over the world who have learned more about animals from zoos than from textbooks.

[Here I need some examples about educational role of zoos in making people aware and concerned about vanishing species. Need some good statistics, too.]

Zoos do a lot of research that benefits animals. They have learned about mating habits and about health needs of different animals. They are able to save baby animals that the mother cannot care for. [Need examples here]

~~Zoos are not bad for animals, either~~. Some species [add stuff here--condor? see Harris] would be extinct if it weren't for zoos. Some species

---

[1]This is rhetorician Maxine Hairston's term for a preliminary exploration of ideas. At this stage, no focused thesis may be apparent. The writer is sorting out her thoughts after reading and taking notes on several sources, and then writing down a list or preliminary outline of the points she thinks she wants to make. Nan Payne wrote her "zero" draft after reading all the sources she would ultimately use except the Jamieson essay, "Against Zoos." [Ed.]

that are in danger in their natural habitats have found a refuge at the great zoos. The animals usually seem to be enjoying themselves. Some of them watch the people as much as the people watch them. One ape at our zoo was so used to his concrete rooms that he wouldn't walk on the sod they put down for him. (They were trying to get him ready to move to the new gorilla habitat.) He would flip it over so he could walk on the concrete he had been used to for 35 years. [read this in Times Herald 3-25-90; look up page ref. on microfilm.] [Add stuff from Harris about how animals "couldn't care less whether they are sitting in an exact replica of a jungle tree or on a shelf in a cage" (162).]

[Make this point?] These animals mostly grew up in captivity (see Harris 162) so it is false sentimentality to say they miss the wild and are being treated inhumanely. [I don't know...seems callous.]

Journal Entry

Possible intro: Zoos kill animals. Zoos keep animals ~~in inhumane concrete boxes~~ inhumanely in concrete and steel cages. Zoos sell animals for experimentation. And yet, ~~anyone who cares about~~ ~~animals~~ many who care deeply about animals will continue to support zoos.

Revised thesis: Despite the ~~dramatic shortcomings~~ ^flaws^
of modern zoos, many who care deeply about animals
will continue to support ~~zoos~~ them.
~~(They make people care)~~

Points to make:

*   Zoos make people interested in animals. They
teach people about animals. They do a lot of
important research about animals. (Do this
second--follows well after "learning about the
animals" in first part)

*   Zoos are constantly improving. They are
learning more about the best ways to take care of
their animals. (Talk about this first, maybe to
refute arguments against zoos.)

*   Zoos preserve endangered species. (Most
important point--save for last)

After reading the Jamieson essay, I don't even want
to make the "entertainment" point. Seems really
trivial, hard to support. Even the "education"
point has problems. In fact, I think now there
should be fewer zoos, or much more limited and
smaller zoos. (Use example of the Arizona zoo.)
Why should both Dallas and Ft. Worth have zoos when
they're just 30 miles apart?

Instructor's Comment

I've always loved zoos. The scruples you raise I find both surprising and fascinating. Like you, I may not have ever given the subject much reflection. Do you think you can support your thesis with conviction? Or have you changed your mind altogether about the morality of zoos?

Journal Entry

I don't think zoos are going to be abolished. And, unlike Jamieson, I really don't think they should be, altogether. But I'm not as firm on the point as I was. I went to the zoo Saturday morning, thinking that might inspire me. The main thing I remember now is Om Bom, the gorilla, staring at me through the bars and glass wall between us.

Student's Journal Notes During Writing Group Discussion

Janice: Says personal illustrations good, but draft too ME-focused. Mothers probably can't care for babies because they were snatched away from their mothers and raised in a cage.

Hassan: Wants to know--where's the evidence, etc., about zoo research? That should strengthen my argument a lot.

Walt: Says it's choppy, and too sketchy for him to be able to say much.

Draft 1 (with additional changes)

Zoos kill animals. Zoos house animals inhumanely in concrete and steel cages. Zoos sell animals for experimentation. And yet, people who care deeply about animals will continue to support zoos.

Some will do so for all the wrong reasons, such as nostalgia. Most of us ∧remember childhood trips
fondly
to the zoo: laughing at the ~~apes~~ hippos, imitating the apes, ~~pulling back~~ recoiling in mock horror from the ~~snakes giant lizards~~ Gila monsters, making ourselves sick on cotton candy and lemonade. But that nostalgia in itself cannot justify keeping animals in confinement.

Others will support zoos because of their
presumed
~~theoretical~~∧educational value. Theoretically, zoos teach us what the other species on earth look like and how they live. And, it is supposed to follow from that that we will become more concerned about these fellow species, maintaining living
them
environments for ~~these species~~∧in the wild. Unfortunately, this appealing argument in favor of zoos is not supported by the evidence. First, we can learn what animals look like from good films shot in the wild. We can learn even more about what they act like. After all, animals in zoos do not act in their normal behavior because they are not in their normal environment [cite sources here--add example or two].

The people who believe in the educational value
of zoos also cite the research carried out by
zoos. Zoos have learned a lot about the eating
habits and health needs of different animals.
[Give example?] But the truth is that most of the
research that is done is carried out away from the
zoos themselves, either in the wild or in preserves
closed to the public. [Give ex.] And the research
that "extra" zoo animals are sold for is often
medical experimentation that may be inhumane [cite
source].

So, not only are several of the common reasons
for supporting zoos not very strong, several of the
common reasons for opposing zoos <u>are</u> strong.
First, many, maybe most, zoos are poorly designed
and poorly run. [Give some specifics here.]
Second, zoos ~~regularly~~ overbreed non-endangered
species and kill the offspring when they pass the
"cute zoo baby" stage [cite source here]. Third,
the surplus animals that are not killed are often
sold to fourth-rate traveling circuses or to labs
that conduct experiments on them [cite sources].

Given all these flaws in zoos, it may be hard to
believe that anyone should continue to support
them. And yet that is the case, and for a reason
that is strong enough to overweigh ~~overcome~~ the drawbacks
of zoos, if some changes are made. That reason is
that zoos do help preserve vanishing species.

The California condor no longer exists in the

wild. But two California zoos are slowly breeding
the ___ condors in their custody, with hopes of
returning some to the wild as early as 199_
[cite]. The [give at least two more examples].

So it isn't that we don't need any zoos. What
we need is fewer and better zoos. We need more
zoos in which, as one writer put it, the people are
in cages (monorail trains) and the animals have the
run of the place [cite]. We need zoos that display
fewer species, and thus are able to do a better job
with the species they have [cite]. We need zoos
that work toward maintaining *both* genetic diversity and
limiting overreproduction by means of birth control
rather than euthanasia.

An example of a zoo that fulfills not only the
aims of preserving endangered species but even the
"nostalgic" functions of providing fun,
entertainment, and education is the [talk about the
zoo in Arizona--cite source].

Another zoo that is doing a superb job is [talk
about the National Zoo and cite source].

Even some zoos that once offered good evidence
for doing away with all zoos are improving. Zoo
Atlanta is one good example [describe and cite].

So, while most cities would spend their money
more effectively by supplying the local library
with lots of first-rate videotapes about animals,

zoos must and will continue to have their place in a changing world.

Journal Entry

Looking over the last draft, I'd say odds are that my thesis won't seem particularly stunning to most readers. I've got to make them see WHY it's a bold claim to say that animal lovers should support zoos. I've got to devote a LOT of my essay to the "other" viewpoint to make the contrast clearer. "Here are all kinds of reasons why zoos are bad. BUT WE MUST SUPPORT THEM! And here's why."

Student's Journal Notes During Writing Group Discussion

Walt: Says it's much better--good to work out core argument before details of supporting evidence-- the illustrations and examples will fill out arg. well if they are strong ones.

Hassan: Thinks point of view in essay really changed! After hearing me talk about Jamieson essay, H. thinks I'm intimidated by it--afraid to really stick up for zoos. (IS HE RIGHT??)

Janice: Says I've got good development so far--good changes in thesis--too much space given to opposing viewpoint? She lost sight of the fact that I really favor zoos.

Nan Payne

English 1302: 021

22 April 1991

The Zoo Paradox

Zoos kill animals. Zoos house animals
inhumanely in concrete and steel cages. Zoos sell
animals for experimentation. And yet, people who
care deeply about animals will continue to support
zoos.

Some will do so for all the wrong reasons,
reasons that do not focus on the animals and their
needs. One such motivation is nostalgia. Most of
us fondly remember childhood trips to the zoo:
laughing at the hippos, imitating the apes,
recoiling in mock horror from the Gila monsters,
making ourselves sick on cotton candy and
lemonade. But nostalgia in itself cannot justify
keeping animals in confinement.

Others will continue to support zoos because of
their presumed educational value. Theoretically,
zoos teach us what the other species on earth look
like and how they live. And, it is supposed to
follow that we will become more concerned about
these fellow species, about maintaining living
environments for them in the wild. Unfortunately,
this appealing argument in support of zoos is not
supported by the evidence. First, we can learn
what animals look like from good films shot in the

wild. We can learn even more about how they act.
After all, animals in zoos do not demonstrate their
normal behavior because they are not in their
normal environment. Autopsies at the San Diego
Zoo, one of the best in the United States, show
"frequent occurrences of cannibalism, infanticide,
and fighting almost certainly caused by overcrowded
conditions" (Jamieson 117). The giant pandas at
the National Zoo in Washington, D.C., another of
the nation's best, have been unable to breed
successfully in the zoo's artificial environment
(Barker C1). And no tiger in a cage has the
freedom to be a tiger.

The people who believe in the educational value
of zoos also cite the research carried out by
zoos. For one thing, zoos have learned a lot about
the eating habits and health needs of different
animals. The tigers at the National Zoo, for
instance, are no longer fed plain horsemeat.
Instead, they are fed a carefully balanced diet of
"beef, horsemeat, fish, eggs, and vitamin and
mineral supplements" (Barker C1). Even the sea
lions get a variety of kinds of fish to choose
from. However, improving animal nutrition in zoos
does little for the species in the wild. Most of
the really important research is conducted away
from the zoos themselves, either in the wild or in
preserves closed to the public. The Bronx Zoo, for
example, conducts research through its "Wildlife
Conservation International, which has some eighty

field projects in thirty-seven countries around the
world, and the Wildlife Survival Center on St.
Catherine's Island, Georgia" (Harris 163). Dale
Jamieson, in "Against Zoos" argues further that

> very few zoos support any real scientific
> research. Fewer still have staff scientists
> with full-time research appointments. Among
> those that do, it is common for their
> scientists to study animals in the wild
> rather than those in zoo collections. (112)

So why have zoos? As Jamieson points out, field
research could be funded by the government (112).

Not only are several of the common reasons for
supporting zoos weak, several of the common reasons
for opposing zoos are strong. First, many, maybe
most, zoos are poorly designed and poorly run. A
former director of the San Jose Zoo, Peter Batten,
studied two hundred American zoos in 1974 and found
most of them to be terrible (Jamieson 117). Even
by 1986, only 9.4% of animal exhibitors in the U.S.
were accredited (Murphy-Hamilton 21). Second, many
zoos overbreed non-endangered species and kill the
offspring when they pass the "cute zoo baby" stage
(Clifton 14). Third, the surplus animals that are
not killed are often sold for research.

Quite a bit of the research involving zoo
animals is done not <u>for</u> them but <u>on</u> them--for human
benefit. "Extra" zoo animals are often sold for

medical experimentation that may be inhumane. University of California researchers could not learn too much from giving elephants LSD, as happened to two Laguna, California, zoo animals in 1984 (Clifton 16). These animals were actually still on the zoo grounds during the experimentation. Zoo sales to labs are such big business that there is actually a monthly newsletter to match available primates with lab needs, Primate Supply Information Clearinghouse (Clifton 53).

Given all these flaws in zoos, it may be hard to believe that anyone should continue to support them. But people will and should continue to support zoos, and for a reason strong enough to outweigh the drawbacks of zoos, if some changes are made. That reason is that zoos help preserve vanishing species.

The California condor no longer exists in the wild. But two California zoos are slowly breeding the fewer than three dozen condors left in the world, all in zoo custody, with hopes of returning some to the wild as early as 1992 or 1993 (Harris 164). Only two of five bird species native to Guam survive, and only in American zoos, which are slowly but successfully breeding them ("Noah's" 44-45). Nearly extinct species such as the red panda, the Sumatran tiger, and the golden lion tamarin (a small monkey) have been salvaged by the National Zoo, and the latter are being prepared to live in their native habitat again ("Noah's" 44). These and many other species would vanish from the earth if it were not for zoos.

This kind of animal preservation will not happen on any useful scale without the contributions of zoos. It is not enough to say that the government could take over animal studies and attempts to preserve species. A government bureaucracy would have no accreditation groups to answer to; we cannot be sure that the government would do a better job than zoos are doing. What is more, practically speaking, people are less likely to support animal preservation efforts (through approving increased taxes or through direct contributions) when they never see the animals. A thrilling monorail ride through a zoo's "Wilds of Africa" may not directly save any species, but it indirectly does. Zoos reach a lot of people: Zoos have a greater annual attendance than all professional sports combined (Harris 162).

Besides, doing away with zoos would mean that a lot of animals, unprepared to live in the wild, would quickly and painfully die if they were returned to their native habitats. Their native habitats may not even exist in a few generations, according to social anthropologist Desmond Morris:

> The human population of Africa is doubling
> with every generation. This means that in
> 60 years' time, when our children have

reached retirement age, the wild animals of
Africa will have only a quarter of the space
they now enjoy. (qtd. in Clifton 19)

In some respects, then, endangered species have
nowhere to go. Morris urges that "perhaps we
should start now to plan our 'ideal zoos' rather
than be emotional about the concept of captivity"
(Clifton 19).

So it isn't that we don't need any zoos. What
we need is better zoos. We need more zoos in
which, as one writer puts it, the people are in
cages (monorail trains) and the animals have the
run of the place (Clifton 162). We need zoos that
display fewer species and thus are able to do a
better job with the species they have. When Warren
Iliff became director of the Dallas Zoo, he sent
the lions, polar bears, and several other species
popular with zoo visitors to other zoos that had
more appropriate facilities for them. Visitors
today can see empty concrete cages. The polar
bears will not again endure the Texas heat; lions
will, however, one day roam the multi-acre African
exhibit recently opened. We need zoos that work
both toward maintaining genetic diversity and
toward limiting overreproduction by means of birth
control rather than euthanasia.

An example of a zoo that fulfills not only the
aims of preserving endangered species but even the
"nostalgic" functions of providing fun,

entertainment, and education is the Arizona-Sonora
Desert Museum. It is a small zoo, and its exhibits
are limited to 220 species native to the region.
Even so, here a visitor "can study seventeen
different species of rattlesnakes and twenty-three
different kinds of hummingbirds" (Harris 163). The
exhibits include a realistic "cave" and a 1920s
mining tunnel. This zoo is universally considered
one of the best, despite--or partly because
of?--its small size.

Another zoo that is doing a superb job is the
Cincinnati Zoo, which has a remarkable success
record in breeding endangered species. While black
rhinoceroses in the wild are fewer than 5,000 in
number, the Cincinnati Zoo has bred fourteen
(Harris 165). And the Brookfield Zoo in Chicago
has a firm commitment to animal conservation and a
policy against exhibiting species they cannot
adequately care for. The Brookfield Zoo's curator
of mammals, Bruce Allan Brewer, is adamant on the
subject:

> We are interested in the ethical questions
> raised by zoo-keeping. We are not in a
> popularity contest.... We will not exhibit
> a pair of koalas merely because they are
> crowd-pleasers. Until we can make a serious
> contribution to the propagation and
> conservation of koalas, we don't want any
> here. (Harris 163)

Even some zoos that once offered good evidence for doing away with all zoos are improving. Zoo Atlanta is one good example. In 1984, it was considered one of the worst zoos in the United States (Murphy-Hamilton 21). Animals were housed in poor conditions, and many died unnecessarily. Now, Zoo Atlanta is considered one of the better zoos in the country (Harris 166). One of its exhibits is a $4.5 million African rain forest in which many of the animals formerly in cages now live.

Zoos kill surplus animals. Zoos sell animals for experimentation. Zoos house animals in small, inhumane cages. Therefore, do away with all zoos? Not at all. Though we should not be naive about their limitations, zoos are an important means to an important end: the preservation of threatened species. Some zoos must go; many must improve what they do. But people will and must continue to support zoos.

Works Cited

Barker, Karlyn. "There's More to the Zoo than the Cuddly Pandas." Washington Post 19 Aug. 1987: C1-2.

Clifton, Merritt. "Chucking Zoo Animals Overboard." The Animals' Agenda Mar. 1988: 14-22, 53-54.

Harris, Leon. "New Life at the American Zoo." Town & Country Mar. 1989: 161-68.

Jamieson, Dale. "Against Zoos." In Defence of

   Animals. Ed. Peter Singer. New York:

   Blackwell, 1985. 108-17.

Murphy-Hamilton, Megan. "America's Worst." The

   Animals' Agenda Mar. 1988: 21.

"Noah's Archive. " The Futurist Jan.-Feb. 1988:

   44-45.

QUESTIONS AND IDEAS FOR DISCUSSION

1.   Reread the assignment for this student essay. Which features are clearly required? List them. Which features seem to be optional, giving the writer some creative leeway? List them. Refer to these lists as you follow the development of the paper. Does the writer always stay on track?

2.   Look again at Payne's preliminary thesis statement on page 30. What advice would *you* have given Payne in response to her preliminary thesis? Next, reread the revised thesis on page 38. Does either thesis strike you as promising an interesting argument? Can you suggest a more effective thesis at this point in the development of the argument?

3.   In your opinion, what are the best elements of this student's "zero" draft? The least promising elements? Notice that Payne brackets ideas that she wants to research further or come back to later. Do you use this method or another when you reach problematic points in your own arguments? Describe your own zero drafts.

4.   Compare the zero draft of Payne's essay to the final draft. What does Payne retain from the zero draft, and how has it been modified in the final essay? What are the effects of the changes?

5.   How consistently does Payne consider her audience as she plans and drafts her essay? What evidence do you find?

6.   How does Payne organize her final argument? Is this ordering of ideas effective? Does it make the reader more likely to be convinced of her conclusions than another ordering might? Discuss.

7.   Even on the final draft, Payne reworked her conclusion three times. Here are the two concluding paragraphs that preceded the one printed in the essay:

So, while many cities would educate their citizens more effectively by supplying the local library with lots of first-rate videotapes about animals, zoos must and will continue to have their place in our ever-changing modern world.

Zoos kill or sell surplus animals for experimentation: So zoos need more careful breeding programs and better contraception. Zoos house animals in cages: So zoos need to reduce the number of their exhibits and improve their quality, creating environments closer to nature. But despite the changes zoos need, people and endangered species need zoos.

Why do you suppose Payne rejected each of these as conclusions to this essay? How effective is the conclusion Payne settled on? What features make a conclusion effective or ineffective?

SUGGESTIONS FOR WRITING AND FURTHER DISCUSSION

1. Describe the "community," or usual audience, for whom you will write arguments in this course. Describe the communities for whom you will write papers in two other courses. What are the differences? What differences (in format, complexity, and other respects) will likely appear in the papers you write for these various communities?

2. Describe some of the prewriting and inventive strategies you use. Even if you believe you have no particular strategies, *something* enables you to put words on paper. Whether deliberate or not, that something is a means of invention, a strategy for discovering what you need to say. Try to recall the experience of beginning the last assigned paper you wrote.

3. When we can accurately and succinctly summarize an essay, we can feel assured that we really comprehend it. Moreover, we tend to remember essays we have summarized in greater and more accurate detail than other essays. Why (if you accept these claims) do you suppose that is the case? Try to break down and identify the process you must go through in order to write a summary. Is the process any harder when the argument is one you find offensive or simply wrong?

4. Here is a claim: It is much harder to read critically when we completely agree with the thesis of an argument than when we completely disagree with it. Discuss this claim, with examples if possible.

5. Write a short essay (perhaps 500 words), addressed to an audience of your rhetoric classmates and arguing a point you strongly believe.

Then write an essay of similar length that argues the opposite position. Your aim is to make it impossible for your classmates to tell which argument you believe and which you do not believe. Exchange essays with members of your writing group or class, and discuss how and why you conclude whether or not the arguments are sincere. Based on your own and your classmates' examples, what are the telltale signs of an insincere argument? Unfortunately, a sincere argument can fail its aims as well. What are the most typical failings of a sincere argument?

6. Consider an issue about which you have strong feelings and about which some of your classmates might have different ideas. How would you go about writing an argument on the subject that those classmates will read? In what specific ways would that argument differ from an essay on the same subject addressed to readers sharing your viewpoint? How do you maintain your integrity while catering to your readers? Is it possible? Discuss these issues as specifically as possible.

7. Strong introductions and conclusions are crucial to effective argument if only because of their positions as beginnings and endings. Introductions draw readers into the argument, engaging their sympathy and interest; conclusions clinch the point with conviction and persuasion. But what makes introductions and conclusions work or fall short? Find in this book one essay with an introduction that particularly intrigues you and makes you want to read on. Just how does the writer engage your interest? Is that essay's conclusion equally effective? If so, why, specifically? If not, how does it come up short?

8. If you have already written an argumentative essay this semester or if you have an essay from another course, try treating it as a first draft and revising it as Nan Payne did hers. Give your argument some new energy: Hone its thesis; support its points with additional or more interesting examples; improve the organization by reordering points if necessary; make sure transitions are clear and logical. Bring both the original essay and the revised draft to class for others to read and discuss. Describe the process that works best for you in revising: Is it similar to your classmates'? To Donald Murray's? Are you able to be, as Murray says, "your own best enemy" (paragraph 2)?

9. Sheridan Baker claims that "the most energetic thesis of all . . . is some tired old truth that you cause to jet with new life, making the old ground green again" (paragraph 7). Below are some "tired old truths." Choose one, and create a thesis for a fresh and compelling argument addressed to an audience that Baker describes as the "loyal opposition consisting of the interested but uninformed" (paragraph 10). Then write the argument!

The grass is always greener on the other side of the fence.

Two wrongs don't make a right.

You can't be all things to all people.

Where there's smoke, there's fire.

10. Turn to the Table of Contents of this book and read the entries under "Pros, Cons, and Maybes." Choose a topic that interests you from those entries. Write the draft of an essay, with your rhetoric class in mind as audience, that narrows, defines, and argues a position that you hold sincerely. Then read the essay in "Pros, Cons, and Maybes" that appears to argue a thesis related to yours. Does it include evidence that might bolster your argument? Does its author make a point that deserves quoting? With your instructor's directions or the Appendix of this book as a guide, incorporate into your argument support from the professional essay. Is your argument strengthened or only lengthened? Discuss with your class the difficulties and the possibilities inherent in using source material in your own arguments.

PART ONE

STRATEGIES FOR ARGUMENT

As the first chapter of this book showed, arguments do not appear whole on the page. Writers must deal with all kinds of concerns and issues, both before writing and as they work. This section will provide strategies for resolving some of the key questions that writers of argument face: What kinds of evidence will best support my claims? How can I be sure I have linked that evidence logically to the claims it supports? Have I overlooked any fallacious arguments that I need to refute—or have I committed any fallacies myself? Would a touch of humor win over my readers—or offend them? How else can I enhance the way I have expressed my argument? And how, if at all, can I argue about nonlogical subjects?

In the first section of each of the following six chapters, experienced writers and teachers of argument suggest some answers to these questions, some strategies for dealing with the issues they raise. The second section of each chapter offers arguments that illustrate the strategies, while at the same time debating a single issue. And the third section of each chapter provides "raw material" for you to evaluate in terms of the chapter's concerns—and possibly for you to draw upon or respond to in your own arguments.

2

SUPPORTING CLAIMS
WITH EVIDENCE

THE STRATEGY

How do we support the claims we make in arguments? First, we consider our readers: Are they likely to be hostile? Sympathetic? Knowledgeable about the subject? Interested or uninterested? If we consider our readers, their needs and preconceptions, we can develop arguments that will reach them and may convince them. We give them reasons; we marshal salient points. Most of all, we offer evidence they can appreciate. We don't just say, for instance, "The college curriculum is not offering students what they need to succeed in the world today, for courses are either narrowly preprofessional or geared more to professors' own esoteric interests than to students' enlightenment." We do more: We cite course descriptions, summarize statistical data on what students actually learn and retain, offer personal anecdotes, quote professors and students taking college courses. The evidence we offer can make our argument both logically convincing and emotionally persuasive to our anticipated readers.

How much evidence does an argument require to support its claims adequately? Your common sense often will tell you: Surprising and unexpected claims will require more and stronger evidence than will conventional and predictable claims. If you argue that a science major is the worst possible choice for a premed student, your fellow undergraduates may be astonished. You will have some convincing to do. If, on the other hand, you assert that working on the college yearbook provides invaluable training for a career in publishing, the same readers will readily grant your conclusion. They may be interested in your evidence and in the statistics and anecdotes you cite, but they will require less convincing. All claims require evidence and examples to qualify as argument, but if the evidence is strong and memorable, it need not be voluminous. You might bear in mind the dangers of what some have called the "Hollywood Elephant Theory"—if one elephant is good, one hundred elephants must be one hundred times better. Not so.

Everything from the loftiest authoritative testimony to the lowliest example can serve as evidence for a claim. And often enough, the example is more illuminating and persuasive than is the testimony, for a good example creates a picture in the reader's mind. To be both effective and logically compelling to critical readers, an example must meet some requirements. These are detailed by Ronald Munson in the first reading selection in this chapter. In the next reading, George Ziegelmueller and Charles Dause offer criteria by which to evaluate a variety of kinds of evidence, notably authorities and statistics. And in the third selection, Michael Gartner cautions against accepting— much less citing—the testimony of unnamed sources.

The Example
RONALD MUNSON

Ronald Munson is a professor of philosophy at the University of Missouri—St. Louis. Munson's lively writing style makes interesting reading even of a treatise as soberly titled as this one. This selection is excerpted from Munson's informal logic text for college students, *The Way of Words* (1978). Notice, as you read, how Munson clarifies and enlivens his own points with examples.

Everyone is bound to bear patiently the results of his own example.

Phaedrus,
Fable 26

If Gaylord complains that Goudge has short-changed him by giv- 1
ing him a nickel instead of a quarter, he won't be satisfied if Goudge tells him not to worry because nickels and quarters are both coins and Gaylord got coins for change. If Gaylord keeps a cool head, he can point out that, though it's true that nickels and quarters are both coins, there's a difference between them. Similarly, analogies and examples are both called "illustrations," but this doesn't mean that they are the same. Examples and analogies are different in a fundamental way which, to avoid confusion, it's good to keep in mind.

An analogy always involves pointing out features that an ana- 2
logue and a primary subject matter have in common. Some points of

resemblance are necessary for there to be an analogy between the two subject matters. But, on the other hand, there must also be significant differences between them. There must be *two* subject matters. Just because two things resemble one another in a few ways doesn't mean they are identical: the President is not really the captain of a ship.

An example, unlike an analogue, doesn't just resemble the pri- 3 mary subject matter. It is *a part of it*—a case, instance, or sample. A sociologist discussing poverty among Chicanos might describe the Juan Martinez family of Brownsville, Texas, as an example of the way many uneducated migrant workers must live. The Martinez family is a *case* of this way of life. A printer talking about typography might illustrate his lecture by presenting examples of different typefaces: Times Modern, Caledonia, Electra, Baskerville, and so on. The typefaces mentioned or shown are part of the subject matter of the talk. They are cases, not part of some other subject matter. Examples involve only one subject matter, and they constitute a portion of it.

Giving examples is often an easy job to do. Someone who is asked 4 to give examples of biological species that are in danger of extinction needs only to list a few of the many: the ocelot, the Indian tiger, the peregrine falcon, the mountain lion, and so on.

Sometimes to give an example is to do more than just name an 5 instance. When a principle, rule, procedure, or method has been discussed, then to give an example is generally to describe in some detail the way in which the principle, etc., applies to a given case or in a concrete situation. Such examples can be quite complex. Here are some examples of such examples:

(a) In heating egg yolks you must always be careful not to let them curdle. If, for example, you were making a hollandaise sauce in a blender, you would want to add the melted butter to the egg yolks in a thin stream of droplets with the blender going at top speed.

(b) The expression $b^x = N$ is a way of representing the assertion that any number N can be expressed as the power of some base. The number 100, for example, can be represented as the second power of base 10 (10^2); 16 as the second power of base 4 or the fourth power of base 2.

(c) Does the law give you the right to protect your property? Yes it does, but only within certain limits. Life is valued above property in the law, and you cannot take measures of protection which would be likely to cause death or grievous bodily harm to a thief or burgler. For example, if you own a barn that is apart from your house, you are justified in locking the doors, installing alarms, and keeping a watchdog. You are not justified, however, in rigging booby-traps which might cause the death of someone who forces entry, though he does it illegally.

A bit of qualification needs to be added to the assertion that 6 examples are part of a subject matter. Particularly in talking about principles and procedures, actual cases are not always used as examples. Rather, suppositious or hypothetical cases are offered for illustration. The advantage of using such cases is that they can be constructed for the purpose they have to serve. Relevant features can be stressed, and irrelevant and complicating features that typically characterize actual instances can be avoided. In the last example given above, it would be possible to find a real instance which illustrates the principle that the law values life more than the protection of property, and whether a real case is chosen or a case is made up depends in part on the purposes of the writer. Students who study law by the so-called case method learn how legal principles have been applied in past instances and thus come to appreciate the connection between laws and actual situations. For the purpose of law students real examples are no doubt best, but for the ordinary reader a suppositious case might be quite enough. He doesn't need to understand the law the way a law student does.

We evaluate and criticize examples as well as analogies. Some of 7 the features we rely on in making appraisals in both cases are similar, but others are quite different. In any event it's useful to raise the same question about examples that we raised about analogies: What are the characteristic marks of a good example? Again, too, it has to be kept in mind that there are really no "rules" for examples. Any criteria we come up with are only rough generalizations based on the fact that we are already able to point to some examples in praise and to others in disgust. We are, as with analogies, only reflecting on the judgments which we typically make.

The Case Should Be an Example

The most obvious instance of a bad example is one in which what 8 is offered as a case illustrating a point or satisfying a description is not one at all. The person who mentions New York as an example of a state with a unicameral legislature has simply made a factual mistake. The same is true of someone who cites Ernest Hemingway as an instance of a nineteenth-century novelist, Malcolm X as a leader of the Ku Klux Klan, and Betty Friedan as a male chauvinist. To show that examples of this kind are faulty, we only have to prove that an error about a matter of fact has been committed.

The Case Should Be Typical

The phrase "typical example" expresses something about what 9
we ordinarily expect of an example. Unless we are explicitly warned
otherwise, we have a right to assume that a case presented to us as
an example is a representative sample of whatever is being exemplified. Most Americans like to eat hamburgers. But if someone is discussing this rather uninteresting fact and he presents us with the
example of John Stubbs of Cedar Rapids, Iowa, who eats five hamburgers a day and has done so for the last twenty-three years, we
have reason to complain. We haven't been offered a typical case, even
though it's true that Stubbs is an American and he likes hamburgers.
"Most Americans don't like hamburgers *that* much," we point out.
Stubbs is peculiar and not representative. His case makes an *odd* example.

When a case is offered as an example of some general fact or 10
principle, as one that satisfies a certain description, it shouldn't be one
marked by some strange feature that clearly sets it apart from cases
that illustrate the same thing but lack that feature. The reason this
shouldn't be done is simply because an untypical example is an invitation to error. It's easy for someone to be misled into accepting the
peculiar feature of the odd example as characteristic of all other cases.
We aren't likely to be shoved into error by the Stubbs example because
it's such an outlandish case that we recognize it for what it is. But
we're often faced with unfamiliar material and sometimes lack the
knowledge and experience necessary to know whether or not a case
given as an example is a representative one. We have to depend upon
the person giving the example to keep our limitations in mind. Conversely, we have to be careful to remember the limitations of others
when it's our job to do the explaining.

Someone who mentioned Isaac Asimov as an example of a 11
foreign-born writer who, after coming to this country, wrote a number
of books in English would be cheating on the truth if he presented
Asimov as a typical case. The fact that Asimov was brought to the
United States as an infant makes his case quite different from that of
foreign-born writers like Nabokov who immigrated as adults and had
to learn to write in English after having grown up speaking and
writing another language.

There is nothing wrong with offering an odd, peculiar, or extreme 12
case so long as it is clearly labeled as such. The trouble starts only
when such a case is given to us without mention of its strangeness. We
are justifiably inclined to take it as typical, and if we're misled, it's
through no fault of our own. Giving fair examples is one of the marks
of honesty in writing and arguing.

The Case Should Be Clear-Cut

The primary reason for offering an example is to supply someone   13
with an illustration of whatever is being discussed. The aim is to
provide him with a definite case in order to get him to see how a rule
applies or to recognize some kind of object or activity. Since examples
are used as aids to understanding, it's important that they should be
clear cases. A *doubtful* case of whatever is being illustrated obviously
makes a bad example. So too does a case that is not doubtful but does
have *extraneous* or *complicating* features that are irrelevant to the matter
being illustrated.

Someone discussing the ways in which the ideas of one thinker   14
influence those of another might take as an example the influence of
George Berkeley on David Hume. If he does, he's making a bad
choice. Whether Hume read Berkeley or was familiar with his ideas is a
matter open to dispute. Much better choices would be the influence of
Plato on Aristotle, Bentham on Mill, Bacon on Hobbes, or Darwin on
John Fiske, for in these cases there is no doubt that there was influence
to some degree. Using a doubtful case as an example sidetracks discussion and argument. Attention centers on the example rather than
upon what it is supposed to illustrate.

A tax lawyer explaining to his client the requirement that all capital   15
gains are subject to taxation best does so by describing a simple case in
which a person gets money from the sale of property owned by him.
There is no need for the lawyer to take a case in which the property
was a gift, was twice mortgaged, and was not sold outright but was
exchanged for other goods of greater value. The complicated case may
be one that falls under the same tax requirement, but the complications add nothing to the illustration. Indeed, they make the example
a bad one, for the extraneous features stand in the way of a clear view
of how the tax requirement applies.

The Case Should Be Fair

Suppose that Victor Fleischkopf is a member of the Association of   16
Friends of Four-Footed Beasts and has been invited to give a talk on
"Animals and Their Lovers" to the local Policemen's Benevolent
group. "The love of animals is widespread," Victor tells the policemen. "The names of animal lovers are, I'm sure, well known to you
all. To mention just a few, there was Adolf Hitler, Heinrich Himmler,
John Christy, and Ian Brady. All of these men were inordinately fond
of dogs." Much to his surprise, Victor was retained for questioning
after his lecture, and an investigation into the Association of Friends of
Four-Footed Beasts was begun immediately.

All of this because of Victor's examples. True, all the people he mentioned were animal lovers, but two of them were also Nazis known to be responsible for the deaths of innumerable people, and the other two were convicted mass murderers. It's hardly strange that the Benevolent Policemen should become curious about Victor and his association.

Victor's error is clear. He gave as examples untypical cases, but more than this, he also presented examples untypical in a special way, since the cases he mentioned are of men who possess traits that we detest or regard as immoral. In talking about analogy, we've already seen that it's possible to mislead people by choosing an analogue toward which everyone feels antipathy, disgust, or disapproval. Attitudes are influenced and manipulated without relevant facts or arguments. There is a parallel to this in choosing examples. Taking as an example of some kind of action, or organization, or principle a case that is atypical in a certain way can do much to influence people's beliefs and attitudes.

Influence works both ways, of course, and an example that will incline people toward approval can be selected as well as one that inclines them toward disapproval. Too, it's always possible to bumble along, like poor Victor, and not realize how people will be affected by the cases chosen for illustration. But fairness demands that cases used as examples should be free from incidental features that encourage people to approve or disapprove of whatever is being exemplified merely because some of the cases have such features.

It may, of course, be the nature of what is being discussed that the majority of people find is detestable or reprehensible. If our friend Victor had been discussing mass murderers and had mentioned Ian Brady as an example of one, his choice would have been perfectly fair. We could hardly accuse him of giving all mass murderers a bad name by choosing Brady, because mass murderers have a bad name already. In such a case, it is just the detestable feature that is being illustrated. As such it is fundamental to the example, not incidental to it. It is for this reason that we can say that Victor, perhaps unwittingly, did give animal lovers a bad name by using Brady's name as an example. The feature Brady has that is incidental to the fact that he was an animal lover also happens to be one that we abominate and thus one that can color attitudes toward animal lovers in general.

QUESTIONS AND IDEAS FOR DISCUSSION

1. Does Ronald Munson practice what he preaches—that is, does he use enough examples to illustrate and support his points? Or does he use too many? What characterizes a good example, in your judgment? Give an example (of course!) of an effective example in Munson's

essay and one that you find less than clear or helpful. If you find a case of the latter, suggest a better illustration for an audience of which you would be a typical member.

2.   Munson begins his discussion of the example by talking about something else, the analogy. What is important about the distinction? Distinguish *example* from *analogy* in your own words and with your own examples. Can you use analogy to prove a point? Explain.

3.   Are examples important to all argument? Or do some subjects of argument (or perhaps some occasions for argument, or some audiences) not require examples? Might examples, even clear and specific ones, sometimes detract from an argument? Explain.

4.   Munson does not talk about the occasional usefulness of what we might call the "negative" example—that is, an example of what something is *not*, or an example that we mean to exclude from a given category. To continue with one of Munson's own illustrations, we might clarify what we mean by "animal lover" by stipulating that hunters cannot be counted in that group, while many vegetarians can be. Similarly, write a negative example and an actual (or hypothetical) example for each of the following:

glasnost   etiquette   affirmative action   argument

Testing Data

GEORGE W. ZIEGELMUELLER AND CHARLES DAUSE

The authors of this excerpt from *Argumentation: Inquiry and Advocacy* (1975) teach speech communication—George Ziegelmueller at Wayne State University and Charles Dause at the University of Detroit. In "Testing Data," they discuss one of the most important principles of logical argument: A claim without supporting data is merely an assertion, not an argument. Moreover, the quality of the supporting data very often determines the quality of the argument. As the authors put it, "If an argument is insufficient at the outset—if the data upon which it is based is inadequate—then the most careful reasoning process and the most clearly phrased conclusions will not salvage it." But on what grounds do we judge examples, statistics, and other evidence? Ziegelmueller and Dause offer specific criteria for evaluating evidence we wish to use in our own arguments and evidence offered in the arguments of others.

Each day we are bombarded with a multitude of facts and opinions concerning the important questions of our society. Whether we are listening to a newscast, chatting with friends, or reading a magazine or newspaper, we are confronted with various types of data which are frequently in conflict with each other. Unfortunately, many people become the mental slaves of what they read or listen to because they do not have criteria by which to measure the accuracy or acceptability of the premises and evidence offered. How does one determine whether or not a given piece of data is logically sufficient to serve as the starting point for argument?

The importance of this task should be obvious. If an argument is   2 insufficient at the outset—if the data upon which it is based is inadequate—then the most careful reasoning process and the most clearly phrased conclusions will not salvage it.

. . . there are three general tests which can be applied to all data.   3 These are the test of internal consistency, the test of external consistency, and the test of relevancy.

The Test of Internal Consistency

The test of internal consistency asks the question, "Is the data   4 consistent with other data from the *same source*?" This test suggests that we must look carefully at the premises, facts, and opinions expressed by a source to determine whether or not they are consistent with each other. Inconsistencies between or among premises, facts, and opinions expressed in a single source raise serious questions concerning the credibility of the source of the data. Unexplained inconsistencies at any level of data suggest that the source of the data is guilty of careless thinking and superficial analysis. Such data are always an inadequate basis for argument and are easily and persuasively refuted by anyone familiar with the consistency problems of the source.

An example of inconsistent opinion data is found in the analysis   5 by the *Tampa Times* of the role of marijuana in a multiple ax-slaying:

> . . . it may or may not be wholly true that the pernicious marijuana cigarette is responsible for the murderous mania of a Tampa young man in exterminating all of the members of his family within his reach—but whether or not the poisonous mind-wrecking weed is mainly accountable for the tragedy, its sale should not be and should never have been permitted here or elsewhere. . . . It required five murders to impress the Tampa public and Tampa officials with the serious effects of the habit.[1]

---

[1] *Tampa Times*, 20 Oct. 1973, 11.

This editorial first admits uncertainty as to the causal connection between marijuana and the killing but then goes on to assume that causality has been established. Such a blatant inconsistency in opinion undermines any assumption of expertness in this matter on the part of the source of the data, the *Tampa Times*.

The Test of External Consistency

The test of external consistency asks the question, "Is the data 6 consistent with other data from *unrelated sources?*" This test suggests that each piece of data must be examined in the light of other known data from other sources. A *New York Times* feature writer once applied the test of external consistency to refute the claim that pollution control costs are causing business failures:

> Headlines such as "Pollution Laws Closing Plants by the Hundreds" and "A Drive to Find Jobs for Victims of the Pollution War" have appeared in both business and lay periodicals. A Department of Commerce publication said recently, "More plant closings are being reported daily from countless small communities throughout the nation."
> However, a nationwide check by *The New York Times*, corroborated by Government reports, provides little substantiation for such assertions and apprehensions.
> To the contrary, the survey yielded indications—supported by a number of officials, economists and other observers—that the costs of pollution control, while they may be causing dislocations in a few specialized situations, could also be a construc ^{7} element in terms of plant modernization and increased efficiency.[2]

The discovery of inconsistencies between unrelated sources does not automatically invalidate the credibility of the data, but it does require that further examination be conducted to determine which of the sources is more credible in the matter under consideration. Such further examination leads to the tests specific to the individual types of data. . . . Problems with external consistency, then, are a tip-off that further testing of the data must be conducted.

The test of external consistency can be used positively to validate 8 data as well as negatively to question the validity of data. When used in the positive sense it becomes the test of "independent corroboration." Historian Louis Gottschalk defines the concept of independent corroboration when he says, "The general rule of historians is to accept as historical only those particulars which rest upon the independent testimony of two or more reliable witnesses."[3] If two unre-

---

[2] Gladwin Hill, "The Cost of Cleanup," *New York Times* 4 June 1972, qtd. from *Congressional Record* 18 July 1972, S11111.
[3] *Understanding History* (New York: Knopf, 1963) 166.

lated (independent) sources provide us with the same premises, facts, or opinions, the credibility of our data is more firmly established.

The Test of Relevancy

The test of relevancy asks the question, "Does the data support 9 the conclusion it is asserted to support?" This test suggests that data can be credible in every other respect but may still be an insufficient basis for argument because it is tangent to the conclusion being forwarded. It is not infrequent for a conclusion to assert one thing and for the data to establish something slightly different. If, for example, an advocate set forth the conclusion that no one in America suffers from hunger or malnutrition and proceeded to cite expert opinion evidence which stated, "No one in America *need* go without adequate food," the evidence would be irrelevant to the claim. In examining the relevancy of data to any given conclusion, then, one must always ask the question, "Does this data really support this conclusion?" If the data is tangential to the conclusion, it provides no probative force and may be dismissed as irrelevant.

Tests of Factual and Expert Opinion Evidence

While the three tests outlined above can be applied to all types of 10 data, there are other tests which are unique to factual and expert opinion evidence. These include the test of recency, the test of source identification, the test of source ability, the test of source willingness, the test of context, and the tests of statistical evidence.

The Test of Recency

The test of recency asks the question, "Is the statement of the 11 evidence based upon recent observations of the real situation?" Since the world is constantly changing, most facts and opinions have maximum validity for only a limited period of time. The test of recency simply asks if the evidence is recent enough so that important facts have not changed in the elapsed time. Factual evidence concerning wage levels in a given profession, for example, can be badly dated in even a year or two. The same is true of data on unemployment, prices, economic growth, etc. Expert opinions which interpret such dated facts must also be carefully examined.

An article in the *Christopher News Notes* used the test of recency in 12 rejecting often-cited statistical estimates of the number of deaths from illegal abortions:

> Estimates widely quoted as recently as 1967, based for the most part on a study by Taussig in 1932, put the number of such deaths each year between 5,000 and 10,000. This study was done before the advent of antibiotics, therapeutic medicine and frequent transfusions—all of which have sharply reduced the medical risks.[4]

Note that in applying the test of recency the author referred both to the fact that the statistics were forty years old and to the fact that conditions had changed during that period.

In applying the test of recency, the advocate should be especially 13 aware of recent statements of old facts. It is not uncommon for current books or articles to base conclusions on evidence from older sources. Books are especially suspect on this count since there is frequently a time lapse of several years between the writing of certain sections of a book and its actual publication.

The Test of Source Identification

The test of source identification asks the question, "Is the source of 14 the evidence identifiable?" This test suggests that each piece of evidence should be traceable to a specific source. Without adequate source identification, complete testing of evidence is impossible. The credibility of factual and expert opinion evidence is, in large part, dependent upon the ability and willingness of a source to perceive and interpret the situation accurately and fairly. Without source identification we cannot make these vital credibility judgments.

Frequently we are confronted with general documentation such as 15 "sources close to the President," or "according to *Newsweek*," or "economists believe." Such general documentation may make arguments easier to read or listen to, but it also renders adequate source evaluation impossible. Every time such general documentation is encountered, one must ask why the documentation was not more specific and must examine whether or not those using the evidence may have reasons for not disclosing the full identification of their sources.

The Test of Source Ability

The test of source ability asks the question, "Is the source of the 16 evidence *able* to report or interpret the situation accurately?" Since the factual and expert opinion evidence used in argumentation must be reported, it is necessary to examine the source of the evidence as well as the fact or expert opinion itself. In questioning a source's ability to

---

[4] Pamphlet #195.

report or interpret the situation accurately it is vital to consider both the source's accessibility to the situation and his expertness.

It is first important to determine a source's geographical and 17 chronological nearness to the elements of the situation which he is reporting or interpreting. Lack of direct accessibility results in a source who is dependent upon other sources for his information. When the source is separated from the situation, the facts and opinions must be sifted through a variety of individual perceptions and interpretations and, therefore, are more subject to distortion and misrepresentation. As a general rule, then, the more a source is separated from direct access to the important elements of a situation, the less accurate his report or interpretation is likely to be. In our courts of law, as well as in society in general, eyewitness accounts are considered more credible than hearsay evidence.

In addition to examining source *accessibility* one must also consider 18 source *expertness*. More specifically, one must question whether or not the source is qualified by experience, training, or position to interpret the situation. These factors of expertness are crucial in determining whether or not the source of the evidence is able to tell the truth. Even superior access to the situation may not be helpful if specialized knowledge or background is necessary to understand the event.

The *experience* test suggests that a source should have worked with 19 the situation sufficiently to enable him to report or interpret the elements of that situation accurately. An experienced diplomat is much better able to interpret the public statements of a foreign power than is a novice news reporter. To the novice reporter, a foreign policy statement may seem to be the same as previous statements. The experienced diplomat, on the other hand, may be able to read between the lines of the statement to see subtle shifts of policy.

In many situations, *specific training* may be necessary to interpret 20 events or even merely to report them. News reporters receive intensive training before being sent to cover combat situations. Military combat situations are so complex that specialized training is necessary in order simply to report events intelligently. In deciding the complex constitutional questions in our society, years of legal training are a vital prerequisite. The layman simply lacks the specialized training necessary to permit an authoritative interpretation of complex legal issues.

Another measure of source expertness is that of *position*. The 21 concept of position is closely related to the test of accessibility. A source's position may give him access to information denied to most people thereby providing him with a degree of expertise. The perfect example, of course, is the position of President of the United States. No matter which individual occupies this office, the position permits access to otherwise classified information. That access enables the President to view and interpret events in a perspective denied to most other people. In much the same way, a Senator who is a member of the Senate Judiciary Committee has access to important information on judicial issues. He becomes an expert on these issues, not because of any personal qualities which he possesses, but rather because of the position he holds.

In examining a source's ability to report or interpret situations 22 accurately, then, we must consider a source's accessibility to the situation and his experience, training, and position with reference to that situation. If a source has problems in any of these areas, it should lead to a search for independent corroboration by sources with superior accessibility, experience, training, or position.

The Test of Source Willingness

The test of source willingness asks the question, "Is the source of 23 the evidence *willing* to report or interpret the situation fairly?" While a source may be in an excellent position to perceive the truth accurately, conditions may exist which may cause him to distort the reporting or interpretation of situations. In examining source willingness to report or interpret accurately, one must consider both the self-interest and writing style of the source.

The first question to ask is, "Does the *self-interest* of the source or 24 his sponsor prejudice the evidence?" If the source of the evidence could profit from a given reporting or interpretation of the situation, we have grounds for questioning the fairness of the source. This was the basis for Senator Frank Moss's rejection of an American Medical Association report on cigarette smoking. "The American Medical Association," he charged, "accepted $10 million for research from the tobacco industry and announced soon afterward that the evidence against smoking was inconclusive."[5] While bias does not automatically negate the validity of the reporting or interpretation, it causes us to doubt objectivity and to look to the other tests of the credibility of the evidence.

We must question not only the self-interest of the source but also 25 the interests of the organization for whom he works. A source may be consciously restrained from telling the whole truth by the organization with which he is associated if the whole truth is deemed in conflict with the interests of that organization. Such restraint is even more likely if the report of a source must be filtered by the organization.

In assessing source willingness to report or interpret events fairly 26

---

[5] *Congressional Record* 25 Jan. 1972, S467.

we must also question whether or not the *writing style* of the source has sacrificed accuracy. Frequently the necessity of writing in a style which is acceptable to given readers results in compromises with accurate reporting and interpreting of the situation. This test is especially important when we evaluate the reporting of sources who write for popular periodicals. The need to make the report simple and interesting to the general reading public frequently leads to overgeneralization of evidence.

The Test of Context

The test of context asks the question, "Is the evidence used in a 27 manner consistent with the *meaning and intent* of the source?" Inevitably, facts and expert opinions exist in a context broader than that used by the advocate. Since evidence gathering and use are selective processes, it is vital to examine the context of any piece of evidence to insure that the meaning or intent of the source is not misrepresented. We frequently hear public figures decry the fact that their words have been taken out of context.

The test of contextual accuracy is one of the more difficult tests of 28 evidence to apply because of its inherent subjectivity. The evidence selected for use by an advocate is almost always an incomplete representation of the total argument of the source. The test of context is used to determine whether or not the advocate has violated the intent of the source in his selection of evidence from that source.

An example of the application of the test of context occurred in the 29 final round of the 1966 National Debate Tournament. The affirmative was arguing that the gambling element of organized crime was careful to avoid engaging in interstate commerce in order to avoid falling within the jurisdiction of federal law-enforcement agencies. The negative, as part of its attempt to refute this argument, challenged the affirmative evidence as being out of context.

> . . . Now Mike came back with a *Wall Street Journal* article that said, "The more knowledgeable gamblers have tailored their operations so they don't become a part of interstate commerce." Mr. Denger, in his eagerness, forgot to read two words in that quotation. "The more knowledgeable gamblers have *attempted* to tailor their operations so they stay out of interstate commerce." I want proof that they have. I want proof that they don't use the telephone, that they don't use the mails, and that they don't use the interstate commerce in any way whatsoever.[6]

---

[6] *Twentieth National Debate Tournament* (West Point, NY: U.S. Military Academy, 1966) 61.

Tests of Statistical Evidence

When evidence takes the form of statistics, a variety of special tests   30
of the measurement procedures must be applied. These special tests
are necessitated by the symbolic nature of statistics. Since items are
collected and given a numerical symbol, the resultant statistic exists on
a higher level of abstraction than the examples it represents. Because
of this symbolic abstraction, statistics are subject to manipulation, and
the underlying truth can be lost or distorted. Therefore, in addition to
applying the general tests of evidence, four special tests should be
considered when evaluating statistical evidence.

Are the statistics based upon adequate sampling techniques? Many peo-   31
ple assume that the figures which they read regarding such matters as
the level of unemployment or the number of new housing starts
represent real numerical counts of those situations. Such statistics are
not, of course, true counts but are rather projections based upon
limited samples. The validity of such statistics, therefore, rests heavily
upon the reasonableness of the sampling techniques used in the
projections.

Unfortunately information concerning the size or representa-   32
tiveness of the sample used to arrive at a statistical statement is not
always provided. Yet, such information must be sought if intelligent
judgments concerning the credibility of statistical evidence are to be
made.

If a sample does not adequately represent all of the elements   33
within a class, the resultant statistic will be quite misleading. When
college debaters discussed the question of compulsory health insurance, many of them came upon a survey of medical financing in the
city of Baltimore. The findings of this study seemed to support the
negative claim that failure to receive adequate medical care was not
related to ability to pay. Because these findings contradicted most
affirmative studies, the better debaters sought to find out more about
the survey. When they examined the survey techniques underlying
the study, they discovered that all people earning less than the national median income had been excluded from the survey sample. An
unrepresentative sample made the survey invalid.

Even if the sample is representative, it must be large enough to   34
guarantee that chance deviation is not operating. The size required
will depend upon the homogeneity of the items being measured and
the representativeness of the items within the sample. It is important,
therefore, to seek explanation and justification of the sampling techniques when examining statistical evidence. The best sources of statistical evidence are sources which provide such explanations and
justifications.

Is the statistical unit an appropriate one? All statistics view phenom- 35
ena from a particular perspective, and the statistical unit selected
determines what that perspective is. The answer to so simple a question as "What is the average income of an American factory worker"
depends, in large part, upon the statistical unit used to measure
"average income." Three statistical measures of average are commonly used: the median, the mean, and the mode. The *median* is the
exact middle point; in the number series one through seven it would
be the number four. The *mean* is the true numerical average; it is
arrived at by adding all the numbers of a series together and dividing
by the number of items in the series. The *mode* is the point around
which the largest number of items cluster; it is the item which occurs
most often. There are no firm rules for determining which of these
measures is most appropriate. In general, if there are a few extreme
numbers in a series which will distort the mean, the median or mode
should be used.

The problem of selecting an appropriate statistical unit is by no 36
means limited to the measurement of averages. There are a variety of
potentially appropriate units which can be used to describe most
situations. If, for example, we wished to discuss poverty or unemployment or crime, we could express the extent of these problems in
absolute terms (1.2 million unemployed), or as percentages of the total
population (6 percent unemployment), or as ratios (one out of every
seventeen adult workers is unemployed), or as a percentage increase
or decrease from a previous period (a 25 percent decrease from last
year), or in a number of other ways.

The selection of the most appropriate statistical unit became the 37
basis of a critical issue in the 1960 presidential election campaign. John
F. Kennedy, the Democratic nominee, charged that under the Republican Eisenhower Administration the United States' rate of economic
growth had not kept pace with the Russians' rate of growth. Richard
Nixon, the Republican candidate, responded that percentage figures
were not a fair measure of growth. He claimed that the Soviet economy was a much poorer one so that even minor economic expansions
sharply increased its rate of growth while the United States' economic
base was so large that even large expansions affected the rate of
growth only slightly. Thus, the two candidates' perspectives and conclusions were affected by their choice of particular statistical measuring units.

In general, the more one knows about what it is he wants to 38
measure and the more one knows about what it is a particular statistical unit measures, the more likely he is to select an appropriate unit.

Do the statistics cover an appropriate time period? Many times statistics 39
are used to describe a situation over a given period of time. It then

becomes critical to know whether the time period selected is appropriate for the purposes at hand. In measuring concepts like economic growth, inflation, and employment, the selection of base years and the length of time measured can have a significant effect upon the impression created by the statistic. By selecting an exceptionally high or an exceptionally low base year, an advocate can sometimes suggest the existence of a trend favorable to his side. The cause of truth, however, dictates that base years be selected not on the basis of personal advantage but on the basis of representativeness and reasonableness.

Are comparisons between comparable units? The old adage that you 40
cannot compare apples and oranges has a significant application to statistical evidence. One of the most common uses of statistical evidence is the attempt to compare conditions. When statistical evidence is used in this comparative sense it is vital to determine whether or not the statistical units are comparable. Before attempting to compare the rates of juvenile crime in two cities, an advocate must determine if the two jurisdictions include the same group of people in the category of juvenile. Some cities define anyone under twenty-one years of age as a juvenile, while others include only those sixteen and under in the class of juveniles. Similarly, when one is comparing the economic growth of two countries it is important to determine whether or not these countries measure economic growth in the same way. If one country measures economic growth using only gross national product statistics while the other country adjusts gross national product statistics to allow for inflation, a comparison between such statistical units is meaningless.

QUESTIONS AND IDEAS FOR DISCUSSION

1.   Summarize what Ziegelmueller and Dause mean by "internal consistency," "external consistency," and "relevancy." Give original examples (they may be hypothetical) of data that would fail each of the tests.

2.   Why do the authors assert that what they identify as the tests of recency, source identification, source ability, source willingness, context, and statistical evidence apply only to "factual and expert opinion evidence" (paragraph 10)? Explain. What *is* "expert opinion evidence"?

3.   How recent are the examples Ziegelmueller and Dause give to support or illustrate their points? Comment.

4.   Does the authors' claim in paragraph 26 mean that we cannot rely on source material that is written in a lively and engaging style? Can we trust *Time* and *Newsweek*? Always? Sometimes? Never? Why?

5. Most of us have not studied the complex science of statistics. We cannot apply, to any thorough extent, tests of statistical data. What *can* we do to minimize the likelihood of misusing or being misled by statistics? How can we best judge whether or not to use any given set of statistics to support our own arguments?

Who Is That "Senior State Department Official" Anyway?

MICHAEL GARTNER

Michael Gartner describes himself as the editor of the *Daily Tribune* in Ames, Iowa, and president of NBC News in New York. The ordering is deliberate; Gartner is first and foremost a "print man" who was formerly an editor at the *Wall Street Journal*. In this essay, first published in Gartner's regular column for the *Wall Street Journal* in 1990, Gartner cautions readers about the examples and particularly the testimony written in newspaper and magazine articles. According to Gartner, "the press is becoming less believable"; he identifies three problems in particular. Two probably will be familiar to you; the third you may never have heard of before. Its name is Nexis.

As you read, decide your answers to these questions in light of Gartner's argument: First, should you use or avoid using newspapers as sources of evidence to support your own arguments? Second, are adjectives acceptable in argumentative writing or not? Third, is it ever appropriate to quote anonymously to support a claim?

Here's a game: 1

Pick a story in your favorite newspaper and read it. Now, go   2 through it and cross out all the descriptive adjectives. Read it again. Did you get a different impression? Now, take out all the facts and quotes and anecdotes attributed to anonymous sources. Do you get a still different meaning?

Now, call up the reporter and ask which "facts" and quotes and   3 anecdotes he got from first-hand interviewing or research. Ask, then, how much came from clips from the library or from something called Nexis, which is a data bank of news stories. Ask, finally, if the reporter then confirmed for himself the truth of those facts and quotes and anecdotes gathered from those secondary sources. Again, eliminate everything that wasn't personally confirmed. Do you get a still different meaning?

Now, reread the original story.   4

Do you believe it now?   5

At best, you'll have doubts.   6

The press is becoming less believable. That's a fact. The Times 7
Mirror Center on the People and the Press has surveyed Americans
about their views of the press. Since 1985, the number of persons who
rate their local newspaper as not believable has doubled—to 32% from
16%. For the media overall, the "not believable" number is 26%, up
from 17% in 1985. (But three national news-gathering organizations,
the Cable News Network, *USA Today* and (self-serving fact) NBC
News, have actually gone up in the "highly believable" rating.)

Theories abound as to why you believe less of what you read and 8
see these days. Some cite the press's preoccupation with scandals.
Others cite tabloid journalism, in print and on television. I blame
adjectives, anonymous sources and Nexis.

Let me tell you about Nexis. Nexis is a wonderful (caution, that's 9
an adjective; but it's okay, for this is a viewpoint column) service from
Mead Data Central Inc., that gathers every word in 650 publications.
Each day, 50,000 documents are added to it and its sister bank, a
legal-research service called Lexis. Each day, 76,000 reporters, lawyers
and others go to Nexis and Lexis for data.

Reporters often go to this data bank first as they embark on a story, 10
calling up everything others have written of late.

That's terrific, if reporters use that information as a guide. It 11
provides names of potential sources. It provides avenues to explore. It
provides anecdotes to check out.

But many reporters don't check the material out. They accept it as 12
fact. It comes from a computer, after all, and computers don't lie. So
they just repeat it, using the wonders of technology to gather, and
then spread, information that is sometimes inaccurate. And the more
it is spread, of course, the more believable it becomes to the next
reporter checking Nexis. If the same anecdote or "fact" has appeared
in a dozen or so newspapers, it must be right, right?

Not always. An example: 13

I am sometimes in the news. Several months ago, a reporter wrote 14
a story that said one of my colleagues and I were in a tiff and weren't
speaking to each other. A few days later, the same anecdote appeared
in another newspaper. By the end of the year, it had appeared in a
score or so of newspapers. The only problem is, it just wasn't true. I
asked my colleague if any reporter had ever called him to check it out.
Not a one, he said. Nor had any ever called me. Why should they? It's
right there in the data base, time and time again.

"If your mother says she loves you, check it out," is the rule young 15
reporters are taught by wise old city editors. But there seems to be a
modern-day exception: If the computer spits it out, print it. Nexis, a
great tool for reporters, is spreading falsehoods at space-age speed.

The Times Mirror survey found that 68% of the public believe that 16 news organizations "tend to favor one side" when presenting the news dealing with political and social issues. That's up 15 percentage points from the 53% who felt that way in 1985.

The survey implies that this is because the public "increasingly 17 sees the press as influenced by powerful people and organizations," a view held by 62% of the 1,507 people surveyed. That's a fact, but I am convinced that one reason readers and viewers—and certainly people who are in the news—view the press as unfair is because so much reporting today is based on anonymous sources, anonymous quotes, anonymous attacks.

Anonymous people lie. Anonymous people pass along unfound- 18 ed stories. Anonymous people launch trial balloons. Anonymous people are not held to account for their statements, their views, their accusations. Names add credibility.

Read almost any newspaper, and you'll find it riddled with 19 quotes, cheap shots, allegations and trial balloons from "a high government official," "a person knowledgeable about the matter," "an insider at the company," "a neighbor," "an industry observer," "an informed source" and the like. Those nameless and gutless people might be providing a titillating quote, but they're also undermining the credibility of the very newspapers that court them. Why do editors continue to allow this?

Not all editors do. *USA Today* will not allow anonymous sources or 20 anonymous quotes. *USA Today* is rising in believability. I think those facts are connected.

USA Today doesn't go in much for adjectives, either. It's a non- 21 judgmental newspaper, a newspaper without a leer, a jeer, a cheer, a sneer. By and large, it just gives the facts. No loaded verbs ("claim," "aver"), no prejudicial nouns ("crony"), few coloring adjectives ("likable," "arrogant"). *USA Today*, as I said, is rising in believability. (For the record, the *Wall Street Journal* remains the most believable medium, according to the Times Mirror survey; its rating was unchanged from 1985.)

A free press is a wonderful thing, something to fight for, to de- 22 fend, to cherish. It is the cornerstone of democracy. And nowhere do we have a freer press than in America.

But a free press that isn't believable isn't worth a lot, either to 23 readers and viewers or to champions of democracy. Credibility is the most important asset of any newspaper or broadcast station. If we lose it, it's our own fault—the fault of those of us who are editors and news directors.

The Times Mirror study makes clear that many of us are losing it. 24 And it makes it clear, to me, that we should start deleting those adjectives and killing those anonymous sources. And if your mother says she loves you, we should still check it out—even if she sends the message modem to modem.

QUESTIONS AND IDEAS FOR DISCUSSION

1. Gartner's essay details the importance of which of Ziegelmueller and Dause's "tests" in the previous essay? Are the two essays in total agreement?

2. "Anonymous people launch trial balloons" (paragraph 18). What does Gartner mean by this statement? Look for an example in your local or campus newspaper, and share it with your writing class.

3. Gartner implies that there is an inherent problem with adjectives (2). What could that problem be? Using an article from your local newspaper, go through the process Gartner describes in paragraph 2. Discuss your findings. (Attach the newspaper clipping to your written comments.)

4. Why does Gartner argue that Nexis, although "wonderful" (9), is at the same time dangerous? Does he persuade you? Comment.

5. Does the biographical information about Michael Gartner, preceding the essay, affect your reception of his argument in any way? Consider your answer carefully.

THE STRATEGY AT WORK:
ARGUMENTS ABOUT COLLEGE EDUCATION

Subjects familiar to us appear to be easy subjects of argument: We can evaluate these arguments from our own knowledge and experience, and we can support them with firsthand information and personal examples. But the same familiarity that lends us authority can also blind us to other viewpoints, to experiences unlike our own, to evidence new to us. The essays in this section all concern college education—and nearly all argue about some problem with either colleges or the students attending them. Just what is wrong varies from essay to essay, as do proposed solutions.

Caroline Bird thinks that perhaps you should not be in college at all; Vermont Royster fears you are something of a *tabula rasa;* Allan Bloom argues that you are a hopeless relativist; William G. Perry, Jr., defends your use of "bull" in essay writing; Henry Rosovsky has high hopes for you, but extremely high standards as well. The students these arguments describe may not be much like you, but they may resemble students you know. And the problems these authors perceive may not be problems at your college, but they may well be problems at another.

As you read the following essays, compare the authors' viewpoints to your own experience of higher education, but do not reject out of hand arguments not borne out in your own experience or in your own college or university. Instead, pay careful attention to the way these writers use evidence, particularly examples and anecdotes, to hold reader interest and gain reader assent. A few good illustrations may not be logically compelling, but they can be wonderfully persuasive.

The Case Against College

CAROLINE BIRD

Caroline Bird worked for many years in public relations. She is the author of many books and essays on business issues, particularly those involving women. Her books include *Born Female* (1970), *Everything a Woman Needs to Know to Get Paid What She's Worth* (1972), and *The Two-Paycheck Marriage* (1979). The following often-anthologized argument is treated at greater length in another of Bird's books written for a general audience, *The Case Against College* (1975). Bird points out that colleges and universities are big businesses. Whether they accomplish much, and at what cost, troubles Bird, writing nearly twenty years ago. The same questions might well trouble you today.

The case *for* college has been accepted without question for more than a generation. All high school graduates ought to go, says Conventional Wisdom and statistical evidence, because college will help them earn more money, become "better" people, and learn to be more responsible citizens than those who don't go.

But college has never been able to work its magic for everyone. And now that close to half our high school graduates are attending, those who don't fit the pattern are becoming more numerous, and more obvious. College graduates are selling shoes and driving taxis; college students sabotage each other's experiments and forge letters of recommendation in the intense competition for admission to graduate school. Others find no stimulation in their studies, and drop out—often encouraged by college administrators.

Some observers say the fault is with the young people themselves—they are spoiled, stoned, overindulged, and expecting too much. But that's mass character assassination, and doesn't explain all campus unhappiness. Others blame the state of the world, and they are partly right. We've been told that young people have to go to college because our economy can't absorb an army of untrained eighteen-year-olds. But disillusioned graduates are learning that it can no longer absorb an army of trained twenty-two-year-olds, either. . . .

The ultimate defense of college has always been that while it may 4 not teach you anything vocationally useful, it will somehow make you a better person, able to do anything better, and those who make it through the process are initiated into the "fellowship of educated men and women." In a study intended to probe what graduates seven years out of college thought their colleges should have done for them, the Carnegie Commission found that most alumni expected the "development of my abilities to think and express myself." But if such respected educational psychologists as Bruner and Piaget are right, specific learning skills have to be acquired very early in life, perhaps even before formal schooling begins.

So, when pressed, liberal-arts defenders speak instead about 5 something more encompassing, and more elusive. "College changed me inside," one graduate told us fervently. The authors of a Carnegie Commission report, who obviously struggled for a definition, concluded that one of the common threads in the perceptions of a liberal education is that it provides "an integrated view of the world which can serve as an inner guide." More simply, alumni say that college should have "helped me to formulate the values and goals of my life."

In theory, a student is taught to develop these values and goals 6 himself, but in practice, it doesn't work quite that way. All but the wayward and the saintly take their sense of the good, the true, and the beautiful from the people around them. When we speak of students acquiring "values" in college, we often mean that they will acquire the values—and sometimes that means only the tastes—of their professors. The values of professors may be "higher" than many students will encounter elsewhere, but they may not be relevant to situations in which students find themselves in college and later.

Of all the forms in which ideas are disseminated, the college 7 professor lecturing a class is the slowest and most expensive. You don't have to go to college to read the great books or learn about the great ideas of Western Man. Today you can find them everywhere—in paperbacks, in the public libraries, in museums, in public lectures, in adult-education courses, in abridged, summarized, or adapted form in magazines, films, and television. The problem is no longer one of access to broadening ideas; the problem is the other way around: how to choose among the many courses of action proposed to us, how to edit the stimulations that pour into our eyes and ears every waking hour. A college experience that piles option on option and stimulation on stimulation merely adds to the contemporary nightmare.

What students and graduates say that they did learn on campus 8 comes under the heading of personal, rather than intellectual, development. Again and again I was told that the real value of college is learning to get along with others, to practice social skills, to "sort out my head," and these have nothing to do with curriculum.

For whatever impact the academic experience used to have on 9 college students, the sheer size of many undergraduate classes . . . dilutes faculty-student dialogue, and, more often than not, they are taught by teachers who were hired when colleges were faced with a shortage of qualified instructors, during their years of expansion and when the big rise in academic pay attracted the mediocre and the less than dedicated.

On the social side, colleges are withdrawing from responsibility 10 for feeding, housing, policing, and protecting students at a time when the environment of college may be the most important service it could render. College officials are reluctant to "intervene" in the personal lives of the students. They no longer expect to take over from parents, but often insist that students—who have, most often, never lived away from home before—take full adult responsibility for their plans, achievements, and behavior.

Most college students do not live in the plush, comfortable 11 country-clublike surroundings their parents envisage, or, in some cases, remember. Open dorms, particularly when they are coeducational, are noisy, usually overcrowded, and often messy. Some students desert the institutional "zoos" (their own word for dorms) and move into run-down, overpriced apartments. Bulletin boards in student centers are littered with notices of apartments to share and the drift of conversation suggests that a lot of money is dissipated in scrounging for food and shelter.

Taxpayers now provide more than half of the astronomical sums 12 that are spent on higher education. But less than half of today's high school graduates go on, raising a new question of equity: Is it fair to make all the taxpayers pay for the minority who actually go to college? We decided long ago that it is fair for childless adults to pay school taxes because everyone, parents and nonparents alike, profits by a literate population. Does the same reasoning hold true for state-supported higher education? There is no conclusive evidence on either side.

Young people cannot be expected to go to college for the general 13 good of mankind. They may be more altruistic than their elders, but no great numbers are going to spend four years at hard intellectual labor, let alone tens of thousands of family dollars, for "the advancement of human capability in society at large," one of the many purposes invoked by the Carnegie Commission report. Nor do any considerable number of them want to go to college to beat the Russians to Jupiter, improve the national defense, increase the Gross National Product, lower the crime rate, improve automobile safety, or create a market for the arts—all of which have been suggested at one time or other as benefits taxpayers get for supporting higher education.

One sociologist said that you don't have to have a reason for 14 going to college because it's an institution. His definition of an institution is something everyone subscribes to without question. The burden of proof is not on why you should go to college, but why anyone thinks there might be a reason for not going. The implication—and some educators express it quite frankly—is that an eighteen-year-old high school graduate is still too young and confused to know what he wants to do, let alone what is good for him.

Mother knows best, in other words.   15

It had always been comfortable for students to believe that au- 16 thorities, like Mother, or outside specialists, like educators, could determine what was best for them. However, specialists and authorities no longer enjoy the credibility former generations accorded them. Patients talk back to doctors and are not struck suddenly dead. Clients question the lawyer's bills and sometimes get them reduced. It is no longer self-evident that all adolescents must study a fixed curriculum that was constructed at a time when all educated men could agree on precisely what it was that made them educated.

The same with college. If high school graduates don't want to 17 continue their education, or don't want to continue it right away, they may perceive more clearly than their elders that college is not for them.

College is an ideal place for those young adults who love learning 18 for its own sake, who would rather read than eat, and who like nothing better than writing research papers. But they are a minority, even at the prestigious colleges, which recruit and attract the intellectually oriented.

The rest of our high school graduates need to look at college more 19 closely and critically, to examine it as a consumer product, and decide if the cost in dollars, in time, in continued dependency, and in future returns, is worth the very large investment each student—and his family—must make.

QUESTIONS AND IDEAS FOR DISCUSSION

1. According to Bird's argument, why do people go to college? According to your own experience and observations, why do people go to college?

2.   What examples and other evidence does Caroline Bird cite to support her claims? Evaluate her use of evidence according to the standards described by Munson and Ziegelmueller and Dause in the readings that begin this chapter.

3.   Bird argues that college disseminates ideas inefficiently. Offer additional illustrations to those she gives, or offer refuting examples.

4.   Is Bird guilty of using statistics inconsistently in paragraphs 2 ("close to half our high school graduates are attending") and 12 ("less than half of today's high school graduates go on") in order to support different points? Comment.

5.   Caroline Bird asserts, "College is an ideal place for those young adults who love learning for its own sake, who would rather read than eat, and who like nothing better than writing research papers" (paragraph 18). Describe her tone here: Is it serious, ironic, or something else? And if Bird has not described you in that sentence, how might you accomplish what you need or want other than by attending college?

6.   In what specific and feasible ways might the college or university you attend be improved? Consider first toward what ends improvements need to be directed. And, of course, give examples!

The Death of Socrates

VERMONT ROYSTER

Vermont Royster worked for the *Wall Street Journal* for nearly all the years between 1936 and 1971, when he retired as its editor. He has continued to write commentary for the *Journal*, receiving his second Pulitzer Prize in 1984 (the first was awarded in 1953). He has also written several books, including *A Pride of Prejudices* (1968) and *My Own, My Country's Time: A Journalist's Journey* (1983). The following essay first appeared in the *Wall Street Journal* in 1984. In it, Royster argues that education, including college education, no longer provides students with a body of common knowledge that enables them to "share in the common Western heritage." Is he right? As you read, note whether or not *you* recognize the events and names Royster cites—and consider whether it matters if you do not.

There was a time when a writer and his readers, even a writer for   1
the daily journalistic audience, had a common plane of reference. If it
was the writer's conceit to drop in a literary allusion, he could feel

some confidence it would not go astray. If he called upon some historical event to illuminate a present argument, he could expect his readers to have at least a general acquaintance with the example.

That was because writer and reader shared a common cultural 2 heritage. Not all the readers of large-circulation periodicals, to be sure, were learned in either history or literature. But even in the little one-room schoolhouses and their city counterparts, if for some reason those classrooms encompassed the whole of many readers' education, the pupils had at least been exposed to the same poetry, novels, drama, or essays. They also shared the same outlines of history, ancient and modern.

This has been less true of late years. The writer today who trusts to 3 some echo phrase from Shakespeare or Dickens—or even the Bible— to make clear his point leans upon a slender reed. He'd best take care to make his point without assuming such common ground between writer and audience.

I've been aware of the change for some time. But only recently was 4 it driven home to me the width of the cultural gap even among those who share the experience of a college education.

I was asked to lead a classroom discussion at one of our major 5 universities on the general topic "The Citizen and Society," examining among other things the question of what obligations, if any, a citizen may owe to the society of which he or she is a part. I thought I might begin an outline of different views by recalling those of Socrates.

My intent was to ask the students, some 40 juniors and seniors in 6 the liberal arts curriculum, their opinion of Socrates' refusal to escape his death sentence by explaining to his friends that while he believed the law which condemned him unjust he had lived his whole life under the protection of the laws of Athens and would not then defy its laws. That, I thought, should spark a lively discussion.

So I began by asking how many knew the story of Socrates. Not a 7 single hand went up. Not one among those advanced university undergraduates.

When I recovered from that shock, I asked how many had *heard* of 8 Socrates. That question brought a dozen or so affirmative answers.

Now I thought myself no innocent about modern education. I 9 didn't expect to find many college students who had read Plato's account (in translation, of course) of that dramatic night in Athens two millennia ago. I did expect, though, that most would know the simple outlines of that story.

I had thought that, simply as a story, it would be as much a part of 10 our educational baggage as, say, the story of Robin Hood, David Copperfield, Hamlet, Lancelot, Nathan Hale, Huck Finn, Christopher Columbus, Hiawatha, or Little Women.

And if I don't expect the average college student today to know 11
much about the thoughts of either Plato or Aristotle—or Emerson or
Burke or Bacon or, for that matter, Jefferson or John Stuart Mill—I did
suppose that somewhere along their educational journey they would
have at least brushed against them.

The more innocent, I! After some years now in a belated career on 12
a university faculty I should have been past surprise. What seems to
have happened in the educational process of late years is that the
umbilical cord to our cultural past has come unraveled if not severed.
It's not so much that Johnny can't read as that he isn't asked to read
very much.

It's startling now to look back on what grammar-school students 13
were once expected to read. At hand is a tattered copy of McGuffey's
Sixth Reader which crossed my childhood path and in a former day was
ubiquitous in the schoolroom. It would leave a modern teacher aghast.
There, for the edification of schoolchildren, are excerpts from Shakespeare, Dryden, Samuel Johnson, Ruskin, Byron, Milton, Dickens,
Disraeli, Jefferson, Daniel Webster, the elder Pitt, Joseph Addison,
and even Sir Humphrey Davy and William Blackstone. McGuffey's
other readers are equally rich.

Moreover, in these excerpts there is no truck with a "simplified 14
vocabulary," a not unknown practice in today's grammar-school
teaching. McGuffey treated children as unshaped but intelligent human beings. They may have gotten only dollops of history, philosophy, or literature, but they got their Samuel Johnson pure. They were
spared the insult of being talked down to.

As a result, those who never went on to college nonetheless 15
shared in the common Western heritage. Those who did had a foundation on which later teachers could build. There was no need to
give college freshmen remedial courses in reading the English language.

Indeed, in some respects a high-school graduate of those times 16
may have had a wider acquaintance with the treasures of his language
than many a college student today.

Of course, if McGuffey were to compile his readers now he would 17
alter some selections. Each generation needs to draw differently from
the reservoir of our cultural heritage. My regret is to see so much of it
left out of sight, out of mind.

I mean no implication that today's college students are less intelli- 18
gent. As a group they are impressive young people. After I had told
the story of that night in Athens in 399 B.C. there was a lively discussion prompted by this man who had so far survived 2,000 years.

I just wish I could have put aside the wonder whether the occasion 19
was at last a funeral service.

QUESTIONS AND IDEAS FOR DISCUSSION

1. Do you find Royster's examples convincing—or if not logically convincing, emotionally persuasive? Other than examples and anecdotes, does Royster offer evidence to support his claims? If so, evaluate his evidence. If not, suggest kinds of evidence that you would have found impressive.

2. From the claims argued in this essay, characterize Royster's basic assumptions about education. Do you share Royster's beliefs? Do students bring to college any kinds of knowledge and experience that Royster discounts or fails to consider? If so, provide specific examples.

3. Without looking up the names in a reference book, briefly identify the following (all mentioned by Royster):

Socrates	Nathan Hale	Plato
Robin Hood	Huck Finn	Aristotle
David Copperfield	Christopher Columbus	Burke
Hamlet	Hiawatha	Bacon
Lancelot	Little Women	John Stuart Mill

Compare your identifications with those of your classmates. Does your class have a shared body of knowledge (at least as far as this list goes)? If not, how does that awareness constrain you as you write arguments for your class? Discuss.

4. How many of the authors mentioned in paragraph 13 have you read? Royster believes that if you have read few or none of them, you have been shortchanged educationally. Do you agree? If not, why not? If so, what do you propose to do about it?

5. Explain the last sentence of Royster's essay. How effectively does it conclude his argument?

The Education of Openness
ALLAN BLOOM

Allan Bloom teaches at the University of Chicago, where he codirects the John M. Olin Center for Inquiry into the Theory and Practice of Democracy. Translator and editor of Plato's *Republic* and Rousseau's *Emile*, and author of many scholarly books and essays, he wrote in 1987 *The Closing of the American Mind*. The following essay is the introduction to that book, which is directed to a highly educated audience familiar with such subjects as philosophy and classical music. Surprisingly, given that rhetorical context, *The Closing of the American Mind* became a best seller. Its core argument, summarized in this essay, evoked passionate responses. Newspaper columnists and television journalists argued for and against Bloom's claims; academic journals devoted entire issues to the debate. Decide for yourself why Bloom's argument inspired fierce argument and frequent condemnation from his colleagues. And decide for yourself if he is right or wrong, in part or in whole.

There is one thing a professor can be absolutely certain of: almost 1 every student entering the university believes, or says he believes, that truth is relative. If this belief is put to the test, one can count on the students' reaction: they will be uncomprehending. That anyone should regard the proposition as not self-evident astonishes them, as though he were calling into question 2 + 2 = 4. These are things you don't think about. The students' backgrounds are as various as America can provide. Some are religious, some atheists; some are to the Left, some to the Right; some intend to be scientists, some humanists or professionals or businessmen; some are poor, some rich. They are unified only in their relativism and in their allegiance to equality. And the two are related in a moral intention. The relativity of truth is not a theoretical insight but a moral postulate, the condition of a free society, or so they see it. They have all been equipped with this framework early on, and it is the modern replacement for the inalienable natural rights that used to be the traditional American grounds for a free society. That it is a moral issue for students is revealed by the character of their response when challenged—a combination of disbelief and indignation: "Are you an absolutist?," the only alternative they know, uttered in the same tone as "Are you a monarchist?" or "Do you really believe in witches?" This latter leads into the indignation, for someone who believes in witches might well be a witchhunter or a Salem judge. The danger they have been taught to fear from absolutism is not error but intolerance. Relativism is necessary to openness; and this is the virtue, the only virtue, which all primary education for more than fifty years has dedicated itself to inculcating. Openness—and the relativism that makes it the only plausible stance in the face of various claims to truth and various ways of life and kinds of human beings—is the great insight of our times. The true believer is the real danger. The study of history and of culture teaches that all the world was mad in the past; men always thought they were right, and that led to wars, persecutions, slavery, xenophobia, racism, and chauvinism. The point is not to correct the mistakes and really be right; rather it is not to think you are right at all.

The students, of course, cannot defend their opinion. It is some- 2 thing with which they have been indoctrinated. The best they can do is point out all the opinions and cultures there are and have been. What right, they ask, do I or anyone else have to say one is better than the others? If I pose the routine questions designed to confute them and make them think, such as, "If you had been a British administrator in India, would you have let the natives under your governance burn the widow at the funeral of a man who had died?," they either remain silent or reply that the British should never have been there in the first place. It is not that they know very much about other nations, or about their own. The purpose of their education is not to make them scholars but to provide them with a moral virtue—openness.

Every educational system has a moral goal that it tries to attain and   3 that informs its curriculum. It wants to produce a certain kind of human being. This intention is more or less explicit, more or less a result of reflection; but even the neutral subjects, like reading and writing and arithmetic, take their place in a vision of the educated person. In some nations the goal was the pious person, in others the warlike, in others the industrious. Always important is the political regime, which needs citizens who are in accord with its fundamental principle. Aristocracies want gentlemen, oligarchies men who respect and pursue money, and democracies lovers of equality. Democratic education, whether it admits it or not, wants and needs to produce men and women who have the tastes, knowledge, and character supportive of a democratic regime. Over the history of our republic, there have obviously been changes of opinion as to what kind of man is best for our regime. We began with the model of the rational and industrious man, who was honest, respected the laws, and was dedicated to the family (his own family—what has in its decay been dubbed the nuclear family). Above all he was to know the rights doctrine; the Constitution, which embodied it; and American history, which presented and celebrated the founding of a nation "conceived in liberty and dedicated to the proposition that all men are created equal." A powerful attachment to the letter and the spirit of the Declaration of Independence gently conveyed, appealing to each man's reason, was the goal of the education of democratic man. This called for something very different from the kinds of attachment required for traditional communities where myth and passion as well as severe discipline, authority, and the extended family produced an instinctive, unqualified, even fanatic patriotism, unlike the reflected, rational, calm, even self-interested loyalty—not so much to the country but to the form of government and its rational principles—required in the United States. This was an entirely new experiment in politics, and with it came a new education. This education has evolved in the last half-century from the education of democratic man to the education of the democratic personality.

The palpable difference between these two can easily be found in 4
the changed understanding of what it means to be an American. The
old view was that, by recognizing and accepting man's natural rights,
men found a fundamental basis of unity and sameness. Class, race,
religion, national origin or culture all disappear or become dim when
bathed in the light of natural rights, which give men common interests
and make them truly brothers. The immigrant had to put behind him
the claims of the Old World in favor of a new and easily acquired
education. This did not necessarily mean abandoning old daily habits
or religions, but it did mean subordinating them to new principles.
There was a tendency, if not a necessity, to homogenize nature itself.

The recent education of openness has rejected all that. It pays no 5
attention to natural rights or the historical origins of our regime, which
are now thought to have been essentially flawed and regressive. It is
progressive and forward-looking. It does not demand fundamental
agreement or the abandonment of old or new beliefs in favor of the
natural ones. It is open to all kinds of men, all kinds of life-styles, all
ideologies. There is no enemy other than the man who is not open to
everything. But when there are no shared goals or vision of the public
good, is the social contract any longer possible? . . .

The upshot of all this for the education of young Americans is that 6
they know much less about American history and those who were
held to be its heroes. This was one of the few things that they used to
come to college with that had something to do with their lives. Nothing has taken its place except a smattering of facts learned about other
nations or cultures and a few social science formulas. None of this
means much, partly because little attention has been paid to what is
required in order truly to convey the spirit of other places and other
times to young people, or for that matter to anyone, partly because the
students see no relevance in any of it to the lives they are going to lead
or to their prevailing passions. It is the rarest of occurrences to find a
youngster who has been infused by this education with a longing to
know all about China or the Romans or the Jews.

All to the contrary. There is an indifference to such things, for 7
relativism has extinguished the real motive of education, the search for
a good life. Young Americans have less and less knowledge of and
interest in foreign places. In the past there were many students who
actually knew something about and loved England, France, Germany,
or Italy, for they dreamed of living there or thought their lives would
be made more interesting by assimilating their languages and litera-
tures. Such students have almost disappeared, replaced at most by
students who are interested in the political problems of Third World
countries and in helping them to modernize, with due respect to their
old cultures, of course. This is not learning from others but condescen-
sion and a disguised form of a new imperialism. It is the Peace Corps

mentality, which is not a spur to learning but to a secularized version of doing good works.

Actually openness results in American conformism—out there in 8 the rest of the world is a drab diversity that teaches only that values are relative, whereas here we can create all the life-styles we want. Our openness means we do not need others. Thus what is advertised as a great opening is a great closing. No longer is there a hope that there are great wise men in other places and times who can reveal the truth about life—except for the few remaining young people who look for a quick fix from a guru. Gone is the real historical sense of a Machiavelli who wrested a few hours from each busy day in which "to don regal and courtly garments, enter the courts of the ancients and speak with them."

None of this concerns those who promote the new curriculum. 9 The point is to propagandize acceptance of different ways, and indifference to their real content is as good a means as any. It was not necessarily the best of times in America when Catholics and Protestants were suspicious of and hated one another; but at least they were taking their beliefs seriously, and the more or less satisfactory accommodations they worked out were not simply the result of apathy about the state of their souls. Practically all that young Americans have today is an insubstantial awareness that there are many cultures, accompanied by a saccharine moral drawn from that awareness: We should all get along. Why fight? In 1980, during the crisis with Iran, the mother of one of the hostages expressed our current educational principles very well. She went to Iran to beg for her son's release, against the express wishes of the government of her country, the very week a rescue of the hostages was attempted. She justified her conduct by explaining that a mother has a right to try to save her son and also to learn a new culture. These are two basic rights, and her trip enabled her to kill two birds with one stone. . . .

One of the techniques of opening young people up is to require a 10 college course in a non-Western culture. Although many of the persons teaching such courses are real scholars and lovers of the areas they study, in every case I have seen this requirement—when there are so many other things that can and should be learned but are not required, when philosophy and religion are no longer required—has a demagogic intention. The point is to force students to recognize that there are other ways of thinking and that Western ways are not better. It is again not the content that counts but the lesson to be drawn. Such requirements are part of the effort to establish a world community and train its member—the person devoid of prejudice. But if the students were really to learn something of the minds of any of these non-Western cultures—which they do not—they would find that each and every one of these cultures is ethnocentric. All of them think their way is the best way, and all others are inferior. Herodotus tells us that the Persians thought that they were the best, that those nations bordering on them were next best, that those nations bordering on the nations bordering on them were third best, and so on, their worth declining as the concentric circles were farther from the Persian center. This is the very definition of ethnocentrism. Something like this is as ubiquitous as the prohibition against incest between mother and son. . . .

It is important to emphasize that the lesson the students are 11 drawing from their studies is simply untrue. History and the study of cultures do not teach or prove that values or cultures are relative. All to the contrary, that is a philosophical premise that we now bring to our study of them. This premise is unproven and dogmatically asserted for what are largely political reasons. History and culture are interpreted in the light of it, and then are said to prove the premise. Yet the fact that there have been different opinions about good and bad in different times and places in no way proves that none is true or superior to others. To say that it does so prove is as absurd as to say that the diversity of points of view expressed in a college bull session proves there is no truth. On the face of it, the difference of opinion would seem to raise the question as to which is true or right rather than to banish it. The natural reaction is to try to resolve the difference, to examine the claims and reasons for each opinion.

Only the unhistorical and inhuman belief that opinions are held 12 for no reason would prevent the undertaking of such an exciting activity. Men and nations always think they have reasons, and it could be understood to be historians' and social scientists' most important responsibility to make explicit and test those reasons. It was always known that there were many and conflicting opinions about the good, and nations embodying each of them. Herodotus was at least as aware as we are of the rich diversity of cultures. But he took that observation to be an invitation to investigate all of them to see what was good and bad about each and find out what he could learn about good and bad from them. Modern relativists take that same observation as proof that such investigation is impossible and that we must be respectful of them all. Thus students, and the rest of us, are deprived of the primary excitement derived from the discovery of diversity, the impulse of Odysseus, who, according to Dante, traveled the world to see the virtues and vices of men. History and anthropology cannot provide the answers, but they can provide the material on which judgment can work. . . .

Thus there are two kinds of openness, the openness of indif- 13 ference—promoted with the twin purposes of humbling our intellectual pride and letting us be whatever we want to be, just as long as we don't want to be knowers—and the openness that invites us to the quest for knowledge and certitude, for which history and the various cultures provide a brilliant array of examples for examination. This second kind of openness encourages the desire that animates and makes interesting every serious student—"I want to know what is good for me, what will make me happy"—while the former stunts that desire.

Openness, as currently conceived, is a way of making surrender to   14 whatever is most powerful, or worship of vulgar success, look principled. It is historicism's ruse to remove all resistance to history, which in our day means public opinion, a day when public opinion already rules. How often I have heard the abandonment of requirements to learn languages or philosophy or science lauded as a progress of openness. Here is where the two kinds of openness clash. To be open to knowing, there are certain kinds of things one must know which most people don't want to bother to learn and which appear boring and irrelevant. Even the life of reason is often unappealing; and useless knowledge, i.e., knowledge that is not obviously useful for a career, has no place in the student's vision of the curriculum. So the university that stands intransigently for humane learning must necessarily look closed and rigid. If openness means to "go with the flow," it is necessarily an accommodation to the present. That present is so closed to doubt about so many things impeding the progress of its principles that unqualified openness to it would mean forgetting the despised alternatives to it, knowledge of which makes us aware of what is doubtful in it. True openness means closedness to all the charms that make us comfortable with the present.

When I was a young teacher at Cornell, I once had a debate about   15 education with a professor of psychology. He said that it was his function to get rid of prejudices in his students. He knocked them down like tenpins. I began to wonder what he replaced those prejudices with. He did not seem to have much of an idea of what the opposite of a prejudice might be. He reminded me of the little boy who gravely informed me when I was four that there is no Santa Claus, who wanted me to bathe in the brilliant light of truth. Did this professor know what those prejudices meant for the students and what effect being deprived of them would have? Did he believe that there are truths that could guide their lives as did their prejudices? Had he considered how to give students the love of the truth necessary to seek unprejudiced beliefs, or would he render them passive, disconsolate, indifferent, and subject to authorities like himself, or the best of contemporary thought? My informant about Santa Claus was just showing off, proving his superiority to me. He had not created the Santa Claus that had to be there in order to be refuted. Think of all we learn about the world from men's belief in Santa Clauses, and all that we learn about the soul from those who believe in them. By contrast, merely methodological excision from the soul of the imagination that projects Gods and heroes onto the wall of the cave does not promote knowledge of the soul; it only lobotomizes it, cripples its powers.

I found myself responding to the professor of psychology that I 16 personally tried to teach my students prejudices, since nowadays—with the general success of his method—they had learned to doubt beliefs even before they believed in anything. Without people like me, he would be out of business. Descartes had a whole wonderful world of old beliefs, of prescientific experience and articulations of the order of things, beliefs firmly and even fanatically held, before he even began his systematic and radical doubt. One has to have the experience of really believing before one can have the thrill of liberation. So I proposed a division of labor in which I would help to grow the flowers in the field and he could mow them down.

Prejudices, strong prejudices, are visions about the way things 17 are. They are divinations of the order of the whole of things, and hence the road to a knowledge of that whole is by way of erroneous opinions about it. Error is indeed our enemy, but it alone points to the truth and therefore deserves our respectful treatment. The mind that has no prejudices at the outset is empty. It can only have been constituted by a method that is unaware of how difficult it is to recognize that a prejudice is a prejudice. Only Socrates knew, after a lifetime of unceasing labor, that he was ignorant. Now every high-school student knows that. How did it become so easy? What accounts for our amazing progress? Could it be that our experience has been so impoverished by our various methods, of which openness is only the latest, that there is nothing substantial enough left there to resist criticism, and we therefore have no world left of which to be really ignorant? Have we so simplified the soul that it is no longer difficult to explain? To an eye of dogmatic skepticism, nature herself, in all her lush profusion of expressions, might appear to be a prejudice. In her place we put a gray network of critical concepts, which were invented to interpret nature's phenomena but which strangled them and therewith destroyed their own *raison d'être*. Perhaps it is our first task to resuscitate those phenomena so that we may again have a world to which we can put our questions and be able to philosophize. This seems to me to be our educational challenge.

QUESTIONS AND IDEAS FOR DISCUSSION

1. In this essay, does Bloom use examples and analogies more often as *support* for his conclusions or as *illustrations* for his claims? How effective are his examples for a reading audience of which you might be a typical member? Explain.

2. In paragraph 9, Bloom uses the example of a woman who went to Iran in 1980 to plead for her hostage son's release. In paragraph 15, he uses the example of the little boy who first told Bloom that there is no Santa Claus. How, and how successfully, do these particular examples illustrate the topics of their respective paragraphs? Characterize an audience that might find these illustrations effective and persuasive. Then describe an audience that might find either example distasteful or difficult to understand.

3. Bloom deplores one kind of "openness" and applauds another. To what extent does he use evidence to clarify the distinctions he draws?

4. Paraphrase Bloom's last paragraph. Were you to argue the same point, what examples and other evidence might you cite to support the value of "prejudices"?

Examsmanship and the Liberal Arts
WILLIAM G. PERRY, JR.

William G. Perry, Jr., is Professor Emeritus of Education at Harvard University. This essay, though dated in its specific details and addressed to an audience of college professors (it was first published in 1963 in a collection of essays for teachers), typically elicits enthusiastic discussion from students. Why? Perhaps the reason is that Perry's argument goes straight to the heart of one prime source of student frustration with higher education: What value has a system in which a conscientious, hard-working student might earn only a mediocre grade on an essay exam, while another, with virtually no study or preparation, makes an *A*? Perry's answer may well surprise you.

"But sir, I don't think I really deserve it, it was mostly bull, really." 1 This disclaimer from a student whose examination we have awarded a straight "A" is wondrously depressing. Alfred North Whitehead invented its only possible rejoinder: "Yes sir, what you wrote is nonsense, utter nonsense. But ah! Sir! It's the right *kind* of nonsense!"

Bull, in this university,[1] is customarily a source of laughter, or a 2 problem in ethics. I shall step a little out of fashion to use the subject as a take-off point for a study in comparative epistemology. The phe-

---

[1] Harvard University. [Ed.]

nomenon of bull, in all the honor and opprobrium with which it is regarded by students and faculty, says something, I think, about our theories of knowledge. So too, the grades which we assign on examinations communicate to students what these theories may be.

We do not have to be out-and-out logical-positivists to suppose 3 that we have something to learn about "what we think knowledge is" by having a good look at "what we do when we go about measuring it." We know the straight "A" examination when we see it, of course, and we have reason to hope that the student will understand why his work receives our recognition. He doesn't always. And those who receive lesser honor? Perhaps an understanding of certain anomalies in our customs of grading good bull will explain the students' confusion.

I must beg patience, then, both of the reader's humor and of his 4 morals. Not that I ask him to suspend his sense of humor but that I shall ask him to go beyond it. In a great university the picture of a bright student attempting to outwit his professor while his professor takes pride in not being outwitted is certainly ridiculous. I shall report just such a scene, for its implications bear upon my point. Its comedy need not present a serious obstacle to thought.

As for the ethics of bull, I must ask for a suspension of judgment. 5 I wish that students could suspend theirs. Unlike humor, moral commitment is hard to think beyond. Too early a moral judgment is precisely what stands between many able students and a liberal education. The stunning realization that the Harvard Faculty will often accept, as evidence of knowledge, the cerebrations of a student who has little data at his disposal, confronts every student with an ethical dilemma. For some it forms an academic focus for what used to be thought of as "adolescent disillusion." It is irrelevant that rumor inflates the phenomenon to mythical proportions. The students know that beneath the myth there remains a solid and haunting reality. The moral "bind" consequent on this awareness appears most poignantly in serious students who are reluctant to concede the competitive advantage to the bullster and who yet feel a deep personal shame when, having succumbed to "temptation," they themselves receive a high grade for work they consider "dishonest."

I have spent many hours with students caught in this unwelcome 6 bitterness. These hours lend an urgency to my theme. I have found that students have been able to come to terms with the ethical problem, to the extent that it is real, only after a refined study of the true nature of bull and its relation to "knowledge." I shall submit grounds for my suspicion that we can be found guilty of sharing the students' confusion of moral and epistemological issues.

I

I present as my "premise," then, an amoral *fabliau*. Its hero-villain 7 is the Abominable Mr. Metzger '47. Since I celebrate his virtuosity, I regret giving him a pseudonym, but the peculiar style of his bravado requires me to honor also his modesty. Bull in pure form is rare; there is usually some contamination by data. The community has reason to be grateful to Mr. Metzger for having created an instance of laboratory purity, free from any adulteration by matter. The more credit is due him, I think, because his act was free from premeditation, deliberation, or hope of personal gain.

Mr. Metzger stood one rainy November day in the lobby of Memo- 8 rial Hall. A junior, concentrating in mathematics, he was fond of diverting himself by taking part in the drama, a penchant which may have had some influence on the events of the next hour. He was waiting to take part in a rehearsal in Sanders Theatre, but, as sometimes happens, no other players appeared. Perhaps the rehearsal had been canceled without his knowledge? He decided to wait another five minutes.

Students, meanwhile, were filing into the Great Hall opposite, 9 and taking seats at the testing tables. Spying a friend crossing the lobby toward the Great Hall's door, Metzger greeted him and extended appropriate condolences. He inquired, too, what course his friend was being tested in. "Oh, Soc. Sci. something-or-other." "What's it all about?" asked Metzger, and this, as Homer remarked of Patroclus, was the beginning of evil for him.

"It's about Modern Perspectives on Man and Society and All 10 That," said his friend. "Pretty interesting, really."

"Always wanted to take a course like that," said Metzger. "Any 11 good reading?"

"Yeah, great. There's this book"—his friend did not have time to 12 finish.

"Take your seats please," said a stern voice beside them. The idle 13 conversation had somehow taken the two friends to one of the tables in the Great Hall. Both students automatically obeyed; the proctor put blue books before them; another proctor presented them with copies of the printed hour-test.

Mr. Metzger remembered afterwards a brief misgiving that was 14 suddenly overwhelmed by a surge of curiosity and puckish glee. He wrote "George Smith" on the blue book, opened it, and addressed the first question.

I must pause to exonerate the Management. The Faculty has a rule 15 that no student may attend an examination in a course in which he is not enrolled. To the wisdom of this rule the outcome of this deplorable story stands witness. The Registrar, charged with the enforcement of the rule, has developed an organization with procedures which are certainly the finest to be devised. In November, however, class rosters are still shaky, and on this particular day another student, named Smith, was absent. As for the culprit, we can reduce his guilt no further than to suppose that he was ignorant of the rule, or, in the face of the momentous challenge before him, forgetful.

We need not be distracted by Metzger's performance on the "ob- 16 jective" or "spot" questions on the test. His D on these sections can be explained by those versed in the theory of probability. Our interest focuses on the quality of his essay. It appears that when Metzger's friend picked up his own blue book a few days later, he found himself in company with a large proportion of his section in having received on the essay a C+. When he quietly picked up "George Smith's" blue book to return it to Metzger, he observed that the grade for the essay was A−. In the margin was a note in the section man's hand. It read "Excellent work. Could you have pinned these observations down a bit more closely? Compare . . . in . . . pp . . . ."

Such news could hardly be kept quiet. There was a leak, and the 17 whole scandal broke on the front page of Tuesday's *Crimson*. With the press Metzger was modest, as becomes a hero. He said that there had been nothing to it at all, really. The essay question had offered a choice of two books, Margaret Mead's *And Keep Your Powder Dry* or Geoffrey Gorer's *The American People*. Metzger reported that having read neither of them, he had chosen the second "because the title gave me some notion as to what the book might be about." On the test, two critical comments were offered on each book, one favorable, one unfavorable. The students were asked to "discuss." Metzger conceded that he had played safe in throwing his lot with the more laudatory of the two comments, "but I did not forget to be balanced."

I do not have Mr. Metzger's essay before me except in vivid 18 memory. As I recall, he took his first cue from the name Geoffrey, and committed his strategy to the premise that Gorer was born into an "Anglo-Saxon" culture, probably English, but certainly "English speaking." Having heard that Margaret Mead was a social anthropologist, he inferred that Gorer was the same. He then entered upon his essay, centering his inquiry upon what he supposed might be the problems inherent in an anthropologist's observation of a culture which was his own, or nearly his own. Drawing in part from memories of table-talk on cultural relativity[2] and in part from creative logic, he rang changes on the relation of observer to observed, and assessed the kind and degree of objectivity which might accrue to an observer

---

[2] "An important part of Harvard's education takes place during meals in the Houses." An Official Publication.—Au.

through training as an anthropologist. He concluded that the book in question did in fact contribute a considerable range of "'objective', and even 'fresh'," insights into the nature of our culture. "At the same time," he warned, "these observations must be understood within the context of their generation by a person only partly freed from his embeddedness in the culture he is observing, and limited in his capacity to transcend those particular tendencies and biases which he has himself developed as a personality in his interaction with this culture since his birth. In this sense the book portrays as much the character of Geoffrey Gorer as it analyzes that of the American people." It is my regrettable duty to report that at this moment of triumph Mr. Metzger was carried away by the temptations of parody and added, "We are thus much the richer."

In any case, this was the essay for which Metzger received his 19 honor grade and his public acclaim. He was now, of course, in serious trouble with the authorities.

I shall leave him for the moment to the mercy of the Administra- 20 tive Board of Harvard College and turn the reader's attention to the section man who ascribed the grade. He was in much worse trouble. All the consternation in his immediate area of the Faculty and all the glee in other areas fell upon his unprotected head. I shall now undertake his defense.

I do so not simply because I was acquainted with him and feel a 21 respect for his intelligence; I believe in the justice of his grade! Well, perhaps "justice" is the wrong word in a situation so manifestly absurd. This is more a case in "equity." That is, the grade is equitable if we accept other aspects of the situation which are equally absurd. My proposition is this: if we accept as valid those C grades which were accorded students who, like Metzger's friend, demonstrated a thorough familiarity with the details of the book without relating their critique to the methodological problems of social anthropology, then "George Smith" deserved not only the same, but better.

The reader may protest that the C's given to students who showed 22 evidence only of diligence were indeed not valid and that both these students and "George Smith" should have received E's. To give the diligent E is of course not in accord with custom. I shall take up this matter later. For now, were I to allow the protest, I could only restate my thesis: that "George Smith's" E would, in a college of liberal arts, be properly a "better" E.

At this point I need a short-hand. It is a curious fact that there is no 23 academic slang for the presentation of evidence of diligence alone. "Parroting" won't do; it is possible to "parrot" bull. I must beg the reader's pardon, and, for reasons almost too obvious to bear, suggest "cow."

Stated as nouns, the concepts look simple enough: 24

cow (pure): data, however relevant, without relevancies.
bull (pure): relevancies, however relevant, without data.

The reader can see all too clearly where this simplicity would lead. 25
I can assure him that I would not have imposed on him this way were I
aiming to say that knowledge in this university is definable as some
neuter compromise between cow and bull, some infertile hermaphro-
dite. This is precisely what many diligent students seem to believe:
that what they must learn to do is to "find the right mean" between
"amounts" of detail and "amounts" of generalities. Of course this is
not the point at all. The problem is not quantitative, nor does its
solution lie on a continuum between the particular and the general.
Cow and bull are not poles of a single dimension. A clear notion of
what they really are is essential to my inquiry, and for heuristic purposes I wish to observe them further in the celibate state.

When the pure concepts are translated into verbs, their complexi- 26
ties become apparent in the assumptions and purposes of the students
as they write:

To cow (*v. intrans.*) or the act of cowing:
    To list data (or perform operations) without awareness of, or com-
ment upon, the contexts, frames of reference, or points of observation which determine the origin, nature, and meaning of the data (or
procedures). To write on the assumption that "a fact is a fact." To
present evidence of hard work as a substitute for understanding,
without any intent to deceive.

To bull (*v. intrans.*) or the act of bulling:
    To discourse upon the contexts, frames of reference and points of
observation which would determine the origin, nature, and meaning
of data if one had any. To present evidence of an understanding of
form in the hope that the reader may be deceived into supposing a
familiarity with content.

At the level of conscious intent, it is evident that cowing is more 27
moral, or less immoral, than bulling. To speculate about unconscious
intent would be either an injustice or a needless elaboration of my
theme. It is enough that the impression left by cow is one of ear-
nestness, diligence, and painful naiveté. The grader may feel disappointment or even irritation, but these feelings are usually balanced by
pity, compassion, and a reluctance to hit a man when he's both down
and moral. We may feel some challenge to his teaching, but none
whatever to his one-ups-manship. He writes in the margin: "See me."

We are now in a position to understand the anomaly of custom: As 28
instructors, we always assign bull an E, *when we detect it;* whereas we
usually give cow a C, *even though it is always obvious.*

After all, we did not ask to be confronted with a choice between 29

morals and understanding (or did we?). We evince a charming humanity, I think, in our decision to grade in favor of morals and pathos.
"I simply *can't* give this student an E after he has *worked* so hard." At
the same time we tacitly express our respect for the bullster's strength.
We recognize a colleague. If he knows so well how to dish it out, we
can be sure that he can also take it.

Of course, it is just possible that we carry with us, perhaps from 30
our own school-days, an assumption that if a student is willing to
work hard and collect "good hard facts" he can always be taught to
understand their relevance, whereas a student who has caught onto
the forms of relevance without working at all is a lost scholar.

But this is not in accord with our experience.   31

It is not in accord either, as far as I can see, with the stated values 32
of a liberal education. If a liberal education should teach students
"how to think," not only in their own fields but in fields outside their
own—that is, to understand "how the other fellow orders knowledge," then bulling, even in its purest form, expresses an important
part of what a pluralist university holds dear, surely a more important
part than the collecting of "facts that are facts" which schoolboys learn
to do. Here then, good bull appears not as ignorance at all but as an
aspect of knowledge. It is both relevant and "true." In a university
setting good bull is therefore of more value than "facts," which,
without a frame of reference, are not even "true" at all.

Perhaps this value accounts for the final anomaly: as instructors, 33
we are inclined to reward bull highly, *where we do not detect its intent,* to
the consternation of the bullster's acquaintances. And often we do not
examine the matter too closely. After a long evening of reading blue
books full of cow, the sudden meeting with a student who at least
understands the problems of one's field provides a lift like a draught of
refreshing wine, and a strong disposition toward trust.

This was, then, the sense of confidence that came to our unfor- 34
tunate section man as he read "George Smith's" sympathetic considerations.

II

In my own years of watching over students' shoulders as they 35
work, I have come to believe that this feeling of trust has a firmer basis
than the confidence generated by evidence of diligence alone. I believe
that the theory of a liberal education holds. Students who have dared
to understand man's real relation to his knowledge have shown themselves to be in a strong position to learn content rapidly and meaning-
fully, and to retain it. I have learned to be less concerned about the
education of a student who has come to understand the nature of

man's knowledge, even though he has not yet committed himself to hard work, than I am about the education of the student who, after one or two terms at Harvard, is working desperately hard and still believes that collected "facts" constitute knowledge. The latter, when I try to explain to him, too often understands me to be saying that he "doesn't *put in enough generalities.*" Surely he has "put in *enough* facts."

I have come to see such quantitative statements as expressions of 36 an entire, coherent epistemology. In grammar school the student is taught that Columbus discovered America in 1492. The *more* such items he gets "right" on a given test the more he is credited with "knowing." From years of this sort of thing it is not unnatural to develop the conviction that knowledge consists of the accretion of hard facts by hard work.

The student learns that the more facts and procedures he can get 37 "right" in a given course, the better will be his grade. The more courses he takes, the more subjects he has "had," the more credits he accumulates, the more diplomas he will get, until, after graduate school, he will emerge with his doctorate, a member of the community of scholars.

The foundation of this entire life is the proposition that a fact is a 38 fact. The necessary correlate of this proposition is that a fact is either right or wrong. This implies that the standard against which the rightness or wrongness of a fact may be judged exists *someplace—*perhaps graven upon a tablet in a Platonic world outside and above *this* cave of tears. In grammar school it is evident that the tablets which enshrine the spelling of a word or the answer to an arithmetic problem are visible to my teacher who need only compare my offerings to it. In high school I observe that my English teachers disagree. This can only mean that the tablets in such matters as the goodness of a poem are distant and obscured by clouds. They surely exist. The pleasing of befuddled English teachers degenerates into assessing their prejudices, a game in which I have no protection against my competitors more glib of tongue. I respect only my science teachers, authorities who *really know.* Later I learn from them that "this is only what we think *now.*" But eventually, surely . . . Into this epistemology of education, apparently shared by teachers in such terms as "credits," "semester hours" and "years of French" the student may invest his ideals, his drive, his competitiveness, his safety, his self-esteem, and even his love.

College raises other questions: by whose calendar is it proper to 39 say that Columbus discovered America in 1492? How, when and by whom was the year 1 established in this calendar? What of other calendars? In view of the evidence for Leif Ericson's previous visit (and the American Indians), what historical ethnocentrism is suggested by the use of the word "discover" in this sentence? As for Leif Ericson, in accord with what assumptions do you order the evidence?

These questions and their answers are not "more" knowledge. 40
They are devastation. I do not need to elaborate upon the epistemology, or rather epistemologies, they imply. A fact has become at last "an observation or an operation performed in a frame of reference." A liberal education is founded in an awareness of frame of reference even in the most immediate and empirical examination of data. Its acquirement involves relinquishing hope of absolutes and of the protection they afford against doubt and the glib-tongued competitor. It demands an ever widening sophistication about systems of thought and observation. It leads, not away from, but *through* the arts of gamesmanship to a new trust.

This trust is in the value and integrity of systems, their varied 41
character, and the way their apparently incompatible metaphors enlighten, from complementary facets, the particulars of human experience. As one student said to me: "I used to be cynical about intellectual games. Now I want to know them thoroughly. You see I came to realize that it was only when I knew the rules of the game cold that I could tell whether what I was saying was tripe."

We too often think of the bullster as cynical. He can be, and not 42
always in a light-hearted way. We have failed to observe that there can lie behind cow the potential of a deeper and more dangerous despair. The moralism of sheer work and obedience can be an ethic that, unwilling to face a despair of its ends, glorifies its means. The implicit refusal to consider the relativity of both ends and means leaves the operator in an unconsidered proprietary absolutism. History bears witness that in the pinches this moral superiority has no recourse to negotiation, only to force.

A liberal education proposes that man's hope lies elsewhere: in 43
the negotiability that can arise from an understanding of the integrity of systems and of their origins in man's address to his universe. The prerequisite is the courage to accept such a definition of knowledge. From then on, of course, there is nothing incompatible between such an epistemology and hard work. Rather the contrary.

I can now at last let bull and cow get together. The reader knows 44
best how a productive wedding is arranged in his own field. This is the nuptial he celebrates with a straight A on examinations. The masculine context must embrace the feminine particular, though itself "born of woman." Such a union is knowledge itself, and it alone can generate new contexts and new data which can unite in their turn to form new knowledge.

In this happy setting we can congratulate in particular the Natural 45
Sciences, long thought to be barren ground to the bullster. I have

indeed drawn my examples of bull from the Social Sciences, and by analogy from the Humanities. Essay-writing in these fields has long been thought to nurture the art of bull to its prime. I feel, however, that the Natural Sciences have no reason to feel slighted. It is perhaps no accident that Metzger was a mathematician. As part of my researches for this paper, furthermore, a student of considerable talent has recently honored me with an impressive analysis of the art of amassing "partial credits" on examinations in advanced physics. Though beyond me in some respects, his presentation confirmed my impression that instructors of Physics frequently honor on examinations operations structurally similar to those requisite in a good essay.

The very qualities that make the Natural Sciences fields of delight for the eager gamesman have been essential to their marvelous fertility. 46

III

As priests of these mysteries, how can we make our rites more precisely expressive? The student who merely cows robs himself, without knowing it, of his education and his soul. The student who only bulls robs himself, as he knows full well, of the joys of inductive discovery—that is, of engagement. The introduction of frames of reference in the new curricula of Mathematics and Physics in the schools is a hopeful experiment. We do not know yet how much of these potent revelations the very young can stand, but I suspect they may rejoice in them more than we have supposed. I can't believe they have never wondered about Leif Ericson and that word "discovered," or even about 1492. They have simply been too wise to inquire. 47

Increasingly in recent years better students in the better high schools and preparatory schools *are* being allowed to inquire. In fact they appear to be receiving both encouragement and training in their inquiry. I have the evidence before me. 48

Each year for the past five years all freshmen entering Harvard and Radcliffe have been asked in freshman week to "grade" two essays answering an examination question in History. They are then asked to give their reasons for their grades. One essay, filled with dates, is 99% cow. The other, with hardly a date in it, is a good essay, easily mistaken for bull. The "official" grades of these essays are, for the first (alas!) C+ "because he has worked so hard," and for the second (soundly, I think) B+. Each year a larger majority of freshmen evaluate these essays as would the majority of the faculty, and for the faculty's reasons, and each year a smaller minority give the higher honor to the essay offering data alone. Most interesting, a larger number of students each year, while not overrating the second essay, 49 award the first the straight E appropriate to it in a college of liberal arts.

For us who must grade such students in a university, these devel- 50 opments imply a new urgency, did we not feel it already. Through our grades we describe for the students, in the showdown, what we believe about the nature of knowledge. The subtleties of bull are not peripheral to our academic concerns. That they penetrate to the center of our core is evident in our feelings when a student whose good work we have awarded a high grade reveals to us that he does not feel he deserves it. Whether he disqualifies himself because "there's too much bull in it," or worse because "I really don't think I've worked that hard," he presents a serious educational problem. Many students feel this sleaziness; only a few reveal it to us.

We can hardly allow a mistaken sense of fraudulence to under- 51 mine our students' achievements. We must lead students beyond their concept of bull so that they may honor relevancies that are really relevant. We can willingly acknowledge that, in lieu of the date 1492, a consideration of calendars and of the word "discovered," may well be offered with intent to deceive. We must insist that this does not make such considerations intrinsically immoral, and that, contrariwise, the date 1492 may be no substitute for them. Most of all, we must convey the impression that we grade understanding qua understanding. To be convincing, I suppose we must concede to ourselves in advance that a bright student's understanding is understanding even if he achieved it by osmosis rather than by hard work in our course.

These are delicate matters. As for cow, its complexities are not 52 what need concern us. Unlike good bull, it does not represent partial knowledge at all. It belongs to a different theory of knowledge entirely. In our theories of knowledge it represents total ignorance, or worse yet, a knowledge downright inimical to understanding. I even go so far as to propose that we award no more C's for cow. To do so is rarely, I feel, the act of mercy it seems. Mercy lies in clarity.

The reader may be afflicted by a lingering curiosity about the fate 53 of Mr. Metzger. I hasten to reassure him. The Administrative Board of Harvard College, whatever its satanic reputations, is a benign body. Its members, to be sure, were on the spot. They delighted in Metzger's exploit, but they were responsible to the Faculty's rule. The hero stood in danger of probation. The debate was painful. Suddenly one member, of a refined legalistic sensibility, observed that the rule applied specifically to "examinations" and that the occasion had been simply an hour-test. Mr. Metzger was merely "admonished."

QUESTIONS AND IDEAS FOR DISCUSSION

1. Did you find Perry's essay enjoyable? Explain why, or why not, as specifically as possible. Like Bloom's essay before it, this argument is

addressed to readers with advanced degrees, many of them professors. Given that limitation, which writer reaches a broader audience,
and how does he manage to do so? How does Perry's use of examples
differ from Bloom's, if at all?

2. The vocabulary in this essay, at least in the first section, may seem
occasionally mystifying. What does Perry mean by "comparative epistemology" (paragraph 2), "logical-positivists" (3), and "certain
anomalies in our grading" (3)? Beyond the terms he uses, what makes
the first six paragraphs harder to follow than section I of the essay?

3. Have you ever known (or been!) a Metzger? Perry defends him:
Defend (or refute) Perry's argument with additional reasons and examples from your own knowledge or experience.

4. Explain and evaluate the reasoning process Metzer follows, as
described in paragraphs 17 and 18, to enable him to write an *A* essay
on the exam.

5. Discuss (that is, support or refute) the following assertions, giving
illustrations from your own experience where possible:

> The phenomenon of bull, in all the honor and opprobrium with
> which it is regarded by students and faculty, says something, I
> think, about our theories of knowledge. (2)

> Bull in pure form is rare; there is usually some contamination by
> data. (7)

> If a liberal education should teach students "how to think," not
> only in their own fields but in fields outside their own—that is, to
> understand "how the other fellow orders knowledge," then
> bulling, even in its purest form, expresses an important part of
> what a pluralist university holds dear . . . (32)

> The student who merely cows robs himself, without knowing it,
> of his education and his soul. The student who only bulls robs
> himself, as he knows full well, of the joys of inductive discovery—
> that is, of engagement. (47)

> Through our grades we describe for the students, in the show-
> down, what we believe about the nature of knowledge. (50)

6. In what ways does this essay reveal the author's sense of humor?
Give several examples. How does Perry's humor affect his persona
(the reader's sense of the writer) and, thereby, the persuasiveness of
his argument?

7. On which issues in their respective essays would Allan Bloom and
William G. Perry likely agree? On which would they probably differ?
Cite specific references. With whom do you agree on each issue? Why?

The Educated Person

HENRY ROSOVSKY

Henry Rosovsky, a specialist in Far East economies, is the Geyser
University Professor of Economics at Harvard University and author
of several books, including *Discord in the Pacific* (1972), *Japanese Economic Growth* (1973), and *Asia's New Giant* (1976). For eleven years
(1973–1984), Rosovsky was dean of the Faculty of Arts and Sciences
at Harvard. It was from that particular vantage point that he wrote
The University: An Owner's Manual (1990), a lively defense of contemporary higher education in America. The book deals with complex
questions such as tenure, admissions, and the core curriculum; it
also, in the excerpt reprinted here, argues a definition of "the educated person." Rosovsky believes that a college-educated person
should have acquired some expertise in critical thinking, an "informed acquaintance" with the major divisions of knowledge and
research, an awareness of "other cultures and other times," an ability
to make sound moral and ethical judgments, and an in-depth grasp
of a particular field.

At every commencement, the president of Harvard University 1
welcomes new graduates of the college "to the fellowship of educated
men and women." Similar greetings are voiced throughout the land
by thousands of college presidents every June. What do they mean?
What should they mean? A bachelor's degree may signify little more
than the satisfactory completion of a fixed number of undergraduate
courses. It is a matter of simple observation that not all college graduates are educated persons, nor are all educated persons necessarily
college graduates. Clearly, we mean—in these ritual greetings—to
imply that students have achieved a certain level of intellectual development. We do not expect them to be learned in the arts, sciences, or
professions; indeed, we will have failed if the bachelor's degree signi-
fied the acme of their intellectual growth. Welcoming graduates to the
company of educated men and women makes sense only if it expresses our belief that their mental skills and powers have met a
reasonable standard.

Some years ago I attempted to formulate a standard for liberal 2
education in our time.

1. An educated person must be able to think and write clearly and 3
effectively. By this I mean that students, when they receive their
bachelor's degrees, must be able to communicate with precision, co-
gency, and force. To put it in yet another way: students should be
trained to think critically.

2. An educated person should have a *critical appreciation* of the 4
ways in which we gain knowledge and understanding of the universe,
of society, and of ourselves. Thus, he or she should have an *informed*

acquaintance with the mathematical and experimental methods of the physical and biological sciences; with the main forms of analysis and the historical and quantitative techniques needed for investigating the workings and development of modern society; with some of the important scholarly, literary, and artistic achievements of the past; and with the major religious and philosophical conceptions of mankind.

This ambitious definition may appear to be impractical. Most 5 members of university faculties would have to confess their own difficulty in measuring up to such a standard. But that is a short-sighted view. First, to have a stated ideal is valuable in itself. Second, the general formulation that I have used does translate into standard areas, for example, physics, history, or English literature. I am not suggesting that each of these areas can be mastered by every educated person. But we are not in search of mastery; the goal is informed acquaintance and that can be adequately achieved—at any historical moment—by a set of requirements that has a sufficiently broad conception.

The leap from informed acquaintance to critical appreciation is 6 more important and more difficult. To achieve that quality, we have to move beyond content to the general applicability of what is taught and how it is taught. The growth of knowledge is very rapid, and we should encourage our students to be lifetime learners. Time constraints are great and only certain subjects can be selected. We can expect a non-scientist to take science courses, but we cannot expect all of these students to study physics, biology, chemistry, geology, and mathematics. Therefore, the general utility of required subjects has to be especially great. Ideally, they should combine significant content with an emphasis on the larger methodology of a specific subject. For example, studying economics is all right from the point of view of liberal education, but considering that field in the general context of the social sciences is of much higher value.

3. An educated American, in the last quarter of this century, 7 cannot be provincial in the sense of being ignorant of other cultures and other times. It is no longer possible to conduct our lives without reference to the wider world or to the historical forces that have shaped the present and will shape the future. Perhaps few educated people will ever possess a sufficiently broad perspective. But it seems clear to me that a crucial difference between the educated and the uneducated is the extent to which one's life experience is viewed in wider contexts.

4. An educated person is expected to have some understanding 8 of, and experience in thinking about, moral and ethical problems. While these issues change very little over the centuries, they acquire a new urgency for each generation when it is personally confronted

with the dilemmas of choice. It may well be that the most significant quality in educated persons is the informed judgment that enables them to make discriminating moral choices.

5. Finally, an educated individual should have achieved depth in 9 some field of knowledge. Here I have in mind something that lies between the levels of professional competence and informed acquaintance. In American college terminology, it is called a "major" or "concentration." The theory is straightforward: cumulative learning is an effective way to develop powers of reasoning and analysis because it requires the consideration of increasingly complex phenomena, techniques, and analytical constructs. It is expected that in every major, students will gain sufficient control of the data, theory, and methods to define the issues in a given problem, develop the evidence and arguments that may reasonably be advanced on the various sides of each issue, and reach conclusions based on a convincing evaluation of the evidence. (As such there is a close overlap with the first goal.)

The "reasonable standard" approach to undergraduate education 10 is not without problems. Occasionally we encounter a student who fits the category of one-sided genius—the mathematical wizard, for example. Similarly, as Bertrand Russell has pointed out, someone with the gifts of a Mozart would gain little from a conservatory. But such occurrences are by definition extremely rare, and need not be central to a broad view of education. Our task can never be the equivalent of custom tailoring, although we should always preserve sufficient flexibility to take care of very special cases.

There could also be political objections. The delineation of a set of 11 standards requires a consensus—normally a faculty consensus— which in turn might be read as imposing conformity or, even more fallaciously, as socializing students on behalf of some ulterior purpose: say, this country's "ruling classes," or a particular religion, say, Christianity. I have never been able to accept this view. The standards I have suggested do not represent or preclude any political or doctrinal point of view; indeed, they favor the broadening of sensibilities and the displacement of conventional wisdom by critical thinking.

William Johnson Cory, a master at Eton, said it very well over a 12 hundred years ago. Addressing a group of young men in 1861, he told them that

> you are not engaged so much in acquiring knowledge as in making mental efforts under criticism. A certain amount of knowledge you can indeed with average faculties acquire so as to retain; nor need you regret the hours that you have spent on much that is forgotten, for the shadow of lost knowledge at least protects you from many illusions.
>
> But you go to a great school, not for knowledge so much as for arts

and habits; for the habit of attention, for the art of expression, for the art of assuming at a moment's notice a new intellectual posture, for the art of entering quickly into another person's thoughts, for the habit of submitting to censure and refutation, for the art of indicating assent or dissent in graduated terms, for the habit of regarding minute points of accuracy, for the habit of working out what is possible in a given time, for taste, for discrimination, for mental courage and mental soberness.

Above all, you go to a great school for self-knowledge.

In my view, these remarks describe some of the central principles 13 for undergraduate education today.

QUESTIONS AND IDEAS FOR DISCUSSION

1. Henry Rosovsky offers examples and reasons for advocating each of the five areas of accomplishment that he deems vital to college education, but he does not offer extensive arguments in their support. Does he provide enough data to make his claims convincing? Comment. What examples or further reasons can you add to any (or all) of the arguments Rosovsky advances?

2. The aim that Rosovsky first identifies is that "students should be trained to think critically" (paragraph 3). As it happens, that is a major aim of the course in which you have been assigned this book. But for college education on the whole, is the ability to think critically first in importance? Why, or why not? If you disagree with the order of Rosovsky's points how would you order them differently? Why?

3. Does Rosovsky make a convincing case for the importance of "informed acquaintance" (4) with the important analytical methods and ideas in several broad fields, such as the sciences, math, art history, literature, and religion? How, or why not? Would additional examples be useful or superfluous?

ADDITIONAL MATERIAL FOR ANALYSIS AND ARGUMENT: STATISTICAL TABLES AND SUMMARIES

As you think about the issues raised in this chapter (and the importance of evidence and examples to support claims), you will find that you can argue about college education with some expertise and plenty of illustrations close at hand. Knowing, however, that you are but one student at one institution of higher learning, you may find it enlightening or thought-provoking to compare your own ideas and experience with those of larger numbers of students. Toward that end, you may poll additional students on your campus, consult the most current *Statistical Abstract of the United States* in a nearby library for recent data, and refer to the following statistical tables and summaries. Here you can see what large numbers of polled undergraduates across the United States thought about academic issues, about their professors, about their majors and career plans. These data offer the opportunity for some historical comparisons as well as for numerical ones: The statistics cover surveys between 1970 and 1989.

Characteristics of Part-Time and Full-Time Undergraduates at Four-Year Institutions

	Percent	
	Part-Time	Full-Time
Age: twenty-five years old or older	67	13
Dropped out for some period since entering college	58	16
Married, divorced, separated, or widowed	53	10
At present employed full time	59	4
Father's occupation: professional or managerial	54	65
skilled or semiskilled	42	32
Father's education: high school or less	55	36
College grade-point average of B or higher	61	55
These goals are "very important": career success	57	63
financial success	40	43
intellectual development	70	69
The chief benefit of a college education is that it increases one's earning power	38	44
College should require all undergraduates to take more courses in: literature	25	26
science	41	32
computer science	73	74
the arts	30	27

Source: The Carnegie Foundation for the Advancement of Teaching, National Survey of Undergraduates, 1984.

What Undergraduates Believe the "Essential" Outcomes from a College Education Should Be (by percentage)

College Outcome	1969	1976	1984	1969–1984
Learning to get along with people	76	69	65	−11
Formulating values and goals for my life	71	63	63	−8
Detailed grasp of a special field	62	68	70	+8
Training and skills for an occupation	59	64	73	+14
Well-rounded general education	57	58	60	+3

Source: The Carnegie Foundation for the Advancement of Teaching, National Surveys of Undergraduates, 1969, 1976, and 1984.

College Freshmen—Summary Characteristics, 1970–1988 [In percent. As of fall for first-time, full-time freshmen. Based on sample survey and subject to sampling error; see source]

CHARACTERISTIC	1970	1975	1980	1982	1983	1984	1985	1986	1987	1988
Sex: Male	55	53	49	49	49	48	48	48	47	46
Female	45	47	51	51	51	52	52	52	53	54
Average grade in high school:										
A− to A+	16	18	21	21	20	20	21	23	21	24
B− to B+	58	60	60	60	59	58	59	56	59	58
C to C+	27	21	19	19	21	21	20	20	19	19
D	1	1	1	1	1	1	1	1	1	1
Political orientation:										
Liberal	34	29	20	19	19	20	21	22	22	22
Middle of the road	45	54	60	60	60	58	57	56	56	54
Conservative	17	15	17	18	18	19	19	19	18	20
Probable field of study:										
Arts and humanities	16	11	9	8	8	8	8	9	9	10
Biological sciences	4	6	4	4	4	4	4	4	4	4
Business	16	19	24	24	24	26	27	26	27	26
Education	11	10	7	5	6	7	7	8	9	9
Engineering	9	8	12	12	12	11	11	11	10	10
Physical science	2	3	3	3	3	3	2	2	2	2
Social science	14	10	7	6	6	7	8	8	9	9
Professional	(NA)	(NA)	15	13	14	14	13	12	11	12
Technical	4	9	6	7	7	5	5	4	3	2
Data processing/computer programming	(NA)	(NA)	2	4	4	2	2	2	1	1
Other[1]	(NA)	(NA)	(NA)	16	16	16	16	15	16	16
Communications	(NA)	(NA)	2	2	2	2	2	2	3	3
Computer science	(NA)	(NA)	1	2	5	3	2	2	2	2
Recipient of financial aid:										
Pell grant	(NA)	27	33	23	26	20	19	17	17	20
Supplemental educational opportunity grant	(NA)	6	8	6	7	6	5	5	6	6
State scholarship or grant	(NA)	19	16	15	16	14	14	14	16	14
College grant	(NA)	[2]9	13	12	13	17	19	18	13	10
Federal guaranteed student loan	(NA)	10	21	11	15	23	23	25	22	22
National direct student loan	(NA)	10	9	6	5	6	6	7	5	3
College loan	(NA)	[2]3	4	4	4	4	4	4	5	6
College work-study grant	(NA)	12	15	12	14	9	10	10	10	7
Attitudes—agree or strongly agree:										
Activities of married women are best confined to home and family	48	28	27	26	25	23	22	20	26	26
Capital punishment should be abolished	56	(NA)	34	28	29	26	27	26	24	23
Legalize marijuana	38	47	39	29	26	23	22	21	20	19
There is too much concern for the rights of criminals	52	53	66	70	69	(NA)	(NA)	(NA)	68	69
Abortion should be legalized	(NA)	(NA)	54	55	55	54	55	59	59	57

NA Not available.   [1] Includes other fields of study, not shown separately.   [2] 1976 data.

Source: The Higher Education Research Institute, University of Califorina, Los Angeles, CA. *The American Freshman: National Norms,* annual.

Student View of General Education Courses at Public and Private Colleges and Universities, 1976 and 1984

	Percent Who Agree					
	Total		Public		Private	
	1976	1984	1976	1984	1976	1984
They add to the enrichment of other courses I have taken	76	73	74	73	81	77
They help prepare me for lifelong learning.	NA	73	NA	72	NA	76
They are *irrelevant* to the subjects that interest me most.	31	38	33	38	26	35
They do *not* help prepare people for jobs.	32	32	32	33	28	28
They are mainly of interest to students planning to teach.	29	NA	30	NA	27	NA

NA: Question not asked in that year.

Note: In 1976, the above questions were addressed to courses in the humanities (e.g., English, history, and philosophy), as opposed to "general education" courses, as was the case in 1984.

Source: The Carnegie Foundation for the Advancement of Teaching, National Surveys of Undergraduates, 1976 and 1984.

General Education Requirements: The Student View

	Percent Agreeing the College Should Require More		
	Total	Public	Private
Computer science	74	75	71
English composition	46	47	43
Mathematics	45	46	40
Science	34	35	28
Foreign language	34	35	30
The arts	28	28	26
Literature	26	27	22
History	24	25	21

Source: The Carnegie Foundation for the Advancement of Teaching, National Survey of Undergraduates, 1984.

Course Requirements for General Education, 1970 and 1985

Course	Percentage of Colleges Requiring at Least One Course in Selected Subjects		
	1970	1985	Change
English composition	77	85	+8
Physical education	59	51	−8
Mathematics	49	67	+18
The arts	44	60	+16
Philosophy/theology	44	50	+6
Foreign languages	42	34	−8
History of Western civilization	40	45	+5
International/global education	4	14	+10
Third world studies	3	7	+4
Computer literacy	1	21	+20

Source: The Carnegie Foundation for the Advancement of Teaching, Survey of Chief Academic Officers, 1985.

Percentages of Entering Freshmen Intending to Major in Selected Fields of Study, 1970–1985

Intended Major	1970	1975	1983	1984	1985	Change 1970 to 1985
Art and humanities	21	13	8	8	8	−13
Biological sciences	4	6	4	4	3	−1
Business	16	19	24	26	27	+11
Education	12	10	6	7	7	−5
Engineering	9	8	12	11	11	+2
Physical science	6	4	3	3	2	−4
Professional occupations*	X	X	14	14	13	−1
Social science	9	6	6	7	8	−1

* Includes architecture, home economics, library science, nursing, and related health professions. Professional occupations category not comparable in years 1970 and 1975 with years later than 1980.

Source: Alexander Astin and associates, *The American Freshman: National Norms for Fall 1970* and other selected years (Los Angeles: Cooperative Institutional Reserach Program), 1970, p. 41; 1975, p. 44; 1983, pp. 46–47; 1984, pp. 48–49; 1985, pp. 48–49.

General Education Graduation Requirements in Colleges and Universities, 1984 and 1989

[Refers to requirements in effect for students entering in the academic year shown. General education is defined as that part of the curriculum that all undergraduates are required to take, regardless of major, in order to graduate. Based on sample data and subject to sampling error. See source for details. Excludes specialized schools such as law and medicine.]

ITEM AND ACADEMIC AREA	FOUR-YEAR SCHOOLS						TWO-YEAR SCHOOLS	
	Total		Control					
			Public		Private			
	1984	1989	1984	1989	1984	1989	1984	1989
Number of schools[1]	1,562	1,504	535	509	1,027	995	1,245	1,120
With general education requirements								
Credits required for graduation[2]	125.9	125.8	125.1	125.0	126.3	126.1	64.4	64.3
General education	49.4	52.1	42.4	45.5	53.0	55.4	28.8	30.5
Humanities	23.5	25.0	17.0	18.3	26.8	28.4	12.0	12.6
SELECTED AREA OF STUDY								
Percent of schools with requirements in—								
Humanities:								
English composition	87.2	87.5	94.2	93.3	83.6	84.6	92.2	93.6
English or American Literature	51.8	54.8	50.6	52.7	52.3	55.8	26.7	28.0
Foreign languages and literature	19.7	23.0	9.0	9.8	25.1	29.8	4.0	4.0
History	57.7	62.5	53.1	57.3	60.1	65.2	33.6	34.6
Philosophy	34.4	37.7	14.1	18.0	44.8	47.7	6.5	7.4
Classics	3.4	4.8	3.8	4.9	3.1	4.7	–	.6
Other humanities fields	49.0	54.1	31.9	33.3	57.7	64.7	28.4	33.6
Unspecified or combination	46.8	50.8	49.7	54.2	45.2	49.1	41.9	48.6

Other selected fields:								
Studio and performing arts	22.4	25.1	24.4	27.3	21.4	23.9	1.3	5.3
Social sciences	73.3	80.2	74.0	76.4	72.9	82.2	63.0	68.5
Mathematics	46.3	58.7	52.4	65.0	43.2	55.5	54.5	64.3
Natural and physical sciences	59.7	66.6	62.2	70.8	58.5	64.5	49.8	55.5
Mathematics and/or science	31.9	32.2	35.1	34.1	30.3	31.3	33.8	36.3
Graduation requirements—minimum credits in—[3]								
Humanities:								
English composition	4.5	4.6	5.0	5.1	4.3	4.4	4.5	4.7
English or American literature	2.3	2.4	2.3	2.4	2.3	2.4	1.1	1.1
Foreign languages and literature	1.8	2.0	.6	.6	2.4	2.7	.2	.2
History	3.2	3.4	2.6	2.9	3.5	3.7	1.8	1.8
Philosophy	1.6	1.8	.4	.5	2.2	2.4	.3	.3
Classics	.1	.2	.1	.2	.1	.3	—	—
Other humanities fields	5.9	6.2	1.8	2.1	8.0	8.4	1.5	1.8
Unspecified or combination	4.1	4.3	4.2	4.6	4.0	4.2	2.5	2.8
Other selected fields:								
Studio and performing arts	4.2	4.1	1.9	2.1	5.4	5.1	.1	.2
Social sciences	5.2	5.6	5.8	6.1	4.9	5.3	4.1	4.3
Mathematics	2.0	2.5	2.3	2.7	1.9	2.4	2.5	2.8
Natural and physical sciences	4.1	4.5	4.7	5.4	3.7	4.0	3.1	3.3
Mathematics and/or science	2.3	2.2	2.4	2.3	2.2	2.2	1.9	2.1

— Represents or rounds to zero. [1] As of spring 1988. [2] Semester hours. [3] Based on all schools with general education requirements, including those with no credit hours required in a particular subject.

Source: U.S. National Science Foundation, U.S. National Endowment for the Humanities, and U.S. Department of Education, *Undergraduate General Education and Humanities Requirements,* January 1989.

Earned Degrees Conferred, by Field of Study and Level of Degree, 1971–1987

Level and Field of Study	1971	1980	1983	1984	1985	1986	1987	Percent Female 1971	Percent Female 1987
Bachelor's, total	**839,730**	**929,417**	**969,510**	**974,309**	**979,477**	**987,823**	**991,339**	**43.4**	**51.5**
Agriculture and natural resources	12,672	22,802	20,909	19,317	18,107	16,823	14,991	4.2	31.2
Architecture and environmental design	5,570	9,132	9,823	9,186	9,325	9,119	8,922	11.9	37.3
Area and ethnic studies	2,582	2,840	2,971	2,879	2,867	3,060	3,340	52.4	61.7
Business and management	114,865	185,361	226,893	230,031	233,351	238,160	241,156	9.1	46.5
Communications	10,802	28,616	38,602	40,165	42,083	43,091	45,408	35.3	60.0
Computer and information sciences	2,388	11,154	24,510	32,172	38,878	41,889	39,664	13.6	34.6
Education	176,614	118,169	97,991	92,382	88,161	87,221	87,115	74.5	76.2
Engineering	50,046	68,893	89,270	94,444	96,105	95,953	93,074	.8	13.7
Foreign languages	19,945	11,133	9,685	9,479	9,954	10,102	10,184	74.6	72.6
Health sciences	25,190	63,607	64,614	64,338	64,513	64,535	63,206	77.1	85.5
Home economics	11,167	18,411	16,705	16,316	15,555	15,288	14,942	97.3	92.5
Law	545	683	1,099	1,272	1,157	1,197	1,178	5.0	68.6
Letters	64,933	33,497	32,743	33,739	34,091	35,434	37,133	65.5	65.8
Liberal/general studies	5,461	20,069	18,524	18,815	19,191	19,248	21,365	29.0	56.4
Library and archival sciences	1,013	398	258	255	202	157	139	92.0	85.6
Life sciences	35,743	46,370	39,982	38,640	38,445	38,524	38,114	29.1	48.5
Mathematics	24,801	11,378	12,453	13,211	15,146	16,306	16,489	38.0	46.4
Military sciences	357	251	267	195	299	256	383	.3	6.8
Multi/interdisciplinary studies	8,306	14,404	17,282	16,734	15,727	15,700	16,402	28.4	53.7
Parks and recreation	1,621	5,753	5,198	4,752	4,593	4,433	4,107	34.7	60.2
Philosophy, religion, and theology	11,890	13,276	12,536	12,349	12,439	11,841	11,686	25.5	30.1
Physical sciences	21,412	23,410	23,405	23,671	23,732	21,731	19,974	13.8	28.4
Psychology	37,880	41,962	40,364	39,872	39,811	40,521	42,868	44.5	68.9
Protective services	2,045	15,015	12,579	12,654	12,510	12,704	12,930	9.2	38.3
Public affairs	6,252	18,422	16,290	14,396	13,838	13,878	14,161	60.2	68.0
Social sciences	155,236	103,519	95,088	93,212	91,461	93,703	96,185	36.8	44.0
Visual and performing arts	30,394	40,892	39,469	39,833	37,936	36,949	36,223	59.7	61.9

Master's, total	230,509	298,081	289,921	284,263	286,251	288,567	289,557	40.1	51.2
Agriculture and natural resources	2,457	3,976	4,254	4,178	3,928	3,801	3,523	5.9	30.1
Architecture and environmental design	1,705	3,139	3,357	3,223	3,275	3,260	3,142	13.8	34.0
Area and ethnic studies	1,032	852	826	888	879	927	851	38.3	46.9
Business and management	26,481	55,006	65,319	66,653	67,527	67,137	67,496	3.9	33.0
Communications	1,856	3,082	3,604	3,656	3,669	3,823	3,937	34.6	59.2
Computer and information sciences	1,588	3,647	5,321	6,190	7,101	8,070	8,491	10.3	29.4
Education	88,952	103,951	84,853	77,187	76,137	76,353	75,501	56.2	74.0
Engineering	16,443	16,243	19,350	20,661	21,557	21,661	22,693	1.1	12.6
Foreign languages	4,755	2,236	1,759	1,773	1,724	1,721	1,746	65.5	70.4
Health sciences	5,445	15,068	17,068	17,443	17,383	18,624	18,426	55.9	78.9
Home economics	1,452	2,690	2,406	2,422	2,383	2,298	2,070	93.9	87.6
Law	955	1,817	2,091	1,802	1,796	1,924	1,943	4.8	26.8
Letters	11,148	6,807	5,767	5,818	5,934	6,291	6,123	60.2	65.0
Liberal/general studies	549	1,373	889	1,173	1,180	1,154	1,126	44.3	59.2
Library and archival sciences	7,001	5,374	3,979	3,805	3,893	3,626	3,815	81.3	79.1
Life sciences	5,728	6,510	5,696	5,406	5,059	5,013	4,954	33.6	48.7
Mathematics	5,191	2,860	2,837	2,741	2,882	3,159	3,321	29.2	39.1
Military sciences	2	46	110	127	119	83	83	–	2.4
Multi/interdisciplinary studies	1,157	3,579	2,930	3,148	3,184	3,104	3,041	10.9	42.0
Parks and recreation	218	647	565	555	544	495	476	29.8	55.3
Philosophy, religion, and theology	4,036	5,126	5,873	6,259	5,519	5,630	5,989	27.1	34.5
Physical sciences	6,367	5,219	5,290	5,576	5,796	5,902	5,652	13.3	24.9
Psychology	4,431	7,806	8,378	8,002	8,408	8,293	8,204	37.2	65.2
Protective services	194	1,805	1,300	1,219	1,235	1,074	1,019	10.3	29.4
Public affairs	8,215	18,413	16,245	15,373	16,045	16,300	17,032	49.2	63.7
Social sciences	16,476	12,101	11,112	10,465	10,380	10,428	10,397	28.5	39.5
Visual and performing arts	6,675	8,708	8,742	8,520	8,714	8,416	8,506	47.4	55.8

(continued)

Earned Degrees Conferred, by Field of Study and Level of Degree, 1971–1987 (continued)

Level and Field of Study	1971	1980	1983	1984	1985	1986	1987	Percent Female 1971	Percent Female 1987
Doctorate's, total	32,107	32,615	32,775	33,209	32,943	33,653	34,120	14.3	35.2
Agriculture and natural resources	1,086	991	1,149	1,172	1,213	1,158	1,049	2.9	17.0
Architecture and environmental design	36	79	97	84	89	73	92	8.3	28.3
Area and ethnic studies	144	151	153	139	137	157	132	16.7	44.7
Business and management	807	792	809	977	866	969	1,098	2.9	23.6
Communications	145	193	214	219	234	223	275	13.1	42.5
Computer and information sciences	128	240	262	251	248	344	374	16.4	13.9
Education	6,403	7,941	7,551	7,473	7,151	7,110	6,909	21.2	54.9
Engineering	3,638	2,507	2,831	2,981	3,230	3,410	3,820	.6	6.9
Foreign languages	781	549	488	462	437	448	441	38.0	58.3
Health sciences	459	771	1,155	1,163	1,199	1,241	1,213	16.3	53.5
Home economics	123	192	255	279	276	311	297	61.0	78.1
Law	20	40	72	121	105	54	120	–	34.2
Letters	1,857	1,500	1,176	1,215	1,239	1,215	1,181	28.0	56.4
Life sciences	3,645	3,636	3,341	3,437	3,432	3,358	3,423	16.3	35.0
Mathematics	1,199	724	698	695	699	742	725	7.8	17.4
Multi/interdisciplinary studies	80	295	387	378	285	319	276	13.8	37.0
Philosophy, religion, and theology	866	1,693	1,612	1,644	1,608	1,660	1,658	5.8	13.3
Physical sciences	4,390	3,089	3,269	3,306	3,403	3,551	3,672	5.6	17.3
Psychology	1,782	2,768	3,108	2,973	2,908	3,088	3,123	24.0	53.3
Public affairs	185	372	347	421	431	385	398	23.8	45.7
Social sciences	3,659	3,219	2,931	2,911	2,851	2,955	2,916	13.9	30.5
Visual and performing arts	621	655	692	728	693	722	792	22.2	43.6
Other	53	218	178	180	209	160	136	28.3	50.0

Source: U.S. National Center for Educational Statistics, *Digest of Education Statistics,* 1989.

SUGGESTIONS FOR WRITING
AND FURTHER DISCUSSION

1.   Truth is a concept that students of argument must consider. Do you agree with Allan Bloom's first sentence ("There is one thing a professor can be absolutely certain of: almost every student entering the university believes, or says he believes, that truth is relative")? What does that statement mean, that "truth is relative")? Relative to what? Do you believe that truth is relative? If not, what do you believe about truth? Explain.

2.   Allan Bloom argues that "the real motive for education [is] the search for a good life" (paragraph 7). What do you suppose he means? Do you agree with him? If so, what specific form should that "search for a good life" take in a college education? That is, what kinds of courses should be included and how much choice should be offered? How should the courses be taught? What should extracurricular life be like? If you disagree with Bloom, what do you believe is the "real motive for education"—either ideally or in practice? In either case, give clear illustrations and examples, and also consider the arguments of other authors in this chapter.

3.   What are the degree requirements under which you are currently enrolled? Do you agree with all of them? Why or why not? What changes would you propose in the course of study leading to a bachelor's degree in your proposed major?

4.   Whether or not your college has such a requirement, argue in favor of or against requiring all students at your college to take a basic "core" of courses in specified areas or subjects. Consider as your audience those students who would be affected (or are now affected) by such a program.

5.   In paragraph 17, Allan Bloom argues in favor of "strong prejudices." Elsewhere, he describes a psychology professor who "did not seem to have much idea of what the opposite of a prejudice might be" (15). Write an argument for your classmates that argues one of the following claims:

Prejudices are destructive.

Prejudices are "the road to knowledge."

The opposite of a prejudice is _____ . (Then argue the merits or demerits of the concept you have chosen.)

6.   Assume that you have been asked, as a student representative, to write a paper for the faculty senate of your college or university in response to the following claim, made by William G. Perry:

> If a liberal education should teach students "how to think," not only in their own fields but in fields outside their own—that is, to understand "how the other fellow orders knowledge," then bulling, even in its purest form, expresses an important part of what a pluralist university holds dear . . . (32)

You may agree with, disagree with, or modify this claim, but you must support your argument with examples and, perhaps, other evidence. You should not assume that all your readers will have read Perry's essay.

7.   Do you agree with Henry Rosovsky's five standards for liberal education? If so, how well will your own college education achieve them? If you disagree with one or more of Rosovsky's standards, explain why. With what (if anything) would you replace the standard(s) on which you differ with Rosovsky? Argue your own viewpoint and conclusions in an essay suitable to be read by the board of trustees and alumni board of your college.

8.   Rosovsky declares, "It is a matter of simple observation that not all college graduates are educated persons, nor are all educated persons necessarily college graduates" (1). Write a short essay that argues and develops this thesis according to examples and evidence of people you know (whom you need not identify by name).

3

SUPPORTING CLAIMS WITH LOGICAL REASONING

THE STRATEGY

If we are interested in arguing soundly as well as persuasively, we must think about *how* we arrive at our conclusions. If we want to reason logically, we need to have a clear sense of what makes some reasoning logical and other reasoning . . . well, unreasonable. In the first part of this chapter, you will read three essays about the process of sound reasoning. These essays provide some standards for reasoning logically and for evaluating others' reasoning, and for the most part, they do so in everyday language. But a few terms may be new to you, and these warrant some words of introduction.

A *claim* is an assertion that may be affirmed or denied. It is not an argument in itself and becomes one only when support is offered for it. Essays may make many claims; the central, most important claim in each is its *thesis*.

The supporting statements that make claims into arguments are called *premises* or *grounds*. Premises are of several kinds. They may offer examples or other evidence (*data*). They may offer reasons to connect ideas or categories. Whatever their content, premises, or grounds, must be directly related to the claim (or *conclusion*) they mean to support.

The grounds and the claim they support must be linked logically; there must be some *reason* for drawing a particular conclusion from a particular set of grounds. This link often is assumed rather than explicitly stated. The philosopher Stephen Toulmin calls it the *warrant*; Aristotle called it the *major premise*. The particular label is much less important, however, than the concept: We must have a logical justification for drawing conclusions from data.

Warrants, in turn, are justified by a general body of information that supplies what Toulmin terms the *backing* for the warrant. The reliability of the warrant hinges on the strength and reliability of its backing.

Sound argument offers true statements that are related logically. An argument may relate its premises to its conclusion logically and yet not be sound—if it contains factual errors. Conversely, an argument may offer nothing but impeccable statements and yet not be sound—if its truths are not logically connected with each other. Logic has to do with the *form* of an argument; truth has to do with the *content* of an argument. A sound argument is both logical and true.

The form of an argument—its logical structure—is either deductive or inductive (and frequently we find an interrelated chain of both kinds of argument). *Deduction* and *induction* are the two basic processes of reasoning. They differ essentially in the relationship between claims and the reasoning and evidence offered to support them. In deduction, the conclusion is implicit within the premises; in induction, the conclusion moves beyond the premises. Accordingly (and the essays in this section will offer many examples of the distinction), in a truly deductive argument, the conclusion is guaranteed; in an inductive argument, the conclusion is speculative. Irving Copi puts the distinction in this way: "If a deductive argument is valid, then its conclusion follows with equal necessity from its premises no matter what else may be the case."[1] If additional information could change the conclusion, the argument would be inductive rather than deductive.

Enthymemes are deductive arguments expressed in ordinary language. Usually, one premise is implicit rather than explicit in an enthymeme; less often, the conclusion may be implied rather than stated. Enthymemes typically deal with the highly probable rather than the certain, for absolute certainty often is not possible. But they remain deductive in the relation between their premises and conclusions as long as the conclusions are expressed with the same degree of certainty as the premises, and as long as their conclusions would be neither strengthened nor weakened by "whatever else may be the case."

These terms are defined here to help you sort them out as the following essays use them. But terminology is relatively unimportant; the concepts in this section, on the other hand, are vitally important. The essays in this section require close attention. Be prepared to read them two or three times—thinking about thinking is hard—but be prepared as well to recognize some principles that were already, even if only instinctively, familiar to you. We don't use the terms *deductive*

---

[1] In "Deductive and Inductive Reasoning," beginning on page 125.

or *inductive*, let alone *reductio ad absurdum* (which you will encounter in the Waring excerpt), every day—but we do use the reasoning processes they represent. In this chapter, you will simply examine in a conscious and structured way how you reason through a problem, whether intellectual or practical. When you become more aware of your own and others' reasoning processes, you will find that you can evaluate either in specific terms rather than only in a general acceptance or rejection.

Deductive and Inductive Reasoning

IRVING COPI

Irving Copi, a professor of philosophy at the University of Hawaii, provides a clear and accurate explanation of deductive and inductive reasoning, without plunging too far into the sometimes esoteric vocabulary of logic. Because we are ordinary people and not logicians, and because we must express our arguments in words rather than in precise mathematical symbols, conclusions rarely are as assured for us as they can be for a philosopher. Ours is informal, not formal, logic. But the *process* is much the same: We do not draw conclusions out of thin air but from directly related premises. We accept or reject conclusions drawn by others based on the soundness of their reasoning. And we determine the soundness of that reasoning according to the basic features of the inductive and deductive processes, as Copi distinguishes them.

Although brief, Copi's explanation merits your close attention—and at least two readings. If you are going to evaluate your own or others' reasoning on specific grounds, you need to grasp the distinctions Copi sets forth. This selection is excerpted from Copi's classic textbook, *Introduction to Logic*, 6th ed. (1982).

Arguments are traditionally divided into two different types, *de-* 1
ductive and *inductive*. Although every argument involves the claim that its premises provide some grounds for the truth of its conclusion, only a *deductive* argument involves the claim that its premises provide *conclusive* grounds. In the case of deductive arguments the technical terms "valid" and "invalid" are used in place of "correct" and "incorrect." A deductive argument is *valid* when its premises, if true, do provide conclusive grounds for its conclusion, that is, when premises and conclusion are so related that it is absolutely impossible for the premises to be true unless the conclusion is true also. Every deductive argument is either valid or invalid; the task of deductive logic is to clarify the nature of the relation between premises and conclusion in

valid arguments, and thus to allow us to discriminate valid from invalid arguments. . . .

An inductive argument, on the other hand, involves the claim, not that its premises give conclusive grounds for the truth of its conclusion, but only that they provide *some* support for it. Inductive arguments are neither "valid" nor "invalid" in the sense in which those terms are applied to deductive arguments. Inductive arguments may, of course, be evaluated as better or worse, according to the strength of the support provided their conclusions by their premisses, that is, by the degree of likelihood or probability which their premisses confer upon their conclusions. . . . 2

Deductive and inductive arguments are sometimes characterized and distinguished from one another in terms of the relative generality of their premises and conclusions. William Whewell wrote in *The Philosophy of the Inductive Sciences* that ". . . in Deduction we infer particular from general truths; while in Induction we infer general from particular. . . ." Thus the classical example of deductive argument 3

All humans are mortal.

Socrates is human.

Therefore Socrates is mortal.

indeed has a *particular* conclusion inferred (validly) from premisses the first of which is a general or universal proposition. By contrast, a fairly standard form of inductive argument is illustrated by

Socrates is human and is mortal.

Xanthippe is human and is mortal.

Sappho is human and is mortal.

Therefore probably all humans are mortal.

in which a general or universal conclusion is inferred from premises all of which are particular propositions. There is some merit to this method of distinguishing between deduction and induction, but it is not universally applicable. For valid deductive arguments may have universal propositions for conclusions as well as for premises, as in

All animals are mortal.

All humans are animals.

Therefore all humans are mortal.

and they may have particular propositions for their premises as well as for their conclusions as in

If Socrates is human then Socrates is mortal.

Socrates is human.

Therefore Socrates is mortal.

And inductive arguments may have universal (i.e., general) propositions for premisses as well as for conclusions, as in

All cows are mammals and have lungs.

All horses are mammals and have lungs.

All humans are mammals and have lungs.

Therefore probably all mammals have lungs.

and they may have particular propositions for their conclusions, as in

Hitler was a dictator and was ruthless.

Stalin was a dictator and was ruthless.

Castro is a dictator.

Therefore Castro is probably ruthless.

So it is not altogether satisfactory to characterize deductive arguments as those which derive particular conclusions from general premisses, or inductive arguments as those which infer general conclusions from particular premisses.

A more adequate insight into the difference between deduction 4 and induction is suggested by the following. If a deductive argument is valid, then its conclusion follows with equal necessity from its premisses no matter what else may be the case. From the two premisses *All humans are mortal* and *Socrates is human* the conclusion *Socrates is mortal* follows necessarily, no matter what else may be true. The argument remains valid no matter what additional premisses may be added to the original pair. Whether we add information that Socrates is ugly, or that angels are immortal, or that cows give milk, the conclusion follows strictly from the enlarged set of premisses because it follows strictly from the two original premisses initially given. And if the argument is valid, nothing can make it *more* valid: if the conclusion follows validly from a given set of premisses it cannot follow from an enlarged set any *more* validly or strictly or logically.

But the case is different for inductive arguments. Consider the 5 following inductive argument:

Most corporation lawyers are Conservatives.

Bernice Malcolm is a corporation lawyer.

Therefore Bernice Malcolm is probably a Conservative.

This is a pretty good inductive argument: if its premises are true, its conclusion is more likely true than false. But adding new premises to the original pair can serve either to weaken or to strengthen the resulting argument. If we enlarge the premises by adding that

Bernice Malcolm is an officer of Americans for Democratic Action.

and

No officers of Americans for Democratic Action are Conservatives.

the conclusion no longer even seems to follow, and in fact the opposite conclusion now follows deductively, that is, validly. On the other hand, if we enlarge the original set of premises by adding the following additional premises instead:

Bernice Malcolm campaigned vigorously for Reagan for president.

and

Bernice Malcolm was a member of President Ford's cabinet.

then the original conclusion follows with much greater likelihood from the enlarged set of premises.

Accordingly, we characterize a deductive argument as one whose 6 conclusion is claimed to follow from its premises with absolute necessity, this necessity not being a matter of degree and not depending in any way upon whatever else may be the case. And in sharp contrast we characterize an inductive argument as one whose conclusion is claimed to follow from its premises only with probability, this probability being a matter of degree and dependent upon what else may be the case.

Typical kinds of inductive argument are the following. First are 7 those that proceed by analogy, in which two or more things acknowledged to resemble each other in some respects are inferred to resemble each other in some further respect also. Second are those that proceed by generalization, in which from the premiss that a number of things of a given kind all have some further characteristic, it is inferred that all things of that kind have that characteristic. Third are those that infer a causal connection between events or characteristics that have been observed to go together regularly.

Two remarks are in order at this point. First, inductive arguments 8 do not always explicitly acknowledge that their conclusions are inferred only with "probability." And, second, the presence of the word "probability" in an argument is no sure indication that the argument is inductive, because there are strictly deductive arguments *about* probabilities themselves, as in the following:

The probability that a tossed coin will come up heads is one-half.

Therefore the probability that it will come up heads on both of two successive tosses is one-fourth.

QUESTIONS AND IDEAS FOR DISCUSSION

1. Because it is part (albeit a complete section) of a textbook and not an essay, this excerpt from Copi's *Introduction to Logic* (6th ed.) begins and ends abruptly. The introduction fails to anticipate a reader's likely thought: So what? Why should I care that "arguments are traditionally divided into two different types"? If you were writing an argument defending the study of logical reasoning for writers, how would you, anticipating the shrugs of *your* readers, begin your essay? Write an introductory paragraph for such an essay.

2. In the broadest sense, what is the difference between deductive and inductive reasoning? Find or invent your own examples of a deductive argument and an inductive argument.

3. While its significance may seem relatively minor at this point, it is crucial that you understand the distinction between *truth* and *validity*. What is the difference? And what is *soundness*? Give original examples of arguments that are (1) true but not valid, (2) valid but not true, (3) sound, and (4) unsound.

4. Copi gives a simple rule for recognizing a valid deductive argument: "If a deductive argument is valid, then its conclusion follows with equal necessity no matter what else may be the case" (paragraph 4). Philosophy professor Ronald Munson, in his textbook *The Way of Words* (1976), gives another rule: "We can say that the conclusion follows from the premises when it would be *contradictory* to assert the premises and deny the conclusion." After locating the conclusions in the following arguments, apply either test to determine if the arguments are valid.

Joe will never graduate with a math major—he can't pass calculus.

Because the U.S.S.R. is moving toward capitalism and increased democracy, the United States can safely dismantle its weapons systems.

The makers of over-the-counter drugs cannot reduce their excess packaging in order to lessen its environmental impact. The remote but very real possibility of tampering prevents such reduction.

In the future, most jobs will require the ability to use a computer. Therefore, typing and basic computer skills must be required in the high schools.

By the early decades of the next century, Hispanics will comprise a large minority of the U.S. population. All the nations to the south of the United States have predominantly Hispanic populations, and all but Brazil use the Spanish language. So it only makes sense that students in the United States should be taught Spanish throughout their school years.

5. Copi identifies three typical forms induction takes: analogy, generalization from examples, and causal relationships. But Copi does not explain *why* each of these reasoning processes is inductive. Give an original example of each, and decide why each relies on an inductive rather than a deductive logical relationship. Explain.

6. You may have heard that "arguing from analogy" is fallacious. But Copi identifies it as a legitimate form of induction. Think about this apparent contradiction, and try to resolve it. Under what circumstances might it be all right to draw a conclusion based on the fact that *x* is like *y*? Under what circumstances might it be ill-advised, or fallacious? Consider the following examples in determining your answer:

Because AIDS is communicable like hepatitis, the names of all persons testing positive for the AIDS virus should be reported to the local health department.

We don't allow amateurs to perform surgery, so by the same token, we shouldn't allow amateurs—juries—to make legal judgments.

If we care enough about our mail to have a national postal service, we should care enough about our health to institute a national health service.

The Method of Scientific Investigation

THOMAS H. HUXLEY

Thomas Henry Huxley (1825–1895) was a renowned English biologist much influenced by the work of his contemporary Charles Darwin. Huxley's many contributions to science included the refinement of the inductive method of research. His contributions to education were also remarkable. A man who had only two years of formal schooling before he began medical studies at age seventeen, Huxley in 1870 created (as a founding member of the London School Board) an elementary education system upon which modern elementary education is based. His interest in education is reflected in the following explanation of deductive and inductive reasoning, first delivered as a lecture to a society of manual laborers in London and published in *On Our Knowledge of the Causes of the Phenomena of Organic Nature* (1863). Huxley does not talk down to his audience, but he does consider its needs and interests. His explanation remains clear and accessible for readers today who are not experts in logic or science.

The method of scientific investigation is nothing but the expression of the necessary mode of working of the human mind. It is simply the mode at which all phenomena are reasoned about, rendered precise and exact. There is no more difference, but there is just the same kind of difference, between the mental operations of a man of science and those of an ordinary person, as there is between the operations and methods of a baker or of a butcher weighing out his goods in common scales, and the operations of a chemist in performing a difficult and complex analysis by means of his balance and finely graduated weights. It is not that the action of the scales in the one case, and the balance in the other, differ in the principles of their construction or manner of working; but the beam of one is set on an infinitely finer axis than the other, and of course turns by the addition of a much smaller weight. 1

You will understand this better, perhaps, if I give you some familiar example. You have all heard it repeated, I dare say, that men of science work by means of induction and deduction, and that by the help of these operations, they, in a sort of sense, wring from Nature certain other things, which are called natural laws, and causes, and that out of these, by some cunning skill of their own, they build up hypotheses and theories. And it is imagined by many, that the operations of the common mind can be by no means compared with these processes, and that they have to be acquired by a sort of special apprenticeship to the craft. To hear all these large words, you would think that the mind of a man of science must be constituted differently from that of his fellow men; but if you will not be frightened by terms, you will discover that you are quite wrong, and that all these terrible apparatus are being used by yourselves every day and every hour of your lives. 2

There is a well-known incident in one of Molière's plays, where the author makes the hero express unbounded delight on being told that he had been talking prose during the whole of his life. In the same way, I trust, that you will take comfort, and be delighted with yourselves, on the discovery that you have been acting on the principles of inductive and deductive philosophy during the same period. Probably there is not one here who has not in the course of the day had occasion to set in motion a complex train of reasoning, of the very same kind, 3 though differing of course in degree, as that which a scientific man goes through in tracing the causes of natural phenomena.

A very trivial circumstance will serve to exemplify this. Suppose 4 you go into a fruiterer's shop, wanting an apple—you take up one, and, on biting it, you find it is sour; you look at it, and see that it is hard and green. You take up another one, and that too is hard, green, and sour. The shopman offers you a third; but, before biting it, you examine it, and find that it is hard and green, and you immediately say that you will not have it, as it must be sour, like those that you have already tried.

Nothing can be more simple than that, you think; but if you will 5 take the trouble to analyze and trace out into its logical elements what has been done by the mind, you will be greatly surprised. In the first place, you have performed the operation of induction. You found that, in two experiences, hardness and greenness in apples went together with sourness. It was so in the first case, and it was confirmed by the second. True, it is a very small basis, but still it is enough to make an induction from; you generalise the facts, and you expect to find sourness in apples where you get hardness and greenness. You found upon that a general law, that all hard and green apples are sour; and that, so far as it goes, is a perfect induction. Well, having got your natural law in this way, when you are offered another apple which you find is hard and green, you say, "All hard and green apples are sour; this apple is hard and green, therefore this apple is sour." That train of reasoning is what logicians call a syllogism, and has all its various parts and terms—its major premiss, its minor premiss, and its conclusion. And, by the help of further reasoning, which, if drawn out, would have to be exhibited in two or three other syllogisms, you arrive at your final determination, "I will not have that apple." So that, you see, you have, in the first place, established a law by induction, and upon that you have founded a deduction, and reasoned out the special conclusion of the particular case. Well now, suppose, having got your law, that at some time afterwards, you are discussing the qualities of apples with a friend: you will say to him, "It is a very curious thing, but I find that all hard and green apples are sour!" Your friend says to you, "But how do you know that?" You at once reply, "Oh, because I have tried them over and over again, and have always found them to be so." Well, if we were talking science instead of common sense, we should call that an experimental verification. And, if still opposed, you go further, and say, "I have heard from the people in Somersetshire and Devonshire, where a large number of apples are grown, that they have observed the same thing. It is also found to be the case in Normandy, and in North America. In short, I find it to be the universal experience of mankind wherever attention has been directed to the subject." Whereupon, your friend, unless he is a very unreasonable man, agrees with you, and is convinced that you are quite right in the conclusion you have drawn. He believes, although perhaps he does not know he believes it, that the more extensive verifications are—that the more frequently experiments have been made, and results of the same kind arrived at—that the more varied the conditions under which the same results are attained, the more certain is the ultimate conclusion, and he disputes the question no further. He sees that the experiment has been tried under all sorts of conditions, as to time, place, and people, with the same result; and he says with you, therefore, that the law you have laid down must be a good one, and he must believe it.

In science we do the same thing; the philosopher exercises pre- 6 cisely the same faculties, though in a much more delicate manner. In scientific inquiry it becomes a matter of duty to expose a supposed law to every possible kind of verification, and to take care, moreover, that this is done intentionally, and not left to a mere accident, as in the case of the apples. And in science, as in common life, our confidence in a law is in exact proportion to the absence of variation in the result of our experimental verifications. For instance, if you let go your grasp of an article you may have in your hand, it will immediately fall to the ground. That is a very common verification of one of the best established laws of nature—that of gravitation. The method by which men of science establish the existence of that law is exactly the same as that by which we have established the trivial proposition about the sourness of hard and green apples. But we believe it in such an extensive, thorough, and unhesitating manner because the universal experience of mankind verifies it, and we can verify it ourselves at any time; and that is the strongest possible foundation on which any natural law can rest.

So much, then, by way of proof that the method of establishing 7 laws in science is exactly the same as that pursued in common life.

QUESTIONS AND IDEAS FOR DISCUSSION

1. How does Huxley show that he has considered his audience carefully? Indicate specific clues in the text.

2. In what ways, if any, is Huxley's essay easier to follow than Copi's on the same subject? What in the choices of words and examples makes it so? In what ways, if any, is Copi's essay clearer than Huxley's—and, again, what makes it so?

3. Huxley does not explain the concept of the syllogism in any great detail. What does he tell us, and what beyond that can we infer about the syllogism from the explanation in paragraph 5?

Logic in Several Flavors

R. H. WARING

Ronald H. Waring was a British design consultant and technical author. Among his books are *Understanding Digital Electronics* and *Understanding Electronics*. His particular interest lay in making complex technical subjects comprehensible to general readers. The following selection is excerpted from the perhaps optimistically but certainly cheerfully titled *Logic Made Easy* (1985), a slim volume aimed at the general reader. In this selection, you will find several types of reasoning described. Some are logical; some, strictly speaking, are not. But all of them show ways we can reason through intellectual puzzles of various kinds. The second part of the selection poses a simple logic problem and shows several ways of arriving at the solution. Work the problem *before* you read the solutions, and then compare your reasoning process with the possibilities Waring describes.

Commonsense Logic

Commonsense logic is deriving conclusions from personal experi- 1
ence and/or knowledge. A conclusion that something makes sense, so it is right; or something does not make sense, so it is wrong. Commonsense does not necessarily produce correct answers, however; and is not necessarily "logical" at all—especially when compared with deductive or mathematical logic, for example; or even established facts.

Commonsense "logic," for example, would maintain that brick, 2
stone, metals are all hard and solid substances. Science establishes that the atomic structure of any solid substance is almost entirely empty space. Commonsense finds it difficult, or impossible, to accept such a fact. It is not understandable, so it is not real. Even less "realistic" is time-dilation in space travel; or the quantum theory which holds that *everything* can be reduced to and analyzed in terms of wave forms.

Yet commonsense is the logic most individuals use for solving 3
ordinary, everyday problems. Applied to pure logic problems it can even provide instant answers which are *known* to be correct, ignoring any rules of logic and avoiding any necessity of positive *proof* that the conclusion is correct.

A person familiar with philosophical logic and deduction would 4
immediately identify the following as a syllogism with an invalid conclusion:

All dogs are animals

All cats are animals

Therefore all cats are dogs.

He could further go on to *prove* that this is an invalid syllogism by drawing a Venn diagram,[1] or by showing that it breaks one or more of the *rules* of deductive logic. Equally, he would probably be prepared to argue this proof at some length.

Commonsense logic has not heard of syllogisms or valid or invalid arguments. It simply affirms, without argument, that cats are *not* dogs. To do this, however, it has to *know* there is a difference between cats and dogs. Without any knowledge at all of the French language, for example, commonsense logic could also maintain that all cats are chats is also wrong (because the spelling is wrong).

This, incidentally, leads to an interesting digression.

All cats are animals

All chats are animals

Therefore: (i) all chats are cats

(ii) all cats are chats.

True or false? (i) is true and (ii) is false. But this is a question of *knowledge,* not logic. (In the case of (ii) all cats are not male (French) cats.)

Here is a classic problem in commonsense logic. A bear walked one mile due South, then turned to the left and walked one mile due East. Then it turned to the left again and walked one mile due North and arrived back at its starting point. . . . What was the color of the bear?

Now apparently the bear walked three legs of a square, like this⌐. But since it ended up where it started from its actual path must have been a triangle△. The only two places in the world where this could happen is if the starting point is either the North Pole or the South Pole. The South Pole is ruled out since it is impossible to travel South from it. So the bear was at the North Pole, i.e., it was a polar bear. So the bear was *white.*

Note again that this problem is solved by *knowledge,* not logic as such—although it needs a logical type of mind to apply that knowledge to a particular problem. So commonsense logic can perhaps best be described as *logical reasoning* based on the available facts, and drawing on additional knowledge or experience to arrive at an answer. It could almost—but not quite—be called inductive logic, which is a

---

[1] A Venn diagram uses circles and squares to represent the logical relationship among terms in a syllogism. [Ed.]

recognized category. It is certainly *not* true deductive logic, which does not permit argument *outside* the facts available.

In this particular example, too, logical reasoning can also be *proved*   11 by geographical fact—except for one thing. There is the remote possibility that a *brown* bear could have been taken to the North Pole by aircraft, say, as an environmental experiment.

Sherlock Holmes's Logic

Almost everyone must be familiar with the infallible reasoning of   12 Sherlock Holmes—his ability to put together a complete picture from the most meager of clues whilst the amiable Watson was simply confused by the situation. Deductive logic at its best—or is it?

In fact it is not, although it is based on the principle of deductive   13 logic. It is fiction, written "backwards" from the answer. Clever, imaginative writing where the answer (conclusion) is first established, the clues (premises) then extracted from the answer and then whittled down to the absolute minimum to be ultimately acceptable for justifying the answer. The possibility of alternative answers is not considered for it does not fit in with the story, or the character of Sherlock Holmes.

Let's face a simple situation which Sherlock Holmes's type logic   14 would answer immediately with ease.

One Spring day you come across two round stones and a carrot   15 lying close together on a grass verge. What do you deduce from that?

The Sherlock Holmes type of mind would immediately answer: 16 "A boy built a snowman there in the second week of February." (Sherlock Holmes himself would probably have gone on to describe the boy in more detail; where he went on holiday last [by the type of stones]; and even the snowman itself.)

Now possibly this answer is right. Why a snowman? Because the   17 stones were used for eyes, and the carrot for a nose. Why a boy? Because a girl would have taken more trouble and molded the nose in snow. Why the second week in February? Because that was when there was the last fall of snow that laid heavily.

None of these conclusions is supported by fact, so it is difficult to   18 justify them on any *logical* basis. Indeed there are many other possible answers, for example:

(i) The two stones just happened to be there, anyway. The carrot fell out of someone's shopping bag at that particular spot.

(ii) Digging up his vegetable plot, a gardener turned up two stones and an old carrot. He threw them all over the hedge, where they landed on the grass verge close together. Neither very interesting, but both equally as plausible as the 'snowman' theory, or even more so.

(iii) One night a burglar approached the house the other side of the grass verge carrying two stones he could use to break a window and force an entry. He thought the house was empty, but it was not; so he turned, ran and jumped over the hedge on to the grass verge, dropping the stones where he landed. The woman who was in the house and saw him was in the kitchen. She picked up the nearest object, which happened to be a carrot and threw it at the burglar. The carrot landed in the same spot as the stones.

That answer has "written a story" around two simple facts. See 19
how many other different stories, or answers, you can think of.

Ordinary Language

Arguments in ordinary language are often difficult to *prove*, even 20
though they may lead to correct conclusions. This is the basic weakness of ordinary language for dealing with problems in logic. Where proof of the validity or otherwise of the conclusion is necessary, the available information may first need changing into what is known as a standard-form categorical syllogism before it can be analyzed fully under the rules of *deductive* logic. The term "standard-form categorical syllogism" is extremely off-putting when first met, but basically means reducing the component propositions into three separate terms. The validity (or otherwise) of the argument is then simple to establish. . . .

As an example, consider the following forms: 21

No wealthy persons are vagrants

All barristers are rich people

Therefore, no high court advocates are tramps.

These contain six terms, but in fact this is because of synonymous 22
descriptions. Thus "wealthy people" and "rich people" are the same; so are "barristers" and "high court advocates"; and so are "vagrants and tramps." Thus, still using ordinary language, here is the same thing in *standard-form* containing just *three* terms.

No rich people are vagrants

All barristers are rich people

Therefore, no barristers are vagrants.

That is now a standard-form categorical syllogism, which is easy to prove as valid argument.

At the same time this demonstrates a basic rule applicable to all 23 types of logic. The information *necessary* to be able to solve the problem, or come to a conclusion, can at first appear obscure because it is wrapped up in a lot of ordinary language. The "facts" of the question have to be extracted and put down in their simplest form, eliminating any ambiguity of duplication (synonymous description).

Reductio ad absurdum

Reductio ad absurdum is a particular type of logic favored by philoso- 24 phers, as well as being applicable to other types of logic. It means, quite simply, showing that an assumption is false by deriving a further conclusion from it which is absurd (i.e., cannot be true). In fact, it can be argued that *reductio ad absurdum* itself is absurd as applied in deductive logic since it argues at length about things which are *not* true. Debating the question rather than seeking the answer. In mathematical logic, however, *reductio ad absurdum* can be quite precise. It can be used to *prove* that something is impossible, i.e., that a particular answer is not a correct solution or method of solution; or that there is no answer to that problem.

Suppose the problem is to complete a series of numbers using each 25 of the ten digits 0,1,2,3,4,5,6,7,8 and 9 once and once only so that the sum of such numbers composed is 100. Can it be done? The *reductio ad absurdum* approach will show that it cannot.

Using the digits as they stand, added together   26

$$0 + 1 + 2 + 3 + 4 + 5 + 6 + 7 + 8 + 9 = 45$$

This is well short of the total required, so some of the numbers will 27 have to be double figures instead of single figures to make up the additional amount in *tens*. Call this sum T for tens. The sum of the remaining figures is then $45 - T$, so we get the following equation expressing the requirement

$$10 \times T + (45 - T) = 100$$

Solving this gives $T = 55/9 = 6.1111. \ . \ . \ .$

This is obviously absurd. You cannot have 6.111 . . . digits denot- 28 ing tens. T *must* be a whole number. So, by *reductio ad absurdum*, the problem is *not* solvable.

By all means apply *reductio ad absurdum* to deductive logic as 29 well—but be prepared for a lengthy debate if discussing it with someone else. In philosophical logic there can be different *opinions* as to what is absurd or not!

Indirect Proof

Indirect proof is closely related to *reductio ad absurdum*, but it works 30
in the opposite sense. It "proves" a deduction or assertion by establishing that the *opposite* assumption is false. A handy trick for politicians, this, to prove their policies right by expounding at length on how the Opposition is wrong.

Even more so than *reductio ad absurdum*, indirect proof is open to 31
objections when applied to philosophical logic, but again in mathematical logic it can be quite positive.

Here is a simple example. If we add all the numbers possible 32
together (i.e., $1 + 2 + 3 + 4 + 5 +$ etc., etc.) we conclude logically
that there is no end to such a series and so the sum of all possible
numbers is an infinitely large quantity—normally called infinity, or
designated ∞. Thus $1 + 2 + 3 + 4 + 5 +$ etc., etc. $= \infty$

Suppose, now, we adopt the *opposite* assumption that there *is* an 33
end to such a series. If that is so, a further 1 can be added to it to give:

$$(1 + 2 + 3 + 4 + 5 + \text{etc., etc.}) + 1 = \infty + 1$$

But there cannot be a quantity $\infty + 1$ because ∞ (infinity) is already an
infinitely large number (there cannot be a larger number). So $\infty + 1$ is
impossible. Thus this second (opposite) assumption is false. Hence
the original assumption must be true.

Lateral Thinking

Lateral thinking is another form of mental discipline which has 34
received considerable recent exposure. . . . Loosely, it is the art of
thinking problems through in more than one direction at a time.
Another form of logical argument, in fact, but only marginally acceptable as a form of logic.

Probably the basic principle involved is best illustrated by exam- 35
ple, where something is being *designed*. The designer develops the
original idea through his own knowledge and experience into something final, which is then built or produced. To complete it, it utilizes
"standard" parts brought in from another company, variation in performance or quality of which may affect the performance of the final
product. Unless the designer has indulged in some degree of "lateral
thinking" to take into account such possible effects (which were outside his immediate design problem), the design could prove unsatisfactory.

Here is a very simple example of this. The call is for a bracket to be 36
designed to hold two parts at a V-angle when screwed or bolted up to
the bracket. Accordingly the design office drew up a V-shaped
bracket, and somebody in the workshop makes it. Then they find that

they cannot possibly get long enough screws or bolts into the holes near the bottom of the V-bracket. So a little "lateral thinking" at the design stage would have taken into account that not only was the shape of the bracket important, but the fact that it had to be *fitted* with bolts. Too bad if they had produced hundreds of brackets before someone found that they were not usable!

Analogy

Analogy can be . . . defined simply as "a sort of similarity." From 37 such similarity it is possible to make an educated guess at possible unknowns. However the application of analagous argument is much broader than simple argument. Analogies can be vague, or clear cut. They can be applied to mathematics, philosophy or other forms of argument. In many cases analogous argument and deduction is the only answer to lack of knowledge in tackling a problem. Probably the clearest example here is the case of a mathematical problem where a solution is quite straightforward (and exact) using calculus, but the person's knowledge of mathematics does not extend to calculus. Using analagous reasoning he (or she) could well derive an acceptable answer, if not necessarily exact.

That, in fact, is the weakness of analogy. It is never exact argument 38 and deduction—it is heuristic reasoning.[2]

Which Type of Logic to Use?

Everyone is born with the inherent ability to do some things well 39 and also to suffer a sort of "mental blank" in dealing with some other subjects. Someone who is good at languages, for example, is often quite hopeless with mathematics, or mechanical subjects. Some people reason best with words, others with "pictures" or diagrams.

It is just the same with logic. Some people will find one type of 40 logic easy to understand and apply, but find other types of logic impossible to comprehend. So the answer to this particular problem is to work with the type of logic you understand best. At the same time, though, it does not necessarily follow that every type of logic can be applied to solving *any* problem in logic. Often the reverse is true. Solving a particular problem may involve a particular type of logic

---

[2] *Heuristic reasoning* is a "speculative formulation serving as a *guide* in the investigation or solution of a problem" (*American Heritage Dictionary;* emphasis added). [Ed.]

being used. Only mathematical logic, for instance, will give *exact* answers to purely mathematical problems.

Let's see how alternative types of logic can be applied to solving 41 the following problem:

> George Brown, Tom Green and Bill White were talking. "Funny thing," said Brown. "I've just noticed we're wearing different colored hats the same as our names." "Yes," said one of the others. "But none of us is wearing a hat the same color as our name. For instance, I'm wearing a green hat."

Solution by Logical Reasoning

First write down the known facts or *premises*.   42

(i) Brown, Green and White are each wearing a colored hat.

(ii) The colors of the hats are brown, green and white.

(iii) Brown pointed out this fact.

(iv) The one wearing the green hat then pointed out that none of the colors of the hats they were wearing was the same as their names.

All these premises are *true*.

Analysis or argument: Since none is wearing the same color as his 43 name:

(a) Brown is wearing either a green or white hat

(b) Green is wearing a brown or white hat

(c) White is wearing either a brown or green hat

(d) Either Brown or White spoke last, and is wearing a green hat.

Conclusion: Since Brown had already spoken, it must have been White who spoke last (consistent with [d]). That means it was *White* who was wearing a *green* hat (consistent with [c]).

That leaves *Brown* wearing a *white* hat (consistent with [a] since the 44 green hat has already been allocated). That leaves *Green* wearing the *brown* hat (consistent with [b] since the white hat has already been allocated).

So—Brown was wearing the *white* hat

Green was wearing the *brown* hat

White was wearing the *green* hat

Solution by Logic Diagram

In this case the problem is set down in the following diagrammatic 45 form:

	brown hat	green hat	white hat
BROWN			
GREEN			
WHITE			

Since the hat colors are not the same as the names we can fill in 46 part of the diagram thus, using "X" to show "not":

	brown hat	green hat	white hat
BROWN	X		
GREEN		X	
WHITE			X

To proceed further we need another diagram to analyze the other 47 available facts:

	spoke first	spoke last
BROWN		
GREEN		
WHITE		

Brown spoke first, so, that completes the first line with a √ and X 48 (√ for "yes" and X for "not"). The person who spoke last was wearing a green hat. He cannot be Green, so he must be White. The second diagram can thus be filled in like this:

	spoke first	spoke last
BROWN	√	X
GREEN		
WHITE	X	√

(Green did not speak at all, so we could fill in his line with X and X, but this is not necessary for solving the problem.)

We can now go back to the original diagram and enter the fact that 49 White has been identified as the last speaker, wearing the green hat:

	brown hat	green hat	white hat
BROWN	X	X	
GREEN		X	
WHITE	X	√	X

That leaves only one possibility for Brown. He must be wearing a 50 white hat. The completed diagram also confirms that Green is wearing the brown hat:

	brown hat	green hat	white hat
BROWN	X	X	√
GREEN	√	X	X
WHITE	X	√	X

Solution by *Reductio ad Absurdum* or Indirect Proof

This could be used to find an answer by assuming an answer and 51 seeing if this contradicts the facts. For example, assume Brown is wearing the green hat. From the facts available, Brown spoke first. But the person who spoke *last* was wearing the green hat. Thus the assumption is not correct, i.e., Brown cannot be wearing a green hat. Equally, from the facts, he is also not wearing a brown hat. Therefore he must be wearing a white hat. The rest of the solution then follows.

This solution has been arrived at surprisingly simply. Note, 52 however, it has used a *mixture* of logic. The final solution, starting with the conclusion that Brown must be wearing a white hat, is derived by deductive logic.

QUESTIONS AND IDEAS FOR DISCUSSION

1. Define "commonsense logic." What are its advantages? Its disadvantages? Do you regard yourself as a person with common sense? Why or why not? (Give specific illustrations if possible.) Can you think

of a situation in which commonsense logic steered you toward the wrong conclusion?

2. Why is Sherlock Holmes always right, according to Waring? And why does he suggest that the first two alternative answers to the problem of the two round stones and the carrot (described in paragraph 18) are "even more" plausible than the "snowman" theory? Explain. Can you, as Waring suggests, propose additional plausible answers? Write two.

3. Arguments must be expressed in ordinary language, not in mathematical symbols. What problems does ordinary language present when we attempt to analyze the reasoning in arguments? How can we minimize those problems?

4. Waring illustrates *reductio ad absurdum* and indirect proof with mathematical examples. Those of use who are not mathematicians might benefit from examples in ordinary language. Give one example for each method.

5. Illustrate the concept of lateral thinking with an example of your own, real or hypothetical.

6. Analogy is logically weak but can provide one of an argument's strongest components. Explain this paradox, giving an example.

THE STRATEGY AT WORK:
ARGUMENTS ABOUT MURDER

Reasoning requires that we examine evidence, draw relationships among facts and reasons, and reach conclusions. Sound reasoning requires that our conclusions be directly related to the grounds, or premises, on which they are based. Moreover, our conclusions must be as strong as our evidence and reasons justify, and no stronger. But when we argue about nuclear energy or time limits on Congressional service or the value of abstract art, we deal with subjects about which there is merit in opposing, even in multiple, viewpoints. There may not be a single "right answer."

Enter Murder, a subject with a particular advantage to the reasoner. While we may never know "the right answer" to a given crime, we may rest assured that there is one. A person who is killed deliberately and with malice is a murder victim. If we can prove or disprove purposeful and malicious killing, we prove or disprove that a murder took place. And for any proven murder, a real murderer exists—or did at the time.

The essays in this section are arguments—with varying degrees of logical plausibility—about murders. In the first essay in this section, Daniel Cohen evaluates the now famous argument that Napoleon was murdered and argues that the evidence is inconclusive. (Sometimes in argument, our conclusions must be less than dramatic!) In the next reading, Anthony Berkeley Cox questions the general assumption that the notorious Englishman, Dr. Crippen, was in fact a murderer. Cox's own assumptions bear some close scrutiny. In the third selection, Michael Harrison argues against the persistent rumor that Prince "Eddy," the Duke of Clarence—and heir to the throne of his grand-mother, Queen Victoria—was the infamous Jack the Ripper. The strength of Harrison's logical reasoning provides a useful contrast to Cox's. And in the last essay in this section, Freeman Wills Crofts reasons through the evidence in a murder case famous in its day, the death of George Henry Storrs, to what Crofts argues is a probable solution.

Because these were real crimes (except, possibly, in Napoleon's case), there must be real solutions. But no one has yet advanced theories that fit all the known facts, that take into account all the evidence, that resolve all the contradictions. There are facts, but many are disputed. There is evidence, but not much. There are plausible theories—perhaps, in some cases, too many. Without a certain culprit in hand, we (and these writers) are thrown back upon our own reasoning to draw a probable conclusion. As you read, be aware that people caught up in their own theories sometimes overlook, misinterpret, or even distort inconvenient evidence. Assess the evidence and evaluate the arguments, and perhaps you will determine that one writer or another has argued the correct solution to a particular crime. Or perhaps, by reasoning to a sounder conclusion from the same evidence, *you* will solve it.

The Death of Napoleon

DANIEL COHEN

Daniel Cohen is an author with a particular interest, as he puts it, in "a variety of mysteries—everything from UFOs to ghosts." Among his many books are *Famous Curses* (1979), *America's Very Own Ghosts* (1985), and *The Encyclopedia of Unsolved Crimes* (1988), from which this essay is taken. Cohen applies logical reasoning to the argument advanced by a Swedish Napoleon buff, Sten Forshufvud, that Napoleon was certainly murdered and *almost* certainly murdered by

Count Charles-Tristan de Montholon, a sometime supporter who joined Napoleon in exile on St. Helena. Cohen evaluates the Forshufvud theory carefully and draws a somewhat different conclusion by challenging one or two of Forshufvud's premises.

The emperor Napoleon was a particularly worrisome prisoner. 1 After conquering much of Europe and terrorizing all of it, he was finally defeated and sent into exile on the island of Elba. But he escaped, gathered another army, and threw another massive scare into the ruling families of Europe until he was finally defeated at the battle of Waterloo and sent into exile on the remote island of St. Helena, from which it was assumed, and hoped, that he would never escape.

Even in his distant exile, Napoleon continued to worry the Eu- 2 ropean governments. There were constant rumors that some plot or the other was being hatched to help the former emperor escape. So long as Napoleon was alive, he remained a threat. It would be so much more convenient for the rulers of Europe if he were dead. But to execute Napoleon would be to create a martyr. Besides, rulers do not like to kill other rulers, even their enemies. It sets a bad precedent. However, there undoubtedly were many powerful people who longed for the former emperor to die quietly and swiftly.

Napoleon was aware that he was in the hands of his enemies—his 3 exile was under control of the British—and that many wished him dead. So he feared, and probably expected, that he would be poisoned.

Napoleon had been depressed and intermittently unwell since his 4 arrival on St. Helena in 1815. The island was not the most cheerful or healthful of places, and while Napoleon was not exactly a prisoner, he certainly wasn't a free man. By 1818, he began suffering from fairly alarming symptoms—sharp pains in the side and chronically cold feet. By January of 1821, Napoleon was feeling very ill, and he told people that he did not think he had long to live. In addition to worrying about poison, Napoleon also worried about cancer. His own father had died of cancer at the age of thirty-five, and Napoleon asked his doctor if the disease could be hereditary.

His symptoms multiplied: a dry cough, constant thirst, weak 5 pulse, nausea, chills, shivering. Until the very end, Napoleon refused to take any medicines, which, in any case, probably wouldn't have done him any good. By mid-April, he made out his will and he expressed the wish that after his death an autopsy should be performed on his body. But he didn't want any English physicians to be involved. On May 5, 1821, after much suffering, Napoleon died.

An autopsy was performed by seven doctors, but contrary to 6

Napoleon's wish, six of the seven were English. The doctors were in sharp disagreement as to what they had found. There was what appeared to be a growth in the stomach, but the doctors could not agree on whether it was cancerous or not, and whether it had been the cause of the emperor's death.

Napoleon was buried in an unmarked grave on St. Helena. Nine- 7 teen years later, the political climate had shifted. Napoleon was once again revered as a hero in France, and his body was removed from St. Helena to be reinterred in the massive crypt of L'Eglise Royale, in the Hotel des Invalides in Paris. Those who witnessed the opening of Napoleon's grave in St. Helena were astonished that the corpse was in a remarkable state of preservation, though no special efforts had been made to preserve it.

From the moment of his death, rumors that Napoleon had been 8 poisoned circulated widely, but there was no solid evidence to support them. There have been rumors of poison around the unexplained death of every prominent person in history.

Among those attracted by the controversy surrounding Napo- 9 leon's death was, improbably, a Swedish dentist and Napoleon buff named Sten Forshufvud. After reading and rereading the accounts of the emperor's final years, he became convinced that Napoleon showed all the signs of arsenic poisoning before his death. The doctors who performed the autopsy on Napoleon had no tests for arsenic, and if they had any suspicions, the English doctors would not have wished to make them public. More than a century later, how could Forshufvud test his theory?

In 1960, Forshufvud learned that a Dr. Hamilton Smith of the 10 University of Glasgow had developed a test that could detect the presence of arsenic in a single strand of hair. It was well known that hair retained arsenic, but previous tests required a considerable quantity of hair. It would be hard enough to get a single strand of the emperor's hair.

It was known that several locks of Napoleon's hair had been cut as 11 souvenirs on the day after his death. Forshufvud finally located one in the possession of Commandant Henri Lachouque, a leading Napoleon expert in Paris. Lachouque was intrigued by the project and was quite happy to part with a strand.

When the hair was tested by Dr. Smith, it showed that Napoleon 12 had been exposed to relatively large amounts of arsenic. More sensitive tests on other strands of hair indicated that Napoleon had received large but not necessarily fatal doses of arsenic at times that corresponded roughly to the times when the emperor fell ill.

When news of Forshufvud's theory was published, he was con- 13 tacted by a descendant of Betsy Balcombe, a girl who had lived on St.

Helena and had become a great friend of the emperor during his years of exile. He learned that it had long been a suspicion in the Balcombe family that Napoleon had been poisoned. He also learned more about the daily life of Napoleon in exile, and of the individuals who had surrounded him in his final years. Forshufvud was not content merely to prove that Napoleon had been poisoned; he wanted to discover exactly who had done the poisoning.

Traces of arsenic began showing up in Napoleon in 1818; thus, everyone who arrived at St. Helena after that year was eliminated. The English, Forshufvud reasoned, would not have risked international scandal by doing the job directly. Some of Napoleon's servants had been with the emperor too long and had proved their loyalty so often they were considered above suspicion. Finally, Forshufvud was left with only one credible suspect—Count Charles-Tristan de Montholon. Montholon was a curious figure. He had been an aristocrat, but had served Napoleon. He switched back to the Bourbons when Napoleon was defeated, but after Waterloo he rejoined the defeated emperor and chose to follow him into lonely exile. His motives were unclear, for he had never been a particularly enthusiastic supporter of Napoleon. On St. Helena, Montholon largely took charge of Napoleon's household, including the food supply. 14

Forshufvud reasoned that Montholon had been sent to St. Helena for the specific purpose of killing Napoleon. The murder plot, Forshufvud believed, had been instigated by the Count d'Artois, known as Monsieur, the younger brother of the newly restored Bourbon king, Louis XVIII, and of Louis XVI, who had been beheaded during the French Revolution. Monsieur was fanatical in his hatred of anything remotely connected with the Revolution, which had deprived him of his power, and he was particularly passionate in his hatred of the usurper Napoleon. While in exile during Napoleon's reign, d'Artois had hatched a long string of unsuccessful plots against Napoleon. He had his own network of spies, and was convinced that even in distant St. Helena, Napoleon represented a grave threat. It would not have been difficult for him to enlist a man like Montholon, who was always in need of money, to slowly poison the menace. 15

D'Artois was to briefly rule France as Charles X, but he was again driven from power and into exile. 16

At the end of his long quest, Sten Forshufvud finally went to St. Helena, the scene of the murder that he believed he had effectively been able to reconstruct. He stood at the gravesite where Napoleon's body had first been buried and thought about the moment, in October 1840, when Napoleon's remains were dug up to be returned in glory to France. Most of those who had shared the emperor's exile and were still alive had returned to the gravesite. Montholon had not. 17

In their book *The Murder of Napoleon,* authors Ben Weider and   18
David Hapgood write:

"It was just as well for Montholon, Forshufvud reflected, that he   19
was not at this spot on that rainy, foggy day when the companions of
the exile watched workmen open the Emperor's grave. The assassin
might have feared that the witnesses would understand the meaning
of the startling sight they saw in that grave. Napoleon's body had not
been embalmed, but merely buried as it was after the autopsy. It was
enclosed in four coffins, two of them of metal, but none of these were
airtight. The witnesses expected, given the normal decay of nineteen
years, that when the innermost coffin was opened they would see a
skeleton.

"Napoleon's body was perfectly preserved. He looked as if he   20
were asleep. His face had changed less in those nineteen years than
the faces of those who were now gazing down into the grave. Napoleon's clothing, the uniform in which he was buried, was decayed, but
not the body itself. Forshufvud knew the explanation for this seeming
miracle—arsenic. Arsenic the destroyer is also a preservative of living
tissue: museums often use it to preserve specimens, and a human
corpse will decay much more slowly if the person is exposed to chronic
arsenic poisoning. And so Napoleon's body was mutely testifying to
the fact of his assassination. It could still testify today if the French
would only agree to open the great tomb at Les Invalides and the
coffins within which the Emperor's remains were sealed."

Forshufvud's findings about the arsenic in Napoleon's hair got a   21
tremendous amount of international publicity, and many people have
come to accept poisoning as the last word on the death of Napoleon.
But it isn't. Sensational, and, yes, logical as this solution may seem, it
is far from proved. First, there is not a single scrap of new documentary evidence supporting the conclusion. There is no deathbed confes-
sion from Montholon; no incriminating papers have turned up in the
archives of Charles X.

There are also the results of the autopsy. The fact that no evidence   22
of poisoning was found by the doctors is not significant, but they did
find that Napoleon had a tumor in his stomach. It is more than probable that the tumor was cancerous, and that Napoleon died of stomach
cancer, just as his father had. Even before the alleged poisoning began, Napoleon had complained of stomach pains. Forshufvud,
however, believes that the condition of Napoleon's stomach was the
result of the corrosive effect of the poison.

What about the arsenic in the emperor's hair? There are many   23
ways that arsenic can get into the human body without assuming that
an unknown poisoner is secretly sprinkling it on the food. A form of
arsenic was once very popular as a pigment for coloring everything

from fabric to wallpaper. In 1982, Dr. David Jones found that Napoleon's wallpaper at St. Helena contained arsenic.

Proponents of the murder theory respond that it is highly unlikely 24 that Napoleon could have absorbed enough arsenic from the wallpaper to account for the quantity found in his body. Forshufvud had considered the possibility of arsenic in the environment, but decided that it was not a possible explanation because others who lived in the house had not come down with the same symptoms. But what if Napoleon had been in the habit of leaning on the wall or tracing the designs with his finger and then putting his finger in his mouth? This might have dramatically increased his risk of exposure. But we really don't know.

Opening the emperor's tomb and examining his remains with the 25 sensitive tools of modern science might enable researchers to answer many of the questions, though probably not to everyone's satisfaction. But no one seriously believes this will be done—so the questions will always remain.

QUESTIONS AND IDEAS FOR DISCUSSION

1.   The second paragraph of this essay tells why Napoleon was exiled rather than executed. Is this an explanation of events or an argument for a particular interpretation of events? Explain your answer.

2.   Paragraph 3 claims that Napoleon "probably expected [to] be poisoned." What support for this claim is stated, and what is implied?

3.   Paragraphs 4 through 7 provide information that we are meant to examine for evidence of foul play. What reasoning and data do you find that clearly support a claim that Napoleon was murdered? What statements *might* lead to such a conclusion? What statements undermine the argument that Napoleon was murdered?

4.   Evaluate the strength of the following statements as support for the claim that Napoleon was murdered:

When the hair was tested by Dr. Smith, it showed that Napoleon had been exposed to relatively large amounts of arsenic. (paragraph 12)

He learned that it had long been a suspicion in the Balcombe family that Napoleon had been poisoned. (13)

5.   Evaluate the strength of the following statements as support for the claim that Napoleon was not murdered:

His own father had died of cancer at the age of thirty-five. . . . (4)

There was what appeared to be a growth in the stomach, but the doctors could not agree on whether it was cancerous or not, and whether it had been the cause of the emperor's death. (6)

6. At what point do you realize toward what conclusion the author is leading you? Are you surprised? Disappointed? Or do you agree with the author that his is the most (or only) reasonable conclusion? Could the evidence the author summarizes in this essay reasonably support another conclusion? Explain the reasons for your answers.

Doctor Crippen: Was He a Murderer?
ANTHONY BERKELEY COX

Writing twelve mystery novels under the pseudonym of Anthony Berkeley and three as Francis Iles, Anthony Berkeley Cox (1893–1971) was a mystery writer of some fame in his day. He was one of the founding members of the Detection Club—along with Dorothy Sayers, G. K. Chesterton, and Agatha Christie. However, Cox wrote no novels after 1939, and his books are no longer in print. This essay is included in Richard Glyn Jones's *The Mammoth Book of Murder* (1989). Its subject is little known in the United States today, and we are puzzled by references to Doctor Crippen in Agatha Christie mysteries. But in England, Crippen is infamous, preserved in waxen image in Madame Tussaud's Chamber of Horrors. Cox here argues a revolutionary assertion: that Doctor Crippen did *not* murder his wife and bury her dismembered body in his cellar.

This essay provides a cautionary reminder that conclusions must be logically drawn from true premises in order to be acceptable, for Cox reasons from premises almost comical in their blithe disregard for fact. Because the essay (though undated) was written in the early decades of this century about a crime that occurred in 1910, it no doubt owes some of its curious assumptions to its era. Nonetheless, the grounds for logical proof were no different then than they are now. As you read, notice which of Cox's assumptions are reasonable and which are not; consider which of his conclusions follow inevitably from his premises and which do not. And decide for yourself whether or not Doctor Crippen was "dreadfully maligned" and unjustly convicted.

It is ironical that the name of the man who, of all the classical murderers, was the least certainly guilty, should have become almost a synonym for the word "murderer." It is no less ironical that a man whose chief characteristics were his kindness and gentle charm, should be remembered only as an inhuman monster.

Few murder cases have remained as famous as that of unfortunate little Hawley Harvey Crippen. Many people to-day have never heard of Seddon, whose case, within a year or two of Crippen's, aroused almost as much interest at the time; yet who is there even now who does not think he knows all about Crippen?

In point of fact he knows very little about Crippen: not even that 3 most important thing of all, namely the very great possibility, amounting almost to probability, that Crippen never committed murder at all.

At the time of his tragedy Hawley Crippen was nearly fifty years 4 old. Here is an interesting point for a beginning. I have never seen any statistics regarding the age of murderers, but one would be inclined to say off-hand that few are as old as this.

If murder is in the blood, it will come out before half a century. 5 Moreover Crippen's alleged crime was one of passion. Is not fifty a little late in life to begin committing murder for love? We may bear the point in mind later.

Crippen is usually referred to as "Dr." Actually, he was not a 6 qualified medical man. He underwent a sketchy kind of training in his own country (he was a native of Michigan, U.S.A.) and in 1883, when he was twenty-one years old, paid a visit to London where he attended several London hospitals in a haphazard way.

The only degree he ever achieved was a diploma in 1883 as an ear 7 and eye specialist at the Ophthalmic Hospital in New York, which may or may not have given him the right to call himself a "doctor," but certainly did not make him one. In view of the profession he was practicing in London at the time of his wife's death, this point will also become important.

After obtaining his diploma, Crippen practiced during the next 8 fifteen years at a variety of places, including Detroit, Santiago, Salt Lake City, New York, Philadelphia, and Toronto, never staying more than two years in any of them; though whether this was due to restlessness of disposition or inability to make a living, we do not know.

In 1887 he married for the first time; his wife died three or four 9 years later leaving a son who, at the time of his father's trial, was living in California. In 1893 he fell in love with a young girl who was not too young to have acquired a bad reputation even at the age of seventeen. This girl passed under the name of Cora Turner. Her mother was a German and her father a Russian Pole, and her real name was Kunigunde Mackamotzki; so that Cora Turner was certainly a change towards simplicity.

Crippen married her and, in 1900, brought her to London, when 10 he obtained the post of manager of the English branch of a patent medicine firm.

If Crippen really did murder his wife, it cannot be denied that Mrs. 11 Crippen almost brought the deed upon herself. She was not a pleasant woman. Possessed of an almost pathologically swollen vanity, she fancied herself for honors on the music-hall stage; at one time indeed, she expected to bring the world to her feet in grand opera, though her voice was no better than that of any of the young women who, at that time, used to sing ballads in the drawing-room after supper.

In any case, arrived in London, Cora Crippen made all prepara- 12 tions to take it by storm. She chose the stage name of "Belle Elmore," she laid in a huge stock of expensive gowns, she joined the Music-hall Ladies' Guild, she did in fact everything except make a success on the stage; for she only appeared on it once, and was then promptly hissed off it by the audience.

Soured by this reception, and the impossibility of obtaining an- 13 other engagement, Mrs. Crippen proceeded to take it out of the indulgent little husband who had paid for all the gowns, the singing-lessons, the agents' fees, and everything else: for at this time Crippen adored his shrewish wife, believing in her talents when no one else did.

She hen-pecked him unmercifully, quarrelled with him, insulted 14 him before his friends, and did not draw the line at assuaging her wounded vanity with the attentions, and more than the attentions, of other men.

In short, Cora Crippen did what so many stupid, shrewish wives 15 have done before her and literally drove her amiable little husband out of love with her.

And to drive out of love with his wife a man who has been 16 accustomed to love is tantamount to driving him into the arms of another woman. Mrs. Crippen drove her husband into the arms of a typist at his office, Ethel Le Neve.

All this, of course, took time. It was 1900 when the Crippens came 17 to London; it was 1910 when Cora Crippen died; and during those ten years there is no doubt that Crippen's home life was becoming more and more intolerable. Between him and Miss Le Neve there sprang up a love which, on Crippen's side at any rate, was to prove stronger than the fear of death.

And then Mrs. Crippen died. 18

There is no need to give the events which followed in any close 19 detail, for they are still well known. Crippen made blunder after blunder—so incredibly foolish that there is surely some inference to be drawn from that very foolishness. He pawned his wife's jewellery quite openly; some of it he gave to Miss Le Neve, and let her wear it openly; he had even bought the hyoscin from which his wife was to die quite openly from a chemist who knew him well and had signed the book in his own name.

If these were indeed the acts of a deliberate murderer then surely a 20 more stupid murderer never existed. I suggest that they were not the acts of a deliberate murderer.

Then, by this small detail and that, an inaccuracy here and there, 21 suspicion was aroused among Mrs. Crippen's friends; information was lodged at Scotland Yard, and a Detective-Inspector went to Hill-drop Crescent to interview Crippen.

The Inspector viewed the visit as a formality; Crippen's demeanor 22 confirmed his expectation that it was all nothing but a mare's nest. But three days later a small point took the Inspector up to Hilldrop Crescent again—and Crippen had fled. If Crippen had stood his ground then, neither you nor I would ever have heard of him.

The events that followed roused the excitement of two continents. 23 It was not merely a case of an insignificant little man being wanted for wife murder; every romantic ingredient was present to turn the affair into the greatest of all classical murder hunts.

There was the identification of the pair on the liner *Montrose* by 24 means of the new-fangled wireless telegraphy; there was the fact that Ethel Le Neve was disguised as a boy; there was the fact that the dead wife's body had been not merely buried under the cellar floor, but dismembered first—and dismemberment invariably rouses [the] public's horror; there was the dramatic chase of the *Montrose* across the Atlantic by Inspector Dew in a faster boat, with the eyes of the whole world on the race except only those of the *Montrose*'s own passengers; there was the love affair which had caused the whole tragedy; and there was finally, the character of Crippen himself as it began to leak out—a gentle, affectionate, mild, precise little man in late middle age, the last little man in the whole world, one would have said, to commit a callous and inhuman murder.

Inspector Dew did reach America first. Crippen was arrested on 25 the *Montrose* when she docked, brought back to England, tried, condemned and hanged. On the evidence before them the jury could have returned no other verdict. Miss Le Neve, tried separately as an accessory after the fact, was acquitted. The letters Crippen wrote to her from prison as he awaited execution are among the most touching documents ever penned.

What, then, is the truth? How can it be asserted, in face of these 26 facts, that Crippen never did commit murder? What considerations, pointing to this conclusion, never came before the jury at all?

It is always easy to argue, on one side or the other. Facts alone 27 can determine truth; and there is one fact in Crippen's case which appears to me insurmountable, in the absence of any greater facts to confute it.

Unfortunately, however, it is a fact of psychology; and psychol- 28 ogy, even psychological fact, carries little or no weight in a court of law. Evidence may be given as to character, but it influences little but the sentence. And yet it is character that determines action.

The insurmountable fact is this: there is overwhelming evidence 29 that Crippen was mild, gentle, and kindly—and mild, gentle, kindly men simply do not commit murder. That is surely incontrovertible. One does not remain gentle and kindly for forty-eight years and then, throwing off the mask, reveal oneself suddenly as a fiend.

That elementary fact of psychology has been recognized for at least 30 two thousand years. It is, after all, a long time since the rule was laid down that *nemo fuit repente turpissimus* (no one ever became vile all of a sudden). And there is no evidence that Crippen ever slid at all down the path of vileness; it is just assumed that he took it in one single bound.

Admit that one psychological fact, if to prove no more than that 31 there is something queer behind the scenes here, and instantly the whole case becomes full of difficulties.

Take, for instance, the choice of poison. Very little was known in 32 1910 about hyoscin, or henbane. It had never been used in a case of murder. It was, I fancy, not even in the British Pharmacopoeia. Why did Crippen choose it?

Consider Crippen's profession. He was not a bona fide doctor, nor 33 did he practice as such. He filled a succession of posts in firms concerned with patent medicines. Almost up to his last moments he was engaged in compiling a formula for a patent medicine of his own, [to] be called *Sans Peine.*

He was, in fact, used to dealing with drugs, but not in the way of 34 the recognized prescriptions: he was used to experimenting with them.

Now put these two considerations together, and look at them in 35 the light of a very curious piece of evidence which was certainly never put forward at the trial, for it was not known then. This evidence takes us from an insignificant villa in London to no less a place than the Royal Palace in St. Petersburg, Russia.

It has been reliably established that, at just about the same time 36 as Crippen was dabbling with hyoscin here, the court Magician, or Conjurer, at St. Petersburg, a man named Papus, was dosing the Tsar and Tsarina with a mixture of hyoscin and hashish, which was said to produce singularly pleasing effects, the admixture of hashish having been found to neutralize much of the toxic properties of hyoscin. What does this give us? It shows us that at this time, the quacks of Europe were experimenting with hyoscin, of which all they knew for certain was that it had properties as a narcotic. And Crippen was a quack.

This seems not only to offer a possible explanation of Crippen's 37 very puzzling choice of a drug; but it goes some way, too, to suggest that his intention was not murderous. That suggestion is more than strengthened by the absence of any concealment of the purchase—the last thing, surely, that one would expect with a guilty intention.

Now, it is a theory of my own that dismemberment seldom enters 38 into any plan of calculated murder. That is to say, when dismemberment occurs it almost amounts to proof that murder had not been planned ahead, and shows that the killing was, if not accidental, at any rate decided only on the spur of the moment.

But a poisoning is never decided on the spur of the moment. 39 Therefore a poisoning, followed by dismemberment, which in turn is followed only by ordinary burial, and not by some such method as a piecemeal burning of the body, carries all the appearances of unexpected instead of expected death.

If, further, we admit dismemberment as indicative of an absence 40 of plan, we see more and more evidence to the same effect. When obvious blunder after obvious blunder is made the conclusion is difficult to resist that nothing was thought out in advance.

Yet the use of poison for purposes of murder is equally strong 41 evidence of premeditated planning. The only way of reconciling these opposing factors in the case of Crippen is that he did not intend to kill with his poison.

What, then, did he intend to do?   42

The late Sir Edward Marshall Hall, who believed strongly in Crip- 43 pen's innocence, propounded a theory to answer this question which seems to me from every point of view convincing. It was his belief that Crippen, knowing of hyoscin only as a narcotic, used it upon his wife, not with any intention of killing her, but in order to put her into a drugged sleep so that he could spend the evening with Miss Le Neve.

This, I think, is what must have happened. But Crippen, in his 44 ignorance, either administered an overdose or perhaps mixed his hyoscin with some agent which did not neutralize it sufficiently. In any case he discovered that he had killed instead of drugged, and lost his head. For plainly he did lose his head. Crippen was not of the stuff of which murderers are made.

There is, actually, a piece of evidence supporting this theory 45 which came out at the trial, though its significance was missed then. On the night before her death Mrs. Crippen had some friends in, who left at about midnight. At Miss Le Neve's trial her landlady gave evidence that one night at the end of January Miss Le Neve came home very late in a state of considerable distress, quite horror-stricken, in fact, as if she had suffered a great shock, and the time mentioned was *two o'clock in the morning.* Mrs. Crippen died on January 31. If Crippen had intended to murder his wife he would not have had Miss Le Neve in the house at the time. If Miss Le Neve was in the house, it may be almost certainly said that murder was not intended.

All these considerations convince me that Crippen was innocent 46 of premeditated murder. That he was responsible for his wife's death is, of course, indubitable, and the defense he adopted, of a blank denial of everything, was the worst possible one. At worst he was guilty only of manslaughter.

Why, then, did he not make a clean breast of the facts and plead 47 manslaughter, or even accident?

The answer to that question is one of the most striking features of 48 the whole case. He was in fact pressed to do this, but he refused. His reason was that to substantiate his plea he would have to admit that Miss Le Neve was in the house that night; and, if anything went wrong with the case and the jury did bring in a verdict of murder, this might have been prejudicial to Miss Le Neve.

He was almost assured of an acquittal from the murder charge if he 49 permitted this defense, but on the quite slender danger of entangling Miss Le Neve he decided upon almost certain death for himself.

I always feel very sorry for Crippen. He has been dreadfully 50 maligned. I cannot believe that he was a monster. Certainly he was, as the late Lord Birkenhead said of him, "a brave man and a true lover."

QUESTIONS AND IDEAS FOR DISCUSSION

1. Anthony Berkeley Cox argues that Doctor Crippen was innocent of murder. State the core argument that comprises Cox's thesis, in your own or his words. How convincing do you find his argument? Why?

2. Consider the following deductive arguments advanced by Cox. What premises (or conclusions) are implied rather than stated? How sound do you find Cox's reasoning? Comment.

> At the time of his tragedy Hawley Crippen was nearly fifty years old. . . . If murder is in the blood, it will come out before half a century. (paragraphs 4, 5)

> Crippen made blunder after blunder—so incredibly foolish that there is surely some inference to be drawn from that very foolishness. (19)

> If these were indeed the acts of a deliberate murderer then surely a more stupid murderer never existed. I suggest that they were not the acts of a deliberate murderer. (20)

> The insurmountable fact is this: there is overwhelming evidence that Crippen was mild, gentle, and kindly—and mild, gentle, kindly men simply do not commit murder. (29)

3. Many of Cox's arguments rely at least in part on the premise that Crippen was "mild, gentle, and kindly" (29). What evidence does Cox offer that sheds light on Crippen's temperament? Discuss.

4. To what extent does the manner of Cora Crippen's death exonerate her husband of murder, according to this essay? Evaluate Cox's reasoning.

5. Examine Cox's statements, claims, and assumptions about Cora Crippen. How, if at all, do they affect the argument about Doctor Crippen's guilt or innocence? Is there a logical relationship? Explain.

6. Which of Cox's arguments are the most reasonable? Why?

The Duke of Clarence: Prince or Ripper?
MICHAEL HARRISON

Michael Harrison is an Irish writer with interests ranging from cookery to crime and with a long list of published books on everything from stamp collecting to the Wright brothers and the beginning of aviation. In 1972, he published a biography of Queen Victoria's grandson, *Clarence: The Life of the Duke of Clarence and Avondale KG, 1864–1892.* Clarence, known to his family as Eddy, was the son of the Prince of Wales and would have become king of England after his father, had he not died at age twenty-eight in 1892. Though *Clarence* is concerned only briefly (primarily in the argument reprinted below) with the suspicions that Prince Eddy might have been Jack the Ripper, the book's subtitle in its American printing was changed to *Was He Jack the Ripper?* Harrison's answer, as you will read, is a firm "no." Harrison is a sympathetic biographer, however, so you must carefully analyze and evaluate his exoneration of Clarence. The Duke of Clarence was heir to England's throne. Surely he could not have been Jack the Ripper. Or could he?

In November, 1970, the extraordinary rumor swept through the world that the Whitechapel mass-murderer, notorious in criminal history as "Jack the Ripper," was none other than Prince Albert Victor, Duke of Clarence and Avondale. The spark which fired this train of blazing scandal was an article by the late Dr. T. E. A. Stowell, C.B.E., M.D., which appeared that month in *The Criminologist.*

The "Ripper" article was "picked up" by a *Sunday Times* staff feature-writer, Mr. Magnus Linklater, who, naturally, set out to interview Dr. Stowell and to pin him down, if possible, to a more detailed statement of the murderer's identity than had appeared in *The Criminologist.* Subsequently interviewed on television, it was inevitable that

Dr. Stowell, whilst refusing to state positively that his "suspect" *was* the Duke of Clarence and Avondale, seemed equally reluctant to state positively that Eddy was *not* the Ripper.

Under a picture of Eddy, *Time* asked the question: *Was this the* 3 *Ripper?* Many other journals were even less sensitive in their approach to the identification of a sadistic and maniac murderer with one who had been in the direct line of succession to the Crown of Great Britain.

If the editors and feature writers had read Stowell's article they 4 would have realized that the author had set out to convey the impression, though without actually committing himself to a positive statement, that he not only believed, but actually knew, that Eddy and the Ripper were the same.

Stowell had, it is clear, convinced himself that a man of whom he 5 had got some particulars *at third hand* was Eddy. It is true that certain dates in the lives of both the real Ripper and of Eddy do tally, but Stowell preferred to believe that he was hearing about Eddy, rather than about someone of lower social rank. It made a better story.

Before considering Dr. Stowell's claims in detail, it is necessary 6 briefly to look at the dreadful crimes whose commission has given Jack the Ripper a dubious immortality as the sadistical murderer *par excellence.*

It is not generally agreed that there were only five murders, and 7 some criminologists include in the series a murder as early as 1887 and another as late as 1892.[1] But *all* agree that five murders were the work of a single killer, the self-styled "Jack the Ripper," since the *modus operandi*, varying only in savagery, but never in type, recurs as the characteristic "signature."

These dominant features may be summarized as follows: 8

1. Although sexually motivated, the murders are not sexual assaults in the ordinary meaning of the phrase. The murderer in no case attempted sexual intercourse, either normally or abnormally, with the victim, and the pudenda were not attacked in any way.

2. The five women were silenced, almost certainly by the clapping of a hand over their mouths, and were killed by having their throats slit with a knife.

3. Once dead, the woman was eviscerated. The extent of this depended upon the amount of time available to the murderer.

---

[1] The five uncontested Ripper murders were those of Mary Ann ("Polly") Nichols, August 31, 1888; Annie Chapman, September 8, 1888; Elizabeth Stride, September 30, 1888; Catherine Eddowes, September 30, 1888; and Mary Jane Kelly, November 9, 1888. Other murders sometimes credited to the Ripper were those of Emma Smith, April 3, 1888; Martha Turner (or Tabram), August 7, 1888; Alice McKenzie, July 16, 1889; and Frances Coles, February 13, 1891. [Ed.]

4. The murderer not only eviscerated his victim, but also took away with him, in most cases, the organs he had removed. His principal interest, according to the evidence of what was missing from the corpses, seems to have been the uterus, although other organs— ovaries, kidneys, bladder—were sometimes cut out. But the focus of the murderer's obsession would appear to have been the uterus.

There is no need to go into the ghastly details of the crimes, for 9 these are readily available in recent books by Colin Wilson, Tom Cullen and Donald McCormick. My tracking down of the murderer has depended not on what he did, but *how he managed to do it*, an awkward question that all the commentators on the Ripper crimes have understandably declined to tackle. The fact that the evisceration of a woman differs only in the minutest detail from the gralloching of a stag has, of course, been noticed. Indeed, it is one of the arguments used by Dr. Stowell for fastening the crime on Eddy. But to accuse a man simply because he knows how to gralloch a stag is as absurd as it is unjust—Stowell might as well have accused almost any landowner of the day or his many guests.

The seriousness with which the Home Office took, not so much 10 the crimes, as the terror inspired by them, is sufficiently indicated by the fact that General Sir Charles Warren, Chief Commissioner of Metropolitan Police, summoned back the Chief of the Criminal Investigation Department from holiday in Switzerland. The latter promptly assigned seven senior C.I.D. officers to assist the six hundred police already serving with H Division and those men of the City Police who had been brought into the case when the last-but-one victim died just within the City limits.

The efforts of all these men were hampered, as they always are in 11 similar circumstances, by lack of any eye-witness evidence and by an overplus of surmise. This latter is hardly surprising in the light of the extensive newspaper coverage of the crimes. Even Queen Victoria was interested in the Ripper—and not, as one writer suggests, because she feared that he might be her beloved grandson, Eddy! The tone of the letters that the Queen wrote, both to the Chief Commissioner of Police and to the Editor of *The Times*, are clearly not those of a woman fearful that her own family was mixed up in these awful crimes.

When modern commentators are spinning their theories about the 12 identity of the Ripper, they make great play with the fact that a man—or men—seen talking to the women victims was—or were— "softly spoken." Dr. Stowell, for example, asks, "What do we know of the murderer? Witnesses stated that he was under medium height—

5 ft. 6 in. to 5 ft. 7 in. He spoke 'softly,' this probably meant that he spoke like a gentleman."

Surmise apart, there is no reason why the "softly spoken" man 13 seen talking to Mary Jane Kelly, most diabolically-mutilated of all the victims, should have been her murderer.

Even assuming that "softly spoken" means "well-spoken," it is 14 not true, as so many assume, that the well-spoken man was a rarity in the East End of the 1880s. Almost as many professional men worked there as in the West End—bank-managers, civil engineers, doctors in both private and hospital practice, senior officials of the Port of London Authority, Trinity House, H. M. Customs.

But—and the significance of this fact appears to have missed most 15 of the investigators—there was also another type of "toff" with which the East End had become familiar in the twenty years or so before Jack the Ripper initiated "the Autumn of Terror." For a non-Socialist, non-political, interest in the "underprivileged" had swept through the upper strata of society, and "social work" became fashionable, not only in the universities, but even with such shallow thinkers as the Prince of Wales.

In February, 1884, during Eddy's first year at Trinity, the Prince of 16 Wales had accepted nomination to membership of a Royal Commission on the Housing of the Working Classes. The membership of the Commission reflects the "pioneering" character of its intentions, and consisted of Lord Brownlow, whose heir, Lionel Cust, was a friend of Eddy's; Lord Carrington; Jesse Collings; G. J. Goschen; Lord Salisbury; and Cardinal Manning; under the chairmanship of Sir Charles Dilke, soon to fall from grace and political power through the notorious Crawford case. As well as attending the regular meetings of the Commission, the Prince, in disguise and accompanied by Lord Carrington, explored some of the Clerkenwell slums.

One thing, however, remains clear, that Eddy was not the Ripper. 17 Such evidence of witnesses as exists, and this was never more than that a victim was seen talking to a man, is so contradictory that it is of no use at all. As all the murdered women were prostitutes, the very nature of their calling would have made them accost men, so that the sight of their talking to a man assumed sinister significance only because of what happened to them later.

One such witness was an ex-night-watchman named Hutchinson, 18 "who saw the Ripper talking to Mary Kelly." This is Colin Wilson's account from his excellent *A Casebook of Murder:*

> After she left [Hutchinson], he saw her picked up by a swarthy-looking man in Commercial Street. He thought the man looked too well-dressed to be hanging around the East End at such an hour, but

he had no suspicion that it was the Ripper. He had a gold watch chain and a heavy moustache that curled up at the ends.

Now Eddy had a moustache which curled up at the ends, but the 19 fact that *Pomade Hongroise* was a best-seller at chemists' and barbers' shops makes it clear that so did most of the moustaches in the 1880s. In any case, Eddy's little moustache could in no way be described as "heavy." Neither was Eddy swarthy nor, going back to earlier "evidence," was he "below the medium height," being, in fact, a little under six feet tall.

Even if the Court Circular did not provide an alibi for Eddy for 20 every one of those nights on which an "unfortunate" was horribly done to death, the evidence of contradictory witnesses shows that no-one resembling Eddy was ever seen talking to any of the women.

But the Court Circular does provide the necessary alibi. If the 21 murders were all the work of a single murderer, then an alibi for only one would prove innocence of all the crimes. For instance, when the woman, Alice McKenzie, was murdered on the night of 16/17th July, 1889, Eddy was accompanying the Shah of Persia on a wearisome tour of the principal centers of commerce and manufacture in England and Scotland. The Shah arrived at Gravesend on 1st July and took his leave of the Queen at Osborne on 29th July. In all that time Eddy was in constant attendance on the Shah. . . .

Since I know, and shall, at the proper time, reveal this unfortunate 22 madman's identity,[2] it is clear that no-one did see him, for otherwise the police and the Whitechapel *vigilantes* would not have been searching for men of so widely different physical type that the huge Polish-Jewish barber, "Chapman"; the shy, neurotic English barrister, Druitt; and "the mad Russian doctor," Michael Ostrog, could all rank as suspects.[3]

Following the publication of Dr. Stowell's article in *The Criminolo-* 23 *gist* and the subsequent publicity, a letter, signed "Loyalist," was printed in *The Times*. Though anonymous, this letter was authoritative, and merely stated what was true: that the innocent movements and activities of the Duke on all the relative dates were on public record and could be checked by anyone interested.

The weakness of Stowell's account is simply explained, in that he 24 was repeating gossip, and not discussing facts whose evidence he could have examined.

---

[2] In a subsequent section of *Clarence*, Harrison argues at length in favor of another suspect, a friend and former tutor of the Duke of Clarence, James K. Stephen. [Ed.]

[3] These suspects are further described in Colin Wilson's "The Crimes of Jack the Ripper" on page 170. [Ed.]

QUESTIONS AND IDEAS FOR DISCUSSION

1. This argument not only summarizes evidence for its readers but also refers to another argument that we do not have access to. Under such circumstances, how are we to decide whether or not to accept the author's restatements and summaries as objective evidence for his claims? Discuss, using the specific details of this essay as illustration.

2. Harrison considers the best approach to solving the question of the Ripper's identity to focus "not on what he did, but *how he managed to do it*" (paragraph 9). What are the advantages of this approach to the problem? Are there any disadvantages?

3. On what grounds does Harrison challenge the claim that Prince Eddy fits eyewitness descriptions of the Ripper? Is this part of Harrison's argument convincing? Explain.

4. In paragraphs 20 and 21, Harrison argues Prince Eddy's innocence in a series of deductive arguments, including this one:

If the murders were all the work of a single murderer, then an alibi for only one would prove innocence of all the crimes. (21)

Earlier (paragraph 7), Harrison states that five murders are universally agreed to be the work of Jack the Ripper, thereby substantiating the "if" clause of this argument and compelling us to accept the "then" clause: an alibi for only one will suffice. Harrison proceeds to offer an alibi. Are we thereby compelled to accept the conclusion that Eddy was innocent? Why or why not?

5. Considering the argument as a whole, does Harrison convince you that Prince Eddy, the Duke of Clarence, was *not* Jack the Ripper? Give specific reasons for your answer.

The Gorse Hall Mystery

FREEMAN WILLS CROFTS

Freeman Wills Crofts (1879–1957) began writing mystery novels to wile away the time when a long illness in midlife took him away from his job as a railway engineer. His first novel, *The Cask*, is considered a classic of its genre. Crofts's Inspector French was the "first and most resolute of the painstaking professionals",[1] and Croft is noted as well

---

[1] Patricia Craig, ed., *The Oxford Book of English Detective Stories* (Oxford: Oxford UP, 1990) 551.

for popularizing the kind of mystery that hinges on railway timetables.

The following essay, which was reprinted in Richard Glyn Jones
(ed.), *Solved!: Famous Mystery Writers on Classic True-Crime Cases*
(1987), is one of Crofts's few accounts of actual crimes. The crime
victim is not particularly noteworthy, for the unfortunate Mr. Storrs
was a person neither famous nor influential beyond his own community. The murderer was probably even less significant in the scheme
of things. But the crime itself had many odd features and many
curious clues—and it was never solved. Crofts proposes a solution.
But he also offers, at two points, the chance to anticipate his reasoning or to come up with your own argument. As you read, pause at the
end of paragraph 17 and at the end of paragraph 25. Reason from the
premises established up to each of those points, and determine for
yourself what may be argued from the premises Crofts provides.

At the beginning of November, 1909, Mr. George Henry Storrs 1
was murdered at his home, near Stalybridge, under circumstances
which have never been cleared up.

Mr. Storrs was a wealthy builder and mill-owner, and lived with 2
his wife and his wife's niece, Miss Lindley, in a large house named
Gorse Hall. There were three servants—a cook and housemaid resident in the building, and a coachman living with his wife over the
stables.

Mr. Storrs was a kindly and popular man, a good employer, and 3
had no known enemies. He and his wife were a devoted couple, and
both were on affectionate terms with Miss Lindley. The household
may, indeed, be called a happy one.

Its peace, however, was destined to be rudely broken. About 9:30 4
on the night of September 10, 1909, when the family were sitting in the
dining-room, a shot was suddenly fired through the window.

Seeing that no one had been hit Mr. Storrs rushed to the window 5
and pulled aside the blind. He could just see a dark figure disappearing into the shrubbery. When the ladies asked if he knew the man
he replied, after a slight hesitation, that he did not.

Mrs. Storrs was more alarmed than her husband, and next day she 6
insisted on the police being informed and asked to keep a special
watch on the house. She also had a large alarm bell put on the roof,
and it was agreed that if this were sounded the police should instantly
hurry over. It was suggested that the man was a homicidal maniac,
and she was afraid that he might return.

Nothing unusual happened, however, for some seven weeks, and 7
then, on the last Saturday of October, Mr. Storrs called on the police
and asked them to be particularly vigilant in their watch. He said he
had no special reason for making the request, but that he "wanted to
be sure."

That night about midnight the alarm bell sounded and the police 8 hurried to the house. But nothing was wrong. Mr. Storrs said apologetically that he had wished to be sure that the alarm was really efficient, and had rung it as a test.

Sunday and Monday passed uneventfully, but on Monday eve- 9 ning tragedy really did visit the house. Some time after dinner the housemaid had to pass the scullery door, when she saw that the gas was alight. She looked in and found that the window had been broken open, but before she could investigate further a man jumped out from behind the door and seized her wrist. He had a revolver in his hand and he swore that if she made a sound he would shoot her.

Instinctively she twisted away from him, running screaming 10 through the house. He did not fire, but followed her till they reached the hall. There Mr. Storrs, attracted by the noise, rushed out of the dining-room. As soon as the man saw him he cried: "I've got you at last!" Again he did not fire, but as Mr. Storrs ran forward he closed with him and a terrible fight began.

In the meantime Mrs. Storrs and Miss Lindley had also rushed 11 out. For a moment they tried to join in the struggle. Mrs. Storrs actually succeeding in tearing away the man's revolver. Then they saw him draw a knife. But Mr. Storrs gasped out: "The bell! Give the alarm!" and Mrs. Storrs rushed off to ring it, while Miss Lindley fled down the drive to summon help from the Stalybridge Central Club, which was close by.

When assistance came the murderer had disappeared and Mr. 12 Storrs was at the point of death. He had received fifteen terrible knife wounds, and died without making a statement.

While neither the ladies nor the servants were able to give a 13 detailed description of the murderer, declaring that there was nothing distinctive about him, they agreed that he was youngish and poorly dressed, with a slight moustache and long fair hair. The revolver was of a cheap type, and yielded no clue.

A young man called Howard was arrested and charged with the 14 murder. He was a cousin of Mr. Storrs, though he was personally unknown to the ladies. The evidence against him seemed purely circumstantial, but the police had a stronger case than was anticipated. When at the trial Mrs. Storrs and Miss Lindley were asked if they could identify the murderer, they pointed dramatically to the prisoner, and swore he was the man.

No possible question of their bona fides arises; at the same time it 15 became evident during the course of the trial that they were mistaken, Howard's innocence being proved beyond question. The verdict of Not Guilty was received with applause, and Howard left the court a popular hero.

Months afterwards a second man named Wilde was charged with   16
the crime, stood his trial at Chester Assizes, and was also acquitted.

Since then the Gorse Hall Tragedy has remained a complete mys-   17
tery, and no trace of the real murderer has ever been found.

In attempting to reconstruct what may have taken place in this   18
strange tragedy, certain facts at once stand out as significant.

First, the murderer, whom for want of a better name I shall call   19
John, had a definite grievance, real or imaginary, against Mr. Storrs.
This is proved by the facts that he said: "I've got you at last," and that
he did not gain materially through his crime.

Second, Mr. Storrs knew of this grievance and of his own danger.   20
From his manner on the occasion of the attempt on September 9, it is
almost certain that he recognized the man, and when he went to the
police on the last Saturday in October, he evidently expected a further
attack. Moreover, when he saw his assailant in the hall on the night of
his death, he gave no exclamation of surprise, but grappled at once as
with a known foe.

Third, Mr. Storrs obviously wished to keep the affair secret. If he   21
knew his own danger, as I have suggested he did, the fact that he
made no statement on the subject proves this. But it is supported by
his other actions. He did not inform the police of the first attack until
the assailant had had time to get away. I will suggest presently that a
second attack was made on the Saturday night on which the alarm was
sounded, and that on this occasion Mr. Storrs suppressed any mention of John's presence for the same reason: to give him time to escape.

Fourth, owing to Mr. Storr's upright character and kindly disposi-   22
tion, the secret was nothing with which he could reproach himself.

Fifthly, certain of John's actions seem to indicate an unbalanced   23
mind. He entered the house on the night of the murder by smashing a
window, and then committed the folly of turning on the gas. When he
was discovered by the housemaid he followed her through the house,
though he must have known her screams would attract attention.
Again, to strike as many as fifteen times with his knife shows a fury
quite abnormal.

With these salient points in mind, can we suggest any circum-   24
stances which might meet the facts?

I think we can.   25

At first sight it might seem as if the crime were committed by some   26
epileptic or homicidal maniac, subject to recurrent fits of illness. But
this theory would not account for the facts that Mr. Storrs undoubtedly recognized his assailant and yet kept his identity secret. If he had
not had some definite and personal reason for silence, he would surely
have told the police who the man was.

Let us then try to fit a theory on to the facts we know. Let us begin 27 by assuming that John is like Howard in personal appearance, and of an extremely unbalanced and excitable temperament. Let us further assume that he nurses a bitter hatred against Mr. Storrs.

The cause of this hatred—that is, the motive for the crime—we do 28 not know. There is not the slightest indication as to its nature in the evidence. All that we really know is that John had some overwhelming but mistaken sense of grievance against Mr. Storrs.

We are probably on firmer ground when we picture John brooding 29 over his fancied wrongs until his desire for revenge grows first into an obsession and then into actual mania.

On going to see Mr. Storrs John blurts out his grievance and 30 threatens vengeance. Mr. Storrs, however, has no ill-feeling towards his visitor; in fact, he is sorry for him.

His kindly disposition makes him regret the young man's sense of 31 injury, and he is willing to discuss the affair. But John, half insane, will not listen to reason, and Mr. Storrs in self-defense is obliged to summon help.

John, seeing his chance gone, hurries away, determined to suc- 32 ceed at the next opportunity. The person who was called does not realize what he has prevented, and Mr. Storrs, finding the whole matter painful, does not discuss it.

This reconstruction is still speculative and unsupported by direct 33 evidence. But it is clear that John and Mr. Storrs must have had some interview of the kind, in order to account for what follows. This interview, further, was probably not at Gorse Hall, as John was not seen by the inmates.

On September 10, John, who has bought a revolver, goes to Gorse 34 Hall to make his attempt. He reaches the house, creeps up to the only lighted window, finds the blind does not exactly fit and that he can see Mr. Storrs, and fires at him through the window. He sees that he has missed, and noticing that there are other people in the room, realizes that if he remains for a further attempt he may be identified. So he hurries off.

Mr. Storrs realizes he is in danger, and asks the police to be 35 specially vigilant. That night John makes his third attempt, but Mr. Storrs sees him and rings the alarm. John again finds that if he remains, he will be caught. Mr. Storrs, full of pity for the misguided youth, and hoping eventually to bring him to reason, tells the police he was only making a test, in order to give the young fellow time to escape.

It is obvious that there must have been some special circumstances 36 about this attempt which enabled Mr. Storrs to ring the alarm before being attacked. Perhaps, for example, he may have discovered John in the act of swarming up a balcony pillar or a waterpipe, or in such other position that the young man could not use his weapon.

On Monday, John again goes to Gorse Hall. Determined this time 37 to make an end of the matter, he breaks in and commits the murder. He escapes from the country and is therefore not found by the police.

The above reconstruction indicates the lines along which I believe 38 the explanation of this mysterious crime must lie.

QUESTIONS AND IDEAS FOR DISCUSSION

1. Describe Crofts's persona in this essay. Is it believable? Do Crofts's words inspire confidence and trust? Explain, with specific reference to the text. How much does the writer's persona affect your reception of his argument?

2. After reading the first section of this essay (paragraphs 1–17), what inferences did *you* draw about the Gorse Hall murder? (An inference, you will recall, is a supposition about the unsaid or unknown based on what is stated.) On what points, if any, do your inferences differ from those Crofts draws in the second section of his argument (paragraphs 18–23)? On which points, if any, do your inferences differ from your classmates'? Together, decide on the inferences that seem most reasonable, given the data in the first part of the essay.

3. Crofts calls the statements in the second section "facts" (paragraph 18). Are they? Explain.

4. Identify two or three arguments in this essay, and either defend them or challenge them (if the latter, indicate in your own words why they are flawed).

5. Is the persuasiveness of Crofts's argument increased or diminished by such statements as "This reconstruction is still speculative and unsupported by direct evidence" (33)? Why?

6. Based on the facts Crofts sets forth, could we reasonably infer that Mrs. Storrs, Miss Lindley, or the housemaid (acting either alone or together) killed Mr. Storrs? Explain why or why not.

ADDITIONAL MATERIAL FOR ANALYSIS AND ARGUMENT: THE IDENTITY OF JACK THE RIPPER

Just over a hundred years ago, at least five women in the White-chapel area of East London died horribly at the hands of an unknown killer. Although our century has seen serial killers just as vicious as Jack the Ripper, nearly all have been identified with reasonable certainty. But the Ripper, the first acknowledged serial killer, remains unknown to this day, despite intensive investigations by the police at the time and by scores of "Ripperologists" since. From the very beginning, the case received intense public scrutiny. Even Queen Victoria took a personal interest in it—and the suspects have included the queen's personal physician, her grandson's tutor, and even her grandson, the Duke of Clarence. Could Jack the Ripper have been heir to the British throne? Or was he a deranged lawyer, a Russian agent, or perhaps (and this would disappoint many theorists) a nobody?

The enduring interest these murders hold for the public is well summed up by columnist John Carey in the *London Sunday Times:*

> Like Dracula or Santa Claus or Robin Hood, he belongs to our cloudy pantheon of immortals, and we are unwilling to see him deposed. We need him. He is Death in pantomime garb: one of the figures we use for coming to terms with our ultimate terror. His semi-fictional nature is what makes him acceptable. Popularised through films, stories and book-illustrations, he has the harmless garishness of romance—a cartoon image pinned protectively over the festering shambles of the Whitechapel corpses. . . . His jaunty name was invented for him. Its fairy-tale ring (evoking Jack the Giant Killer) helps to remove him from the human sphere.
>
> Qtd. in Richard Whittington-Egan, "The Ripper Report:
> A Hundred-Year Stocktaking," Contemporary Review
> Aug. 1988: 84

All the same, the Whitechapel villain was no fairy-tale character but one of the most infamous murderers of all time; the crimes were real and have never been conclusively solved. Earlier in this chapter, Michael Harrison set himself the task of exonerating one suspect.[1] The readings that follow will challenge you to do more and to use all the reasoning powers you have. Reasoning from the evidence here, your task is to draw some conclusions about the identity of Jack the Ripper. The first selection describes the crimes and the evidence found at the various scenes. The second quotes the key documentary evidence. Do not attempt to name a specific individual, but argue the necessary and the probable characteristics of the murderer as fully as the data here permit.

---

[1] To give Harrison credit, however, we should note that he did not let himself off that easily. Following the argument reprinted here as "The Duke of Clarence: Prince or Ripper?" Harrison argues at length the guilt of a particular person: James K. Stephen, friend and onetime tutor of the Prince, son of the eminent jurist Sir James Fitzjames Stephen, and cousin of Virginia Woolf. [Ed.]

The Crimes of Jack the Ripper

COLIN WILSON

Colin Wilson is an English writer who specializes in crime and is regarded as among the most knowledgeable and unbiased Jack-the-Ripper experts, or "Ripperologists." The following essay, first published as a series in the London *Evening Standard* in 1960, summarizes the series of vicious murders in London in 1888 that were attributed to a killer known to history only as Jack the Ripper. The crimes of Jack the Ripper were truly horrific, as Wilson makes clear in this narration of the killings. Read carefully for information that might help identify the Ripper: For example, note the leather apron that gave rise to the theory that the killer might have been a butcher; consider the fact that the killer must have been bloodied and yet vanished after each killing without attracting attention. And read critically: While this account is fairly accurate, it is not totally free of bias. Wilson repeats twice the testimony that the Ripper had to have medical skill to commit the crimes as he did but fails to mention conflicting medical testimony that such skill might not have been needed. Additionally, many Ripper theorists believe that Martha Turner could not have been the first victim. Can you determine why, from the data in Wilson's own essay?

When I was about eight, someone lent my father a great red 1 volume called *The Fifty Most Amazing Crimes of the Last 100 Years*—I'm not sure why, for I've never yet caught my father reading a book. I was strictly forbidden to read it, in case it gave me nightmares. So I seized on it every time I was left alone in the house, and read it from cover to cover.

I have a copy of it beside me as I write. At the top of every article 2 there is a sketch of the criminal. Landru looks villainous and intellectual; Smith, who drowned his wives in the bath, is an unattractive nondescript. But there is no drawing of Jack the Ripper—only a large black question mark. That question mark started me on my search for Jack the Ripper. It is not logical, or course, but the mind of a child is romantic and not logical. Why should the Ripper be more interesting than Landru, just because he was never caught? No-one has yet discovered how Landru destroyed every trace of his victims' bodies, and, in its way, this mystery is far more interesting than guessing at the identity of Jack the Ripper. And yet it is the Ripper who exercises a fascination beyond that of any other mass murderer.

Most of them are boring little men, like Christie and Haigh— 3 shifty, weak and unimpressive. Many of them have had long criminal records—petty theft, swindling, burglary or confidence trickery— like Heath, Kurten and Dr. Marcel Petiot. Murder has not yet produced its Caesar, its Napoleon. Murderers are a dull lot.

Perhaps the Ripper was a sneak-thief, with many prison sentences 4
behind him; perhaps it was only Wormwood Scrubs, and not death,
that put an end to his amazing career. We shall never be certain. And
that is enough to make the Ripper almost unique in the annals of mass
murder. We know almost nothing about him.

How many murders did he commit? Even that is the subject of 5
debate. All that we do know is that at least five murders of unparal-
leled brutality were committed in the latter part of the year 1888. Four
of them took place in the Whitechapel district of London, at night; the
victims were all prostitutes, although none of them was what we
would call "professionals." All London panicked. There were meetings in the streets; bands of citizens formed themselves into vigilante
groups to patrol Whitechapel at night; thousands of men were questioned, and released; men carrying black bags were attacked by mobs;
the Commissioner of Police resigned. And finally, after a lull of more
than a month, the Ripper committed yet another crime, this time
indoors. The pieces of the victim—a girl in her early twenties—were
left spread around the room like bits of a jigsaw puzzle. The panic
reached new proportions; there were so many blue uniforms in Whitechapel that the place resembled a police barracks. And then nothing
more happened. The murders stopped.

In the following year, 1889, there were two more murders of 6
prostitutes in the Whitechapel area, but without the same appalling
mutilations; we shall never know whether the same man was responsible for these. . . .

Who was the first victim of the Ripper? It might have been Emma 7
Smith, of George Street, Spitalfield, who was stabbed to death in
Osborn Street.

Osborn Street is a sinister little thoroughfare that runs between 8
Old Montague Street and the Whitechapel Road. Emma Smith lived
for twenty-four hours after the attack, and stated positively that she
had been assaulted and robbed by four men, one of whom had stabbed her with an iron spike in the abdomen. It was a brutal and stupid
murder, and its victim was a pathetic, drunken prostitute of forty-five,
who had never had more than a few shillings in her purse. She was
staggering home drunk at four in the morning when the attack took
place. (There were no licensing hours in those days, and many pubs
stayed open all night.) An hour later, she was admitted to the hospital,
her head bruised, her right ear almost torn off. Her death was due to
peritonitis.

At the time of the murders, many journalists stated that this was 9
the Ripper's first crime. It seems unlikely, but the murder is worth
mentioning for the insight it gives into the Whitechapel of the 1880's.
A man or woman might be found like this almost any morning, robbed

and battered; it was too commonplace to be reported in the daily press.

Many criminologists believe that the murder of Martha Turner 10 was quite definitely the first Ripper crime. This took place on August Bank Holiday, 1888.

Martha Turner was a prostitute who lived in George Yard Build- 11 ings, Commercial Street. In the early hours of the morning, she was found on one of the outside landings of the lodging-house; the post mortem revealed that she had been stabbed thirty-nine times with some weapon like a bayonet, and the coroner stated that the wounds had been inflicted by a left-handed man. Martha Turner had been seen talking to a guardsman on the evening before the murder, and since the injuries resembled bayonet wounds, the police started to look for a left-handed soldier. All the guards in the Tower of London were paraded, but no arrest was made. Within a few weeks, the murder had been forgotten. How could anyone guess that a super-criminal was starting on a series of the most sensational murders of all time? . . .

In the early hours of the morning of August 31st, 1888, a carter 12 named William Cross was walking along Buck's Row, on his way to work. Buck's Row is another street that has not changed since 1888, although its name is now Durward Street. On one side of the road are small houses, all absolutely uniform, and on the other are blocks of warehouses. Cross noticed something on the other side of the street—a bundle which he took to be a tarpaulin. Then he saw that it was a woman, apparently drunk. She was sprawled in the entrance to an old stable-yard, with her head in the gutter. Another man walked up as he stood there, looking down at her, and the newcomer said: "Come on, let's get her on her feet."

They bent down to turn her over, and Cross jumped back, ex- 13 claiming: "Blimey, she's bleeding!"

The other man confirmed this, and commented: "She's not 14 drunk—she's perishing well dead."

The two men ran off to find a policeman, and while they were 15 away the body was discovered by another policeman. Within a few minutes, four men were standing around the body. It was about four o'clock in the morning. . . .

Both the policemen were puzzled; they had beats that took them 16 past where the body was now lying, and both of them had been in the street, at either end of Bucks Row, for the past quarter of an hour. Neither had seen anyone. Someone summoned Dr. Ralph Llewellyn, who felt the woman's pulse, commented that she had been dead about half an hour, and told the police to take her to the mortuary at the Old Montague Street workhouse. The noise of the discussion attracted several people from the nearby houses. A Mrs. Emma Green, whose bedroom was within ten yards of the spot where the body had been found remarked that "whoever had done it" must have been very quiet, since she had been lying awake for several hours, and had heard no sound.

In the morgue, a young policeman lifted the woman's clothes to 17 gain some idea of the extent of her injuries. What he saw made him vomit. The woman's body had been ripped open from the throat to the stomach. The policeman rushed off to find Dr. Llewellyn, who had to give him first aid before he hurried to the morgue.

The first problem was that of identification. This was quickly 18 solved: the woman's name was Mary Anne Nichols, she was forty-two years old, and was known to her friends and acquaintances as Polly. She had been married to a printer's machinist and had borne him five children, but they had been separated for seven years; her love of the gin bottle, and the slovenliness that resulted from it, had made him leave her. But as he stood over her body in the mortuary, he was heard to say: "I forgive you for everything now that I see you like this." . . .

A week after the murder of Mary Anne Nichols the murderer 19 found his third victim, and the pattern of the crime was curiously similar to that in the previous case. Mary Nichols had been turned away from a doss house in Thrawl Street and went off to seek a "customer." Annie Chapman was turned out of a doss house in Dorset Street by the keeper, a man named Donovan, and, like Mary Nichols, her life was sacrificed for fourpence, the cost of a bed.

If you walk up Commercial Street from Aldgate, you will pass 20 Dorset Street on your left-hand side. Since 1888, its name had been changed to Duval Street. An extension of Spitalfields market now stands on the site of the lodging-house from which Annie Chapman was turned away in the early hours of Saturday, September 8th. When she left number 35, Dorset Street, she had only a few hundred yards to walk to her death. . . . As it happened, 29 Hanbury Street was a convenient meeting-place for a prostitute and a prospective client, for a passage runs by the side of the house, with a door at each end. These doors were never kept closed. And at the far end of the passage was a back-yard—a yard that looked exactly as it did 72 years before, when the Ripper entered it with Annie Chapman.

They tiptoed down the passageway, and crept into a corner of the 21 yard by the fence. The man moved closer; she was not even aware of the knife he held in his left hand. A moment later she was dead; the first thrust had severed her windpipe. The man allowed her to slide down the fence. He slipped out of his dark overcoat, and bent over the woman.

The sight of the blood roused in him a kind of frenzy, and for five 22 minutes he remained there, crouched over her. Then he wiped the knife on her skirt, and cleaned some of the blood off his shoes. It was already getting light. He pulled on the overcoat, and crossed to the tap that projected from the fence three feet to the left of the body. From his overcoat he pulled a bundle, which he soaked in water and used to wipe his hands, then he dropped it under the tap. It was a leather apron.

As he pulled it out of his pocket, an envelope dropped out too. 23 The man picked this up, tore off its corner, which was marked with the crest of the Sussex Regiment, and dropped it into Annie Chapman's blood. It would be another false trail for the police to follow. Before leaving the yard, another idea struck him. He searched the pockets of the dead woman's jacket, and removed two brass rings, a few pennies and some farthings, then arranged these carefully by her feet.

A few pennies! Annie Chapman had actually possessed just 24 enough money to stay in the lodging-house! Did she know this? Or could it be that my reconstruction is wrong, and the Ripper took the pennies from his own pocket, as a sort of ironical payment for the pleasure she had given him?

An hour went by, and one of the inhabitants of the house, John 25 Davies, came downstairs and looked into the yard. The body was huddled against a fence. He rushed to Spitalfields Market, where he worked as a porter, and brought two of his fellow-workmen back with him. A few minutes later the police arrived, and the divisional surgeon, Mr. Philips, was summoned. His first act was to remove the handkerchief tied around the woman's throat; immediately, the head rolled sideways—it was only just attached to the body. By now, the windows of all the surrounding houses were crowded with sightseers, and some of the local householders even charged a small fee for access to their windows.

Finally, the body was removed to the mortuary, where Mr. Philips 26 discovered that the injuries were even more extensive than they had been in the case of Mary Nichols. In addition to numerous stab wounds, there were incisions in the woman's back and abdomen. Moreover, a careful examination of the body revealed that certain internal organs had been removed and taken away by the murderer. So too had two of her front teeth—a curious touch that repeated a feature of the murder of Mary Nichols.

At the inquest, Dr. Philips expressed the opinion that the mur- 27 derer must have been a man with some anatomical knowledge and medical skill. And the weapon must have been some kind of long-bladed knife, at least eight inches long, which might have been "an instrument such as a doctor would use for surgery." . . .

Children sing and play today on the spot where the Ripper's next 28 victim was killed. It was in the back-yard of the International Working Men's Club at 40, Berners Street, where the Ripper began the most sensational night's work in English criminal history. The yard is now part of the playground of a London council school. . . .

The story of that remarkable night begins at 1 A.M., when the 29 steward of the club tried to guide his pony and trap into the back-yard. He had some difficulty, for the pony was obviously unwilling to enter. The cart blocked the gateway, and the man—Louis Delmschutz— dismounted and peered into the darkness, trying to find out what was frightening the pony.

He did not know it, but he was very close to death. A few feet 30 behind him, still holding a knife, was the Whitechapel murderer. But Delmschutz was not aware of this, for he saw the body of a woman lying against the way, and rushed into the club to raise the alarm.

The man who would soon be known as Jack the Ripper clambered 31 over the wheel of the cart and slipped out into Berners Street. A moment later, he had disappeared into an alleyway.

Delmschutz emerged from the club followed by a crowd of men 32 who babbled in Polish and Russian. Someone struck a light. The body was that of a tall woman, shabbily dressed. Her throat had been cut, and one of her ears was slightly torn. The ripper had been interrupted. The doctor who was called verified that the woman had been killed very recently indeed.

At the moment that the murderer walked out of Berners Street into 33 the Commercial Road, a prostitute named Catherine Eddowes was released from Bishopsgate Police Station, where she had been in charge for drunkenness since 8 o'clock. Five hours in a cell had not sobered her appreciably; she walked down Bishopsgate towards Aldgate, and the man who had just left Berners Street was walking along the Commercial Road towards his usual haunts. Berners Street was the farthest afield that he had yet ventured; it is on the right as you go down the Commercial Road towards the East India Dock Road—a good half-mile from Commercial Street, the Ripper's usual hunting-ground. Perhaps he was finding the narrow streets of Spitalfields too hot for him; policemen in rubber-soled boots walked through his alleys, and the tradesmen of Whitechapel also prowled around in bands of "vigilantes" in the hope of catching the murderer. At all events, the Ripper avoided Spitalfields and walked on towards Bishopsgate.

At the corner of Houndsditch he met Catherine Eddowes. After a 34 brief conversation, the two of them turned off to the right, into Duke Street. Half-way up Duke Street there is a narrow alleyway called St. James Passage; in 1888 it had been known as Church Passage. At its far end lies Mitre Square, which looks today almost exactly as it looked in 1888. On its north side stands a warehouse.

The Ripper was standing on the south side of the square, near 35

Church Passage, when P. C. Watkins walked through the square on his beat; as the policeman walked by, he pressed back into the shadow of a doorway, and, as soon as the steps were out of earshot, he placed a hand over Eddowes' mouth and cut her throat.

Exactly a quarter of an hour later, P. C. Watkins again walked 36 through Mitre Square, but this time a mutilated body lay in the right-hand corner, near Church Passage. There was no doubt about the identity of the killer, for the body had been stabbed and cut ferociously, and the face had also been mutilated beyond recognition. And two of the woman's internal organs were missing.

The murderer had not given himself much time. The doctor who 37 examined the body agreed that it must have taken at least ten minutes to inflict so many injuries; besides, the removal of the organs revealed some medical skill. And yet the man walked off without fear into Duke Street and right across Whitechapel into Dorset Street, where he found a convenient sink in which to wash his hands. He had torn off a fragment of the woman's apron, and used this to wipe off the blood. Major Smith, of the City Police, actually saw the sink before the bloodstained water had had time to drain away. Possibly some noise frightened the killer there, for he hurried off without finishing the wash, and continued to wipe off the blood as he walked towards Aldgate again. He finally dropped the piece of bloodstained apron in Goulston Street, within a short distance of the scene of the murder.

Although the Ripper did not know it then, Dorset Street was to be 38 the scene of his most horrible murder, six weeks later.

Early the following morning, the Central News Agency received a 39 letter written in red ink, signed "Jack the Ripper." It was their second letter bearing this signature. The first had arrived two days before the murder, and promised "some more work" in the near future. It also promised to clip off the ladies' ears and send them to the police. No-one had taken the first letter seriously—it was assumed to be another practical joke—but this second letter altered the complexion of things. To begin with, it arrived early in the day, before the news of the murders was generally known. Secondly, there *had* been an attempt to cut off the ear of the first victim in Berners Street, and in his second letter the Ripper apologized for not sending it, saying that he had been interrupted!

The murder of Annie Chapman in Hanbury Street had caused a 40 sensation, but it was nothing to the furor that followed the double murder. Hysteria swept the country. Sir Charles Warren, the unpopular Commissioner of Police, was bombarded with furious telegrams demanding his resignation. (He did, in fact, finally resign.) He was also bombarded with letters full of theories about the identity of the murderer and how to catch him.

It is almost impossible to give an adequate idea of the commotion 41 caused by the murders, but the newspapers of the day devoted more space to them than our own journalists give to a royal wedding.

The police arrested about a dozen men a day, but all of them were 42 released after questioning. Sometimes cranks gave themselves up as Jack the Ripper, for after the two letters had been made public the name had caught the popular imagination.

It took the police some time to identify the two women who had 43 been killed that night. The woman who had been killed in Berners Street was finally identified as Elizabeth Stride, a Swedish woman who had taken to drink and prostitution after some emotional tragedy. (One story has it that she saw her children drowned in an accident on a Thames steamer.) The second victim was less easy to trace, because the mutilations to her face made recognition difficult, and there was one stage when she was identified as an Irishwoman named Mary Anne Kelly—an astounding coincidence in view of what was to come. Eventually, the evidence of her clothes established that she was Catherine Eddowes, aged forty-five, and that she had been in police custody only three-quarters of an hour before she was murdered. . . .

In 1888, Dorset Street was a narrow and shabby thoroughfare 44 running parallel with Spitalfields market, in Brushfield Street. On its north side, extending towards the market, was an entry labelled Millers Court. It was in a house in Millers Court that the Whitechapel murderer killed and dismembered his last victim, a twenty-four-year-old prostitute called Mary Jeanette Kelly.

Five weeks had elapsed since the double murder, and London had 45 begun to hope that the Ripper had left town. The police and vigilante groups began to relax a little. Then, on the morning of November 9th, a man knocked on the door of Mary Kelly to ask for the rent. Getting no reply, he went round to the window and peered through the half-open curtains. What he saw was probably the most appalling sight in London's violent criminal history.

The body that lay on the bed had been taken to pieces like a jigsaw 46 puzzle, and the pieces had been scattered around the room, draped over a picture, or piled upon the sideboard. The heart lay on the pillow, beside the head. The hysteria in London reached new heights.

At some time after two o'clock on the morning of November 9th, 47 the Ripper had been solicited by Mary Kelly outside her room in Millers Court. A man named Hutchinson had actually watched the "pick-up" and described the man as a "toff," a short, thickset man with a curling moustache, and carrying a parcel of some sort. A short time later, a neighbor heard Mary Kelly singing "Sweet Violets." At 3:10 the same neighbor heard a cry of "Murder!" And for the next two hours there was silence, as Jack the Ripper dissected the body. Then the Ripper left, and the great mystery begins.

For how did he walk through London in clothes that must have 48 been soaked in blood? Why did he burn a pile of clothes in the grate of Mary Kelly's room? Above all, what happened to the murderer after November 9th? There is no case in history of a maniacal killer who simply stopped of his own accord. Why did he stop?

These questions have puzzled students of crime ever since. There 49 are theories by the dozen, but no shred of evidence. Is it possible, at this late date, that someone will prove the identity of Jack the Ripper? Are there papers somewhere in police files, or in some mental home, that tell the whole story?

The Key Documents

DONALD RUMBELOW

Donald Rumbelow, an author and a City of London policeman, is former chair of the Crime Writers Association of England. His books include *I Spy Blue* (1971) and *The Houndsditch Murders* (1973). The following excerpt from his *Jack the Ripper: The Complete Casebook* (1988) quotes the major documents associated with the 1888 murders. In his foreword, Rumbelow notes that a few more documents have been made public since his book was written, including the coroner's inquest records on Catherine Eddowes. But most of the theories about the case rely to some extent on the following documents: the "Macnaghten papers" and a report by Dr. Thomas Bond, who conducted the post-mortem on Mary Kelly (as well as that on Alice McKenzie, regarded by some as a Ripper victim). You should consider, as you read, the difference between primary evidence and secondary evidence—and hearsay. All will figure to some extent in these "reports."

The best known of all the Ripper documents are the legendary 1 Macnaghten papers. These are not a large manuscript collection, as is often supposed, but a single document written by Sir Melville Macnaghten several years after he joined Scotland Yard as an assistant chief constable in 1889 and before he was appointed head of the CID in 1903.[1] There are two versions of these notes. One forms part of the Ripper case papers which are deposited in the MEPOL (Metropolitan Police) papers in the Public Records Office. The other set of papers is in the possession of Lady Aberconway, Sir Melville Macnaghten's

---

[1] Sir Melville Macnaghten joined Scotland Yard in 1889, the year after the undisputed Ripper killings, and wrote this report in 1894. Rumbelow speculates that Macnaghten based his secondhand report on the reports made by Detective Inspector Frederick Abberline, who headed the actual investigation, to Robert Anderson, head of the CID (Criminal Investigation Department) at the time of the Ripper murders. [Ed.]

daughter, who made them available to Dan Farson in 1959 and to Tom Cullen in 1965. The former quoted from them in a television documentary which he made at the time, although only the initials of leading suspects were given. Tom Cullen was more fortunate, and was able to print the names in full. Farson was able to do the same thing eight years later when he published his own account of the same story. . . .

Anyone who is hoping for startling revelations from the Jack the 2 Ripper file will be very disappointed with what they find. They are incomplete. There are three bundles of loose-leaf papers in brown wrap-round files tied up with tapes.

Two of the Ripper files contain letters from the general public 3 offering advice on the best way to catch the Whitechapel murderer. They contain nothing of any real importance. The third file has a number of thin brown folders—some of them very thin—which relate not only to the five definite Ripper murders but to others such as Alice McKenzie and Frances Coles which some contemporaries attributed to him. Each of these folders has the victim's, or alleged victim's, name across the top. There are very few documents in each file. The Eddowes murder was investigated by the City of London Police and contains only a single newspaper cutting. Some of the other files contain very little more. . . .

In general, the documents are a haphazard collection and their 4 very haphazardness suggests that they have been well picked over in the past hundred years. The only recorded destruction of any part of them is attributed to Sir Melville Macnaghten who is alleged to have burned the most incriminating of the papers to protect the murderer's family. His daughter denies this story and says that her father probably said that he had done this to stop himself from being pestered by people at his club.

His notes are reproduced below in full for the first time any- 5 where. . . .

*   *   *

Confidential

The case referred to in the sensational story told in *The Sun* in its 6 issue of 13th inst,[2] & following dates, is that of Thomas Cutbush who was arraigned at the London County Sessions in April 1891 on a

---

[2] Inst: abbreviation of *instans,* meaning "the current month." [Ed.]

charge of maliciously wounding Florence Grace Johnson, and attempting to wound Isabella Fraser Anderson in Kennington. He was found to be insane, and sentenced to be detained during Her Majesty's Pleasure.

This Cutbush, who lived with his mother and aunt at 14 Albert   7
Street, Kennington, escaped from the Lambeth Infirmary (after he had been detained only a few hours, as a lunatic) at noon on 5th March 1891. He was rearrested on 9th idem.[3] A few weeks before this, several cases of stabbing, or jobbing, from behind had occurred in the vicinity, and a man named Colicott was arrested, but subsequently discharged owing to faulty identification. The cuts in the girl's dresses made by Colicott were quite different to the cut(s) made by Cutbush (when he wounded Miss Johnson) who was no doubt influenced by a wild desire of morbid imitation. Cutbush's antecedents were enquired into by C. Insp. (now Supt.) Chis(?), by Inspector Hale, and by P. S. McCarthy CID—(the last named officer had been specially employed in Whitechapel at the time of the murders there)—and it was ascertained that he was born, and had lived, in Kennington all his life. His father died when he was quite young and he was always a "spoilt" child. He had been employed as a clerk and traveller in the Tea trade at the Minories, and subsequently canvassed for a Directory in the East End, during which time he bore a good character. He apparently contracted syphilis about 1888, and,—since that time,—led an idle and useless life. His brain seems to have become affected, and he believed that people were trying to poison him. He wrote to Lord Grimthorpe and others,—and also to the Treasury—complaining to Dr. Brooks, of Westminster Bridge Road, whom he threatened to shoot for having supplied him with bad medicines. He is said to have studied medical books by day, and to have rambled about at night, returning frequently with his clothes covered with mud; but little reliance could be placed on the statements made by his mother or his aunt, who both appear to have been of a very excitable disposition. It was found impossible to ascertain his movements on the nights of the Whitechapel murders. The knife found on him was bought in Houndsditch about a week before he was detained in the Infirmary. Cutbush was the nephew of the late Supt. Executive.

Now the Whitechapel murderer had 5 victims—& 5 victims   8
only,—his murders were

1. 31st August '88. Mary Ann Nichols—at Buck's Row—who was found with her throat cut—& with (slight) stomach mutilation.

---

[3] Idem: in Latin, "the same," meaning "the same month." [Ed.]

2. 8th Sept. '88. Annie Chapman—Hanbury St.—throat cut—
   stomach & private parts badly mutilated & some of the entrails
   placed round the neck.

3. 30th Sept. '88. Elizabeth Stride—Berner's Street—throat cut, but
   nothing in shape of mutilation attempted, & *on same date*
       Catherine Eddowes—Mitre Square, throat cut & very bad muti-
   lation, both of face & stomach.
       9th November. Mary Jane Kelly—Miller's Court, throat cut, and
   the whole of the body mutilated in the most ghastly manner—

The last murder is the only one that took place in a *room,* and the   9
murderer must have been at least 2 hours engaged. A photo was taken
of the woman, as she was found lying on the bed, without seeing
which it is impossible to imagine the awful mutilation.

With regard to the *double* murder which took place on 30th Sep-   10
tember, there is no doubt but that the man was disturbed by some
Jews who drove up to a Club (close to which the body of Elizabeth
Stride was found) and that he then, "mordum satiatus," went in
search of a further victim who he found at Mitre Square.

It will be noticed that the fury of the mutilations *increased* in each   11
case, and, seemingly, the appetite only became sharpened by indulgence. It seems, then, highly improbable that the murderer would
have suddenly stopped in November '88, and been content to recom-
mence operations by merely prodding a girl's behind some 2 years and
4 months afterwards. A much more rational theory is that the murderer's brain gave way altogether after his awful glut in Miller's Court,
and that he immediately committed suicide, or, as a possible alternative, was found to be so hopelessly mad by his relations, that he was
by them confined in some asylum.

No one ever saw the Whitechapel murderer; many homicidal   12
maniacs were suspected, but no shadow of proof could be thrown on
any one. I may mention the cases of 3 men, any one of whom would
have been more likely than Cutbush to have committed this series of
murders:

1. A Mr. M. J. Druitt, said to be a doctor & of good family—who
   disappeared at the time of the Miller's Court murder, & whose
   body (which was said to have been upwards of a month in the
   water) was found in the Thames on 31st December—or about 7
   weeks after that murder. He was sexually insane and from private
   information I have little doubt but that his own family believed
   him to have been the murderer.

2. Kosminski—a Polish Jew—& resident in Whitechapel. This man
   became insane owing to many years indulgence in solitary vices.

He had a great hatred of women, specially of the prostitute class, & had strong homicidal tendencies: he was removed to a lunatic asylum about March 1889. There were many circumstances connected with this man which made him a strong "suspect."

3. Michael Ostrog, a Russian doctor, and a convict, who was subsequently detained in a lunatic asylum as a homicidal maniac. This man's antecedents were of the worst possible type, and his whereabouts at the time of the murders could never be ascertained.

And now with regard to a few of the other inaccuracies and   13
misleading statements made by *The Sun*. In its issue of 14th February, it is stated that the writer has in his possession a facsimile of the knife with which the murders were committed. This knife (which for some unexplained reason has, for the last 3 years, been kept by Inspector Hale, instead of being sent to Prisoner's Property Store) was traced, and it was found to have been purchased in Houndsditch in February '91 or 2 years and 3 months *after* the Whitechapel murders ceased!

The statement, too, that Cutbush "spent a portion of the day in   14
making rough drawings of the bodies of women, and of their mutilations" is based solely on the fact that 2 *scribble* drawings of women in indecent postures were found torn up in Cutbush's room. The head and body of one of these had been cut from some fashion plate, and legs were added to shew a woman's naked thighs and pink stockings.

In the issue of 15th inst. it is said that a *light overcoat* was among the   15
things found in Cutbush's house, and that a man in a *light* overcoat was seen talking to a woman at Backchurch Lane whose body with arms attached was found in Pinchin Street. This is hopelessly incorrect! On 10th Sept. '89 the naked body, with arms, of a woman was found wrapped in some sacking under a Railway arch in Pinchin Street: the head and legs were never found nor was the woman ever identified. She had been killed at least 24 hours before the remains which had seemingly been brought from a distance, were discovered. The stomach was split up by a cut, and the head and legs had been severed in a manner identical with that of the woman whose remains were discovered in the Thames, in Battersea Park, and on the Chelsea Embankment on 4th June of the same year; and these murders had no connection whatever with the Whitechapel horrors. The Rainham mystery in 1887 and the Whitehall mystery (when portions of a woman's body were found under what is now New Scotland Yard) in 1888 were of a similar type to the Thames and Pinchin Street crimes.

It is perfectly untrue to say that Cutbush stabbed 6 girls behind.   16
This is confounding his case with that of Colicott. The theory that the Whitechapel murderer was left-handed, or, at any rate, "ambidexter," had its origin in the remark made by a doctor who examined

the corpse of one of the earliest victims; *other doctors did not agree with him.*

With regard to the 4 additional murders ascribed by the writer in 17 the Sun to the Whitechapel fiend:

1. The body of Martha Tabram,[4] a prostitute, was found on a common staircase in George Yard buildings on 7th August 1888; the body had been repeatedly *pierced,* probably with a *bayonet.* This woman had, with a fellow prostitute, been in company of 2 soldiers in the early part of the evening: these men were arrested, but the second prostitute failed, or refused, to identify, and the soldiers were eventually discharged.

2. Alice McKenzie was found with her throat cut (or rather *stabbed*) in Castle Alley on 17th July 1889; no evidence was forthcoming and no arrests were made in connection with this case. The *stab* in the throat was of the same nature as in the case of the murder of

3. Frances Coles in Swallow Gardens, on 13th February 1891—for which Thomas Saddler, a fireman, was arrested, and, after several remands, discharged. It was ascertained at the time that Saddler had sailed for the Baltic on 19th July '89 and was in Whitechapel on the nights of 17th idem. He was a man of ungovernable temper and entirely addicted to drink, and the company of the lowest prostitutes.

4. The case of the unidentified woman whose trunk was found in Pinchin Street: on 10th September 1889—which has already been dealt with.

M. L. Macnaghten
23rd February 1894

As Macnaghten did not join the Yard until 1889 he had no first hand experience of the case and must, one assumes, have been drawing on Abberline's reports to compile this particular document some six years after the events. Unlike some of the other policemen involved, Abberline never published any account of the murders—or of his subsequent investigations into the Cleveland Street scandal centering on a homosexual brothel in the West End to which Clarence was supposed to have gone, and which implicated some of the highest in the land.

Soon after completion of this case Abberline resigned, having 18 completed twenty-nine years service, on 7 February 1892. . . .

*   *   *

---

[4] Also known as Emma, also known as Martha Turner. The Whitechapel prostitutes often went by more than one name. [Ed.]

The following document, which is also reproduced for the first 19 time, was written by Dr. Thomas Bond, who carried out the post-mortems on both Alice McKenzie and Mary Kelly. Besides being a lecturer on Forensic Medicine and consulting surgeon to "A" division and to the Great Western Railway, he was also the author of several publications, including one on the "Diagnosis and Treatment of Primary Syphilis."

7 THE SANCTUARY,
WESTMINSTER ABBEY
November 10th '88

Dear Sir,
   Whitechapel Murders
   I beg to report that I have read the notes of the four Whitechapel 20 Murders viz-:

1. Buck's Row
2. Hanbury Street
3. Berners Street
4. Mitre Square

I have also made a Post Mortem Examination of the mutilated remains of a woman found yesterday in a small room in Dorset Street—:
   1. All five murders were no doubt committed by the same hand. 21 In the first four the throats appear to have been cut from left to right, in the last case owing to the extensive mutilation it is impossible to say in what direction the fatal cut was made, but arterial blood was found on the wall in splashes close to where the woman's head must have been lying.
   2. All the circumstances surrounding the murders lead me to form 22 the opinion that the women must have been lying down when murdered and in every case the throat was first cut.
   3. In the four murders of which I have seen the notes only, I 23 cannot form a very definite opinion as to the time that had elapsed between the murder and the discovery of the body. In one case, that of Berners Street, the discovery appears to have been immediately after the deed. In Buck's Row, Hanbury St., and Mitre Square three or four hours only could have elapsed. In the Dorset Street case the body was lying on the bed at the time of my visit two o'clock quite naked and mutilated as in the annexed report. Rigor Mortis had set in but increased during the progress of the examination. From this it is difficult to say with any degree of certainty the exact time that had elapsed since death as the period varies from six to twelve hours before rigidity

sets in. The body was comparatively cold at two o'clock and the remains of a recently taken meal were found in the stomach and scattered about over the intestines. It is therefore, pretty certain that the woman must have been dead about twelve hours and the partly digested food would indicate that death took place about three or four hours after food was taken, so one or two o'clock in the morning would be the probable time of the murder.

4. In all the cases there appears to be no evidence of struggling 24 and the attacks were probably so sudden and made in such a position that the women could neither resist nor cry out. In the Dorset St. case the corner of the sheet to the right of the woman's head was much cut and saturated with blood, indicating that the face may have been covered with the sheet at the time of the attack.

5. In the first four cases the murderer must have attacked from the 25 right side of the victim. In the Dorset Street case, he must have attacked from in front or from the left, as there would be no room for him between the wall and the part of the bed on which the woman was lying. Again the blood had flowed down on the right side of the woman and spurted on to the wall.

6. The murderer would not necessarily be splashed or deluged 26 with blood, but his hands and arms must have been covered and parts of his clothing must certainly have been smeared with blood.

7. The mutilations in each case excepting the Berners Street one 27 were all of the same character and showed clearly that in all the murders the object was mutilation.

8. In each case the mutilation was inflicted by a person who had 28 no scientific nor anatomical knowledge. In my opinion he does not even possess the technical knowledge of a butcher or horse slaughterer or any person accustomed to cut up dead animals.

9. The instrument must have been a strong knife at least six inches 29 long, very sharp, pointed at the top and about an inch in width. It may have been a clasp knife, a butcher's knife or a surgeon's knife, I think it was no doubt a straight knife.

10. The murderer must have been a man of physical strength and 30 of great coolness and daring. There is no evidence that he had an accomplice. He must in my opinion be a man subject to periodical attacks of Homicidal and erotic mania. The character of the mutilations indicates that the man may be in a condition sexually, that may be called Satyriasis. It is of course possible that the Homicidal impulse may have developed from a revengeful or brooding condition of the mind, or that religious mania may have been the original disease but I do not think either hypothesis is likely. The murderer in external appearance is quite likely to be a quiet inoffensive looking man proba-

bly middle-aged and neatly and respectably dressed. I think he must be in the habit of wearing a cloak or overcoat or he could hardly have escaped notice in the streets if the blood on his hands or clothes were visible.

11. Assuming the murderer to be such a person as I have just 31 described, he would be solitary and eccentric in his habits, also he is most likely to be a man without regular occupation, but with some small income or pension. He is possibly living among respectable persons who have some knowledge of his character and habits and who may have grounds for suspicion that he isn't quite right in his mind at times. Such persons would probably be unwilling to communicate suspicions to the Police for fear of trouble or notoriety, whereas if there were prospect of reward it might overcome their scruples.

This letter went to Robert Anderson, head of CID

*   *   *

These are the two major documents and most of the arguments for 32 or against the respective theories hinge on them to some extent.

SUGGESTIONS FOR WRITING
AND FURTHER DISCUSSION

1. Whether or not you have studied formal or informal logic, you judge the arguments of others—at least in part—according to logical standards. What are those standards for reasoning? Are they universal? To work toward an answer to these questions, assume that you have encountered an argument in favor of increasing the number of nuclear energy facilities in this country. No matter what the specific premises (reasons) the argument offers, what specific standards would you require of both premises and conclusion in order to accept them as reasonable? Suppose that you personally oppose the expansion of nuclear energy resources. Would the standards by which you judge the pronuclear energy argument be different, more numerous, or applied more stringently than those by which you judge antinuclear energy arguments? Finally, compare your "standards for reasonableness" to those of your classmates. To what extent do you share the same standards for evaluating argument? If you find any substantive differences, discuss why they exist.

2. What is logically arguable and what is not? Identify some of the particular subjects (and categories of subjects) about which logical argument is possible and the kinds of subjects about which logical argument is not possible. When people try to argue about the latter, what are the typical results?

3. In logical argument we must prove some of our premises, but others we take as "given"—we assume that they are familiar and acceptable to our readers. To make such assumptions, we need to have a clear sense of our audience: its knowledge about the subject, its likely preconceptions and biases. Some assumptions are safe enough for almost any audience: "Murder is wrong." "People have a right to privacy." "The Los Angeles freeways are congested." But we sometimes make assumptions that, in fact, our audience may *not* accept: "Capital punishment is wrong." "The right to privacy extends to the right to have an abortion." "Autos entering freeways with only one occupant should be ticketed." Accordingly, it is in our assumptions, not in the premises for which we offer evidence and support, that our arguments most often go astray. List ten assumptions that you could safely make in arguments that will be read by an audience consisting of your rhetoric class. Is there disagreement within the class about any of those assumptions?

4. Select one assumption about which your class was unable to agree in question 3, and write an essay arguing your point of view with that same audience in mind. Of course, you will have to make some assumptions, but do so with care!

5. We can argue about what our subject is, thereby correcting misconceptions (definition); what its significance or worth is (value); what our attitudes and actions in regard to the subject should be (policy); and what the influences leading to or consequences arising from the subject may be (causation). Write a tentative thesis from each of these perspectives for one of the following subjects. Discuss which thesis would be easiest to develop into a sound argument and which would be most difficult—and why. Select one of your tentative theses to develop into an argument suitable for publication in your campus newspaper.

- required courses in science and math
- volunteer service in the local community
- AIDS education in secondary schools
- the censorship of obscenity
- lab research involving experimentation on animals
- affirmative action in college admissions
- the punishment of convicted white-collar criminals

6. Real murders are often straightforward matters, with eyewitnesses and obvious suspects—with motive, opportunity, and fingerprints on the murder weapon. Fictional murder mysteries are never straightforward; they typically have no witnesses and multiple plausible suspects. Nonetheless, as the readings in this chapter show, a real murder can present reasoning challenges well beyond those that a fictional crime offers. Given the distinctions Irving Copi explains between inductive and deductive reasoning, which kind of reasoning is required of you most often in attempting to determine the identity (or at least the identifying characteristics) of a real murderer? Give examples from your analyses of one or more of the crimes discussed in this chapter.

7. Write an essay in which you argue that one of the readings in this chapter reasons incorrectly to its conclusion. Show the problems in the reasoning. You may suggest a more likely suspect than its writer does; or you may content yourself, as the argument about the Duke of Clarence does, with disproving the solution offered.

8. Based on the evidence available to you in Michael Harrison's essay and in the section of the chapter entitled "Additional Material for Analysis and Argument," argue a solution to the Ripper murders in terms of necessary and likely characteristics of the criminal.

9. What, according to Colin Wilson, accounts for the public's enduring fascination with the Ripper crimes? Do you find this fascination comprehensible—or reprehensible? Argue your viewpoint in a brief essay.

10. Why are some murders widely publicized and others all but ignored? What criteria do newspapers and television stations appear to have for deciding which murders to publicize? Do those decisions reflect the interests and concerns of the reading and viewing public—and should they? Argue your viewpoint.

4

RECOGNIZING AND AVOIDING FALLACIES

THE STRATEGY

While the previous chapter had much to say—and to show—about reasoning, it showed as well that reasoning does not always follow logical and reliable paths. Reasoning gone astray is called *fallacy;* and, while this term is popularly equated with *lie,* it means in rhetorical terms only logical error. Fallacies may not be deliberate, and they may not be lies. They can occur either in the process of reasoning, of linking one idea to another, or in the ideas or statements themselves. The former are called "formal" fallacies; the latter, "material" fallacies. In either case, the effect is to make an argument unsound.

The first selection that follows, Monroe Beardsley's discussion of fallacious emotional appeals, identifies some of the various wrong directions reasoning can take. To be able to apply specific labels to fallacious arguments can simplify the task of refuting them, but labels are not always necessary. Indeed, fallacies sometimes go by several names, and some that logicians and rhetoricians carefully delineate are virtually indistinguishable from one another. What is important is to understand and recognize problems in reasoning, not to shout fancy Latin epithets at your opponents in argument.

The second essay gives James Thurber's indictment-by-example of one of the most common fallacies—the sweeping generalization. While we must generalize in order to reason, when we do so unfairly or too hastily we can do harm far greater than a mere infraction of logic rules. That sober truth underlies Thurber's humor in this essay.

The third selection, an essay by Sylvia Wright, offers a tongue-in-cheek criticism of advertising and its dependence on deliberate but unwarranted implications. That kind of fallacy, known nowhere else but in this essay as "ompremity," is one of the most common errors in reasoning in all contexts: the begged question.

Emotional Appeals

MONROE BEARDSLEY

Monroe Beardsley (1915–1985) was a philosopher, an educator (at Swarthmore College and Temple University), and the author of many works on logic, aesthetics, and the history of philosophical thought. Among the latter are *Aesthetics: Problems in the Philosophy of Criticism* (1958) and *The Possibility of Criticism* (1970). Beardsley had a gift for clear writing and explanation that the following excerpt from his *Practical Logic* (1950) illustrates. He describes in this selection some of the fallacious emotional appeals that we often associate with advertising but that are by no means limited to that arena. We find them in political rhetoric and in arguments of all kinds.

At the same time, we must remember that emotional appeals are not always fallacious. There are appropriate occasions for such appeals. How else would the Salvation Army gather donations for needy people at holiday time? How else would CARE finance its work in developing countries? But, as Beardsley notes, "to get at the truth about anything, you have to do something more than feel strongly about it. You have to think." Thus is the line drawn: An emotional appeal cannot be offered as a substitute for reasoning.

Terms with marked emotive force (positive or negative) make up 1 our vocabulary of praise and blame, glorification and vilification. They are the means by which discourse makes a strong appeal to our emotions. We shall use the term "emotion" in a fairly popular sense. Feelings like fear, hate, and love are usually called "emotions" because they are rather *specific*. They are directed toward an object; there is fear of fire, of poverty, of tigers, of revolution. They involve some degree of belief: that fire burns, that tigers bite, that revolutions produce a redistribution of property. The variety of emotions to which discourse appeals is, of course, considerable. But it will be useful for us to label briefly six very common types of emotional appeal. They are not sharply separable, but it is important to be aware of them when they turn up. Note that they operate through words with strong connotations, and also that they depend a good deal upon suggestion.

1. *Identification with audience.* "You and I are just plain folks . . . 2 we understand each other . . . we ain't gonna let them fool us. . . ." By such phrases as these, a speaker seeks to make us identify ourselves with him, to feel friendly toward him, and to trust what he says. What he *suggests* is that he has our true interests at heart; but the only evidence he gives is that he dresses like his audience, uses colloquial grammar and diction, and speaks in a hearty and confidential manner. He suggests that he is "one of the boys," a "man of the people," a "great Commoner," and so on through many variations. The speaker

uses identification as an *emotional appeal,* instead of giving *reasons* (say, by quoting from his record in Congress) for believing that he has the interests of his audience at heart.

2. *Flattery.* "Your great state of Oregon . . . your lovely New 3 England village . . . our country, the greatest in the world." By such phrases as these, ranging from the gentlest pat on the back to the wildest flag-waving, the speaker makes us feel pleased with ourselves, with our possessions, our achievements, or our heritage. What he *suggests* is that he is well disposed toward us, and also that he is particularly smart because he recognizes our virtues. But he does this only by catering to our trained responses, our smugness, our self-satisfaction, or our legitimate pride in our work. The speaker uses flattery as an *emotional* appeal, instead of giving *reasons* for believing that what he praises is really praiseworthy.

3. *Alarm.* "A cloud is on the horizon . . . Asiatic hordes . . . the 4 Yellow Peril . . . a world laid waste by atheism and anti-Christ . . . crime waves sweeping across the nation." By calling up such spectres, the speaker seeks to make us feel unreasonably afraid. What he *suggests* is that the policy he opposes will inevitably lead to these fearful consequences; but he does not stop to *prove* that these consequences will follow. He merely makes the consequences so frightening that we will be unwilling to try any policy even remotely suggestive of the possibility of such consequences. So with the advertisements: very often they don't give reasons to show that we will lose our jobs, or be left alone to sulk at beach-parties, or be laughed at by our guests— they merely try to make us so unhappy at the very thought of these things that we will do anything to avoid them, even if we have no good reason to believe it will help. This is using alarm as an *emotional appeal,* instead of giving *reasons* for believing that the consequences will actually follow, and that they are undesirable.

4. *Appeal to pity.* "Those unhappy people . . . the homeless of the 5 world . . . a child torn from his mother's arms." By presenting us with scenes about which we are naturally inclined to feel sad, the speaker seeks to make us feel unreasonable pity toward those whom his policy is supposed to help. A story can be a "tearjerker" even when we don't believe it really happened; and once our sympathies are aroused, we are more open to subtle suggestion. What the speaker *suggests* is that those people are really deserving of pity, and that his policy will actually help them. But he does not give any reasons for these statements; again, he hopes that the very strength of our sympathy will make us willing to try any policy that is vaguely associated with charity, generosity, and an honest desire to help. If the bill has the word "housing" in its title, and if its preamble makes well-worded references to "homeless veterans," "the ill-housed," "tearing down

disgraceful slums," perhaps we shall read no further. Yet maybe further down in the bill these purposes are so hedged with restrictions that the effect of the bill is nullified. This is appealing to pity, instead of giving *reasons* for believing that the people need help, and that the policy recommended will actually help them.

5. *The argument from illegitimate authority.* "As the atomic scientists say . . . as great men of the past agree . . . as I was taught at my mother's knee. . . ." By such appeals to authority, by invoking our willingness to be guided by those who really know more than we do, the speaker seeks to bolster up his claims. What he *suggests* is that the authority he quotes is a legitimate one—that is, one whom we have good reason to trust on the matter at hand. But his appeal is based on the hope that we can easily be led to transfer the reverence and respect we may feel for an authority on one matter to other matters on which he is not an authority. Thus our reasonable affection and respect for doctors and surgeons have made them a national symbol of authoritative guidance on a host of irrelevant questions, and the advertising pages are peopled with men in white brandishing stethoscopes or test tubes. They are quoted on psychology (though they may not have been trained in this field), on cigarette-smoking (though they may have done no research on it), on economics, on ethics, or on international affairs.

A speaker with a certain amount of prestige, based on a high batting average, a Hollywood contract, or a Ph.D., uses the same appeal when he poses as an expert outside his own field. And if he merely repeats his view, over and over again, in a confident tone, the repetition will go far to suggest that his view is really authoritative. But a speaker is not relying on illegitimate authority when he gives *reasons* for believing that the opinion he quotes was reached by someone (*a*) who had access to the relevant information, (*b*) who was capable, by training and ability, of thinking about it, and (*c*) who was fair and unbiased in his thinking. For these are the marks of a *legitimate* authority.

6. *The ad hominem argument.* "My opponent says that we should return the municipal garbage-disposal plant to private hands. But why does he say this? What are his underlying motives? Could it be that he and his friends want to get in on a profitable little monopoly?" We all know how hard it is to keep personalities out of a serious discussion. The *ad hominem* argument (sometimes called "poisoning the well") is perhaps the most natural emotional appeal. The speaker seeks to discredit the character, motives, family, friends, pronunciation, grammar, or some other characteristic of the person who disagrees with him. The argument is not "to the thing" (*ad rem:* to the statement at issue), but "to the man" (*ad hominem*). It ranges from mild ridicule to

sharp invective; but the principle is always the same. The speaker *suggests* that if something is wrong with a person, then what that person says cannot be true.

Now, obviously, the most villainous and despicable character in 9 the world can say that fire is hot and that statement will still be true. But by arousing mistrust in the *source* of the statement, the *ad hominem* arguer hopes to make us reject the statement itself. That is his technique. Of course, when a witness is giving *testimony* in a trial, the question at issue is, precisely, the reliability of the witness. Here it is legitimate to impeach the evidence by raising doubts about its source. The appeal is *ad hominem* when the question at issue is the *truth* of a statement, but we are asked to disbelieve it because we do not approve of the person who uttered the statement.

It would be a mistake to condemn, or even to mistrust, all dis- 10 course that contains these emotional appeals. A statement can arouse emotions and still be true. Some facts are delightful, and some facts are damnable. But to get at the truth about anything, you have to do something more than feel strongly about it. You have to think. That is why you should be able to recognize these emotional appeals. It is the only way you can, so to speak, back off from a discourse and get a little perspective.

QUESTIONS AND IDEAS FOR DISCUSSION

1.   The headnote to this essay claims that emotional appeals are not always fallacious. Under what kinds of circumstances might an emotional appeal be legitimate? Discuss.

2.   Of the six specific emotional appeals that Beardsley describes, which do you find the most prevalent in advertising? In political rhetoric? In other contexts? Give examples.

3.   Beardsley's examples of six emotional appeals are drawn mostly from the political arena. Give an example of each (it may be of your own invention) about more everyday issues and arguments.

What a Lovely Generalization!
JAMES THURBER

James Thurber (1894–1961) was a renowned American humorist and cartoonist who was on the staff of the *New Yorker* for most of his career. He wrote a number of books, including *My Life and Hard Times* (1933) and *Fables for Our Time* (1940). This essay is reprinted from one of Thurber's many collections, *Thurber Country* (1953). It describes one of the most common, often cruelest, and sometimes funniest types of fallacies—the sweeping generalization. We generalize all the time, of course, and we must. In order to function, we need to generalize from what we experience or learn. Otherwise, we would have to encounter our world each day as if for the first time. The problems arise when we generalize broadly from too few or untypical examples. This essay provides an enjoyable reminder of the absurdity of the sweeping generalization, even as —tongue in cheek— the author commits a few himself.

I have collected, in my time, derringers, snowstorm paper- 1
weights, and china and porcelain dogs, and perhaps I should explain what happened to these old collections before I go on to my newest hobby, which is the true subject of this monograph. My derringer collection may be regarded as having been discontinued, since I collected only two, the second and last item as long ago as 1935. There were originally seventeen snowstorm paperweights, but only four or five are left. This kind of collection is known to the expert as a "diminished collection," and it is not considered cricket to list it in your *Who's Who* biography. The snowstorm paperweight suffers from its easy appeal to the eye and the hand. House guests like to play with paperweights and to slip them into their luggage while packing up to leave. As for my china and porcelain dogs, I disposed of that collection some two years ago. I had decided that the collection of actual objects, of any kind, was too much of a strain, and I determined to devote myself, instead, to the impalpable and the intangible.

Nothing in my new collection can be broken or stolen or juggled or 2
thrown at cats. What I collect now is a certain kind of Broad Generalization, or Sweeping Statement. You will see what I mean when I bring out some of my rare and cherished pieces. All you need to start a collection of generalizations like mine is an attentive ear. Listen in particular to women, whose average generalization is from three to five times as broad as a man's. Generalizations, male or female, may be true ("Women don't sleep very well"), untrue ("There are no pianos in Japan"), half true ("People would rather drink than go to the theater"), debatable ("Architects have the wrong idea"), libelous ("Doctors don't know what they're doing"), ridiculous ("You never see foreigners fishing"), fascinating but undemonstrable ("People who break into houses don't drink wine"), or idiosyncratic ("Peach ice cream is never as good as you think it's going to be").

"There are no pianos in Japan" was the first item in my collection. 3
I picked it up at a reception while discussing an old movie called "The Battle," or "Thunder in the East," which starred Charles Boyer, Merle Oberon, and John Loder, some twenty years ago. In one scene, Boyer,

as a Japanese naval captain, comes upon Miss Oberon, as his wife, Matsuko, playing an Old Japanese air on the piano for the entertainment of Loder, a British naval officer with a dimple, who has forgotten more about fire control, range finding, marksmanship, and lovemaking than the Japanese commander is ever going to know. "Matsuko," says the latter, "why do you play that silly little song? It may be tedious for our fran." Their fran, John Loder, says, "No, it is, as a matter of—" But I don't know why I have to go into the whole plot. The lady with whom I was discussing the movie, at the reception, said that the detail about Matsuko and the piano was absurd, since "there are no pianos in Japan." It seems that this lady was an authority on the musical setup in Japan because her great-uncle had married a singsong girl in Tokyo in 1912.

Now, I might have accepted the declarations that there are no 4 saxophones in Bessarabia, no banjo-mandolins in Mozambique, no double basses in Zanzibar, no jews'-harps in Rhodesia, no zithers in Madagascar, and no dulcimers in Milwaukee, but I could not believe that Japan, made out in the movie as a great imitator of Western culture, would not have any pianos. Some months after the reception, I picked up an old copy of the *Saturday Evening Post* and, in an article on Japan, read that there were, before the war, some fifteen thousand pianos in Japan. It just happened to say that, right there in the article.

You may wonder where I heard some of the other Sweeping 5 Statements I have mentioned above. Well, the one about peach ice cream was contributed to my collection by a fifteen-year-old girl. I am a chocolate man myself, but the few times I have eaten peach ice cream it tasted exactly the way I figured it was going to taste, which is why I classify this statement as idiosyncratic; that is, peculiar to one individual. The item about foreigners never fishing, or, at any rate, never fishing where you can see them, was given to me last summer by a lady who had just returned from a motor trip through New England. The charming generalization about people who break into houses popped out of a conversation I overheard between two women, one of whom said it was not safe to leave rye, Scotch or bourbon in your summer house when you closed it for the winter, but it was perfectly all right to leave your wine, since intruders are notoriously men of insensitive palate, who cannot tell the difference between Nuits-St.-Georges and saddle polish. I would not repose too much confidence in this theory if I were you, however. It is one of those Comfortable Conclusions that can cost you a whole case of Château Lafite.

I haven't got space here to go through my entire collection, but 6 there is room to examine a few more items. I'm not sure where I got hold of "Gamblers hate women"—possibly at Bleeck's—but, like "Sopranos drive men crazy," it has an authentic ring. This is not true, I'm afraid, of "You can't trust an electrician" or "Cops off duty always shoot somebody." There may be something in "Dogs know when you're despondent" and "Sick people hear everything," but I sharply question the validity of "Nobody taps his fingers if he's all right" and "People who like birds are queer."

Some twenty years ago, a Pittsburgh city editor came out with the generalization that "Rewrite men go crazy when the moon is full," but this is perhaps a little too special for the layman, who probably doesn't know what a rewrite man is. Besides, it is the abusive type of Sweeping Statement and should not be dignified by analysis or classification. 7

In conclusion, let us briefly explore "Generals are afraid of their daughters," vouchsafed by a lady after I had told her my General Wavell anecdote. It happens, for the sake of our present record, that the late General Wavell, of His Britannic Majesty's forces, discussed his three daughters during an interview a few years ago. He said that whereas he had millions of men under his command who leaped at his every order, he couldn't get his daughters down to breakfast on time when he was home on leave, in spite of stern directives issued the night before. As I have imagined it, his ordeal went something like this. It would get to be 7 A.M., and then 7:05, and General Wavell would shout up the stairs demanding to know where everybody was, and why the girls were not at table. Presently, one of them would call back sharply, as a girl has to when her father gets out of hand, "For heaven's sake, Daddy, will you be quiet! Do you want to wake the neighbors?" The General, his flanks rashly exposed, so to speak, would fall back in orderly retreat and eat his kippers by himself. Now, I submit that there is nothing in this to prove that the General was afraid of his daughters. The story merely establishes the fact that his daughters were not afraid of him. 8

If you are going to start collecting Sweeping Statements on your own, I must warn you that certain drawbacks are involved. You will be inclined to miss the meaning of conversations while lying in wait for generalizations. Your mouth will hang open slightly, your posture will grow rigid, and your eyes will take on the rapt expression of a person listening for the faint sound of distant sleigh bells. People will avoid your company and whisper that you are probably an old rewrite man yourself or, at best, a finger tapper who is a long way from being all right. But your collection will be a source of comfort in your declining years, when you can sit in the chimney corner cackling the evening away over some such gems, let us say, as my own two latest acquisitions: "Jewelers never go anywhere" and "Intellectual women dress funny." 9

Good hunting. 10

QUESTIONS AND IDEAS FOR DISCUSSION

1.   The headnote to this essay asserts that we must generalize in order to function. Discuss this claim.

2.   Thurber treats sweeping generalizations lightly. However, in their darker forms, they can reflect and worsen all kinds of prejudices. Give some examples. Have you ever been the victim of an unfounded sweeping generalization? Discuss.

3.   Is James Thurber guilty of sexism only in the sweeping generalization that women's generalizations are "from three to five times as broad as a man's" (paragraph 2)? There, his sexism is deliberately ironic. Do you find unconscious sexism in this essay? Comment.

4.   During the next day or two, notice and record all the sweeping generalizations that you read or overhear. Do you find them as common as the headnote suggests? Do they tend to fall into typical categories (not necessarily Thurber's) or not? What can you generalize about the sweeping generalizations you encounter?

Quit It, Ompremitywise
SYLVIA WRIGHT

Sylvia Wright (1917–1981) was an editor and author who worked for Farrar and Rinehart Publishing Company and for *Harper's Bazaar* magazine. This essay first appeared in *Get Away from Me with Those Christmas Gifts* (1959). Although dated in some of its details, the essay describes what remains probably the most common fallacy in argument of all kinds: the begged question. To "beg the question" is simply to make a claim on the basis of an an unwarranted assumption, to take as given what in fact needs to be proven. Advertisers are certainly guilty of this fallacy often enough—but so are most of us! Wright has her own tongue-in-cheek reasons for assigning a new name to this fallacy, as you will see.

I feel tolerant about advertising but there is one device of the   1
advertisers that I would like to call their attention to. I think it may get them into trouble.

I am calling this device Omitted Premise Superiority, and, since I   2
am a real American, advertised at regularly, in the flow, the swim, and the drink of our national life, and not an outsider or an egghead

(unless you lay the egg flat—my hat size is 23), I am going to be like the advertising copy writers and hereinafter (a word I have always wanted to use) call this device Ompremity.

Here is an example of ompremity: Gallo wine; picture of lush   3 grapes. "These grapes are only squeezed once."

What, I want to know, is wrong with squeezing grapes twice, or   4 three times, or as many times as it takes to get every bit of juice out of them? There may be a perfectly good reason, such as that if you go on squeezing, you get crushed seeds in your wine. But I want to be told. I don't automatically know why squeezing grapes once is superior.

"The only mustard made with two kinds of specially grown mus-   5 tard seed." Why are two kinds of mustard seed better than one? You could sell me just as badly if you said, "The only mustard made with only one specially grown mustard seed."

"The only cereal with two whole grains." Do all the other cereals   6 have one whole and one half grain? If the bulk were the same, mightn't half grains be easier to chew and not stick in the teeth as much? I'm not questioning the veracity of the statement. I simply want that omitted premise.

Ompremity, as you see, is often associated with the word "only."   7 It is also often associated with a made-up word, as in "the only tooth paste that contains gardol." Gardol and irium and such don't irritate me quite as much, because by their very vagueness they give my inquiring mind something to work on. I can picture to myself some extraordinary substance, a great technical advance, developed in our clean, modern laboratories by a new process, which could certainly do whatever they say it does. My only quarrel with these words is that they aren't alluring. I am told not to buy a chicken unless it is acronized. Does this make my mouth water? Am I yummyized? I'm not, because acronized does not sound like what I would want done to a chicken. It sounds like what I would want done to a hot-water bottle.

Pillsbury tells me that if I use their Hot Roll Mix, I will have the   8 "excitement of working with living dough." What is living dough, and do I want it? Is all dough but Pillsbury's dead? Who's that there in Pillsbury's dough, trying to get out?

If you are not alert, ompremity can trick you into belief. There is a   9 deodorant which is better because it rolls on. At first reading, this seemed to me obvious: of course a deodorant that rolls on is better than one that—well, what? Scrunches in? But mightn't scrunching in be more thorough?

"Roto-roasting" is the "secret that brings out all the golden good-   10 ness of the peanuts" used in Big Top peanut butter. (By the way, why is goodness always golden? What about bisque goodness, as in lobster bisque, or chartreuse goodness, as in chartreuse?) Roto comes from the Latin, *rota*, a wheel. Because of having a dictionary, I can get a little further with this ompremity than with most, but I can't get very far. The implication is that these peanuts are roasted on all sides. How do you suppose they do this? Do they spit each peanut with a fine sewing needle?

The point is that if they don't watch it, the advertisers will be hoist 11 with their own ompremity. I am thinking of the face powder which is proofed against moisture discoloration because it is triple-creamed. I am, as I mentioned above, a regular American, and I have been advertised at to the point where I take it for granted that I am entitled to the very best. Why should I be satisfied with face powder that is only triple-creamed? I want face powder that is at least quintuple-creamed, and now that I think of the very delicate skin I have, I think I should have face powder that is centuple-creamed.

In this country one person is just as special as the next one, except 12 that I am more so. I have just written the *only* article that contains ompremity.

QUESTIONS AND IDEAS FOR DISCUSSION

1. Given that "omitted premise superiority," or "ompremity," refers to the long-recognized fallacy of the begged question, why does Wright make up her own name for it?

2. Wright claims that "ompremity" in advertising "is often associated with the word 'only' " (paragraph 7). She gives examples but not reasons. Give reasons.

3. "If you are not alert, ompremity can trick you into belief" (9). Think about any recent advertisements or commercials that led you to try a new product. Did any of them use "ompremity" to win you over? Discuss.

4. Give some illustrations of begged questions from recent advertisements, including the ones reprinted in this chapter. Are the omissions obvious or subtle? Do they seem seriously misleading or relatively minor? Discuss your findings and conclusions.

5. Give some illustrations of begged questions from nonadvertising contexts, such as letters to the editor of your local or campus newspaper, magazine editorials, or political speeches. In each case, discuss what has been unjustifiably assumed.

6. If to beg the question is to assume what really needs to be proven, how can we best avoid committing this fallacy in our own arguments?

THE STRATEGY AT WORK:
ARGUMENTS ABOUT ADVERTISING

It is almost too easy to criticize advertising. We often feel that advertisers intend to trick us into buying, using, or supporting products or causes that are either useless or bad. We feel that they attempt to make us materialistic, that their sole aim is to promote needless consumption. Political advertising we discount as wholly misleading and untruthful. Solicitations from charitable organizations arouse our suspicions even as they play on our sympathies. We do not trust advertising.

And many advertisements confirm our fears. More than a few are fallacious and deceptive. Many promote image over substance.

But advertising also informs us: We learn who has the best price on green beans and who has the toys in stock that our nephews and nieces want for their birthdays. We learn about new and useful products that we would otherwise know nothing about. If it is true that people will buy a bad product only once, then advertising promotes quality. Moreover, advertising pays for the television programs we want to watch and the magazine articles we want to read; without advertising, we would have to pay dearly for both.

From another point of view, some people scoff at the idea that advertising has even enough influence to warrant attack. People flip past the ads in newspapers and magazines, and wander off to the refrigerator during advertisements on television. Nobody pays much attention to ads, no matter how catchy the jingle or how clever the headline.

The essays in this section focus on the merits and demerits, virtues and fallacious appeals of advertising. Michael Parenti, a left-wing critic of politics and culture, argues that advertising is "the big sell" of much more than products: Advertising promotes consumerism as the whole aim of life. Advertising dispenses ideology along with information—and advertising is omnipresent. John O'Toole, an advertiser, counters such claims with the argument that advertising is simply salesmanship. People understand both its uses and its limitations. Even Ralph Nader would not mention a worn fan belt in an ad to sell his own car. "Positive" advertising is not fallacious, O'Toole argues. People who want full disclosure in ads are paternalistic and fail to credit consumers' good sense.

In the third essay, James Playsted Wood, a former advertiser and an authority on advertising and communications, defends advertising more broadly. Wood argues that advertising, because it makes no pretenses of being unbiased, is the most honest form of journalism that exists. Moreover, he reasons, all the other forms of journalism exist only because of the advertising that pays their way. Last, Michael Schudson, a sociologist who grew up in an advertising family, finds ads to be powerful and dangerous. Schudson acknowledges the good uses of advertising but argues that today it also tends to promote bad products, bad values, and the stratification of society.

These writers raise issues well worth considering. Advertising is neither entirely good nor entirely bad, entirely innocent nor entirely manipulative. It is a complex component of a complex society, one we would do well to understand better. Michael Schudson, in arguing for a middle position on advertising and the material culture it represents, concludes his essay with this hope: "It is time for a study that will not be a reflexlike intellectual revulsion at the world of goods but an effort to understand what place material culture might hold in a good world."

The Big Sell

MICHAEL PARENTI

Michael Parenti is a writer who has articulated a leftist viewpoint about political and cultural issues in many publications over the last twenty-five years. He has also written a number of books, including *Power and the Powerless* (1978), *Democracy for the Few,* 5th ed. (1987), and *The Sword and the Dollar: Imperialism, Revolution and the Arms Race* (1988). The following essay comprises a brief chapter in Parenti's *Inventing Reality: The Politics of the Mass Media* (1986). The book is directed both to an academic audience, with as many as eighty-six footnotes to a chapter, and to a general audience, aiming to "reeducate and enrage" the reading public. In the introduction to the book, Parenti anticipates an objection to his arguments: "Some readers will complain of this book's 'one-sidedness.' But if it is true that 'we need to hear all sides and not just one,' then all the more reason why the criticisms and information usually suppressed or downplayed by the American press deserve the attention accorded them in the pages to follow." In Parenti's view, advertising is fallacious in several ways. It leads readers and viewers to draw wrong conclusions—about products, about society, and about themselves. It equivocates, shifting from "nutrition" to "nutrients" (that is, calories), from ostensibly public-service Ad Council spots to private interests. It oversimplifies problems, and then offers "cosmetic solutions." Most of all, advertising deceives because it sells not so much products as a way of life—the life of the consumer.

Much of our media experience is neither news nor entertainment.   1 .
Some 60 to 80 percent of newspaper space and about 22 percent of

television time (even more on radio) is devoted to advertising. The average viewer who watches four hours of television daily, sees at least 100 to 120 commercials a day, or 36,400 to 43,680 a year. Many of the images in our heads, the expressions in our conversation, the jingles and tunes we hum, and, of course, the products we find ourselves using, are from the world of the Big Sell. Advertising not only urges products upon us, we in part become one of its products. We are, if anything, consumers. And even if we have learned to turn away from the television set when commercials come on and pass over the eye-catching ads in our newspapers and magazines, we cannot hope to remain untouched by the persistent, ubiquitous bombardment.

Most of us think of advertising as the sideshow we must tolerate in 2 order to experience the media's more substantial offerings. Advertising picks up most of the costs of newspapers and magazines and all the costs of radio and television. Thus it is thought of as a means to an end. But a moment's reflection should tell us it is the other way round: The media's content, the news and entertainment, the features and "specials," are really the *means*, the lures to get us exposed to the advertisements. ("Journalists," said one press representative, "are just people who write on the back of advertisements."[1]) The *end* is the advertising, the process of inducing people to spend as much money as possible on consumer products and services. Entertainment and news are merely instrumental to the goal of the advertiser. They are there to win audiences for the advertisers, to keep people tuned in and turned on. The objective is commercial gain, the sale of mass-produced goods to a mass market; only for that reason are advertisers willing to pay enormous sums for what passes as entertainment and news.

Mass advertising has not always been with us. It grew with mass 3 media, or rather mass media grew with *it*. Mass advertising was a response to significant transformations in the productive system. The growth of modern technology and mass production brought changes in the lives of millions of Americans. The small community with its local economy and homebred recreational and cultural life gave way to an urbanized, industrial society of people who were obliged to turn more and more to a mass commodity market.[2]

The age of mass consumption came to the United States most 4 visibly in the 1920s, interrupted by the Great Depression and World

---

[1] Charles Clark quoted in *City Paper* (Washington, D.C.), June 24, 1983.
[2] For a good discussion of advertising and the creation of consumer culture, see Stuart Ewen, *Captains of Consciousness* (New York: McGraw-Hill, 1976).

War II, then exploding upon us with accumulated vigor in the postwar era. With it came the advertising industry, called into being by the economic imperative of having to market vast quantities of consumer goods and services. Among the new products were those that enabled advertising itself to happen: the penny-press newspaper, the low-priced slick magazine, the radio, and finally the television set—all in their turn were to become both mass consumption items and prime conduits for mass consumption advertising. Today the family and local community are no longer the primary units for production, recreation, self-definition, or even personal loyalty. Self-images, role models, and emotional attachments are increasingly sought from those whose specialty is to produce and manipulate images and from the images themselves.

The Consumer Ideology

The obvious purpose of ads and commercials is to sell goods and 5 services, but advertisers do more than that. Over and above any particular product, they sell an entire way of life, a way of experiencing social reality that is compatible with the needs of a mass-production, mass-consumption, capitalist society. Media advertising is both a propagator and a product of a consumer ideology.

People have always had to consume in order to live, and in every 6 class society, consumption styles have been a measure of one's status. But modern consumerism is a relatively recent development in which masses of people seek to accumulate things other than what they need and often other than what they can truly enjoy. Consumption is no longer just a means to life but a meaning for life. This is the essence of the consumer ideology. As propagated through mass advertising, the ideology standardizes tastes and legitimizes both the products of the system and the system itself, representing the commodity-ridden life as "the good life" and "the American Way." The consumer ideology, or consumerism, builds a mass psychology of "moreness" that knows no limit; hence the increase in material abundance ironically also can bring a heightened sense of scarcity and a sense of unfulfilled acquisition.

Advertisements often do not explicitly urge the consumer to buy a 7 given product, rather they promise that the product will enhance a person's life, opening a whole range of desiderata including youthfulness, attractiveness, social grace, security, success, conviviality, sex, romance, and the admiration of others. Strictly speaking the advertisement does not *sell* the product as such. Rarely does the television commerical say "Buy Pepsi"; instead it urges us to "Join the Pepsi Generation."

Most consumers, if questioned on the matter, would agree that 8
many commercials are exaggerated, unrealistic, and even untrue; but
this skepticism does not immunize them from the advertisement
hype. One can be critical of a particular commercial yet be swayed by it
at some subliminal level, or by the overall impact of watching a thousand commercials a week. Thus millions of people bought high-priced
designer jeans even if few actually believed the product would win
them entry into that never-never world of slim-hipped glamorous
people who joyfully wiggled their blue-denim posteriors into the TV
camera, in an endless succession of commercials during the early
1980s.

The consumer ideology not only fabricates false needs, it panders 9
in a false way to real ones. The desire for companionship, love, approval, and pleasure, the need to escape from drudgery and boredom,
the search for security for oneself and one's family, such things are
vital human concerns. The consumer ideology does something more
pernicious than just activate our urge for conspicuous consumption;
like so much else in the media and like other forms of false consciousness, consumerism plays on real human needs in deceptive and ultimately unfulfilling ways.

One of the goals of advertising is to turn the consumer's critical 10
perception away from the product—and away from the system that
produces it—and toward herself or himself.[3] Many commercials characterize people as loudmouthed imbeciles whose problems are solved
when they encounter the right medication, cosmetic, cleanser, or
gadget. In this way industry confines the social imagination and cultural experience of millions, teaching people to define their needs and
life styles according to the dictates of the commodity market.

The reader of advertising copy and the viewer of commercials 11
discover that they are not doing right for baby's needs or hubby's or
wifey's desires; that they are failing in their careers because of poor
appearance, sloppy dress, or bad breath; that they are not treating
their complexion, hair, or nails properly; that they suffer unnecessary
cold misery and headache pains; that they don't know how to make
the tastiest coffee, pie, pudding, or chicken dinner; nor, if left to their
own devices, would they be able to clean their floors, sinks, and toilets
correctly or tend to their lawns, gardens, appliances, and automobiles.
In order to live well and live properly, consumers need corporate
producers to guide them. Consumers are taught personal incompetence and dependence on mass-market producers.

Are people worried about the security of their homes and families? 12
No need to fear. Prudential or All-State will watch over them. Are

---

[3] Ibid.

people experiencing loneliness? Ma Bell brings distant loved ones to them with a telephone call. The corporate system knows what formulas to feed your infants, what foods to feed your family, what medication to feed your cold, what gas to feed your engine, and how best to please your spouse, your boss, or your peers. Just as the mass market replaced family and community as provider of goods and services, so now corporations replace parents, grandparents, midwives, neighbors, craftspeople, and oneself in knowing what is best. Big business enhances its legitimacy and social hegemony by portraying itself as society's Grand Provider.[4]

The world of mass advertising teaches us that want and frustra-   13
tion are caused by our own deficiencies. The goods are within easy reach, before our very eyes in dazzling abundance, available not only to the rich but to millions of ordinary citizens. Those unable to partake of this cornucopia have only themselves to blame. If you cannot afford to buy these things, goes the implicit message, the failure is yours and not the system's. The advertisement of consumer wares, then, is also an advertisement for a whole capitalist system, a demonstration that the system can deliver both the goods and the good life to everyone save laggards and incompetents.

Selling the System

Along with products, the corporations sell themselves. By the   14
1970s, for the first time since the Great Depression, the legitimacy of big business was being called into question by large sectors of the public. Enduring inflation, unemployment, and a decline in real wages, the American people became increasingly skeptical about the blessings of the corporate economy. In response, corporations intensified their efforts at the kind of "advocacy advertising," designed to sell the entire capitalist system rather than just one of its products. Between 1971 and 1977, the spending on "nonproduct-related" advertisements more than doubled, from $230 million to over $474 million, showing a far greater growth rate than advertising expenditures as a whole.[5] *Today, one-third of all corporate advertising is directed at influencing the public on political and ideological issues as opposed to pushing consumer goods.* (That portion is tax deductible as a "business expense," like all other advertising costs.) Led by the oil, chemical, and steel companies, big business fills the airwaves and printed media with celebrations of

---

[4] Ibid.

[5] J. S. Henry, "From Soap to Soapbox: The Corporate Merchandising of Ideas," *Working papers,* May/June, 1980, p. 55.

the "free market," and warnings of the baneful effects of government regulation. "What this outpouring of eloquence seems to represent . . . is a sweeping reactionary movement that has outgrown its earlier roots in the special interests of particular firms and become readily class-wide."[6]

Mobil Oil, probably the forerunner in this area, ran ad campaigns, [15] with an annual budget of $5 million, to inform readers that Mobile "gave employment" to thousands of persons, contributed to charities, and brought prosperity to local communities. More signficantly, as some of the Mobil ads note, business firms all across America do their part to create prosperity for all. One Mobil "Observations" column in the *Washington Post* put it this way:

> Business, generally, is a good neighbor, and most communities recognize this fact.
> From time to time, out of political motivations or for reasons of radical chic, individuals may try to chill the business climate. On such occasions we try to set the record straight. . . . And the American system, of which business is an integral part, usually adapts.
> So when it comes to the business climate, we're glad that most people recognize there's little need to tinker with the American system.[7]

Thus capitalism and Americanism are inseparably joined in something called "the American system." A few faddish radicals or individual malcontents may criticize business but Mobil and the American system are pretty near perfect.

Newsweek ran a series of ideological advertisements sponsored by [16] "The SmithKline Forum for a Healthier American Society." The November 9, 1981, four-page ad on "The Heroes of Growth" featured the headline: "SALUTE THE CAPITALIST ENTREPRENEURS, SAYS SOCIAL PHILOSOPHER GEORGE GILDER. THEY DREAM, THEN ACT, AND ENRICH OUR LIVES." The text has Gilder informing us that, contrary to Adam Smith's view, "capitalism is good and successful not because it miraculously transmutes personal avarice and ambition into collective prosperity but because it calls forth, propagates, and relies upon the best and most generous of human qualities. The process of capitalist investment, for all the obvious differences, bears a close relationship to the ritual gift-giving that anthropologists have discovered to be universal in primitive life."

Other ideological ads, like the one run by United Technologies, as [17] an open letter to Ronald Reagan entitled "Godspeed, Mr. President,"

---

[6] Ibid., p. 56.
[7] *Washington Post*, October 25, 1981.

call for "a revitalized system of free enterprise" with more reliance on "the competitive forces of the marketplace," along with "controlling the growth and cost of government and its intrusion into our lives and liberties."[8]

One prime-time television commercial (October 1981) offers foot- 18 age of a skier going down a beautiful mountain slope, with a deep, male, off-screen voice saying: "Freedom. We Americans have the freedom to choose. The freedom to live our lives the way we want as individuals. The freedom to take risks [skier leaps over a precipitous embankment]. The freedom to succeed [skier makes a skillful maneuver] and the freedom to fail [skier takes a mild spill into the powdery snow]. When government comes into our lives, things change. When people look to government for protection, they get protection but they lose some of their precious freedom [skier at the end of the trail on less precipitous ground, moving along slowly with his hands hanging down and his poles dragging behind him]. Just something to think about from the people at Getty."

Business as a providential social force was the theme of a full page 19 ad by Conoco Inc. in the *Christian Science Monitor* (August 29, 1980). It read:

WHAT WILL CAPITAL BE DOING ON LABOR DAY?
Working.
Building new plants. Starting new businesses. Funding innovation and growth. Developing more energy to fuel the economy.
Part of the capital that creates jobs comes from the earnings of American industry . . .
Throughout the economy, stronger earnings can provide the capital to create more and better jobs. So as we celebrate Labor Day, let's not forget capital.
It works, too.

American readers are not likely to be treated to an alternative view. No newspaper would run an advertisement pointing out that capital cannot build an industry, plant, or commodity without labor, and that when labor takes off on Labor Day, nothing is produced. Capital is the surplus value created by labor. "Putting one's money to work" means mixing it with labor to create more capital. Purely on its own, without labor, capital is incapable of building a woodshed, let alone "new plants." But the message we get is that capital creates, rather than *is* created.

Business is also depicted as society's Grand Protector. Defense 20 companies spend millions in weeklies like *Time* and *Newsweek* and in

---

[8] This appeared as a full-page ad in the *Columbia Journalism Review*, March/April 1981, and other publications.

the major newspapers to advertise their accomplishments in weap-
onry and to assure the reader that America's defenses are growing
stronger thanks to the military hardware produced by this or that
contractor. An advertisement in the *Washington Post* by "McDonnell
Douglas, prime contractor," and "Northrop Corporation, principal
subcontractor" displays a photo of the latest U.S. navy and marine
corps fighter plane, along with the statement (reproduced here in its
entirety): "We are convinced that we have in the F/A-18A a superior
aircraft. One day we use it as a fighter, and that same afternoon we use
it as an attack aircraft."[9] Fortified with this Dr. Strangelove pronouncement, Americans are supposed to sleep easier.

A full-page advertisement in the *Washington Post*, paid for by Bath   21
Iron Works Corporation, pictures a U.S. navy officer's hat sitting next
to a Soviet navy officer's hat (complete with hammer and sickle em-
blem). The Soviet cap looks easily ten times larger. Under the picture is
the headline: "When the other fellow's four times bigger, it's not
enough to be right." The text warns:

> . . . U.S. naval strength has been declining while the Russians
> have been building in such numbers that they now have four times
> the number of ships we have.
> Our new administration has recently asserted that it's time to
> change the ratio. Quality ships in quantity are what we need. Ships
> like the guided missile frigates (FFGs) designed and built on a pro-
> duction line basis by Bath Iron Works.[10]

For the next few years, almost on a weekly basis, Bath Iron Works ran
full-page advertisements in the *New York Times* and *Washington Post*,
with variations of this same warning, accompanied by photos or illustrations showing a massive line-up of Soviet ships (each with hammer
and sickle emblems) next to a few paltry American vessels, or a Soviet
admiral dominating the entire page, peering through his binoculars at
an American vessel that presumably is his intended prey.

Neither the *Times* nor *Post* expressed an obligation to inform their   22
readers that these advertisements might be offering something less
than the truth. According to the Center for Strategic and International
Studies, the U.S. navy has twice the tonnage of the Soviet navy, with
ships that are more modern, better equipped and designed to transport military forces anywhere in the world. As of 1984 the United
States had thirteen operational aircraft carriers equipped with 1200
combat aircraft, the USSR had one full-size carrier, and a few minia-

---

[9] *Washington Post*, October 25, 1981; similar kinds of McDonnell Douglas and other defense
company ads have appeared in the *New York Times, U.S. News and World Report, Business Week*, and
other such publications.
[10] *Washington Post*, October 6, 1981.

ture ones designed for antisubmarine warfare, specifically to try to
locate U.S. nuclear missile submarines that target Soviet cities. The
Soviet navy also has a very limited amphibious capacity, unlike
the U.S. navy which is designed to deliver troops anywhere in the
world.[11]

What the defense contractors sell to the public is an ideology, a   23
fear of being harmed by some sinister foreign threat—most usually the
Russian Bear, a promise of security through strength, an assurance
that we can go on living safely as long as we don't skimp on military
spending. The defense firms present benign facades: "Where science
gets down to business," says Rockwell , whose business is making the
plutonium triggers for atomic warheads. "We bring good things to
life," says General Electric, who makes such good things as the neu-
tron generators that activate thermonuclear devices. "We'll show you
a better way," says Honeywell, whose electronic components show
nuclear missiles a better way to designated targets.[12]

Another area targeted by corporate propaganda is environmen-   24
talism. The 1970s witnessed a surge in ecological consciousness in the
United States. Industry responded by spending millions of dollars in a
propaganda campaign designed to convince the public that business
was caring for the environment. At the same time, the big corporations spent next to nothing on actual conservation and pollution controls. Were one to judge strictly from the ads, however, business does
everything it can to avoid dumping raw industrial effusion and
chemical toxins into our rivers and atmosphere. An ad by Chemical
Manufacturer's Association in the *New York Times* (May 4, 1982) shows
an attractive woman being hugged by a smiling little girl. The woman
is saying: "My job is managing chemical industry wastes. What I do
helps make the environment safer today—and for generations to
come." Of the many similar ads that have appeared regularly on
television and in various newspapers and news magazines, none
alters the truth that the chemical industry has a dreadful record of
poisoning the environment with toxic wastes.

Sometimes Money Isn't Enough

Advertisements by public interest groups and labor unions de-   25
signed to counter the perpetual pro-business propaganda fail to gain
exposure, mostly for lack of the millions of dollars needed to buy

---

[11] Albert Szymanski, *Is the Red Flag Flying?* (London: Zed, 1979), pp. 114–115; also Center for
Strategic and International Studies, *Soviet Sea Power*, cited in Szymanski.
[12] Robert Friedman, "How America Gets Up In Arms," *Nuclear Times*, March 1983, p. 19.

television time and print space. As of 1983 a full-page ad in the *Washington Post* costs $23,916 a day—and substantially more on Sunday.

On the infrequent occasions when unions and public interest 26 groups muster enough money to buy broadcasting time or newspaper space, they still may be denied access to the media. Liberal-minded commentators have been refused radio spots even when they had sponsors who would pay. A group of scientists, politicians and celebrities opposing the Pentagon's antiballistic missile (ABM) program was denied a half hour on television by all three major networks even though they had the required $250,000 to buy time. On various occasions during the Vietnam era, the *New York Times* would not sell space to citizens' groups that wanted to run advertisements against war taxes or against the purchase of defense bonds. A *Times* executive turned down the antibond advertisement because he judged it not to be in the "best interests of the country."[13] In 1983, the American Council, a Washington-based public foundation concerned with foreign policy issues, tried to buy commercial time on local affiliates of the three networks in order to run a 28-second commercial critical of U.S. involvement in El Salvador. The ABC affiliate sold three spots, but the NBC and CBS affiliates refused to carry it.

Broadcasters and publishers can refuse to run any political mes- 27 sage for any reason, or no reason at all, regardless of how factually accurate or important it might be. During the 1980 electoral campaign, the airwaves were crowded with political commercials, many sponsored by probusiness, conservative, and New Right organizations. In contrast, a citizen's group, Common Sense in National Defense, prepared a 99-word spot commercial dealing with the danger of nuclear war by computer error and calling for a freeze on nuclear weapons. In the last week of the campaign, the group set out to buy air time for the commercial in three senatorial and seven House races in an effort to defeat incumbents who had opposed the nuclear freeze. Some stations did not respond; others agreed to carry the spot, then canceled at the last moment. In the end, voters in only three of the ten electoral contests got to see the commerical. Among the reasons given by broadcasters for turning down the message were:

"Too controversial."

"How an incumbent voted on the nuclear freeze does not constitute a controversial issue of public importance."

"Not in the best interest of the station to run it."

---

[13] Robert Cirino, *Don't Blame the People* (New York: Vintage, 1972), pp. 90, 302.

"I don't think this is the style that the people of Wyoming like. In my judgment it is not in the interest of the populace of Wyoming. They would not understand."[14]

All the stations were acting within their court-given rights: non- 28 candidates have no guaranteed right of access to the airwaves. Broadcasters can run any political commercials they might want, no matter how emotionally raw and derogatory, and they can refuse to run any spot without having to give a reason.

Public Service for Private Interests

Not all air time is given to commercial gain. The Federal Commu- 29 nications Commission (FCC) requires broadcasters to set time aside for "public service announcements." The obligation is a vague one; the FCC has never denied any station its license for failing to live up to it, despite complaints from community and public interest groups. About 3 percent of air time, worth a half billion dollars annually, is given to public service announcements. This free time, like the millions of dollars worth of free space donated by newspapers and magazines, is monopolized by the Advertising Council, a nonprofit corporation funded and directed by corporations, bankers, and network officials. Its board of directors reads like a who's who of big business, with representatives from such major advertisers as Procter and Gamble, General Motors, General Mills, General Electric, and General Foods. A subcommittee of the Advertising Council, the Industries Advisory Committee (at one count composed of twenty-eight bankers and fifty-four major corporate executives), sets the ideological tone for all advertising campaigns. No public interest groups are represented on the Council's board.[15]

The Advertising Council is the second largest advertiser in the 30 world (behind Procter and Gamble). Since its formation in 1941, it has used more than $10 billion worth of free "public service" advertising donated by radio, television, newspapers, and magazines. While supposedly nonpartisan and nonpolitical, the Council's public service commercials laud the blessings of free enterprise and urge viewers to buy U.S. Savings Bonds. The ads tell us that business is "doing its job" in hiring the handicapped, veterans, minorities, and the poor—when in fact, business makes little voluntary effort on behalf of such groups.

---

[14] Philip Stern, "How TV Gagged Our Freeze Ads," *Washington Post*, November 21, 1982.
[15] Bruce Howard, "The Advertising Council: Selling Lies," *Ramparts*, December 1974/January 1975, pp. 26–32; also "The State and Corporations: Public Service Ads," *Guardian*, May 26, 1976.

Workers are exhorted to take pride in their work and produce more for their employers, but nothing is said about employers paying more to their workers.

The Advertising Council has waged a "Food, Nutrition and 31 Health" campaign, whose ads urge viewers to send in for a free booklet entitled "Food is More than Just Something to Eat." The booklet fails to mention that Americans eat too much processed food, sugar, and junk food. Instead it cheerily announces: "Fresh or frozen? Canned or dried? Instant or from scratch? Which foods have the nutrients? Which do not? They all do."[16]

Council ads offer cosmetic solutions to serious social problems, 32 thereby trivializing the nature of the problems. Unemployment? It can be reduced with "better job training." Crime? Lock your car after parking it and secure your front door. Hazardous and costly automobile transportation? Fasten your safety belts. Ecology and conservation? Listen to Smokey Bear and prevent forest fires. Industry's devastation of the environment? Do not litter. The Council's slogan is "People start pollution, and people can stop it." The ads blame pollution on everyone in general—thus avoiding placing any blame on industry in particular. The Council's "Keep America Beautiful" campaign of 1983 was coordinated by the public relations director of Union Carbide, a chemical manufacturer and a major polluter.

Throughout the Council's diverse range of messages runs one 33 underlying theme: personal charity, individual effort, and neighborly good will can solve any mess; collectivist, class-oriented, political actions, and governmental regulations are not needed in a land of self-reliant volunteers.[17]

In the 1970s, with funds from the U.S. Department of Commerce, 34 the Advertising Council launched campaigns to educate Americans about the blessings of private enterprise and the evils of inflation. Some 13 million booklets, distributed to schools, workplaces, and communities and reprinted in newspapers across the nation, informed readers that only *they* could whip inflation and make the system work better by themselves working harder, producing more, and shopping smarter. The anti-inflation campaign, reaching some 70 million Americans, listed government regulation as the primary cause of inflation. The solution was to keep the lid on wages and prices and roll back regulations.

The Ad Council's campaign seemed to have an effect on public 35 opinion. In 1975, 22 percent of those polled thought there was too

---

[16] Howard, "The Advertising Council . . . ," p. 31.
[17] Kennen Peck, "Ad Nauseam," *Progressive*, May 1983, p. 44.

much government regulation; by 1979, 50 percent; and in 1980, 60 percent.[18] By the 1980 electoral campaign, "deregulation" had become a widespread, ready-made theme utilized to advantage by presidential candidate Ronald Reagan.

Those who wished to make monopoly profits, occupational 36 safety, unemployment, and environmental protection the central themes of popular debate have no way of reaching mass audiences. The public service air time that could be used by conservationists, labor, consumer, and other public interest groups has been preempted by a business-dominated Advertising Council that passes off its one-sided, ideological ads as noncontroversial, nonpolitical, and in the public interest. As one liberal Congressman complained, "The Ad Council and the networks have corrupted the original intent of public service time by turning it into a free bonus for the special interests. The Ad Council is a propagandist for business and government, and with staggering control of the media, it not only makes sure its own side of the story is told, but that the other side isn't. The public has no meaningful access to the media."[19]

QUESTIONS AND IDEAS FOR DISCUSSION

1. Given the author's avowed leftist perspective, some politically conservative readers might be disinclined to heed his argument. Does Parenti strike you as contemptuous of those readers, or do you find that he aims to win their attention and respect, if not their agreement? Give examples.

2. From your own experience of advertising, do you agree or disagree with the following claims? Give your reasons.

Advertising not only urges products upon us, we in part become one of its products. (paragraph 1)

Consumption is no longer just a means to life but a meaning for life. (6)

Consumers are taught personal incompetence and dependence on mass-market producers. (11)

The world of mass advertising teaches us that want and frustration are caused by our own deficiencies. (13)

Business is . . . depicted as society's Grand Protector. (20)

---

[18] Ibid., p. 45.
[19] Congressman Benjamin Rosenthal (D-N.Y.) quoted in Howard, "The Advertising Council . . . ," p. 32.

3.   In paragraph 8, Parenti asserts, "One can be critical of a particular commercial yet be swayed by it at some subliminal level, or by the overall impact of watching a thousand commercials a week." Does Parenti offer evidence sufficient to substantiate this claim? Is it a "knowable" generalization? Does it correspond to your own experience or your observation of others' behavior? Explain, with specific illustrations if possible.

4.   The advertisements cited in this essay go back about a decade. Discuss how, if at all, print and television advertisements have changed from those Parenti describes. Are they different in their tactics? In their "hidden agendas"? Do they still (if indeed they ever did) attempt to make consumers insecure and dependent on mass-market producers?

5.   Do you agree with Parenti that nonproduct advertising, advertising with political and ideological aims, is largely or perhaps exclusively right-wing? Examine six to ten recent magazines for a sampling of such advertisements. Are the ads right-wing, centrist, or left-wing—and how did you decide? Are opposing viewpoints represented or not? If possible, bring some examples (or photocopies) for class discussion, along with your assessment of their political or ideological bent.

6.   One question inevitably arises when we read an argument exposing the fallacious appeals made by others: Does the author commit any fallacies himself? Discuss.

What Advertising Isn't

JOHN O'TOOLE

John O'Toole is the former chairman of the board of Foote, Cone, and Belding Communications, Inc., one of the world's largest advertising agencies. Since 1988, he has served as president of the American Association of Advertising Agencies. O'Toole argues here, in an essay from his *The Trouble with Advertising*, 2nd ed. (1985), that advertising is not so much fallacious in its appeals as simply (and sometimes willfully) misunderstood by its critics. He asserts that the critics of advertising distort its nature and function and then knock down the easily vanquished "straw man" they have created: It is the critics, claims O'Toole, who argue fallaciously. As students of logical argument know, attacks on a straw man do not address the actual issue under debate. To clarify the actual issues here, O'Toole argues a corrective definition of what advertising is and how it should be judged. Is his definition a fair one?

Advertising . . . is salesmanship functioning in the paid space 1
and time of mass media. To criticize it for being that, for being true to
its nature, is to question whether it should be permitted—a position
taken by only the most rabid, none of whom has come up with a
reasonable substitute for its role in the economy. And to criticize it for
not being something else—something it might resemble but by definition can never be—is equally fruitless. Yet much of the professional
criticism I spoke of has its feet planted solidly on those two pieces of
shaky ground.

As a format for conveying information, advertising shares certain 2
characteristics with journalism, education, entertainment and other
modes of communication. But it cannot be judged by the same standards because it is essentially something else. This point is missed by
many in government, both the regulators and the elected representatives who oversee the regulators.

The Federal Trade Commission was pushing not too long ago for 3
one of those quasi-laws they call a Trade Regulation Ruling (when
they were empowered to write the law of the land, I don't know; but
that's another argument). This particular TRR would have required an
ad or commercial for any product claiming to be nutritious to list all its
nutritive elements. For two reasons advertising cannot comply with
such a requirement and still end up as advertising.

One, advertising is salesmanship, and good salesmanship does 4
not countenance boring the prospect into glassy-eyed semiconscious-
ness. Yet I am sure—and consumers on whom sample ads and
commercials were tested agreed—that a lengthy litany of niacin,
riboflavin, ascorbic acid and so on is as interesting as watching
paint dry.

Less subjective is the fact that such a listing can't be given for 5
many good, wholesome products within the confines of a thirty-
second commercial. Since that's the standard length today, the end
result of the proposed TRR would have been to ban those products
from television advertising. The FTC staff did not consider that advertising necessarily functions in the paid space and time of mass
media. Adding twenty or more seconds of Latin makes that impossible.

This example illustrates the problems that can arise when regula- 6
tors try to dictate what must go into advertising. An FTC attorney
named Donald F. Turner was quoted by Professor Raymond Bauer in a
piece for the *Harvard Business Review* as saying, "There are three steps
to informed choice. (1) The consumer must know the product exists.
(2) The consumer must know how the product performs. (3) He must
know how it performs compared to other products. If advertising only
performs step one and appeals on other than a performance basis,
informed choice cannot be made."

This is probably true in an ad for a new floor wax from S. C. 7
Johnson or an antiperspirant from Bristol-Myers. But what about a
new fragrance from Max Factor? How do you describe how Halston
performs compared to other products? Is it important for anyone to
know? Is it salesmanship to make the attempt? Or suppose you're
advertising Coca-Cola. There can't be many people left in the world
who don't know Coke exists or how it performs. Granted, there may
be a few monks or aborigines who don't know how it performs in
relation to other products, but you can't reach them through advertising. So why waste the time or space?

The reason Coca-Cola advertises is to maintain or increase a level 8
of awareness about itself among people who know full well it exists
and what it tastes like, people whom other beverage makers are con-
tacting with similar messages about their products. Simple information about its existence and its popularity—information that triggers
residual knowledge in the recipient about its taste and other characteristics—is legitimate and sufficient. It does what a salesman would do.

On the other hand, advertising for a big-ticket item—an automo- 9
bile, for instance—would seemingly have to include a lot of information in order to achieve its end. But the advertising is not attempting to
sell the car. It is an advance salesman trying to persuade the prospect
to visit a showroom. Only there can the principal salesman do the
complete job. Turner's definition is neither pertinent nor possible in
the case of automobiles. In such cases mass communications media
cannot convey the kind of information one needs in order to "know
how the product performs" or to "know how it performs compared to
other products." You have to see it, kick the tires, ask the salesman
questions about it, let the kids try out the windshield wipers. And
surely you have to drive it.

In the paid space and time of mass media, the purpose of automo- 10
bile advertising is to select the prospect for a particular car and, on the
basis of its appeal to his income, life-style or basic attitudes, to persuade him he's the person the designers and engineers had in mind
when they created this model. If the information is properly chosen
and skillfully presented, it will point out the relevance of the car to his
needs and self-image sufficiently to get him into the showroom. Then
it's up to the salesman to sell him the car—but with a different package
of information, including the tactile and experiential, than could be
provided in the ad.

From time to time some government regulator will suggest that 11
advertising information should be limited to price and function. But
consider how paleolithic that kind of thinking is. Restricting advertising to a discussion of price and function would eliminate, among other
things, an equally essential piece of information: what kind of people
make and market this product or provide this service.

The reputation, quality standards, taste and responsibility of the 12
people who put out a product is information that's not only important
to the consumer but is increasingly demanded by the consumer. It's
information that can often outweigh price and function as these differences narrow among products within the same category. It's information that is critical to the advertising my agency prepares for clients like
Johnson's Wax, Sunkist Growers, Hallmark, Sears and many others.
Advertising would not be salesmanship without it. Put it this way: if
surgeons advertised and you had a hot appendix, would you want the
ads to be limited to price and function information?

The government regulators, and the consumer advocates dedi- 13
cated to influencing them, do not understand what advertising is and
how it is perceived by the consumer. And their overwhelming fear
that the one is always trying to deceive the other leads them to demand from advertising the kind of product information that characterizes *Consumer Reports*. They expect advertising to be journalism, and
they evaluate it by journalistic standards. Since it is not, advertising,
like the ugly duckling, is found wanting.

It is not in the nature of advertising to be journalistic, to present 14
both sides, to include information that shows the product negatively
in comparison with other entries in the category (unless, of course, the
exclusion of such information would make the ad misleading or product usage hazardous). For example, advertising for Sunkist lemons,
which might point out the flavor advantages of fresh lemons over
bottled juice, should not be expected to remind people that fresh
lemons can't be kept as long as a bottle of concentrate. Information is
selected for journalism—or should be—to provide the recipient with
as complete and objective an account as possible. Information is selected for advertising to persuade the recipient to go to a showroom or
make a mental pledge to find the product on a store shelf.

Advertising, like the personal salesman, unabashedly presents 15
products in their most favorable light. I doubt that there's a consumer
around who doesn't understand that. For instance, would you, in a
classified ad offering your house for sale, mention the toilet on the
second floor that doesn't flush? I doubt that even a conscience as
rigorous as Ralph Nader's would insist, in an ad to sell his own used
car, on information about that worn fan belt or leaky gasket. No reader
would expect it. Nor does anyone expect it from our clients.

Information, as far as advertising is concerned, is anything that 16
helps a genuine prospect to perceive the applicability of a product to
his or her individual life, to understand how the product will solve a
problem, make life easier or better, or in some way provide a benefit.
When the knowledge can't safely be assumed, it also explains how to
get the product. In other words, it's salesmanship.

It is not witchcraft, another craft government regulators and oth- 17
erwise responsible writers are forever confusing with mine. For the
same reasons people like to believe that someone is poisoning our
water supply or, as in the Joseph McCarthy era, that pinkos proliferate
in our government and are trying to bring it down, someone is always
rejuvenating the idea of subliminal advertising.

Subliminal advertising is defined as advertising that employs 18
stimuli operating below the threshold of consciousness. It is supposed
to influence the recipient's behavior without his being aware of any
communication taking place. The most freqently cited example, never
fully verified, involved a movie theater where the words "Drink
Coke" were flashed on the screen so briefly that while the mind
recorded the message, it was not conscious of receiving it. The result
was said to be greatly increased sales of Coca-Cola at the vending
counter.

I don't like to destroy cherished illusions, but I must state un- 19
equivocally that there is no such thing as subliminal advertising. I
have never seen an example of it, nor have I ever heard it seriously
discussed as a technique by advertising people. Salesmanship is persuasion involving rational and emotional tools that must be employed
on a conscious level in order to effect a conscious decision in favor of
one product over its competitive counterparts, and in order to have
that decision remembered and acted upon at a later time. Furthermore, it's demeaning to assume that the human mind is so easily
controlled that anyone can be made to act against his will or better
judgement by peremptory commands he doesn't realize are present.

Even more absurd is the theory proposed by Wilson Bryan Key in 20
a sleazy book entitled *Subliminal Seduction.* From whatever dark motivations, Key finds sexual symbolism in every ad and commercial. He
points it out to his readers with no little relish, explaining how, after
reducing the prospect to a pliant mass of sexual arousal, advertising can get him to buy anything. There are some who might envy
Mr. Key his ability to get turned on by a photograph of a Sunkist
orange.

Most professional critics are much less bizarre in their condem- 21
nations. Uninformed about the real nature of advertising, perhaps,
but not mad. For instance, they often ascribe recondite powers to
advertising—powers that it does not have and that they cannot adequately define—because it is not solely verbal. Being for the most part
lawyers and academics, they are uncomfortable with information conveyed by means other than words. They want things spelled out, even
in television commercials, despite the fact that television is primarily a
visual medium. They do not trust graphic and musical information
because they aren't sure that the meaning they receive is the same one

the consumer is receiving. And since they consider the consumer much more gullible and much less astute than they, they sound the alarm and then charge to the the the rescue. Sorcery is afoot.

Well, from time immemorial, graphics and music have been with 22 us. I suspect each has been part of the salesman's tool kit for as long as there have been salesmen. The songs of medieval street vendors and Toulouse-Lautrec's Jane Avril attest.

A mouth-watering cake presented photographically as the end 23 benefit of Betty Crocker Cake Mix is just as legitimate as and more effective than a verbal description. The mysteriously exuberant musical communication "I Love New York" honestly conveys the variety of experiences offered by New York State; it is not witchcraft. It is not to be feared unless you fear yourself. But perhaps that is the cradle that spawns consumer advocates and government regulators. There is something murky in that psyche, some kink in the mentality of those who feel others are incapable of making mundane decisions for themselves, something Kafka-like in the need to take over the personal lives of Americans in order to protect them from themselves.

I read with growing disquiet a document put out by the staff of the 24 Federal Trade Commission in 1979 entitled *Consumer Information Remedies*. In discussing how to evaluate consumer information, they wrote,

> The Task Force members struggled long and hard to come up with a universally satisfactory definition of the *value* of consumer information. Should the Commission consider a mandatory disclosure to be a valuable piece of information, for instance, if it were later shown that although consumers understood the information, they did not use it when making purchase decisions? Is there a value in improving the *quality* of market decisions through the provision of relevant information, or is it necessary for the information to change behavior to have value?

The ensuing "remedies" make it clear that the staff really judges the value of a mandatory disclaimer by the degree to which it changes consumer behavior in the direction they are seeking.

But wait a minute. I'm a consumer, too. Who are they to be 25 wondering what to do with me next if I understand but choose to ignore some dumb disclaimer they've forced an advertiser to put in his ad? It's my God-given right to ignore any information any salesman presents me with—and an ad, remember, is a salesman. And what's this about changing behavior? Well, mine is going to change if the employees of a government I'm paying for start talking like that out loud. It's going to get violent.

Later in the same document, the staff addresses "Sub-Optional 26 Purchases." While I have no quarrel with their intent, I find my hackles rising as they define the problem in terms of people "misallocating resources," consumers wasting their dollars on "products that do not best safisfy their needs." Listen, fellows, those are *my* resources you're talking about. Those are *my* dollars, what there is of them after you guys in Washington have had your way with my paycheck. I'm going to allocate them as I damn well please. And if I want to waste a few on products that do not best satisfy my needs—an unnutritious but thoroughly delicious hotdog at the ball park, for example—try to stop me.

Perhaps I, in turn, am seeking evidence of conspiracy. Perhaps 27 I'm looking under beds. But I think I understand the true nature of government bureaucrats. They, on the other hand, do not understand that of advertising. They and other professional critics—the journalists, consumerists, academicians—don't understand that it's not journalism or education and cannot be judged on the basis of objectivity and exhaustive, in-depth treatment. Thorough knowledge of a subject cannot be derived from an advertisement but only from a synthesis of all relevant sources: the advertising of competitors, the opinions of others, the more impartial reports in newspapers, magazines and, increasingly, television.

The critics also don't understand that advertising isn't witchcraft, 28 that it cannot wash the brain or coerce someone to buy what he doesn't want. It shouldn't be castigated for what it cannot and does not purport to do. And it isn't entertainment, either. A commercial should offer some reward to the viewer in return for his time, but that reward need not always take the form of entertainment. Sometimes the tone should be serious, even about seemingly frivolous subjects. Hemorrhoids are not funny to those who have them.

Advertising sometimes resembles other fields, just as an elephant 29 resembles a snake to the blind man who feels its trunk, and a tree to another who feels its leg. But advertising is really salesmanship functioning in the paid space and time of mass media. . . . We can find enough reasons to criticize advertising without flailing it for not being what it isn't.

QUESTIONS AND IDEAS FOR DISCUSSION

1.   How reasonable do you find O'Toole's argument in paragraphs 3 through 5? Has he convincingly demonstrated that "advertising cannot comply with such a requirement [to list nutritive elements when making claims of nutritional value] and still end up as advertising" (paragraph 3)? Explain.

2.   In terms of his overall argument and persuasive aims, what does O'Toole accomplish through his discussion of subliminal advertising?

3. Agree or disagree with the following assertions, giving specific reasons for your conclusions:

It is not in the nature of advertising to be journalistic, to present both sides . . . . (paragraph 14)

Salesmanship is persuasion involving rational and emotional tools that must be employed on a conscious level in order to [work]. (19)

And it [advertising] isn't entertainment, either. (28)

4. The essay identifies (in paragraph 7) some categories of consumer goods for which Donald F. Turner's "three steps to informed choice" (6) are inapplicable. Suggest others. Are advertisements for such products inevitably bound to rely on fallacious (irrelevant or misleading) claims? Why or why not?

5. In paragraph 11, O'Toole argues against limiting advertising to price and function on the grounds that such advertising "would eliminate, among other things, an equally essential piece of information: what kind of people make and market this product or provide this service." Do you agree or disagree? Is O'Toole's argument logical? Evaluate this argument.

6. Is O'Toole guilty of any fallacious emotional appeals? Defend your answer with specific reference to the essay.

7. How would O'Toole answer Michael Parenti's charges against advertising? What would Parenti likely object to in O'Toole's arguments? On what basic premises do the two authors disagree, as revealed in these two essays?

The Merits of Advertising
JAMES PLAYSTED WOOD

It seems that advertising is subject to attack on all fronts: Here James Playsted Wood defends advertising against charges ranging from dishonesty to price inflation to the manipulation of behavior. Wood has written some fifty books in the last fifty years, including novels, biographies, nonfiction for young readers, and several college textbooks on advertising. His professional experience in advertising includes working as an advertising copywriter and as a marketing and advertising researcher. This essay comprises the first chapter in Wood's *This Is Advertising* (1968). Wood argues that advertising, far from being deceptive or fallacious, is in fact "the most honest form of major present-day journalism"—a statement that directly contradicts one of John O'Toole's key arguments in the previous essay. Wood further asserts that the rest of the journalistic media could not exist without advertising. Consider Wood's arguments with care: Are they logical? Does he reason fallaciously at any point? Does he beg any questions?

At least once a day and twice on Tuesdays—or so it seems—we are 1 told that we live in a mass-communications world. We hardly need to be warned. The global reporting of wars and disasters, and of fact, rumor, opinion, and prophecy is now almost immediate. Discussion, explanation, and interpretation of them all is almost as swift.

The sneeze of a newsworthy man or woman in some distant part 2 of the world is given public notice even before the sound of the sneeze has died out. Conjecture as to the significance of the sneeze is head-lined in large type or broadcast in earnest voices in time for breakfast or dinner, depending upon whether it was an A.M. or a P.M. sneeze.

We live in a din of news, not all of it news and not all of it accurate. 3 In self-defense, the belabored reader, listener, and viewer must try to discriminate between what is fact and what is fancy, between what is intended primarily to inform and what is concocted to influence and direct his reactions and opinions.

An increasingly large proportion of the news is based on press 4 releases and reports prepared and distributed by governments, gov-ernment departments and agencies, corporations, labor unions, edu-cational institutions, and many other organizations. Each organization has its special interests and objectives. Its press handouts are always prepared so as to place it in the most favorable light. Usually the objective is not so much to inform as to gain approval. The intent may be to win votes, influence legislation, swell governmental appropri-ations, obtain financial contributions for a cause, gain public support for a position or merely to curry favor. Press conferences are often held for the same or comparable reasons.

The governmental, educational, commercial, industrial, religious, 5 and labor and management groups responsible for so much of the news that reaches us do not release their statements carelessly. Most employ or retain public-relations experts. It is the business of these men and women to create and circulate material favorable to their employers, and they are very good at it.

Completely accurate and objective reporting is, in any event, an 6 ideal, seldom an accomplishment. Everything reported is reported through the senses and the intelligence of some individual or group of individuals. Even when no distortion is intended, the impressions conveyed may not greatly resemble the facts. A backyard bonfire can appear as a holocaust, or some harmless incident a threatening por-tent, or some disaster a bagatelle. The selection of what to report, how much time or space to give it and how much or how little to display can make what is taken to the public seem trivial or world-shaking. Reporting battlefield casualties, for instance, as if they were the box scores of sporting events effectively hides the human tragedy behind the numbers.

By comparison with some of the other forms of mass commu- 7 nications advertising seems honest and reliable. In its open declaration of intent it is perhaps the most honest form of major present-day journalism.

On the face of it, an advertisement says what it is. It says: I am an 8 advertisement. I have been bought and paid for. I make no pretense to objectivity. I am not a disinterested and impartial observer. I am a deeply interested and wholly partial pleader. My object is gain. I want to sell you something. I will persuade you by every means I can devise to buy what I have for sale.

What the advertisement has to sell may be a jet airplane, a pen, an 9 automobile, a lipstick, a new food, an old food, a fad, or a trip from wherever you are to wherever you can be persuaded to spend your money to go. It may try to sell you an idea, a dream, a fact, an opinion, or a prejudice. The advertisement may entice. It may soothe or excite. It may try to frighten you. It may order or coax. Whatever it does and in whatever way it tries to do it, it is directed at you.

The advertisement wants to affect your mind or your emotions. It 10 wants to separate you from your money. It offers delights for hard cash or the promise of hard cash. Come buy! Come buy! Always you are the target. You are the concern of giant corporations, big department stores, and little neighborhood shops—everybody who has something to sell. There is flattery in this. It is pleasant to be offered goodies, even when you know you have to pay. It is pleasant to be tempted. It is wonderful to be the center of attention, and you are the center of attention when you enjoy or detest a television commercial or look at a page of glamorous advertising in a slick magazine.

This is an advertisement. You have been warned. It may have the 11 dignity of the Declaration of Independence or the winsomeness of a small child telling Mummy he loves her, but it is an advertisment. You know you are flirting with danger when you stop, look, or listen. There is excitement in that. Be self-indulgent and buy yourself a diamond, an almost-Paris frock, a garden tractor, or a double-edged, triple-plated, 496 hp, all-weather guarantee of attractiveness to the other sex.

Advertising in reputable media is honest in its declaration of 12 intent. It is almost always honest in the claims it makes for the product or service it brings to what it hopes will be your favorable attention. Generally the nationally advertised item is all that it claims to be.

Usually it is better and less expensive than a comparable product or service not advertised. Advertising is not masquerading propaganda or disguised publicity. It blazons its intent, and it offers sound value for your approval and purchase.

Why all this virtue? Advertising is not created and used just to 13 provide a smug example of public morality. Advertising is honest because it has to be.

Advertising is subject to all of the laws against fraud. Advertisers 14 can be found guilty and prosecuted if they are proven to have defrauded or attempted to defraud. Advertising is scrutinized continually by Better Business Bureaus, and it comes under the jurisdiction of the Federal Trade Commisssion, which was set up in 1915 to enforce prohibition of unfair methods of competition in interstate commerce. The Food and Drug Administration, the Federal Communications Commission, the Alcohol and Tobacco Tax Division of the Internal Revenue Service, and the United States Post Office also have some regulatory power over advertising.

In 1906, with the strong backing of reputable advertisers and 15 advertising media, the Food and Drug Act—the "Wiley Law"—was passed. This law made it a misdemeanor to make or sell misbranded or adulterated foods, drugs, medicines, or liquors. Control was greatly extended by the passage of the Pure Food and Drug Act of 1938, known as the Wheeler-Lea Act. This forbade dissemination of false advertising about foods, drugs, related products, and cosmetics.

Advertising is policed by government, but the strongest controls 16 are exerted by advertisers and advertising media themselves. Like most other successful activities, advertising is largely self-regulatory. It has to be. Advertising is basically honest in its own self-interest. There is no satisfactory alternative.

Advertised products are branded products. It is a particular brand 17 of oats, hair dye, or detergent that is advertised. It carries the advertiser's name or mark. As in the craft guilds of the Middle Ages, where the practice originated, the maker is responsible for what he makes. The name or trademark is the maker's guarantee of the worth of what he has produced. If what he has made is good, the credit is all his. If it is bad, the blame is his and he must accept it. He can make good, or he can go out of business.

If the public finds a brand good, it buys and, persuaded through 18 continuous advertising and satisfactory experience with the product, continues to buy. If people find the brand poor, they will not continue to buy. No amount of advertising blandishment can sell an unsatisfactory product. In the case of an inferior product, advertising only enables more people to discover its inferiority. The market for the product disappears and so does the advertiser and his enterprise.

Only the manufacturer or distributor who intends to stay in busi- 19
ness can afford to face the testing through use of what he sells that
advertising provokes. He must make a good product, and he must
continually improve his brand. He is manufacturing and selling in
tight competition with others whose advertising as well as product
brands compete with his. To maintain and expand his markets, to
make a profit, he has to make certain that his product will prove the
accuracy of his advertising claims.

The consumer—and every man, woman, and child is a consumer, 20
the guise under which advertisers see them—gets not only a better,
but also usually a more inexpensive product when he buys an advertised brand. The reason is simple. Advertising creates quantity consumption. This allows quantity production. The manufacturer can
make more of what he sells. Thus he can take advantage of the low-
ered costs made possible through quantity production, offer his product at lower cost, and still make a profit.

One automobile produced for one man would cost a huge amount 21
of money. Few people could own an automobile. For that matter, one
tube of toothpaste made for an individual or a family would cost
enough to make daily dental scrubbing an expensive luxury. When
automobiles and toothpaste can be produced in the millions, the price
is brought within the range of the average purchaser.

The United States is a mass country. It is governed by and for the 22
mass of the people. Mass production is made possible through mass
purchase and use. In turn, mass production makes mass employment
possible. As a means of creating and maintaining mass consumption,
advertising is thus a basic support of high levels of sustained employment in this country. The ability of advertising to create mass markets
is its economic reason for being.

There are reasons for the existence of advertising which transcend 23
the economic. One of the basic impulses behind it is psychological.
Advertising is as natural as the impulse of man to boast of what he is,
what he does, what he makes, and what he wants to show others for
their approval and applause.

Heeding advertising is as natural as people's wish to gratify their 24
curiosity. It is as natural as their susceptibility to persuasion and their
eagerness to possess what attracts them.

Some people react to mere suggestion and hurry to buy what they 25
see dangled before them with all the forethought and excitement of a
magpie darting on a shiny pebble, flashing off with it, and carefully
adding it to his hoard of accumulated treasures. Others react far
differently to very different kinds of advertising.

A large utility contractor will study the advertisements in a trade 26
journal in search of just the machine he needs to use on a particular

job. (I know one who not only bought the machine but, to make sure he got what he needed, bought the company which made it.) A paper manufacturer or the executives of a textile mill will weigh the advertised specifications of a piece of equipment against their requirements, investigate further, then spend perhaps a hundred thousand dollars or more to buy it. To men like these, advertising pertinent to their business is a necessary source of information. Through it they acquire what they need for the successful operation of their companies.

If advertising has a basic economic reason for being and springs 27 from psychological causes, it also has a strong social effect. It is one of the vital forces which sustain and continually elevate the already high (and well-advertised) standard of living in the United States. It was in large part advertising which supplanted the household broom with the carpet sweeper and then the vacuum cleaner. Largely through advertising, people were persuaded to part with their old iceboxes and the overflowing pans of melted ice beneath them and to risk trying electric or gas refrigerators. Housewives were taught to stop buying foodstuffs in bulk from open bins and to buy instead food conveniently packaged in sanitary containers. The flour bin has disappeared from the pantry. In its place, advertising has installed the freezer, and shelves of prepared mixes for almost any baked good the housewife wishes to serve her family.

Advertising sold the phonograph, then radio, then television. It 28 replaced coal with oil, gas, and electricity for home heating. As advertising men like to point out, advertising has changed and is continually changing people's way of life. It operates to create new needs and new desires. It keeps people dissatisfied with what they have and avid for what is newer, bigger, shinier, easier. Advertising helped turn the no-car family into the one-car family, the one-car family into the two-car family. Now, with little perceptible hesitation, it is trying for three.

Whether this is always a good thing entails a moral judgment 29 beyond the capacity of any but the most self-assured to make. Certainly the force of advertising is vital in American life as we now live it. We still live in a free-enterprise economy in an industrial civilization where the job of the entrepreneur is not finished until he has successfully distributed what he makes, until what begins on the drawing board and passes through the assembly line reaches the people for whom it was made.

Advertising is literally of consuming importance in this entire situ- 30 ation. It is the spokesman for business and industry. It is responsible for the noise. It is also the consuming public's chief source of information about the availability of goods and services. It functions to serve both the advertiser and those to whom the advertising is directed.

There is another point. Advertising is not only pervasive public 31 communication. It is also part, parcel, and primary support of all the major forms of public communication.

Newspapers, magazines, radio, and television are not maintained 32 by government subsidies or charitable foundations. They are private business enterprises that must pay their own way in order to function. As business enterprises, they do not exist primarily to keep the public informed and amused. They exist to carry advertising. It is advertising which makes possible this communication on which people depend. As things are presently arranged, none of these sources of news and entertainment could exist without the income which advertising provides.

If any of them could survive at all, the cost to the purchaser of a 33 newspaper or magazine would be prohibitive. If it was felt they are worth retaining, newspapers, magazines, radio, and television would have to be supported by governmental appropriations out of tax money—government has no other kind—or by philanthropy which would soon bankrupt the philanthropist. People would have to pay substantial fees to listen to radio or watch television. Neither would there be comparable newspapers, magazines, or electronic programs. An essential element would be lacking. The advertising upon which people depend would be missing. Some other way of telling people where to find and buy the necessities of life, the luxuries they have come to expect, and the new products and services they will need as soon as they can learn of them would have to be devised.

Advertising is like that, and so are people. 34

QUESTIONS AND IDEAS FOR DISCUSSION

1. What are the several virtues of advertising, in Wood's estimation? Evaluate the strength of his arguments in defense of each. Which is his weakest argument? Could it be made stronger? If so, suggest what he might have added to or changed in his argument.

2. Wood claims that advertising is honest, and much of his argument hinges on that claim. Does he shift ground from the ordinary meaning of "honest," or does he use the adjective as you would? Comment, with reference to the text.

3. Evaluate the argument in paragraph 16. Is it reasonable or fallacious? Explain your answer.

4. How would you respond to Wood's claim, in paragraph 29, that we cannot make moral judgments about the consumerism that advertising promotes?

5. In what respects does Wood's defense of advertising resemble O'Toole's? On what points do they differ? Which argument do you find to be stronger rhetorically, freer of fallacious claims?

An Evaluation of Advertising
MICHAEL SCHUDSON

Michael Schudson is a professor of sociology and communications at the University of California, San Diego. In addition to a number of scholarly essays and magazine articles on communication and society, Schudson has written *Discovering the News* (1978), a book about American journalism. The following essay is the concluding chapter in his *Advertising: The Uneasy Persuasion* (1984), a book written for both an academic audience and the general public. Schudson argues that advertising is neither as misleading and manipulative as its critics claim nor as worthwhile and effective as its advocates assert.

Advertising was barely a speck on the screen of American culture 1 when Alexis de Tocqueville visited America in 1830 and observed "a kind of decent materialism" emerging. Restrained as it was, Tocqueville assured his readers that it "will not corrupt souls" but he worried that it would "soften and imperceptibly loosen the springs of action."[1] By 1900, with advertising established as a business institution of modest but growing proportion, concern about the materialism of the modern world had achieved great intensity. Max Weber expressed the passion well in the final pages of *The Protestant Ethic and the Spirit of Capitalism,* an essay focusing on Europe but strongly influenced by his recent trip to America. Weber wrote that "material goods have gained an increasing and finally an inexorable power over the lives of men as at no previous period in history." For him, material goods that had served the early Puritan as a sign of grace had come to be not sign but final substance, the goal that personal striving sought to attain. A world of spirit was losing out to a world of matter and the human project seemed encased in the leaden-ness of things.[2]

That is still the indictment a consumer culture must face. Advertis- 2 ing and marketing, as part of the cultural complex of materialism, are

---

[1] Alexis de Tocqueville, *Democracy in America,* trans. J. P. Mayer (Garden City, N.Y.: Doubleday Anchor, 1969), p. 534.
[2] Max Weber, *The Protestant Ethic and the Spirit of Capitalism* (New York: Charles Scribner's, 1958), p. 181.

codefendants. The indictment is strengthened by ecological concern that human *life*, as well as human spirit, is threatened by the headlong rush to produce and to consume.

The defenders of marketing and advertising seek a separate trial. 3 Perhaps, they admit, there are things wrong with a consumer culture, but advertising is not responsible for them. Marketing, they say, merely identifies and responds to human needs and does not—cannot—create the motivations that propel the race of consumption. They are appalled that critics imagine they have such overwhelming powers. They easily brush off criticism that attributes to advertising untold magical influence, extraordinary psychological sophistication, or primary responsibility for creating a consumer culture. They show that they work to reach people already predisposed to the product they are selling, that their appeals stress solid product information as often as they engage in emotional manipulation, and that the consumer is so fickle and the world so complex that their best-laid plans go astray as often as not.

All of this is true. But it is a much less sturdy defense of marketing 4 than it appears. The pseudopopulist rhetoric of "discovering needs" and giving the public what it says it wants is misleading on at least four counts.

First, marketers do not actually seek to discover what consumers 5 "want" but what consumers want *from among commercially viable choices*. One can hardly blame marketers for this, but because of it, one cannot accept the rhetoric of "we have the consumer always in mind." Marketers keep the consumer in mind only to the degree that the consumer defines his or her own prospects in terms agreeable to marketers. Thus consumers are not asked if they would prefer public television to advertising-supported television or public transportation to private automobiles or government-supported health care to private physicians. Developers survey consumers to find out what kind of housing project they prefer, but they do not ask if a public park would be more desirable.

Nor do they ask consumers if they prefer long-term consumer 6 benefits to short-term. Nor do they ask if consumers would like a role in corporate decision making, some representation of consumer interests on the boards of private firms. As marketers read people's preferences for particular products, they take everything else in society as settled—the legitimacy of a market economy, the good sense of devoting the nation's wealth to things that can be commercialized in the short-run, the justice of focusing commercial development on the needs of consumers with the majority of dollars rather than on the needs of the majority of consumers, and the rightness of leaving the task of identifying needs and desires in private hands not responsible to public oversight. In short, the consumers the marketers listen to are not persons, not citizens, but thin voices choosing from among a set of predetermined options. The "people" the marketers are concerned with are only those people or those parts of people that fit into the image of the consumer the marketer has created.

Second, marketers do not listen to all people equally. There is 7 nothing democratic or populist about an approach that listens ten times as carefully to the person with $10,000 in discretionary income as to the person with $1,000. But that is what marketers do. The point is to make money, not to please people. The marketers keep their eyes on the main prize—pocketbooks, not persons. This yields an array of consumer choices top heavy in luxury, and it sometimes works directly to diminish the array of goods available to the person of modest means. For instance, in the competition for the affluent person's dollar, more and more extras become standard equipment on automobiles and other products, and the low-income consumer has no choice but to go deeper into debt to pay for the simplest model, now weighted with superfluous "standard" equipment. In Third World countries, national and multinational corporations provide a highly inappropriate array of products for local needs because they serve largely the very small affluent population in those nations. This is especially noticeable and dangerous in an area like that of health care: "Since middle-income and rich consumers represent the main market for modern drugs, pharmaceutical companies concentrate on furnishing remedies for middle-class ailments like general fatigue, headaches, and constipation rather than for low-income diseases like leprosy, filariasis, and tuberculosis."[3]

Third, marketers wrongly assume that since "good advertising 8 kills a bad product," they can do little harm; people will only buy what they find satisfying. This works, as I have argued, only if people have enough information available to know what the range of possibilities is and how to purchase wisely. This is not true for many populations: poor people, children, Third World peoples, people entering new social roles, people with limited time or uncertain emotional stability for making decisions. Even with educated, middle-class adults, where the product sold is complex and where the normal adult is not able to make informed comparisons among products, advertising or other

---

[3] Gary Gereffi, *The Pharmaceutical Industry and Dependency in the Third World* (Princeton: Princeton University Press, 1983), p. 201. Sometimes marketers direct their products not only *toward* the affluent but *away from* the poor or other "undesirable" consumers. If a product becomes too popular among a stigmatized social group, say, an ethnic minority group, this may drive away potential customers in the dominant population group. Then marketers seek methods of "demarketing." See Philip Kotler and Sidney J. Levy, "Demarketing, Yes, Demarketing," *Harvard Business Review* 49 (November–December 1971): 74–80.

marketing practices can lead people to buy things that they do not need, things that will not "satisfy" their desires, and things that are not good for them. Financial institutions that advertise adjustable-rate mortgages have in some instances been guilty of an old-fashioned "bait and switch" tactic addressed to consumers smart enough not to fall for the practice when it concerns less complex products. The ads emphasize the below-market "teaser" interest rates and play down the true cost of the loan.[4] Life insurance is another case in point. Middle-class, educated people who want both some security and some savings buy whole life insurance when many of them would be better off buying cheaper term life insurance and investing the difference in an ordinary passbook savings account. People are unusually anxious about and ill informed about life insurance; tens of thousands have unwisely turned over their money to insurance companies.[5]

Finally, the marketing ideology mistakenly assumes that responding to discovered, felt needs among consumers is an innocuous activity—that "the people say they want it" is defense enough of a business practice. Obviously, a conscientious marketer would want to circumscribe such a view to say that some goods are harmful and should not be sold or promoted even if people want them. Drug pushers who claim they sell only to people who are already heavy users, are not likely to gain one's sympathy. Marketers and advertisers understand this and while they do not *collectively* take positions on the worth of products, they find ways to accommodate individual moral views. Thus many advertising agencies gracefully excuse employees from working on accounts such as those for cigarettes or liquor if their personal moral positions forbid it. 9

But responding to consumers' expressed desires is potentially harmful even when the product in question is within the bounds of acceptable usage. Even when advertising and other marketing practices respond to expressed desires, they surely reinforce those desires, give them life, embodiment, and provide them a permanence they might not otherwise attain. If there is an infrastructure of consumption—a set of social conditions that predispose one toward certain patterns of consuming, there is also a superstructure of consumption, a set of consuming images, that does its part, too, to make a given product normal, acceptable, convenient, manageable, and popular. There is no proof of this hypothesis and no way to specify the 10

---

[4] Tom Furlong, "Adjustable-Rate Loan Marketing Triggers Concern," *Los Angeles Times*, March 25, 1984, p. V–1.

[5] Bureau of Consumer Protection and Bureau of Economics, Federal Trade Commission, *Life Insurance Cost Disclosure* (Washington, D.C.: U.S. Government Printing Office, 1979).

precise effects of promotional efforts. But that they play a role is as obvious as their provable demonstration is elusive.

Advertising not only promotes specific products but also fosters a 11 consumer way of life. As I have insisted, there are many other factors that also promote consumerism, but this does not mean advertising's contribution can be overlooked.

However misconceived the arguments of advertising's critics, the 12 defense of advertising has been obtuse and disturbingly indifferent to genuine concerns about the morality of marketing. There is plenty to be concerned about. If American materialism has often been decent and virtuous, as Tocqueville observed, it has not always been so, and the key institutions in the cultural complex of materialism are implicated in its failings. What degree of responsibility should one ascribe to advertising? It is not possible to say. But nor is it possible to think through the role of advertising in society without coming to some views about the rights and wrongs of the institution and stating them clearly. A few concluding remarks, then, in evaluation of the role of advertising in American society:

1. Advertising serves a useful informational function that will not 13 and should not be abandoned. It helps people know about available consumer choices and helps them make more rational consumer judgments. This is especially true of price advertising and strongly informational advertising. Even when advertising is not very informative, it can be a modest form of consumer protection, providing consumers some knowledge of the availability of products and so making them less dependent on the local retailer.

2. Advertising probably has a socially democratizing influence 14 but one with an ultimately inegalitarian outcome. It lets the people who are not in-the-know in the know. It helps people to recognize what external signs have currency and helps them know how to move in social circles they may not otherwise have access to or knowledge about. The distribution of consumer goods is much more egalitarian than the distribution of wealth in the form of stocks, bonds, and Swiss bank accounts.[6] This may lead people to imagine the world to be more genuinely egalitarian than it is. This may make people more acquiescent, accommodating them to a stratified society whose degree of inequality is protected by its relative invisibility.

3. The most offensive advertising tends to have the least informa- 15 tional content. It thus has the slightest defense as a legitimate feature

---

[6] See Marcus Felson, "Invidious Distinctions Among Cars, Clothes and Suburbs," *Public Opinion Quarterly* 42 (Spring 1978): 49–58 and Marcus Felson, "The Masking of Material Inequality in the Contemporary United States," *Public Opinion Quarterly* 43 (Spring 1979): 120–22.

of the economic system. However, it helps sustain the media. Until we devise some better way of supporting a relatively free and relatively varied media system, this is an incidental but important virtue of advertising. If advertising were more informative and espoused a more diverse set of values, it would support the media just as well. What is defended by this argument is advertising in the abstract, not the actual advertising we have. Further, advertising does not support the media in a way well designed to foster a healthy democracy. Advertising is skewed toward upscale audiences. Large circulation newspapers with working-class or general readerships have suffered as advertisers have shifted to television and specialized upscale print publications. Advertising supports the media but by no means in a way ideal for the democratic process.[7]

4. Some advertising promotes dangerous products or promotes potentially dangerous products to groups unlikely to be able to use them wisely. Liquor advertising to the young or to the heavy drinker, if it is effective even in the slightest, is socially costly and morally questionable.[8] The advertising and marketing of infant formula in Third World countries where poverty and ignorance guarantee widespread abuse of the product is a grotesque case of the pursuit of profit gone berserk. It is the kind of savagery that people of some future generations may look back on as we look back to slavery, witch burning, or infanticide.

5. Nonprice advertising often promotes bad values, whether it effectively sells products or not. It peppers the airwaves with the insouciant promotion of values that, on a personal basis, few advertisers or copywriters or artists would affirm for themselves or their children. It speaks to people as no decent person would talk to a friend or neighbor or customer. An egregious instance in the past year is the advertising for home computers which, on negligible evidence of the importance of computers in children's educational development, encourages parents to believe they will be ruining their children's lives if they do not shell out a few thousand dollars now for a computer. This advertising, and too much other advertising, takes advantage of peo-

---

[7] See, for instance, Felix Gutierrez and Clint C. Wilson II, "The Demographic Dilemma," *Columbia Journalism Review* 17 (January-February 1979): 53–55.

[8] The question of the morality of liquor advertising is at present a growing public issue, spurred in particular by a report from the Center for Science in the Public Interest: Michael Jacobson, George Hacker, and Robert Atkins. *The Booze Merchants: The Inebriating of America* (Washington, D.C.: Center for Science in the Public Interest, 1983). The controversy has an international dimension, too, with concern in activist circles about why the World Health Organization shelved its plan to study the world liquor industry. See Kathleen Selvaggio, "WHO Bottles Up Alcohol Study," *Multinational Monitor* 4 (November 1983): 9–11.

ple's anxieties or fondly held hopes in order to make money. Whether it works or not, it is indecent.[9]

Advertising often incorporates key values of family, love, and friendship, but it all too often promotes values that our religious traditions, our schools, and our most respected counselors urge us to reject. Too much advertising winks at sexism or encourages it. Too much advertising encourages and legitimates self-indulgence while executives from the corporations that do the advertising self-righteously bemoan the decline of the work ethic in America.   18

6. Advertising could survive and sell goods without promoting values as bad as those it favors now. Some liquor companies promote "moderate drinking" in their ads. These ads provide information at the same time that they promote a product. Some cereal companies now provide information about balanced meals in their ads while still plugging their brand of cereal. This seems to me a step forward. Automobile ads that stressed the dangers of driving and the advantages of safety features would not be taken amiss. Perhaps marketing departments and advertising agencies could even encourage auto manufacturers to install safety equipment that for decades they have resisted. It is certainly possible to harness the techniques of advertising for prosocial ends without making commercials anti-business. Advertising techniques in the Third World, for instance, have been employed not only to sell infant formula in a way that guarantees infant deaths but also to instruct people in boiling water and other practices that help preserve health and life.[10]   19

7. Advertising is but one factor among many in shaping consumer choice and human values. The question, ultimately, is not one of how people independently arrive at a set of desires. Desires are never independently arrived at, but are socially constructed. The important question is what social conditions will be most conducive to autonomous, rational choice. What is the sum of the influence of advertising, family, school, government policy, and the promotional efforts of   20

---

[9] Richard Hoggart puts the case this way: "The overriding fact is that much of the work of this profession [advertising], as it is at present practised, consists of exploiting human weakness through language. Anyone who thinks it is better to try to understand one's weaknesses than to indulge them, anyone who thinks that language (the articulation of our thoughts and feelings in communicable form) can help in that better grasp, anyone with these two premises must regard modern advertising as, at the best, a stupid waste of good human resources and at the worst, a wicked misuse of other people." Richard Hoggart, "Where Is It All Leading Us?" in *Advertising and the Community*, ed. Alexander Wilson (Manchester, England: Manchester University Press, 1968), p. 54. On the hope behind the home computer market, see Douglas Noble, "The Underside of Computer Literacy," *Raritan* 3 (Spring, 1984): pp. 37–64.

[10] A good example is the work of Richard K. Manoff on behalf of various United Nations and other international agencies. See Richard K. Manoff, "When the 'Client' Is Human Life Itself," *Advertising Age*, August 22, 1983, pp. M-4, M-5.

private industries on personal values? How does a nation that assigns more independent decision-making authority to private enterprise than does any other developed country in the world shape desire and form or deform human preferences?

Although advertising is but one factor among many, there are 21 serious objections to it that do not apply to some of the other forces in the formation of need and desire. Advertising comes from *outside* the community whereas parents and often (though not always) teachers are a part of a person's community. The objection to advertising is an objection to a "foreign power" and critics from both left and right object to advertising for much the same reason that critics from both ends of the political spectrum have supported local control of schooling. One's children are going to be influenced by forces outside the family—how can one hold those forces responsible? Can the outside forces be made answerable to the community? There are ways for a community to exercise some control over its school system or over government policy, but there is scarcely any effective way to regulate the messages that come into the community from the mass media, especially the broadcast media. Where one's exposure to advertising is relatively "voluntary" as it is with print advertising, objections to advertising as a "foreign power" are modest. But where exposure is largely unavoidable, as it is with billboards, radio and television, advertising is objectionable as an outside, literally unaccountable influence.

Advertisements are a ripe object for analysis. They are too vivid a 22 body of evidence about what is base in American life to be overlooked. But I hope that critics of advertising will not misspend their energies by taking symbol for substance and believing that the analysis of advertising can substitute for an understanding of the economic, political, social and cultural forces that give rise to it and contribute to the social phenomena often attributed to it.

I hope that people who work in advertising will consider my 23 suggestions for making their activities less "the single most value-destroying activity of a business civilization" in Robert Heilbroner's overblown but still troubling words.[11] Advertising can be, in some measure, an art that enhances human and humane values. Some individual advertising workers would fervently welcome any opportunity to make their craft one they could be proud of, not just aesthetically, but morally. But there is very little that professional associations in the business have done to make this possible. There are

---

[11] Robert Heilbroner, *Business Civilization in Decline* (New York: W. W. Norton, 976).

responsible voices in advertising, to be sure. The generally liberal, "good government" tone of *Advertising Age* is a case in point. But it seems to me that the professional associations in advertising have been more concerned to defend the worth of advertising than to worry about creating an activity they would not need to be so defensive about. Despite the existence of the Advertising Council, there is no tradition of *pro bono* work in advertising as there is in law; despite the National Advertising Review Board, there are no serious standards of condemnation for work that promotes products or values that advertising workers would not accept in their own homes. Nor is there a sense that all communication is an interaction and, potentially, an education. The range of educative possibilities in a page of print or a thirty-second spot is limited, but the opportunity, however small, remains—and remains largely untapped.

Having criticized the advertising industry, I should also say that 24 there is not much that the universities, including the business schools, have done to make advertising better understood, let alone more responsible and responsive to other institutions of moral leadership. As for my own world of social science, I hope that more of my colleagues will take up the suggestions here and in other recent works for a new sociology of consumption. It is time for a study that will not be a reflexlike intellectual revulsion at the world of goods but an effort to understand what place material culture might hold in a good world.

QUESTIONS AND IDEAS FOR DISCUSSION

1. What is the core argument, or thesis, of this essay? Is the thesis adequately supported by reasons or evidence? Does Schudson consider opposing viewpoints fairly? Is the essay guilty of fallacious reasoning? Evaluate the essay's credibility on these bases.

2. Of the four counts on which Schudson challenges the notion that advertising simply responds to public desires, which strikes you as the most serious charge, and why? Give examples from your own experience as a consumer.

3. Paragraph 18 asserts that advertising "all too often promotes values that our religious traditions, our schools, and our most respected counselors urge us to reject." Schudson does not detail what those values are. What are some of them? Do you agree that advertising is often guilty of promoting what these institutions deplore? If so, do you see that as a serious problem? Discuss.

4. Schudson claims that "too much advertising winks at sexism or encourages it" (paragraph 18). Give reasons and examples to support or challenge this claim.

5. Discuss the following claims in light of your own knowledge and experience:

Advertising serves a useful informational function that will not and should not be abandoned. (13)

Advertising probably has a socially democratizing influence but one with an ultimately inegalitarian outcome. (14)

Advertising supports the media but by no means in a way ideal for the democratic process. (15)

The objection to advertising is an objection to a "foreign power" . . . . (21)

ADDITIONAL MATERIAL FOR ANALYSIS AND ARGUMENT: ADVERTISEMENTS AND SOLICITATIONS

Advertisers have never limited their attention to toothpaste and laundry detergent. If we define advertising as solicitation intended to persuade us to part with money for some perceived good, even requests for donations by charities fall under the category of advertising. Certainly, recruitment ads for the armed services do—though they ask not for money but for an even more valuable commodity, time (and sometimes life itself). Historically, advertisements have provided easy pickings for the harvester of fallacies. That is still true today. But not all products are snake oil, and not all advertisements are rampantly fallacious. Some even offer a sound argument for a good product.

Evaluate the following advertisements and solicitations skeptically but not with a closed mind. Decide which are the most persuasive, and why. Decide which is the most fallacious and what makes it so. Consider the advertisers' choices of words and phrases; what is included, what omitted. Which product, if any, are you tempted to buy after reading about it? Which cause are you inclined to support?

"These Are Not...Sunglasses!"

Nationally Advertised Ambervision™ Super Glasses For Only...

$10?

(Not $59.99)

Ambervision™
REVOLUTIONIZES EYEWEAR

As part of an enormous publicity campaign to prove that we have the absolute lowest prices available in the nation, "U.S. Buyers Network" will give away one milion pair of its most expensive vision enhancement glasses — the nationally advertised Ambervision™ Super-Glasses, for the unbelievable "compeition-buster" price of just $10 only to those who respond to this ad before Midnight, May 5, 1991.

Not $100, Not $59.99 — Incredible Give Away For Only $10!

Vision enhancement eyeglasses have been nationally advertised by others in leading media at many times this price. In fact, you would think that high-tech vision enhancement Super-Glasses like these would sell for well over $100.00. But during this nationwide publicity campaign, you don't pay $100.00 — or even half that much. You pay an incredible give away price of just $10! But this offer is for a limited time and only available through THIS nationwide publicity campaign if you respond before the deadline above.

High Technology Disguised As High Fashion

Don't be fooled by the appearance of these glasses! These are not ordinary sunglasses. They may look like high fashion sunglasses (in fact, they are designed after some of the most expensive brand names on the market today — e.g.Porsche™,Carrera™,etc.) — but are actually the latest breakthrough in sunglass technology. Ambervision'S™ scientific design filters out blue and ultraviolet portions of the light spectrum

Allow up to 60 days for shipment. © *Direct Marketing of Virginia, Inc. 1987, (2515)*

that have been proven to be harmful to your eyes. By filtering out these dangerous rays, not only are your eyes protected from damage, but your vision is enhanced to a new level of percep tual eyesight!

A New World Through New Eyes

Just imagine what it would be like to look through glasses that make the world seem sharper, more vibrant, more alive and more cheerful. Slip on a pair of these sleek designer sunglass "look alikes" and you'll notice a marked improvement in your vision. The world will seem so crisp, so clear, that you'll feel as if someone had just given you a new set of eyes. This vision enhancement experience is so incredibly phenomenal that you literally "won't believe your eyes!" Thousands of professional golfers, hunters, and skiers have already discovered and reaped the benefits of these indispensable Super-Glasses — now you too can experience the excitement of ENHANCED EYESIGHT!

What About Sunglasses

The unbelievable truth is that ORDINARY sunglasses may be dangerous to your eyes. Everybody knows that your eyes automatically adjust to light. When you wear plain darkened lenses, your pupils open wider to adjust for darkness — but this becomes harmful because your eyes are now letting MORE dangerous UV rays in. Ambervision™ lenses are gradiated to help shield against overhead light. These remarkable glasses also offer 100% UV protection. The lightweight frames are designed for ultra comfortable wear and tear and the molded nose rest is designed to rest comfortably on your nose. The

hinge design of these frames allows them to be the perfect "one size fits all" eyeglasses. Your "Super-Glasses" even come complete with a luxurious black suede-like protective pouch. No wonder these are the most popular and fastest selling sunglasses ever sold by this company!

These Ambervision™ Super-Glasses will not be sold to any wholesalers, dealers, or retailers at this price. They are only available through this special publicity campaign for a limited time. There is a limit of two (2) pairs per address at this price, but requests that are mailed early enough (before May 1) may request up to five. Each pair of SuperGlasses is covered by a full one year money back guarantee.

PRENTICE HALL
Business Information & Publishing Division
Englewood Cliffs, NJ 07632
Simon & Schuster   A Paramount Communications Company

Increase Your Memory Powers

> Studies have shown that police who are trained to report their observations have better memories than Phi Betta Kappa college seniors who have had no training.
>
> A young man with just ordinary levels of memory and intelligence, learned a special memory technique that enabled him to remember *any* sequence of numbers up to a *world record* 82 digits!
>
> A famous Russian newspaper reporter amazed people by remembering and reciting incredibly long lists of household items. When he finally explained how he did it, it turned out he used a simple technique even a five-year-old child could master.

By 300% to 400%—Immediately!

Dear Friend:

The examples above prove that ordinary people -- with just a little training -- can activate the huge untapped resource we all possess ... memory.

Now there's startling good news: You can increase your memory powers by 300% to 400% immediately -- simply and easily -- with a breakthrough program developed by internationally-known memory trainer Robert L. Montgomery. It's called -

MEMORY MADE EASY
a unique 3-audio cassette program packed with techniques
to develop your memory and concentration
and put it to practical use

During the past 25 years over 100,000 people -- businessmen, doc-tors, lawyers, scientists, teachers, artists and musicians -- have found in this program the invaluable aid they needed to do their jobs better. Thousands have also improved themselves socially and intellectually by discovering how to easily remember the names of people they have met, the cards they have played at bridge, the information necessary for intel-ligent conversation about history or current events, to give just a few examples.

And MEMORY MADE EASY can do all this for you and much more!

* You'll be able to retain more of what you read in newspapers, magazines and books ... all the latest trends in art, music, fashion will be at the tip of your tongue for you to discuss at business meetings and social events.

* You'll recall, immediately and accurately, those facts and dates so essential to your business and personal life.

* You'll be able to access your memory like a computer and pull out, word for word, speeches you have to make ... poems you've always loved ... famous quotes ... excerpts from plays and movies ... and much more.

Whatever your personal memory goals, the way to achieve them is with

(Continued)

the simple-to-learn techniques in the MEMORY MADE EASY program. It's based on a _proven_ _system_ that will enable you to commit to memory anything and everything you wish to remember in your business or social life.

The MEMORY MADE EASY program will strengthen your powers of observation, concentration and classification so that you will lock into your memory whatever you want to remember -- _without_ _effort_. With the MEMORY MADE EASY program, you will be able to:

* Impress your boss with your ability to pull statistics out of the air during meetings -- such as sales figures, quarterly results, stock prices. And your colleagues will turn to you as an unerring source of vital information.

* Become an interesting and much sought after conversationalist, since you'll be able to recall with ease people's names, facts about them, and details about both current and past events.

* Escape from your reliance on notes or cards to deliver a presentation or speech ... with MEMORY MADE EASY techniques you can confidently deliver a flawless speech and you won't forget a single topic.

* Learn enough of a foreign language _in_ _one_ _hour_ to get you through a business or vacation trip.

* Score higher than you ever have on standardized tests given by the government for promotions - or any new job testing - or advanced field of study requirements.

* Significantly increase your chances of winning games that require a powerful memory ... from blackjack to bridge.

You're living in a world of information, and becoming successful in it requires that you master a great deal of knowledge. With the MEMORY MADE EASY program, you'll discover how to develop a memory which is both accurate and effective, and be the envy of your co-workers and friends.

With the MEMORY MADE EASY program you'll be able to remember names, faces, addresses, telephone numbers, speeches, printed materials, languages, and much more - effortlessly!

SEND NO MONEY NOW -
TRY THESE PROVEN TECHNIQUES FIRST ABSOLUTELY _FREE_

Just fill out and mail the enclosed postpaid Reservation Card, and we will send you the complete MEMORY MADE EASY audio cassette program to try FREE for 15 days.

At the end of that time, you can either honor our invoice for only $39.95 plus local sales tax, postage and handling, or you can return the program and pay nothing.

Why not mail the Reservation Card right now while it's handy? You've got nothing to lose.

Sincerely,

Robert Spencer

B-MC/A

Every day is Earth Day with nuclear energy.

Nuclear energy is America's second-leading source of electricity. Every day, nuclear energy generates one-fifth of America's electricity—enough to light over half the homes in the U.S.

Nuclear energy doesn't emit greenhouse gases. Because nuclear plants generate electricity cleanly, every day nuclear energy helps reduce greenhouse gas emissions from utilities by 20%.

Nuclear energy helps reduce air pollution. Every day, by using nuclear-generated electricity Americans help reduce airborne pollutants by over 19,000 tons.

Nuclear energy helps reduce our dependence on foreign oil. Every day, nuclear energy helps cut our foreign oil use by over 850,000 barrels and reduce our foreign oil payments by $16 million.

For more complete information on nuclear energy, send for this free booklet.
Write to: U.S. Council for Energy Awareness
P.O. Box 66080, Dept. ED01, Washington, D.C. 20035

Slow road to glory

The Story of the Lands' End Rugby Shirt

by Red Mulcahy

We had high hopes for our original Rugby Shirt when we introduced it in 1980.

After all, it was <u>heavyweight</u> cotton. Not a bit flimsy. And darn good-looking too, with its jaunty stripes. (We called 'em Team Stripes, which we thought had a real ring of authenticity.)

So we mailed out our catalogs, and waited for the applause.

Setback Number One.

What we got was more like a sustained Bronx cheer. Our customers complained that our rugby shirts shrank too much. Up to 20%. Went in the dryer a Large, came out a Medium.

We were embarrassed. Took the shirts out of our catalog, and even wondered whether we should leave rugby shirts to the sporting goods companies.

But our feisty nature got the best of us. We went back to the drawing board and developed a preshrunk 100% cotton jersey fabric. A beefy fabric, 10.5 oz. versus the usual 5 to 9 oz. A fabric that reduced shrinkage to a tolerable 3%.

So far, so good. But we wanted to be sure our improved shirts were the real thing. Especially since about this time, lots of "rugby shirts" were appearing on the market that were really nothing more than colorful sportshirts.

We figured a "field test" was in order. And gave our shirts to the University of Chicago rugby team. (They happened to be close at hand.)

Setbacks Number Two and Three.

The results were disastrous. While our new fabric stood up, almost nothing else did. A particular problem was the two-piece placket, which the ruggers consistently tore asunder.

Again, we went back to the drawing board, and developed a more rugged continuous placket—all one piece, with no weak point.

Would this make our shirt tough enough for rugby? We decided to submit our latest shirts to the ultimate test— international rugby—giving them to the USA Eagles, America's national team. The biggest, toughest rugby players in the country. (Some of these guys were <u>born</u> with five o'clock shadow.)

OUR SHIRTS FAILED AGAIN! Seams came apart. Buttons popped off. In a Hong Kong match, one Eagle came off the field wearing nothing above the waist but a collar.

We went (no, we <u>trudged</u>) back to the drawing board. But this time, we had the help of the Eagles. We switched to stronger thread. Developed deeper biting seams. Beefed up our shirt at collar, placket. And added other indomitable (we hoped) features.

The Eagles took our shirts into action in June 1984 against Canada. And we held our breath.

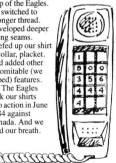

243

The problem isn't how little we care.
The problem is how little we do about it.

We think of ourselves as a nation of caring people. And, in principle, it's absolutely true.

Most of us contribute money to at least one cause. Nearly half of us contribute time. Confronted with a direct appeal, we respond instinctively with help.

The trouble is that, too often, it's not much more than token help. A dollar here, an hour there, and then it's back to the concerns of our own lives.

But think about it, for a minute. If we all gave just five hours a week to the causes we care about, it would be like mobilizing a force of more than 20 million full-time volunteers. If we all gave just 5% of what we earn, it would come to $175 billion a year.

It has to start with somebody, though. And not somebody else. Us.

So take a look around your own community and find something that needs doing. Or make that next donation a little bigger than usual. But, whatever you do, do something.

After all, one person may not be able to make that much difference.

But 200 million people can make all the difference in the world.

**What you give is five.
What you get back is immeasurable.**

SUGGESTIONS FOR WRITING
AND FURTHER DISCUSSION

1. Choose one advertisement reprinted in this chapter that relies on fallacious reasoning. Revise the ad copy, making your text both persuasive and nonfallacious. Discuss the difficulties involved, if you encountered any. How important were your word choices?

2. Are there any issues about which you feel strongly, as Monroe Beardsley puts it, but have never fully thought through or attempted to support with logical argument? Write an argument that articulates your position on an issue for someone who does not share either your view or the strength of your emotions about it.

3. Turning your attention to James Thurber's introduction to his essay on sweeping generalizations, argue the benefits and value of collecting something (whatever you collect—or would like to). Alternatively, argue the pointlessness of collecting things. Whether serious or tongue-in-cheek like Thurber's essay, your essay should make a strong case for your position, well supported by examples. And by all means, avoid committing any fallacies yourself, however many you expose in the opposing viewpoint.

4. Sylvia Wright says, "I feel tolerant about advertising . . ." (paragraph 1). Do you? Argue your answer in a brief essay addressed (if you agree with Wright) to individuals enrolled in an ethics course or (if you feel *in*tolerant about advertising) to individuals enrolled in an introductory advertising course at your college.

5. Do you agree with John O'Toole that even Ralph Nader wouldn't mention "that worn fan belt or leaky gasket" (15) in a classified ad to sell his own car? Have you ever placed a classified ad in a newspaper in order to sell something? How did you describe the car, musical instrument, or other item for sale? Was your description at all misleading or fallacious? Whether or not you have written such an ad in the past, write one now. The item you want to sell has the following characteristics:

> Tan 1985 Oldsmobile Delta 88, four-door, vinyl roof, paint peeling a bit on the hood, dent (paint rusted off) over right rear tire, good repair record, 49,000 miles, upholstery in good condition but somewhat dirty, adequate stereo radio-cassette player, air conditioning, rear window defroster, cruise control, big trunk, about 14 miles to the gallon, almost new whitewall tires.

You plan to ask $2,000 for the car. Owing to the low rates for classified ads in your campus paper, you can write up to one hundred words if you like. Write an ad that is both persuasive and honest—without fallacious appeals.

6. Does advertising still "wink at sexism or encourage it," as Michael Schudson and others have argued? Argue your answer, supporting your reasons with evidence gleaned by examining a substantial number of recent advertisements. Alternatively, ask the same question with regard to racism.

7. In the introduction to *Advertising: The Uneasy Persuasion,* Michael Schudson makes the following assertions:

> We live and shall live, barring nuclear or other disaster, in what has been called a "promotional culture." America has long been a nation of salesmen, and the "shoeshine and a smile" that were Willy Loman's stock-in-trade are now the tools of politicians and religious evangelists and hospital administrators as much as of advertising agents and public-relations directors. The promotional culture has worked its way into what we read, what we care about, the ways we raise our children, our ideas of right and wrong conduct, our attribution of significance to "image" in both public and private life. The promotional culture has been celebrated and indulged in. It has been ridiculed and reviled. It still needs to be understood. (page 13)

Do you agree that the "promotional culture" associated with advertising has become an integral part of (1) "what we read," (2) "what we care about," (3) "the ways we raise our children," (4) "our ideas of right and wrong conduct," or (5) the importance we ascribe to any given person's "image"? If so, write an essay, suitable for the editorial page of your local newspaper, in which you consider *one* of these areas and argue the impact that advertising (including "public relations") has had on it in your community.

8. John O'Toole says that consumers understand and expect that advertising will focus on positive, not negative, features. In your view, is that position on the part of advertisers morally defensible? Argue your answer in a brief essay that would be suitable for inclusion in a pamphlet to be distributed by a newspaper's classified ads department to individuals interested in placing ads.

9. In Chapter 11 of *Confessions of an Advertising Man* (1963), veteran advertiser David Ogilvy addresses several questions asked (often in attack) of advertising. Among them are

- Does advertising encourage monopoly?
- Does advertising corrupt editors?
- Does advertising make people want to buy products they don't need?
- Should advertising be used in politics?

Choose one of these questions to consider and investigate. Argue your conclusions in an essay with your class in mind as an audience. Whether or not you cite secondary sources, use current advertising to support the points you made.

10. The readings in this chapter by no means exhaust the ways in which arguments and appeals can be fallacious. Another fallacy of which advertising is often accused is that of suppressed evidence. That is, evidence is deliberately omitted that would affect the conclusion of an argument. If someone were to claim that "suppressed evidence is the hardest fallacy to detect," would you agree or disagree? Argue your answer, with examples.

5

Using Humor in Argument

THE STRATEGY

You can read stacks of books on argument without finding more than a mention of the significant role humor plays in it. Humor, after all, can persuade—that is, it can affect people's attitudes and actions—but it does not logically convince. It can make a writer's persona seem warmer and friendlier, so that we pay closer attention to the argument, but it cannot make the reasoning and evidence any stronger. It is easy to dismiss humor as trivial, particularly in serious business or academic contexts.

But what better way is there to get the attention of a reader who is uninterested in your subject matter or to disarm a reader's hostile predisposition toward it—or toward you? This editor has sat at academic conferences and watched weary professors—slumped in their seats, brows furrowed—respond to a speaker's relevant humor by sitting up attentively and looking receptive, even at the end of a long day. The same thing happens in undergraduate classrooms. Humor can win you an audience for your argument, whether you are speaking or writing.

Humor has a wide range, from subtle ironies and incongruities to outright slapstick and broad pun. It can make the reader laugh out loud or cringe inwardly in reaction to bitter sarcasm—for humor can be deliberately unfunny, as Jonathan Swift taught us.[1] Unfortunately, humor can also be inadvertently unfunny or appeal to one reader and not another. For humor cuts both ways: As well as being a powerful tool of the arguer, it is the tool most likely to injure the unskilled user.

---

[1] You may have read Swift's "A Modest Proposal," in which Swift argues that the starving Irish might remedy their problem by eating their babies. [Ed.]

So perhaps we should not be surprised that textbooks are silent on humor. Most shun humor because, first, nothing so destroys a writer's persona as ineffectual, heavyhanded humor. Second, as E. B. White once said, "Humor can be dissected, as a frog can, but the thing dies in the process and the innards are discouraging to any but the pure scientific mind."[2] In the two essays that follow, Mark Twain and William Zinsser both argue that humor is itself always a form of argument, or "preaching." Zinsser also offers some suggestions on how to use humor wisely and well.

Humor and Honesty

MARK TWAIN

Mark Twain (1835–1910) is the pseudonym of Samuel Clemens, who adopted the name during his steamboating days on the Mississippi River. ("Mark twain" was the signal that a depth of two fathoms had been sounded.) A journalist and humorous lecturer as well as novelist and storyteller, Twain is today most famous for his classic novels *Tom Sawyer* and *Huckleberry Finn*. The story of Huck, in Twain's masterpiece, well illustrates the use of humor to argue serious issues such as racism and religious bigotry. We may laugh when Huck believes he will go to hell for helping the runaway slave Jim, who is the epitome of human goodness, but we cannot help but see the absurdity of laws and doctrines that would teach Huck such nonsense.

Twain wrote the following piece in reaction to word that F. A. Duneka, vice president of Twain's publishers, Harper and Brothers, had discovered that someone had printed an unauthorized edition of *Mark Twain's Library of Humor* (and was, of course, pocketing the illicit profits). This undated selection appears in a posthumous volume, *Mark Twain in Eruption* (1940).

Mark Twain's Library of Humor was a collection of humorous stories and essays by Twain and seventy-eight other writers. Looking over a copy of the spurious reprint, Twain was struck by the fact that so many of the humorists had vanished from the literary scene, their names and their humor forgotten. (They are today almost entirely unknown.) Musing over that fact, Twain here argues the purpose of humor—and the reasons for its transient quality. But Twain's humor has endured and is enjoyed to this day. Does his own success prove him wrong?

The Western pirate of whom Duneka had heard rumor has really 1 published his book and my copyright lawyer has sent me a copy of

---

[2] Quoted by William Zinsser in *On Writing Well*, 3rd ed. (New York: Harper, 1985), 190. [Ed.]

it—a great fat, coarse, offensive volume, not with my name on it as perpetrator but with its back inflamed with a big picture of me in lurid colors, placed there, of course, to indicate that I am the author of the crime. This book is a very interesting curiosity, in one way. It reveals the surprising fact that within the compass of these forty years wherein I have been playing professional humorist before the public, I have had for company seventy-eight other American humorists. Each and every one of the seventy-eight rose in my time, became conspicuous and popular, and by and by vanished. A number of these names were as familiar in their day as are the names of George Ade and Dooley today—yet they have all so completely passed from sight now that there is probably not a youth of fifteen years of age in the country whose eye would light with recognition at the mention of any one of the seventy-eight names.

This book is a cemetery; and as I glance through it I am reminded 2 of my visit to the cemetery in Hannibal, Missouri, four years ago, where almost every tombstone recorded a forgotten name that had been familiar and pleasant to my ear when I was a boy there fifty years before. In this mortuary volume I find Nasby, Artemus Ward, Yawcob Strauss, Derby, Burdette, Eli Perkins, the "Danbury News Man," Orpheus C. Kerr, Smith O'Brien, Josh Billings, and a score of others, maybe two score, whose writings and sayings were once in everybody's mouth but are now heard of no more and are no longer mentioned. Seventy-eight seems an incredible crop of well-known humorists for one forty-year period to have produced, and yet this book has not harvested the entire crop—far from it. It has no mention of Ike Partington, once so welcome and so well known; it has no mention of Doesticks, nor of the Pfaff crowd, nor of Artemus Ward's numerous and perishable imitators, nor of three very popular Southern humorists whose names I am not able to recall, nor of a dozen other sparkling transients whose light shone for a time but has now, years ago, gone out.

Why have they perished? Because they were merely humorists. 3 Humorists of the "mere" sort cannot survive. Humor is only a fragrance, a decoration. Often it is merely an odd trick of speech and of spelling, as in the case of Ward and Billings and Nasby and the "Disbanded Volunteer," and presently the fashion passes and the fame along with it. There are those who say a novel should be a work of art solely, and you must not preach in it, you must not teach in it. That may be true as regards novels but it is not true as regards humor. Humor must not professedly teach, and it must not professedly preach, but it must do both if it would live forever. By forever, I mean thirty years. With all its preaching it is not likely to outlive so long a term as that. The very things it preaches about, and which are novelties when it preaches about them, can cease to be novelties and become commonplaces in thirty years. Then that sermon can thenceforth interest no one.

I have always preached. That is the reason that I have lasted thirty 4 years. If the humor came of its own accord and uninvited, I have allowed it a place in my sermon, but I was not writing the sermon for the sake of the humor. I should have written the sermon just the same, whether any humor applied for admission or not. I am saying these vain things in this frank way because I am a dead person speaking from the grave. Even I would be too modest to say them in life. I think we never become really and genuinely our entire and honest selves until we are dead—and not then until we have been dead years and years. People ought to start dead, and then they would be honest so much earlier.

QUESTIONS AND IDEAS FOR DISCUSSION

1. Analyze Twain's argument that humor is not likely to endure more than a few decades (paragraph 3). Is the argument reasonable? Why or why not?

2. Does Twain's enduring appeal prove him wrong in the claims he makes about the transient quality of humor? Explain. Name other "humorists" whose work has also endured. Does the humor share any features that might account for the writers' staying power? Discuss.

3. If you have read any of Twain's fiction, such as *Huckleberry Finn*, identify the subjects Twain "preaches" about most often. Taking into account his subjects and his original audience, what makes humor a suitable vehicle for Twain's "sermons"? Why has his humor aged so well? Or has it? (*Huckleberry Finn* has been taken off some high school reading lists because it offends some African-Americans with its language and portrayal of black characters.)

4. *Must* humor both teach and preach? Support or challenge Twain's assertion with examples from television comedians such as Jay Leno or Joan Rivers and humorous newspaper and magazine writers such as Dave Barry, Calvin Trillin, Erma Bombeck, Art Buchwald, or Lewis Grizzard. Do these people teach and preach? Always? Sometimes? Never? Discuss.

5. This is not a humorous essay but rather an essay about humor. Nonetheless, the essay has its humorous moments. Identify them. How does Twain achieve humor here? Through what strategy or choices of words? How would you characterize the humor—broad, subtle, ironic, or _____?

The Power of Humor

WILLIAM ZINSSER

William Zinnser taught writing at Yale University before becoming general editor of Book-of-the-Month Club, Inc., where he worked from 1979 to 1986. Among his recent works are *Spiritual Quests* (1988), *Paths of Resistance* (1989), and *Worlds of Childhood* (1990). Zinsser is a writer, a teacher, and an editor, not a professional humorist. But he does not overlook, and would not have us overlook, the importance of humor to persuasion. Zinsser devotes an entire chapter of *On Writing Well* (3rd ed.), from which this excerpt is taken, to the subject of humor and how to use it effectively in argument. The advice contained in *On Writing Well* developed out of a course in writing nonfiction that Zinsser started at Yale in the seventies. Zinsser argues that "if you're trying to write humor, almost everthing that you do is serious." Decide as you read whether or not he convinces you of that claim.

Humor is the secret weapon of the nonfiction writer. It is secret 1 because so few writers realize that it is often their best tool—and sometimes their only tool—for making an important point.

If this strikes you as a paradox, you are not alone. The professional 2 writer of humor lives with the knowledge that half of his readers never know what he is trying to do. I remember a reporter calling to ask how I happened to write a certain parody in *Life*. At the end he said, "Should I refer to you as a humorist? Or have you also written anything serious?"

The answer, of course, is that if you're trying to write humor, 3 almost everything that you do is serious. Few Americans understand this. We dismiss our humorists as triflers because they have never settled down to "real" work. So the Pulitzer Prizes go to authors like Ernest Hemingway and William Faulkner who are (God knows) serious and are therefore certified as men of literature. The prize has never gone to people like George Ade, H. L. Mencken, Ring Lardner, Robert Benchley, S. J. Perelman, Art Buchwald, Jules Feiffer and Woody Allen, who seem to be just fooling around.

They're not just fooling around. They are as serious in purpose as 4 Hemingway or Faulkner—in fact, a national asset in forcing the country to see itself clearly. To them humor is urgent work. It's an attempt to say important things in a special way that regular writers aren't getting said in a regular way—or, if they are, it's so regular that nobody is reading it.

One cartoon by Herblock or Bill Mauldin is worth a hundred 5 solemn editorials. One *Doonesbury* comic strip by Garry Trudeau—on journalism's exploitation of the "Son of Sam" killings, or on the tendency of voters to re-elect convicted Congressmen—is worth a thou sand words of moralizing. One pop art painting of our neon landscape is worth a hundred earnest pieces deploring urban sprawl. It takes us by surprise and says "Look again!"

One *Catch-22* or *Dr. Strangelove* is more powerful than all the books 6 and movies that try to show war "as it is." They are two works of comic imagination, but they are still the standard points of reference for anyone trying to warn us about the military mentality that could blow us all up tomorrow. Joseph Heller and Stanley Kubrick heightened the truth about war just enough to catch its essential lunacy, and we recognize it as lunacy. The joke is no joke. . . .

The columns that I wrote for *Life* made people laugh. But they all 7 had a serious purpose, which was to say: "Something grotesque is going on here—some erosion in the quality of life, or some threat to life itself, and yet everyone assumes that it's normal." Today in America the outlandish becomes routine overnight. The humorist is trying to say that it really is still outlandish.

I remember a cartoon by Bill Mauldin during the student turmoil 8 of the late 1960s, when infantrymen and tanks were summoned to keep peace at a college in North Carolina and undergraduates at Berkeley were dispersed by a helicopter spraying them with Mace. The cartoon showed a mother pleading with her son's draft board: "He's an only child—please get him off the campus." It was Mauldin's way of pinning down this particular lunacy, and he was right on target. In fact, he was at the center of the bull's-eye, as Kent State and Jackson State subsequently proved.

Obviously the targets will change from week to week and from 9 year to year. But there will never be a dearth of new lunacies—and dangers—for the humorist to detect and to fight. Lyndon Johnson in the years of his Vietnamization was brought down partly by Jules Feiffer and Art Buchwald. Joseph McCarthy and Spiro Agnew were brought down partly by Walt Kelly in the comic strip *Pogo*. H. L. Mencken brought down a whole galaxy of hypocrities in high places, and "Boss" Tweed was partly toppled by the cartoons of Thomas Nast.

Mort Sahl, a comic, was the only person who stayed awake during 10 the Eisenhower years, when all of America was under sedation and didn't want to be roused. Many people regarded Sahl as a cynic, but he thought of himself as an idealist. "If I criticize somebody," he said, "it's because I have higher hopes for the world, something good to replace the bad. I'm not saying what the Beat Generation says: 'Go away because I'm not involved.' I'm here and I'm involved."

"I'm here and I'm involved"—make this your creed if you seri- 11 ously want to write serious humor. The humorist operates on a deeper current than most people suspect. He must not only make a strong point; he must be willing to go against the grain, to state what the populace and the Presidents may not want to hear. Herblock and Art Buchwald perform an act of courage at least once a week. They say things which need to be said but which a regular columnist couldn't get away with. What saves them is that politicians are not known for humor and are therefore even more befuddled by it than the citizenry.

It is a lonely and perilous calling. No other kind of writer risks his   12 neck so visibly on the high wire of public approval. It is the thinnest wire in all nonfiction, and the humorist knows that he will frequently fall off. Yet he is in dead earnest, this acrobat bobbing over our heads, trying to startle us with nonsense into seeing our lives with sense.

But of course humor has many uses besides the merely topical.   13 They are not as urgent because they don't address problems of the day. But they are equally important because they help us to look at far older problems of the heart, the home, the job and all the other frustrations of just getting from morning to night.

In 1970 I interviewed the late Chic Young, creator of *Blondie*, when   14 he had been writing and drawing that strip—daily and Sunday—for forty years, or 14,500 strips. It was the most popular of all comic strips, reaching 60 million readers in every corner of the world and in seventeen languages, and I asked him the secret of its durability.

"It's durable because it's simple," he said. "It's built on four things   15 that everybody does: sleeping, eating, raising a family and making money." The comic twists on these four themes have been as various in the strip as they are in life. Dagwood's efforts to get money from his boss, Mr. Dithers, have their perpetual counterweight in Blondie's efforts to spend it. "I try to keep Dagwood in a world that people are used to," Young said. "He never does anything as special as playing golf, and the people who come to the door are just the people that an average family has to deal with."

I cite Young's four themes as a reminder that most humor,   16 however freakish it may seem, is based on fundamental truths. Humor is not a separate organism that can survive on its own frail metabolism. It is a special angle of vision granted to certain writers who already write good English. They are not writing about life that is essentially ludicrous. They are writing about life that is essentially serious, but their vision focuses on the areas where serious hopes are mocked by some ironic turn of fate—"the strange incongruity," as Stephen Leacock put it, "between our aspiration and our achievement."

QUESTIONS AND IDEAS FOR DISCUSSION

1. Do you agree with Zinsser's argument that humor creates more powerful arguments than does "serious" prose—or with his argument that "most humor . . . is based on fundamental truths" (paragraph 16)? What further arguments or examples could you offer to support Zinsser's contention? How might you refute it?

2. Often it is not so much the point we make but how we phrase it that creates humor. Find some examples of humorous phrases or sentences (or even a short paragraph) in a current syndicated column in a newspaper. Reword the phrases or sentences in such a way that they convey the same point humorlessly. Analyze what the writer did to add a light or ironic touch to his or her point.

3. Suggest aspects of the following topics that might be treated humorously for persuasive ends in writing to a group of professional people. That is, what's funny about any of these? For example, if you supported reinstating prayer in public schools, what light touch could you add to disarm an uniterested or possibly hostile audience?

- Reinstating the AT & T regulated telephone monopoly
- The need for home computers
- Legislating the right to pray in public schools
- The value of television commericals

4. Does Zinsser employ humor as he discusses humor? Give examples. How would you characterize Zinsser's style of humor?

5. In the same chapter from which this excerpt is drawn, Zinsser offers the following advice for the writer of humor:

> Master the craft of writing good "straight" English; humorists from Mark Twain to Russell Baker are, first of all, superb writers. Don't search high and low for the outlandish and scorn what seems ordinary; you will touch more chords by finding what is funny in what you know to be true. Finally, don't strain for laughs; humor is built on surprise, and you can surprise the reader only so often. (page 190)

Find examples of nonfiction prose, advertisements, and political cartoons that use humor for persuasive ends. Do the ones that you find effective adhere to Zinsser's principles? Comment.

THE STRATEGY AT WORK: ARGUMENTS ABOUT MARRIAGE

All the essays in this section argue claims about marriage, and all employ humor (or at least irony) to do so. Marriage is a subject about which most people have opinions, whether or not they are themselves married. Marriage is also a subject about which the humor of even ten years ago can sound sexist and profoundly unfunny. And, like humor about babies or computers, some humor about marriage can escape the uninitiated. These complications, however, make "humorous" essays about marriage particularly interesting to analyze.

The writers of the following essays all recognize the possibilities for making their points with humor. Much of the humor in these selections is still fresh—and not only in the most recent (despite Mark Twain's claim about humor's short lifespan). Some of the humor in these selections is curiously dated—and not necessarily in the oldest piece. One writer uses humor with a subtle, light touch; another employs an irony verging on bitterness. Still another applies broad strokes of comic truth: "If any man truly believes that he is the boss of his house, then let him do this: pick up the phone, call a wallpaper store, order new wallpaper for one of the rooms in his house, and then put it on. He would have a longer life expectancy sprinkling arsenic on his eggs." Humor has a wide range—and even, in skillful hands, a long life.

Notice what these writers do well, and consider the uses to which humor can be put in argument. In your own arguments, use humor where it will enhance your persona and warm your reader to your claims, but use it with restraint. Subtle humor that is overlooked is not a problem; broad humor that misses its mark can be an embarrassing liability.

Marriage Is Belonging

KATHERINE ANNE PORTER

Katherine Anne Porter (1890–1980) is one of the outstanding American writers of this century, best known for her novellas, short stories, and her one long novel, *Ship of Fools*, on which she worked for twenty years. Porter received two Pulitzer Prizes, for *Pale Horse, Pale Rider* (1938) and for *Collected Short Stories* (1965). This essay, first published in 1951 in *Mademoiselle* magazine, eloquently defends the institution of marriage and its possibilities for good. Porter had some expertise on the subject of marriage, having embarked on that adventure several times, beginning at age sixteen. Her own experiences do not seem to have soured her on marriage, as this essay makes clear. The essay is not "funny." "How could we call any essay funny that ends with the death of Elizabeth Barrett Browning and contains such conceptually dense sentences as "The task of regulating its [marriage's] unruly impulses is a thorn in the soul of theologians, its social needs and uses the insoluble riddle of law-makers"? But the light touch of humor that recurs throughout the essay engages our interest and endears to us the persona of the arguer. After more than forty years, this essay—and its humor—remains remarkably fresh. How Porter achieves this quality is well worth considering.

Having never written a word about marriage, so far as I remem- 1
ber, and being now at the point where I have learned better than to
have any theories about it, if I ever had; and believing as I do that most
of the stuff written and talked about it is more or less nonsense; and
having little hope that I shall add luster to the topic, it is only logical
and natural that I should venture to write a few words on the subject.

My theme is marriage as the art of belonging—which should not 2
be confused with possessing—all too often the art, or perhaps only the
strategy, and a risky one, of surrendering gracefully with an air of pure
disinterestedness as much of your living self as you can spare without
incurring total extinction; in return for which you will, at least in
theory, receive a more than compensatory share of another life, the life
in fact presumably dearest to you, equally whittled down in your favor
to the barest margin of survival. This arrangement with variations to
suit the circumstances is of course the basis of many contracts besides
that of marriage; but nowhere more than in marriage does the real
good of the relationship depend on intangibles not named in the
bond.

The trouble with me is—always was—that if you say "marriage" 3
to me, instantly the word translates itself into "love," for only in such
terms can I grasp the idea at all, or make any sense of it. The two are
hopelessly associated, or rather identified, in my mind; that is to say,
love is the only excuse for marriage, if any excuse is necessary. I often
feel one should be offered. Love without marriage can sometimes be
very awkward for all concerned; but marriage without love simply
removes that institution from the territory of the humanly admissible,
to my mind. Love is a state in which one lives who loves, and whoever
loves has given himself away; love then, and not marriage, is belonging. Marriage is the public declaration of a man and a woman that
they have formed a secret alliance, with the intention to belong to, and
share with each other, a mystical estate; mystical exactly in the sense
that the real experience cannot be communicated to others, nor explained even to oneself on rational grounds.

By love let me make it clear, I do not refer only to that ecstatic 4
reciprocal cannibalism which goes popularly under the name, and
which is indeed commonly one of the earliest biological symptoms
(Boy Eats Girl and vice versa), for, like all truly mystical things, love is
rooted deeply and rightly in this world and this flesh. This phase is
natural, dangerous but not necessarily fatal; so remarkably educational it would be a great pity to miss it; further, of great importance,
for the flesh in real love is one of the many bridges to the spirit; still, a
phase only, which being passed is too often mistaken for the whole
thing, and the end of it. This is an error based on lack of imagination,
or the simple incapacity for further and deeper exploration of life,
there being always on hand great numbers of people who are unwill-

ing or unable to grow up, no matter what happens to them. It leads to early divorce, or worse. Like that young man whose downward career began with mere murder, this error can lead to infidelity, lying, eavesdropping, gambling, drinking, and finally to procrastination and incivility. These two last can easily have destroyed more marriages than any amount of murder, or even lying.

Let us recall a few generalities about marriage in its practical 5 aspects which are common knowledge, such as: it is one of the most prevalent conditions of the human adult, heading the list of vital statistics, I believe. It has been made very easy to assume, and fairly easy in the legal sense, at least, to abandon; and it is famous for its random assortment of surprises of every kind—leaf-covered booby traps, spiders lurking in cups, pots of gold under rainbows, triplets, poltergeists in the stair closet, and flights of cupids lolling on the breakfast table—anything can happen. Every young married pair believes their marriage is going to be quite different from the others, and they are right—it always is. The task of regulating its unruly impulses is a thorn in the souls of theologians, its social needs and uses the insoluble riddle of law-makers. Through all ages known to man almost everybody, even those who wouldn't be seen dead wearing a wedding ring, having agreed that somehow, in some way, at some time or another, marriage has simply got to be made to work better than it does, or ever has, for that matter. Yet on the whole, my guess is that it works about as well as any other human institution, and rather better than a great many. The drawback is, it is the merciless revealer, the great white searchlight turned on the darkest places of human nature; it demands of all who enter it the two most difficult achievements possible: that each must be honest with himself, and faithful to another. I am speaking here only of the internal reality of marriage, not its legal or even its social aspects.

In its present form it is comparatively modern. As an idea, it must 6 have begun fairly soon after the human male discovered his highly important role in the bringing forth of young. For countless aeons, we are told by those who pretend to know, it was believed that the powers of generation were vested in women alone, people having never been very bright about sex, right from the start. When men at last discovered, who knows how? that they were fathers, their pride in their discovery must have been equaled only by their indignation at having worshiped women as vessels of the Great Mystery when all along they should have been worshiping themselves. Pride and wrath and no doubt the awful new problem of what to do with the children, which had never bothered them before, drove them on to an infinite number of complicated and contradictory steps toward getting human affairs on a sounder basis. And, after all this time (skipping lightly over the first few hundred thousand years of total confusion), in our fine big new busy Western world, we have succeeded in establishing not only as the ideal, but in religious and legal fact (if not altogether in practice), as the very crown and glory of human ties, a one-man-one-woman-until-death sort of marriage, rivaling the swans for purity, with a ritual oath exchanged not only to stick to each other through thick and thin, to practice perfect fidelity, flawless forbearance, a modified bodily servitude, but to love each other dearly and kindly to the end.

All this is to be accomplished in a physical situation of the direst 7 intimacy, in which all claims to the most ordinary privacy may be disregarded by either, or both. I shall not attempt to catalogue the daily accounting for acts, words, states of feeling and even thoughts, the perpetual balance and check between individual wills and points of view, the unbelievable amount of tact, intelligence, flexibility, generosity, and God knows what, it requires for two people to go on growing together and in the same directions instead of cracking up and falling apart.

Take the single point of fidelity: It is very hard to be entirely 8 faithful, even to things, ideas, above all, persons one loves. There is no such thing as perfect faithfulness any more than there is perfect love or perfect beauty. But it is fun trying. And if I say faithfulness consists of a great many things beside the physical, never let it be dreamed that I hold with the shabby nonsense that physical infidelity is a mere peccadillo beneath the notice of enlightened minds. Physical infidelity is the signal, the notice given, that all the fidelities are undermined. It is complete betrayal of the very principle on which love and marriage are based, and besides, a vulgar handing over of one's partner to public shame. It is exactly as stupid as that, to say nothing more.

Yet every day quite by the thousands delightfully honest young 9 couples, promising, capable, sometimes gifted, but in no way superhuman, leap gaily into marriage—a condition which, for even reasonable success and happiness (both words seem rather trivial in this connection), would tax the virtues and resources and staying powers of a regiment of angels. But what else would you suggest that they do?

Then there come the children. Gladly, willingly (if you do not 10 think so, I refer you to the birth records of this country for the past ten years. There haven't been so many young wives having so many babies so fast for at least four generations!) these pairs proceed to populate their houses, or flats—often very small flats, and mother with a job she means to keep, too—with perfect strangers, often hostile, whose habits even to the most adoring gaze are often messy and unattractive. They lie flat on their noses at first in what appears to be a drunken slumber, then flat on their backs kicking and screaming, demanding impossibilities in a foreign language. They are human nature in essence, without conscience, without pity, without love, without a trace of consideration for others, just one seething cauldron of primitive appetites and needs; and what do they really need? We are back where we started. They need love, first; without it everything worth saving is lost or damaged in them; and they have to be taught love, pity, conscience, courage—everything. And what becomes of them? If they are lucky, among all the million possibilities of their fates, along with the innumerable employments, careers, talents, ways of life, they will learn the nature of love, and they will marry and have children.

If this all sounds a little monotonous, and gregarious, well, some-   11 times it is, and most people like that sort of thing. They always have. It is hardly possible to exaggerate the need of a human being, not a madman, or a saint, or a beast, or a self-alienated genius who is all of these in one, and therefore the scapegoat for all the rest, to live at peace—and by peace I mean in reconciliation, not easy contentment— with another human being, and with that one in a group or society where he feels he belongs. The best, the very best, of all these relation- ships is that one in marriage between a man and a woman who are good lovers, good friends, and good parents; who belong to each other, and to their children, and whose children belong to them: that is the meaning of the blood tie that binds them, and may bind them sometimes to the bone. Children cut their teeth on their parents and their parents cut their wisdom teeth on each other: that is what they are there for. It is never really dull, and can sometimes be very memo- rably exciting for everybody. In any case, the blood-bond, however painful, is the condition of human life in this world, the absolute point of all departure and return. The ancient biological laws are still in force, the difference being merely in the way human beings regard them, and though I am not one to say all change is progress, in this one thing, a kind of freedom and ease of mind between men and women in marriage—or at least the possibility of it, change has been all for the better. At least they are able now to fight out their differences on something nearer equal terms.

We have the bad habit, some of us, of looking back to a time—   12 almost any time will do—when society was stable and orderly, family ties stronger and deeper, love more lasting and faithful, and so on. Let me be your Cassandra prophesying after the fact, and a long study of the documents in the case: it was never true, that is, no truer than it is now. Above all, it was not true of domestic life in the nineteenth century. Then, as now, it was just as good in individual instances as the married pairs involved were able to make it, privately, between themselves. The less attention they paid to what they were expected to think and feel about marriage, and the more attention to each other as loved and loving, the better they did, for themselves and for everybody. The laws of public decorum were easy to observe, for they had another and better understanding. The Victorian marriage feather bed was in fact set upon the shaky foundation of the wavering human heart, the inconsistent human mind, and was the roiling hotbed of every dislocation and disorder not only in marriage but all society, which we of the past two generations have lived through. Yet in love—this is what I have been talking about all the time—a certain number of well-endowed spirits, and there are surprisingly quite a lot of them in every generation, have always been able to take their world in stride, to live and die together, and to keep all their strange marriage vows not because they spoke them, but because like centuries of lovers before them, they were prepared to live them in the first place.

Example: A certain woman was apparently a prisoner for life in 13 several ways: already thirty-five or -six years old, supposed to be an incurable invalid, whose father had forbidden any of his children to marry; and above all, a poet at a time when literary women were regarded as monsters, almost. Yet she was able to write, in the first flush of a bride's joy: "He preferred . . . of free and deliberate choice, to be allowed to sit only an hour a day by my side, to the fulfillment of the brightest dream which should exclude me in any possible world."

This could be illusion, but the proof of reality came fifteen years 14 later. Just after her death her husband wrote to a friend: "Then came what my heart will keep till I see her again and longer—the most perfect expression of her love to me within my whole knowledge of her. Always smilingly, and happily, and with a face like a girl's; and in a few minutes she died in my arms, her head on my cheek."

If you exclaim that this is not fair, for, after all, these two were, of 15 course, the Robert Brownings, I can only reply that it is because I sincerely believe they were not so very special that I cite them. Don't be thrown off by that lyrical nineteenth-century speech, nor their fearless confidence not only in their own feelings, but the sympathy of their friends; it is the kind of love that makes real marriage, and there is more of it in the world than you might think, though the ways of expressing it follow the fashions of the times; and we certainly do not find much trace of it in our contemporary literature. It is *very* old-style, and it was, long before the Brownings. It is new, too, it is the very newest thing, every day renewed in an endless series of those fortunate people who may not have one point in common with the Brownings except that they know, or are capable of learning, the nature of love, and of living by it.

QUESTIONS AND IDEAS FOR DISCUSSION

1.   The persona, you will recall from previous discussions in this book and perhaps elsewhere, is the reader's sense of the writer. Is the writer believable? Bright? Likeable? A careful arguer will work hard to create a persona that the anticipated audience will find appealing and trustworthy. How does Porter use humor in the first paragraph to establish an appealing persona? Her original audience was the readers of *Mademoiselle* more than forty years ago. How does her humor strike readers of an entirely different generation?

2.   Does Porter contradict her avowed "theme" when she says, in paragraph 3, that "love then, and not marriage, is belonging"? Explain.

3.   Much of the humor in this essay is tossed out as if in passing, in dependent clauses and parenthetical phrases. Find several examples of "throwaway" humor in the essay. Why does Porter risk readers' missing those quick smiles? Why doesn't she make a stronger point of them?

4.   Another subtle touch of humor is found in Porter's lists. We expect lists to include parallel elements or to build in importance or intensity. But Porter begins one list with murder and infidelity and "builds" to incivility! In a mostly poetic listing of the surprises possible in marriage, she tosses in "triplets." Discuss the several ways in which humor arises in this essay.

5.   Humor also comes through fidelity to truth: showing things as they are and not as we idealize them. Porter's description of babies in paragraph 10 is funny because it is fundamentally *true*. Find an example from another source (in this chapter or elsewhere) of humor created through describing things accurately and not as sentiment would color them. Discuss the importance (if any) of this kind of humor to argument.

Why I Want a Wife

JUDY BRADY

Judy Brady, a freelance writer, wrote "Why I Want a Wife" for the inaugural issue of *Ms.* magazine, Spring 1972. The essay has been anthologized many times since—and, more than twenty years later, it still describes many aspects of marriage for many women. The humor in this essay depends on obvious irony. What the essay really argues for is not what it purports to argue for. Brady makes no pretense of offering a balanced argument or considering both sides; exaggeration for effect is key to the humor. Consider, though, how much of what follows actually *is* exaggerated.

I belong to that classification of people known as wives. I am A 1
Wife. And, not altogether incidentally, I am a mother.

Not too long ago a male friend of mine appeared on the scene fresh 2
from a recent divorce. He had one child, who is, of course, with his
ex-wife. He is looking for another wife. As I thought about him while I
was ironing one evening, it suddenly occurred to me that I, too, would
like to have a wife. Why do I want a wife?

I would like to go back to school so that I can become economically 3
independent, support myself, and, if need be, support those dependent upon me. I want a wife who will work and send me to school.
And while I am going to school I want a wife to take care of my
children. I want a wife to keep track of the children's doctor and
dentist appointments. And to keep track of mine, too. I want a wife to
make sure my children eat properly and are kept clean. I want a wife
who will wash the children's clothes and keep them mended. I want a
wife who is a good nurturant attendant to my children, who arranges
for their schooling, makes sure that they have an adequate social life
with their peers, takes them to the park, the zoo, etc. I want a wife who
takes care of the children when they are sick, a wife who arranges to be
around when the children need special care, because, of course, I
cannot miss classes at school. My wife must arrange to lose time at
work and not lose the job. It may mean a small cut in my wife's income
from time to time, but I guess I can tolerate that. Needless to say, my
wife will arrange and pay for the care of the children while my wife is
working.

I want a wife who will take care of *my* physical needs. I want a wife 4
who will keep my house clean. A wife who will pick up after my
children, a wife who will pick up after me. I want a wife who will keep
my clothes clean, ironed, mended, replaced when need be, and who
will see to it that my personal things are kept in their proper place so
that I can find what I need the minute I need it. I want a wife who
cooks the meals, a wife who is a *good* cook. I want a wife who will plan
the menus, do the necessary grocery shopping, prepare the meals,
serve them pleasantly, and then do the cleaning up while I do my
studying. I want a wife who will care for me when I am sick and
sympathize with my pain and loss of time from school. I want a wife to
go along when our family takes a vacation so that someone can continue to care for me and my children when I need a rest and change of
scene.

I want a wife who will not bother me with rambling complaints 5
about a wife's duties. But I want a wife who will listen to me when I
feel the need to explain a rather difficult point I have come across in my
course of studies. And I want a wife who will type my papers for me
when I have written them.

I want a wife who will take care of the details of my social life. 6 When my wife and I are invited out by my friends, I want a wife who will take care of the babysitting arrangements. When I meet people at school that I like and want to entertain, I want a wife who will have the house clean, will prepare a special meal, serve it to me and my friends, and not interrupt when I talk about things that interest me and my friends. I want a wife who will have arranged that the children are fed and ready for bed before my guests arrive so that the children do not bother us. I want a wife who takes care of the needs of my guests so that they feel comfortable, who makes sure that they have an ashtray, that they are passed the hors d'oeuvres, that they are offered a second helping of the food, that their wine glasses are replenished when necessary, that their coffee is served to them as they like it. And I want a wife who knows that sometimes I need a night out by myself.

I want a wife who is sensitive to my sexual needs, a wife who 7 makes love passionately and eagerly when I feel like it, a wife who makes sure that I am satisfied. And, of course, I want a wife who will not demand sexual attention when I am not in the mood for it. I want a wife who assumes the complete responsibility for birth control, because I do not want more children. I want a wife who will remain sexually faithful to me so that I do not have to clutter up my intellectual life with jealousies. And I want a wife who understands that *my* sexual needs may entail more than strict adherence to monogamy. I must, after all, be able to relate to people as fully as possible.

If, by chance, I find another person more suitable as a wife than 8 the wife I already have, I want the liberty to replace my present wife with another one. Naturally, I will expect a fresh, new life; my wife will take the children and be solely responsible for them so that I am left free.

When I am through with school and have a job, I want my wife to 9 quit working and remain at home so that my wife can more fully and completely take care of a wife's duties.

My God, who *wouldn't* want a wife?   10

QUESTIONS AND IDEAS FOR DISCUSSION

1. What does this essay really argue for? Is Brady's tactic effective? Comment.

2. Discuss the distinctions to be drawn among the following kinds and derivatives of humor: exaggeration, irony, sarcasm. Locate examples of each type of humor in this essay. Can humor be unfunny and still be effective?

3. Porter (in the previous essay) and Brady argue very different theses about marriage. Whose do you believe is more accurate? Why? Whose argument is more persuasive? Explain.

Incompatible, with One L

CALVIN TRILLIN

Calvin Trillin is an American journalist, novelist, and humorist, best known for his witty essays in the *New Yorker* and the *Nation*. Trillin's books include *Alice, Let's Eat* (1978), *Killings* (1984), and *With All Disrespect* (1985). "Incompatible, with One L" first appeared in the *Nation*, a highly regarded periodical of politically liberal bent, and was included in a collection, *Uncivil Liberties* (1982). This essay is not political; indeed, it is not even a conventional argumentative essay. But it does argue an implicit thesis, and the thesis certainly is not that Trillin and his wife, Alice, are incompatible. Nor has it anything to do with spelling—or does it?

September 16, 1978

I married Alice under the assumption that she could spell "oc-   1
curred." She now insists that nothing specific was mentioned about "occurred" in prenuptial discussions. It seems to me, though, that implicit in someone's making a living as a college English teacher is the representation that she is a speller with a repertoire adequate to any occasion. She must have known that the only person in her line of work I had any experience being related to, my Cousin Keith from Salina, once reached the finals of the Kansas State Spelling Bee. She now says Cousin Keith's spelling triumph was never spoken of between us. I distinctly remember, though, that I listed for Alice the highlights of our family's history, as any prospective bridegroom might for his future wife, and Cousin Keith has always been part of my standard Family History recitation—along with my Cousin Neil, who was once the head drum major of the University of Nebraska marching band, and my Uncle Benny Daynofsky, who in his early eighties was knocked down by a car while planting tomatoes in his own backyard in St. Jo. It is significant that she does not deny knowing about Uncle Benny.

Is spelling the sort of thing that modern young couples get   2
straightened out beforehand in marriage contracts? I wouldn't bring it up after all of these years, except that, as it happens, I can't spell "occurred" either. I was forced to look it up twice in order to write the first paragraph, and once more to get this far in the second. Somehow, I had expected to marry someone whose spelling would be, if not perfect, at least complementary to mine. We would face the future with heads held high, and maybe a short song on our lips—confident

that together we could spell anything they dished out. Before we had been married a month, the real world started to eat away at that fantasy: It turned out that Alice was not very good on "commitment." I don't mean she didn't have any; she couldn't spell it. I have never been able to spell "commitment" myself.

I know how to spell "embarrass"—usually considered by double- 3 letter specialists to be a much more difficult word. I have been able to spell it for years. I planted "embarrass" in my mind at an early age through a rather brilliant mnemonic device having to do with bar-stools. In fact, not to make a lot out of it, I had always thought of my ability to spell "embarrass" as a nice little facility to bring to a marriage—the sort of minor bonus that is sometimes found in a husband's ability to rewire lamps. (I don't mean it was the only facility I was able to contribute: Although I can't rewire a lamp, I can bark like a dog and I can blow a hard-boiled egg out of its shell seven times out of ten.) We have now been married thirteen years, and Alice still has not asked me how to spell "embarrass." Apparently, she has a mnemonic device of her own. I have never inquired. That sort of thing doesn't interest me.

For a while, our reformist friends used to urge us to make a list of 4 the words that troubled both of us—their theory being that some wretched consistency in the American educational system would be further documented by the fact that a husband and wife who went to public schools 1,300 miles apart were left without the ability to spell precisely the same words. Not long ago, an analytically inclined East-erner who came over for a drink when Alice happened to be out of town tried to establish some psychological significance in which words Alice and I were able to spell and which ones we weren't. "Is it really an accident that neither of you can spell 'commitment' but both of you can spell 'embarrass'?" he said. It has been my experience that when analytically inclined Easterners ask a question that begins "Is it really an accident . . ." the answer is always yes. I wanted to write Alice to describe the psychological analysis of our spelling problem, but, as it happens, the one word she can spell and I can't is "cocka-mamie."

Converts to the new politics of lowered expectations have told me 5 that I should simply accept Alice's spelling limitations and comfort myself with thoughts of the many splendid qualities she does have— the way Americans are now supposed to settle for only two gigantic automobiles, reminding themselves that some people in Chad have none at all. I have tried that. I have reminded myself that Alice can explain foreign movies and decipher road maps. I suspect that in a pinch she might be able to rewire a lamp. But, having come of drink-ing age in the 1950s, I may be culturally immune to the politics of low-ered expectations. I can't get over the suspicion that a politician who preaches that doctrine is really arguing that we ought to settle for him. I still find myself thinking back on the old-fashioned scenes I had envisioned for our marriage: We are sitting peacefully in the parlor—after having kissed the little ones goodnight—and I glance up from the desk, where I have been polishing off a letter to the *Times* on our policy in the Far East, and say, "Alice, how do you spell 'referred'?" Alice tells me. Or, on another evening, Alice looks over from her side of the desk (in this version of our marriage, the custodian of an abandoned courthouse in Pennsylvania had sold us an 18th-century double-desk for $85 including delivery to New York in his brother's pickup), where she has been composing a letter to her parents saying how sublimely happy she is. She asks me how to spell "embarrass." I tell her.

QUESTIONS AND IDEAS FOR DISCUSSION

1. What is Trillin's thesis—his central, underlying point—and what makes humor the ideal vehicle for it? How does Trillin support his point(s)? Are you convinced, or at least persuaded, by the essay's thesis? Implicit theses, as in this essay, are common in humorous writing. Why?

2. Analyze the "logic" of Trillin's argument in the first paragraph. Why, according to his tongue-in-cheek reasoning, is it "significant that she does not deny knowing about Uncle Benny"?

3. Discuss the significance—in their context—of the particular words Trillin claims not to be able to spell. Or is there any significance? They are, after all, words that people often do have trouble spelling.

4. How does Trillin use humorous details and examples to engage our interest and winningly make his points? Give examples.

5. Basing your judgment on the persona Trillin establishes in this essay and the details he cites, what can you infer about him and about his marriage? Do you base your inferences largely on logical reasoning or on your personal preconceptions and experience—or on both?

The Wife Is in Charge

BILL COSBY

Bill Cosby is a comedian (and a well-educated one, having earned a doctorate in education) and the author of best-selling books of humorous essays, including *Fatherhood* (1986), *Time Flies* (1987), and *Love and Marriage* (1989), from which the following selection is taken. Given his credentials, we should not be surprised to find that an essay written by Bill Cosby is funny. But like all good humorists (if we are to believe Mark Twain's and William Zinsser's claims), Cosby uses humor in order to make a point. Here he argues, tongue-in-cheek, that in a marriage the wife is in charge. But is that Cosby's "real" argument about marriage? What makes a good relationship in marriage? In what ways does the Cosbys' marriage resemble the Trillins'? In what ways does it resemble (or fail to) other marriages you have observed—or experienced?

1   If the amusement park called Great Adventure had been created by me, it would have no slides or rides: it would simply have one married couple trying to sustain the glow of their love while the wife gave the husband's favorite suits to the Salvation Army. For the last twenty-five years, since a certain wedding in Olney, Maryland, in 1964, the Salvation Army has been fighting Satan not only with the cross of Jesus but the cream of my coats and pants.

2   When I got married, one of the many things I didn't know was that Camille would grow tired of looking at some of my suits, even two I hadn't worn; but I loved her so much that I didn't mind her secretly recycling my wardrobe. I rejoiced that I now was married to the most beautiful woman I had ever seen, a woman who suddenly made Jane Russell no more alluring to me than Nipsey. My instinct was to break the rules of marriage and be honest with her about everything. I quickly realized, however, that even the deepest love doesn't stop a marriage from being a constant struggle for control. Any husband who says "My wife and I are completely equal partners" is talking about either a law firm or a hand of bridge.

3   Yes, let us now set forth one of the fundamental truths about marriage: the wife is in charge. Or, to put it another way, the husband is not. Now I can hear your voices crying out:

What patronizing nonsense.

What a dumb generalization.

What a great jacket for the Salvation Army.

4   Well, my proof of the point is a simple one. If any man truly believes that he is the boss of his house, then let him do this: pick up the phone, call a wallpaper store, order new wallpaper for one of the rooms in his house, and then put it on. He would have a longer life expectancy sprinkling arsenic on his eggs. Any husband who buys wallpaper, drapes, or even a prayer rug on his own is auditioning for the Bureau of Missing Persons.

5   Therefore, in spite of what Thomas Jefferson wrote, all men may

be created equal, but not to all women, and the loveliest love affair must bear the strain of this inequality once the ceremony is over. When a husband and wife settle down together, there is a natural struggle for power (I wonder why he bothers); and in this struggle, the husband cannot avoid giving up a few things—for example, dinner.

To be fair, I must admit that Camille did wait a few years before 6 allowing me to make this particular sacrifice. I had just sat down at the table one night with her and our three children when I happened to notice that my plate contained only collard greens and brown rice.

"Would you please donate this to the Hare Krishna and bring me 7 my real meal," I said to the gentleman serving the food.

"You have it all," he replied.   8

"No, what I have is a snack for the North Korean Army. The meat 9 must have slipped off somewhere. Why don't we try to find it together?"

"Mrs. Cosby said we are no longer eating meat."   10

"She *did*?" I looked down the table at Camille. "Dear, if I got a 11 letter from the Pope, do you think I could—"

"Bill, meat is bad for us and we just have to cut it out. It's full of fat 12 that could kill you. I'm sorry I forgot to tell you."

"So am I. I could've started eating out at a place where they don't 13 mind who they kill."

"Honey, *lots* of people are vegetarians."   14

"And lots of people like to get hit with whips, but I've managed to 15 be happy not joining them."

Nevertheless, I became a vegetarian. A husband should go with 16 the flow of his marriage, even when that flow leads over a cliff.

About two years later, however, I sat down to dinner one night 17 and a steak suddenly appeared on my plate.

"Look at this," I said to the gentleman serving the food. "Some- 18 one has lost a steak. Would you please return it to its owner."

"Mrs. Cosby said we are eating meat again," he told me.   19

"How nice to see the cows come home," I said.   20

QUESTIONS AND IDEAS FOR DISCUSSION

1. What is Cosby's thesis, and with what arguments and evidence does he support it?

2. Cosby's humor is broader than that of some of the other writers in this chapter, but it, too, often turns on unexpected and even subtle deviations from what the reader expects to come next. Find examples of this strategy in the essay.

3. This essay comprises one section in a chapter, so it does not conclude as tidily as we might expect from an essay standing alone. Were it such an essay, how might Cosby effectively conclude it? Write a conclusion for the essay, and compare versions with other members of your class. Decide which ending works best, and why.

4. Basing your judgment on the persona Cosby establishes and the details he cites, what can you infer about him *and* about his marriage? As you did with the Trillin essay, think about whether you base your inferences largely on logical reasoning or on your personal preconceptions and experience—or on both.

Ease Up, Please, on Single Women . . .

MARY CAROLYN MORGAN

Writing for the *New York Times* in 1990, journalist Mary Carolyn Morgan defends the rights of the unmarried to be treated with courtesy—not to be pounced on and embarrassed by well-meaning friends intent on matching them up with some equally embarrassed member of the opposite sex. Even more important, Morgan argues, is for singles not to "be treated as half-people because they do not have a spouse, fiancé, live-in companion, significant other or date." Her claim is supported with examples of match-making do-gooders ranging from an acquaintance who resembles a priggish character on "Saturday Night Live" to a zealous middle-aged male relative. There is humor in the images Morgan creates and in an occasional turn of phrase ("trying to prod me into the chutes of matrimonial bliss"), but hers is a serious argument nonetheless.

It has happened again: Some conscientious soul more concerned 1 with my business than her own managed in the course of polite conversation to suggest that as a 29-year-old single woman, I must be ready to pounce on any unattached man who crosses my path. We had just left a church service and were exchanging pleasantries, when she spied a man without a wedding ring in the coffee-hour crowd and suggested that I hurry over to put in a bid on him. It was embarrassing. I reminded this second cousin of Dana Carvey's church lady that meeting men is not the sole reason single women attend church, and I began to ponder why single women are shabbily treated when they venture out in public.

For some reason my marital status is of immense interest and 2 concern to various friends and acquaintances. Certainly, it seems to occupy more of their time than it does mine. Granted, I would not be averse to meeting Prince Charming, but it does not occupy my every waking hour.

For the last five years, a married friend has made a point of trying 3 to prod me into the chutes of matrimonial bliss. Every communication with her involves a reference to the dating game. For two years after I had broken up with a boyfriend, she kept asking, "When are you two going to get back together?" And, at the last party she threw, she gathered the three dateless single women together and announced cheerily and loudly that she had invited a few single men for our consideration. I wish she would discover that discretion exercised with fewer decibels would make everyone more comfortable.

The people who aggressively try to fix you up tend to be the most 4 annoying. One zealous relative used to threaten to introduce me to unattached colleagues of his. He kept it up until, during one of his sales pitches, his very pretty 15-year-old daughter announced that the bachelor co-worker had tried to bridge a 20-year generation gap by asking her out while she waited for Dad at his office. The co-worker's name was never again mentioned in that house in a favorable light.

And then there was the elderly lady who in the interest of pro- 5 moting what she thought would be a "nice friendship between two agreeable young people" managed to cause immeasurable embarrassment by saying so much that neither one can face the other without going beet red. Etiquette and her advanced age prevent me from informing her of her indiscretion.

Then there is the story of my aunt. When she was in her 20's, a 6 young, unmarried curate was hired by the church she attended. If she shook his hand at the end of the service, people gossiped that she was after him. If someone wanted to know why she wasn't married, his name would be suggested, sometimes within earshot. She barely knew him and was dating the man she eventually married.

Therefore I should like to say several things on behalf of single 7 women everywhere. Just because a man is single and available does not mean those are the only criteria he needs to be considered attractive.

Every unmarried woman should not be viewed as a predatory 8 man-hungry creature whose only quest in life is to bag elusive male prey.

Single women should not be treated as half-people because they 9 do not have a spouse, fiancé, live-in companion, significant other or date.

If people kept meddlesome plans to themselves, single women 10 would breathe a sigh of relief.

QUESTIONS AND IDEAS FOR DISCUSSION

1. Just what is Morgan's thesis in this essay: that she wants to be left alone or that she and other single people are—and should not be— shabbily treated? Or is it something else? State the thesis in your own words. Does Morgan make a good case for it? What points, if any, could you add?

2. Characterize the humor in this essay: Is it subtle? Ironic? Broad? Is it meant to be funny or to point up some unfunny incongruities? Suggest another illustration or claim in support of Morgan's thesis that employs humor in a similar vein.

3. In paragraph 1, Morgan calls one interfering friend a "second cousin of Dana Carvey's church lady," a reference to a simpering, hat-and-gloves-clad character portrayed by actor Dana Carvey on "Saturday Night Live." In paragraph 3, Morgan describes a friend's efforts to "prod me into the chutes of matrimonial bliss." In what different ways does Morgan achieve humor in these two examples?

. . . And Don't Push Single Men, Either
THOMAS CANGELOSI

Thomas Cangelosi writes for the *New York Times* and other publications. This essay first appeared as a companion piece to Mary
Carolyn Morgan's "Ease Up, Please, on Single Women . . ." in the
New York Times, July 15, 1990. A more fully developed argument than
Morgan's, it argues that single people are subjected by married people to so much unwarranted pressure, both subtle and overt, because
singles represent a kind of threat. They create, claims Cangelosi, an
uncomfortable doubt in the hearts of the married. Is he pessimistic or
realistic?

At a recent party, I overheard a woman ask, "What's wrong with   1
him?" She was referring to me, and her tone suggested she had just
learned I was a 36-year-old bachelor. These days, the word prompts a
litany of unpopular possibilities: Gay? Divorced? Disturbed? It wasn't
always so.

I remember summer evenings in the 1950's, when we boys played   2
hide-and-seek in my backyard, before we and the day were put to
sleep. One evening, as I crouched behind the throne-shaped barbecue
pit, anticipating my brother's call to "come in free," and dreading my
father's call to "get in here," a young, dark-haired woman in a white
summer dress appeared like some latter-day Juliet at my uncle's porch

railing. She was one of a string of women who mysteriously showed up that summer upon his return from the Army.

My uncle escorted her down the stairs, her hand resting in the 3 crook of his elbow. His usually curly hair gleamed straight with Wildroot, and his sunburned cheeks dimpled in what seemed a permanent smile that summer.

As they passed my hiding spot, I inhaled the sweet bouquet of her 4 perfume, and my uncle flashed me a conspiratorial wink before disappearing into the neon night. At that moment, I longed for the day when I, too, would be a man, single and free.

It hasn't been easy. There seems to be a subtle movement in 5 society to close its ranks, economically, racially and now even matrimonially. There is an implied demand for single people to marry, an almost irrestistible but emphatic pull, hard to recognize but undeniable in impact.

I received a phone call from a woman I had dated for 10 years and 6 lived with for 2. The relationship had ended when she wanted children and marriage, and I reiterated that I wanted neither. She called on the eve of her wedding, bubbling with joy.

"It's like going through a door where a party is going on," she 7 said. "In a way it seems unfair to those left out." She didn't say this to make me feel bad; she said it because it was the truth. She was joining a large but exclusive club.

The holidays perennially serve as the rush season of the marriage 8 membership drive, a most trying time for single people. The social wagons circle, and married men rope me aside, slap my back a bit too hard and ask me when I will "tie the knot," "settle down" or "put on the old ball and chain."

Though their verbal fusillade may sound lighthearted, I suspect 9 their motives are as much sympathetic as defensive. My English professor once described America's love-hate relationship with its alien heroes: "We identify and sympathize with the hero who breaks with convention, but we don't want him to move into the house next door."

A single man, especially if divorced, represents to the married 10 man the same kind of threat the career woman brought to the traditional housewife: doubt. One generation after the rebellious 60's, the connotation of "different" has changed from "special" to "alien."

In the march up the aisle, the bachelor has been unceremoniously 11 cast out like a heathen from the church of the American dream, along with his much maligned feminine counterpart, the spinster. (Unmarried women have always been blackballed by society, labeled "witch," "old maid," and much worse, primarily by insulted men and frightened wives who could not fathom why anyone would not join a club of which they were a member.)

To many, a bachelor represents a narcissistic hedonist, a victim of 12 Peter Pan syndrome or an AIDS time bomb. But to most, he is someone with a dark secret. Or, as a woman who had consumed one glass of champagne too many at a wedding bluntly asked recently, "Are you one of those men who fears commitment?"

"Commitment to what?" I asked.   13

"I knew it," she said and waved me off with a knowing nod.   14

I wasn't trying to be coy. I consider myself very committed—to 15 work, to friends, to everything I do, from travel to sports to writing.

Probably due to my commitment to these loves, I have decided not 16 to marry. Marriage I take quite seriously. But its success rate these days can be determined by the flip of a coin. I blame this hit-or-miss record on a whole generation of baby boomers whose expectations of marriage rivals in fantasy a child's vision of heaven.

My parents recently celebrated their golden wedding anniversary, 17 and standing together at the head of the table, surrounded by friends and family, they were a living portrait of the kind of fulfillment that comes from raising a family and living with each other for 50 years.

For their generation, however, the matter was clear and simple: 18 marriage was the only path. It carried a lifelong commitment, til death do us part, a vow taken quite literally.

The divorced or the ones who "lived in sin" were failures, but the 19 bachelor still enjoyed respect, probably for not making a promise that he did not know if he could keep.

In more than two decades the raison d'être of marriage has 20 changed dramatically. With the explosion of the nuclear family, the advent of the AIDS virus, and a cultural drug habit heavy on our backs, there seems sufficient reason to marry and pursue the innocent ways of the '50s.

But the sexual revolution of the 1960's and the proliferation of 21 alternative life styles, including live-in lovers, has now made the march up the aisle a choice instead of a certainty, one undertaken by those who are well aware of the paths not taken.

I have chosen to take the path less traveled. If it is true that some 22 people are born to some things, I believe I was born to be single. Raised in a close-knit family in a close-knit neighborhood in a close-knit town, with relatives upstairs, downstairs, next door and down the street, I had to leave town just to get a good look at myself. Consequently, I have worked to loosen the weave in the fabric of my life.

As far back as grammar school, I wagered with my fellow students 23 and the Sisters of Mercy that I would never get married. They laughed, but I plan on collecting a bundle at our next reunion.

Recently, I read an article in the health section of the newspaper 24
that said single men have significantly shorter lives than married men,
because they don't receive the emotional support conducive to longer
life. This fact alone raises martial status to a life-and-death issue.

Why would anyone choose to be single in the face of a shortened 25
life, a loss of friends and a black-sheep label? It seems to me that
bachelors, far from their insecure and immature stereotype, may represent a spirit of adventure, independence and honor. Socially speaking, a bachelor is one who goes alone. Morally speaking, he may do so
merely to keep his integrity.

Despite what Frost said about the path less traveled having made 26
all the difference, I believe both paths can lead to the same place. There
may be as much enjoyment in the silence of solitude as in the voices of
communion, in the mobility of the open road as the stability of home
sweet home, in a trip abroad as in a family vacation.

And can't a weekend hike—as much as a child's first step—lift my 27
heart? Can't life be learned equally from the rushing stream and the
calm pool, nourished by the fruits of variety, as well as those of
intimacy? These paths may not be mutually exclusive, but bache-
lorhood is more conducive to one and marriage to the other.

People no doubt will continue to ask me whether I will ever marry. 28
In our culture, this seems a natural question. But the reverse is seldom
asked of the betrothed: why are you married? It sounds impertinent,
doesn't it? That, in itself, is revealing.

QUESTIONS AND IDEAS FOR DISCUSSION

1. How do Cangelosi's and Morgan's theses differ? Compare the
tone of the two essays. Which uses humor more—or more effectively?
Which writer seems to argue the thesis with greater conviction? On
what basis do you say so?

2. What function does the anecdote about Cangelosi's uncle (paragraphs 2–4) serve in this essay?

3. Explain how Cangelosi creates humor in the following passage:

Raised in a close-knit family in a close-knit neighborhood in a
close-knit town, with relatives upstairs, downstairs, next door and
down the street, I had to leave town just to get a good look at
myself. Consequently, I have worked to loosen the weave in the
fabric of my life. (paragraph 22)

4. Like Katherine Anne Porter, Cangelosi ends his essay seriously.
Analyze and explain his final paragraph.

ADDITIONAL MATERIAL FOR ANALYSIS AND ARGUMENT:
EDITORIAL CARTOONS

The editorial cartoonist must create an entire argument in a single panel with often no more than a few words of text—and sometimes none at all. He (for reasons unknown, rarely *she*) reveals absurdities and uncovers truths. As William Zinsser declares in his essay earlier in this chapter, "One cartoon by Herblock or Bill Mauldin is worth a hundred solemn editorials." When we laugh at such cartoons, it is the laughter of sometimes startled recognition. The following editorial cartoons, some of them prize winners (Doug Marlette's "Front Runner" received a Pulitzer Prize in 1988), cut right to the bone of pressing political and social issues. You may choose to analyze the cartoons themselves (what makes them funny, if they are?), to compare the techniques of the cartoonists (which demand the most of their readers?), or to use the cartoons as starting points for arguments about the issues they represent. Your own arguments may use humor, as these do, to argue serious matters.

"PRESIDENT?... NO, CHILD, BUT YOU CAN GROW UP TO BE FRONT-RUNNER!"

"I'M SENTENCING YOU TO 25 YEARS IN PRISON WITH NO HOPE OF PAROLE UNTIL AFTER 3 P.M. TOMORROW AFTERNOON!"

Geriatrics dilemma

SUGGESTIONS FOR WRITING
AND FURTHER DISCUSSION

1. Pulitzer Prize–winning humorist Dave Barry, who writes a syndicated column for the *Miami Herald*, says this about the writing of humor:

> The theory I go on . . . is that nothing you could ever make up is as funny as what real people actually do, especially if these people work for enormous, rich, powerful, chronically bone-headed institutions such as the United States government. . . . The funniest stuff is usually the truest stuff, if you ask me, and one of the great mysteries of journalism is how we so often take astoundingly comical events such as the presidential election campaigns, and, through enormous expenditures of manpower and money, render them boring.[1]

With these words, Barry joins Twain, Zinsser, and a host of other writers on the role of effective humor: "The funniest stuff is usually the truest stuff. . . ." Do these writers take humor too seriously? Analyze their claims as if you were refuting them. If, however, the claims hold up, support them with additional examples from current magazines or newspapers.

2. What subject interests you that your classmates might regard as trivial or silly? What do you appreciate that no one else does? What subject do you understand (the theory of relativity? what happens to socks in a dryer?) that no one else grasps? Write an essay in which you argue a case for your particular interest or your particular understanding of a subject everyone else dismisses or takes for granted as proven. Don't choose a wholly frivolous subject (forget the socks in the dryer), and don't write about how hard it is to write a funny essay. Don't even make humor your first objective. Recall instead the words of Mark Twain, and write "the sermon just the same, whether any humor applie[s] for admission or not." If you strain for humor, the humor will be strained.

3. List as many ways to create humor through words as you can, illustrating each with an example of your own or one from an essay in this section. Incongruous metaphors, emphatic repetition, understatement, exaggeration should be on the list—and more as well.

---

[1] *The Pulitzer Prizes, 1988,* ed. Kendall J. Wills (New York: Simon, 1988) 379–80.

Discuss the extent to which you are comfortable using these various tactics to drive home a point with humor.

4.   When you use humor to make a point, don't you run the risk that your audience will take you literally and miss the real point? The seventies' television program "All in the Family" and its central character, Archie Bunker—which you can still view, in syndication—were enjoyed both by political liberals and by racists. Wasn't somebody missing the point? Discuss the dangers and pitfalls of humor, with examples from your own reading, viewing, or experience.

5.   Humor has another drawback besides the chance of being overlooked: Humor cannot increase the persuasiveness of an argument if it offends readers. On the other hand, if we are to believe the writers in this section, no strategy can beat appropriate humor for actually changing people's attitudes. Argue for or against using humor to underscore arguments with serious aims.

6.   If you are not quite the fan of editorial cartoons that William Zinsser is, argue your reasons why.

7.   The six examples of argument employing humor in this chapter were written by three women and three men. Which writer has created the most appealing persona for an audience of which you would be a typical member? Or to put the question in a somewhat different way: Judging from their writing alone (not even from their sexes), to which author would you prefer to be married? Why?

8.   By consulting the *Readers' Guide to Periodical Literature,* find essays on the subject of marriage written during a particular decade (the thirties, fifties, sixties, or eighties, perhaps). Do you find much or little writing on marriage that is humorous during that decade (judging from the sampling you find)? Analyze the humorous (or intended-to-be-humorous) essays and articles to see what conclusions may be drawn: What kinds of humor do you find—what typical approaches to marriage? Does the humor seem dated? Why? How much of it now strikes you as being sexist? Does women's writing use humor more or less often than men's writing? Can you draw any conclusions about or from that? Does the writing by women strike you as more or less humorous than that by men? (Consider to what extent your own biases and preconceptions about marriage might affect your analyses.)

Determine an arguable thesis on some aspect of your research, and write a documented essay for the enlightenment—and perhaps entertainment—of your class. Should you be inspired to include a humorous touch, let your own humor be subtle—not sophomoric!

6

ARGUING WITH STYLE

THE STRATEGY

This chapter by no means begins our consideration of style in writing. Because style is simply *how* writers say *what* they say, we are concerned with style from the first paragraph we read or, when we are the writers, the first paragraph we write. Style is not mere affectation: If our arguments are not well written, they may not be understood—or even read. Nor is there one "right" style of writing. Voltaire once said, "All styles are good save the boresome kind." We should take that as encouragement. On the other hand, while true, Voltaire's pronouncement is stunningly unhelpful. We may recognize "the boresome kind" of style when we see it, but how do we avoid *writing* it? This is a particular problem for the required writing we do at work or for academic courses.

The previous chapter offered some advice about and examples of one stylistic (and persuasive) strategy: humor. But for most writers, it is almost as hard to be serious without being stuffy as it is to be funny without being absurd. It is as hard to be clear and concise as it is to be logically convincing. The readings that follow offer advice well worth heeding on just these concerns. It is not coincidental that these essays are themselves written with style. F. L. Lucas and Walker Gibson practice what they preach.

As you read the essays in this chapter, think about the elements that give our arguments style: the length and grammatical structure of sentences, the level of vocabulary, the choice of words, the use of metaphor. There is surely no one right style, as the semiliterate, ungrammatical, but eloquent and moving prose of Bartolomeo Vanzetti will show in the subsequent section. Perhaps F. L. Lucas is right: If our writing shows honesty and courtesy—and "good humor, good sense, vitality, imagination"—it cannot help but have style.

On Style

F. L. LUCAS

F. L. Lucas (1894–1967), an Englishman, was a Fellow of Kings
College, Cambridge, and a classics scholar—whose scholarship extended to Victorian literature, French literature, modern drama, and
eighteenth-century philosophy, among other interests. Lucas also
wrote poetry, novels, short stories, and plays. His many published
works include *Seneca and Elizabethan Tragedy* (1922), *The Decline and
Fall of the Romantic Ideal* (1936), and *Literature and Psychology* (1951).
Among writers and scholars, Lucas has always been noted for the
grace and clarity of his prose—perhaps one reason why many of his
books have been reprinted decades after their original writing. Lucas
wrote a book on the subject that his own writing so well exemplifies,
Style (1955). The short piece that follows, which first appeared in
Holiday magazine in 1960, offers a wealth of good advice in a short
space—and does so with style.

No man was less of a literary aesthete than Benjamin Franklin; yet 1
this tallow-chandler's son, who changed world history, regarded as "a
principal means of my advancement" that pungent style which he
acquired partly by working in youth over old *Spectators;* but mainly by
being Benjamin Franklin. The squinting demagogue, John Wilkes, as
ugly as his many sins, had yet a tongue so winning that he asked only
half an hour's start (to counteract his face) against any rival for a
woman's favor. "Vote for you!" growled a surly elector in his constituency. "I'd sooner vote for the devil!" "But in case your friend should
not stand . . . ?" Cleopatra, that ensnarer of world conquerors, owed
less to the shape of her nose than to the charm of her tongue. Shakespeare himself has often poor plots and thin ideas; even his mastery of
character has been questioned; what does remain unchallenged is his
verbal magic. Men are often taken, like rabbits, by the ears. And
though the tongue has no bones, it can sometimes break millions of
them. . . .

Words can be more powerful, and more treacherous, than we 2
sometimes suspect; communication more difficult than we may think.
We are all serving life sentences of solitary confinement within our
own bodies; like prisoners, we have, as it were, to tap in awkward
code to our fellowmen in their neighboring cells. Further, when A and
B converse, there take part in their dialogue not two characters, as they
suppose, but six. For there is A's real self—call it A_1; there is also A's
picture of himself—A_2; there is also B's picture of A—A_3. And there
are three corresponding personalities of B. With six characters involved even in a simple tête-à-tête, no wonder we fall into muddles
and misunderstandings.

Perhaps, then, there are five main reasons for trying to gain some 3
mastery of language:

We have no other way of understanding, informing, misin- 4
forming, or persuading one another.

Even alone, we think mainly in words; if our language is muddy, 5
so will our thinking be.

By our handling of words we are often revealed and judged. "Has 6
he written anything?" said Napoleon of a candidate for an appointment. "Let me see his *style.*"

Without a feeling for language one remains half-blind and deaf to 7
literature.

Our mother tongue is bettered or worsened by the way each 8
generation uses it. Languages evolve like species. They can de-
generate; just as oysters and barnacles have lost their heads. Compare
ancient Greek with modern. A heavy responsibility, though often
forgotten. . . .

The writer should respect truth and himself; therefore honesty. 9
He should respect his readers; therefore courtesy. These are two of the
cornerstones of style. Confucius saw it, twenty-five centuries ago:
"The Master said, The gentleman is courteous, but not pliable: common men are pliable, but not courteous."

First, honesty. In literature, as in life, one of the fundamentals is to 10
find, and be, one's true self. One's true self may indeed be unpleasant
(though one can try to better it); but a false self, sooner or later,
becomes disgusting—just as a nice plain woman, painted to the eye-
brows, can become horrid. In writing, in the long run, pretense does
not work. As the police put it, anything you say may be used as
evidence against you. If handwriting reveals character, writing reveals
it still more. You cannot fool *all* your judges *all* the time.

Most style is not honest enough. Easy to say, but hard to practice. 11
A writer may take to long words, as young men to beards—to impress. But long words, like long beards, are often the badge of char-
latans. Or a writer may cultivate the obscure, to seem profound. But
even carefully muddied puddles are soon fathomed. Or he may cultivate eccentricity, to seem original. But really original people do not
have to think about being original—they can no more help it than they
can help breathing. They do not need to dye their hair green. The fame
of Meredith, Wilde or Bernard Shaw might now shine brighter, had
they struggled less to be brilliant; whereas Johnson remains great, not
merely because his gifts were formidable but also because, with all his
prejudice and passion, he fought no less passionately to "clear his
mind of cant."

Secondly, courtesy—respect for the reader. From this follow sev- 12
eral other basic principles of style. Clarity is one. For it is boorish to

make your reader rack his brains to understand. One should aim at being impossible to misunderstand—though men's capacity for mis-understanding approaches infinity. Hence Molière and Po Chü-i tried their work on their cooks; and Swift his on his menservants—"which, if they did not comprehend, he would alter and amend, until they understood it perfectly." Our bureaucrats and pundits, unfortunately, are less considerate.

Brevity is another basic principle. For it is boorish, also, to waste   13 your reader's time. People who would not dream of stealing a penny of one's money turn not a hair at stealing hours of one's life. But that does not make them less exasperating. Therefore there is no excuse for the sort of writer who takes as long as a marching army corps to pass a given point. Besides, brevity is often more effective; the half can say more than the whole, and to imply things may strike far deeper than to state them at length. And because one is particularly apt to waste words on preambles before coming to the substance, there was sense in the Scots professor who always asked his pupils—"Did ye remember to tear up that fir-r-st page?" . . .

Clarity comes before even brevity. But it is a fallacy that wordiness   14 is necessarily clearer. Metternich when he thought something he had written was obscure would simply go through it crossing out everything irrelevant. What remained, he found, often became clear. Wellington, asked to recommend three names for the post of Commander-in-Chief, India, took a piece of paper and wrote three times —"Napier." Pages could not have been clearer—or as forcible. On the other hand the lectures, and the sentences, of Coleridge became at times bewildering because his mind was often "wiggle-waggle"; just as he could not even walk straight on a path.

But clarity and brevity, though a good beginning, are only a   15 beginning. By themselves, they may remain bare and bleak. When Calvin Coolidge, asked by his wife what the preacher had preached on, replied "Sin," and, asked what the preacher had said, replied "He was against it," he was brief enough. But one hardly envies Mrs. Coolidge.

An attractive style requires, of course, all kinds of further gifts—   16 such as variety, good humor, good sense, vitality, imagination. Variety means avoiding monotony or rhythm, of language, of mood. One needs to vary one's sentence length (this present article has too many short sentences; but so vast a subject grows here as cramped as a djin in a bottle); to amplify one's vocabulary; to diversify one's tone. There are books that petrify one throughout, with the rigidly pompous solemnity of an owl perched on a leafless tree. But ceaseless face-tiousness can be as bad; or perpetual irony. Even the smile of Voltaire can seem at times a fixed grin, a disagreeable wrinkle. Constant peevishness is far worse, as often in Swift; even on the stage too much irritable dialogue may irritate an audience, without its knowing why.

Still more are vitality, energy, imagination—gifts that must be 17 inborn before they can be cultivated. But under the head of imagination two common devices may be mentioned that have been the making of many a style—metaphor and simile. Why such magic power should reside in simply saying, or implying, that A is like B remains a little mysterious. But even our unconscious seems to love symbols; again, language often tends to lose itself in clouds of vaporous abstraction, and simile or metaphor can bring it back to concrete solidity; and, again, such imagery can gild the gray flats of prose with sudden sunglints of poetry.

QUESTIONS AND IDEAS FOR DISCUSSION

1. Lucas argues the importance of style and offers "five main reasons for trying to gain some mastery of language" (paragraph 3). Does he equate "mastery of language" with "style"? Discuss. Does his argument persuade you? Is style really important in *all* the ways Lucas claims? Has Lucas overstated the case? Evaluate his argument.

2. Style is indisputably nonlogical. Can it then be as important to argumentative writing as it may be to narrative or descriptive writing? Discuss. Which of Lucas's "five main reasons for trying to gain some mastery of language" strike you as most relevant to the writing of arguments? Expand on the points you have chosen. Has Lucas overlooked any others?

3. This essay begins with a list of examples, not with a thesis paragraph. Comment on the pros and cons of beginning an argument (or any essay) in this way. Identify words and phrases in the first paragraph that help create Lucas's own style.

4. Lucas says that metaphor and simile "have been the making of many a style" (17). Create one or two metaphors or similes for each of the following items. Discuss the contexts in which the metaphors you have created might be appropriate.

- the current state of relations between eastern Europe and Russia
- the current state of relations between you and your roommate
- the place where you would most like to live
- the place where you would least like to return
- the importance (or lack of it) of sending a satellite to Mars
- science fiction
- portable cellular telephones

Being Serious Without Being Stuffy

WALKER GIBSON

Walker Gibson, Professor of English at the University of Massachusetts, has written several books, among them *The Limits of Language*
(1962), *Poems in the Making* (1963), and *Persona* (1969). In addition, his
poetry has appeared in the *New Yorker, Harper's,* and the *Nation,* and
in two collections. The following piece is taken from Gibson's book
on style, *Tough, Sweet, and Stuffy* (1965). In it, Gibson offers some
advice that will help you avoid "stuffiness" when you write serious
arguments. As Gibson characterizes the broad categories of poor
writing styles, the "Tough" writer "pushes us around." Tough
writing is curt—characterized by short words, few modifers, and few
subordinate clauses. The "Sweet" writer "cuddles up to us" with
longer words, many adjectives and adverbs, and quite a few noun
adjuncts.[1] Gibson regards advertising prose as the essence of
"sweet" writing. The "Stuffy" writer, finally, "holds us off" with
pretentious, polysyllabic words, complicated sentence structures,
passive voice, and "to be" verb forms rather than verbs showing
specific action. The Stuffy writer is "remote from both subject and
audience."

   You will find all three prose styles illustrated in this excerpt, but
Gibson is particularly concerned here with the difficulty many
writers have in being serious without being stuffy. We would do well
to heed Gibson's concern, for writing in academic contexts, and
much "serious" argument, often lapses into "Stuffiness."

   In the last few years there have appeared on the textbook market a   1
number of anthologies of essays about language and usage. These
have been extraordinarily similar in purpose, they have been aimed at
an identical audience, and they share current fashionable attitudes of
the modern linguistic scholar. They provide us, therefore, with something of a laboratory situation for measuring difference in style. What
kinds of voice can we identify in the styles of the anthologists themselves? How do they share the difficulties of self-expression that we
have been observing in novelists, journalists, ad writers, and committee spokesmen? All we need, for a tentative answer, is a look at the
first hundred words or so of their prefaces.

   Here is one: 2

   From the early grades through the first year of college, the textbooks in grammar and usage scarcely change. The repetition is well

---

[1] In Gibson's words, "One of the traditional ways in which modifiers have come into being
historically is of course by transfer from other parts of speech, notably from nouns. Children who
attend school become school children; trees that bear fruit become fruit trees. . . . By this process a
clumsy phrase can be shortened, perhaps strengthened. The technical name for this use of words is
the 'noun adjunct.'" (*Tough, Sweet, and Stuffy* 77) [Ed.]

meant and apparently necessary: if they won't learn what's good for them, make them do it again. Certainly habits are formed and re-formed by repetitive drill, but it is clear from the record that repetition is not enough.

This book is based on the conviction that knowledge must be added to drill so that repetition may open into growth. Everyone aims at this, at confidence and pleasure in the use of language rather than at anxiety about being correct; the problem has been to get the liberating knowledge, which is scattered through books and jour-nals, into the hands of the students.

A reader who thinks first about details of grammar, and only 3 second of his impression of the whole voice, may too quickly assume that we have a Stuffy Talker here. The reader . . . might tick off those verbs in the passive voice and say, There it is—Stuffy. For there they are: *is well meant, are formed and re-formed, is based, must be added, is scattered.* Nevertheless, as any sensible reader will point out, this is *not* a Stuffy voice at all—quite the contrary. Perhaps it is almost too breezy. In any case the barrage of passive verbs here is simply not enough to overcome all the other stylistic tricks in this passage which propel the tone in quite another direction, toward Toughness and Sweetness.

What are they? For one thing, the wry half-quotation, *if they won't* 4 *learn what's good for them . . .* , with its colloquial flavor, serves to disarm the reader in the very second sentence. The willingness to include such talk, in a kind of jocular spirit, is part of a general modesty on the part of the speaker, who is at pains to remind us that there is something to be said for the opposition. "The repetition is well meant," he acknowledges. "Everyone aims at this, at confidence and pleasure in the use of language"—not just I in my wisdom. In sum, the voice here is not that of a Stuffy lecturer at all, but represents some mixture of my three styles.

A short time after the anthology prefaced in this manner ap- 5 peared, another similar collection was published whose preface be-gins as follows:

The basic premise of this collection of essays is that language in and of itself is an important subject for study. The second, and equally important, premise is that one can learn about language by reading a variety of essays oriented to the best that modern scholars have thought and said about it.

Because the study of English is often atomized, it is effectively divorced from the broad and scholarly concerns that it is uniquely able to illuminate. In his study of language under the guise of compo-sition, grammar, rhetoric, or poetics, the student is seldom made to think about the nature of language itself.

I hope my reader may sense the difference in that voice, before he   6
stops to take note of details that may account for the difference. The
voice here, as I hope we may agree, is less brisk, more removed from
the reader, with an academic manner of address that suggests some
lack of excitement about what it's saying. If that judgment is at all fair,
we may then ask, where does this manner come from? Why is this
man so different, even though in realistic fact he is attempting to talk
to the same audience for an almost identical purpose?

There are plenty of concrete differences; some of them may be   7
persuasive. The vocabulary of our second speaker is more pretentious,
with more longer words and far fewer monosyllables. There are fewer
independent verbs, resulting in more subordination, both clauses and
other dependent structures. (Half the passage occurs inside subordinate clauses.) There is a tendency to interrupt normal sentence patterns, to make the reader wait for further modification. "The basic
premise *of this collection of essays is.* . . . The second, *and equally
important*, premise is. . . ." The tag about the best thought and said
may be deliberately ironic, but it's a tired tag for all that. These and
other habits of speech may partially justify our feeling that the second
anthologist is more dryly professorial (if not plain duller) than the first.

Now here is a third, introducing still another collection of similar   8
essays, aimed at the same audience. It may be his sense of the competition that makes this writer speak as he does.

> The growth of interest in language study, in linguistics, has been
> one of the interesting intellectual developments of the twentieth
> century. Linguistics must now be viewed as an established and inde-
> pendent branch of study. Under the circumstances it would be odd if
> there were not a number of books issued to introduce this study to
> the general public and to the university undergraduate. Many excel-
> lent collections of language articles and selections for the under-
> graduate—especially for the freshman—have appeared in recent
> years. The compiler of still another collection is consequently obliged
> to indicate why he adds his product to the number available.[2]

Anyone who begins a book by telling us that "the growth of   9
interest" in something is an "interesting development" cannot himself be overwhelmingly interested in what he has to say. In any event,
those rhetorical habits of Stuffiness that we associate with a remote-
ness from both subject and audience are here apparent. The vocabulary is now even more multisyllabic. There are fewer finite verbs, with

---

[2] The three passages in this chapter were taken from prefaces of the following anthologies:
Leonard F. Dean and Kenneth G. Wilson, *Essays on Language and Usage* (New York, 1959); John A.
Rycenga and Joseph Schwartz, *Perspectives on Language* (New York, 1963); Donald W. Lee, *English
Language Reader* (New York, 1963).

consequent subordination of much of the language. Passive verbs are actually less frequent than in our first passage, but other significant habits appear—for instance the noun adjunct. We have *language study, university undergraduates, language articles*—clear hints that we are approaching the jargon of officialese. The interrupted sentence patterns are interesting; here the writer habitually places modifying phrases between his subject and verb, letting his reader wait patiently until he is all through qualifying. The writer's reference to himself as "the compiler of still another collection" may be taken as a symptom of his nervous self-consciousness. His reaction to his nervousness is withdrawal.

The paragraph I have quoted is followed by a sentence beginning 10 "It is hoped that this book may be welcome for three main reasons. . . ." It is to be wondered who's doing the hoping. Could it be by any chance the author himself? Is there then some good reason why he shouldn't say so? This man seems to be running scared.

The major fault in modern prose generally is Stuffiness. . . . For 11 most people, . . . in most situations, in the writing of everyday serious expository prose, it is the Stuffy voice that gets in the way. The reason it gets in the way, I submit, is that the writer is scared. If this is an age of anxiety, one way we react to our anxiety is to withdraw into omniscient and multisyllabic detachment where nobody can get us.

No book . . . can remove a person's anxiety for him. But it may be 12 that, through a study of style, one might remove some *symptoms* of anxiety from one's prose. Therefore it may not be utterly useless to offer a little Practical Advice, most of it fairly obvious, for avoiding the symptoms of Stuffiness. To follow such advice may amount to little more than taking aspirin: it may reduce the headache without touching the anxiety. And yet, if anxiety is found in the style of our language, perhaps changing our style may be the best thing we can do. In any case, here are some Rules, deduced from this study, for avoiding the Stuffy voice. . . .

How to Avoid Being Stuffy

1. Make about two-thirds of your total vocabulary monosyllabic; keep words of three syllables or more down to under 20 percent.
2. Try making some of the subjects of your verbs *people*, not neuter nouns.
3. Manage a *finite verb* about every ten words, on the average. (Which is more than that sentence does.)
4. Don't overuse the *passive voice*. (But don't avoid it altogether either.)

5. Keep down the *noun adjuncts.*

6. Keep the average length of *subordinate clauses* down to ten words or so, and see to it that the total proportion of subordinate clauses runs to no more than a third of the whole.

7. Most marks of *punctuation* (except commas and semicolons) serve to lighten tone. Consider question marks, parentheses, italics, dashes, and of course exclamations.

8. Don't *interrupt* subject and verb with intervening subordinate constructions and modifiers.

9. If really desperate, try a *contraction* or two, or a *fragment* (verbless sentence).

10. Whatever you do, *don't obey all these rules at once,* for to do so would be to emerge with something disastrously cute, probably on the Sweet side. The careful writer, in fact, carefully *dis*obeys some of these rules, precisely to avoid the pose of sickly Sweetness. He includes a passive verb, now and then, a lengthy subordinate clause, an elegant interruption between subject and verb. Perhaps his skill in making such choices is what we mean by a *balanced style.*

It remains to say a word about the moral side of rhetoric. The three 13 styles I have been trying to describe can be called ways of making believe. Any style, any way of thinking, can be regarded as a make-believe performance, and it is always possible to take comfort by distinguishing between the performance on the one hand and the Real Person that stands behind all the play-acting on the other. That's not me, that's just my voice of the moment. But such a distinction breaks down very soon; even in the writing of fiction . . . it produces difficulties. And in the course of our day-to-day lives, we have to live with the effects of our performances. The voices I choose are mine, my responsibility, and the belief I own up to is the make-believe I have made. Serious play-acting. The world is not a stage, nor ever was.

QUESTIONS AND IDEAS FOR DISCUSSION

1. You may need to review some grammatical terms in a writing handbook in order to benefit from Gibson's advice in writing your argumentative essays. If you can, give an example of each of the following, or look up the terms and *then* give examples:

- finite verb
- passive voice
- noun adjunct
- subordinate clause

2. According to Gibson, verbs dramatically affect style. Why are passive verbs "stuffy"? Why does a lively prose style typically have more independent clauses than dependent clauses? *Why* are verbs so important, anyway?

3. Gibson argues that stuffy writing occurs because "the writer is scared" (paragraph 10). Do you agree? Discuss, with specific examples if possible.

4. Find an example of a serious argumentative passage (perhaps a paragraph in length) in one of your assigned texts. Photocopy the passage to bring for class discussion. Does the writer avoid "Stuffiness"? If so, how? Give specific examples. If not, rewrite the passage, preserving the meaning while enlivening the prose.

5. Gibson does not address argumentative writing specifically. Can it be argued that argumentative writing is particularly susceptible to stuffiness? Can it be argued that stuffiness is even more destructive to argumentative writing than to "ordinary" expository writing? Why or why not?

THE STRATEGY AT WORK:
ARGUMENTS FAVORING CAPITAL PUNISHMENT

The subject of capital punishment is familiar to anyone who has studied argument or participated in debate—or to anyone who watches the evening news regularly. In some respects, the death penalty is easy to argue because it is so far removed from the experiences of most who argue it. Typically, we examine arguments for and against capital punishment and discuss their relative merits. But, in part because usually we are not personally involved in the issue and in part because we have *a priori* beliefs about justice, rarely do our opinions change as a result of the debate.

So, in this section, you will not be asked to take a position on the death penalty. Nor will you be asked to agree or disagree with the arguments you read (although you certainly may do so). Indeed, you will find that the arguments included here do not differ substantially in their conclusions: All these writers *favor* capital punishment, and often for quite similar reasons. Yet it is unlikely that you will find all the arguments equally engaging or similarly persuasive. You may object to the brusque self-assurance of H. L. Mencken's voice, or you may find him refreshingly blunt. You may find William F. Buckley's summary of Ernest van den Haag's argument lucid and logical, or you may be put off by Buckley's continual list-making (*a*'s and *b*'s, *one*'s and *two*'s). You may regard George Bernard Shaw's frequent irony as masterful or as unpleasantly sarcastic. And Jacques Barzun's scorn— of egotistical killers, of "inconsistent" and "blind" abolitionists, even of psychiatry—may make you uncomfortable or angry. Or perhaps you will find Barzun's graceful turns of phrase and his sharp wit engaging.

What you *will* be asked to do in this section is to consider the ways in which these writers' styles vary and the ways in which their varied styles affect the persuasiveness of their arguments. You will need to note as well the elements of style that appeal to you personally and those that might appeal more to a different audience. You will also need to observe the elements of your own writing style that characterize how you argue an issue. Only by being conscious of your own writing style can you take charge of it so that the voice that speaks through your prose is both authentic and compelling.

The Penalty of Death

H. L. MENCKEN

H. L. Mencken (1880–1956) was a journalist famed for his incisive wit and curmudgeonly outlook. Throughout his long career, he wrote irreverent columns for the *Baltimore Sun* and essays and reviews for many periodicals, including *The Smart Set* (an important magazine in its day in whose pages Mencken became an enormously influential literary critic) and the *New Yorker*. His particular talent, as *New Republic* contributor Alfred Kazin put it, was that "by prodigious skill he managed to insult everyone but his readers." One of Mencken's most important works had little to do with his literary, political, and social criticism. It was a serious scholarly study, *The American Language*, first published in 1919, revised throughout Mencken's life, and still in print. A stirrer of controversy in life, Mencken has continued to be one after death—notably when his private diaries, revealing ethnic and racial prejudices, were published by Knopf in 1990.

"The Penalty of Death" is an essay Mencken wrote in 1926. In it, he responds to the movement of the day to abolish the death penalty. One of Mencken's great talents, as this essay shows, is to compel us to re-examine our assumptions—the questions we thought were settled, the issues we thought we understood. Having done that, he is satisfied. He is not in the least concerned about whether we like him or not.

Of the arguments against capital punishment that issue from up 1
lifters, two are commonly heard most often, to wit:

1. That hanging a man (or frying him or gassing him) is a dreadful business, degrading to those who have to do it and revolting to those who have to witness it.
2. That it is useless, for it does not deter others from the same crime.

The first of these arguments, it seems to me, is plainly too weak to 2 need serious refutation. All it says, in brief, is that the work of the hangman is unpleasant. Granted. But suppose it is? It may be quite necessary to society for all that. There are, indeed, many other jobs that are unpleasant, and yet no one thinks of abolishing them—that of the plumber, that of the soldier, that of the garbage-man, that of the priest hearing confessions, that of the sand-hog, and so on. Moreover, what evidence is there that any actual hangman complains of his work? I have heard none. On the contrary, I have known many who delighted in their ancient art, and practised it proudly.

In the second argument of the abolitionists there is rather more 3 force, but even here, I believe, the ground under them is shaky. Their fundamental error consists in assuming that the whole aim of punishing criminals is to deter other (potential) criminals—that we hang or electrocute A simply in order to so alarm B that he will not kill C. This, I believe, is an assumption which confuses a part with the whole. Deterence, obviously, is *one* of the aims of punishment, but it is surely not the only one. On the contrary, there are at least half a dozen, and some are probably quite as important. At least one of them, practically considered, is *more* important. Commonly, it is described as revenge, but revenge is really not the word for it. I borrow a better term from the late Aristotle: *katharsis*. *Katharsis*, so used, means a salubrious discharge of emotions, a healthy letting off of steam. A school-boy, disliking his teacher, deposits a tack upon the pedagogical chair; the teacher jumps and the boy laughs. This is *katharsis*. What I contend is that one of the prime objects of all judicial punishments is to afford the same grateful relief (*a*) to the immediate victims of the criminal punished, and (*b*) to the general body of moral and timorous men.

These persons, and particularly the first group, are concerned 4 only indirectly with deterring other criminals. The thing they crave primarily is the satisfaction of seeing the criminal actually before them suffer as he made them suffer. What they want is the peace of mind that goes with the feeling that accounts are squared. Until they get that satisfaction they are in a state of emotional tension, and hence unhappy. The instant they get it they are comfortable. I do not argue that this yearning is noble; I simply argue that it is almost universal among human beings. In the face of injuries that are unimportant and can be borne without damage it may yield to higher impulses; that is to say, it may yield to what is called Christian charity. But when the injury is serious, Christianity is adjourned, and even saints reach for their sidearms. It is plainly asking too much of human nature to expect it to conquer so natural an impulse. A keeps a store and has a bookkeeper, B. B steals $700, employs it in playing at dice or bingo, and is cleaned out. What is A to do? Let B go? If he does so he will be unable to sleep at night. The sense of injury, of injustice, of frustration will haunt him like pruritus. So he turns B over to the police, and they hustle B to prison. Thereafter A can sleep. More, he has pleasant dreams. He pictures B chained to the wall of a dungeon a hundred feet underground, devoured by rats and scorpions. It is so agreeable that it makes him forget his $700. He has got his *katharsis*.

This same thing precisely takes place on a larger scale when there 5 is a crime which destroys a whole community's sense of security. Every law-abiding citizen feels menaced and frustrated until the criminals have been struck down—until the communal capacity to get even with them, and more than even, has been dramatically demonstrated. Here, manifestly, the business of deterring others is no more than an afterthought. The main thing is to destroy the concrete scoundrels whose act has alarmed everyone, and thus made everyone unhappy. Until they are brought to book that unhappiness continues; when the law has been executed upon them there is a sigh of relief. In other words, there is *katharsis*.

I know of no public demand for the death penalty for ordinary 6 crimes, even for ordinary homicides. Its infliction would shock all men of normal decency of feeling. But for crimes involving the deliberate and inexcusable taking of human life, by men openly defiant of all civilized order—for such crimes it seems, to nine men out of ten, a just and proper punishment. Any lesser penalty leaves them feeling that the criminal has got the better of society—that he is free to add insult to injury by laughing. That feeling can be dissipated only by a recourse to *katharsis*, the invention of the aforesaid Aristotle. It is more effectively and economically achieved, as human nature now is, by wafting the criminal to realms of bliss.

The real objection to capital punishment doesn't lie against the 7 actual extermination of the condemned, but against our brutal American habit of putting it off so long. After all, every one of us must die soon or late, and a murderer, it must be assumed, is one who makes that sad fact the cornerstone of his metaphysic. But it is one thing to die, and quite another thing to lie for long months and even years under the shadow of death. No sane man would choose such a finish. All of us, despite the Prayer Book, long for a swift and unexpected end. Unhappily, a murderer, under the irrational American system, is tortured for what, to him, must seem a whole series of eternities. For months on end he sits in prison while his lawyers carry on their idiotic buffoonery with writs, injunctions, mandamuses[1], and appeals. In order to get his money (or that of his friends) they have to feed him with hope. Now and then, by the imbecility of a judge or some trick of juridic science, they actually justify it. But let us say that, his money all gone, they finally throw up their hands. Their client is now ready for the rope or the chair. But he must still wait for months before it fetches him.

That wait, I believe, it horribly cruel. I have seen more than one 8 man sitting in the death-house, and I don't want to see any more. Worse, it is wholly useless. Why should he wait at all? Why not hang him the day after the last court dissipates his last hope? Why torture him as not even cannibals would torture their victims? The common answer is that he must have time to make his peace with God. But how long does that take? It may be accomplished, I believe, in two hours quite as comfortably as in two years. There are, indeed, no temporal limitations upon God. He could forgive a whole herd of murderers in a millionth of a second. More, it has been done.

QUESTIONS AND IDEAS FOR DISCUSSION

1.   What does the very short first paragraph lead us to expect from this essay in terms of style and content?

2.   How does Mencken organize his essay? Is this organization effective for the purposes of his argument? Explain.

3.   Explain how the concept of *katharis* figures in Mencken's reasoning. Toward what stylistic effect does the Greek term also work in the essay?

4.   How would Walker Gibson characterize Mencken's style? On what basis?

5.   Mencken's final argument is for *swift* execution of death penalties. But some might regard his last paragraph as enigmatic. Explain it. The conclusion is as abrupt as the beginning of the essay. Does Mencken's conclusion mar the style or weaken the argument? Why, or why not?

---

[1] Mandamus: A judicial writ compelling the performance of some public duty by a lower court, corporation, or public official. [Ed.]

Capital Punishment

WILLIAM F. BUCKLEY, JR.

William F. Buckley, Jr., is a well-known conservative political com-
mentator who founded the *National Review* and edited it from 1955
until 1990. He has hosted the PBS weekly program "Firing Line"
since 1966. In addition, he is a syndicated newspaper columnist ("On
the Right") and novelist. His novels include *High Jinx* (1986) and
Mongoose, R.I.P. (1988). In 1989, he wrote *On the Firing Line: The Public
Life of Our Public Figures.* While Buckley is sometimes accused of being
long-winded in speech, his writing is usually airtight: clear and succinct. Certainly, that is true in this essay, an appreciative recapitula-
tion of an argument made by New York University professor Ernest
van den Haag to the House Judiciary Committee. At the time (1972),
the national abolition of the death penalty seemed imminent, and the
issue was hotly debated. Capital punishment was declared unconsti-
tutional by the Supreme Court later that year in *Furman v. Georgia.*
While thirty-five states responded to the Court decision by legislating
the death penalty in their own jurisdictions, no further executions
took place in the United States until that of Gary Gilmore in Utah in
1977.

Compare Buckley's argument to Mencken's as you read: Whose
argument do you find more logically convincing? More persuasive?
Has the writer's style anything to do with your response?

There is national suspense over whether capital punishment is 1
about to be abolished, and the assumption is that when it comes it will
come from the Supreme Court. Meanwhile, (a) the prestigious State
Supreme Court of California has interrupted executions, giving constitutional reasons for doing so; (b) the death wings are overflowing with
convicted prisoners; (c) executions are a remote memory; and—for the
first time in years—(d) the opinion polls show that there is sentiment
for what amounts to the restoration of capital punishment.

The case for abolition is popularly known. The other case less so, 2
and (without wholeheartedly endorsing it) I give it as it was given
recently to the Committee of the Judiciary of the House of Representatives by Professor Ernest van den Haag, under whose thinking cap
groweth no moss. Mr. van den Haag, a professor of social philosophy
at New York University, ambushed the most popular arguments of the
abolitionists, taking no prisoners.

(1) The business about the poor and the black suffering exces- 3
sively from capital punishment is no argument against capital punishment. It is an argument against the *administration* of justice, not against
the penalty. Any punishment can be unfairly or unjustly applied. Go
ahead and reform the processes by which capital punishment is inflicted, if you wish; but don't confuse maladministration with the merits
of capital punishment.

(2) The argument that the death penalty is "unusual" is circular. 4
Capital punishment continues on the books of a majority of states, the
people continue to sanction the concept of capital punishment, and
indeed capital sentences are routinely handed down. What has made
capital punishment "unusual" is that the courts and, primarily, gover-
nors have intervened in the process so as to collaborate in the frustration of the execution of the law. To argue that capital punishment is
unusual, when in fact it has been made unusual by extra-legislative
authority, is an argument to expedite, not eliminate, executions.

(3) Capital punishment is cruel. That is a historical judgment. But 5
the Constitution suggests that what must be proscribed as cruel is (a) a
particularly painful way of inflicting death, or (b) a particularly un-
deserved death; and the death penalty, as such, offends neither of
these criteria and cannot therefore be regarded as objectively "cruel."

Viewed the other way, the question is whether capital punish- 6
ment can be regarded as useful, and the question of deterrence arises.

(4) Those who believe that the death penalty does not intensify 7
the disinclination to commit certain crimes need to wrestle with statistics that disclose that, in fact, it can't be proved that *any* punishment
does that to any particular crime. One would rationally suppose that
two years in jail would cut the commission of a crime if not exactly by
100 percent more than a penalty of one year in jail, at least that it would
further discourage crime to a certain extent. The proof is unavailing.
On the other hand, the statistics, although ambiguous, do not show
either (a) that capital punishment net discourages; or (b) that capital
punishment fails net to discourage. "The absence of proof for the
additional deterrent effect of the death penalty must not be confused
with the presence of proof for the absence of this effect."

The argument that most capital crimes are crimes of passion com- 8
mitted by irrational persons is no argument against the death penalty,
because it does not reveal how many crimes might, but for the death
penalty, have been committed by rational persons who are now deterred.

And the clincher. (5) Since we do not know for certain whether or 9
not the death penalty adds deterrence, we have in effect the choice of
two risks.

Risk One: If we execute convicted murderers without thereby 10
deterring prospective murderers beyond the deterrence that could
have been achieved by life imprisonment, we may have vainly sacrificed the life of the convicted murderer.

Risk Two: If we fail to execute a convicted murderer whose execu- 11
tion might have deterred an indefinite number of prospective murderers, our failure sacrifices an indefinite number of victims of future
murderers.

"If we had certainty, we would not have risks. We do not have 12
certainty. If we have risks—and we do—better to risk the life of the
convicted man than risk the life of an indefinite number of innocent
victims who might survive if he were executed."

QUESTIONS AND IDEAS FOR DISCUSSION

1.   Does Buckley here argue in favor of the death penalty or against its
abolition? Or does he argue for both? What is his thesis?

2.   What particular elements does Buckley's style share with Mencken's? In what ways are the two quite different? Give specific examples.

3.   Buckley's argument largely summarizes another person's. To
what extent does that fact make analyzing Buckley's own style more
difficult? To what extent is that fact not a problem in a stylistic analysis? Explain.

4.   In paragraph 4, Buckley writes, "The argument that the death
penalty is 'unusual' is circular." What does he mean by this claim? Is
he right? Give an original illustration of a circular argument.

5.   Choose three or four phrases (or sentences) that Buckley might
have written more simply, and revise them. For example, you could
try simplifying "the death penalty does not intensify the disinclination
to commit certain crimes" (paragraph 7). If "simpler" is usually considered "better" style, does your phrase sound better than Buckley's?
Why, or why not?

6.   Does the style and conviction of Buckley's essay suffer because the
argument ends in another person's voice—with a quotation? Explain.

Incorrigible Villains
GEORGE BERNARD SHAW

George Bernard Shaw (1856–1950), an Englishman, is acclaimed
today as the chief English-language dramatist of the modern age. He
was also one of the most prolific. In 1925, he was awarded the Nobel
Prize in Literature—and joked that it was because he had not written
a play that year. Although Shaw is best remembered for his plays—
Man and Superman (1905), *Major Barbara* (1905), *Pygmalion* (1913),

Heartbreak House (1920), *Saint Joan* (1923), and many others—he wrote
volumes of literary and political criticism as well. Among these is *The
Crime of Imprisonment* (1922), from which this selection is taken.
Shaw, while totally opposed to imprisonment, favors the death penalty for certain "nuisances and monsters." Compare his style—and
his thesis—to the two preceding arguments.

It will be seen that I am prepared to go to lengths which still seem 1
fantastic as to the possibility of changing a criminal into an honest
man. And I have more faith than most prison chaplains seem to have
in the possibilities of religious conversion. But I cannot add too emphatically that the people who imagine that all criminals can be re-
formed by setting chaplains to preach at them, by giving them pious
books and tracts to read, by separating them from their companions in
crime and locking them up in solitude to reflect on their sins and
repent, are far worse enemies both to the criminal and to Society than
those who face the fact that these are merely additional cruelties which
make their victims worse, or even than those who frankly use them as
a means of "giving them hell." But when this is recognized, and the
bigoted reformers with their sermons, their tracts, their horrors of
separation, silence, and solitude to avoid contamination, are bundled
out of our prisons as nuisances, the problem remains, how are you to
deal with your incorrigibles? Here you have a man who supports
himself by gaining the confidence and affection of lonely women;
seducing them; spending all their money; and then burning them in a
stove or drowning them in a bath. He is "quite an attractive" fellow,
with a genuine taste for women and no taste at all for murder, which is
only his way of getting rid of them when their money is spent and they
are in the way of the next woman. There is no more malice or Sadism
about the final operation than there is about tearing up a letter when it
is done with, and throwing it into the waste paper basket. You electrocute him or hang him or chop his head off. But presently you have to
deal with a man who lives in exactly the same way, but has not
executive force or courage enough to commit murder. He only aban-
dons his victims and turns up in a fresh place with a fresh name. He
generally marries them, as it is easier to seduce them so.

Alongside him you have a married couple united by a passion for 2
cruelty. They amuse themselves by tying their children to the bed-
stead; thrashing them with straps; and branding them with red-hot
pokers. You also have to deal with a man who on the slightest irritation flings his wife under a dray, or smashes a lighted kerosene lamp
into her face. He has been in prison again and again for outbursts of
this kind; and always, within a week of his release, or within a few
hours of it, he has done it again.

Now you cannot get rid of these nuisances and monsters by 3
simply cataloguing them as subthyroidics and superadrenals or the
like. At present you torment them for a fixed period, at the end of
which they are set free to resume their operations with a savage
grudge against the community which has tormented them. That is
stupid. Nothing is gained by punishing people who cannot help themselves, and on whom deterrence is thrown away. Releasing them is
like releasing the tigers from the Zoo to find their next meal in the
nearest children's playing ground.

The most obvious course is to kill them. Some of the popular 4
objections to this may be considered for a moment. Death, it is said, is
irrevocable; and after all, they may turn out to be innocent. But really
you cannot handle criminals on the assumption that they may be
innocent. You are not supposed to handle them at all until you have
convinced yourself by an elaborate trial that they are guilty. Besides,
imprisonment is as irrevocable as hanging. Each is a method of taking
a criminal's life; and when he prefers hanging or suicide to imprisonment for life, as he sometimes does, he says, in effect, that he had
rather you took his life all at once, painlessly, than minute by minute
in long-drawn-out torture. You can give a prisoner a pardon; but you
cannot give him back a moment of his imprisonment. He may accept a
reprieve willingly in the hope of a pardon or an escape or a revolution
or an earthquake or what not; but as you do not mean him to evade his
sentence in any way whatever, it is not for you to take such clutchings
at straws into account.

Another argument against the death penalty for anything short of 5
murder is the practical one of the policeman and the householder,
who plead that if you hang burglars they will shoot to avoid capture on
the ground that they may as well be hanged for a sheep as for a lamb.
But this can be disposed of by pointing out, first, that even under
existing circumstances the burgler occasionally shoots, and, second,
that acquittals, recommendations to mercy, verdicts of manslaughter,
successful pleas of insanity and so forth, already make the death
penalty so uncertain that even red-handed murderers shoot no oftener
than burglars—less often, in fact. This uncertainty would be actually
increased if the death sentence were, as it should be, made applicable
to other criminals than those convicted of wilful murder, and no
longer made compulsory in any case.

Then comes the plea for the sacredness of human life. The State 6
should not set the example of killing, or of clubbing a rioter with a
policeman's baton, or of dropping bombs on a sleeping city, or of
doing many things that States nevertheless have to do. But let us take
the plea on its own ground, which is, fundamentally, that life is the
most precious of all things, and its waste the worst of crimes. We have

already seen that imprisonment does not spare the life of the criminal: it takes it and wastes it in the most cruel way. But there are others to be considered beside the criminal and the citizens who fear him so much that they cannot sleep in peace unless he is locked up. There are the people who have to lock him up, and fetch him his food, and watch him. Why are their lives to be wasted? Warders, and especially ward-resses, are almost as much tied to the prison by their occupation, and by their pensions, which they dare not forfeit by seeking other employment, as the criminals are. If I had to choose between a spell under preventive detention among hardened criminals in Camp Hill and one as warder in an ordinary prison, I think I should vote for Camp Hill. Warders suffer in body and mind from their employment; and if it be true, as our examination seems to prove, that they are doing no good to society, but very active harm, their lives are wasted more completely than those of the criminals; for most criminals are discharged after a few weeks or months; but the warder never escapes until he is superannuated, by which time he is an older gaolbird than any Lifer in the cells.

How then does the case stand with your incurable pathological 7 case of crime? If you treat the life of the criminal as sacred, you find yourself not only taking his life but sacrificing the lives of innocent men and women to keep him locked up. There is no sort of sense or humanity in such a course. The moment we face it frankly we are driven to the conclusion that the community has a right to put a price on the right to live in it. That price must be sufficient self-control to live without wasting and destroying the lives of others, whether by direct attack like a tiger, parasitic exploitation like a leech, or having to be held in a leash with another person at the end of it. Persons lacking such self-control have been thrust out into the sage-brush to wander there until they die of thirst, a cruel and cowardly way of killing them. The dread of clean and wilful killing often leads to evasions of the commandment "Thou shalt not kill" which are far more cruel than its frank violation. It has never been possible to obey it unreservedly, either with men or with animals; and the attempts to keep the letter of it have led to burying vestal virgins and nuns alive, crushing men to death in the press-yard, handing heretics over to the secular arm, and the like, instead of killing them humanely and without any evasion of the heavy responsibility involved. It was a horrible thing to build a vestal virgin into a wall with food and water enough for a day; but to build her into a prison for years as we do, with just enough loathsome food to prevent her from dying, is more than horrible: it is diabolical. If no better alternatives to death can be found than these, then who will not vote for death? If people are fit to live, let them live under decent human conditions. If they are not fit to live, kill them in a decent human way. Is it any wonder that some of us are driven to prescribe the lethal chamber as the solution for the hard cases which are at present made the excuse for dragging all the other cases down to their level, and the only solution that will create a sense of full social responsibility in modern populations?

QUESTIONS AND IDEAS FOR DISCUSSION

1. Shaw opposes imprisonment as being more than inhumane, as being "diabolical." How then does he argue in favor of capital punishment? Does the distinction he draws make sense? Explain.

2. Describe Shaw's style in terms of sentence length and complexity, vocabulary, and figures of speech such as metaphor. In what specific ways does Shaw's style differ from Mencken's or Buckley's?

3. In paragraph 6, Shaw challenges the "sacredness of life" argument against the death penalty. Analyze Shaw's reasoning. Is it sound?

4. Shaw from time to time employs an ironic humor verging on sarcasm. Identify two or three examples. Does this stylistic element make you uncomfortable, or do you find it effective? Comment.

5. Is Shaw's style vivid and his arguments memorable? Or is his style overblown and his arguments confusing? Give reasons for your answer, with specific examples from the text.

In Favor of Capital Punishment
JACQUES BARZUN

Jacques Barzun, a native of France, is an eminent historian and cultural critic, and the author of works ranging from translations of French works and studies of Darwin, Marx, and William James to studies of detective novels. His particular interest is the evolution of the modern mind from 1750 to the present. Barzun spent his long and distinguished academic career at his alma mater, Columbia University, where he was University Professor of History and then Dean of Faculties and Provost. In addition, he is a Fellow of Churchill College, Cambridge University.

The following argument is an excerpt from a longer essay of the same title, first published in the *American Scholar*, the journal of Phi Beta Kappa, in 1962. You will find its argument much the same as the others in this section (one in particular), but—again!—distinctive in its style and emphases. After a rather dry beginning, with the same dispassionate enumerations that appear in some of the other essays, the argument heats up considerably. Notice the frequency of quotations marks, the invented comments and parenthetical remarks that give a conversational quality to this essay: It is as if Barzun's opponents sat across from him as he wrote.

I readily concede at the outset that present ways of dealing out 1 capital punishment are as revolting as Mr. Koestler says in his harrowing volume, *Hanged by the Neck.* Like many of our prisons, our modes of execution should change. But this objection to barbarity does not mean that capital punishment—or rather, judicial homicide—should not go on. The illicit jump we find here, on the threshold of the inquiry, is characteristic of the abolitionist and must be disallowed at every point. Let us bear in mind the possibility of devising a painless, sudden and dignified death, and see whether its administration is justifiable.

The four main arguments advanced against the death penalty are: 2 1. punishment for crime is a primitive idea rooted in revenge; 2. capital punishment does not deter; 3. judicial error being possible, taking life is an appalling risk; 4. a civilized state, to deserve its name, must uphold, not violate, the sanctity of human life.

I entirely agree with the first pair of propositions, which is why, a 3 moment ago, I replaced the term capital punishment with "judicial homicide." The uncontrollable brute whom I want put out of the way is not to be punished for his misdeeds, nor used as an example or a warning; he is to be killed for the protection of others, like the wolf that escaped not long ago in a Connecticut suburb. No anger, vindictiveness or moral conceit need preside over the removal of such dangers. But a man's inability to control his violent impulses or to imagine the fatal consequences of his acts should be a presumptive reason for his elimination from society. This generality covers drunken driving and teen-age racing on public highways, as well as incurable obsessive violence; it might be extended (as I shall suggest later) to other acts that destroy, precisely, the moral basis of civilization.

But why kill? I am ready to believe the statistics tending to show 4 that the prospect of his own death does not stop the murderer. For one thing he is often a blind egotist, who cannot conceive the possibility of his own death. For another, detection would have to be infallible to deter the more imaginative who, although afraid, think they can escape discovery. Lastly, as Shaw long ago pointed out, hanging the wrong man will deter as effectively as hanging the right one. So, once again, why kill? If I agree that moral progress means an increasing respect for human life, how can I oppose abolition?

I do so because on this subject of human life, which is to me the 5 heart of the controversy, I find the abolitionist inconsistent, narrow or blind. The propaganda for abolition speaks in hushed tones of the sanctity of human life, as if the mere statement of it as an absolute should silence all opponents who have any moral sense. But most of the abolitionists belong to nations that spend half their annual income on weapons of war and that honor research to perfect means of killing. These good people vote without a qualm for the political parties that quite sensibly arm their country to the teeth. The West today does not seem to be the time or place to invoke the absolute sanctity of human life. As for the clergymen in the movement, we may be sure from the experience of two previous world wars that they will bless our arms and pray for victory when called upon, the sixth commandment notwithstanding.

"Oh, but we mean the sanctity of life *within* the nation!" Very well: 6 is the movement then campaigning also against the principle of self-defense? Absolute sanctity means letting the cutthroat have his sweet will of you, even if you have a poker handy to bash him with, for you might kill. And again, do we hear any protest against the police firing at criminals on the street—mere bank robbers usually—and doing this, often enough, with an excited marksmanship that misses the artist and hits the bystander? The absolute sanctity of human life is, for the abolitionist, a slogan rather than a considered proposition.

Yet it deserves examination, for upon our acceptance or rejection 7 of it depend such other highly civilized possibilities as euthanasia and seemly suicide. The inquiring mind also wants to know, why the sanctity of *human* life alone? My tastes do not run to household pets, but I find something less than admirable in the uses to which we put animals—in zoos, laboratories and space machines—without the excuse of the ancient law, "Eat or be eaten."

It should moreover be borne in mind that this argument about 8 sanctity applies—or would apply—to about ten persons a year in Great Britain and to between fifty and seventy-five in the United States. These are the average numbers of those executed in recent years. The count by itself should not, of course, affect our judgment of the principle: one life spared or forfeited is as important, morally, as a hundred thousand. But it should inspire a comparative judgment: there are hundreds and indeed thousands whom, in our concern with the horrors of execution, we forget: on the one hand, the victims of violence; on the other, the prisoners in our jails.

The victims are easy to forget. Social science tends steadily to mark 9 a preference for the troubled, the abnormal, the problem case. Whether it is poverty, mental disorder, delinquency or crime, the "patient material" monopolizes the interest of increasing groups of people among the most generous and learned. Psychiatry and moral liberalism go together; the application of law as we have known it is thus coming to be regarded as an historic prelude to social work, which may replace it entirely. Modern literature makes the most of this same outlook, caring only for the disturbed spirit, scorning as bourgeois those who pay their way and do *not* stab their friends. All the while the determinism of natural science reinforces the assumption that society causes its own evils. A French jurist, for example, says that in order to understand crime we must first brush aside all ideas of Responsibility. He means the criminal's and takes for granted that of society. The murderer kills because reared in a broken home or, conversely, because at an early age he witnessed his parents making love. Out of such cases, which make pathetic reading in the literature of modern criminology, is born the abolitionist's state of mind: we dare not kill those we are beginning to understand so well.

If, moreover, we turn to the accounts of the crimes committed by 10 these unfortunates, who are the victims? Only dull ordinary people going about their business. We are sorry, of course, but they do not interest science on its march. Balancing, for example, the sixty to seventy criminals executed annually in the United States, there were the seventy to eighty housewives whom George Cvek robbed, raped and usually killed during the months of a career devoted to proving his virility. "It is too bad." Cvek alone seems instructive, even though one of the law officers who helped track him down quietly remarks: "As to the extent that his villainies disturbed family relationships, or how many women are still haunted by the specter of an experience they have never disclosed to another living soul, these questions can only lend themselves to sterile conjecture."

The remote results are beyond our ken, but it is not idle to specu- 11 late about those whose death by violence fills the daily two inches at the back of respectable newspapers—the old man sunning himself on a park bench and beaten to death by four hoodlums, the small children abused and strangled, the middle-aged ladies on a hike assaulted and killed, the family terrorized by a released or escaped lunatic, the half-dozen working people massacred by the sudden maniac, the boatload of persons dispatched by the skipper, the mindless assaults upon schoolteachers and shopkeepers by the increasing horde of dedicated killers in our great cities. Where does the sanctity of life begin?

It is all very well to say that many of these killers are themselves 12 "children," that is, minors. Doubtless a nine-year-old mind is housed in that 150 pounds of unguided muscle. Grant, for argument's sake, that the misdeed is "the fault of society," trot out the broken home and the slum environment. The question then is, What shall we do, not in the Utopian city of tomorrow, but here and now? The "scientific" means of cure are more than uncertain. The apparatus of detention only increases the killer's antisocial animus. Reformatories and mental hospitals are full and have an understandable bias toward discharging their inmates. Some of these are indeed "cured"—so long as they stay under a rule. The stress of the social free-for-all throws them back on their violent modes of self-expression. At that point I agree that society has failed—twice: it has twice failed the victims, whatever may be its guilt toward the killer.

As in all great questions, the moralist must choose, and choosing 13 has a price. I happen to think that if a person of adult body has not been endowed with adequate controls against irrationally taking the life of another, that person must be judicially, painlessly, regretfully killed before that mindless body's horrible automation repeats.

QUESTIONS AND IDEAS FOR DISCUSSION

1. Describe the person Barzun creates in this essay. What is your reaction to it, and why?

2. Is Barzun's argument emotionally persuasive? If so, what features of style contribute to its persuasiveness? Is it logically convincing? Why, or why not?

3. How did bank robbers and lab animals find their way into this argument? Evaluate Barzun's use of analogy to create vivid images. Do these images support his argument and enhance his style? Comment.

ADDITIONAL MATERIAL FOR ANALYSIS AND ARGUMENT: DEFENSES OF THE CONDEMNED

As rare as it is to hear a series of arguments all favoring capital punishment, it is even rarer, when we encounter essays on the subject, to hear anything from the people most personally and directly involved: those who have been condemned to death. And yet, from Joan of Arc to Sidney Carton, some of the most eloquent and persuasive speeches in history and in literature have come from people facing execution. Here, for your consideration of their eloquent and very distinct styles, are three famous arguments by three famous prisoners: Socrates, Saint Paul, and Bartolomeo Vanzetti.

The Apology of Socrates

PLATO

Plato (427?–347? B.C.) was a pupil of Socrates, and the two were among the greatest philosophers of the ancient world. While no writings from Socrates are known to exist, all of Plato's known works have been preserved, including thirty-five dialogues in which Socrates is featured prominently. How much of the philosophy reflected in the dialogues is Socrates's, and how much Plato's, is the subject of scholarly speculation. Plato taught the objective reality of "Ideas." His explanation in the "parable of the cave" in the *Republic* is among his most famous writings. The selection reprinted here is from the *Apology of Socrates,* which records Socrates's defense against charges of impiety and the corruption of youth, which had led to his death sentence. Anytus, whom Socrates mentions several times, is one of his three principal accusers.

Some one will say: And are you not ashamed, Socrates, of a course 1 of life which is likely to bring you to an untimely end? To him I may fairly answer: There you are mistaken: a man who is good for anything ought not to calculate the chance of living or dying; he ought only to consider whether in doing anything he is doing right or wrong— acting the part of a good man or of a bad. Whereas, upon your view, the heroes who fell at Troy were not good for much, and the son of Thetis above all, who altogether despised danger in comparison with disgrace; and when he was so eager to slay Hector, his goddess mother said to him, that if he avenged his companion Patroclus, and slew Hector, he would die himself— "Fate," she said, in these or the like words, "waits for you next after Hector"; he, receiving this warning, utterly despised danger and death, and instead of fearing them, feared rather to live in dishonor, and not to avenge his friend. "Let me die forthwith," he replies, "and be avenged of my enemy, rather than abide here by the beaked ships, a laughing stock and a burden of the earth." Had Achilles any thought of death and danger? For wherever a man's place is, whether the place which he has chosen or that in which he has been placed by a commander, there he ought to remain in the hour of danger; he should not think of death or of anything but of disgrace. And this, O men of Athens, is a true saying.

Strange, indeed, would be my conduct, O men of Athens, if I, 2 who, when I was ordered by the generals whom you chose to command me at Potidaea and Amphipolis and Delium, remained where they placed me, like any other man, facing death—if now, when, as I conceive and imagine, God orders me to fulfil the philosopher's mission of searching into myself and other men, I were to desert my post through fear of death, or any other fear; that would indeed be strange, and I might justly be arraigned in court for denying the existence of the gods, if I disobeyed the oracle because I was afraid of death, fancying that I was wise when I was not wise. For the fear of death is indeed the pretense of wisdom, and not real wisdom, being a pretense of knowing the unknown; and no one knows whether death, which men in their fear apprehend to be the greatest evil, may not be the greatest good. Is not this ignorance of a disgraceful sort, the ignorance which is the conceit that a man knows what he does not know? And in this respect only I believe myself to differ from men in general, and may perhaps claim to be wiser than they are:—that whereas I know but little of the world below, I do not suppose that I know: but I do know that injustice and disobedience to a better, whether God or man, is evil and dishonorable, and I will never fear or avoid a possible good rather than a certain evil. And therefore if you let me go now, and are not convinced by Anytus, who said that since I had been prosecuted I must be put to death; (or if not that I ought never to have been prosecuted at all); and that if I escape now, your sons will all be utterly ruined by listening to my words—if you say to me, Socrates, this time we will not mind Anytus, and you shall be let off, but upon one condition, that you are not to enquire and speculate in this way any more, and that if you are caught doing so again you shall die;—if this was the condition on which you let me go, I should reply: Men of Athens, I honor and love you; but I shall obey God rather than you, and while I have life and strength I shall never cease from the practice and teaching of philosophy, exhorting any one whom I meet and saying to him after my manner: You, my friend,—a citizen of the great and mighty and wise city of Athens,—are you not ashamed of heaping up the greatest amount of money and honor and reputation, and caring so little about wisdom and truth and the greatest improvement of the soul, which you never regard or heed at all? And if the person with whom I am arguing, says: Yes, but I do care; then I do not leave him or let him go at once; but I proceed to interrogate and examine and cross-examine him, and if I think that he has no virtue in him, but only says that he has, I reproach him with undervaluing the greater, and overvaluing the less. And I shall repeat the same words to every one whom I meet, young and old, citizen and alien, but especially to the citizens, inasmuch as they are my brethren. For know that this is the command of God; and I believe that no greater good has ever happened in the State than my service to the God. For I do nothing but go about persuading you all, old and young alike, not to take thought for your persons or your properties, but first and chiefly to care about the greatest improvement of the soul. I tell you that virtue is not given by money, but that from virtue comes money and every other good of man, public as well as private. This is my teaching, and if this is the doctrine which corrupts the youth, I am a mischievous person. But if any one says that this is not my teaching, he is speaking an untruth. Wherefore, O men of Athens, I say to you, do as Anytus bids or not as Anytus bids, and either acquit me or not; but whichever you do, understand that I shall never alter my ways, not even if I have to die many times.

Men of Athens, do not interrupt, but hear me; there was an 3 understanding between us that you should hear me to the end: I have something more to say, at which you may be inclined to cry out; but I believe that to hear me will be good for you, and therefore I beg that you will not cry out. I would have you know, that if you kill such an one as I am, you will injure yourselves more than you will injure me. Nothing will injure me, not Meletus nor yet Anytus—they cannot, for a bad man is not permitted to injure a better than himself. I do not deny that Anytus may, perhaps, kill him, or drive him into exile, or deprive him of civil rights; and he may imagine, and others may imagine, that he is inflicting a great injury upon him; but there I do not agree. For the evil of doing as he is doing—the evil of unjustly taking away the life of another—is greater far.

And now, Athenians, I am not going to argue for my own sake, as 4 you may think, but for yours, that you may not sin against the God by condemning me, who am his gift to you. For if you kill me you will not easily find a successor to me, who, if I may use such a ludicrous figure of speech, am a sort of gadfly, given to the State by God; and the State is a great and noble steed who is tardy in his motions owing to his very size, and requires to be stirred into life. I am that gadfly which God has attached to the State, and all day long and in all places am always fastening upon you, arousing and persuading and reproaching you. You will not easily find another like me, and therefore I would advise you to spare me. I dare say that you may feel out of temper (like a person who is suddenly awakened from sleep), and you think that you might easily strike me dead as Anytus advises, and then you would sleep on for the remainder of your lives, unless God in his care of you sent you another gadfly. When I say that I am given to you by God, the proof of my mission is this:—if I had been like other men, I should not have neglected all my own concerns or patiently seen the neglect of them during all these years, and have been doing yours, coming to you individually like a father or elder brother, exhorting you to regard virtue; such conduct, I say, would be unlike human nature. If I had gained anything, or if my exhortations had been paid, there would have been some sense in my doing so; but now, as you will perceive, not even the impudence of my accusers dares to say that I have ever exacted or sought pay of any one; of that they have no witness. And I have a sufficient witness to the truth of what I say—my poverty.

Some one may wonder why I go about in private giving advice and   5 busying myself with the concerns of others, but do not venture to come forward in public and advise the State. I will tell you why. You have heard me speak at sundry times and in divers places of an oracle or sign which comes to me, and is the divinity which Meletus ridicules in the indictment. This sign, which is a kind of voice, first began to come to me when I was a child; it always forbids but never commands me to do anything which I am going to do. This is what deters me from being a politician. And rightly, as I think. For I am certain, O men of Athens, that if I had engaged in politics, I should have perished long ago, and done no good either to you or to myself. And do not be offended at my telling you the truth: for the truth is, that no man who goes to war with you or any other multitude, honestly striving against the many lawless and unrighteous deeds which are done in a State, will save his life; he who will fight for the right, if he would live even for a brief space, must have a private station and not a public one.

Speech to King Agrippa

SAINT PAUL

Paul (a.d. 1?–67?), one of the earliest Christian missionaries and author of several books of the New Testament, was born a Jew in Tarsus and originally named Saul. Before his conversion to Christianity, he was a strong opponent of the Christian religion. Paul speaks here at a moment of crisis. Like Socrates, he faces death (much like Socrates, for endangering public order through his teachings and fostering treason against the imperial cult). But unlike Socrates, Paul has not yet exhausted his appeals. Because he is a Roman citizen as well as a Jew, Paul has appealed his case to Rome. Ultimately, he will be exonerated and freed, not to die until several years later in a persecution under Nero. This passage, Acts 26.1–28, is taken from the seventeenth-century King James translation of the New Testament. The paragraph breaks are this editor's; neither the original Greek texts nor the King James translation marks paragraphs.

Then Agrippa said unto Paul, "Thou art permitted to speak for 1 thyself." Then Paul stretched forth the hand, and answered for himself:

"I think myself happy, King Agrippa, because I shall answer for 2 myself this day before thee concerning all the things of which I am accused of the Jews, especially because I know thee to be expert in all customs and questions which are among the Jews; wherefore, I beseech thee to hear me patiently.

"My manner of life from my youth, which was at the first among 3 mine own nation at Jerusalem, know all the Jews, who knew me from the beginning, if they would testify, that after the strictest sect of our religion I lived a Pharisee.

"And now I stand and am judged for the hope of the promise 4 made of God unto our fathers, unto which promise our twelve tribes, earnestly serving God day and night, hope to come. For which hope's sake, King Agrippa, I am accused by the Jews.

"Why should it be thought a thing incredible with you, that God 5 should raise the dead?

"I verily thought within myself, that I ought to do many things 6 contrary to the name of Jesus of Nazareth, which thing I also did in Jerusalem; and many of the saints did I shut up in prison, having received authority from the chief priests. And when they were put to death, I gave my voice against them. And I punished them often in every synagogue, and compelled them to blaspheme; and being exceedingly mad against them, I persecuted them even unto foreign cities.

"Whereupon, as I went to Damascus with authority and commis- 7 sion from the chief priests, at midday, O king, I saw in the way a light from heaven, above the brightness of the sun, shining round about me and them who journeyed with me. And when we were all fallen to the earth, I heard a voice speaking unto me, and saying in the Hebrew tongue, 'Saul, Saul, why persecutest thou me? It is hard for thee to kick against the goads.'

"And I said, 'Who art thou, Lord?'   8

"And he said, 'I am Jesus, whom thou persecutest. But rise, and 9 stand upon thy feet; for I have appeared unto thee for this purpose, to make thee a minister and a witness both of these things which thou hast seen, and of those things in which I will appear to thee; delivering thee from the people, and from the Gentiles, unto whom now I send thee, to open their eyes, and to turn them from darkness to light, and from the power of Satan unto God, that they may receive forgiveness of sins, and inheritance among them who are sanctified by faith that is in me.'

"Whereupon, O King Agrippa, I was not disobedient unto the 10 heavenly vision, but showed first unto them of Damascus, and at Jerusalem, and throughout all the borders of Judaea, and then to the Gentiles, that they should repent and turn to God, and do works fit for repentance. For these causes the Jews caught me in the temple, and went about to kill me.

"Having, therefore, obtained help from God, I continue unto this 11 day, witnessing both to small and great, saying no other things than those which the prophets and Moses did say should come: That Christ should suffer, and that he should be the first and should rise from the dead, and should show light unto the people, and to the Gentiles."

And as he thus spoke for himself, Festus said with a loud voice, 12 "Paul, thou art beside thyself; much learning doth make thee mad."

But he said, "I am not mad, most noble Festus, but speak forth the 13 words of truth and soberness. For the king knoweth of these things, before whom also I speak freely; for I am persuaded that none of these things are hidden from him; for this thing was not done in a corner.

"King Agrippa, believest thou the prophets? I know that thou 14 believest."

Then Agrippa said unto Paul, "Almost thou persuadest me to be a 15 Christian."

Speech to the Court

BARTOLOMEO VANZETTI

Bartolomeo Vanzetti (1888–1927), an Italian immigrant fish peddler in Massachusetts, was a defendant in one of the most famous trials of the twentieth century. Along with codefendant Nicola Sacco, Vanzetti was convicted in 1921 of the armed payroll robbbery and murder of Frederick Parmenter, the paymaster of a South Braintree, Massachusetts, shoe factory, and Alessandro Berardelli, a bodyguard. A week earlier, there had been a similar, failed attempt to rob the paymaster of a shoe factory in nearby Bridgewater (to which Vanzetti here refers, and in which he was implicated). Because Sacco and Vanzetti were Italian anarchists, many people thought—both at the time and in the decades since—that the two were unjustly accused of the South Braintree crimes and unfairly convicted. The case stirred a furor of international interest from the beginning; entire books have been devoted to it and to the question of the defendants' guilt or innocence.

Before the sentencing, on April 9, 1927, Vanzetti spoke in his own defense, as excerpted here. His eloquence was to no avail: Sacco and Vanzetti were executed on August 23, 1927.

What I say is that I am innocent, not only of the Braintree crime, 1 but also of the Bridgewater crime. That I am not only innocent of these two crimes, but in all my life I have never stole and I have never killed and I have never spilled blood. That is what I want to say. And it is not all. Not only am I innocent of these two crimes, not only in all my life I have never stole, never killed, never spilled blood, but I have struggled all my life, since I began to reason, to eliminate crime from the earth.

Everybody that knows these two arms knows very well that I did 2 not need to go in between the street and kill a man to take the money. I can live with my two arms and live well. But besides that, I can live even without work with my arm for other people. I have had plenty of chance to live independently and to live what the world conceives to be a higher life than not to gain our bread with the sweat of our brow. . . .

Well, I want to reach a little point farther, and it is this,—that not 3 only have I not been trying to steal in Bridgewater, not only have I not been in Braintree to steal and kill and have never steal or kill or spilt blood in all my life, not only have I struggled hard against crimes, but I have refused myself the commodity or glory of life, the pride of life of a good position, because in my consideration it is not right to exploit man. I have refused to go in business because I understand that business is a speculation on profit upon certain people that must depend upon the business man, and I do not consider that that is right and therefore I refuse to do that.

Now, I should say that I am not only innocent of all these things, 4 not only have I never committed a real crime in my life—though some sins but not crimes—not only have I struggled all my life to eliminate crimes, the crimes that the official law and the official moral condemns, but also the crime that the official moral and the official law sanctions and sanctifies,—the exploitation and the oppression of the man by the man, and if there is a reason why I am here as a guilty man, if there is a reason why you in a few minutes can doom me, it is this reason and none else.

I beg your pardon. (Referring to paper) There is the more good 5 man I ever cast my eyes upon since I lived, a man that will last and will grow always more near and more dear to the people, as far as into the heart of the people, so long as admiration for goodness and for sacrifice will last. I mean Eugene Debs. I will say that even a dog that killed the chickens would not have found an American jury to convict it with the proof that the Commonwealth produced against us. That man was not with me in Plymouth or with Sacco where he was on the day of the crime. You can say that it is arbitrary, what we are saying, that he is good and he applied to the other his own goodness, that he is incapable of crime, and he believed that everybody is incapable of crime.

Well, it may be like that but it is not, it could be like that but it is 6 not, and that man has a real experience of court, of prison and of jury. Just because he want the world a little better he was persecuted and slandered from his boyhood to his old age, and indeed he was murdered by the prison. He know, and not only he but every man of understanding in the world, not only in his country but also in the other countries, men that we have provided a certain amount of a record of the times, they all still stick with us, the flower of mankind of Europe, the better writers, the greatest thinkers of Europe, have pleaded in our favor. The scientists, the greatest scientists, the greatest statesmen of Europe, have pleaded in our favor. The people of foreign nations have pleaded in our favor.

Is it possible that only a few on the jury, only two or three men, 7 who would condemn their mother for worldly honor and for earthly fortune; is it possible that they are right against what the world, the whole world has say it is wrong and that I know that it is wrong? If there is one that I should know it, if it is right or if it is wrong, it is I and this man. You see it is seven years that we are in jail. What we have suffered during these seven years no human tongue can say, and yet you see me before you, not trembling, you see me looking you in your eyes straight, not blushing, not changing color, not ashamed or in fear. . . .

We were tried during a time that has now passed into history. I 8 mean by that, a time when there was a hysteria of resentment and hate against the people of our principles, against the foreigner, against slackers, and it seems to me—rather, I am positive of it, that both you and Mr. Katzmann has done all what it were in your power in order to work out, in order to agitate still more the passion of the juror, the prejudice of the juror, against us.

I remember that Mr. Katzmann has introduced a witness against 9 us, a certain Ricci. Well, I have heard that witness. It seems that he has nothing to say. It seemed that it was foolishness to produce a witness that has nothing to say. And it seemed if he were called by the Commonwealth to tell the jury that he was the foreman of that laborer that was near the scene of the crime and who claimed, and it was testified in our behalf, that we were not the men and that this man, the witness Ricci, was his foreman, and he has tried to keep the man on the job instead of going to see what was happening so as to give the impression that it was not true that the man went towards the street to see what happened. But that was not very important. The real importance is that that man say that it was not true. That a certain witness that was the water boy of the gang of the laborers testified that he take a pail and go to a certain spring, a water spring, to take water for the gang—it was not true that he go to that spring, and therefore it was not true that he see the bandit, and therefore it was not true that he can tell that neither I nor Sacco were the men. But it was introduced to show that it was not true that that man go to that spring, because they know that the Germans has poisoned the water in that spring. That is what he say on that stand over there. Now, in the world chronicle of the time there is not a single happening of that nature. Nobody in America—we have read plenty things bad that the Germans have done in Europe during the war, but nobody can prove and nobody will say that the Germans are bad enough to poison the spring water in this country during the war.

Now, this, it seems, has nothing to do with us directly. It seems to 10 be a thing by incident on the stand between the other thing that is the essence here. But the jury were hating us because we were against the war, and the jury don't know that it makes any difference between a man that is against the war because he believes that the war is unjust, because he hate no country, because he is a cosmopolitan, and a man that is against the war because he is in favor of the other country that fights against the country in which he is, and therefore a spy, and he commits any crime in the country in which he is in behalf of the other country in order to serve the other country. We are not men of that kind. Katzmann know very well that. Katzmann know that we were against the war because we did not believe in the purpose for which they say that the war was done. We believe it that the war is wrong, and we believe this more now after ten years that we understood it day by day,—the consequences and the result of the after war. We believe more now than ever that the war was wrong, and we are against war more now than ever, and I am glad to be on the doomed scaffold if I can say to mankind. "Look out; you are in a catacomb of the flower of mankind. For what? All that they say to you, all thay they have promised to you—it was a lie, it was an illusion, it was a cheat, it was a fraud, it was a crime. They promised you liberty. Where is liberty? They promised you prosperity. Where is prosperity? They have promised you elevation. Where is the elevation?

From the day that I went to Charlestown, the misfortune, the 11 population of Charlestown has doubled in number. Where is the moral good that the War has given to the world? Where is the spiritual progress that we have achieved from the War? Where are the security of life, the security of the things that we possess for our necessity? Where are the respect for human life? Where are the respect and the admiration for the good characteristics and the good of the human nature? Never as now before the war there have been so many crimes, so many corruptions, so many degeneration as there is now.

In the best of my recollection and of my good faith, during the trial   12 Katzmann has told to the jury that a certain Coacci has brought in Italy the money that, according to the State theory, I and Sacco have stole in Braintree. We never steal that money. But Katzmann, when he told that to the jury, he know already that that was not true. He know already that that man was deported in Italy with the Federal policeman after our arrest. I remember well that the Federal policeman with him in their possession—that the Federal policeman has taken away the trunks from the very boarding where he was, and bring the trunks over here and look them over and found not a single money.

Now, I call that murder, to tell to the jury that a friend or comrade   13 or a relative or acquaintance of the charged man, of the indicted man, has carried the money to Italy, when he knows it is not true. I can call that nothing else but a murder, a plain murder. . . .

Well, I have already say that I not only am not guilty of these two   14 crimes, but I never commit a crime in my life,—I have never steal and I have never kill and I have never spilt blood, and I have fought against the crime, and I have fought and I have sacrificed myself even to eliminate the crimes that the law and the church legitimate and sanctify.

This is what I say: I would not wish to a dog or to a snake, to the   15 most low and misfortunate creature of the earth—I would not wish to any of them what I have had to suffer for things that I am not guilty of. But my conviction is that I have suffered for things that I am guilty of. I am suffering because I am a radical and indeed I am a radical: I have suffered because I was an Italian, and indeed I am an Italian; I have suffered more for my family and for my beloved than for myself; but I am so convinced to be right that if you could execute me two times, and if I could be reborn two other times, I would live again to do what I have done already.

I have finished. Thank you.   16

The next day Vanzetti handed to friends the notes of what he had wished to   17 say further to Judge Thayer when he interrupted the pronouncement of sentence. Included in those notes was this estimate of Sacco:

I have talk a great deal of myself but I even forgot to name Sacco. 18
Sacco too is a worker from his boyhood, a skilled worker lover of work,
with a good job and pay, a bank account, a good and lovely wife, two
beautiful children and a neat little home at the verge of a wood, near a
brook. Sacco is a heart, a faith, a character, a man; a man lover of
nature and of mankind. A man who gave all, who sacrifice all to the
cause of Liberty and to his love for mankind; money, rest, mundain
ambitions, his own wife, his children, himself and his own life. Sacco
has never dreamt to steal, never to assassinate. He and I have never
brought a morsel of bread to our mouths, from our childhood to
to-day—which has not been gained by the sweat of our brows. Never.
His people also are in good position and of good reputation.

Oh, yes, I may be more witful, as some have put it, I am a better 19
babbler than he is, but many, many times in hearing his heartful voice
ringing a faith sublime, in considering his supreme sacrifice, remembering his heroism I felt small at the presence of his greatness and
found myself compelled to fight back from my eyes the tears, and
quanch my heart trobling to my throat to not weep before him—this
man called thief and assassin and doomed. But Sacco's name will live
in the hearts of the people and in their gratitude when Katzmann's
and yours bones will be dispersed by time, when your name, his
name, your laws, institutions, and your false god are but a *deem
rememoring of a cursed past in which man was wolf to the man. . . .*

SUGGESTIONS FOR WRITING
AND FURTHER DISCUSSION

1. F. L. Lucas asserts, "If handwriting reveals character, writing
reveals it still more" (paragraph 10). Discuss. If that is indeed so, how
would you characterize one or two of the authors included in this
chapter, based on the limited sampling of their prose available here?
Support your points with references to the writing. What do we learn
about capital punishment in these essays—and what do we learn
about Mencken, Buckley, Shaw, and Barzun?

2. Find an example of an argumentative passage that seems "stuffy"
and rewrite it, improving the style.

3. Is there any writer among those names in F. L. Lucas's essay
whose work—and therefore whose style—is unfamiliar to you? Look
up some short pieces by that writer, and consider the writing in

relation to the characteristics of style that Lucas identifies. Try to find examples to illustrate Lucas's point. For instance, you might look for an example of Bernard Shaw "struggling to be brilliant," or of Coleridge's sentences becoming "bewildering." Or look for Ben Franklin's "pungent style." Do you see features of style in the writer you examine that bear resemblance to any of your own strengths or weaknesses as a writer? Discuss.

4.   The essays by Mencken, Buckley, Shaw, and Barzun are written on the same topic, and the writers are more or less on the same side of the issue. The differences lie chiefly in the emphases of their respective theses, the methods of development, their styles, and the persona that each projects. How do the essays differ in rhetorical stance—the writers' apparent attitude toward subject and audience—and in content? Discuss the differences in style and content, giving examples from the essays. Attempt to define the style of one writer by comparing it to the others.

5.   Perhaps in light of all the arguments in this chapter favoring the death penalty, you would feel a sense of relief to challenge that position, to oppose capital punishment. Write an essay that does so, with people who think like Mencken, Buckley, Shaw, and Barzun as your intended audience. You need not refer to Mencken, Shaw, or Buckley in your essay; you may quote Socrates, Saint Paul, or Vanzetti if you wish. Your eloquence must be matched by the soundness of your reasoning, for your audience (consisting of your classmates) may be skeptical.

6.   None of the three speeches included in this chapter is written in the standard English of the late twentieth century. Could a person facing the death penalty today argue in ordinary English as eloquently as Socrates, Paul, and Bartolomeo Vanzetti do? Suppose that you have been wrongly condemned to death for treason (perhaps you were framed by your cousin, who was the real spy). Write a speech defending your character and loyalty, the eloquence of which would move a jury and judge to believe you. But be careful: Bathos (strained pathetic effect and obvious attempts to play on emotions) would likely offend your audience and might work against you.

7.   Was Bartolomeo Vanzetti guilty or innocent of the crimes for which he was executed? Impassioned arguments have been offered on both sides of the question. Which is right? Research the question and decide; then write a documented essay arguing your conclusions.

8. Jacques Barzun declares that "one life spared or forfeited is as important, morally, as a hundred thousand" (paragraph 8). He does not argue this point, taking it as one his audience will readily grant. What are the implications, both favorable and unfavorable, of the principle Barzun here declares? Could it be challenged on moral grounds or only on pragmatic ones? Discuss.

7

REASONING ABOUT
THE AESTHETIC

THE STRATEGY

It is a truth universally acknowledged that matters of taste are not appropriate subjects for argument. Unfortunately, like so many declarations, this one is but half true. While it may be the case that someone is entitled to prefer red to yellow without having to defend his or her preference, matters of taste and aesthetics are daily the subjects of argument. And it is appropriate that they should be. If you prefer Raphael to Rubens, Remington to Russell, Roethke to James Whitcomb Riley, you are entitled not only to do so but also to argue your reasons. In so doing, you may enlighten others, helping us to understand and appreciate the aesthetic just as we do the rational.

When you argue about the nonlogical, you may make comparative or hierarchical arguments: Shakespeare is greater than Milton who is greater than Jonson; abstract sculpture engages the imagination more than does representational sculpture; Frank Lloyd Wright's furniture designs are unsatisfactory because they are less comfortable than the Shakers'. But you may also argue about meaning: that Georgia O'Keeffe's flower paintings are overtly sexual in their appeal. You may argue about execution: that Gerard Manley Hopkins's "sprung" rhythm scans regularly if you disregard Hopkins's marked accents—thereby discounting Hopkins's claimed innovation. You may argue about classification: that Henry James the realist is a Gothic writer at heart. You may argue about interpretation and significance. You may assert, as John Updike does in an essay in this chapter, that two very different paintings both celebrate the independence of American children. All that is required of you, as Marya Mannes argues in the first essay, is that you articulate clear standards and apply them.

In other readings in this section, the renowned American art critic Clement Greenberg argues "The Case for Abstract Art," with suggestions about how to understand and argue about nonrepresentational art. And English poet and critic Vernon Scannell shows some specific ways we can talk, as ordinary readers, about the relative merits of poems. We *can* argue about the nonlogical, and being able to do so can heighten both our enjoyment and appreciation of a wealth of subjects, from architecture to Thai cooking. These essays will show you some of the possibilities.

How Do You Know It's Good?

MARYA MANNES

Marya Mannes (1904–1990) was a novelist and social critic who wrote extensively for magazines such as the *New Yorker* and the *Reporter*. Her books include an autobiography, *Out of My Time* (1971), and two novels. In this essay taken from her *But Will It Sell?* (1962), Mannes argues that standards of judgment in aesthetic matters are not only possible but crucial. Moreover, she believes that sound judgments can be made by ordinary readers, viewers, and hearers of the arts—if we are willing to invest some time and attention in reading, viewing, and listening. We should not abandon the arts, and we should not be intimidated by them. Even if our judgments are finally deemed wrong by history, they need not be deemed baseless.

Suppose there were no critics to tell us how to react to a picture, a 1
play, or a new composition of music. Suppose we wandered innocent as the dawn into an art exhibition of unsigned paintings. By what standards, by what values would we decide whether they were good or bad, talented or untalented, successes or failures? How can we ever know that what we think is right?

For the last fifteen or twenty years the fashion in criticism or 2
appreciation of the arts has been to deny the existence of any valid criteria and to make the words "good" or "bad" irrelevant, immaterial, and inapplicable. There is no such thing, we are told, as a set of standards, first acquired through experience and knowledge and later imposed on the subject under discussion. This has been a popular approach, for it relieves the critic of the responsibility of judgment and the public of the necessity of knowledge. It pleases those resentful of disciplines, it flatters the empty-minded by calling them open-minded, it comforts the confused. Under the banner of democracy and the kind of equality which our forefathers did *not* mean, it says, in effect, "Who are you to tell us what is good or bad?" This is the same cry used so long and so effectively by the producers of mass media

who insist that it is the public, not they, who decides what it wants to hear and see, and that for a critic to say that *this* program is bad and *this* program is good is purely a reflection of personal taste. Nobody recently has expressed this philosophy more succinctly than Dr. Frank Stanton, the highly intelligent president of CBS television. At a hearing before the Federal Communications Commission, this phrase escaped him under questioning: "One man's mediocrity is another man's good program."

There is no better way of saying "No values are absolute." There is 3 another important aspect to this philosophy of *laissez faire*: It is the fear, in all observers of all forms of art, of guessing wrong. This fear is well come by, for who has not heard of the contemporary outcries against artists who later were called great? Every age has its arbiters who do not grow with their times, who cannot tell evolution from revolution or the difference between frivolous faddism, amateurish experimentation, and profound and necessary change. Who wants to be caught *flagrante delicto* with an error of judgment as serious as this? It is far safer, and certainly easier, to look at a picture or a play or a poem and to say "This is hard to understand, but it may be good," or simply to welcome it as a new form. The word "new"—in our country especially—has magical connotations. What is new must be good; what is old is probably bad, and if a critic can describe the new in language that nobody can understand, he's safer still. If he has mastered the art of saying nothing with exquisite complexity, nobody can quote him later as saying anything.

But all these, I maintain, are forms of abdication from the responsi- 4 bility of judgment. In creating, the artist commits himself; in appreciating, you have a commitment of your own. For after all, it is the audience which makes the arts. A climate of appreciation is essential to its flowering, and the higher the expectations of the public, the better the performance of the artist. Conversely, only a public ill-served by its critics could have accepted as art and literature so much in these last years that has been neither. If anything goes, everything goes; and at the bottom of the junkpile lie the discarded standards too.

But what are these standards? How do you get them? How do you 5 know they're the right ones? How can you make a clear pattern out of so many intangibles, including that greatest one, the very private I?

Well for one thing, it's fairly obvious that the more you read and 6 see and hear, the more equipped you'll be to practice that art of association which is at the basis of all understanding and judgment. The more you live and the more you look, the more aware you are of a consistent pattern—as universal as the stars, as the tides, as breathing, as night and day—underlying everything. I would call this pattern and this rhythm an order. Not order—*an* order. Within it exists an incredible diversity of forms. Without it lies chaos. I would further call this order—this incredible diversity held within one pattern—health. And I would call chaos—the wild cells of destruction—sickness. It is in the end up to you to distinguish between the diversity that is health and the chaos that is sickness, and you can't do this without a process of association that can link a bar of Mozart with the corner of a Vermeer painting, or a Stravinsky score with a Picasso abstraction; or that can relate an aggressive act with a Franz Kline painting and a fit of coughing with a John Cage composition.

There is no accident in the fact that certain expressions of art live 7 for all time and that others die with the moment, and although you may not always define the reasons, you can ask the questions. What does an artist say that is timeless; how does he say it? How much is fashion, how much is merely reflection? Why is Sir Walter Scott so hard to read now, and Jane Austen not? Why is baroque right for one age and too effulgent for another?

Can a standard of craftsmanship apply to art of all ages, or does 8 each have its own, and different, definitions? You may have been aware, inadvertently, that craftsmanship has become a dirty word these years because, again, it implies standard—something done well or done badly. The result of this convenient avoidance is a plenitude of actors who can't project their voices, singers who can't phrase their songs, poets who can't communicate emotion, and writers who have no vocabulary—not to speak of painters who can't draw. The dogma now is that craftsmanship gets in the way of expression. You can do better if you don't know *how* you do it, let alone *what* you're doing.

I think it is time you helped reverse this trend by trying to redis- 9 cover craft: the command of the chosen instrument, whether it is a brush, a word, or a voice. When you begin to detect the difference between freedom and sloppiness, between serious experimentation and ego-therapy, between skill and slickness, between strength and violence, you are on your way to separating the sheep from the goats, a form of segregation denied us for quite a while. All you need to restore it is a small bundle of standards and a Geiger counter that detects fraud, and we might begin our tour of the arts in an area where both are urgently needed: contemporary painting.

I don't know what's worse: to have to look at acres of bad art to 10 find the little good, or to read what the critics say about it all. In no other field of expression has so much double-talk flourished, so much confusion prevailed, and so much nonsense been circulated: further evidence of the close interdependence between the arts and the critical climate they inhabit. It will be my pleasure to share with you some of this double-talk so typical of our times.

Item one: preface for a catalogue of an abstract painter: 11

"Time-bound meditation experiencing a life; sincere with plastic 12 piety at the threshold of hallowed arcana; a striving for pure ideation giving shape to inner drive; formalized patterns where neural balances reach a fiction." End of quote. Know what this artist paints like now?

Item two: A review in the *Art News*:   13

". . . a weird and disparate assortment of material, but the mon-   14
strosity which bloomed into his most recent cancer of aggregations is present in some form everywhere. . . ." Then, later, "A gluttony of things and processes terminated by a glorious constipation."

Item three, same magazine, review of an artist who welds automo- 15
bile fragments into abstract shapes:

"Each fragment . . . is made an extreme of human exasperation,   16
torn at and fought all the way, and has its rightness of form as if by accident. *Any technique that requires order or discipline would just be the human ego.* No, these must be egoless, uncontrolled, undesigned and different enough to give you a bang—fifty miles an hour around a telephone pole. . . ."

"Any technique that requires order or discipline would just be the   17
human ego." What does he mean—"just be"? What are they really talking about? Is this journalism? Is it criticism? Or is it that other convenient abdication from standards of performance and judgment practiced by so many artists and critics that they, like certain writers who deal only in sickness and depravity, "reflect the chaos about them". . . ? Again, whose chaos? Whose depravity?

I had always thought that the prime function of art was to create 18
order *out* of chaos—again, not the order of neatness or rigidity or convention or artifice, but the order of clarity by which one will and one vision could draw the essential truth out of apparent confusion. I still do. It is not enough to use parts of a car to convey the brutality of the machine. This is as slavishly representative, and just as easy, as arranging dried flowers under glass to convey nature.

Speaking of which, i.e., the use of real materials (burlap, old   19
gloves, bottletops) in lieu of pigment, this is what one critic had to say about an exhibition of Assemblage at the Museum of Modern Art last year:

"Spotted throughout the show are indisputable works of art, ac-   20
counting for a quarter or even half of the total display. But the remainder are works of non-art, anti-art, and art substitutes that are the aesthetic counterparts of the social deficiencies that land people in the clink on charges of vagrancy. These aesthetic bankrupts . . . have no legitimate ideological roof over their heads and not the price of a square intellectual meal, much less a spiritual sandwich, in their pockets."

I quote these words of John Canaday of *The New York Times* as an 21
example of the kind of criticism which puts responsibility to an intelligent public above popularity with an intellectual coterie. Canaday has

the courage to say what he thinks and the capacity to say it clearly: two qualities notably absent from his profession.

Next to art, I would say that appreciation and evaluation in the field of music is the most difficult. For it is rarely possible to judge a new composition at one hearing only. What seems confusing or fragmented at first might well become clear and organic a third time. Or it might not. The only salvation here for the listener is, again, an instinct born of experience and association which allows him to separate intent from accident, design from experimentation, and pretense from conviction. Much of contemporary music is, like its sister art, merely a reflection of the composer's own fragmentation: an absorption in self and symbols at the expense of communication with others. The artist, in short, says to the public: If you don't understand this, it's because you're dumb. I maintain that you are not. You may have to go part way or even halfway to meet the artist, but if you must go the whole way, it's his fault, not yours. Hold fast to that. And remember it too when you read new poetry, that estranged sister of music. 22

"A multitude of causes, unknown to former times, are now acting with a combined force to blunt the discriminating powers of the mind, and, unfitting it for all voluntary exertion, to reduce it to a state of almost savage torpor. The most effective of these causes are the great national events which are daily taking place and the increasing accumulation of men in cities, where the uniformity of their occupations produces a craving for extraordinary incident, which the rapid communication of intelligence hourly gratifies. To this tendency of life and manners, the literature and theatrical exhibitions of the country have conformed themselves." 23

This startlingly applicable comment was written in the year 1800 by William Wordsworth in the preface to his "Lyrical Ballads"; and it has been cited by Edwin Muir in his recently published book, *The Estate of Poetry*. Muir states that poetry's effective range and influence have diminished alarmingly in the modern world. He believes in the inherent and indestructible qualities of the human mind and the great and permanent objects that act upon it, and suggests that the audience will increase when "poetry loses what obscurity is left in it by attempting greater themes, for great themes have to be stated clearly." If you keep that firmly in mind and resist, in Muir's words, "the vast dissemination of secondary objects that isolate us from the natural world," you have gone a long way toward equipping yourself for the examination of any work of art. 24

When you come to theatre, in this extremely hasty tour of the arts, you can approach it on two different levels. You can bring to it anticipation and innocence, giving yourself up, as it were, to the life on the stage and reacting to it emotionally, if the play is good, or listlessly, if 25 the play is boring; a part of the audience organism that expresses its favor by silence or laughter and its disfavor by coughing and rustling. Or you can bring to it certain critical faculties that may heighten, rather than diminish, your enjoyment.

You can ask yourselves whether the actors are truly in their parts 26 or merely projecting themselves; whether the scenery helps or hurts the mood; whether the playwright is honest with himself, the characters, and you. Somewhere along the line you can learn to distinguish between the true creative act and the false arbitrary gesture; between fresh observation and stale cliché; between the avant-garde play that is pretentious drivel and the avant-garde play that finds new ways to say old truths.

Purpose and craftsmanship—end and means—these are the keys 27 to your judgment in all the arts. What is this painter trying to say when he slashed a broad band of black across a white canvas and lets the edges dribble down? Is it a statement of violence? Is it a self-portrait? If it is *one* of these, has he made you believe it? Or is this a gesture of the ego or a form of therapy? If it shocks you, what does it shock you into?

And what of this tight little painting of bright flowers in a vase? Is 28 the painter saying anything new about flowers? Is it different from a million other canvases of flowers? Has it any life, any meaning, beyond its statement? Is there any pleasure in its forms or texture? The question is not whether a thing is abstract or representational, whether it is "modern" or conventional. The question, inexorably, is whether it is good. And this is a decision which only you, on the basis of instinct, experience, and association, can make for yourself. It takes independence and courage. It involves, moreover, the risk of wrong decision and the humility, after the passage of time, of recognizing it as such. As we grow and change and learn, out attitudes can change too, and what we once thought obscure or "difficult" can later emerge as coherent and illuminating. Entrenched prejudices, obdurate opinions are as sterile as no opinions at all.

Yet standards there are, timeless as the universe itself. And when 29 you have committed yourself to them, you have acquired a passport to that elusive but immutable realm of truth. Keep it with you in the forest of bewilderment. And never be afraid to speak up.

QUESTIONS AND IDEAS FOR DISCUSSION

1.   Discuss how you would answer Mannes's question in paragraph 1: "By what standards, by what values would we decide whether they [unsigned paintings in an exhibition] were good or bad, talented or untalented, successes or failures?"

2.   Mannes's argument in paragraph 2 echoes the concerns of another essay in this book, Allan Bloom's "The Education of Openness" (page

88). Where, if at all, would the two writers differ in their attitudes about openness and judgment?

3. Mannes's thesis is that judgment is a responsibility—"For after all, it is the audience which makes the arts" (paragraph 4)—and that judgment must be based on standards. How, according to Mannes, do we acquire the ability to judge with standards? Can you add anything to Mannes's suggestions?

4. "All you need to restore it [craft] is a small bundle of standards and a Geiger counter that detects fraud . . ." (9). Just what *is* "fraud" in art or literature? Do you feel confident that you can detect fraud when you encounter it? How? If not, why? How might you best acquire an internal fraud detector?

5. What are the problems, in Mannes's view, with much contemporary music and poetry? Do you agree? Comment. For what reasons might Mannes call new poetry "that estranged sister of music" (22)?

6. Locate a reproduction of a contemporary nonrepresentational painting with broad bands of color (perhaps a Mark Rothko), and answer Mannes's questions in paragraph 27. Then, find a "tight little painting of bright flowers in a vase" *and* Van Gogh's "Sunflowers," and answer Mannes's questions in paragraph 28. Are you *able* to answer all of the questions? Discuss any problems you may have encountered, and possible reasons and remedies for them.

The Case for Abstract Art

CLEMENT GREENBERG

Clement Greenberg is an American, one of the great art critics of the twentieth century. His fame results in part from his usually unerring judgments about which new artists would achieve renown. Greenberg has written extensively on nearly all the important modern artists, including Pablo Picasso, Joan Miro, Henri Matisse, and Jackson Pollock. In 1961, some of his essays and reviews were published as *Art and Culture,* a book that remains influential among artists and art lovers. Greenberg's *Collected Essays and Criticism,* in two volumes, was published in 1986. What Greenberg says about abstract art in this essay, first published in 1959, bears on our appreciation of representational art, as well. And, indeed, "Abstract art is not a special kind of art; no hard-and-fast lines separate it from representational art. . . ." But many people find abstract art the hardest kind of art to appreciate, so it is well that we hear a few eloquent words in its defense. Not only does Greenberg make a case for abstract art, he shows us ways to consider and discuss art in general.

Many people say that the kind of art our age produces is one of the 1
major symptoms of what's wrong with the age. The disintegration
and, finally, the disappearance of recognizable images in painting and
sculpture, like the obscurity in advanced literature, are supposed to
reflect a disintegration of values in society itself. Some people go
further and say that abstract, nonrepresentational art is pathological
art, crazy art, and that those who practice it and those who admire and
buy it are either sick or silly. The kindest critics are those who say it's
all a joke, a hoax, and a fad, and that modernist art in general, or
abstract art in particular, will soon pass. This sort of thing is heard or
read pretty constantly, but in some years more often than others.

There seems to be a certain rhythm in the advance in popularity of 2
modernist art, and a certain rhythm in the counter-attacks which try to
stem it. More or less the same words or arguments are used in all the
polemics, but the targets usually change. Once it was the impressionists who were a scandal, next it was Van Gogh and Cézanne, then it
was Matisse, then it was cubism and Picasso, after that Mondrian, and
now it is Jackson Pollock. The fact that Pollock was an American
shows, in a backhanded way, how important American art has lately
become.

Some of the same people who attack modernist art in general, or 3
abstract art in particular, happen also to complain that our age has lost
those habits of disinterested contemplation, and that capacity for enjoying things as ends in themselves and for their own sake, which
former ages are supposed to have cultivated. This idea has been
advanced often enough to convert it into a cliché. I hate to give assent
to a cliché, for it is almost always an oversimplification, but I have to
make an exception in this case. While I strongly doubt that disinterested contemplation was as unalloyed or as popular in ages past as is
supposed, I do tend to agree that we could do with more of it in this
time, and especially in this country.

I think a poor life is lived by anyone who doesn't regularly take 4
time out to stand and gaze, or sit and listen, or touch, or smell, or
brood, without any further end in mind, simply for the satisfaction
gotten from that which is gazed at, listened to, touched, smelled or
brooded upon. We all know, however, that the climate of Western life,
and particularly of American life, is not conducive to this kind of thing;
we are all too busy making a living. This is another cliché, of course.
And still a third cliché says that we should learn from Oriental society
how to give more of ourselves to the life of the spirit, to contemplation
and meditation, and to the appreciation of what is satisfying or beautiful in its own sole right. This last is not only a cliché, but a fallacy, since
most Orientals are even more preoccupied than we are with making a
living. I hope that I myself am not making a gross and reductive

simplification when I say that so much of Oriental contemplative and aesthetic discipline strikes me as a technique for keeping one's eyes averted from ugliness and misery.

Every civilization and every tradition of culture seem to possess 5 capacities for self-cure and self-correction that go into operation automatically, unbidden. If the given tradition goes too far in one direction it will usually try to right itself by going equally far in the opposite one. There is no question but that our Western civilization, especially in its American variant, devotes more mental energy than any other to the production of material things and services; and that, more than any other, it puts stress on interested, purposeful activity in general. This is reflected in our art, which, as has been frequently observed, puts such great emphasis on movement and development and resolution, on beginnings, middles, and endings—that is, on dynamics. Compare Western music with any other kind, or look at Western literature, for that matter, with its relatively great concern with plot and over-all structure and its relatively small concern with tropes and figures and ornamental elaborations; think of how slow-moving Chinese and Japanese poetry is by comparison with ours, and how much it delights in static situations; and how uncertain the narrational logic of non-Western fiction tends to be. Think of how encrusted and convoluted Arabic poetry is by contrast even with our most euphuistic lyrical verse. And as for non-Western music, does it not almost always, and literally, strike us as more monotonous than ours?

Well, how does Western art compensate for, correct, or at least 6 qualify its emphasis on the dynamic—an emphasis that may or may not be excessive? And how does Western life itself compensate for, correct, or at least qualify its obsession with material production and purposeful activity? I shall not here attempt to answer the latter question. But in the realm of art an answer is beginning to emerge of its own accord, and the shape of part of that answer is abstract art.

Abstract decoration is almost universal, and Chinese and Japanese 7 calligraphy is quasi-abstract—abstract to the extent that few occidentals can read the characters of Chinese or Japanese writing. But only in the West, and only in the last fifty years, have such things as abstract pictures and free-standing pieces of abstract sculpture appeared. What makes the big difference between these and abstract decoration is that they are, exactly, pictures and free-standing sculpture—solo works of art meant to be looked at for their own sake and with full attention, and not as the adjuncts, incidental aspects, or settings of things other than themselves. These abstract pictures and pieces of sculpture challenge our capacity for disinterested contemplation in a way that is more concentrated and, I daresay, more conscious than anything else I know of in art. Music is an essentially abstract art, but even at its most rarefied and abstract, and whether it's Bach's or the middle-period Schoenberg's music, it does not offer this challenge in quite the same way or degree. Music tends from a beginning through a middle toward an ending. We wait to see how it "comes out"—which is what we also do with literature. Of course, the *total* experience of literature and music is completely disinterested, but it becomes that only at a further remove. While undergoing the experience we are caught up and expectant as well as detached—disinterested and at the same time interested in a way resembling that in which we are interested in how things turn out in real life. I exaggerate to make my point—aesthetic experience *has* to be disinterested, and when it is genuine it always is, even when bad works of art are involved—but the distinctions I've made and those I've still to make are valid nevertheless.

With representational painting it is something like what it is with 8 literature. This has been said before, many times before, but usually in order to criticize representational painting in what I think is a wrong-headed when not downright silly way. What I mean when I say, in this context, that representational painting is like literature, is that it tends to involve us in the interested as well as the disinterested by presenting us with the images of things that are inconceivable outside time and action. This goes even for landscapes and flower pieces and still lifes. It is not simply that we sometimes tend to confuse the attractiveness of the things represented in a picture with the quality of the picture itself. And it is not only that attractiveness as such has nothing to do with the abiding success of a work of art. What is more fundamental is that the meaning—as distinct from the attractiveness—of what is represented becomes truly inseparable from the representation itself. That Rembrandt confined impasto—thick paint, that is—to his highlights, and that in his later portraits especially these coincide with the ridges of the noses of his subjects is important to the artistic effect of these portraits. And that the effectiveness of the impasto, as impasto—as an abstract element of technique—coincides with its effectiveness as a means of showing just how a nose looks under a certain kind of light is also genuinely important. And that the lifelike delineation of the nose contributes to the evocation of the personality of the individual to whom the nose belongs is likewise important. And the manner and degree of insight into that individual's personality which Rembrandt exhibits in his portrait is important too. None of these factors can be, or ought to be, separated from the legitimate effect of the portrait as a picture pure and simple.

But once we have to do with personalities and lifelikeness we have 9 to do with things from which we cannot keep as secure a distance for the sake of disinterestedness as we can, say, from abstract decoration.

As it happens, the whole tendency of our Western painting, up until the later stages of impressionism, was to make distance and detachment on the part of the spectator as insecure as possible. It laid more of a stress than any other tradition on creating a sculpture-like, or photographic, illusion of the third dimension, on thrusting images at the eye with a lifelikeness that brought them as close as possible to their originals. Because of their sculptural vividness, Western paintings tend to be far less quiet, far more agitated and active—in short, far more explicitly dynamic—than most non-Western paintings do. And they involve the spectator to a much greater extent in the practical and actual aspects of the things they depict and represent.

We begin to wonder what we think of the people shown in   10
Rembrandt's portraits, *as* people; whether or not we would like to walk through the terrain shown in a Corot landscape; about the life stories of the burghers we see in a Steen painting; we react in a less than disinterested way to the attractiveness of the models, real or ideal, of the personages in a Renaissance painting. And once we begin to do this we begin to participate in the work of art in a so-to-speak practical way. In itself this participation may not be improper, but it does become so when it begins to shut out all other factors. This it has done and does, all too often. Even though the connoisseurs have usually been able in the long run to prefer the picture of a dwarf by Velásquez to that of a pretty girl by Howard Chandler Christy, the enjoyment of pictorial and sculptural art in our society has tended, on every other level than that of professional connoisseurship, to be excessively "literary," and to center too much on merely technical feats of copying.

But, as I've said, every tradition of culture tends to try to correct   11
one extreme by going to its opposite. And when our Western tradition of painting came up at last with reservations about its forthright naturalism, these quickly took the form of an equally forthright antinaturalism. These reservations started with late impressionism, and have now culminated in abstract art. I don't at all wish to be understood as saying that it all happened because some artist or artists decided it was time to curb the excesses of realistic painting, and that the main historical significance of abstract art lies in its function as an antidote to these. Nor do I wish to be understood as assuming that realistic or naturalistic art inherently needs, or ever needed, such a thing as an antidote. The motivations, conscious and unconscious, of the first modernist artists, and of present modernists as well, were and are quite different. Impressionism itself started as an effort to push naturalism further than ever before. And all through the history of art— not only in recent times—consequences have escaped intentions.

It is on a different, and more impersonal and far more general level   12 of meaning and history that our culture has generated abstract art as an antidote. On that level this seemingly new kind of art has emerged as an epitome of almost everything that disinterested contemplation requires, and as both a challenge and a reproof to a society that exaggerates, not the necessity, but the intrinsic value of purposeful and interested activity. Abstract art comes, on this level, as a relief, an archexample of something that does not have to mean, or be useful for, anything other than itself. And it seems fitting, too, that abstract art should at present flourish most in this country. If American society is indeed given over as no other society has been to purposeful activity and material production, then it is right that it should be reminded, in extreme terms, of the essential nature of disinterested activity.

Abstract art does this in very literal and also in very imaginative 13 ways. First, it does not exhibit the illusion or semblance of things we are already familiar with in real life; it gives us no imaginary space through which to walk with the mind's eye; no imaginary objects to desire or not desire; no imaginary people to like or dislike. We are left alone with shapes and colors. These may or may not remind us of real things; but if they do, they usually do so incidentally or accidentally—on our own responsibility as it were; and the genuine enjoyment of an abstract picture does not ordinarily depend on such resemblances.

Second, pictorial art in its highest definition is static; it tries to 14 overcome movement in space or time. This is not to say that the eye does not wander over a painted surface, and thus travel in both space and time. When a picture presents us with an illusion of real space, there is all the more inducement for the eye to do such wandering. But ideally the whole of a picture should be taken in at a glance; its unity should be immediately evident, and the supreme quality of a picture, the highest measure of its power to move and control the visual imagination, should reside in its unity. And this is something to be grasped only in an indivisible instant of time. No expectancy is involved in the true and pertinent experience of a painting; a picture, I repeat, does not "come out" the way a story, or a poem, or a piece of music does. It's all there at once, like a sudden revelation. This "at-onceness" an abstract picture usually drives home to us with greater singleness and clarity than a representational painting does. And to apprehend this "at-onceness" demands a freedom of mind and un-trammeledness of eye that constitute "at-onceness" in their own right. Those who have grown capable of experiencing this know what I mean. You are summoned and gathered into one point in the continuum of duration. The picture does this to you, willy-nilly, regardless of whatever else is on your mind: a mere glance at it creates the attitude required for its appreciation, like a stimulus that elicits an automatic response. You become all attention, which means that you become, for the moment, selfless and in a sense entirely identified with the object of your attention.

The "at-onceness" which a picture or a piece of sculpture enforces 15 on you is not, however, single or isolated. It can be repeated in a succession of instants, in each one remaining an "at-onceness," an instant all by itself. For the cultivated eye, the picture repeats its instantaneous unity like a mouth repeating a single word.

This pinpointing of the attention, this complete liberation and 16 concentration of it, offers what is largely a new experience to most people in our sort of society. And it is, I think, a hunger for this particular kind of experience that helps account for the growing popularity of abstract art in this country: for the way it is taking over in the art schools, the galleries, and the museums. The fact that fad and fashion are also involved does not invalidate what I say. I know that abstract art of the latest variety—that originating with painters like Pollock and Georges Mathieu—has gotten associated with progressive jazz and its cultists; but what of it? That Wagner's music became associated with German ultranationalism and that Wagner was Hitler's favorite composer, still doesn't detract from its sheer quality as music. That the present vogue for folk music started, back in the 1930's, among the Communists doesn't make our liking for it any the less genuine, or take anything away from folk music itself. Nor does the fact that so much gibberish gets talked and written about abstract art compromise it, just as the gibberish in which art criticism in general abounds, and abounds increasingly, doesn't compromise art in general.

One point, however, I want to make glaringly clear. Abstract art is 17 not a special kind of art; no hard-and-fast line separates it from representational art; it is only the latest phase in the development of Western art as a whole, and almost every "technical" device of abstract painting is already to be found in the realistic painting that preceded it. Nor is it a superior kind of art. I still know of nothing in abstract painting, aside perhaps from some of the near-abstract cubist works that Picasso, Braque and Léger executed between 1910 and 1914, which matches the highest achievements of the old masters. Abstract painting may be a purer, more quintessential form of pictorial art than the representational kind, but this does not of itself confer quality upon an abstract picture. The ratio of bad abstract painting to good is actually much greater than the ratio of bad to good representational painting. Nonetheless, the very best painting, the major painting, of our age is almost exclusively abstract. Only on the middle and lower levels of quality, on the levels below the first-rate—which is, of course, where most of the art that gets produced places itself—only there is the better painting preponderantly representational.

On the plane of culture in general, the special, unique value of 18 abstract art, I repeat, lies in the high degree of detached contemplativeness that its appreciation requires. Contemplativeness is demanded in greater or lesser degree for the appreciation of every kind of art, but abstract art tends to present this requirement in quintessential form, at its purest, least diluted, most immediate. If abstract art— as does happen nowadays—should chance to be the first kind of pictorial art we learn to appreciate, the chances are that when we go to other kinds of pictorial art—to the old masters, say, and I hope we all do go to the old masters eventually—we shall find ourselves all the better able to enjoy them. That is, we shall be able to experience them with less intrusion of irrelevancies, therefore more fully and more intensely.

The old masters stand or fall, their pictures succeed or fail, on the 19 same ultimate basis as do those of Mondrian or any other abstract artist. The abstract formal unity of a picture by Titian is more important to its quality than what that picture images. To return to what I said about Rembrandt's portraits, the whatness of what is imaged is not unimportant—far from it—and cannot be separated, really, from the formal qualities that result from the way it is imaged. But it is a fact, in my experience, that representational paintings are essentially and most fully appreciated when the identities of what they represent are only secondarily present to our consciousness. Baudelaire said he could grasp the quality of a painting by Delacroix when he was still too far away from it to make out the images it contained, when it was still only a blur of colors. I think it was really on this kind of evidence that critics and connoisseurs, though they were almost always unaware of it, discriminated between the good and the bad in the past. Put to it, they more or less unconsciously dismissed from their minds the connotations of Reubens' nudes when assessing and experiencing the final worth of his art. They may have remained aware of the pinkness as a *nude* pinkness, but it was a pinkness and a nudity devoid of most of their usual associations.

Abstract paintings do not confront us with such problems. Or at 20 least the frequenting of abstract art can train us to relegate them automatically to their proper place; and in doing this we refine our eyes for the appreciation of non-abstract art. That has been my own experience. That it is still relatively rare can be explained perhaps by the fact that most people continue to come to painting through academic art—the kind of art they see in ads and in magazines—and when and if they discover abstract art it comes as such an overwhelming experience that they tend to forget everything produced before. This is to be deplored, but it does not negate the value, actual or potential, of abstract art as an introduction to the fine arts in general, and as an introduction, too, to habits of disinterested contemplation. In this respect, the value of abstract art will, I hope, prove far greater in the future than it has yet. Not only can it confirm instead of subverting tradition; it can teach us, by example, how valuable so much in life can be made without being invested with ulterior meanings. How many people I know who have hung abstract pictures on their walls and found themselves gazing at them endlessly, and then exclaiming, "I don't know what there is in that painting, but I can't take my eyes off it." This kind of bewilderment is salutary. It does us good not to be able to explain, either to ourselves or to others, what we enjoy or love; it expands our capacity for experience.

QUESTIONS AND IDEAS FOR DISCUSSION

1. Does Greenberg's essay answer any of Marya Mannes's objections to abstract art in the previous essay? Comment. On what matters would they agree?

2. How do Rembrandt's noses help Greenberg argue that representational painting has qualities akin to literature? Explain Greenberg's argument in paragraphs 8 through 10 in your own words.

3. Discuss the paradox of Greenberg's argument in paragraph 17:

   Abstract painting may be a purer, more quintessential form of pictorial art than the representational kind, but this does not of itself confer quality upon an abstract picture. The ratio of bad abstract painting to good is actually much greater than the ratio of bad to good representational painting. Nonetheless, the very best painting, the major painting, of our age is almost exclusively abstract.

4. Surely few of us can bring to our appreciation of and arguments about art the same breadth and depth of knowledge that Clement Greenberg brings. We cannot speak with such familiarity or confidence about dozens of painters and musicians. But Greenberg makes us understand his argument through the use of analogies that we can understand and appreciate. Identify some of those analogies, and discuss how you might use analogy in arguments of your own about art.

5. Greenberg's last sentence seems to be an argument *against* trying to argue one's opinions about works of art. Is it? Do you agree or disagree with Greenberg? Why?

Making Judgments about Poetry
VERNON SCANNELL

Vernon Scannell is a well-known English poet whose work has been recognized in Great Britain by such awards as the Heinemann Award for Literature (1960), the Cholmondeley Poetry Prize (1974), and a Civil List Pension for Services to Literature (1981). Scannell is a fellow of the Royal Society of Literature. In addition to poetry, he has written fiction, literary criticism, and autobiography, and he is particularly interested in enabling ordinary readers to enjoy and appreciate poetry. Toward that end, he created a popular series of radio talks on poetry, "A Closer Look," and wrote *How to Enjoy Poetry* (1983), from which the following selection is excerpted. In it, Scannell uses two poems by a single author, Wilfred Owen, to show how readers who are not literary scholars can confidently judge the relative merits of different poems.

The more first-rate poetry you read and listen to, the more discer- 1 ning your taste will become, but . . . you may reasonably ask: "How can I know what is first-rate from what is second-, third- or even tenth-rate?" Judgments of the relative merits of poems must ultimately be subjective and therefore, in the absolute scientific sense, their soundness cannot be proved. However, no one could possibly doubt that Keats's "Ode to a Nightingale," for instance, is a better poem than T. E. Brown's "My Garden" (both to be found in the first *Oxford Book of English Verse* edited by Quiller-Couch) or that *Hamlet* or *King Lear* contain infinitely greater poetry than Christopher Fry's "The Lady's Not for Burning." Furthermore, I believe that it is demonstrably possible to distinguish between the excellent and the slightly flawed, taking two works by the same poet. Here, for example, are two poems by Wilfred Owen who, at the age of twenty-six, was killed in the First World War just one week before the Armistice in 1918:

Greater Love

Red lips are not so red
   As the stained stones kissed by the English dead.
Kindness of wooed and wooer
Seems shame to their love pure.
O Love, your eyes lose lure   5
   When I behold eyes blinded in my stead!

Your slender attitude
   Trembles not exquisite like limbs knife-skewed,
Rolling and rolling there
Where God seems not to care;   10
Till the fierce love they bear
   Cramps them in death's extreme decrepitude.

Your voice sings not so soft,—
   Though even as wind murmuring through raftered loft,
Your dear voice is not dear,   *15*
Gentle, and evening clear,
As theirs whom none now hear,
   Now earth has stopped their piteous mouths that coughed.

Heart, you were never hot
   Nor large, nor full like hearts made great with shot;   *20*
And though your hand be pale,
Paler are all which trail
Your cross through flame and hail:
   Weep, you may weep, for you may touch them not.

The Send-Off

Down the close, darkening lanes they sang their way
   To the siding-shed,
And lined the train with faces grimly gay.

Their breasts were stuck all white with wreath and spray
   As men's are, dead.   *5*

Dull porters watched them, and a casual tramp
   Stood staring hard,
Sorry to miss them from the upland camp.
Then, unmoved, signals nodded, and a lamp
   Winked to the guard.   *10*

So secretly, like wrongs hushed-up, they went.
They were not ours:
We never heard to which front these were sent.

Nor there if they yet mock what women meant
Who gave them flowers.   *15*

Shall they return to beatings of great bells
In wild train-loads?
A few, a few, too few for drums and yells,
May creep back, silent, to still village wells
Up half-known roads.   *20*

First we should take "Greater Love" and read it slowly and carefully, straight through. . . . This first reading gives me a sense of the poet's anguish and guilt at being alive when his comrades have died horribly on the battlefields. It seems that he is addressing a woman whom he loves, and he contrasts the physical details of their loving with those of the soldiers in their death throes. However, the final stanza, with its reference to "Your cross . . ." puzzled me, for it seemed to suggest that he was here apostrophising Christ. The second, more concentrated reading corrected this impression: it becomes clear now that, though he is indeed addressing a beloved woman, she is not only a specific person but also a representative of womankind. The lines "Paler are all which trail/Your cross through flame and hail . . ." refer, I think, to those who have sacrificed their lives for the women, who are literally women, but could also symbolize home, the Motherland, domestic certainties, peace.

A third examination of the poem, paying attention to structure 2 and form, confirmed what my ear had been rather distressed by on the first reading: the repetition of the sibilant in "As the stained stones kissed by the English dead . . ." is clumsily handled. It may well be that the poet wished to enact the sound of kissing onomatopoeically, but those repeated "s" sounds create an unfortunate hissing effect. The stanza form, with the varying line length, is resourcefully handled, but the rhymes "wooer" and "pure" strike my ear as inaccurate and dreadfully false. The juxtaposing of soft, sensuous language with harsh, staccato words—"slender" . . . "trembles" . . . "limbs" . . . "with knife-skewed" . . .—is, I am sure, deliberate, but the total effect is one of an ambiguity that I do not think the poet intended to convey. There is an uncomfortable sense of the poet almost revelling in the images of carnage, which are presented in terms of physical love and sexuality.

"The Send-Off" strikes me as a far more consistently satisfactory 3 poem. Here the language is restrained and the poet shows a marked preference for the simplest rather than the most sonorous word. There are no troubling ambiguities in this poem. The troops in the evening march to the station from which they are to be transported to the Front. Some are wearing flowers which have been pinned on to them by the women who watch them march past. The tramp, who has no doubt received tit-bits from the cookhouse of their camp, seems the only bystander who is moved by their departure. The poet, obviously a soldier from another camp and unit—"they were not ours"— speculates on their future, knowing that many will be killed and that the survivors will return, not to a hero's welcome, but to a sad, bereaved and almost alien place.

While "Greater Love" possesses some fine qualities, I would claim 4 with some confidence that "The Send-Off" is the better poem. Where the first is straining to elicit a sense of the waste of war through generalization and highly colored, dramatic language and images, "The Send-Off" deals with a particular event and does not attempt to extract from it, or to inject into it, more drama and emotional force than the situation actually contains. The second is the better poem because it is completely truthful. Here Owen does not try to bludgeon his reader into a shocked state of horror at the cruelties of war: he simply presents one simple scene, but one which contains in a muted way all the pathos of loss and futility that the First World War has come to symbolize for succeeding generations.

QUESTIONS AND IDEAS FOR DISCUSSION

1. Some students distrust poetry because they fear that it is written in some kind of code, accessible only to the initiated. They fear that everything is a symbol; reading a poem becomes a name-that-symbol guessing contest. What would Scannell say to such fears? What other fears do ordinary readers have when they approach poetry?

2. One standard by which Scannell tests poetry is truth; he likes Owen's "The Send-Off" because "it is completely truthful" (paragraph 4). But how do we judge whether or not a poem is "truthful"? Discuss.

3. Scannell acknowledges that the judgment of poetry is ultimately subjective and that equally strong arguments might be advanced for several interpretations of a single poem or for the superior merits of each of two poems in comparison to the other. But he also points out that some broad judgments are universally shared, that we cannot argue just *anything* about poetry. Discuss what some of those broad, shared standards for judgment are, based on your experience in reading poetry over the years.

4. Do you agree with Scannell's judgment of the relative merits of the two Owen poems? If you agree, offer a reason in addition to those Scannell argues. If you disagree, show why an appreciative reader might prefer "Greater Love" to "The Send-Off."

5. American poet Mark Van Doren has argued in an essay titled "What Is a Poet?" that poetry "speaks for itself." Do you agree or disagree? Is interpretation helpful or unnecessary? Does it further appreciation or destroy poetry's music? Give your reasons.

THE STRATEGY AT WORK:
ARGUMENTS ABOUT PAINTING AND POETRY

In this section, you will find reproductions of two paintings and the text of one poem. Look at the paintings (pages 341 and 342) and read the poem (page 344) before you read the selections. How—and why—do you think John Updike chose to discuss these two paintings? What could be the connection between them? What is John Donne's poem about? What idea does it argue? Is it appealing? Mysterious? What makes it so? Your responses to these works, if they are reasoned and not merely dismissive, give you a right to evaluate them and to interpret their significance or their meaning. You are as entitled to argue about painting as is John Updike, to argue about poetry as is Norman Cousins.

To enjoy and evaluate and even argue your opinions about art and literature does not mean that you must have a scholar's expertise, as three of the selections in this section will show. One is written by a prominent novelist (not an art critic), writing here about two paintings he enjoys and unites in an unexpected thesis. Another is written by a magazine editor (not a poetry editor, however) and nonfiction writer. A third is written by a college student. Only one of these four essays is written by an expert in the field. But all the writers argue theses that offer insights into art and poetry. Even the two writers who pointedly disagree with each other can help a reader better understand and even better appreciate the poem about which they disagree.

American Children: Two Declarations of Independence for Youth

JOHN UPDIKE

John Updike, an American novelist, poet, and critic, concluded his famed series of novels about Harry ("Rabbit") Angstrom with the 1990 publication of *Rabbit at Rest.* Among Updike's more recent publications are *Trust Me,* a short-story collection (1986); *S.,* a novel (1988); and *Self-Consciousness,* a memoir (1989). The following essay appears in Updike's book of essays about his favorite paintings, *Just Looking* (1989). Reproductions of the paintings are included with Updike's essay. If possible, look in your college's fine arts library for color reproductions in order to fully appreciate both the paintings and Updike's prose. Although not impossible, it is harder to appreciate "Greek drapery in the color-gouged fold of the sunlit white sleeve" in black and white.

Updike's essay shows how a layperson without formal training or recourse to technical jargon can argue a thesis about art. Updike claims that American art treats children with particular respect, and he offers as evidence two widely reprinted portraits of American youth. As you read, consider how you might use some of Updike's strategies in your own arguments about art. Like Updike, you might use interpretive description, so a reader sees the paintings as the writer sees them, or unexpected comparisons and a deferred statement of thesis, so a reader's curiosity is aroused.

The boys and girls depicted here might not mix very well if they 1 were released from their frames, but separately they compose two peaceful groups and two beautiful paintings. Winslow Homer's anonymous lads are taking their ease in a pasture; the daughters of the prosperous Edward Boit are scattered through two fine rooms, and all

BOYS IN A PASTURE

WINSLOW HOMER

Courtesy, Museum of Fine Arts, Boston, Hayden Collection.

but one of them gaze with respectful curiosity at the busy bearded intruder into their home, the fashionable painter John Singer Sargent. The dashing impressionism of Sargent's technique carries a generation farther Homer's flickering grasses and dabs of sunny red, and the triangular pose of the little girl in the foreground mirrors the unified shape of the two country idlers. Both painters surround their childish subjects with surprisingly large margins of environment. The effect is of silence: silent vases, silent sky, silent carpet and turf underfoot. A great hushed world waits around these children to be tasted, explored, grown into.

They take themselves seriously, and are taken seriously. Homer 2 gives his little subjects a monumental dignity; there is something of Greek drapery in the color-gouged fold of the sunlit white sleeve, and something angelically graceful in the extended, self-shadowed feet. And Sargent, catching his subjects where they have alighted like white butterflies, displays deep spaces about them, and permits them all the gravity their young femininity warrants. They recede, from youngest

DAUGHTERS OF EDWARD D. BOIT

JOHN SINGER SARGENT

Courtesy, Museum of Fine Arts, Boston, Marianne Brimmer Fund.

to oldest, toward a dark other room; beyond the toddler with her doll a girl no longer quite childish stands on the edge of shadow while her sister, a little taller and older still, is half-turned into it. The huge vase she leans against suggests a woman's shape. These young ladies are watching, not just the painter, but us, to see what we will do next, and whether what we do will be worthy of their responding. Like butterflies, they will elude us if we startle them.

Sargent's painting could have been a mere commission, an expert 3 piece of toadying within the upper classes, but the jaunty eccentricity of its composition, and a wit within its deference, save it for art.

Winslow Homer's could have been a bit of calendar art, falsely bucolic, but for the abstract power of a severe and stately composition that locks the barefoot pair as if forever into the center of the canvas and that lends solemn substance to a fleeting summer day. There is a mystery to the faces; the painter has declined all opportunity for easy anecdote within the ruddy shade of those hats.

Both artists have attempted honest portraits of children, as per-   4
haps only Americans could have done. Though the Declaration of Independence nowhere promises a better deal for children, the American child does appear freer than his European counterpart and is taken more seriously—as a source of opinion, as a market for sales, and as not just a future inheritor but an independent entity now, while still a child. Childhood and then youth are seen in our democracy as classes that cut across class distinctions. Within their frames these two sets of children are similarly pensive. Responsible but powerless, childhood does not smile; it watches and waits, amid shadows and sun.

QUESTIONS AND IDEAS FOR DISCUSSION

1.   What is Updike's thesis, and where is it most explicitly stated?

2.   Why has Updike chosen to link these two particular paintings to make his point about the particular qualities of paintings of American children? Does he succeed in making the kinds of unexpected but enlightening associations of which Marya Mannes speaks in "How Do You Know It's Good?" Comment.

3.   What about Sargent's composition (his arrangement of elements within the painting) is "jauntily eccentric"? What specifically in the painting shows "a wit within its deference"? And why does Updike claim that those qualities make this painting art, and not a "mere commission" (paragraph 3)?

4.   Specifically, what saves Homer's painting from being "a bit of calendar art" (3)? (You will have to decide what constitutes "calendar art." What are its characteristics?) Do you agree with Updike's assessment?

5.   Locate a reproduction of a European painting of children from about the same time period as the Homer and Sargent paintings. Does it substantiate Updike's claim that European children—and portraits of them—are less "free" and are taken less seriously than American children? Discuss, with specific reference to details.

Confined Love

JOHN DONNE

An Anglican clergyman famous during his lifetime for his sermons, John Donne (1571–1631) is today remembered chiefly as a poet. Ironically, the poetry that ranks him among the greatest Renaissance poets was not published until two years after his death. Donne's poetry is renowned for its wit and its rich imagery, and ranges in scope from satire to religious sonnets. "Confined Love" argues for free love. But who is arguing? As you read the poem, consider the likely identity of the speaker. The two essays following the poem will argue different answers to that question.

> Some man unworthy to be possessor
> Of old or new love, himselfe being false or weake,
>   Thought his paine and shame would be lesser,
> If on womankind he might his anger wreake,
>   And thence a law did grow,   5
>   One should but one man know;
>   But are other creatures so?
>
>   Are Sunne, Moone, or Starres by law forbidden,
> To smile where they list, or lend away their light?
>   Are birds divorc'd, or are they chidden   10
> If they leave their mate, or lie abroad a night?
>   Beasts doe no joyntures lose
>   Though they new lovers choose,
>   But we are made worse than those.
>
>   Who e'r rigg'd faire ship to lie in harbors,   15
> And not to seek new lands, or not to deale withall?
>   Or built fair houses, set trees, and arbours,
> Only to lock up, or else to let them fall?
>   Good is not good, unless
>   A thousand it possesse,   20
>   But doth wast with greedinesse.

Donne's "Confined Love"
(Student Essay)

SALLY DE WITT

This essay was written years ago when this editor was fortunate enough to be the student of an extraordinary teacher, Laurence Perrine, the author of *Sound and Sense* and other books, and essays of poetry interpretation too numerous to recount. Professor Perrine would ask one student at each meeting to read aloud his or her analysis of a particular poem; on one occasion, the task fell to me, and this was the essay I read. You may imagine my dismay when Professor Perrine quietly remarked that my assumptions and (therefore) my argument were entirely wrong, and that he would write a refutation and read it to the class at the next meeting! He did, and I was impressed but not convinced. Though I would change several things about my own essay today, I stand by my argument: The speaker is a man. See if you agree.

Donne's "Confined Love" is a seduction poem, but one skillfully 1 covert in its plea. The lover speaks as if to himself, ② but his five questions are not merely rhetorical. Too pointed is the progression and direction of the speaker's plaint; too clear is the image of a particular woman. The lady must be married, for the lover makes his principal argument against the moral stricture that "One should but one man know." She must pride herself on her generosity and goodness ② if her lover's conclusion is to touch her (lines 19–21); he flatters that predictable vanity by equating his lady (or her favors!) with all good. However, she must be more worldly than religious for the lover to dare his opening heresy.

For who can that false (both in the sense of "faithless" and of 2 "erroneous"), weak creature be who, unable to consummate or win love, devised a cruel law to vent his frustration upon womankind? ③ Who, indeed, but that "man" who decreed that "thy husband shall rule over thee" (Genesis 3:16): Jehovah God. The speaker, aware of the lady's apparently minimal regard for religious niceties, appeals rather to her sense of justice: "But are other creatures so?"

The lover fuels his argument quickly with a second and a third 3 question, naming some among the "other creatures" who are not restricted as women are in "lending," generously giving away, their "smiles" and their "light." Little birds are not ostracized or divorced if they "lie abroad a night." Man, or more particularly, woman, is not made a little lower than the angels but, by virtue of moral restrictions, lower even than the beasts. Nor, claims our intrepid lover, are man-made things designed for limited, "confined" use. It is contrary, finally, to nature and to man to restrict the scope of "good"—to limit the use of one's possessions, including oneself: "Good is not good, unless / A thousand it possesse, / But doth wast with greedinesse." Unless many may enjoy it, good will atrophy from its (and its would-be recipients') thwarted and spent eagerness—"greedinesse"— to share it. ④

The imagery in this poem is remarkable in its delicate skirting of 4 Biblical allusions: house, ship, arbors, the birds of the field—even the law ⑤ (cf. Galatians 5:14) might be turned to the lover's advantage, had he not invented so great a heresy for the premise of his plea. Slight connotations must, and do, suffice; the Bible and the Church are too given to exhortation to chastity, after all. The pun on "jointure" in the second stanza is as subtle: if the danger of losing her husband's "jointure" (property set aside for her support after his death) has not occurred to her, the hint is not alarmingly emphatic; if it has, the question is so phrased as to rouse her indignation. Birds are not "unjoined" or divorced; neither are they disinherited: "But we are made worse than those." The rhythm of the stanzas serves the same purpose of selective emphasis: where arguments are made and questions put, the rhythm is the irregular beat of prose speech (albeit rhymed and loosely pentametric), emphatic but less memorable than the singsong three-beat lines concluding each stanza. The seduction is subtle, as befits the wooing of a married lady by her courtly suitor; we are left to guess whether it proved successful.

Instructor's Comments

This is a subtle and sophisticated paper, I think over-subtle, and I think wrong, as I shall argue in my class "rebuttal." I shall confine myself to just a few remarks here.   5

1. Yes, the speaker speaks "as if to himself." If it were truly a seduction poem, I think he would be speaking pretty clearly to the lady.   6

2. The poem ends with a generalization about what philosophers call "a good" (something desirable for man to have, cf. economic "goods"). But the specific good being referred to in the context of the poem is sexual pleasure. That is, the last lines are not about her "goodness" (some moral quality) but about her capacity to afford sexual pleasure.   7

3. The conception of Jehovah as a weak, false creature (and of course he wasn't a "creature" but a Creator) unable to consummate or win love and thus moved to devise a cruel law to vent his frustration upon womankind is so bizarre that I don't think even Donne would have thought of it. Whom did Jehovah woo? Who turned him down?—We do think of the Greek gods in those terms, but not of Jehovah (and of course the Greek gods mostly got whomever they wanted).   8

4. No. What I think is meant here is: Unless many may enjoy it, good will atrophy from the "greediness" of its *owner* or *possessor* (the husband) who wants it all to himself and refuses to share it. The house falls to ruin in the lines preceding because its builder locks it up and refuses to let others enter.   9

5. I would myself say, I think, that there are no Biblical allusions 10
in the poem. The mention of a ship or of a house is not sufficient to
constitute an allusion. Genesis 3:16 gives man dominion over woman
in the family, but that is not quite the same as the law "One should but
one man know": it just means that man is the boss. The Biblical rule on
sex is that one shalt not commit adultery, and this refers to both men
and women. Thus the law referred to in line 6 is more likely a social
law, not a Biblical law—the social law permitting a double standard—
a law indeed devised by men, not by Jehovah.

QUESTIONS AND IDEAS FOR DISCUSSION

1. This essay's first argument is that "Confined Love" is a seduction
poem—that is, a poem with a dramatic context in which the male
speaker argues that the woman he addresses should agree to have sex
with him for several compelling (and fallacious!) reasons. Much about
the identity of the speaker hinges on the accuracy of that claim. Why?
Evaluate the argument.

2. At least one claim in this essay is thoroughly refuted in the instructor's notes: that God is the "man" in line 1. Evaluate the other claims
and the evidence offered for them.

3. At this point (after reading the student essay and the instructor's
comments), do you believe the speaker of the poem is a man or a
woman? Give *your* reasons, based on evidence in the poem.

4. Characterize the style of this essay. Does it avoid what Walker
Gibson describes in the previous chapter as "stuffiness"? Give examples (of stuffiness or passages that avoid it) from the text.

Donne's "Confined Love"

LAURENCE PERRINE

Laurence Perrine is Professor Emeritus of English at Southern Methodist University and author of *Sound and Sense* (7th ed.), a classic
introduction to the study of poetry; *Story and Structure* (7th ed.), a
literature anthology; and countless journal articles. The following
argument is a slightly revised version of the essay Professor Perrine
read to refute mine; it was published in the *Explicator* several years
later, in 1980. I can attest that Laurence Perrine is an exemplary
teacher, a sound scholar, and a writer of wicked limericks. But I still
don't think the persona of "Confined Love" is female. You decide.

In John Donne's "Confined Love" the speaker argues that women   1
should have greater freedom in love. Specifically, protest is made
against the social law that "One should but one man know" (6),
paraphrasable as "A woman should have carnal knowledge of but one
man." The argument is organized on quasi-logical lines. In stanza 1
the law is said to have an irrational origin. It was invented by some
man who, unsuccessful in love, wanted revenge on womankind. In
stanza 2 the law is declared unnatural. Heavenly bodies are not forbidden to shine on more than one object; birds are not blamed or divorced
for taking more than one sexual partner; animals are not forced to
surrender their "joyntures" if they take new lovers. In stanza 3 the law
is held to be illogical. No reasonable person would build a fair ship and
confine it to one harbor, or construct a fair house, pleasantly land-
scaped, only to lock it up and prevent its being used and enjoyed.
Good things, argues the speaker, are wasted when confined in their
use; their benefits should be widely distributed.

Much of the poem's argument could be taken simply as a plea for   2
free love for both sexes. Stanza 1, however, clearly aims it at a restric-
tion placed upon women by men, and stanzas 2 and 3 subtly support
this intention. In stanza 2 a "joynture" in Donne's time was an estate
settled upon a wife for her use after her husband's death but forfeit if
she married again. In stanza 3 ships were objects referred to by feminine pronouns, and houses were domains of feminine or domestic
activity though built and owned (like ships) by men. The speaker is
specifically arguing for a freedom for women which men, by operation
of the double standard, already enjoyed.

Who is the poem's speaker? N. J. C. Andreasen, in *John Donne:*   3
Conservative Revolutionary (Princeton Univ. Press, 1967), p. 85, takes
the speaker as a libertine male attempting to seduce "a woman who
has scruples about being unfaithful to her husband." Judah Stampfer,
Joan Bennett, and A. J. Smith agree that the speaker is male.[1] Helen
Gardner, John T. Shawcross, and Patrick Cruttwell take the speaker as
being a woman, but do not argue the point.[2] I intend to argue it.

It is significant that nothing in the poem indicates a dramatic   4
situation. We do not know where the speaker is, or (Andreasen to the
contrary) whom the speaker is addressing (whether one person or

---

[1] Stampfer, in *John Donne and the Metaphysical Gesture* (New York: Funk and Wagnalls, 1970),
p. 79, says of the speaker that "his perverse logic is pugnacious." Joan Bennett, in *Five Metaphysical
Poets* (Cambridge Univ. Press, 1964), p. 19, and A. J. Smith, ed., John Donne, *The Complete English
Poems* (Harmondsworth: Penguin Books, 1971), p. 359, both state that "Break of Day" is the only one
of Donne's authenticated poems to have a woman speaker.
[2] John Donne, *The Elegies and The Songs and Sonnets*, ed. Helen Gardner (Oxford: Clarendon
Press, 1965), p. 157; *The Complete Poetry of John Donne*, ed. John T. Shawcross (New York: New York
Univ. Press, 1968), p. 123; "The Love Poetry of John Donne," *Metaphysical Poetry*, ed. David Palmer
and Malcolm Bradbury (London: Edward Arnold, 1970), p. 20. Shawcross mis-glosses line 6.

many or any), or on what occasion. The poem contains no vocatives; it does not once use the pronoun "you" (or even "I" or "me"). Its content consists of a philosophical argument divorced from dramatic context.

To read the poem as a seduction poem, we must hypothesize (as 5 Andreasen does) a dramatic context not supplied by the poem. We must also make other assumptions. First, we must assume that the lady is willing to be seduced except for this social law, for the speaker's entire effort is directed at discrediting the law. He does not declare his passion for the woman, or attempt to praise or flatter her; the argument is pitched on a logical, not an emotional level. Second, we must assume that he neither has nor pretends to have (as most seducers would) an enduring interest in the lady: his argument is directed not at securing her favors exclusively for himself; he suggests she should share them with others. "Good is not good," he argues (no doubt with some overstatement), unless a thousand possess it. Each of these assumptions, since it has no foundation *within* the poem, makes more questionable the reading which requires it. There is an additional objection. In stanza 3 the presumed seducer clumsily reminds the woman that she risks divorce and loss of her jointure if she takes another lover. This reminder (which works against his own interest) is inconsistent with his cleverness in the rest of the poem.

If we examine the poem on its own terms, devoid of dramatic 6 context, the evidence strongly favors a woman speaker. The speaker argues against the social law that a woman should be confined to one man. Women, she believes, should have sexual parity with men. She blames the existence of the restrictive social law upon a man, not upon God or a woman. It is natural for men and women to blame the opposite sex for their ills. Men blame Eve, or Pandora. Donne's speaker, with considerable historical justice, blames man for the restrictions of the double standard. The elements of self-interest and of psychological plausibility both support the probability of a woman speaker. A libertine woman would be much more likely than a man to argue that one woman should a "thousand" know.

Helen Gardner traces the reasoning of the poem to Ovid's *Meta-* 7 *morphoses* (X. 320–355). Andreasen traces it to Ovid's *Amores* (I. VIII. 49–54). In both suggested "sources" the speaker is a woman.

QUESTIONS AND IDEAS FOR DISCUSSION

1. Why does Perrine regard it as "significant that nothing in the poem indicates a dramatic situation" (paragraph 4)? Is he right on both counts—that there is no dramatic situation and that the fact is significant? Evaluate Perrine's argument.

2. "If we examine the poem on its own terms, devoid of dramatic context, the evidence strongly favors a woman speaker" (6). Evaluate the argument that supports this claim.

3. Perrine uses the conclusions of other scholars as a departure point for his own argument. Does his doing so enhance his persona? Explain.

4. Characterize the style of this essay. Does Perrine avoid stuffiness (as Walker Gibson describes it in Chapter 6)? Comment on the reasons for your aesthetic judgment of the essay.

The Poet and the Computer

NORMAN COUSINS

Norman Cousins (1915–1990), long-time editor of the *Saturday Review*, received the United Nations Peace Medal in recognition of his efforts to "foster the good of the world community." One of the best known of Cousins's many best-selling books is his *Anatomy of an Illness* (1979), in which he recounts taking charge of his own treatment—prescribing large doses of laughter and cheer—in order to recover from a life-threatening infection acquired during a visit to Russia. His last book, in a similar vein, was *Head First: The Biology of Hope* (1989). The following essay first appeared in *Beyond Literacy: The Second Gutenberg Revolution* (1990), a collection of essays, edited by R. Patton Howell, on the place of language and literature at the end of the twentieth century. In this essay, Cousins argues the value of "poetry"—all imaginative literature, and imagination itself—in an age of technology. To Cousins, poetry is not only *as* valuable as "electronic intelligence," it is *more* valuable.

"A poet," said Aristotle, "has the advantage of expressing the 1 universal; the specialist expresses only the particular." The poet, moreover, can remind us that man's greatest energy comes not from his dynamos but from his dreams. The notion of where a man ought to be instead of where he is; the liberation from cramped prospects; the intimations of immortality through art, all these proceed naturally out of dreams. But the quality of man's dreams can only be a reflection of his subconscious. What he puts into his subconscious, therefore, is quite literally the most important nourishment in the world.

Nothing really happens to a man except as it is registered in the 2 subconscious. This is where event and feeling become memory and where the proof of life is stored. The poet, and I use the term to include all those who have respect for and speak to the human spirit, can help to supply the subconscious with material to enhance its sensitivity, thus safeguarding it. The poet, too, can help to keep man from making himself over in the image of his electronic marvels. The danger is not so much that man will be controlled by the computer as that he may imitate it.

There once was a time, in the history of this society, when the 3 ability of people to convey meaning was enriched by their knowledge of and access to the work of creative minds from across the centuries. No more. Conversation and letters today, like education, have become enfeebled by emphasis on the functional and the purely contemporary. The result is a mechanization not just of the way we live but of the way we think and of the human spirit itself.

The delegates to the United States Constitutional Convention 4 were able to undergird their arguments with allusions to historical situations and to the ideas of philosophers, essayists, and dramatists. Names such as Thucydides, Aristotle, Herodotus, Plutarch, or Seneca were commonly cited to support their positions. They alluded to fictional characters from Aristophanes, Marlowe, or Shakespeare to lend color to the exploration of ideas. The analytical essays by Hamilton, Madison, and Jay that appeared in *The Federalist Papers* were an excursion into the remote corners of history.

Men such as Jefferson, Adams, Franklin, and Rush could summon 5 pertinent quotations from Suetonius or Machiavelli or Montaigne to illustrate a principle. If they referred to Bacon's opinion of Aristotle, they didn't have to cite particulars; they assumed such details were common knowledge. Their allusions were not the product of intellectual ostentation or ornamentation but the natural condiments of discourse, bringing out the full flavor of the cultivated intelligence.

The same was true of correspondence. People regarded letters as 6 an art form and a highly satisfying way of engaging in civilized exchange. The correspondence of Jefferson and Adams and Priestley was not so much a display of personal matters as a review of the human condition. It was not unusual for the writers to range across the entire arena of human thought as a way of sharing perceptions. Allusion was common currency. Today, we rarely turn to letters as a way of embarking on voyages of intellectual discovery.

The essential problem of man in a computerized age remains the 7 same as it has always been. That problem is not solely how to be more productive, more comfortable, more content, but how to be more sensitive, more sensible, more proportionate, more alive. The computer makes possible a phenomenal leap in human proficiency; it demolishes the fences around the practical and even the theoretical intelligence. But the question persists, and indeed grows, whether the computer makes it easier or harder for human beings to know who they really are, to identify their real problems, to respond more fully to beauty, to place adequate value on life, and to make their world safer than it now is.

Electronic brains can reduce the profusion of dead ends involved 8 in vital research. But they can't eliminate the foolishness and decay that come from the unexamined life. Nor do they connect a man to the things he has to be connected to, the reality of pain in others; the possibilities of creative growth in himself; the memory of the race; and the rights of the next generation.

The reason these matters are important in a computerized age is 9 that there may be a tendency to mistake data for wisdom, just as there has always been a tendency to confuse logic with values and intelligence with insight. Unobstructed access to facts can produce unlimited good only if it is matched by the desire and ability to find out what they mean and where they would lead.

Facts are terrible things if left sprawling and unattended. They are 10 too easily regarded as evaluated certainties rather than as the rawest of raw materials crying to be processed into the texture of logic. It requires a very unusual mind, Whitehead said, to undertake the analysis of a fact. The computer can provide a correct number, but it may be an irrelevant number until judgment is pronounced.

To the extent, then, that man fails to make the distinction between 11 the intermediate operations of electronic intelligence and the ultimate responsibilities of human decision and conscience, the computer could obscure man's awareness of the need to come to terms with himself. It may foster the illusion that he is asking fundamental questions when actually he is asking only functional ones. It may be regarded as a substitute for intelligence instead of an extension of it. It may promote undue confidence in concrete answers. "If we begin with certainties," Bacon said, "we shall end in doubts; but if we begin with doubts, and we are patient with them, we shall end in certainties."

The computer knows how to vanquish error, but before we lose 12 ourselves in celebration of victory, we might reflect on the great advances in the human situation that have come about because men were challenged by error and would not stop thinking and probing until they found better approaches for dealing with it. "Give me a good fruitful error, full of seeds, bursting with its own corrections," Ferris Greenslet wrote. "You can keep your sterile truth for yourself."

Without taking anything away from the technicians, it might be 13 fruitful to effect some sort of junction between the computer technologist and the poet. A genuine purpose may be served by turning loose the wonders of the creative imagination on the kinds of problems being put to electronic tubes and transistors. The company of poets may enable the men who tend the machines to see a larger panorama of possibilities than technology alone may inspire.

Poets remind men of their uniqueness. It is not necessary to 14 possess the ultimate definition of this uniqueness. Even to speculate on it is a gain.

QUESTIONS AND IDEAS FOR DISCUSSION

1. Are we, as Cousins claims (paragraph 3), "mechanized" in how we live and think? Discuss. With what examples might you support (or counter) Cousins's argument?

2. How did the framers of the United States Constitution get into this essay? Is Cousins making the "need for cultural literacy" argument as we are growing accustomed to seeing it? How do paragraphs 3 through 6 contribute to Cousins's argument?

3. Discuss the following two assertions, offering examples if possible:

The danger is not so much that man will be controlled by the computer as that he may imitate it. (paragraph 2)

Facts are terrible things if left sprawling and unattended. (10)

4. How could Cousins's proposal in paragraph 13 be effected? What "sort of junction between the computer technologist and the poet" is possible—or desirable? Discuss.

ADDITIONAL MATERIAL FOR ANALYSIS AND ARGUMENT: PAINTINGS AND POEMS

The paintings and poems that follow provide but a small sampling of the analytical and argumentative possibilities art offers. To begin, you might choose to compare Sargent's *Two Girls Fishing* on page 355 to his more formal portrait of the Boit daughters on page 342, or you might consider *Two Girls Fishing* in relation to Homer's *Boys in a Pasture* (page 341)—which resembles it in its natural, outdoor setting. Comparisons offer a starting point, but you might even consider *Two Girls Fishing*—or any other work included in this section—and argue its merits without making comparisons.

In the two portraits of Mary Cassatt, we see the differences between an artist's vision of herself and another artist's vision of her. Do the two portraits seem to be of different women? You might look at other pairs (many Impressionists painted themselves and each other), if you want to decide whether artists can paint themselves with as clear an eye as they portray others.

The poems in this section concern love and war—hardly small issues, though with one exception these are small (that is, brief) poems. The first offers the classic *carpe diem* arguments, the second is a rebuttal, and the third is a modern parody. Each is an argument in poetry—but the arguments support entirely different conclusions. The last two poems share only one element. Both argue a point about war, but their poetic treatment of war could not be more different. You might find it interesting to consider, along with these two, one of the Wilfred Owen poems about war quoted by Vernon Scannell on pages 336 and 337.

You can draw upon this material in creating your own arguments about the nonlogical. You can also, if time permits, go beyond these paintings and poems: to your college art library, your local library, a nearby art museum. As more than one writer in this chapter has suggested, the more you see and read, the more confident you will become in your judgments and your ability to give reasons for them. As the essays in this chapter demonstrate, to argue about the aesthetic is not only possible but important.

Two Girls Fishing

JOHN SINGER SARGENT

John Singer Sargent (1856–1925) was an artist both popular and gifted. Sargent was an American Impressionist painter who was born in Italy and lived most of his life in London. He was much in demand for his unusual and brilliant portraits. He painted *Two Girls Fishing* (1912) exactly thirty years after *Daughters of Edward D. Boit.* In 1910, Sargent had given up portrait painting, but not his interest in human subjects. These girls are older than the Boit daughters, and in some respects this painting is even more intriguing. Does it show the same feeling for American youth that John Updike describes in his essay on page 340? Would *Two Girls Fishing* have been a more appropriate, or less appropriate, painting to discuss in conjunction with Winslow Homer's *Boys in a Pasture*?

Courtesy, Cincinnati Art Museum, John J. Emery Fund.

Portrait of the Artist

MARY CASSATT

Portrait of the Artist (ca. 1878) was painted by master American Impressionist Mary Cassatt during her early years in Paris, at a time when she was particularly influenced by Edgar Degas. It is not much like the later paintings Cassatt is most famous for, the idyllic portraits of sweet round-faced mothers with their children. This woman, dressed in white except for a bright bonnet, shows in her bearing and expression little enough of sweetness. What *does* she show?

Courtesy, The Metropolitan Museum of Art, Bequest of Edith H. Proskauer, 1975 (1975. 319.1).

Seated Portrait of Mary Cassatt

EDGAR DEGAS

French Impressionist Edgar Degas (1834–1917) is probably most familiar to you for his paintings and bronzes of ballerinas, but his subjects were not limited to dancers. *Seated Portrait of Mary Cassatt* (ca. 1884) was one of several paintings and etchings Degas did of his pupil Cassatt beginning in about 1876. In this painting, Cassatt holds a group of photographs, fanned out like playing cards. The painting contrasts in intriguing ways with Cassatt's self-portrait of a few years earlier. Think, as you consider the two, about how the artist sees herself and how a fellow artist sees her. This question is underscored by the fact that Mary Cassatt came to dislike Degas's portrait intensely. She asked a dealer to sell it as the portrait of an unknown person, and thus the portrait was lost until 1951. It is now in a private collection. Can you detect in Degas's portrait the intense energy for which Cassatt was known among her circle of friends?

Courtesy, National Portrait Gallery, Smithsonian Institution, Washington, D.C./Art Resource.

The Passionate Shepherd to His Love

CHRISTOPHER MARLOWE

Christopher Marlowe (1564–1593) is regarded as the father of English tragedy. He wrote six heroic tragedies, the first ever written for the public stage, and the long poem *Hero and Leander*. But he may be at least as well known today for "The Passionate Shepherd to his Love," the quintessential *carpe diem* (literally, "seize the day," or seduction) poem. It offers an argument calculated for emotional, not logical, impact. Read it several times before you go on to the more cynical outlook of Raleigh's "Reply." Marlowe's poem is worth appreciating on its own terms.

> Come live with mee, and be my love,
> And we will all the pleasures prove,
> That Vallies, groves, hills and fieldes,
> Woods, or steepie mountaine yeeldes.
>
> And wee will sit upon the Rocks,   5
> Seeing the Sheepheards feede theyr flocks
> By shallow Rivers, to whose falls
> Melodious byrds sings Madrigalls.
>
> And I will make thee beds of Roses,
> And a thousand fragrant poesies,   10
> A cap of flowers, and a kirtle,
> Imbroydred all with leaves of Mirtle.
>
> A gowne made of the finest wooll,
> Which from our pretty Lambes we pull,
> Fayre lined slippers for the cold,   15
> With buckles of the purest gold.
>
> A belt of straw and Ivie buds,
> With Corall clasps and Amber studs,
> And if these pleasures may thee move,
> Come live with mee, and be my love.   20
>
> The Sheepheards Swaines shall daunce & sing
> For thy delight each May-morning.
> If these delights thy minde may move,
> Then live with mee, and be my love.

The Nymph's Reply to the Shepherd
SIR WALTER RALEIGH

Sir Walter Raleigh (1552?–1618) explored the New World under the auspices of Queen Elizabeth I and is credited with introducing both the potato and tobacco to England. He was executed by the Queen's successor, King James I, for conspiracy. A true Renaissance man, Raleigh also wrote poetry and, while in prison, his *History of the World* (1614). Of his poetry, this ironic poem is best known. It refutes Marlowe with a vengeance.

If all the world and love were young,
And truth in every Sheepheards tongue,
These pretty pleasures might me move,
To live with thee, and be thy love.

Time drives the flocks from field to fold,   5
When Rivers rage, and Rocks grow cold,
And Philomell becommeth dombe,
The rest complaines of cares to come.

The flowers doe fade, and wanton fieldes,
To wayward winter reckoning yeeldes,   10
A honny tongue, a hart of gall,
Is fancies spring, but sorrowes fall.

Thy gownes, thy shooes, thy beds of Roses,
Thy cap, thy kirtle, and thy poesies,
Soone breake, soone wither, soone forgotten: 15
In follie ripe, in reason rotten.

Thy belt of straw and Ivie buddes,
Thy Corall claspes and Amber studdes,
All these in mee no meanes can move,
To come to thee, and be thy love.   20

But could youth last, and love still breede,
Had joyes no date, nor age no neede,
Then these delights my minde might move,
To live with thee, and be thy love.

Dooley Is a Traitor

JAMES MICHIE

James Michie is both a poet and a publisher, the editorial director of the British publishing company Bodley Head. He is author of two volumes of poetry: *Possible Laughter* (1959), from which this poem is taken, and *New and Selected Poems* (1983). Michie's poem and the one following it move away from the subject of love—to war. "Dooley" is a narrative poem that argues a moral difference between murder and war. Perhaps unexpectedly, however, it argues that killing in battle is worse than murder. Also unexpectedly, the speaker is a man of no great personal appeal, himself an admitted killer of "a good many." Why do you suppose Michie created a character as blemished as Dooley to argue against war?

"So then you won't fight?"
"Yes, your Honour," I said, "that's right."
"Now is it that you simply aren't willing,
Or have you a fundamental moral objection to killing?"
Says the judge, blowing his nose   5
And making his words stand to attention in long rows.
I stand to attention too, but with half a grin
(In my time I've done a good many in).
"No objection at all, sir," I said.
"There's a deal of the world I'd rather see dead—   10
Such as Johnny Stubbs or Fred Settle or my last landlord, Mr.
      Syme.
Give me a gun and your blessing, your Honour, and I'll be
      killing them all the time.
But my conscience says a clear no
To killing a crowd of gentlemen I don't know.
Why, I'd as soon think of killing a worshipful judge,   15
High-court, like yourself (against whom, God knows, I've got
      no grudge—
So far), as murder a heap of foreign folk.
If you've got no grudge, you've got no joke
To laugh at after."
                        Now the words never come flowing   20
Proper for me till I get the old pipe going.
And just as I was poking
Down baccy, the judge looks up sharp with "No smoking,
Mr. Dooley. We're not fighting this war for fun.
And we want a clearer reason why you refuse to carry a gun.   25
This war is not a personal feud, it's a fight

Against wrong ideas on behalf of the Right.
Mr. Dooley, won't you help to destroy evil ideas?"
"Ah, your Honour, here's
The tragedy," I said. "I'm not a man of the mind.   30
I couldn't find it in my heart to be unkind
To an idea. I wouldn't know one if I saw one. I haven't one of
    my own.
So I'd best be leaving other people's alone."
"Indeed," he sneers at me, "this defence is
Curious for someone with convictions in two senses.   35
A criminal invokes conscience to his aid
To support an individual withdrawal from a communal crusade
Sanctioned by God, led by the Church, against a godless,
    churchless nation!"
I asked his Honour for a translation.
"You talk of conscience," he said, "What do you know of the
    Christian creed?"   40
"Nothing, sir, except what I can read,
That's the most you can hope for from us jail-birds.
I just open the Book here and there and look at the words.
And I find when the Lord himself misliked an evil notion
He turned it into a pig and drove it squealing over a cliff into
    the ocean,   45
And the loony ran away
And lived to think another day.
There was a clean job done and no blood shed!
Everybody happy and forty wicked thoughts drowned dead.
A neat and Christian murder. None of your mad slaughter   50
Throwing away the brains with the blood and the baby with
    the bathwater.
Now I look at the war as a sportsman. It's a matter of choosing
The decentest way of losing.
Heads or tails, losers or winners,
We all lose, we're all damned sinners.   55
And I'd rather be with the poor cold people at the wall that's
    shot
Than the bloody guilty devils in the firing-line, in Hell and
    keeping hot."
"But what right, Dooley, what right," he cried,
"Have you to say the Lord is on your side?"
"That's a dirty crooked question," back I roared.   60
"I said not the Lord was on my side, but I was on the side of
    the Lord."
Then he was up at me and shouting,

But by and by he calms: "Now we're not doubting
Your sincerity, Dooley, only your arguments,
Which don't make sense." 65
('Hullo,' I thought, 'that's the wrong way round.
I may be skylarking a bit, but my brainpan's sound.')
Then biting his nail and sugaring his words sweet:
"Keep your head, Mr. Dooley. Religion is clearly not up your
 street.
But let me ask you as a plain patriotic fellow 70
Whether you'd stand there so smug and yellow
If the foe were attacking your own dear sister."
"I'd knock their brains out, mister,
On the floor," I said. "There," he says kindly, "I knew you
 were no pacifist.
It's your straight duty as a man to enlist. 75
The enemy is at the door." You could have downed
Me with a feather. "Where?" I gasp, looking round.
"Not this door," he says angered. "Don't play the clown.
But they're two thousand miles away planning to do us down.
Why, the news is full of the deeds of those murderers and
 rapers." 80
"Your Eminence," I said, "my father told me never to believe
 the papers
But to go by my eyes,
And at two thousand miles the poor things can't tell truth from
 lies."
His fearful spectacles glittered like the moon: "For the last time
 what right
Has a man like you to refuse to fight?" 85
"More right," I said, "than you.
You've never murdered a man, so you don't know what it is I
 won't do.
I've done it in good hot blood, so haven't I the right to make
 bold
To declare that I shan't do it in cold?"
Then the judge rises in a great rage 90
And writes DOOLEY IS A TRAITOR in black upon a page
And tells me I must die.
"What, me?" says I.
"If you still won't fight."
"Well, yes, your Honour," I said, "that's right." 95

Buttons

CARL SANDBURG

Carl Sandburg (1878–1967) was the Illinois-born son of Swedish immigrants. Although also a biographer and folklorist, Sandburg is best remembered for his poetry, especially his famous poem "Chicago." His *Complete Poems* (1950) was awarded the Pulitzer Prize for poetry in 1951. Sandburg's greatest poetic debt is to Walt Whitman, and like Whitman, Sandburg is decisively American in his outlook and his language. The following poem offers an implicit argument: Is it against war? Against complacency? Or against something else?

I have been watching the war map slammed up for
    advertising in front of the newspaper office.
Buttons—red and yellow buttons—blue and black
    buttons—are shoved back and forth across the
    map.
A laughing young man, sunny with freckles,
Climbs a ladder, yells a joke to somebody in the crowd,
And then fixes a yellow button one inch west   5
And follows the yellow button with a black button one
    inch west.
(Ten thousand men and boys twist on their bodies in a
    red soak along a river edge,
Gasping of wounds, calling for water, some rattling
    death in their throats.)
Who would guess what it cost to move two buttons one
    inch on the war map here in front of the newspaper
    office where the freckle-faced young man is
    laughing to us?

SUGGESTIONS FOR WRITING
AND FURTHER DISCUSSION

1. How comfortable are you with the arts? Do you ever read poetry or classic fiction for enjoyment? Do you visit art museums? Often? How many different kinds of music do you enjoy? What kinds of concerts do you attend, and how often?

Think about these questions in light of the readings for this chapter. Most people probably do not turn to art, literature, or classical poetry for pleasure, and yet, giving pleasure is arguably art's most important purpose. Analyze this paradoxical situation, and write an essay for an audience of your peers—the readers of your campus newspaper, perhaps—that argues your conclusions (and, if possible, solutions). You may find it useful to poll students on your campus to determine their feelings about the arts.

2. Argue a layperson's defense of your own favorite art (whether modern sculpture, old master portraits, nineteenth-century sea-scapes, pop art, or what have you) by creating clear analogies as Clement Greenberg does, so that a reader who has never valued that type of work will understand why you do.

3. Visit a nearby museum or gallery where contemporary art is displayed. Sit quietly for an hour, and observe the reactions and comments of people viewing the art. Note how long they linger, how close or far away they stand from individual works, whether or not they read the cards identifying and discussing the works. Record your observations carefully. Later, decide what sorts of conclusions you can draw about this limited sampling of responses to contemporary art. Do you find Clement Greenberg's arguments confirmed or challenged?

4. Research the development of the Impressionist movement in art. Greenberg asserts, "Impressionism itself started as an effort to push naturalism further than ever before" (paragraph 11). Is this claim borne out by your investigations? Write a documented essay that either supports Greenberg's claim or offers another reason for the rise of the Impressionist movement.

5. Many artists paint self-portraits, if for no other reason than that the model works cheap. Examine reproductions of self-portraits by a single artist (Van Gogh, perhaps) to see how the artist's view of himself or herself evolved over time. Or look at self-portraits and compare them to portraits of the same person by other artists (for example, see the two portraits of Mary Cassatt reprinted in this chapter). A ready supply of comparisons can be found in the nineteenth-century Impressionists, who were forever painting each other's portraits—for example, Morisot, Manet, Matisse, Renoir. Write an essay on the paintings, based on your conclusions about the chances of really "seeing ourselves as others see us." Your audience will be a group of people who in a literal sense never have seen themselves (for a mirror offers only a mirror image, after all): your classmates.

6. At your library, find several reproductions of paintings of a person reading. Four possibilities are listed below, but many artists have painted at least one reader. (You might find it intriguing to speculate on the reasons for *that.*) How does the artist seem to regard the subject, the reader? How does the reader appear to regard the artist, or the viewer? Does the reader fit into the setting comfortably? Incongruously? What strikes you as significant about the work or your response to it? You may choose to argue the merits or meaning of a single painting, to compare two, or to locate as many as possible over a given span of time and decide what conclusions a group of paintings suggests. Your audience will be your classmates, a group not necessarily knowledgeable about art, but interested and willing to learn.

- Cassatt, *Woman Reading in a Garden* (1880). Chicago Art Institute.
- Manet, *The Illustrated Newspaper* (1878–79). Chicago Art Institute.
- Matisse, *Reader Against a Black Background* (1939). Musée d'Art Moderne, Paris.
- Picasso, *Woman Reading* (1935). Musée Picasso.

7. What does *Two Girls Fishing* suggest about the girls who are its subject? About American youth? Discuss this painting and your responses to it. Do you prefer it to Sargent's *Daughters of Edward D. Boit?* Why, or why not?

8. Look through a poetry anthology, and find a poem that is also an argument—whether on the subject of love or war or something in between. Evaluate the argument of the poem. Is the poem persuasive? If so, how much of that quality is based on the language and the rhythm, and how much on the reasoning? Discuss your conclusions.

9. Is there any poem that you know more or less by heart? Perhaps your grandmother used to recite it to you, or you had to memorize it for a school program and now find it popping into your head at odd moments. Write an essay in which you argue for or against requiring students to memorize poems. Assume that three of your high school English teachers, along with all the students now in their classes, will read your essay.

10. Have you ever written a poem? What makes a poem, especially a "good" poem? Argue a set of criteria and standards, using two or three poems you particularly enjoy as examples. If no favorites come immediately to mind, here are three that you might read and consider. You can find them in many anthologies of poetry.

- Matthew Arnold, "Dover Beach"
- Theodore Roethke, "Elegy for Jane"
- William Shakespeare, Sonnet 73, "That Time of Year . . ."

PART TWO

PROS, CONS, AND MAYBES

In "The Strategy at Work" in chapters two through seven, you read arguments on six topics—college education, murder, advertising, marriage, capital punishment, and art—as examples of important strategies of argument. In this section you will confront arguments on six more topics, ranging from AIDS to zoos. These essays show how thirty-one writers justify their positions on important issues. They demonstrate as well the possibilities argument holds for the discovery of ideas—and occasionally, the discovery of truth. Some of the arguments directly oppose each other, and some are concerned with different aspects of related subjects. Whatever their stance, they argue their points energetically and often compellingly. Try, as you read, to put aside your own preconceptions on each subject and read each argument for its own merits. By doing so, you may gain as a writer, seeing what can be argued, and how. And you may gain as a thinker, seeing what can be thought, and why.

These essays by no means exhaust the possibilities of the subjects they discuss. They do not cover every viewpoint or every aspect of these often complex subjects. It may remain for you to find a stronger argument, a better way, a clearer vision, a more fitting solution. Even to try is worthwhile.

8

RECYCLING AND
WASTE DISPOSAL

It's hard to find anyone who will argue in favor of styrofoam or toxic waste dumps—almost as hard as it is to find someone who faithfully recycles, buys only minimally packaged products (and not too many of them), and properly disposes of all wastes. Recycling is noncontroversial—or is it? At least one essay in the following selections challenges what its writer views as unnecessary alarmism. Another argument reminds us that recycling is less desirable than *precycling*—using fewer materials and resources in the first place. Yet another essay argues practical concerns rather than moral ones: Companies can better compete in the marketplace if they are good stewards of the environment, minimizing their wastes through improved operating practices, recycling to generate useful byproducts and avoid the costs of disposal, and using alternate materials that will generate less toxic waste. And the final essay in the section announces in its first paragraph: "Without toxic wastes, life would still be possible, but it certainly would be bleaker."

So there is still room for disagreement and even controversy over how we should deal with the huge quantities of waste materials our consumer society generates and how troubled we should be about the environmental impact of our disposable diapers, our old auto batteries, our telephone books. But however great or small the problem, surely we are responsible and contributing parties to it. And surely the problem is worth our careful and reasoned consideration. As you read and evaluate these essays, notice in particular the writers' use of numbers and statistics. Which are we to believe, and why? How well do these writers support their claims?

Cut the Garbage

LAURENCE SOMBKE

Laurence Sombke has written essays and a book, *The Solution to Pollution* (1990), on environmental concerns. He has also produced a radio program, "Energy Issues," and has been a newswriter for ABC Radio News in New York. "Cut the Garbage" was first published in a nationally distributed newspaper supplement, *USA Weekend,* in 1989. Aware that he is writing to a broad audience with a brief attention span, Sombke takes a practical and direct approach. No hand wringing over the pollution problem here: Sombke argues that we must take individual action if we truly wish to have a collective impact on the environment, and he makes many specific recommendations. He also paints vivid pictures: "Every two weeks we throw away enough glass to fill the twin towers of the World Trade Center in New York." This essay accomplishes more than some more elegant arguments: It may make some of us change our ways.

Call it enviro-guilt. 1

Causes: The hole in the ozone, the greenhouse effect, garbage 2 barges, hypodermic needles washing ashore, last summer's beastly heat and drought.

Symptoms: A vague feeling that each of us may be contributing to 3 this mess.

Cure: Do a little every day to use up, recycle, renew. And here are 4 easy, at home ways to help the world instead of hurting it. . . .

Each person in the USA creates 3.5 pounds of garbage a day and 5 only about 10 percent is recycled. We need to recycle 25 percent by 1992, says the Environmental Protection Agency. That's a modest goal: Washington, D.C., soon will require 45 percent recycling.

In any case, your paper, metal, glass and plastic shouldn't just be 6 carted to the curb anymore. To get organized, you might try a three-container system recommended by Environmental Action. It began in Rhode Island a year ago and quickly is being copied around the country. The first container, maybe a cardboard box, holds newspapers to be recycled. A sturdy second container holds all other recyclables (aluminum, glass, tin cans, plastic bottles) to be sorted at the recycling center later. The third container is for regular trash.

Each town has its own recycling routine. For information about 7 your area, call the Environmental Defense Fund's hotline, 1-800-CALLEDF.

Mandatory recycling is working in 10 states (Florida, Pennsylva- 8 nia, New Jersey, Rhode Island, Oregon, Wisconsin, Connecticut, Massachusetts, New York, Maryland) and more than 600 communities outside those states. Some sanitation trucks in Seattle now have separate bins for each recycled material. In upstate Columbia County, New York, people are charged $2 for each bag of unseparated garbage, but recyclable items are free.

Why recycle? Because a third of our landfills will be overflowing in 9 five years. Even now, "The highest points in South Florida are our high-rise landfills," says Bill Hinkley, administrator of solid waste for Florida.

What's going to waste: 10

- Each Sunday, 500,000 trees are made into newspapers that aren't recycled.
- Every two weeks we throw away enough glass to fill the twin towers of the World Trade Center in New York.
- Every three months, we throw away enough aluminum cans to rebuild our entire commercial air fleet.
- Every hour, we throw away 2.5 million plastic bottles.

A chemical soup of potentially hazardous, toxic and corrosive 11 waste is cooking under your kitchen sink or wherever you store your household cleaners. When you toss out unused portions, they go to the landfill, the landfill leaks and the toxic wastes come back home in drinking water.

Labels tell you what's toxic. Highly toxic products must be labeled 12 "Danger," medium toxicity gets "Warning" and low toxicity gets "Caution."

The best solution: Find a non-toxic alternative. Replace toxic oven 13 cleaners, for instance, with a mixture of salt and baking soda, both natural abrasives. Vinegar for cleansing, lemon for cutting grease and plain soap are other staples in a clean *and* non-toxic house. . . .

If you insist on using chemical products, be careful and take 14 unused portions to a household hazardous waste center. To find a center, call your local sanitation or public works department.

Old cans of oil-based paints, thinners, turpentine, furniture strip- 15 per or stain also belong in your area's household hazardous waste center, not in your trash or down your drain.

Phosphates, added to powdered laundry soaps as a water soft- 16 ener, are banned in areas around the Great Lakes, the Chesapeake Bay and Florida; they could be a problem anywhere. Soap powders like Cheer and Tide mark their phosphate contents on the box.

To eliminate confusion and phosphates, use liquid laundry 17 soap—none of them has phosphates.

Chlorine bleach is a powerful chemical that can be used well and 18 wisely. But too much chlorine dumped into a small stream kills fish.

Use your chlorine bleach sparingly, or switch to a nonchlorine bleach like borax.

The USA used 16 billion disposable diapers last year. And they're 19 still around—they don't break down, especially the plastic outer coatings and tabs. You could switch to cloth diapers, but 85 percent of diaper-changers prefer disposables.

Enter the biodegradable diaper, with its plastic made with corn- 20 starch. (This is better than regular plastic, but not the final answer. Industry is looking for a real solution.) There are several brands of biodegradable diapers now, but the pioneer was TenderCares, developed by the Rocky Mountain Medical Corp., a group of pediatricians in Montrose, Colo. TenderCares are sold in health food stores and by mail and cost $1 to $1.50 more a bag than regular diapers. Information: 1-800-344-6379.

Supermarkets have switched to plastic bags to pack groceries, bag 21 veggies and display foods. As markets move into the prepared food take-out business, they use more plastic containers. But you don't have to.

Ask for paper bags at the check-out. 22

Buy eggs and milk in cardboard cartons, not plastic. 23

Buy concentrated, multi-purpose products—like a laundry soap 24 that is also a bleach or a fabric softener—to cut down on packaging.

Buy products in cardboard: 50 percent of cardboard supermarket 25 packages are recycled paper. Kellogg, Ralston Purina and General Foods all use recycled paper packaging.

Don't put your tomatoes and potatoes in plastic bags: They'll 26 make it home OK unwrapped.

Always buy plain white toilet paper or paper towels. Dyed paper 27 pollutes water when disposed of.

If you have a choice, buy non-aerosol sprays. All aerosols now 28 meet legal requirements for levels of cfc's (chlorofluorocarbons) but all cfc's still destroy the ozone that filters the sun's rays. Some aerosols substitute other chemicals, which have questionable effects.

Buy rechargeable batteries for flashlights and other household 29 gear. They'll cost a bit more but last longer. And you won't have as many batteries to take to your hazardous waste center.

Also, scout your local health food stores for recyclable, biodegrad- 30 able and renewable products. If you can't find special products—like 30-gallon heavy-duty paper garbage bags, biodegradable sanitary napkins, toilet paper made from 100 percent recycled paper, non-toxic household cleansers—there's a mail-order catalog that carries a variety of goods. Send $2 to Seventh Generation catalog, 10 Farrell St., South Burlington, VT 05403.

Some of you (maybe 20 percent) use leaded gas when your car is 31
meant for unleaded. That fouls your catalytic converter and spews out
lead and nitrogen oxides, contributing to smog, acid rain and de-
pletion of the ozone layer.

If you change your own oil, and an estimated 50 percent of you do, 32
do not pour it down your city sewer system. Just one quart of oil can
contaminate up to 2 million gallons of drinking water. The four quarts
of oil you just drained from your crankcase can form an oil slick nearly
8 acres across. These not-so-fun facts come from the Chesapeake Bay
Foundation, an environmental group that has taken to printing sten-
cils near drains that warn: "This drain leads directly to the bay."

That used battery you left in the garage is made of lead and full of 33
sulfuric acid. If it cracks, those toxins go onto the soil and into the
water system.

Tires are a major disposal problem, very difficult to recycle. Buy 34
the longest-wearing tires you can, keep them properly inflated and
make them last.

In each case, you should take your old oil, batteries and tires to a 35
local household hazardous waste center. Or ask around for a garage or
gas station that will add your mess to its own and properly dispose of
it all later. . . .

Yard waste, lawn clippings, tree limbs and leaves are 18 percent of 36
the garbage that gets hauled to the dump, unnecessarily overloading
landfills. You should put yard waste in a compost, and then recycle it
as natural fertilizer. Your local county agent or cooperative extension
office can show you how. Also, you can get a free booklet on non-toxic
gardens from Safer Gardens, P.O. Box 1665, New York, N.Y. 10116.

When you spread fertilizers on your lawn, some chemicals can be 37
washed into local water supplies. One fertilizer element, nitrogen, is
linked to brown and red tides (actually algae blooms) that cause
massive fish and shellfish kills. Pesticides and herbicides can pollute,
too. Prevent this by using the correct amounts of fertilizers and sprays
and reducing runoff with good grass cover, shrubs and trees.

For every tree you plant in your yard, you'll save $100-$200 a year 38
in heating, cooling, soil erosion and air pollution costs. So why not
plant an extra tree—or two—to celebrate this Earth Day?

QUESTIONS AND IDEAS FOR DISCUSSION

1.   Summarize the argument of Sombke's essay. What is his thesis? Is
it explicitly stated in the essay? If so, where?

2.   Does Sombke make you feel that you are part of his intended
audience? Does he make you care about his subject? How, or why not?

Do you believe that what Sombke argues applies to you? If so, how do you plan to respond? If not, why not? Be specific.

3.   Sombke interrupts his essay at frequent intervals to include addresses and telephone numbers. What rhetorical effect do these intrusions have on the essay? Why?

4.   Sombke declares, "Every three months, we throw away enough aluminum cans to rebuild our entire commercial air fleet" (paragraph 10). This is an impressive statistic; is it a "knowable" statistic? What is Sombke's source of this information? Comment.

5.   In the months after this essay first appeared in 1989, environmental researchers publicized a serious problem with "biodegradable" garbage bags and diapers of the kind Sombke recommends. Biodegradable products require exposure to light and air in order to break down, and most of these products end up buried in landfills where neither light nor air can reach them. What other possibilities remain available to us as environmentally conscious consumers? Sombke indicates some; can you suggest others?

Rubbish!

WILLIAM L. RATHJE

William L. Rathje, a professor of anthropology at the University of Arizona in Tucson, is a knowledgeable authority on waste and recycling. His is more than book knowledge: Since 1973, Rathje has headed the "Garbage Project" at Arizona. The aim of this project has been to learn from what is thrown away. Rathje and his students have sifted through literally tons of trash—in the process, discovering a great deal about people. The researchers have accumulated a wealth of data on everything from the quantity of grass clippings a yard generates and the amount of junk mail a mailbox attracts to nutrition (what people really buy to eat as opposed to what they say or think they eat) and drug abuse. Just as significantly, Rathje has seen firsthand what typical urban refuse consists of and how effectively it decomposes. "Rubbish!" first appeared in a longer version as the cover story in the *Atlantic,* December 1989. The writer knows his subject, but you may find his conclusions unorthodox and even startling.

Newspapers. Telephone books. Soiled diapers. Half-empty cans of   1
paint, motor oil and herbicide. Broken furniture and forsaken toys. Americans produce a lot of garbage. Recently, the press has paid

much attention to the filling up (and closing down) of landfills and to the apparent inadequacy of our recycling efforts. The word *crisis* has become routine. For all the publicity, however, it may be that misinformation constitutes the real garbage crisis.

Since the early 1970s, the University of Arizona's Garbage Project 2 has been looking at landfills and garbage fresh out of the can. As director of the program, I have talked extensively with people who think about garbage every day—city officials, junkyard owners, landfill operators, civil engineers, microbiologists. Our garbage woes turn out to be serious, but not exceptional. And they can be dealt with by disposal methods that are safe and already available.

How much garbage is there? I have seen figures ranging from 2.9 3 to eight pounds discarded per person per day. But Garbage Project studies of refuse reveal that even three pounds of garbage per person per day may be too high an estimate for much of the country. Americans are wasteful, but we think of ourselves as more wasteful than we are.

What's more, we forget everything we no longer see: as much as 4 1200 pounds per year of wood or coal ash that every American generated at home at the turn of the century; the tens of thousands of dead horses that once had to be disposed of every year; the food waste that modern packaging has prevented. Consider the difference in terms of garbage generation between making orange juice from concentrate and orange juice from scratch, keeping in mind that producers of the concentrate sell the leftover orange rinds as feed, while households don't. In reality, Americans, as individuals, are not suddenly producing more garbage. Per capita our record seems to be one of relative stability.

Landfills. In the northeastern United States, there is an acute short- 5 age of sanitary landfills. Nationwide some 3000 landfills reached capacity and were shut down between 1982 and 1987. Articles on the subject often warn that 50 percent of the landfills now in use will likely close down within five years. But that has always been true because most landfills are designed to be in use for only about ten years. The real problem is that in many areas old landfills are not being replaced. Texas, for example, awarded some 250 permits a year for municipal solid-waste landfills in the mid-'70s, but only 13 last year.

The landfill movement that matured after World War II intended 6 not only to dispose of mountains of garbage but also to reclaim thousands of acres of "waste" land. Its proponents argued that the ideal sites for landfills were the very places that most scientists now believe to be the worst: along rivers or in wetlands. It is in unlined landfills in places like these that chemical "leachates"—solubles removed by percolating water—have posed a grave concern.

Environmental scientists now know enough to design and locate 7
safe landfills. Places such as Long Island, N.Y., where the water table
is high, should never have landfills again and should continue to ship
garbage elsewhere. But the country at large still has room aplenty.

The obstacles to the sanitary landfill these days are monetary 8
(transporting the garbage) and psychological: no one wants a garbage
dump in his back yard. But these problems are not insuperable. Few
nations have the enormous, and enormously safe, landfill capabilities
that America has.

Fast Foods and Diapers. Another idea that persists about landfills is 9
that certain products are disproportionately responsible for filling
them up. I recently ran across articles in an Oregon newspaper that
blame disposable diapers. An editorial in the New York *Times* singled
out fast-food packaging, almost everyone's villain of choice, for straining the capacity of the nation's landfills. I have asked many people
who have never seen the inside of a landfill to estimate what percentage consists of fast-food packaging. Most estimated either 20 or 30
percent.

The reality is considerably different. Over the past two years, the 10
Garbage Project team has dug into seven landfills: two outside Chicago, two in the San Francisco Bay Area, two in Tucson and one in
Phoenix. In eight tons of garbage and dirt cover, there were fewer than
16 pounds of fast-food packaging—about a tenth of one percent of the
landfills' contents by weight. Less than one percent by weight was
disposable diapers. Things made from plastic accounted for less than
five percent by weight.

The real "culprit" in every landfill is plain old paper—non-fast- 11
food paper—which accounts for 40 to 50 percent by weight. Yet, in all
the hand-wringing, has a single voice been raised against the proliferation of telephone books? Each two-volume set of these books distributed in Phoenix last year—to be thrown out this year—weighed 7.95
pounds, for a total of more than 5000 tons of wastepaper. Dig a trench
through a landfill and you will see layers of phone books, like geological strata. Just as conspicuous are newspapers, which, according to
my research, make up ten to 18 percent of a typical municipal landfill
by volume. During a recent dig in Phoenix, I found newspapers dating
back to 1952 that looked so fresh you might read one over breakfast.

Biodegrading. The notion that paper rapidly biodegrades inside 12
lined landfills is largely a myth. This may be a blessing, because if
paper did degrade quickly, the result would be an enormous amount
of ink and paint that could leach into ground water.

The fact that plastic hardly biodegrades at all, often cited as one of 13
its great defects, may actually be a great virtue. Being inert, it doesn't
introduce toxic chemicals into the environment. The senior staff scien-

tist of the National Audubon Society, Jan Beyea, contends that plastics in landfills are no problem. The plastics that marine animals sometimes swallow or become enmeshed in generally come from ocean dumping.

Recycling. There is a big split between those who would recycle to 14 make money and those who would recycle to do good. When I described the city of Tucson's successful newspaper-recycling program to a wastepaper dealer, he looked at me in horror. "You're telling me how well the competition is doing—the ones who are subsidized by the taxpayers to take away our livelihood," he said. "Don't you understand? There never has been a shortage of recycled newspapers. There just isn't enough demand. The more Tucson recycles, the less business I do."

Recycling by anyone should be encouraged. But it is important to 15 understand what kind of recycling works and what kind may do more harm than good. Newsprint illustrates one potential problem. Only about ten percent of old newspapers are recycled into new newspapers. What newspapers are really good for is making cereal boxes and other containers (if the box is gray on the inside, it's from recycled stock), the insides of automobiles (the average car contains about 60 pounds of recycled paperboard containing newsprint), wallboard and insulation. All these end uses seem to be near saturation.

What happens when the market is suddenly flooded with news- 16 print? Two years ago the state of New Jersey began implementing legislation requiring every community to separate at curbside and collect at least three categories of recyclables. As a result, the price of used newspaper in some parts of New Jersey has plummeted from as much as $40 a ton to minus $25 a ton—in other words, you have to pay to have it taken away. If legislation like this became widespread, without measures to increase demand for recycled-paper products, the effects could be precisely the opposite of those intended.

The fact is that we are currently recycling about as much paper as 17 the market can bear. The demand for recyclable plastic and aluminum has not yet been fully met, but Americans have been doing a pretty good job of returning their aluminum cans. And whatever people say about their willingness to recycle, the only reliable predictor of recycling is the price paid at buy-back centers. The Garbage Project's research showed that as prices rose for, say, newsprint, the number of newspapers found in local refuse declined.

Source Reduction. Not long ago I stopped at the University of 18 California at Berkeley, where a ban was being considered on expanded-polystyrene foam—the substance used in coffee cups, hamburger boxes and meat trays. It was lunch time, and Sproul Plaza was filled with some 700 or 800 students, virtually all of whom held large foam clamshells containing hot food. I asked one group of lunchers what they thought about a ban on polystyrene. Great idea, they said between mouthfuls and without irony.

Source reduction is to garbage what preventive medicine is to 19 health—a means of eliminating a problem before it can happen. But the utility of legislated source reduction is in many respects an illusion. Most consumer industries already have made products as compact and light as possible for ease of distribution and to conserve costly resources. In 1970 a typical plastic soda bottle weighed 60 grams; today it weighs 48 grams and is more easily crushed. And source-reduction measures don't eliminate much garbage; hamburgers, eggs and VCRs still have to be put in something.

America *can* manage its garbage. Safely designed landfills should 20 be employed where there is still room for them. Incinerators with appropriate safety devices can be sited anywhere, but make the most sense in the Northeast. States and municipalities need to cut deals with wastepaper and scrap dealers on splitting the money to be made from recycling.

Additional steps could be taken to reduce the biggest component 21 of garbage: paper. Freight rates could be revised to make the transport of paper for recycling cheaper than the transport of wood for pulp to make new paper. And to increase the demand for recycled paper, the federal government—which uses more paper by far than any other institution in America—could insist that most federal paper work be done on recycled paper.

Finally, we need to expand our knowledge. Many of us are better 22 informed about Neptune than we are about this country's garbage.

But even if present trends continue, I am not worried that we will 23 be buried in our garbage. Perhaps the biggest challenge we face is to recognize that the conventional wisdom about garbage is often wrong.

QUESTIONS AND IDEAS FOR DISCUSSION

1.   What is Rathje's thesis? With what major points does he support it? Why do you suppose Rathje's thesis is explicitly stated at the point where it is, and not, as we might expect, at the end of the first paragraph? Discuss the organization of Rathje's argument and possible reasons for it.

2.   How does Rathje support his claim (paragraph 4) that "Americans, as individuals, are not suddenly producing more garbage"? Are you convinced? Comment.

3.   Why does Rathje include the anecdote about the students eating lunch at Berkeley (18)? What argument does the anecdote illustrate?

4.   Whatever your views on recycling and the environment, do you find yourself more likely to accept all or part of Rathje's argument because of his persona—that of the scholar with firsthand knowledge? Discuss the role persona plays in this essay and your response to it.

5.   Compare Rathje's essay with Laurence Sombke's. Which strikes you as logically more convincing? Which is emotionally more persuasive? Why?

Recycling/Precycling

JOHN ELKINGTON, JULIA HAILES, AND JOEL MAKOWER

John Elkington is an English authority on ecological issues in industry. He has served as a consultant to British Petroleum, the Nature Conservancy Council, and the United Nations Environment Programme. Julia Hailes, who is also English, is a founder and co-owner of Sustain-Ability, a company that "aims to promote environmentally sustainable economic growth." Joel Makower is an American writer on consumer and business subjects and a former consumer columnist for the *Washington Star*. Elkington and Makower are authors and co-authors of numerous books. All three share a concern for the environment that led to the writing of *The Green Consumer* (1990), a book that argues the importance of our being "green consumers"— that is, people who try to minimize their impact on the environment in the purchasing choices they make. "Green consumers" will choose minimally packaged products, recycled products, products that do not cause pollution in their manufacture, and—not least important— only as many products as they really need. In this selection from *The Green Consumer*, the authors argue that we must not only recycle—we must *precycle*, too.

The newspaper and TV news stories a few years back about the 1 trash-filled barge with no place to dock didn't even begin to describe the extent of the garbage crisis we are facing. Some cities are virtually choking on their citizens' refuse, and solutions are few and far between. The simple fact is that Americans generate so much garbage that we are rapidly running out of places to put it.

Although the problem has been around for years, the problem 2 seems to be getting worse. Between 1960 and 1986, the amount of American garbage discarded annually grew by 80 percent, to between one and two tons of melon rinds, grass clippings, plastic hamburger boxes, and discarded toasters for every living soul in the country. All told, Americans throw away an average 3.5 pounds of solid waste every day, although some estimates range as high as 6.5 pounds a day.

By comparison, the average West German or Japanese throws away about half as much.

The obvious problem is where to put it all. Sanitary landfills— what we used to call "dumps"—are rapidly filling up, sometimes turning away trash generated by those in other regions, as the barge-to-nowhere episode so graphically illustrated. There's good reason for this glut of garbage: 80 percent of all our trash goes into landfills; of the remaining 20 percent, half is incinerated and half is recycled. The U.S. Conference of Mayors predicts that over half of the nation's 9,300 landfills will face closure within ten years. 3

But where to put the trash is only part of the problem. An equally serious question has to do with what is contained in our trash. Experts believe that somewhere between 5 percent and 15 percent of municipal solid waste contains hazardous substances—garbage that can injure living things and is sometimes even life-threatening. Such hazardous wastes go well beyond the leaky drums of industrial chemicals we've seen on television. They include many of our most common household items. . . . 4

The tragic fact behind such hazards is that most of what we throw into landfills can be recycled, turned into compost, or otherwise disposed of safely. Recycling in particular makes sense. A sizable portion of our trash contains valuable resources—metals, glass, paper, and wood—that can be reprocessed and used again. Cities and states throughout the United States are adopting voluntary or mandatory recycling programs, usually with great success. . . . 5

Americans currently recycle only about 10 percent of their household trash. In the process, they throw away incalculable amounts of raw materials—and the energy it takes to convert these materials into finished goods. Part of the problem may be that many people don't understand what can and what cannot be recycled. According to a poll by the Gallup Organization, Inc., 54 percent of Americans said that if they knew a certain food or beverage container was not recyclable, they would switch to a container that was. 6

There are at present some 8,000 community recycling programs in the United States. These range from voluntary drop-off programs, in which individuals bring recyclable materials to central locations, to mandatory curbside pickup programs, in which citizens are required by law to separate their garbage and prepare it in a prescribed manner for pickup by the local trash company. In addition, a growing number of business recycling programs are emerging, including some mandated by state or local law, in which companies save, reuse, and recycle the massive amounts of paper, cardboard, metals, and other materials used in our information and manufacturing society. . . . 7

There's no doubt that recycling is the single most important step in 8
easing the garbage crisis. But even before that comes *precycling*—your
decision to avoid buying materials that are overpackaged or that are
packaged in harmful plastics or other materials. . . .

That's right: *precycling*. Precycling means making intelligent, en- 9
vironmentally sound decisions at the store, and reducing waste *before*
you buy. In other words, by precycling you will reduce waste by
avoiding buying those things that will need to be disposed of or
recycled.

In 1989, the city of Berkeley, California, launched an innovative 10
citywide precycling campaign, complete with posters, brochures, and
newspaper ads. Other communities and organizations have examined
this relatively simple notion—which is known more formally as
"source reduction." By whatever name, in whatever form, the idea
makes good environmental sense.

Clearly, you won't be able to precycle all your products. There 11
simply aren't reasonable alternatives for some purchases. But the
more you do precycle, the less trash you will generate.

How do you precycle? Here are six basic guidelines: 12

1. *Be picky about packaging.* At the store, consider more than just the
   contents of a package; consider the package itself. Can it be re-
   used, refilled, or recycled? Whenever possible, choose products
   packaged in recyclable materials such as paper, cardboard, glass,
   and aluminum.

2. *Don't pay for overpackaging.* If the packaging isn't necessary to
   protect the product, buy the less-packaged alternative. There's a
   good chance it will cost less, too.

3. *Avoid plastic.* Even the plastic that is recyclable has a limited life
   compared with glass, aluminum, and cardboard. Eventually, even
   recycled plastic products will contribute to environmental problems. Be particularly wary of polystyrene foam (Styrofoam is one
   brand), which can be harmful to the stratospheric ozone layer.

4. *Don't buy disposables.* The longer the life span of a product, the
   better. Disposable razors, diapers, lighters, cameras, cups, and
   plates are a waste of resources and contribute to disposal
   problems.

5. *Buy in bulk.* Whenever practical, purchase larger packages. You'll
   save money and avoid excess containers. Especially avoid "convenience" packaging—single-serving meals, for example—which
   are both overpackaged and overpriced.

6. *Look for products in refillable containers.* A growing number of prod-

ucts include reusable containers. From cleaners to cake mixes, manufacturers are creating new products that require you to purchase the container during the first purchase, then buy only refills or concentrates after that, eliminating the need to purchase unneeded packaging.

Recycling is really only part of what has become known as "integrated waste management"—a bureaucratic term that refers to a four-part strategy for effectively dealing with landfill and pollution problems: *reducing* the amount of trash generated; *incinerating* refuse, preferably turning the heat into energy; *recycling* as much as possible; and *landfilling* whatever is left. The federal government has actively been promoting these integrated programs, which can be made flexible enough to meet each community's needs.   13

QUESTIONS AND IDEAS FOR DISCUSSION

1.   This selection argues not only for recycling but for *precycling*. Summarize the authors' argument in favor of precycling. Is it logically convincing? Will it affect your behavior? Explain.

2.   Many language authorities tell us that what we call something affects our attitude toward it. This essay reminds us that "sanitary landfills" used to be called "dumps." What happens to our perceptions of the thing described when we alter its name in this way? Should we resume using the label "dump"? Why, or why not?

3.   Evaluate the authors' use of statistics. Compare the statistics presented in this essay with the statistics in other essays in this chapter. Discuss your findings.

The Art of Minimizing Waste
DOUGLAS E. OLESEN

Douglas E. Olesen is the president and chief executive officer of Battelle Memorial Institute, a scientific research and development company. The following essay was originally presented as a speech to a national meeting of the Society of American Military Engineers in May 1990. Many in the audience were owners or managers of industrial manufacturing companies—some of them major polluters. Olesen speaks to both the moral and financial concerns of his audience in arguing for reducing pollution and waste in manufacture. Every word reflects his careful consideration of his audience and its interests and needs, without blunting the argument he makes. Notice in particular Olesen's organization and use of examples to support each claim.

In just a few years, the most widely viewed artwork in the world 1 may not be the Mona Lisa, or the Statue of Liberty, or even the Mapplethorpe exhibit. No, it just might be a landfill in Kearny, New Jersey.

The state recently closed the landfill, and now it's considering one 2 artist's idea to beautify this one-hundred-foot high mountain of buried garbage. The artist wants to turn the dump into an enormous celestial calendar and call it "Sky Mound." Really. It will have steel posts, earthen mounds, a plume of burning methane, and radiating gravel paths aligned with the seasonal movements of the sun, the moon, and the stars.

Why might that be the most widely viewed artwork in the world? 3 Well, I'm not sure how many people will go out of their way to visit, but it just so happens that the site is bordered by the New Jersey Turnpike and an Amtrak commuter line. Also, Newark Airport is nearby.

So, we're going to have millions of commuters driving, riding, and 4 flying by wondering if they're looking at art or at trash, or both.

That certainly is going to be one of the more creative site remedia- 5 tion solutions we'll see. But it represents innovation, and that's what we'll need to meet the waste challenge ahead of us. Like any artist, we'll need to view the big picture; we'll need to imagine creative solutions; and we'll need to develop innovative processes.

For the past 20 years, our policy for dealing with waste has pri- 6 marily had two components. First, we've tried to clean up pollution already in the environment. That's the approach right now with the groundwater remediation at Wright-Patterson.

Our second effort has been to cut pollution with control devices 7 installed on the product or at the end of the production line. Two of the best examples are catalytic converters in automobiles and coal scrubbers in power plants.

The first step, cleaning up, is one we're going to be working on for 8 a long time. The EPA, for instance, estimates there are leaks in 189,000 underground storage tanks at retail fuel outlets across the country. Some of that fuel may be seeping into groundwater. Cleaning up that and other waste in the environment is going to be one of the major technological challenges of this decade.

But waiting until the damage has been done and the waste has 9 been released into the environment is by far the most expensive and time-consuming method of cutting pollution.

Around the world, and right in our own backyards, we have sites 10 contaminated with fuels, with PCBs, with cleaning solvents, with heavy metals. To clean up these areas, we have to put more effort into developing new techniques that get the job done more effectively, and at lower costs. Often, the quickest and least expensive way to develop these new techniques is through existing technology. Creating entirely new technologies can be a slow and risky endeavor, and it sometimes won't do when you need to get results *right now.*

Let me give you an example. A few years ago, a group of our 11 scientists and engineers at Battelle developed a technology called "electro-acoustic dewatering." It employs electric currents and acoustic waves to remove the water from materials. It was originally intended for use with foods, but it was adapted later to remove water from sewage sludge. Now, we're adapting the technology as an *in situ* method for removing contaminants from soil.

The electric currents and acoustic waves moving through the 12 ground extract contaminants from the soil and direct them through the water to withdraw wells. The water can then be pumped out and treated with conventional methods to remove the pollutants. Then the clean water can be returned to the ground. You can clean up the site without ever digging it up.

That's the kind of technology adaptation we need to concentrate 13 on to solve our immediate waste remediation problems.

Of course, many of our remediation techniques *will* require that 14 we dig up the ground. For instance, the EPA recently developed a new technique to remove the toxicity of PCBs by chemically stripping the chlorine off them. The technology was originally developed to treat PCB transformer oils, but it's since been modified to treat soil contaminated with PCBs. We'll be field testing the new system at a 5,500-ton test site in Guam next spring.

This type of technique, though, where we must dig up the ground 15 to treat it, presents us with the single most difficult engineering problem in the entire remediation field: handling soils. With every soil remediation process we develop, we must consider how we're going to excavate the soil, separate it, mix in chemicals, and get it into a reactor. Soils are terribly difficult to work with. And once you develop a technique to work with the clay soils in Ohio, chances are, it's not going to work with sandy soils in California.

Again, we're going to have to concentrate on adapting current 16 technology to meet this soil-handling challenge.

I'm sometimes amazed at the speed with which we're adapting 17 and developing new cleanup and soil-handling methods. But obviously, we can't continue to rely on removing waste after the fact. It's too expensive, and the liability is too great. We have to reduce, and preferably eliminate, waste at its source.

So far, we've focused those efforts on eliminating waste only on 18 the very end of the production line, and it's been only marginally successful. We've installed emission-control devices on cars; we've added coal scrubbers to our power plants; and we've found better ways to store manufacturing waste. But unfortunately, that hasn't been enough. For example, with new automobile exhaust controls, we reduced carbon monoxide emissions only 19 percent between 1975 and 1985. And nitrogen oxides actually *increased* 4 percent in that time.

But in those same 10 years, we cut emissions of lead into the air by 19 94 percent. We've had the same kind of success with DDT, with PCBs, and with strontium 90.[1] The difference is that we didn't tack on a device to *control* these pollutants. No, we *eliminated* them from the production process itself. And that's where we must focus our efforts in the future. Our environmental policy today must be one of waste minimization. We must work to eliminate environmentally hazardous materials where possible and redesign systems that don't leave behind hazardous byproducts.

In this effort, we need to think about *how* we manufacture as well 20 as *what* we manufacture. We must consider what happens during the entire production chain, from the origins of the material through the end of the assembly line. To cut waste at its source, maybe we'll have to change the way we make products. Maybe we'll even need to change the products themselves.

There's a four-step process in this waste-minimization chain. The 21 four steps encompass a complete and systematic analysis of a manufacturer's production lines and processes.

The first step, which is the easiest, the least expensive, and in 22 some ways the most effective, is simply good housekeeping. I'm talking about better inventory management and improved operating practices. This approach focuses on making existing processes work more efficiently. And that means less waste.

Better housekeeping might mean finding more efficient ways to 23 handle a particular hazardous waste. It might mean developing better training programs for workers who handle hazardous waste. It might mean softening water before it's mixed with chemicals. And it might mean making fundamental changes in how a company thinks about waste management.

We've seen that companies taking these kinds of actions can 24 sometimes cut their waste by as much as 80 percent!

---

[1] Strontium 90: a metallic element used in certain nuclear electric power sources. It constitutes a radiation hazard. [Ed.]

The benefits from cutting that much waste can be tremendous. It 25 can translate into dramatically lower costs, decreased liability, healthier work environments, improved community and customer relations, and, ultimately, increased competitiveness.

And companies that do more are often going to be gaining an even 26 bigger competitive edge. They'll make the effort and the investment to go beyond good housekeeping, and they'll use technology to make modifications throughout the production chain to eliminate waste wherever possible, and increase productivity.

The next three waste minimization steps are increasingly more 27 expensive, and they normally operate under the law of diminishing returns. With the first—and cheapest—step, a company may cut out 70 or 80 percent of its waste. But the steps needed to eliminate that last 20 percent can become expensive. And cutting out the final 5 to 10 percent can be very costly.

Nevertheless, inaction in this area may be the most expensive 28 decision a company ever makes. Money spent now to eliminate waste will also eliminate the need to spend even more later on to store the waste, to dispose of it, and to cover the liability if it should ever escape into the environment.

These next three steps toward minimizing waste are: 1) recycling 29 and reuse, 2) material substitution, 3) process modification.

First, let's take a look at recycling. It can be the least expensive of 30 these three steps, and it can give companies useful byproducts. And, it works.

In the metal-finishing area, for example, one of the biggest waste 31 problems is the large volume of waste from electroplating baths that are contaminated with heavy metals like copper, iron, and chrome. Well, the Air Force now has a new selective ion-exchange technology that can extract the metal from the baths—while they're operating. That allows them to reuse the plating solution. The new process reduces downtime for tank cleaning. It improves plating quality. And it dramatically reduces the waste stream.

In other fields, recycling's not only cutting waste but also opening 32 new markets for reprocessed materials. The U.S. Navy, for instance, has had an enormous challenge in disposing of hundreds of thousands of cubic yards of sandblasting grit every year. And the problem's especially tough in California, where the grit is classified as a hazardous waste.

Well, the Navy now has a recycling technology that is going to 33 save it a lot of money, and may also give it a product to use or sell. Very soon, the Navy is going to be recycling its sandblasting grit into asphalt. The grit is basically sand with a very low concentration of metal. Turning it into asphalt traps the metals in place and keeps them from leaching away. It gives the Navy a useful product. And it saves a lot of money and landfill space.

Industries all over are turning to recycling as part of their waste 34 minimization strategy. We've even developed a way now to recycle disposable diapers into pots for plants. Clearly, the opportunities we have for turning waste into economically viable products are limited only by our imaginations.

In the next step beyond recycling, companies should determine if 35 they can use alternate materials in their manufacturing processes to reduce waste and still maintain performance and quality.

That's what's happening with furniture manufacturers in Califor- 36 nia right now. Here's their problem: Solvents, like those in paints and coatings we put on wood furniture, are responsible for nearly a third of all hydrocarbon emissions in southern California. Furniture making is big business in that area, but air quality is an enormous issue there.

The answer to the problem will likely be ultraviolet-curable 37 coatings that are environmentally acceptable. These coatings will be applied to the wood and then exposed to UV light. The light will accelerate a chain reaction that instantly cures the coating on the wood. There's no harmful spraying, and no dangerous emissions.

These new coatings are going to have to be safe for the environ- 38 ment, but they're also going to have to provide superior performance. And they're going to have to be inexpensive enough for the companies to maintain their competitive edge. That's a tall order. But it's one we must meet.

Going one step beyond finding new materials, we can modify the 39 entire production process in order to minimize waste. By modifying their production processes, many firms can meet several objectives. (1) They can improve product quality. (2) They can eliminate pollutant emissions. (3) And they can trim expenses for waste management, treatment, and disposal.

The U.S. Navy achieved all three of those objectives recently when 40 it adopted a new method for stripping paint. The conventional way to strip paint is with chemicals. That leads to a lot of hazardous waste. And, the paint stripping solutions release a lot of vapors, and that leads to concerns about health and about air quality.

But now, the Navy can strip paint with a technique called "media 41 blasting." It works basically by shooting thousands of tiny plastic pellets at an object, and the pellets chip off the paint. The technique eliminates all liquid and gas wastes. So instead of having maybe 30 barrels of liquid waste, all you have is about 4 barrels of tiny paint chips and plastic beads.

Another process that's produced a lot of waste in the past has been 42 putting metal plating on a molded plastic part. Normally, that takes a

25-to-30-step process. There's a lot of labor involved, a lot of materials, and a lot of waste. And all that adds up to a lot of cost.

Rather than trying to run the conventional process as cleanly as 43
possible, we've recently developed several methods to eliminate about 25 steps in the plating process. The most successful method is called "in-mold plating," and it's being used now in about six different firms. The idea behind in-mold plating is to directly electro-plate the surface of the mold. Then you put the plastic into the mold, and it comes out a plated part.

This process can cut total manufacturing costs by 30 to 50 percent. 44
But perhaps even more importantly, it eliminates a lot of hazardous waste associated with the conventional plating process.

Of course, completely changing your manufacturing process is a 45
costly endeavor. But in the long run, the savings you'll achieve, the waste you'll eliminate, the positive reaction you'll gain from consumers will more than make up for your initial investment.

Those benefits are going to add up to a real, long-term competitive 46
advantage for many firms. The environmental issue is not just a fad; it's not going to go away. The companies that use the full capability of technology to meet the new environmental challenges will gain a strong advantage over their competition. They will comply with new environmental guidelines in their production processes, and they will be meeting the market call for environmentally compatible products.

Clearly, there are many options open to us as we all face critical 47
decisions on how to invest in waste minimization. But whatever direction we take, whether it's to go with recycling, substituting new materials, or modifying processes, we still must make our decisions as part of a systematic analysis of the production lines and processes involved. We have to consider how we get the materials we're going to use; how the materials hold up; how we manufacture them; how the products react when used; and how they react when discarded. We can make no change at any point along this chain without considering what impact it will have on the entire system.

For example, if we change the material we're working with, we 48
may need to change the way the material arrives or how it's processed upstream. And downstream, we may need to change the processes for receiving the new product or wastes.

This same type of broad vision is going to help us eliminate waste 49
from the production chain, and it will help us clean up the waste that's already out there. Like the creative artist who finds new ways to use paints or metals, we need to find new waste treatment and minimization techniques from the vast array of technologies already at our disposal. And we must continue working on new technologies that will give us a competitive edge in an environmentally conscious marketplace.

Unlike our friends from the landfill in New Jersey, we're not trying 50 to create art from waste. What we're trying to do is create the competitive advantage we need to succeed in the tough global marketplace of today and tomorrow.

QUESTIONS AND IDEAS FOR DISCUSSION

1. Olesen's is the only argument in this chapter for which we— ordinary citizens and consumers—are clearly *not* the target audience. How is that difference made evident in the essay? Does it lessen your interest in the essay's claims? Or do you find it instructive to "listen in" to an argument directed to another audience? Comment.

2. Olesen begins and ends his essay with a description of a proposed landfill art project in Kearny, New Jersey. How does Olesen connect the New Jersey project with his concerns? How well does the reference work as the introduction and conclusion to his argument? Explain.

3. Some of the kinds of changes Olesen advocates are expensive and time consuming to implement. How does he organize his argument with the aim of lowering audience resistance to the remedies he proposes?

Beyond Dumping

BRUCE PIASECKI

Bruce Piasecki is a writer whose particular interest is environmental issues. He has published a volume of poetry, *Stray Prayers* (1976), and several books on the environment, including *Beyond Dumping: New Strategies for Controlling Toxic Wastes* (1984), *America's Future in Toxic Waste Management* (1987), and *In Search of Environmental Excellence* (1990). Piasecki is a contributor to several journals, including *Washington Monthly,* in which this essay first appeared in 1983. Piasecki argues to the pocketbook: If companies continue to dump wastes, they will have to pay skyrocketing fees; if they learn to recycle and to detoxify (and sell the harmless and useful substances produced thereby), they will profit financially.

A familiar advertisement by Monsanto proclaims, "Without 1 chemicals, life itself would be impossible." Without toxic wastes, life would still be possible, but it certainly would be bleaker.

This isn't an apology for the 77 billion pounds of these wastes that 2 are produced each year in the United States, but a realization that they have become an integral part of our daily life. Sulfuric acid and mercury are inevitable by-products of the pulp and paper industry. The manufacture of life-saving drugs produces zinc and other heavy metals. The textile industry generates toxic dyes and organic chlorine. Even the common doorknob requires electroplating, which generates large volumes of rinse waters and sludges laced with cyanide. For America's major industries, toxic wastes are as ubiquitous and inevitable as the garbage trucks that prowl through America's neighborhoods each morning to cart away old newspapers, broken egg shells, and other assorted trash.

Just because we generate toxic wastes doesn't mean they have to   3
kill us. But as Love Canal and a host of other examples demonstrate, they're doing just that, though that should come as no surprise when you consider what we do with our lead, mercury, chlorinated hydrocarbons, PCBs, benzene, cyanides, and various other poisons. For the most part we simply dump them—into landfills, abandoned wells, holding ponds, open fields, and even old Titan missile silos. And then we cross our fingers and hope for the best.

This dump-and-hope approach has prompted people like former   4
California Congressman John Moss to call the problem of toxic wastes "the sleeping giant of the decade" and has led to widespread calls for better dumps. Dumps that are properly identified and policed 24 hours a day—and monitored for generations. Dumps that confine waste in corrosion-resistant containers. Dumps with impermeable liners to prevent groundwater contamination. Dumps that aren't right next door to housing developments, drinking water supplies, and children's playgrounds.

But dumps nevertheless. Yet as the toxic waste cognoscenti know,   5
the search for the perfect dump is about as fruitful as trying to build a perpetual motion machine. Containers corrode and leak. Rainwater seeps into underground storage areas. Aquifers supplying drinking water eventually become contaminated. In one case in Texas, for example, wastes supposedly pumped into a 9,000-foot-deep well came back to haunt nearby residents in their kitchen sinks. A report by Princeton University's Hazardous Waste Research Program last summer graphically illustrated the problem: among state-of-the-art landfills that far exceeded current federal standards, some were leaking large amounts of contaminants after only two years of use.

The lesson in all this is obvious but usually overlooked. The last   6
thing we should do with our toxic wastes is figure out the best way to dump them. Instead, we should do something safer and far more sensible: turn them into harmless chemicals and make some money selling what's left over.

Before dismissing this as a modern day version of the alchemist's   7
lead-into-gold fantasy, consider one thing: detoxification of hazardous

waste happens to be standard operating procedure in much of the rest of the industrial world. In the Netherlands, the Chemical Waste Act of 1976 explicitly prohibited the dumping of a wide range of toxic wastes, a ban that has since spawned a thriving waste detoxification business. In Denmark, the Kommunekemi plant handles every toxic waste in the country. And if it can't destroy or recycle a particular waste, the Danes don't dump it—they put it in storage until they can find a way to treat it.

Holland and Denmark are not exactly world-class industrial 8 powers—like West Germany, for example. But those who doubt that detoxification is both effective and economical need only visit any of that country's 15 waste treatment facilities, which are operated as part of a coordinated national program. The West Germans detoxify 85 percent of all their hazardous wastes. To them, detoxification has virtues beyond merely protecting their citizens. For example, through a process known as "chlorinolysis" the Farbwerke Hoechst company converts chlorinated hydrocarbons (a group of chemicals that includes PCBs, a known carcinogen; DDT-related pesticides; and kepone) and other toxic residues from organic chemical production into useful substances such as carbon tetrachloride, a valuable solvent used as a degreaser for machine parts and in other industrial processes. The company detoxifies about 8,000 tons of waste each year through chlorinolysis, but it has even grander ambitions. Hoechst recently began construction of a new plant that can handle 50,000 tons per year—allowing it to start *importing* wastes from other European producers.

West Germany's example hasn't gone unnoticed in at least one 9 corner of the United States. In 1981 California Governor Jerry Brown appointed a special Toxic Waste Group to examine alternatives for the 1.3 million tons of hazardous wastes disposed annually in the state's landfills. Prepared in cooperation with representatives from Dow Chemical, Friends of the Earth, and various academic institutions, the report concluded that 75 percent of California's toxic wastes could economically be recycled, treated, or detoxified. Brown since has established a low-interest loan program for building detoxification facilities; to discourage dumping he has instituted new dumping rules and increased the state's landfill tax by 600 percent. Hit with additional charges of $4 million, Chevron and Getty are now dumping far less waste. "We don't like to refer to these regulations as *banning* dumping," explains Gary Davis, a waste management specialist for the state. "But that is what they are meant to do eventually for California."

Before you assume California's anti-dumping crusade will cause 10 many beleaguered manufacturers to throw in the towel, consider the numbers. California industry now spends about $17 million to dispose of its high-priority wastes in landfills, and that will increase in the next two years to about $30 million. Using alternative treatment technology for this high-priority waste will cost only about $50 million a year, the state estimates. The additional $20–30 million annual cost will be spread among almost 4,000 California businesses with gross sales exceeding $30 billion. The two biggest waste generators—the chemical and petroleum industries—also have the highest profit margins of all other manufacturers. "There are no good reasons why the entire nation shouldn't rectify its toxic predicament by the end of this decade," Governor Brown says. "The knowledge is there. The tools have been developed. All that is required now is the political will."

Toxic-Change Operations

California still dumps most of its toxic wastes, but compared to the 11 rest of the United States, it's a pioneer. After producing three times as much toxic waste per citizen as West Germany, American industry proceeds to dump 80 percent of it into unlined surface impoundments (pits, ponds and lagoons) and unsecured landfills. Less than 20 percent is treated in any way, and the most common method—incineration—is often conducted under uncontrolled conditions that transfer the toxics into the atmosphere.

For a country that prides itself on its technological sophistication, 12 this enthusiasm for dumping is not only appalling, but downright mystifying. It's especially so when one considers how relatively simple, inexpensive, and elegant some of the best detoxification techniques are.

For example, until recently waste water and sludges contaminated 13 with heavy metals such as lead, nickel, and mercury could be detoxified only at exorbitant cost. These wastes were usually dumped in holding ponds and landfills, but because of their persistence often worked their way into water supplies and the food chain.

In 1978 L. J. Bailin of Lockheed Missiles and Space Company, Inc., 14 developed a technique called microwave plasma detoxification that treats heavy metals with the same ease that microwave ovens handle baked potatoes. A neutral gas, usually pure oxygen, is irradiated with microwaves. This transforms the gas molecules into a highly reactive state, causing them to combine with the heavy metals, which break into harmless compounds and marketable grades of scarce metals. The MWP [microwave plasma] process can also be applied to deadly wastes such as kepone, DDT-related pesticides, and dioxin, and recent research endorses this process for the detoxification of cancer-causing nitrosamines and nerve poisons from the military.

The real beauty of MWP is both its ease and its relatively low cost. 15
The process produces no troublesome emissions and eliminates
unnecessary transportation of wastes; prototype trucks have been
developed that can detoxify 50–100 pounds of these wastes per hour at
the dump site. At a cost of about $400 per wet metric ton, MWP at first
might seem uncompetitive with landfill costs of about $40 a ton. But
the $400/ton figure is for a very early prototype; a recent EPA report
estimated the widespread use of MWP and the resulting improvements in design could decrease costs "by a factor of 10." The cost of
dumping will move in the opposite direction as regulations get
tougher and existing landfills reach capacity.

Other wastes can be treated biologically. This approach has been 16
of limited value until recently because most biological agents have
been appropriate only for very dilute wastes. But new mutant
bacteria—known as "superbugs"—can now handle several thousand
times the toxic concentration of their precursors. One new culture can
remove cyanide wastes from coking operations at steel mills for only
two cents per thousand gallons of waste water. A mixture of several
other microbes feeds on 2,4,5-T, the toxic component of the defoliant
Agent Orange. Yet another superbug eats benzene, the ubiquitous
carcinogen once used as a chemical feedstock to produce PCBs, pesticides, linoleum, and varnishes.

Unfortunately, these new superbugs are doing little while the 17
wastes they could render harmless remain a hazard. The Air Force
spends more than $100,000 a year monitoring 2.3 million gallons of
stockpiled Agent Orange; each day an estimated fifteen 55-gallon
drums develop new leaks. Massive stockpiles of benzene are now
being dumped into landfills, even though the chemical quickly vapor-
izes and, when exposed to sunlight, produces a toxic smog.

Dumping Über Alles

So where are all the MWP trucks, the chlorinolysis plants, the new 18
superbugs? For the most part, they're stuck on the drawing boards or
in the laboratory while hazardous waste dumping continues to increase at a distinctly unhealthy clip. This would be dismaying enough
were it not for another thing: the very federal agency ostensibly responsible for doing something to solve the hazardous waste problem
is working to make sure things stay that way.

The particular agency is the Environmental Protection Agency, 19
which, in all fairness, had almost nothing to do with hazardous wastes
until 1978. Before then, dumping was largely the responsibility of
individual states, some of which regulated toxic waste dumping and

some of which made it clear to dumpers that as long as their enforcers didn't see anything, no one would make any trouble.

But by 1978, shamed by disclosures about Love Canal, Congress 20 had ordered the EPA to set up uniform federal standards governing toxic waste dumping. The purpose of the law went beyond cleaning up old, contaminated dumps and making new ones more secure. Congress hoped stricter regulations, by forcing toxic waste producers to pay higher dumping costs, would spur detoxification efforts.

Congress was thus addressing the major reason detoxification has 21 been virtually ignored by American producers while the Europeans have been busy building integrated treatment centers. Dumping is too cheap and too easy. A good example of the problem is found in the textile industry, which annually produces nearly 200,000 wet metric tons of hazardous waste laced with toxic dyes, organic chlorine, and heavy metals. A recent analysis of the textile industry by Booz-Allen and Hamilton, EPA's major consulting firm, estimated that these wastes could be reduced nearly 80 percent while adding less than one percent to total production costs. Yet textile companies have done almost nothing; as the report subtly suggests, a company would have to be foolish to add this burden in the absence of any EPA regulations restricting dumping.

For the same reason, no commercial-scale chlorinolysis plant ex- 22 ists in America, despite the process's proven track record in Europe. Chlorinolysis detoxifies chlorinated hydrocarbons (a family of chemicals that are usually used in agriculture) by subjecting them to high pressure and low temperatures. The EPA estimates the process would add less than one percent to manufacturing costs. Yet while these wastes pose one of the greatest hazards in landfills—and some, like Agent Orange, are considered *too* toxic for existing landfills—in the absence of stiffer federal regulations there is little economic incentive for a company to use this technique. . . .

It's always dismaying when a court is forced to order a govern- 23 ment agency to obey the law. But in the case of toxic wastes, there are additional reasons for dismay. The obstacle to detoxification is not a lack of technology, nor is it cost. Over the long run detoxification is actually cheaper than watching landfills for decades and trying to clean up after the inevitable leaks and spills. Nor are EPA's professionals ignorant of the alternatives to dumping. Scientists usually avoid politics, but occasionally they show a remarkable frankness in their comments, which was certainly the case when William Sanjour, chief of the EPA's Hazardous Waste Implementation Branch, wrote to congratulate Jerry Brown on California's program. "We have known for a decade that hazardous wastes can be managed properly . . . yet we have had to watch the unfolding of one horror story after another while solutions are sought in every direction but the right one," he wrote.

But having defied the laws of Congress, the EPA now appears 24 willing to take on the laws of nature. The United States has less than 18 years of landfill capacity left; if nothing were done at all, the increasing shortage of dumping space would ultimately give detoxification a future. But EPA feels compelled to do something about this shortage, as was revealed in a notice in the October 18, 1982 issue of *Inside EPA*, an internal agency newsletter. The notice revealed that EPA officials are considering changing existing regulations to permit toxic waste dumping in 100-year flood plains if dikes are built around the dumpsites—or if the waste handler files an emergency removal plan with the EPA. It's a terrifying vision: as the flood waters slowly rise, one can imagine the bulldozers frantically trying to remove the corroded drums of PCBs and cyanides—no doubt so they can then be dumped somewhere else.

QUESTIONS AND IDEAS FOR DISCUSSION

1. The first paragraph of this essay makes an astonishing claim: "Without toxic wastes, life would still be possible, but it certainly would be bleaker." What effect does this introduction have on you, the reader, and on your receptivity to Piasecki's argument? Discuss.

2. How does Piasecki enliven his essay on a subject as unglamorous as waste disposal? Indicate some specific strategies in the text.

3. How effective is Piasecki's use of examples to support his claims? Discuss.

4. This essay was originally addressed to an audience interested in (and many of them professionally active in) political matters—not to manufacturers and others who produce toxic wastes. Why then does Piasecki bother to couch his argument in terms of the economic advantages to polluters of improving their performance environmentally? How well does he consider his audience here?

SUGGESTIONS FOR WRITING
AND FURTHER DISCUSSION

1. Based on the essays in this section and your own experience and knowledge, argue for or against *mandatory* recycling in your community. If you favor recycling, what specific actions can you recommend in addition to those recommended by Laurence Sombke? If you write an essay on this topic, regard the citizens of your community as your target audience.

2. As William Rathje points out, ordinary paper is a major component of landfills. Paper is a major byproduct of college education: Consider how much waste paper the students, faculty, researchers, and staff at your college generate each day. Visit the computer center; study a few wastebaskets in the photocopying rooms of department offices; glance in a few dumpsters behind dormitories and academic buildings. In a brief essay suitable for publication in your campus newspaper (yet another source of waste paper!), argue the extent of the problem as you perceive it on your campus and suggest ways to improve the situation through recycling and "precycling."

3. Could it be argued that William Rathje's unconventional arguments about refuse and recycling, even if sound, are dangerous? That is, might they lead to complacency and a real deterioration of the quality of life in the future? Should writers like Rathje withhold arguments and evidence that might be misinterpreted or misused? Argue your answer, with examples. Assume that your readers will include both staunch environmentalists and free speech advocates.

4. Decide which of the essays in this chapter argues its claims most effectively—whether or not you like or agree with its conclusions. Argue the reasons for your choice. (You may choose to comment on the difficulty, if any, of putting aside your own ideas about the issues while you judge the arguments.) Is the most effective argument the best written and the most clearly organized? The most logical? The best documented? Or is it more emotional than logical in its argument? What does the essay show you as a writer about ways to make a point well?

9

THE COSTS OF AIDS

When AIDS first imposed itself on the collective consciousness of the developed countries of the world, roughly in 1982, it was treated with a kind of detached horror. Regarded as a disease of homosexual men, most people did not feel personally threatened. They certainly did not rush to demand extensive funding for research. Then people who had received blood transfusions began to contract AIDS. People who had had sexual relations with drug-abusing prostitutes began to contract AIDS. Some babies and spouses of hemophiliacs developed AIDS. Some famous and talented people died of AIDS. And public support for AIDS research skyrocketed.

Many of the issues of AIDS once hotly debated are now all but settled. We know what causes the syndrome and to what diseases its victims typically succumb. We know how the virus is transmitted and how best to avoid contracting it. The chances for exposure through casual contact, from a cough or a kiss, are no longer much debated—nor is the issue of quarantining victims, or of requiring AIDS testing of the entire population.

But some issues do remain unsettled, and chief among them are the questions of the costs of AIDS—both in a literal and a figurative sense. Most of the following arguments deal with the literal question. Where should the money for research and care come from, and how much money is enough? But some of the arguments also deal with the equally hard questions about what AIDS has cost and will cost society—in terms of lives and talent lost, confidence in the future and in each other jeopardized. As B. D. Colen says in his essay, "We will *all*, in some way, have to pay for AIDS." How, and how much, are the issues raised in this chapter.

Who Should Foot the AIDS Bill?

ANDREA SACHS

Andrea Sachs is a writer for Time *magazine. In this essay, first pub-lished in* Time *in October 1989, Sachs argues that American society is—and should not be—"shrinking from the task" of caring for AIDS patients. Sachs uses quotations from patients, AIDS counselors, gov-ernment officials, and doctors to make her case that society needs to assume fuller financial responsibility for AIDS-related care. What Sachs and New York City Health Commissioner Stephen Joseph advocate as the best solution is nationalized health care, available to all.*

When Robert Simpson tested positive for the AIDS virus last 1 November, medical bills were the least of his worries. As a court reporter, Simpson, 44, was earning $48,000 a year and was covered by group health insurance. In addition, he had planned ahead by buying three disability policies. Less than a year later, however, he has fallen through the widening cracks in the U.S. medical-care system. Too weak to work, he has lost the insurance coverage from his job; moreover, he has yet to see a penny from his disability policies, although he filed six months ago. "I'm just tired of being a victim," the pale, bushy-haired Simpson says slowly, pausing to gather strength in his San Francisco apartment.

Like Simpson, many of those caught up in the spiraling AIDS 2 epidemic are awash in medical expenses they cannot afford. And the safety net beneath them has proved less than reassuring. Since the AIDS crisis began in the early 1980s, the nation's private health-care industry—hospitals, insurance companies and pharmaceutical firms—has engaged in quiet combat with government agencies over who should foot the bill for the disease, which now afflicts an esti-mated 44,000 Americans. And the tab is rising. This year the cost for AIDS medical care is expected to be $3.75 billion; by 1992 that figure is likely to more than double. Whose responsibility is it to pay for AIDS-related care? And why does American society, on the whole, seem to be shrinking from the task?

No one is rushing in to assume the financial burden. "Everyone is 3 playing duck and cover while trying to shield themselves from the costs," observes Ronald Brunk of AIDS Benefits Counselors in San Francisco. This year federal and state programs will pay 40% of the bill, with private insurers taking care of another 40%. The remaining 20% falls in the "self pay"—often meaning "no pay"—category. The most important government program, Medicaid, is available only to impoverished patients. As a result, those infected with the AIDS virus frequently must "spend down" into poverty, demonstrating that they hold assets of less than $2,000. This low level of federal coverage portends future problems, since the number of people with AIDS continues to rise. "Federal health planners have been acting as if AIDS will go away," says Congressman Henry Waxman of California. "It won't."

The thicket of state insurance laws makes it possible in some cases 4 for private insurers to find ways to keep profits up and payments for AIDS care down. In 1985 one firm, the Great Republic Insurance Co., even issued an "AIDS profile" to its agents, instructing them to treat differently applications from "single males without dependents that are engaged in occupations that do not require physical exertion." These applicants were usually denied insurance. While such major insurers as Blue Cross/Blue Shield and the Travelers deny discriminating on the basis of AIDS, others still use information about living arrangements, residences and Zip Codes to try to identify gay or bisexual men at risk for the disease. Testing applicants for the AIDS virus gives companies additional protection against insuring infected individuals who will have high medical costs. As a result, a number of jurisdictions, including Washington and the states of Florida, Maine, Wisconsin and California, have legislatively limited such testing.

Despite the substantial costs (average lifetime care for a person 5 with AIDS: about $83,000), a fifth of those infected with the AIDS virus have no insurance at all. Increasingly, these people are flooding into overburdened public hospitals, raising fears of bankruptcies. In August the National Public Health and Hospital Institute reported that in 1987 only 5% of the nation's hospitals, most of them in inner cities, were treating 50% of the country's AIDS patients. Bellevue Hospital Center, which has one of the biggest emergency rooms in New York City, is overwhelmed to the point that care for other patients is threatened. Says Bellevue's Dr. Lewis Goldfrank: "There is going to be hospital gridlock by 1990, because there's not enough long-term, short-term or emergency-care space for AIDS patients. I think they're eventually going to fill every hospital bed in the big cities."

The stigma attached to the groups primarily afflicted by AIDS— 6 gays, minorities and intravenous drug users—has unfairly limited the degree of economic assistance offered. "If this disease struck only the presidents of major corporations, the effort to evade responsibility would not have been tolerated by society," says Earl Shelp, executive director of Houston's Foundation for Interfaith Research and Ministry. Additionally, society's sense of financial obligation—not to mention its compassion—has been diminished by a blame-the-victim syndrome. "I think that there is a tendency to discount a situation if one feels that an infected person's condition could have been avoided," says Dr. Kathleen Nolan of the Hastings Center in Briarcliff,

N.Y. Alluding to the disease's long incubation period—frequently ten years or more—she adds that "the vast majority of individuals who are seropositive or who have AIDS had never heard of the virus before they engaged in the behavior that resulted in their infection."

The mounting bills for AIDS patients have renewed a call in some 7 quarters for a national medical-care system. "Optimistically, AIDS will push this country into getting universal health insurance," says New York City Health Commissioner Stephen Joseph. "Or we may be reduced to narrow-minded scrambling to see who gets what piece of the pie." However, the current budget crisis, plus resistance to socialized medicine, makes that prospect a far-off solution. In the short run, a combination of public- and private-sector responsibility, translated into cash, seems to offer the best hope for coping with this ongoing human crisis.

QUESTIONS AND IDEAS FOR DISCUSSION

1.   On first reading, this essay might appear to be simply a report. Why? What makes it an argument?

2.   How rhetorically effective is the introduction to this essay? Does it engage your interest and attention? How, or why not? Does it predispose you to read the rest of the essay sympathetically, or not? Would it have been better to describe and quote a well-known person with AIDS?

3.   Sach's concluding sentence appears to advocate precisely what is the present case—a combination of government and private insurers paying most of the financial costs of AIDS. Why then does she bother to write the argument? What does this essay aim to accomplish? Does it succeed? Discuss.

The AIDS Lobby: Are We Giving It Too Much Money?

MICHAEL FUMENTO

Michael Fumento is by training a political scientist and lawyer who has written extensively about AIDS and formerly worked as an AIDS analyst for the U.S. Commission on Civil Rights. His forced resignation from the Commission came after his August 1988 *New Republic* essay on the "conservative alarmists." That essay appears as part of Fumento's 1990 book, *The Myth of Heterosexual AIDS: How a Tragedy*

Has Been Distorted by the Media and Partisan Politics. The book argues that AIDS is not now nor will it be in the future epidemic among heterosexuals who do not abuse intravenous drugs. Another claim Fumento argues is that homosexuals, who comprise the largest percentage of AIDS victims, make up a much smaller percentage of the U.S. population than gay lobbyists assert. Still another of Fumento's claims is that AIDS research is receiving too much money. That argument is advanced in the following essay, which appears as a chapter in *The Myth of Heterosexual AIDS.*

The evidence continues to come in that the scope of the [AIDS] 1 epidemic—including its effect on homosexuals, its effect on sexually active heterosexuals, its effect on persons in neither category, and its effect on the economy—has been grossly overplayed. The time has come to ask whether spiraling increases in AIDS funding are justified.

It would be nice to live in a world where one could simply assign 2 more money, more personnel, more resources in general to any given problem without worrying about any other problem being short-changed. But we live in a world of scarce resources. Money and attention devoted to one cause means resources pulled off another. And there's the rub. Clearly, there is a connection between the perception of AIDS as a world catastrophe and the willingness to fund the campaign against it. It is not the present caseload; there are still fourteen causes of death in America that are ahead of AIDS. It was the predictions of millions or tens of millions or hundreds of millions of future cases that had many of us rating AIDS as the number-one health priority. As AIDS activists are well aware, to challenge those predictions could be tantamount to challenging the pouring of massive amounts of resources into the anti-AIDS fight.

Indeed, rumblings are being heard. Dr. Vincent T. DeVita, Jr., just 3 before stepping down from his position as director of the National Cancer Institute (NCI), bemoaned the loss of resources to the AIDS industry: "[AIDS] has been an extraordinary drain on the energy of the scientific establishment. . . . It's been a big stress. It's taken a lot of intellectual energy away from the cancer program."[1] The American Heart Association, for its part, in order to trigger more donations for heart research, began running advertisements in early 1989 showing the risk of getting AIDS versus that of getting heart disease.

Despite the far greater health threat posed by cancer, federal AIDS 4 funding allocated to the Public Health Service at $1,300,000,000 (of which about $400,000,000 goes to education, not research) now nearly matches cancer funding. In President Bush's budget proposal for fiscal year 1990, this figure rises to $1,600,000,000. Cancer funding, by

---

[1] Susan Okie, "Assessing the War on Cancer." *Washington Post,* 22 August 1988, p. A13.

contrast, with the AIDS portion pulled out, comes to about $1,450,000,000. Even if the AIDs epidemic kept up with the CDC [Centers for Disease Control] projection and did not peak until 1993, AIDS cases diagnosed that year would be but a fourth of all 1993 cancer deaths. Each year a million cases of cancer are diagnosed, almost half of which end in death. This will be the case the next year and the year after that, with no peaking or decline anticipated until scientists bring one about. Heart disease kills more people than even cancer, over 750,000 Americans a year; yet funding to fight it is two thirds that of AIDS.[2]

AIDS research has now drained cancer research to a point where the NCI's ability to fund promising new research proposals is less than at any time in the past two decades. During fiscal year 1989, only 25 percent of cancer grant applications approved by review committees will receive funding. During the 1970s, between 43 percent and 60 percent of such approved grants were funded. Two top NCI doctors left the agency in 1988, partly in frustration over this. "They bled cancer to feed AIDS in terms of people's time," complained one.[3]

Perhaps we could just trade funds earmarked for F-16s or MX missiles for AIDS research, as some have suggested, but even this would not alleviate the problem that when it comes to researchers, this is pretty much a zero-sum game. It takes up to a decade to put a high school graduate through medical school. Thus, in the short run, AIDS researchers must come from and have come from other research areas, primarily but not exclusively cancer. In a medical newspaper editorial asking "Are We Spending Too Much Money on AIDS?" two young psychiatric researchers spoke of having to resist the "seduction" of AIDS research money. "Unfortunately," wrote the researchers, "many other young scientists may have no choice but to go into the field that offers the most easily obtained funding. If this happens, other areas of research important to the welfare of the U.S. public will be neglected for years to come."[4] One of the two retiring top NCI officials exclaimed that NCI "is withering away."[5] Further, the 1989 appropriations bill signed into law by President Reagan expressly called for hiring an additional 780 AIDS researchers. Where will they

---

[2] Spending figures are for fiscal year 1989, were allocated in the Labor, Health and Human Services and Education Appropriations Act of 1989, and were relayed to me by the Health and Human Services and Education Subcommittee. Cancer and heart disease death rates are from the Bureau of the Census.

[3] Susan Okie, "Cutbacks, AIDS Emphasis Seen Slowing Cancer Fight," *Washington Post*, 28 December 1988, p. A9.

[4] Stephen Dilsaver and Jeffrey Coffman, "Are We Spending Too Much Money on AIDS?" *The Scientist* 2 (11 July 1988): 11.

[5] Okie, "Cutbacks," p. A9.

come from? They'll come from where they've *been* coming from. For non-AIDS work, the National Institutes of Health has lost almost 1,100 employees since 1984. At the same time, the number of employees engaged in AIDS work has increased by more than 400 to 580 workers or their full-time equivalents, according to *Science* magazine.[6]

Terrible as it sounds, there will never be enough researchers or money to go around. Hard decisions have to be made about what programs should be emphasized and what ones de-emphasized. AIDS has prompted a general de-emphasis of other medical problems. The blunt fact is that people will die of these other diseases because of the overemphasis on AIDS. We will never know their names, and those names will never be sewn into a giant quilt. We will never know their exact number. But they will die nonetheless.

Of course, a comparison of death counts is not the only appropriate factor in allocating funding and researchers. Another argument used to advocate massive AIDS spending is to look at federal spending for patient care; in other words, "pay me now or pay me later." But when the preceding two researchers did just that, they found that in terms of both persons affected and patient costs, direct and indirect, the toll caused by psychiatric disorders swamps that of AIDS. The ratio of AIDS research and development spending to federal patient costs is vastly out of proportion to other deadly diseases. For example, cancer research expenditures will equal about 4.5 percent of cancer patient costs. For heart disease, it is about 2.9 percent; and for Alzheimer's disease, federal research expenditures will equal less than 1 percent of federal patient costs. But with AIDS, using a conservatively high estimate for federal patient costs, federal research expenditures will be an astounding 230 percent greater than federal patient costs for AIDS patients this year.[7]

Aside from death rates and patient costs, there may be some justification to spend more for AIDS. Perhaps AIDS research will lead to new discoveries in other areas. However, direct research is generally more efficient than spinoff research. As it happens, of the only five drugs approved for treatment of AIDS or its conditions, two (AZT and alpha interferon) are spinoffs of *cancer* research. Dr. Robert Gallo, co-discoverer of the AIDS virus, began his research as a cancer specialist. So the "overlap" argument really comes to something of a wash. Further, only about a fourth of the PHS AIDS budget goes for the kind of hard research that could even have the possibility of aiding

7

8

9

---

[6] William Booth, "No Longer Ignored, AIDS Funds Just Keep Growing," *Science* 242 (4880 [11 November 1988]): 859.

[7] Figures for federal patient costs are from a personal communication with Hay.

other research. About $385 million out of the fiscal year 1989 budget of $1.3 billion. Nevertheless, perhaps a breakthrough for AIDS is closer than for other diseases. Perhaps AIDS deserves more money because it is a more horrible way to die. Perhaps it deserves more money because its victims tend to be younger than those of heart disease and cancer. Perhaps. But if the case for disproportionate AIDS spending is to be made, it must be done with realistic numbers, not projections driven by ignorance or political concerns.

Finally, such a massive increase in one area is begging for boon- 10 doggles. And while the media, undoubtedly out of a sense of national purpose, has circumspectly avoided reporting on these, they exist nonetheless. In December 1988, the National Institute of Allergies and Infectious Diseases announced two grants totaling $22,800,000 to, as the Associated Press put it, study non-IVDA heterosexuals in order to "prevent a huge new epidemic."[8] Speaking on condition of anonymity, one prominent federal epidemiologist said of the study, "I think it's complete bullshit." He said, "That amount of money is ridiculous. You can do a good study for a tenth of that amount; in fact, PHS already is. Plus, it's an area that's being studied intensively and my sense is they're not asking very good questions." He told me, "My sense was that a huge amount of money got dumped on NIAID and that by the time they got around to awarding the money a lot of good institutions had already been funded and all that was left was schlock." Alas, this "schlock" adds up to one third of the entire yearly federal allocation for Alzheimer's disease, a cruel, debilitating malady that wipes away memory and that, because people are living longer, will continue to take an ever-higher yearly toll unless medical intervention becomes possible. Indeed, if scientists do not find a way to treat Alzheimer's by the middle of the next century, there will be five times as many victims of this disease in the United States as there are now. Up to 6,000,000 older Americans will be living in nursing homes, instead of the 1,000,000 there today.[9] The increased costs, of course, will be tremendous.

While writers like Randy Shilts have made an excellent case that 11 too little was spent on the AIDS epidemic early on because its scope was understated, does that justify too much now being spent because it was subsequently overstated? Should there be an affirmative action program for AIDS spending? Put another way, while it's a tragedy that in the first two years of AIDS appropriations the federal government allocated only $34,000,000 to be spent on the disease, are we going to

---

[8] "Major AIDS Study on Drug-free Heterosexuals," AP, 16 December 1988.
[9] Daniel Perry and Robert N. Butler, "Aim Not Just for Longer Life, But Extended 'Health Span,'" *Washington Post*, 20 December 1988, p. H20.

make amends for that by wasting $22,000,000 on a single project at this much later date?

Homosexuals have learned to use their victim status as a powerful 12 lobbying tool. Their pink triangles are ubiquitous in major cities, slapped on everything from newspaper boxes to telephone booths to stoplights, with superadhesive that will probably keep some of the stickers stuck for longer than the AIDS epidemic will last. In the 1940s, the pink triangle was used to send homosexuals to German concentration camps, and often to their deaths. In the 1970s, the pink triangle became a symbol of Gay Liberation, of a demand to be treated with the same rights and respect given to heterosexuals. By the late 1980s, the pink triangle was used like an American Express Platinum Card, as a means of getting special privileges available only to the bearer. AIDS victims began the 1980s by asking to be treated no worse than victims of other fatal diseases. But within a few years they were demanding funding and other treatment far superior to that received by sufferers of any other disease.

Likewise, the problems AIDS victims had with the Food and Drug 13 Administration were no different from the problems other disease sufferers have had for decades. The FDA has established testing procedures for all food additives and drugs. These procedures, which have been developed to ensure that these products are both safe and effective, are controversial because they can substantially delay the marketing of an important product. Nobody has established that the FDA slowed AIDS drug development any more than it had slowed up everything from life-saving beta blockers for heart disease to fat substitutes for food to a formula for growing hair. AIDS victims demanded preferential treatment. Like all special interests, the AIDS victims and their fellows wanted us to believe theirs was especially special. Yet why did the government have "blood on its hands" for AIDS, as some of the stickers claim, but for no other cause of death? It might have been because AIDS did not receive as much funding early on as it is now agreed it should have gotten. This was a strong theme in Randy Shilts's book. In hindsight, it is easy to see that much more money should have been spent much more quickly on AIDS than was the case. For that matter, though, hindsight also tells us that those same public health authorities strongly overreacted to the swine-flu scare in the mid-1970s. But would funding have been substantially different if the afflicted had been, to use one congressman's comparison, tennis players instead of homosexuals?[10] This is something that Shilts's ex-

---

[10] "Kaposi's Sarcoma and Related Opportunistic Infection," hearings before House of Representatives Subcommittee on Health and the Environment, 13 April 1982, p. 2, as cited in Dennis Altman, *AIDS in the Mind of America* (New York: Anchor/Doubleday, 1986), p. 113.

haustive research and his memos obtained under the Freedom of Information Act did not reveal. The conclusion is left more to conjecture and occasional conversational tidbits than anything else. If early funding had been made available, how greatly would this have affected the course of the epidemic? Again, this is a matter of conjecture.

AIDS advocates have said it is wrong to treat victims of this disease 14 differently from victims of other diseases. After all, heart disease and cancer, especially lung cancer, are often behaviorally linked as well. Nobody lectures the dying cigarette smoker, we are reminded. Fair enough. But nobody exalts him, either. If AIDS victims want to be treated as well as victims of other diseases, that is their right. But they have no right to be treated any better, either. There is no national guilt for AIDS, and there is no excuse for condescending to AIDS activists as if there were.

AIDS is a terrible disease that, even though the worst will soon be 15 over, is not going to go away on its own. But there are many other terrible diseases that will not go away. All deserve our attention, and all their victims deserve our compassion. But compassion begins with allocating resources on the basis of where they can do the most good, not on the basis of oiling the wheel that squeaks the loudest. It is not fair to penalize victims of cancer and other life-threatening illnesses because they do not knit quilts or blockade the Golden Gate Bridge or picket magazines that say things they don't believe should be allowed in print. And lest they forget, homosexuals get cancer, too.

Dennis Altman, chronicler of the Gay Liberation movement, 16 wrote in *AIDS in the Mind of America,*

> The real test posed by AIDS was expressed by Jesse Jackson in a speech to the Human Rights Campaign Fund dinner in New York in 1983 when he said: "Gay health issues, such as a cure for AIDS, *are* important. But I suggest to you this night that when you give life you gain life. If there is a commitment to health care for *whatever* the disease, based upon need and not based upon wealth or class—then within health care is encompassed the issue of AIDS. AIDS is not the only disease in the nation tonight. Be concerned about AIDS but also sickle cell. Never let it be said that you are a one-agenda, self-centered, narcissistic movement."[11]

If that was the test of AIDS, then clearly the test was failed. AIDS activists, homosexual and otherwise, have become exactly what the Reverend Jackson warned against.

---

[11] Altman, *AIDS in the Mind of America,* p. 190.

QUESTIONS AND IDEAS FOR DISCUSSION

1. How does Fumento answer the question that is the title of his essay? How would you answer it? How would you answer Fumento, if you disagree with his conclusion?

2. Evaluate Fumento's argument: Is it logical? Is the evidence convincing? Does the argument avoid fallacious appeals? Discuss.

3. Statistically, most of Fumento's readers are likely to be heterosexuals who do not use intravenous drugs. If Fumento is correct, few people in that category have any chance of contracting AIDS. Is it possible that arguments such as his could make people complacent about AIDS? Could it, by indicating that AIDS research is being done at the expense of more prevalent killers, make people oppose funding AIDS research? Discuss the implications of Fumento's argument.

4. Discuss the rhetorical effectiveness of the concluding paragraph.

AIDS: *Getting More Than Its Share?*
CHARLES KRAUTHAMMER

Charles Krauthammer came to writing by way of medicine and to medicine by way of political theory, a circuitous and fascinating journey he describes in the introduction to his collection of essays, *Cutting Edges* (1985). He ultimately chose, after studying political theory at Oxford and medicine at Harvard Medical School, to write, because "there was no shortage of hands to take up my work in medicine, but there was a shortage of hands, voices actually, advancing the things I believed in outside." Krauthammer is today a widely published author and columnist for the *New Republic, Time,* and many other periodicals. In this 1990 essay, Krauthammer advances an argument very similar to Michael Fumento's, although briefer. Krauthammer's essay is included here so that you may compare the styles and degrees of persuasiveness of two essays whose arguments are in substance much the same. Emphases and effects are different, however, as you will see.

Last month [May 1990] a thousand demonstrators camped outside 1
the National Institutes of Health near Washington and with a talented display of street theater protested governmental and scientific neglect of AIDS. If not the angriest demonstration Washington has seen in a long time, it was certainly the most misdirected. The idea that Ameri-

can government or American society has been inattentive or unresponsive to AIDS is quite simply absurd. Consider:

Treatment. Congress is about to do something extremely rare: 2
allocate money specifically for the treatment of one disease. The Senate voted $2.9 billion, the House $4 billion over five years for treating AIDS. And only AIDS. When Senator Malcolm Wallop introduced an amendment allowing rural districts with few AIDS patients to spend the money on other diseases, the amendment was voted down, 2 to 1.

Research. Except for cancer, AIDS now receives more Government 3
research money than any other illness in America. AIDS gets $1.2 billion to $1.3 billion. Heart disease, for example, receives about half as much, $700 billion. The AIDS research allocation is not just huge, it is hugely disproportionate. AIDS has killed 83,000 Americans in nine years. Heart disease kills that many every six weeks.

Testing. Under pressure from AIDS activists, the FDA has radically 4
changed its regulations for testing new drugs. The Administration has proposed "parallel track" legislation that would make drugs available to certain patients before the usual testing process is complete. Nothing wrong with this. But this exception is for AIDS patients only—a fact that hardly supports the thesis that government is holding back an AIDS cure or discriminating against AIDS patients.

The suffering caused by AIDS is enormous. Sufferers deserve 5
compassion, and their disease deserves scientific inquiry. But AIDS has got far more. AIDS has become the most privileged disease in America. Why? Mainly because its victims are young, in many cases creative and famous. Their deaths are therefore particularly poignant and public. And because one of the two groups that AIDS disproportionately affects (gay men) is highly organized. This combination of conspicuousness and constituency has allowed AIDS activists to get more research funding, more treatment money and looser drug-testing restrictions than any comparable disease.

Nothing wrong with that. The system for allocating research and 6
treatment money in American medicine is archaic, chaotic and almost random anyway. Under the "Disease of the Month Club" syndrome, any disease that has in some way affected a Congressman or some relation gets special treatment. There is rough justice in this method of allocation because after a while Congressmen and their kin get to experience most of the medical tragedies that life has to offer. At the end of the day, therefore, funds tend to get allocated in a fairly proportionate way.

AIDS is now riding a crest of public support, won in the rough and 7
tumble of politics. All perfectly legitimate, and a tribute to the passion and commitment of AIDS activists. But that passion turns to mere stridency when they take to the streets to protest that a homophobic

society has been ungenerous and stinting in its response to the tragedy of AIDS. In fact, American society is giving overwhelming and
indeed disproportionate attention and resources to the fight.

At first the homosexual community was disoriented and defensive   8
in reaction to AIDS. In the quite understandable attempt to get public
support, it fixed on a strategy of claiming that AIDS was everyone's
problem. Since we were all potential sufferers—anyone can get AIDS,
went the slogan—society as an act of self-protection should go all out
for cure and care.

This campaign was initially successful. But then it ran into an   9
obstacle. It wasn't true. AIDS is not everyone's problem. It is extremely difficult to get AIDS. It requires the carrying out of specific and
quite intentional acts. Nine out of ten people with AIDS have got it
through homosexual sex and/or intravenous drug use. The NIH
demonstrators, therefore, now appeal less to solidarity than to guilt:
every person who dies is more blood on the hands of a society unwilling to give every dollar demanded for a cure.

But society has blood on its hands every time it refuses to give   10
every dollar demanded by the cancer lobby, the heart disease lobby,
the diabetes lobby. So now a different tack: the claim that the AIDS
epidemic is, of course, not an act of government but an act of God—
and government has not done enough to help its helpless victims.   11

In fact, AIDS is far less an act of God than is, say, cancer or
diabetes. Apart from a small number of relentlessly exploited Ryan
White–like exceptions, the overwhelming majority of sufferers get
AIDS through some voluntary action: sex or drug abuse. You don't get
AIDS the way you used to get TB, by having someone on the trolley
cough in your face. You don't get it the way you get, say, brain cancer,
which is through some act of God that we don't understand at all.

AIDS is in the class of diseases whose origins we understand quite   12
well. It is behaviorally induced and behaviorally preventable. In that
sense it is in the same moral class as lung cancer, the majority of whose
victims get it through voluntary behavior well known to be highly
dangerous. For lung cancer the behavior is smoking; for AIDS, unsafe
sex (not, it might be noted, homosexuality) and IV drug use.

As a society we do not refuse either to treat or research lung cancer   13
simply because its sufferers brought it on themselves. But we would
find it somewhat perverse and distasteful if lung cancer sufferers
began demonstrating wildly, blaming society and government for
their problems, and demanding that they be first in line for a cure.

Many people contracted AIDS before its causes became known,   14
about six years ago. For them it is truly an act of God. For the rest (as
the word has gone out, an ever increasing percentage), it is an act of
man. They, of course, deserve our care and treatment. But it is hard to

see from where they derive the claim to be first in line—ahead of those dying of leukemia and breast cancer and stroke—for the resources and compassion of a nation.

QUESTIONS AND IDEAS FOR DISCUSSION

1.   Compare Krauthammer's core argument with Fumento's. On what substantive points, if any, do they differ? On what points do they differ in emphasis?

2.   Compare Fumento's persona with Krauthammer's. Which writer—if either—do you find more trustworthy and believable? Why?

3.   *Slanting* is choosing words, phrases, and examples to achieve a particular emotional response in readers. Do you find any evidence of slanting in Krauthammer's word choices? If so, in what direction? Give examples. If not, what specific underlying assumptions does this argument reveal (as all arguments do)?

No, Spending More on AIDS Isn't Unfair

NAOMI FREUNDLICH

Naomi Freundlich is the science and technology editor for *Business Week* magazine, in which this essay first appeared in September 1990. Freundlich opposes the views expressed by Michael Fumento and Charles Krauthammer, which she characterizes as a "backlash" against the amount of money allocated in recent years to AIDS research. Freundlich acknowledges that more people die of cancer and heart disease than of AIDS, but she argues that the AIDS epidemic differs from those health problems in significant ways that require extensive and immediate funding—and that the real issue is not so much AIDS as an even broader problem.

Just a year or so ago, it would have been political suicide for a   1 scientist, politician, or journalist to speak out against increased spending for AIDS research. After a regrettably slow start, the federal government took up the campaign in 1983 and has steadily increased research funding in an effort to curb the deadly epidemic. By the end of fiscal 1989, AIDS had garnered nearly $2.5 billion in government funds. And this year, the National Institutes of Health will kick in

$740 million more. Last month, Congress allocated an additional $875 million for states to use for AIDS treatment.

Now, as activists stage protests demanding even more money for AIDS, a backlash is forming. For a few critics, the attack is a value judgment on the lifestyles of AIDS sufferers. Other critics just question whether AIDS research should be such a high priority. Politicians from rural states, for instance, complain that the funds Congress is allocating for AIDS can't be used to fight other diseases. And there is growing resentment among some cancer and other non-AIDS researchers. 2

They charge that a project without a mention of AIDS in the title runs an unfair risk of getting turned down. An Office of Technology Assessment report released last April [1990] shows how pervasive that feeling is. Of some 148 scientists who answered a poll on AIDS research, nearly half complained that too much funding has been diverted to AIDS. This year, some 1 million people will die of heart disease, and an additional 500,000 or so of cancer. So why, the argument goes, spend so much on a disease that has killed just 83,000 Americans in nine years? 3

It doesn't take much digging to come up with the answer. Heart disease and cancer occur at a fairly stable rate. AIDS, by contrast, is an infectious disease and can spread rapidly through a population. In fact, the number of cases is expected to triple in the U.S. by 1993. And in the next decade alone, doctors will be treating a million or more people who are already infected with HIV, the virus that leads to AIDS. 4

Beyond that, the most recent figures from the Centers for Disease Control in Atlanta show that the malady is no longer confined to gays and drug users. Countrywide, the ratio of men to women who carry the HIV virus has dropped from 11 to 1 early in the epidemic to close to 3 to 1 today. In some rural areas, says Dr. June E. Osborn, dean of the University of Michigan's School of Public Health and chairwoman of the National Commission on AIDS, the ratio is closer to 1 to 1. Because the number of people infected with HIV in these rural areas is growing faster than in urban centers, that raises the specter of a heterosexual epidemic such as is now sweeping parts of Africa. And unlike cancer and heart disease, which usually strike older people, AIDS is a disease of the young. Some 82% of its victims are below the age of 44—in the most productive years of their lives. 5

If all this isn't reason enough to fund AIDS work, there is one more factor. According to Osborn, AIDS research is yielding a wealth of knowledge about viruses, cancer, the brain, and, most important, the immune system. "We have already learned many broadly important facts about how the body works, and there have been more 6 spin-offs for cancer and other diseases than for AIDS directly," she says. For example, she adds, before AIDS, there was only speculation that the immune system helps fight off cancer. Now, boosting the body's defenses has become a key part of cancer research. The [Office of Technology Assessment] OTA report came to the same conclusion, citing benefits in public health, epidemiology, and basic science from AIDS research.

If there is a problem of scarce resources, moreover, it's not that 7 money used for AIDS is being taken away from cancer and heart disease. It's true that the AIDS share of the NIH budget is rising rapidly. Funding for AIDS is growing 23% this fiscal year, while support for non-AIDS research is rising by only 4.4%. But William F. Raub, acting director of the NIH, says there is no guarantee that AIDS money would have gone to other diseases. More likely, it would have been used elsewhere in the federal budget, he says.

The problem he and others see is too little funding for biomedical 8 research in general. The U.S. spent $600 billion last year on health care—but just 2% of it went to research on disease. Only one-quarter of the research grants submitted to NIH are now approved, compared with 60% in 1975. That's because the funding pie is growing slower than both the cost of research and the number of scientists clamoring for a slice. As a result, young investigators are less able to get research funds, and even established researchers are leaving basic science to work in industry or to practice medicine.

For many researchers and other critics, AIDS funding is a conve- 9 nient target. But ultimately, the real issue is how much should be spent on biomedical research. Giving AIDS short shrift while that question is hashed out would be a tragic mistake.

QUESTIONS AND IDEAS FOR DISCUSSION

1. Characterize Freundlich's persona in this essay, citing evidence from the text for the inferences you draw. Is Fruendlich persuasive?

2. Is Freundlich's argument logically convincing? Why, or why not?

3. Do you find any evidence of slanting—of choosing words for their emotional value more than their meaning—in Freundlich's word choices? If so, in what direction? Give examples. If not, what specific underlying assumptions does this argument reveal (as all arguments do)?

4. What does this essay aim to accomplish—that is, what action does Freundlich want us to take, or what attitudes does she want us to adopt toward her subject? Does the essay succeed in this respect? How, or why not?

Paying the Price of AIDS

B. D. COLEN

B. D. Colen is the Pulitzer Prize–winning senior correspondent for science and medicine for *Newsday* (New York) and the author of nine books, including *Born at Risk* (1981), *Hard Choices* (1986), and *The Essential Guide to Living Wills* (1991). This essay first appeared in *Health,* a magazine on health issues written for the general public, in 1988. Colen works from the same starting point as Michael Fumento—that "white, middle-class, heterosexual Americans" do not face a major AIDS outbreak—to a substantially different conclusion.

For the six years I've been covering AIDS, I have been continually 1 amazed and depressed by the public's—and the media's—willingness to ignore the unfolding story. Sure, there have been flurries of interest, primarily centered on the deaths from AIDS of celebrities like Rock Hudson and Perry Ellis. But in general, the level of media and public attention has remained far below what I'd expect for an incurable, epidemic, killer disease.

You don't think the public has turned its back on AIDS? You say, 2 "Every time I turn around there's another story about AIDS in the paper or on TV"? Yes, AIDS *does* get in the news. But as the scourge enters its eighth year in the public consciousness, I find public awareness is at a much lower level than the disease's importance demands. Evidence: At the newspaper where I work, I can program my computer to build directories listing the stories coming into the paper— from various news sources, including The Associated Press, Reuters, the Los Angeles Times–Washington Post News Service and our own reporters—containing the word "AIDS." Until about nine months ago, I'd get a listing of 25 to 50 AIDS stories on any given day. However, since then and up until a week before the Fourth International Conference on AIDS in Stockholm in June, I found between *three* and *six* AIDS stories per day. The Monday after the conference ended, there were *no* stories in the file.

What has happened? I suspect there are at least two explanations. 3 In the first place, most reporters have had to write about AIDS far more than they'd care to. "Enough, already!" they are saying. "Give us some *good* news for a change. No more plagues. No more death." They imagine—and they're probably correct—that their readers are starting to feel the same way. Additionally, at this point there are no major medical breakthroughs or real changes in the story, so its coverage naturally shrinks as it falls victim to the old journalists' dictum, "Old news is no news."

The second reason for the drop-off in coverage is that since the 4
vast majority of Americans don't feel threatened by AIDS, they no
longer feel very concerned about its victims. It has become more and
more obvious that the epidemiologic evidence does not add up to a
major outbreak of AIDS among white, middle-class, heterosexual
Americans. Instead, most of those affected are male homosexuals, or
poor, black or Hispanic drug abusers (or the sexual partners or children of these groups of people). And since we are an essentially racist,
classist society, the prevailing attitude toward AIDS has become "It's
their problem, not mine."

Unfortunately, the media often reflect those biases. With rare 5
exceptions, they've done an abysmal job of covering what Michael
Harrington termed "the other America"—the poverty-stricken under-
class that peoples our inner cities and rural hollows.

But turning our backs on AIDS and its victims causes us to miss 6
the same point that we miss when we ignore other societal ills: *We* are
they. Beyond the philosophical argument that we all are affected by the
misfortunes of those less fortunate than ourselves—and that includes
the millions of AIDS cases worldwide, not just the tens of thousands of
Americans—we will *all,* in some way, have to pay for AIDS.

"How?" you may ask. After all, most of us will never get AIDS, 7
and many of us have never even known someone who had or has it.
But we will pay in many ways. First, we will literally pay for the
disease's ever-escalating medical costs. While there is no agreement
on the present (or the ultimate) price tag for the AIDS epidemic, all
agree that it will be astronomical. It's not unusual for a single person
with AIDS to rack up medical bills in excess of $125,000. And we are
now told that within the next five years the United States will record
more than a third of a million AIDS cases. A little simple arithmetic
shows that with that number the total adds up to more than 41 *billion*
dollars. The most conservative cost estimate I've heard is $40,000 per
patient (a figure many experts consider absurdly low), which still
brings the total to a whopping $13 billion. And while the cost of the
treatment of the average case is shrinking, this is largely because more
people are receiving care at home. The cost of hospital treatment
continues to *increase* because people who require this kind of care are
the sickest of all. In many cases, they remain hospitalized because they
are homeless and have nowhere else to go. (You know, *them* again.)

So where will these billions of dollars for treatment come from? 8
Not from private insurance carriers because more and more people
with AIDS come from the ranks of those who either receive public
assistance such as Medicaid or are part of the working poor, who make
too much to qualify for Medicaid and don't have private health insur-

ance. Federal, state and local governments will pay for this care, and of course *we* are the government. Certainly in states like New York, California and Florida, which have the majority of AIDS cases, state and city taxes will rise. And the same thing may well occur at the Federal level—if a new administration finally faces up to the magnitude of the crisis.

We will all pay for AIDS in other ways as well. Residents of cities   9 where the disease has hit the hardest may soon find themselves waiting longer to be admitted to hospitals, as AIDS patients occupy more of the available beds. The ever-increasing pressures exerted by AIDS on the urban poor may exacerbate racial and ethnic tensions in cities such as New York, Newark and Los Angeles.

Costs of basic scientific research—the vitally important, time- and   10 resource-intensive searches for better diagnoses, treatments and a cure—undoubtedly will continue to rise. So will the costs of AIDS support services, which have been financed largely by charitable organizations. And let's not forget the undeniable effects AIDS has had on the social lives and interactions of those who aren't even at major risk of contracting it.

Of course, these costs don't touch upon the steepest cost of all,   11 that which we'll pay in the loss of human life until some way is found to prevent AIDS or cure those already afflicted.

All this is meant not as a complaint but as a reminder. While most   12 of us, thankfully, are at low risk of becoming *infected,* we are all at extremely high risk of having our lives *affected* by this viral killer. The costs of AIDS are not going to go away, and as a society, we cannot afford to ignore them.

QUESTIONS AND IDEAS FOR DISCUSSION

1.   Colen's thesis is that "everybody pays for AIDS." Why then does he begin his essay with a lengthy anecdote about something else, the decline in the number of news stories on AIDS? How effective is the introduction rhetorically?

2.   In what ways will "we all pay for AIDS," according to Colen? For which claims does he offer supporting evidence? Is he justified in assuming that we will accept the other claims without evidence? (That is, has he considered his audience well?)

3.   Colen does not directly advocate either increasing *or* decreasing funding for AIDS. From the points he *does* make, which would you infer to be his preference? Would his argument have been stronger had he spelled it out? Discuss.

SUGGESTIONS FOR WRITING
AND FURTHER DISCUSSION

1. Do arguments about AIDS focus on readers' presumed self-interests and fears to an unusual degree? Or is such the case with arguments about any health-related issue? Argue your answer.

2. Defend or oppose the claim that the best way to find a cure for AIDS (and other diseases) is in long-term rather than short-term allocation of funds. That is, the best strategy is not to allocate all funds for immediate research but to fund publicity and scholarships to encourage students to major in biology and biochemistry and pursue careers in research medicine.

3. Defend or oppose the claim that the U.S. Food and Drug Administration rules requiring extensive testing of new drugs should be made less stringent in order to give dangerously ill people quick access to promising drugs and treatments. Your audience will probably include animal rights activists (who may oppose such testing anyway) and people with dangerously ill family members, but not pharmacists or others with specialized knowledge about drug testing.

4. Defend or oppose the claim that the United States should adopt universal health insurance ("socialized medicine") so that catastrophic illnesses such as AIDS will not impoverish their victims and families. Your audience will be members of your class, many of whom have not experienced major illnesses either personally or in their families. Whichever position you choose, you must convince your audience that the issue *matters*—and that it matters for *them*. Either they are now or they will be taxpayers; either they have been or they will be patients or relatives of patients in hospitals.

5. Suppose that Michael Fumento and the 1970 Kinsey report he quotes in *The Myth of Heterosexual AIDS* (207) are right in claiming that men who are exclusively homosexual constitute only 1.4 percent of the adult U.S. population. Should that knowledge affect funding for AIDS research? Discuss.

6. Do you find AIDS more or less in the news today than when B. D. Colen lamented the decline of publicity in 1988? What reasons can you suggest for the current trend? Discuss.

7. Decide which of the essays in this chapter argues its claims most effectively—whether or not you like or agree with its conclusions.

Argue the reasons for your choice. (You may choose to comment on the difficulty, if any, of putting aside your own ideas about the issues while you judge the arguments.) Is the most effective argument the best written and the most clearly organized? The most logical? The best documented? Or is it more emotional than logical in its argument? What does the essay show you as a writer about ways to make a point well?

10

OVERPOPULATION

Is the earth overpopulated? If it is not at present, what about the near future? Will there be too many inhabitants for the planet to support within the next decade or two? And if so, what can and should be done about it? Our answers to these questions depend upon all kinds of assumptions: about the definition of "a good quality of life," about what constitutes overcrowding, about the degree to which governments can legitimately interfere in the lives of their citizens, about the sanctity of life itself.

As you read the essays in this chapter, be aware of the assumptions the writers have made about these questions. Think as well about your own assumptions. And consider the implications of the several and conflicting claims these writers earnestly argue. Some authors will call attention to unwarranted assumptions and to issues that may surprise you.

Growth Means Progress

JULIAN SIMON

Julian Simon, a professor of marketing at the University of Illinois, is the author of *The Ultimate Resource* (1982), *The Resourceful Earth: Population and Economic Growth Theory* (co-author, 1985), *Effort, Opportunity, and Wealth* (1987), and a number of other works. He has been described (by the editors of *Science Digest,* in which the following essay first appeared in 1983) as "the most outspoken critic of the doom-and-destruction prophecies of many population experts." In "Growth Means Progress," Simon offers an unconventional but provocative argument that population growth is not the specter we have feared. His original audience was the readers of *Science Digest* in general and Donald Mann, whose argument in response to this one follows it, in particular. But before you read Mann's essay and the others in this chapter, make your own assessment of Simon's argument.

In the short run, an additional person—baby or immigrant— 1
inevitably means a lower standard of living for everyone. More consumers mean less of the fixed available stock of goods to be divided
among more people. And more workers laboring with the same fixed
current stock of capital means that there will be less output per
worker. The latter effect, known as "the law of diminishing returns,"
is the essence of Malthus's theory as he first set it out. This extraordinarily powerful idea brought me to work in the field of population
economics and population control because it led me to worry about the
effects of population growth.

But if the resources with which men work are *not* fixed over the 2
period being analyzed, then the Malthusian logic of diminishing returns does not apply. And the plain fact is that, given some time to
adjust to shortages, the resource base does not remain fixed—because
people create more resources of all kinds.

Extraordinary as it may seem, raw-material scarcity, that is, the 3
cost of materials—which is the relevant economic measure of scarcity—has tended to diminish and resource availability has tended to
increase over all of history. The idea that scarcity is diminishing is
mind-boggling because it defies commonsense reasoning, which says
that when one starts out with a fixed stock and uses some up, there is
less left. But for all practical purposes there are no resources until we
find them, identify their possible uses and develop ways to obtain and
process them. We do these tasks with increasing skill as technology
develops. Hence, scarcity diminishes.

This idea is fairly easy to accept for trees and food, which are alive. 4
The idea of increasing availability for metals seems harder to accept,
until one remembers that metals are not used up but, rather, are
recycled and that we constantly find substitutes for metals; plastics
replace tin cans, satellites replace copper telephone wire. The idea of
increasing availability seems hardest to accept for energy, but it is
nonetheless true that the cost of energy in general has been falling
over the years.

Nor is there any identifiable limit to this process.   5

This becomes clear when we recognize that the sun is very much 6
part of our energy world, and any notion of finite resources that
excludes the sun would be ridiculous. The sun's future life is so long as
to make nonsense of any worries about "ultimately" running out of
energy. A little closer in time, even the future supply of oil is seen not
to be measurable (and hence not finite), when we remember that we
will be creating new oil in the future, just as we already create oil from
coal, soybeans and other "renewable" resources. Therefore, there is
no solid reason to believe that in the future natural-resource scarcity
will necessarily be a brake on population growth any more than in the

past. And the evidence of the past suggests that even more people
imply even more resource availability in the long run, without limit.

The most extraordinary part of the resource-creation process is 7
that temporary or expected shortages—whether due to population
growth, income growth or other causes—tend to leave us even better
off than if the shortage had never arisen because of the continuing
benefit of the intellectual and physical capital created to meet the
shortage. For example, when people settle in an area more densely,
they eradicate the malaria mosquito by cultivating the places where it
breeds. This is the only successful way of preventing malaria in the
long run, in contrast to DDT and other mosquito-fighting chemicals
that the mosquito eventually surmounts. Or when a generation runs
short of copper, it finds new materials such as aluminum or plastic to
replace it.

Of course it is not logically inevitable that positive responses to a 8
shortage will dominate the short-run negative effects of Malthusian
capital dilution. Which force is stronger differs at different times in
history and in different stages of culture. The only way to find out
which dominates is to check data on the overall relationship between
the growth rates of population and per capita income. And it is such
data that converted me from a fighter for lower population growth to a
believer in the long-run benefits of more people.

Cross-national comparisons of recent rates of population growth 9
and economic growth show a lack of negative impact of population
growth on living standards in the long run. More generally, in less
developed countries per capita income has been growing as fast as or
faster than in the developed countries, according to a World Bank
survey for the years 1950 to 1975, despite the fact that population has
grown faster in developing countries than in developed countries.

Two frequently raised questions can be dealt with quickly. First, 10
"untrammeled copulation" is hardly more true of the poor and uneducated than it is of us; marriage and sex are subject to rational
decision-making and tight social control everywhere, and to think
otherwise is ignorant or arrogant. Second, population growth is not
"inexorable." Historically, population size has fallen as well as risen,
and has stayed constant for long centuries; rapid rises have been
temporary and due to sudden improvements in the basis for human
life. And growth in human numbers will probably ebb and flow in the
future, as material and cultural changes occur.

Immigrants are an even better deal for Americans than are native 11
babies because the benefits come sooner. Even immigrants with relatively little education pay more into the public coffers in taxes soon
after arrival than they take out in welfare services, because, on average, immigrants come when they are young and strong and do not

need (and are not eligible for) Social Security. Nor do immigrants reduce the public capital available to natives; rather, they pay more than their share of "rent" for schools and other facilities whose capacities are affected by the number of Americans. And when the positive effects on productivity are also brought in the calculation, immigrants are seen to be an "investment" for natives that brings a high rate of return.

One can raise assorted noneconomic social and cultural argu- 12 ments against more immigrants and babies, but one can also raise persuasive noneconomic arguments in their favor.

QUESTIONS AND IDEAS FOR DISCUSSION

1. Does Simon make any claim that strikes you on first reading as incredible? If so, what is it? How does he attempt to convince you of his claims? *Does* he convince you? Explain.

2. Simon argues that "scarcity is diminishing" (paragraph 3). Is this a contradiction in terms? Summarize Simon's support for this key claim. Does he make a strong case?

3. "The idea of increasing availability seems hardest to accept for energy, but it is nonetheless true that the cost of energy in general has been falling over the years" (4). What ideas does Simon link here? What implicit assumptions does he make?

4. Does Simon claim that the earth has an infinite supply of oil? How would you respond to his argument in paragraph 6?

5. Evaluate Simon's argument concerning the benefits of population growth and immigration: Is it logical? Is it humane?

Growth Means Doom

DONALD MANN

Donald Mann is president and one of the founders of Negative Population Growth, Inc., and the author of *Urgently Needed Now: A National Policy to Reduce U.S. Population.* His essay here, first published in *Science Digest* in 1983, was paired there with the preceding essay by Julian Simon. Mann argues the position on population growth most familiar to us: that it threatens to doom the planet. Even though the argument is familiar, it merits careful evaluation. Does the author make reasonable claims and draw a defensible conclusion?

There is a growing consensus that further population growth in 1
our already vastly overpopulated world threatens to destroy man's
ancient dream of a good life for all, free from material want.

At the beginning of the century, world population was about 1.6 2
billion, a figure it had taken millions of years to reach. Today, world
population is increasing by that number every 15 to 20 years. There are
now 4.6 billion people on Earth; it is projected that there will be 6
billion by the end of the century and 10 to 15 billion before the population *possibly* levels off sometime in the next 100 years.

These are staggering figures, difficult to appreciate because of 3
their sheer magnitude. The consequences of such population growth,
however, are now well understood.

It is generally accepted that the planet's resources and the ability 4
of the environment to absorb pollution are finite. We depend on a
complex ecosystem that is already being strained beyond the limits of
tolerance by the pressure of human numbers. Many reliable studies
have depicted in stark terms the alarming consequences of too many
people.

The Global 2000 Report to the President was released several years ago 5
after more than two years of study. The report, made by a committee
of experts from the departments of State, Energy and the Interior and
other government agencies, spells out the frightening deterioration of
the environment that is projected to occur over the next two decades if
present trends continue. In just 17 more years, hundreds of thousands
of plant and animal species will have become extinct; half the world's
forests will be gone; severe energy and water shortages will reduce
agriculture production. "The problems of preserving the carrying capacity of the Earth and sustaining the possibility of a decent life for the
human beings that inhabit it are enormous," the report concludes.

The report deals primarily with three problems: population 6
growth, resource scarcity and environmental deterioration. It is clear
that by controlling one—population growth—we can remove the
cause of the other two.

But it is becoming increasingly apparent that population stabili- 7
zation at projected or even at present levels would not be sufficient if a
good life for all and a sustainable economy are our goals. And why
should humankind settle for anything less?

More and more, informed individuals believe that the only possi- 8
ble solution for our planet lies in halting and then reversing population growth so that population size can eventually be stabilized at
some reasonable fraction of today's numbers.

We at Negative Population Growth [NPG] believe the optimum 9
number of people that the United States can support is 100 million; the
entire world, 2 billion. These recommended levels, which were

reached and passed roughly a half century ago, are less than 50 percent of the current population burden.

It can be argued that modern technology, as well as overcrowding, 10 has contributed to the deterioration of our planet. But technology and our modern industrial society are here to stay, and we must accommodate ourselves to their requirements. We can and we should reduce per capita consumption of energy and materials, and reduce per capita pollution, by improving technology and simplifying life-styles. But these measures will not create a healthy *sustainable* society without a substantial reduction in numbers as well. The impact of sheer numbers on resources and our environment cannot be denied. The great lesson of the Industrial Revolution, largely unheeded until now, is that vast numbers of people are simply incompatible with a healthy and prosperous industrial society.

Is a goal of 100 million Americans and a world population of 2 11 billion realistic? Absolutely. There is no reason why population cannot decline as well as increase.

There are many possible paths to a smaller population. In the 12 United States, for example, our present total fertility rate (the average number of children per completed family) is now roughly 1.8. That is slightly below the rate of 2.1 that is needed to maintain our present population size on a long-term basis (immigration excepted). Nevertheless, the U.S. population still continues to grow because of the preponderance of young people in the nation, the result of the baby boom.

If the present rate of 1.8 could be maintained long enough, 13 however, our population would eventually stabilize and begin a very slow decline. This path to a smaller population would require centuries to achieve a *substantial* reduction of numbers. It should be noted that if immigration into the United States is not drastically curtailed, population growth will never end, even with such a fertility pattern.

NPG recommends a somewhat faster transition to optimum popu- 14 lation size, a transition that—based on computer projections—would take about 100 years. Such a path would entail gradually lowering the total fertility rate to 1.0 (an average one-child family) and maintaining it at that low level for only a decade. At that time, it could be allowed to rise slowly, over a 20-year period, to the long term replacement rate of 2.1 and then be carefully maintained at that rate thereafter.

If the fertility rate followed such a path, after a decade or so the 15 U.S. population would stop growing (immigration excepted) and start a slow decline. A century later, there would be about 100 million Americans.

NPG opposes any compulsory measures or mandatory limitation 16 of family size. We believe that the recommended reduction in numbers could be achieved voluntarily, with the aid of tax incentives and disincentives to encourage couples to have small families. In brief, the path NPG recommends to a smaller population represents a realistic and painless option. It would not require major sacrifices on the part of the American public, nor would it require a major change in life-style.

Humankind today stands at a crossroads. One road, that of fur- 17 ther population growth, leads inevitably to starvation, poverty, social and political chaos and war. It leads to the certain destruction of all that we hold dear, including personal freedom, political liberty, peace and security, a decent standard of living and a healthy environment. The other road—that of population stabilization after a period of population decrease—is the road that humanity must start down *now*.

QUESTIONS AND IDEAS FOR DISCUSSION

1. Does Mann make any claims that strike you on first reading as incredible? If so, which? How does he attempt to convince us of his claims? Are you convinced? Explain.

2. On what does Mann base his claim that "the optimum number of people that the United States can support is 100 million" (paragraph 9)? (As Mann notes, our present population is well over double that number.) Evaluate the claim. Is it reasonable? Is it well supported by evidence or reasoning?

3. Evaluate the proposal Mann offers for achieving a 50 percent population reduction.

4. Does Mann's last paragraph effectively round out or sum up his argument? Compare the effectiveness of Mann's concluding paragraph with that of Simon's. Does either author particularly strengthen or weaken his argument with his conclusion? Explain.

The People Threat

FLORA LEWIS

Flora Lewis has spent more than fifty years as a foreign correspondent, including eight years (1972–1980) as Paris bureau chief for the *New York Times*. She is the author of four books on international issues and since 1980 has written a biweekly column on foreign affairs for the *New York Times*, in which this essay appeared in 1990. Flora Lewis approaches the issues of overpopulation from a pragmatic perspective: She argues in favor of allowing the so-called "abortion pill," RU486, to be imported into the United States and other countries as a means of fighting overpopulation. She begins by painting a menacing picture of a world with "peace at risk" because of far too many people—primarily immigrants from third-world countries—competing for far too few jobs. RU486 is a drug she regards as "an urgently needed safeguard" to help control the world's population.

Lucien Paye, head of the O.E.C.D., which groups 24 industrial- 1 ized countries was asked what worried him most on the horizon. U.S. budget and trade deficits? Protectionism? Recession?

"It depends if you talk short-term or long-term," he answered. 2 The serious concern, out about a decade, "is demography." Third-world countries are building up population at a rate no imaginable economic development effort could accommodate.

As things are going, pressures will become explosive, launching 3 invasion tides of desperate people trying to throw themselves on labor markets. They won't be armed, but will set forth in overwhelming multitudes.

Mr. Paye is a Frenchman, and he was thinking mainly of burgeon- 4 ing African populations. Already immigration from the south is the most abrasive political issue in France, strengthening the nationalist ultraright. The issue is sharpening in Italy, a country with no tradition of absorbing the poor from abroad.

For the U.S., the push will mount primarily from Latin America. 5 But the stakes are global because development, environment, peace will be put at risk if the number of people and capacity to sustain them is thrown into such imbalance.

That is why deliberate restraint of science in providing reproduc- 6 tive choice is beyond comprehension. The U.S. is hobbling a humane approach by its obsession with abortion. In the name of "right to life," American militants are disregarding conditions of life for children around the world: nutrition, health care, education at home, famine, disease, war abroad.

During the Reagan Administration, funds for United Nations pop- 7 ulation control programs were cut because they might be used for abortions. In the last couple of years, threats from American groups have blocked distribution of a pill that prevents development of a fertilized egg.

It is RU486, called the "French pill" because it was developed by a 8 French biochemist, Etienne-Emile Baulieu, who won a 1989 Lasker Award for his discovery. The citation said it provided a "safe, effective" means for preventing pregnancy and avoiding surgical abortion. Made by the French company Roussel Uclaf, RU486 has been widely tested in France and other European countries. In April, reports on

40,000 cases of use listed only two "incidents," without damaging consequences.

The anti-abortion lobby in the U.S. succeeded in preventing legal 9 importation of the drug under Federal law. Worse, by threatening a general boycott of pharmaceuticals from the German company Hoechst, which controls Roussel Uclaf, the lobby persuaded Hoechst to shut down production. The order was reversed in France by the Government, which had a minority share, so the pill is available here under medical supervision, but not much elsewhere.

Now, a group of San Francisco doctors has decided to test a 10 California law that permits import of banned drugs for experimental purposes, passed to enable investigation of as-yet uncertified treatments for AIDS. The French newspaper *Libération* quotes Dr. Bernard Gore as saying, "Like your Minister of Health, we think this revolutionary discovery is the moral property of women."

He pointed out that some 300,000 women die yearly of botched 11 abortions, mostly in the third world, and that law or no law, some 300,000 women in California undergo abortions every year.

The difference between a contraceptive pill and RU486 is that it 12 can be taken after insemination. It works in the early stage of pregnancy by countering the hormone progesterone, which serves to attach the fertilized egg to the uterus.

The World Development Forum called RU486 a "breakthrough for 13 developing countries." Dr. Baulieu said, "It is a far safer method of abortion than any operation in countries where medical facilities are limited."

But, the Forum said, Hoechst has refused to license production in 14 China, and the World Health Organization is ducking the issue. "We have no position," a spokesman said. A Hoechst spokesman said his company had yet to make a final decision, which would be based on medical reports, chemical trials, "and other issues, such as opinions in society. We will take note of their wishes."

That is a way of saying that the threat from American militants of 15 commercial loss on its other products has intimidated Hoechst to the point of depriving the world of an urgently needed safeguard. The San Francisco doctors have a chance to prove the pill should be legalized in the U.S., and open the possibility of worldwide distribution. They deserve support.

QUESTIONS AND IDEAS FOR DISCUSSION

1. What is Lewis's thesis? Evaluate its logic.

2. Discuss the emotional appeals in this essay. Does Lewis appeal to

racial and ethnic prejudices? Does she appeal to compassion and fairness? Be specific.

3.   What policy does Lewis advocate as a means of putting her thesis into action? Does the policy strike you as reasonable, based on this argument? Explain.

The Myth of Overpopulation
GERMAINE GREER

Germaine Greer, currently a special lecturer at Newnham College, Cambridge, may be best known for her feminist work, *The Female Eunuch*, an international best seller following its publication in 1970. Among her many other publications are *The Obstacle Race* (1979), *The Madwoman's Underclothes* (1986), and *Daddy, We Hardly Knew You* (1990). In this excerpt from her book *Sex and Destiny: The Politics of Human Fertility* (1984), Greer challenges almost all of our assumptions about overpopulation. In this respect, her argument has some points in common with Julian Simon's essay; in other respects, her argument shares some ideas with Donald Mann's essay. Finally, however, it is radically different from both—and from Flora Lewis's. You will see why as you read.

Whether we believe the world is overpopulated depends to some extent on how we think people should live. If we in the West think that only our kind of life is worth living, then clearly the numbers that the Earth supports will have to be substantially reduced. The world could become a vast luxury hotel, complete with recreational space for us to hunt and ski and mountaineer in.

But it must not be forgotten that our luxurious lifestyle demands the services of a huge number of helots,[1] who cannot be paid so much that they can afford rooms in the hotels for themselves. Like Ricardo,[2] we would like to see the supply of helots kept constant, neither falling so low that we have to take out the trash ourselves nor becoming so high that we shake in our shoes, fearing insurrection in the compound.

The official ideology is that the guests in the hotel create all the wealth; only by the extraordinary efficiency of their wealth-creation are all the rest able to survive by merely drudging in the kitchens and

---

[1] Helots: neither slave nor free; after a class of serfs in ancient Sparta. [Ed.]
[2] Ricardo: David Ricardo (1772–1823) was a British economist who predicted that eventually food supply would fail to keep up with population growth. [Ed.]

the lavatories and the market gardens. At very little cost to himself, the guest creates the wealth that is apportioned to them for these worthless but indispensable and time-consuming activities.

If this is so, if the capitalist system is actually the best system for creating wealth ever devised, perhaps it could be made less spectacularly unjust. Perhaps the cultivation of inessentials regarded as essentials, but for which we will not pay a price commensurate with the human labor that they absorb, should be made illegal. 4

Perhaps we should impose the same penalties on the consumption of sugar, tobacco and tea as we do on heroin, so that people brutalized by this kind of cultivation could go back to farming food crops. Perhaps we should outlaw speculation in commodities, which, if it is a way to maintain a "fair" market price, seems to have a very odd idea of fairness. 5

I don't know how many people the Earth can support, and I don't believe that anybody else does; it can certainly support more people on a low-calorie intake than it can on a high-calorie intake, but as the world is not a huge soup kitchen, the fact is irrelevant. It is quite probable that the world is overpopulated and has been for some time, but getting into a tizzy about it will not help. 6

Nothing good can come of fear eating the soul. We do not have access to our imagination if we are convinced that catastrophe lurks just around the corner. 7

We may be living in catastrophe now; perhaps we shall have to adapt to it, or go under. Perhaps catastrophe is the natural for humans, and even though we spend a good deal of energy trying to get away from it, we are programmed for survival amid catastrophe. It is an odd thing that people living precariously have more commitment to the continuity of their line than people ensconced in plenty. 8

If this is true, there is not much we can do about it, for we cannot design a political system that will supply the right proportions of potential catastrophe. If we are to deal with the problem of people at all gracefully, we will have to stop rushing into situations we do not understand, encumbered with all kinds of non-solutions. 9

In the past we have tried to avoid this by undertaking cunningly designed research that cost many times what practical help would have cost. 10

What I have tried to show[3] is how false reasoning and obtuseness have distorted an important development in human affairs. I do believe that the crashing blunders of family planning programs, espe- 11

---

[3] In the book *Sex and Destiny*. [Ed.]

cially in India, have actually delayed smaller families. I also believe that unwanted children have been born because of inept family planning, and that some people have died.

In the spectrum of global cruelty and mismanagement, the crimes 12 of family planning are small indeed. The money spent, although it is more than the entire international budget for health aid, is a piffling sum compared with the billions spent on "defense." Nevertheless, family planning mismanagement matters, if only because so many thoughtful people in the field have put so much hard work into it. It is not fair to them that they become the tools of half-baked right-wing theory, for their motives are usually very different.

The statistics so ingeniously amassed by the rich research institu- 13 tions are no help in the field. Every field worker eventually realizes that overpopulation is not our problem to define and solve; that there may be an alternative, coming from the community with whom he is working.

The blind conviction that we have to do something about other 14 people's reproductive behavior, and that we may have to do it whether they like it or not, derives from the assumption that the world belongs to us, who have so expertly depleted its resources, rather than to them, who have not. Put in this way, the ZPG (Zero Population Growth) intellectual position is seen as totally illiberal, yet some, I would even say most, liberals hold some such belief.

The only possible coherent motivation in offering family planning 15 services around the world is a desire to help people, families, individuals, to do what they want, not what we think they ought to want. If we allow the recipients to define their needs, we would save all the millions of dollars we squander in defining needs. In practice, this is what the field worker has to do, for the the information he has from the secretariat or the regional office is useless.

There is very little satisfaction to be had in averting births, partly 16 because one is never sure of having actually averted one. There is much more satisfaction from keeping alive the babies who are already there, and in improving the health of their mothers.

There is even more satisfaction in learning from the people just 17 how amazing human beings are, how graceful, how resilient, how funny and how sad. Strange to relate, the poor get more opportunity to develop all these sides of themselves than do the rich, who are much the same the world over.

Let us therefore abandon the rhetoric of crisis, for we are the crisis. 18 Let us stop wasting energy in worrying about a world crammed with people standing shoulder to shoulder and counting the babies born every minute, and begin to use our imagination to understand how it is that poverty is created and maintained. Let us get to know Lady Poverty up close, so we lose our phobia about the poor.

If we must be afraid, let us rather be afraid that man, the ecological 19 disaster, now has no enemy but his own kind. Rather than being afraid of the powerless, let us be afraid of the powerful, the rich sterile nations, who, whether they be of the Eastern or the Western variety, have no stake in the future.

The birth of every unwanted child is a tragedy, for itself and for 20 the unwilling parents, but in spite of all the attention we have given to the matter, more unwanted children are born to us, the rich, than to them, the poor. This may seem a paradox, but the time gives it proof.

QUESTIONS AND IDEAS FOR DISCUSSION

1. What is Greer's thesis? Is it developed consistently and logically? Comment.

2. From the very first paragraph of this argument, Greer challenges common Western preconceptions and attitudes. List the major claims she makes in this essay. Do any of these claims surprise or offend you? How does Greer support those points? What might be said to counter these claims? On the other hand, what might be said to further support them?

3. Greer asserts that "we are the crisis" (paragraph 18). On what reasoning does she base that assertion? Do you agree with her? Discuss.

SUGGESTIONS FOR WRITING
AND FURTHER DISCUSSION

1. Could it be argued that Simon's and Greer's arguments about overpopulation, even if sound, are dangerous? That is, might widespread acceptance of either viewpoint lead to complacency and a deterioration of the quality of life in the future? Discuss. Should writers withhold arguments and evidence that might be misused?

2. Germaine Greer argues that we—the educated, prosperous citizens of the Western world—have few children not out of virtuous concern about overpopulation but because we don't really like children. Greer goes so far as to assert that "more unwanted children are born to us, the rich, than to them, the poor" (paragraph 20). Do you believe that she is right or wrong? Consider this claim in light of your firsthand knowledge of contemporary Western society, and argue your answer for an audience of middle-class, educated readers.

3.   In an essay of your own, argue one of the following claims or an opposing claim. You may support your argument with quotations from and references to the readings in this chapter. Consider as your audience people who have completed high school.

> Arguments about overpopulation tend to succumb to racist and nationalist stereotypes and assumptions.
>
> Arguments about overpopulation often show more concern for the environment than for humans.
>
> Opposition to population controls demonstrates a lack of real concern about children and about society.

4.   Based on your readings, do you believe that poverty is the cause of overpopulation, that overpopulation is the cause of poverty, or that poverty and overpopulation are not as intrinsically related as some people claim? Argue your position, supporting it with evidence from the essays in this section.

5.   Should the FDA approve RU486 for use in the United States under medical supervision? Why, or why not? Argue your answer in an essay suitable to be read to a Congressional committee considering this question. Keep in mind that your audience (and the voters who comprise its constituency) will have widely varying religious beliefs.

6.   Decide which of the essays in this chapter argues its claims most effectively—whether or not you like or agree with its conclusions. Argue the reasons for your choice. (You may choose to comment on the difficulty, if any, of putting aside your own ideas about the issues while you judge the arguments.) Is the most effective argument the best written and the most clearly organized? The most logical? The best documented? Or is it more emotional than logical in its argument? What does the essay show you as a writer about ways to make a point well?

11

PORNOGRAPHY, OBSCENITY, AND CENSORSHIP

Arguments about pornography, obscenity, and censorship nearly always are arguments from definition, and nearly always they come up short in some way, for we cannot agree on the definitions. Then we cannot agree on the solutions—and so the controversies rage on. Books are taken off shelves and then returned to them. Exhibitions at art galleries are scheduled and then canceled. Everyone—or nearly everyone—agrees that pornography is exploitive and obscenity is wrong, but the consensus ends there, abruptly. And not even that much consensus is available on censorship.

Nevertheless, these are issues that must be dealt with. We cannot turn our backs if people are being cruelly exploited; we cannot overlook the censorship of literary or artistic works of great merit. There are also variations on the problem: What if we are asked to finance, as taxpayers, the creation of artistic works that we consider obscene?

The first three essays in this chapter deal with the general problem of censoring pornography and obscenity, and the last two readings center on a particular case, a traveling exhibit of photographs by artist Robert Mapplethorpe. The controversy of 1989, when the Corcoran Gallery canceled the exhibit, paled by comparison with the controversy of 1990, when the Cincinnati Art Museum showed it. The Museum and its director, Dennis Barrie, were tried—and acquitted—on obscenity charges for exhibiting the Mapplethorpe photographs. But the issues, not surprisingly, were not settled by the trial (or by Andrew Ferguson or Arthur C. Danto, in the arguments reprinted here): What *is* obscene? Is obscenity dangerous or merely distasteful? Should taxpayers have to support art that they may find obscene? *Will* people refuse to support the arts if they are offended by artistic works? Should art that is deemed obscene (and by whom?) be publicly exhibited? These are by no means the only issues, but they are more than enough with which to begin your consideration of these essays.

Let's Put Pornography Back in the Closet

SUSAN BROWNMILLER

Susan Brownmiller, founder of Women Against Pornography and a leader in the feminist movement since 1968, published her first novel, *Waverly Place: A Novel,* in 1989. *Against Our Will: Men, Women, and Rape* (1975), is her best known work. In the following essay, first published in *Newsday* magazine in 1979 and reprinted in Laura Lederer's anthology of feminist essays on pornography, *Take Back the Night* (1980), Brownmiller eloquently argues in favor of an abridgement of free speech. In so doing, she distinguishes the feminist opposition to pornography from that of "old-line conservatives." Definitions of key terms are crucial to Brownmiller's argument; note them carefully as you read.

Free speech is one of the great foundations on which our democ- 1 racy rests. I am old enough to remember the Hollywood Ten, the screenwriters who went to jail in the late 1940s because they refused to testify before a congressional committee about their political affiliations. They tried to use the First Amendment as a defense, but they went to jail because in those days there were few civil liberties lawyers around who cared to champion the First Amendment right to free speech, when the speech concerned the Communist Party.

The Hollywood Ten were correct in claiming the First Amend- 2 ment. Its high purpose is the protection of unpopular ideas and political dissent. In the dark, cold days of the 1950s, few civil libertarians were willing to declare themselves First Amendment absolutists. But in the brighter, though frantic, days of the 1960s, the principle of protecting unpopular political speech was gradually strengthened.

It is fair to say now that the battle has largely been won. Even the 3 American Nazi Party has found itself the beneficiary of the dedicated, tireless work of the American Civil Liberties Union. But—and please notice the quotation marks coming up—"To equate the free and robust exchange of ideas and political debate with commercial exploitation of obscene material demeans the grand conception of the First Amendment and its high purposes in the historic struggle for freedom. It is a misuse of the great guarantees of free speech and free press."

I didn't say that, although I wish I had, for I think the words are 4 thrilling. Chief Justice Warren Burger said it in 1973, in the United States Supreme Court's majority opinion in *Miller v. California.* During the same decades that the right to political free speech was being strengthened in the courts, the nation's obscenity laws also were undergoing extensive revision.

It's amazing to recall that in 1934 the question of whether James 5
Joyce's *Ulysses* should be banned as pornographic actually went before
the Court. The battle to protect *Ulysses* as a work of literature with
redeeming social value was won. In later decades, Henry Miller's
Tropic books, *Lady Chatterley's Lover* and the *Memoirs of Fanny Hill* also
were adjudged not obscene. These decisions have been important to
me. As the author of *Against Our Will*, a study of the history of rape
that does contain explicit sexual material, I shudder to think how my
book would have fared if James Joyce, D. H. Lawrence and Henry
Miller hadn't gone before me.

I am not a fan of *Chatterley* or the *Tropic* books, I should quickly 6
mention. They are not to my literary taste, nor do I think they represent female sexuality with any degree of accuracy. But I would hardly
suggest that we ban them. Such a suggestion wouldn't get very far
anyway. The battle to protect these books is ancient history. Time does
march on, quite methodically. What, then, is unlawfully obscene, and
what does the First Amendment have to do with it?

In the Miller case of 1973 (not Henry Miller, by the way, but a porn 7
distributor who sent unsolicited stuff through the mails), the Court
came up with new guidelines that it hoped would strengthen obscenity laws by giving more power to the states. What it did in actuality
was throw everything into confusion. It set up a three-part test by
which materials can be adjudged obscene. The materials are obscene if
they depict patently offensive, hard-core sexual conduct; lack serious
scientific, literary, artistic or political value; and appeal to the prurient
interest of an average person—as measured by contemporary community standards.

"Patently offensive," "prurient interest" and "hard-core" are in- 8
deed words to conjure with. "Contemporary community standards"
are what we're trying to redefine. The feminist objection to pornography is not based on prurience, which the dictionary defines as lustful,
itching desire. We are not opposed to sex and desire, with or without
the itch, and we certainly believe that explicit sexual material has its
place in literature, art, science and education. Here we part company
rather swiftly with old-line conservatives who don't want sex education in the high schools, for example.

No, the feminist objection to pornography is based on our belief 9
that pornography represents hatred of women, that pornography's
intent is to humiliate, degrade and dehumanize the female body for
the purpose of erotic stimulation and pleasure. We are unalterably
opposed to the presentation of the female body being stripped,
bound, raped, tortured, mutilated and murdered in the name of commercial entertainment and free speech.

These images, which are standard pornographic fare, have nothing to do with the hallowed right of political dissent. They have everything to do with the creation of a cultural climate in which a rapist feels he is merely giving in to a normal urge and a woman is encouraged to believe that sexual masochism is healthy, liberated fun. Justice Potter Stewart once said about hard-core pornography, "You know it when you see it," and that certainly used to be true. In the good old days, pornography looked awful. It was cheap and sleazy, and there was no mistaking it for art. 10

Nowadays, since the porn industry has become a multimillion dollar business, visual technology has been employed in its service. Pornographic movies are skillfully filmed and edited, pornographic still shots using the newest tenets of good design artfully grace the covers of *Hustler, Penthouse* and *Playboy*, and the public—and the courts—are sadly confused. 11

The Supreme Court neglected to define "hard-core" in the Miller decision. This was a mistake. If "hard-core" refers only to explicit sexual intercourse, then that isn't good enough. When women or children or men—no matter how artfully—are shown tortured or terrorized in the service of sex, that's obscene. And "patently offensive," I would hope, to our "contemporary community standards." 12

Justice William O. Douglas wrote in his dissent to the Miller case that no one is "compelled to look." This is hardly true. To buy a paper at the corner newsstand is to subject oneself to a forcible immersion in pornography, to be demeaned by an array of dehumanized, chopped-up parts of the female anatomy, packaged like cuts of meat at the supermarket. I happen to like my body and I work hard at the gym to keep it in good shape, but I am embarrassed for my body and the bodies of all women when I see the fragmented parts of us so frivolously, and so flagrantly, displayed. 13

Some constitutional theorists (Justice Douglas was one) have maintained that any obscenity law is a serious abridgement of free speech. Others (and Justice Earl Warren was one) have maintained that the First Amendment was never intended to protect obscenity. We live quite compatibly with a host of free-speech abridgements. There are restraints against false and misleading advertising or statements—shouting "fire" without cause in a crowded movie theater, etc.—that do not threaten, but strengthen, our societal values. Restrictions on the public display of pornography belong in this category. 14

The distinction between permission to publish and permission to display publicly is an essential one and one which I think consonant with First Amendment principles. Justice Burger's words which I 15 quoted above support this without question. We are not saying "Smash the presses" or "Ban the bad ones," but simply "Get the stuff out of our sight." Let the legislatures decide—using realistic and humane contemporary community standards—what can be displayed and what cannot. The courts, after all, will be the final arbiters.

QUESTIONS AND IDEAS FOR DISCUSSION

1.   What is Brownmiller's thesis? Evaluate her argument in support of that thesis. Do the supporting points lead logically and inexorably to the thesis? Or is the argument emotionally compelling at the expense of reason? Give your reasons.

2.   Discuss the meaning of the following terms as you understand them. Do you agree with Brownmiller's understanding of them?

- First Amendment
- civil libertarian
- pornography
- obscenity

3.   Brownmiller identifies four descriptive terms from the 1973 *Miller* decision that she finds problematic: "patently offensive," "prurient interest," "hard-core," and "contemporary community standards" (paragraph 8). What are the problems with these terms? Discuss their meaning in the context of Brownmiller's argument. Does her discussion of them enhance or detract from her argument?

4.   In paragraph 13, Brownmiller refutes Justice Douglas's statement that "no one is compelled to look" at pornography. Discuss Douglas's statement and Brownmiller's refutation. With whom do you agree, and why?

Pornography Through the Looking Glass

CHARLES KRAUTHAMMER

Charles Krauthammer is a political theorist turned medical doctor turned journalist who writes on current issues for the *New Republic, Time,* and other periodicals. In Chapter 9 you may have read his essay on AIDS funding; in this essay he turns his attention to pornography. Krauthammer acknowledges the distastefulness of pornography and at the same time deplores—on the grounds of civil liberty—the effort to ban it. Would he be opposed to banning pornography on other grounds? Or does Krauthammer regard the abridgment of free speech as more dangerous than pornography?

Television ushered in the new year [1984] by cracking what it 1 breathlessly billed as "the last taboo": incest. Liberal Minneapolis celebrated by backtracking a couple of taboos and considering a ban on pornography. One would have thought that that particular hang-up had been overcome. But even though the ban voted by the Minneapolis city council was eventually vetoed by Mayor Donald Fraser, pornography is evidently a hang-up of considerable tenacity. And according to the proposed law it is more than that: it is a violation of civil rights.

Now that seems like a peculiar notion, but one has to read the 2 proposed ordinance to see just how peculiar it is. The city council proposed banning "discrimination . . . based on race, color, creed, religion, ancestry, national origin, sex, including . . . pornography." What can that possibly mean? How can one discriminate based on pornography?

Anticipating such questions, the bill helpfully provides "special 3 findings on pornography." If it ever passes (immediately after the mayor's veto proponents vowed to bring it up again), the findings are destined to be the most famous gifts from social science to law since footnote eleven of *Brown* vs. *Board of Education*.[1] The *Brown* findings, however, were based on real empirical data. The Minneapolis findings are of a more metaphysical nature. They begin: "The council finds that pornography is central in creating and maintaining the civil inequality of the sexes." If that were true, then it would follow that where pornography is banned—as in the U.S. of 50 years ago or the Tehran of today—one should not expect to find civil inequality of the sexes. Next finding. "Pornography is a systematic practice of exploitation and subordination based on sex which differentially harms women." While it is true that some pornography subordinates women, some does not, and none is "systematic" or a "practice." Outside the Minneapolis city council chambers, pornography means the traffic in obscenity. Inside, as in Alice's Wonderland, words will mean what the council wants them to mean.

The liberal mayor of Minneapolis was sympathetic with the pro- 4 posal's aims, but vetoed it nonetheless. He found it too vague and ambiguous, a classic complaint against obscenity laws, old and new.

---

[1] The Supreme Court's 1954 ruling cited seven scholars to prove that separate-but-equal schooling harmed black children, and led one critic to complain that it thus needlessly gave ammunition to those who wished to see the *Brown* decision not as an expression of civilized truth but as a brand of sociology.

In simpler times Justice Potter Stewart answered the question what is pornography with a succinct "I know it when I see it." But would even he know "subordination based on sex which differentially harms women" when he saw it? After all, the new dispensation seems to exclude homosexual pornography. And only embarrassment, not logic, would prevent including those weddings at which the bride is old-fashioned enough to vow "to love, honor, and *obey*."

The head of the Minneapolis Civil Liberties Union says, unkindly,   5 that the ordinance "has no redeeming social value." That seems a bit harsh. Set aside for a moment the pseudo findings, the creative definitions, the ambiguities. The intent of the bill is to do away with the blight of pornography. What can be wrong with that?

A good question, and an important one. Over the decades it has   6 spawned a fierce debate between a certain kind of conservative (usually called cultural conservative) on the one hand and civil libertarians on the other. The argument went like this. The conservative gave the intuitive case against pornography based on an overriding concern for, it now sounds almost too quaint to say, public morality. Pornography is an affront to decency; it coarsens society. As Susan Sontag, not a conservative, writing in defense of pornography says, it serves to "drive a wedge between one's existence as a full human being and one's existence as a sexual being." The ordinary person, of course, does not need a philosopher, conservative or otherwise, to tell him why he wants to run pornography out of his neighborhood. It cheapens and demeans. Even though he may occasionally be tempted by it, that temptation is almost invariably accompanied by a feeling of shame and a desire to shield his children from the fleshy come-ons of the magazine rack.

That may be so, say the civil libertarians, but it is irrelevant.   7 Government has no business regulating morality. The First Amendment guarantees freedom of expression, and though you may prefer not to express yourself by dancing naked on a runway in a bar, some people do, and you have no business stopping them. Nor do you have any business trying to stop those who like to sit by the runway and imbibe this form of expression. It may not be *Swan Lake*, but the First Amendment does not hinge on judgments of artistic merit or even redeeming value.

Now this traditional debate over pornography is clear and com-   8 prehensible. It involves the clash of two important values: public morality *vs.* individual liberty. The conservative is prepared to admit that his restrictions curtail liberty, though a kind of liberty he does not think is particularly worth having. The civil libertarian admits that a price of liberty is that it stands to be misused, and that pornography may be one of those misuses; public morality may suffer, but freedom is more precious. Both sides agree, however, that one cannot have everything and may sometimes have to trade one political good for another.

Not the Minneapolis bill, and that is what made it so audacious— 9 and perverse. It manages the amazing feat of restoring censorship, which after all is a form of coercion, while at the same time claiming not to restrict rights but expand them. The logic is a bit tortuous. It finds that pornography promotes bigotry and fosters acts of aggression against women, both of which, in turn, "harm women's opportunities for equality of rights in employment, education, property rights, . . . contribute significantly to restricting women from full exercise of citizenship . . . and undermine women's equal exercise of rights to speech and action."

Apart from the questionable logical leaps required at every step of 10 the syllogism, the more immediate question is: Why take this remote and improbable route to arrive at a point—banning pornography— that one can reach directly by citing the venerable argument that pornography damages the moral fiber of society? Why go from St. Paul to Minneapolis by way of Peking?

The answer is simple. As a rallying cry, public morality has no sex 11 appeal; civil rights has. Use words like moral fiber and people think of Jerry Falwell. Use words like rights and they think of Thomas Jefferson. Use civil rights and they think of Martin Luther King, Jr. Because civil rights is justly considered among the most sacred of political values, appropriating it for partisan advantage can be very useful. (The fiercest battle in the fight over affirmative action, for example, is over which side has rightful claim to the mantle of civil rights.) Convince people that censorship is really a right, and you can win them over. It won over the Minneapolis city council. And if to do so, you have to pretend that fewer rights are more, so be it.

Civil rights will not be the first political value to have its meaning 12 reversed. The use of the term *freedom* to describe unfreedom goes back at least as far as Rousseau, who wrote, without irony, of an ideal republic in which men would be "forced to be free." In our day, the word *democracy* is so beloved of tyrants that some have named their countries after it, as in the German Democratic Republic (a.k.a. East Germany). And from Beirut to San Salvador, every gang of political thugs makes sure to kneel at least five times a day in the direction of "peace." So why not abuse civil rights?

The virtue of calling a spade a spade is that when it is traded in, 13 accountants can still make sense of the books. The virtue of calling political values by their real names is that when social policy is to be made, citizens can make sense of the choices. That used to be the case in the debate about pornography. If Minneapolis is any indication of where that debate is heading, it will not be the case for long.

That is a pity, because while it is easy to quarrel with the method of   14 the Minneapolis ban, it is hard to quarrel with the motive. After a decade's experience with permissiveness, many Americans have become acutely aware that there is a worm in the apple of sexual liberation. That a community with a reputation for liberalism should decide that things have gone too far is not really news. The call for a pause in the frantic assault on the limits of decency (beyond which lies the terra cognita of what used to be taboos) is the quite natural expression of a profound disappointment with the reality, as opposed to the promise, of unrestricted freedom. There are pushes and pulls in the life of the national superego, and now there is a pulling—back. Many are prepared to make expression a bit less free in order to make their community a bit more whole, or, as skeptics might say, wholesome.

That is nothing to be ashamed of. So why disguise it as a campaign   15 for civil rights? (True, liberals may be somewhat embarrassed to be found in bed with bluenoses, but the Minneapolis case is easily explained away as a one-issue marriage of convenience.) In an age when the most private of human activities is everywhere called by its most common name, why be so coy about giving censorship its proper name, too?

QUESTIONS AND IDEAS FOR DISCUSSION

1.   How does Krauthammer use his introductory paragraph to influence reader opinion even before we understand his argument?

2.   What is Krauthammer's thesis, and how does it differ from Brownmiller's?

3.   At what points does Krauthammer make concessions to the opposing viewpoint? Do his concessions strengthen the appeal of his persona or merely confuse his argument? Comment.

4.   In paragraphs 8 through 11, Krauthammer challenges the logic of the Minneapolis pornography ordinance. Summarize his refutation, and evaluate both his logic and the city council's.

I Am a First Amendment Junkie

SUSAN JACOBY

Susan Jacoby is a writer with a special interest in feminist issues. Her books include *Inside Soviet Schools* (1974), which was based on research conducted from 1969–71 when Jacoby was a foreign correspondent based in Moscow, and *The Possible She* (1979). Jacoby has written for such magazines as *McCalls* and the *Nation* and was a columnist for the *Washington Post* and the *New York Times.* This essay, first published in Jacoby's weekly *New York Times* column ("Hers") in 1978, takes on all comers who would abridge the First Amendment right to freedom of speech in any degree. Notice, as you read, how Jacoby concedes what she must to opposing viewpoints, then challenges the conclusions and implications of those viewpoints. She even turns a criticism of herself ("a First Amendment junkie") to her own advantage.

It is no news that many women are defecting from the ranks of civil libertarians on the issue of obscenity. The conviction of Larry Flynt, publisher of *Hustler* magazine—before his metamorphosis into a born-again Christian—was greeted with unabashed feminist approval. Harry Reems, the unknown actor who was convicted by a Memphis jury for conspiring to distribute the movie *Deep Throat,* has carried on his legal battles with almost no support from women who ordinarily regard themselves as supporters of the First Amendment. Feminist writers and scholars have even discussed the possibility of making common cause against pornography with adversaries of the women's movement—including opponents of the equal rights amendment and "right-to-life" forces.

All of this is deeply disturbing to a woman writer who believes, as I always have and still do, in an absolute interpretation of the First Amendment. Nothing in Larry Flynt's garbage convinces me that the late Justice Hugo L. Black was wrong in his opinion that "the Federal Government is without any power whatsoever under the Constitution to put any type of burden on free speech and expression of ideas of any kind (as distinguished from conduct)." Many women I like and respect tell me I am wrong; I cannot remember having become involved in so many heated discussions of a public issue since the end of the Vietnam War. A feminist writer described my views as those of a "First Amendment junkie."

Many feminist arguments for controls on pornography carry the implicit conviction that porn books, magazines and movies pose a greater threat to women than similarly repulsive exercises of free speech pose to other offended groups. This conviction has, of course, been shared by everyone—regardless of race, creed or sex—who has ever argued in favor of abridging the First Amendment. It is the argument used by some Jews who have withdrawn their support from the American Civil Liberties Union because it has defended the right of American Nazis to march through a community inhabited by survivors of Hitler's concentration camps.

If feminists want to argue that the protection of the Constitution 4 should not be extended to *any* particularly odious or threatening form of speech, they have a reasonable argument (although I don't agree with it). But it is ridiculous to suggest that the porn shops on 42d Street are more disgusting to women than a march of neo-Nazis is to survivors of the extermination camps.

The arguments over pornography also blur the vital distinction 5 between expression of ideas and conduct. When I say I believe unreservedly in the First Amendment, someone always comes back to me with the issue of "kiddie porn." But kiddie porn is not a First Amendment issue. It is an issue of the abuse of power—the power adults have over children—and not of obscenity. Parents and promoters have no more right to use their children to make porn movies than they do to send them to work in coal mines. The responsible adults should be prosecuted, just as adults who use children for back-breaking farm labor should be prosecuted.

Susan Brownmiller, in *Against Our Will: Men, Women, and Rape,* 6 has described pornography as "the undiluted essence of anti-female propaganda." I think this is a fair description of some types of pornography, especially of the brutish subspecies that equates sex with death and portrays women primarily as objects of violence.

The equation of sex and violence, personified by some glossy rock 7 record album covers as well as by *Hustler,* has fed the illusion that censorship of pornography can be conducted on a more rational basis than other types of censorship. Are all pictures of naked women obscene? Clearly not, says a friend. A Renoir nude is art, she says, and *Hustler* is trash. "Any reasonable person" knows that.

But what about something between art and trash—something, 8 say, along the lines of *Playboy* or *Penthouse* magazines? I asked five women for their reactions to one picture in *Penthouse* and got responses that ranged from "lovely" and "sensuous" to "revolting" and "demeaning." Feminists, like everyone else, seldom have rational reasons for their preferences in erotica. Like members of juries, they tend to disagree when confronted with something that falls short of 100 percent vulgarity.

In any case, feminists will not be the arbiters of good taste if it 9 becomes easier to harass, prosecute and convict people on obscenity charges. Most of the people who want to censor girlie magazines are equally opposed to open discussion of issues that are of vital concern

to women: rape, abortion, menstruation, contraception, lesbianism—
in fact, the entire range of sexual experience from a woman's viewpoint.

Feminist writers and editors and film makers have limited finan- 10
cial resources: Confronted by a determined prosecutor, Hugh Hefner
will fare better than Susan Brownmiller. Would the Memphis jurors
who convicted Harry Reems for his role in *Deep Throat* be inclined to
take a more positive view of paintings of female genitalia done by
sensitive feminist artists? *Ms.* magazine has printed color reproductions of some of those art works; *Ms.* is already banned from a number
of high school libraries because someone considers it threatening and/
or obscene.

Feminists who want to censor what they regard as harmful por- 11
nography have essentially the same motivation as other would-be
censors. They want to use the power of the state to accomplish what
they have been unable to achieve in the marketplace of ideas and
images. The impulse to censor places no faith in the possibilities of
democratic persuasion.

It isn't easy to persuade certain men that they have better uses for 12
$1.95 each month than to spend it on a copy of *Hustler*? Well, then,
give the men no choice in the matter.

I believe there is also a connection between the impulse toward 13
censorship on the part of people who used to consider themselves civil
libertarians and a more general desire to shift responsibility from
individuals to institutions. When I saw the movie *Looking for Mr.
Goodbar*, I was stunned by its series of visual images equating sex and
violence, coupled with what seems to me the mindless message (a
distortion of the fine Judith Rossner novel) that casual sex equals
death. When I came out of the movie, I was even more shocked to see
parents standing in line with children between the ages of 10 and 14.

I simply don't know why a parent would take a child to see such a 14
movie, any more than I understand why people feel they can't turn off
a television set their child is watching. Whenever I say that, my friends
tell me I don't know how it is because I don't have children. True, but I
do have parents. When I was a child, they did turn off the TV. They
didn't expect the Federal Communications Commission to do their job
for them.

I am a First Amendment junkie. You can't OD on the First Amend- 15
ment, because free speech is its own best antidote.

QUESTIONS AND IDEAS FOR DISCUSSION

1.   Much of Jacoby's argument refutes opposing positions on the
pornography versus free speech issue. Where and to what extent does

Jacoby explain and support her own belief in "an absolute interpretation of the First Amendment" (paragraph 2)? What is the effect of this ordering on the persuasiveness of the essay?

2.   How does Jacoby counter the argument that First Amendment rights must be abridged to eliminate the exploitation of children in "kiddie porn" (5)? Is her argument logical, or does she shift ground? Explain your answer.

3.   Explain the metaphor in the last sentence of the essay: "You can't OD on the First Amendment, because free speech is its own best antidote?" How can anything be "its own best antidote"?

4.   How would Jacoby respond to Charles Krauthammer's argument in the preceding essay? What would he say to hers?

Mad about Mapplethorpe

ANDREW FERGUSON

Andrew Ferguson is an editorial writer for the Scripps-Howard News service and was formerly the assistant managing editor of the *American Spectator*, a politically conservative periodical. The following essay was first published in the *National Review*, also a politically conservative publication, in 1989. It centers on the heated debate in 1989 (which continued into 1990) over government funding of controversial artists and art exhibits, especially those that many viewers regarded as obscene. In particular, Ferguson discusses the exhibit of works by photographer Robert Mapplethorpe. As you read Ferguson's argument, characterize the audience to whom he writes: Are you part of it? To what extent do you find the argument emotionally persuasive? Logically convincing?

Bureaucrats in the arts, like their brethren elsewhere, are the Greta 1 Garbos of democratic society: all they want is to be left alone. They labor in a tiny vineyard, a hermetic subculture of thousands of artists and dozens of customers; here a show of fingerpainted toilet seats hung on the walls of a county welfare office; there, a nude dance performed in the basement of a Presbyterian church. Their obscurity is their happiness—that, and the $150 million they annually dispense through the National Endowment for the Arts.

Every so often, however, there's a leak in security. Controversy— 2 the bureaucrat's nightmare of nightmares—inevitably ensues. There was the flap this spring, for example, when Senator Alfonse D'Amato discovered that a photographer called Andres Serrano had used

$15,000 of NEA money to finance *Piss Christ,* a photograph of a crucifix submerged in urine. And then Congressman Dick Armey of Texas heard about Robert Mapplethorpe.

Mapplethorpe died in March [1989] of AIDS, celebrated, as he had 3 been for a dozen years or more, as a major artist. The *Christian Science Monitor* (even!) had early tagged him "one of the most original of America's younger photographers." Mary Baker Eddy, phone your arts desk: Mapplethorpe's leitmotif was "homoerotic and sadomasochistic imagery"—one of his more celebrated pieces, for example, showed a man urinating into a pal's mouth, while another featured the artist himself, doubled over and pantless, with a bullwhip dangling from his orifice of choice—as well as photos of "children in erotic poses," a form of personal expression more commonly known, when not federally funded, as child pornography. These pictures and more coagulated in a traveling show sponsored in part by the NEA, to the tune of $30,000. The exhibit—which also included, for aesthetic effect, scores of pictures of flowers—was scheduled to arrive at Washington, D.C.'s, Corcoran Gallery in July.

On June 8, Congressman Armey and 108 co-signers sent a letter to 4 Hugh Southern, the acting chairman of NEA, asking, in effect, what the hell was going on. Noting "this is not the first time we have had concerns about the NEA funding inappropriate materials," the congressmen said they understood that "the interpretation of art is a subjective evaluation, but there is a very clear and unambiguous line that exists between what can be classified as art and what must be called morally reprehensible trash."

Had it not been backed up by the power of the purse, the letter 5 would surely have been laughed off as the thundering of Neanderthal lunatics or the posturing of pols (which in some cases it doubtlessly was). Under the circumstances, however, the Corcoran decided not to show the Mapplethorpe exhibit after all, reasoning that the proximity of Mapplethorpe's subsidized shutterbuggery to irate congressmen might endanger NEA funding.

The Corcoran's decision sparked the predictable outrage from 6 the Washington arts crowd: "appalled . . . right-wing . . . outright cave-in . . . censorship of the most vulgar kind . . . McCarthyism . . . muzzle freedom of expression"—the heavy breathing almost drowned out the clichés. A hardy amalgamation of artists and gays and lesbians and aesthetes gathered outside the gallery, chorusing, "Shame! Shame!" Cocktail parties were held. There was talk of boycotts, although of what, precisely, no one seemed sure. The directors of the hapless Corcoran seemed at first surprised, and finally hurt: all they had tried to do, after all, was keep the money flowing to the very same people who now reviled them for their prudence.

In the wake of Mr. Armey's objections, Sidney Yates (D., Ill.), the 7
art establishment's mouthpiece in Congress, has undertaken to ban
indirect funding from the NEA, a practice which he blames for the
Serrano and Mapplethorpe contretemps. Conservatives on the Hill
have greeted the reforms, along with the Corcoran's self-censorship,
as a small victory.

But do they understand how small it really is? There was some- 8
thing almost quaint about Mr. Armey's letter, with its talk of a "very
clear and unambiguous line" separating art from rubbish. For it is one
of the primary premises of the art world that this line doesn't really
exist—that it is in fact a kind of cramp in the consciousness of the
unenlightened (read: middle-class American) mind. "If art is to remain
something other than a blue-chip commodity," hollered one of the
speakers at the rally outside the Corcoran, "it will challenge and
offend, especially those whose power rests in the status quo."

Given such a premise, questions of taste are by definition beside 9
the point: those who are offended are *supposed* to be offended. The
concerns of the people whom Mr. Armey is charged with representing
and the values of the art establishment that wants to receive their
subsidies are utterly incompatible. Arguments from taste and merit
can never be won because they can never be joined.

In the end the only argument that will work is the libertarian one: 10
artists can do whatever they wish in the privacy of their own galleries
so long as the rest of us don't have to pay for it. Mr. Armey says that
although he is "philosophically opposed" to federal funding of the
arts, the position is politically unrealistic: "You can't get there from
here," he says. But with a few more Mapplethorpes and Serranos—
and there will be more—the case will become easier to make.

QUESTIONS AND IDEAS FOR DISCUSSION

1. Ferguson does not make his thesis entirely explicit until the last
paragraph of his essay. What is the rhetorical effect of this delay?
How does he hold the argument together when the reader does not
begin with the thesis clearly in mind?

2. Indicate several examples of emotionally colored words and
phrases in Ferguson's argument. Are these effective? How, or why
not? Next, suggest "neutral" substitutes. Would you find the argument more persuasive, or less so, had the author used more neutral
language? Why? Finally, create a third list of substitute words or
phrases with connotations opposite to Ferguson's own. What happens to the argument when the labels are changed in these ways?
Discuss the importance of—and the rhetorical problems connected
with—word choices in argument.

3. Identify some of the unexpected links and juxtapositions through which Ferguson creates humor, notably in paragraph 6. Do you find the humor effective or distasteful? Why?

Art and Taxpayers

ARTHUR C. DANTO

Arthur C. Danto is the art critic of the *Nation,* a politically liberal journal of current events and issues. In this essay, first published in the *Nation* in 1989, Danto uses the Corcoran Gallery's cancellation of the Robert Mapplethorpe exhibit as a starting point for considering the interrelation of art, freedom, and tax money. In a more subdued tone than Andrew Ferguson's in the previous essay, but with no less conviction, Danto argues, "It is very much in the interest of every taxpayer that freedom be supported, even—or especially—in its most extreme expressions." At the same time, he supports people's right to be indignant at offensive works: "It is also not an offense to counter outrage with outrage." Danto's argument is complex, grounded in the paradoxes he finds central to these issues.

The Corcoran Gallery's pre-emptive decision in June to cancel a 1 planned exhibition of Robert Mapplethorpe's photographs in order to forestall Congressional indignation at their content brought far greater notoriety to the now-famous images than showing them would have. Many of the same photographs of men who engage in the sexual domination of other willing men were presented at the Whitney Museum in New York City last year to no greater stir than some isolated tongue-clucking and wonderment as to what the museum thought it was doing. Indeed, the *Nation* was nearly alone in drawing attention to the homoerotic content of those explicit images in a show whose works conveyed a homoerotic sensibility whatever the subject, even when flowers or faces. . . . The issue that had to be raised was how to respond to such charged representations in works of the highest photographic beauty. Mapplethorpe was still alive, although his sickness with AIDS was common knowledge in the art world, and that gave a certain solemn urgency to the showing of those sexually unsettling pictures. It was Mapplethorpe's wish that they be shown, as if he regarded them as an artistic testament.

The position of many neoconservatives is that this is not the kind 2 of art taxpayers want to support. Hilton Kramer advanced this view in the *New York Times* recently. And this is now the position of the United States Senate—as a result of the July 26 passage of Jesse Helms's amendment banning Federal support for "obscene or indecent" art. But the issue could not be more obscurely framed. It is imperative to distinguish taxpayers from individuals who pay taxes, as we distinguish the uniform from the individual who wears it. As individuals, we have divergent aesthetic preferences. Kramer has little interest in supporting art that others find of great interest. But aesthetic preference does not enter into the concept of the taxpayer, which is a civic category. What does enter into it is freedom. It is very much in the interest of every taxpayer that freedom be supported, even—or especially—in its most extreme expressions. However divided individuals are on matters of taste, freedom is in the interest of every citizen. The taxpayer does not support one form of art and withhold support from another as a taxpayer, except in the special case of public art. The taxpayer supports the freedom to make or show art, even when it is art of a kind this or that *individual* finds repugnant.

Mapplethorpe did not make these photographs to test his free- 3 doms. They are disturbing images for many, exciting images for some, but were not intended to strike a blow for artistic liberty (though perhaps for sexual liberty). They very much belong to an intersection of the art world and a certain erotic underground, and they have never been easy to view. The Whitney demonstrated that they could be shown to a wide audience without inducing riots.

Although there may never come a time when one can look at their 4 subjects as commonplace, like female nudes or landscapes or still lifes, these works contrast completely with the now-also-notorious photograph by Andres Serrano of a plastic Jesus in a pool of pee. They contrast as well with the recent gesture, by a senior at the School of the Art Institute of Chicago, of laying a U.S. flag on the floor in a student exhibition so that visitors found it necessary to walk on it. Both works were intended to offend, and did offend. People responded indignantly and directly, by confrontations, demonstrations, protests. It would have been absurd to argue that they ought not to have done this on the ground that the objects were art. Art has the privileges of freedom only because it is a form of expression. And to be seriously interested in making an expression is to be seriously prepared to endure the consequences of making it. It is also not an offense to counter outrage with outrage. On the contrary, it is taking art seriously to do so. One cannot distance the flag and think of it as an arresting composition of stars and bands. One cannot distance one of the powerful religious symbols of the West and view a derogatory photograph of it merely as a formal composition.

It is healthy for art to vacate the position of pure aestheticism in 5 which conservative critics seek to imprison it and to try to affect the way viewers respond to the most meaningful matters of their lives. It is healthy for the museum to play a role in the life of its time rather than to stand outside as a cloister for aesthetic delectations. Art has been primarily aesthetic only throughout a very brief interval of its history of political, moral and religious engagement. As taxpayers our interest is solely in everyone's freedom to participate in the thought of the age.

Whatever grave reservations regarding Congress may have moti- 6 vated the directors of the Corcoran, they weakened the entire social fabric by yielding their freedom. Their decision should have been to show the work, whose merit they must have believed in to have scheduled the exhibition. Since then individual members of Congress have revealed themselves as enemies of freedom by letting their aesthetic attitudes corrupt their political integrity as custodians of the deepest values of a democratic society.

QUESTIONS AND IDEAS FOR DISCUSSION

1.   Restate Danto's core argument in paragraph 2, and evaluate its logic. What assumptions underlie it? Are they justifiable, or should they be argued as well? If you grant Danto's assumptions, is his conclusion compelling? Discuss.

2.   How does Danto ask us to regard Andres Serrano's photograph and the Chicago Art Institute student's work? Do you agree with his reasoning? Why, or why not?

3.   Danto declares that only recently in all its long history has art been regarded and treated as solely aesthetic. How does this historical reminder affect your reception of his argument and the works about which he argues? Does it undermine his argument or support it? Comment.

SUGGESTIONS FOR WRITING
AND FURTHER DISCUSSION

1.   Brownmiller describes the fifties as "dark" and "cold" for civil libertarians. The sixties she calls "brighter, though frantic" (paragraph 2). Based on recent cultural and legal issues concerning obscenity and civil liberties, how would you characterize—so far—the nineties? Write an argument that justifies your assessment in terms of current events.

2.   Justice Douglas's statement that "no one is compelled to look" at pornography is an often argued viewpoint. Write an essay in which you either agree or disagree with this assertion, offering reasons in addition to or other than those advanced in the essays in this section. Do not assume that your readers have themselves viewed much pornography. You may have to overcome some reader indifference about pornography, obscenity, and free-speech issues.

3.   If you agree with Representative Dick Armey (and, for that matter, Justice Potter Stewart, as quoted by Susan Brownmiller) that there is a " 'very clear and unambiguous line' separating art from rubbish" (Ferguson, paragraph 8), write an essay in which you define (and defend) that line. Consider as your audience the fine arts majors at your college.

4.   Are the expensively photographed covers of *Playboy*, *Penthouse*, and *Hustler* pornographic? Are the carefully composed photographs of Robert Mapplethorpe pornographic? How do we decide what is art and what is pornography? Must we decide? Discuss.

5.   When debates such as the Mapplethorpe question arise, is the controversy fundamentally about free speech? Morality? Money? Argue your answer in an essay suitable for publication on the editorial page of your local newspaper.

6.   Charles Krauthammer asserts, "Government has no business regulating morality" (7). Do you agree or disagree, either entirely or in part, with this claim? Defend your viewpoint. You may elect to expand the focus of your argument beyond pornography and obscenity or to argue concerning some other aspect of morality entirely.

7.   Andrew Ferguson argues that "the concerns of [ordinary citizens] . . . and the values of the art establishment that wants to receive their subsidies are utterly incompatible" (9). If you can, argue that Ferguson suggests a cultural gulf that either does not exist or that can be spanned. Assume that your readers are "ordinary citizens," not members of the "art establishment."

8.   In light of the arguments these essays develop and your own knowledge (backed up by additional research you may be asked or wish to do), just how unlimited is the right to free speech? How unlimited should it be? Argue this question for a hypothetical audience of newspaper editors, elementary school librarians, and PTA (Parent-Teacher Association) presidents.

9. Decide which of the essays in this chapter argues its claims most effectively—whether or not you like or agree with its conclusions. Argue the reasons for your choice. (You may choose to comment on the difficulty, if any, of putting aside your own ideas about the issues while you judge the arguments.) Is the most effective argument the best written and the most clearly organized? The most logical? The best documented? Or is it more emotional than logical in its argument? What does the essay show you as a writer about ways to make a point well?

12

THE JURY SYSTEM

If you are a registered voter, you are subject to being summoned for jury duty; indeed, you may already have served. And you may have found the experience profoundly stirring, profoundly troubling,—or perhaps, just plain dull. Regardless of our individual experiences as jurors, the fact remains that the jury lies at the heart of our judicial system. Many attorneys and judges defend the system heartily. Others, however, are not so sure, their objections ranging from complaints over minor irritations to horror at major travesties of justice. Some few would abolish the jury system altogether. But because more people want to reform the system than do away with it, the arguments in this chapter address several issues about juries, rather than countering each other on a single issue.

In the following arguments, then, you will find claims that jury selection has been tainted by the use of psychological and sociological analyses of prospective jurors, that jurors should not be excluded from service because of their knowledge about a case, that anonymous juries all but destroy a defendant's chance for a fair trial, and that to expect ordinary jurors to evaluate highly technical evidence is absurd. One last voice—but a strong one—answers all these complaints with a firm declaration: The jury works. But that is for you to judge.

Creating an Imbalance
AMITAI ETZIONI

Amitai Etzioni is a professor of sociology at Columbia University and Director of the Center for Policy Research. This essay, first published in the *Washington Post* in 1974, concerns the practice of using paid psychological experts to help seat the jury most predisposed toward a given side (invariably the defense, according to Etzioni). Etzioni proposes several solutions to the problem—but first decide, as you read, whether or not he has proven that there is indeed a problem.

Man has taken a new bite from the apple of knowledge, and it is 1 doubtful whether we all will be better for it. We may not choke on the mouthful, but it will take quite a bit of collective chewing until our system comes to terms with this latest ingestion of scientific bounty. This time it is not religion, the family, or the village community that is being challenged by a new application of science; instead, it is that venerable traditional institution of being judged by a jury of one's peers.

The impartiality of the jury is threatened because defense attor- 2 neys have recently discovered that they can manipulate the composition of the jury by the use of social science techniques, so as to significantly increase the likelihood that the defendants will be acquitted.

An example of how such social teams work is the jury selection 3 accomplished by Jay Schulman and Richard Christie at the trial of Indian militants at Wounded Knee. First, a detailed profile of the community's sociological composition was assembled through interviews with 576 persons chosen at random from voter lists. The interviews allowed the research team to cross-tabulate social background characteristics (such as occupation, level of education, etc.) with attitudes favorable to the defense (especially towards the Indians) and select out the best "predictor variables." Such analysis is vital because people of the same social background hold different attitudes in different parts of the country and, hence, a generalized sociological model does not suffice (e.g., women in Harrisburg, where the Berrigan trial was held, proved to be more friendly toward the defense than men, but the reverse was true in Gainesville).

Next, observers were placed in the courtroom to "psych out" the 4 prospective jurors, using anything from the extent to which they talked with other prospective jurors to their mode of dress to evaluate each individual juror, rather than relying only on the sociological category of which he or she was a member. (In the Angela Davis case,[1] handwriting experts were used to analyze the signatures of prospective jurors.)

Information gained in this way was compared to what a computer 5 predicted about the same "type" of person, on the basis of the interview data fed into it. This double reading was further checked, especially when the two sources of information did not concur, by field

---

[1] Angela Davis is an African-American political activist who in 1972 was acquitted by an all-white jury of charges of attempted murder, kidnapping, and conspiracy connected with the attempted bombing of the Marin County (CA) Civic Center. [Ed.]

investigators who interviewed people acquainted with the prospective jurors. The results were used by the defense attorneys to question jurors and to challenge them, as well as to provide the judge with questions he or she may have wished to ask prospective jurors.

Now, social scientists did not invent the idea of using challenges 6 to help obtain a favorable jury. Lawyers have used it as far back as records go. But, until recently, lawyers commonly could not use much more than rule of thumb, hunches and some experience.

The new method, while quite a bit more accurate, is also far from 7 foolproof. People do not always act out their dispositions. Social science data is statistical, not absolute. At best, survey techniques—even when supplemented with psychological analysis—can produce only "probabilistic" profiles, not determinate results. Nevertheless, the recent spate of acquittals—Harrisburg Seven, Camden 28, Mitchell-Stans—demonstrates that the impact can be very considerable. Over scores of cases, on an averaging basis, the method will work well for those who employ it. Hence, we are assuredly in for much more frequent use of this technique. What are the dangers? Are there any remedies?

It might be said that soon both sides to all trials will be equipped 8 with the same techniques—and so long as the granting of an uneven number of challenges is curbed, giving both sides similar selection power, the edge of the social science helpers will be dulled. But the extent to which this takes place will be limited by the costliness of the technique. The radical defendants have benefited from the free labor of scores of volunteers and time donations of high power consultants, although even they needed expensive computers. As Howard Moore, Jr., Angela Davis's chief counsel, put it: "We can send men to the moon, but not everyone can afford to go. Every unpopular person who becomes a defendant will not have the resources we used in the Davis case."

Clearly, the average defendant cannot avail himself of such aid 9 and, therefore, the net effect of the new technique, as is so often the case with new technology, will be to give a leg up to the wealthy or those who command a dedicated following. This is hardly what the founders of the American judicial system had in mind.

Also, it should be noted that up to now the procedure has been 10 used, as far as we know, solely by defense attorneys. The state has not provided any district attorneys with social science teams and computers. However, what would happen if the state *did* resort to systematic reliance on such techniques? Could any but the most affluent Americans compete with the state, once it began to apply these procedures to the prosecution?

Unfortunately, one cannot unbite the apple of knowledge, return 11 to the innocence of not knowing. Even sadder is that we see here, as we have seen so often before, that attempting to contain the side effects of the application of science is costly, at best partially effective and far from uncontroversial itself.

Probably the best place to start is with the list of the prospective 12 jurors. If fewer persons were allowed to excuse themselves from jury duty (and fewer asked to be on it), the universe from which jurors are drawn would be more representative of the community and, to a degree, less easy to manipulate. Next, serious consideration could be given to reducing the number of permissible challenges, especially the preemptory ones.

More powerful, but even more problematic, action is to extend the 13 ban on tampering with the jury, a taboo both sides usually observe, to all out-of-courtroom investigations of jurors. It would thus be defined as a serious violation of the law to collect data about prospective jurors, investigate their handwriting, interview their neighbors, etc., and any discovery of such data gathering would be grounds for a mistrial.

Another potent-yet-controversial solution is for the judge alone to 14 be allowed to question and remove prospective jurors. In this way, the judge could seek both an open-minded jury and one that is a cross section of the community, not sociologically loaded dice. To the extent that the judges themselves are free from social bias (in racial, class, and sex terms), this alternative would probably work quite well.

Until one remedy or another is applied, the state will almost surely 15 have to do its own research if only to even the odds. District attorneys cannot be expected to stand by doing nothing while the most serious offenders buy themselves a significant edge in case after case. The champions of the technique will have to realize that the days it could be reserved for their favorite defendants are over.

QUESTIONS AND IDEAS FOR DISCUSSION

1. How well does Etzioni organize his argument? Does he give appropriate attention to the points he most needs to prove? On what points is his argument most susceptible to challenge? Discuss.

2. In paragraph 11, Etzioni acknowledges that "one cannot unbite the apple of knowledge, return to the innocence of not knowing." To what does he refer here, and what are its implications for his argument?

3. Consider the following facts about jury selection:

- Prospective jurors' names are drawn from lists of registered voters.

- In many jurisdictions, certain groups—notably doctors, law-yers, teachers, ministers, government officials—are routinely excused from jury duty.
- Anyone for whom jury duty constitutes "undue hardship" may be excused.
- Questions about prospective jurors' racial biases may be limited by the judge and may be asked by the judge.
- Attorneys for both sides in a trial are permitted a certain number of "peremptory challenges," by which they can reject a prospec-tive juror without stating any reason.

How, if at all, do these facts (any or all of them) affect the points argued in this essay? Discuss.

Impartial—Not Ignorant— Juries Needed

NEWTON MINOW AND FRED H. CATE

Newton Minow, formerly head of the Federal Communications Commission, directs Northwestern University's Annenberg Wash-ington Program in communications policy studies. Fred H. Cate is a fellow in that program. Together they wrote this essay, first pub-lished in the *Los Angeles Times* in 1990. In it, the authors challenge the assumption, all but taken for granted today, that juries need to be untainted by any prior knowledge about a case. If you have served on a jury, you may have encountered this assumption in the courtroom; if not, you may in the future experience firsthand the difficult situa-tion the authors describe. Do you agree with their conclusions?

Defense lawyers for deposed Panamanian dictator Manuel A. 1 Noriega are already claiming that it will be impossible to find a jury of 12 people who have not been influenced by the publicity surrounding his indictment and arrest. "We're going to have to look on the dark side of the moon for people who haven't heard bad things about the general," Noriega defense counsel Frank Rubino said.

The claim is not original. On the day that almost any newsworthy 2 criminal trial begins, if not the day of the indictment, or arrest, the defense argues: "My client can't get a fair trial because the prospective jurors have been prejudiced by press reports about the case."

But the justice system's frequent response to the problem of pre- 3 trial publicity—banning informed citizens from a jury—is obsolete in our news-saturated society.

According to the Sixth Amendment, every person accused of a 4 crime has the right to a trial "by an impartial jury of the State and district wherein the crime shall have been committed." The standard for selecting jurors is impartiality, not ignorance. As described in the common law that underlies our legal system, it must be a jury of "peers." In fact, in 12th-century England, the earliest juries were chosen for their knowledge of the case, not their lack of it. In this country, the criterion has long since been reversed.

If the court excludes potential jurors who follow the news, it 5 excludes a vast segment of the population—ironically leaving those who are presumably less interested in the civic principles that a jury is expected to uphold. This exclusion, intended to prevent prejudice, substitutes a different kind of prejudice.

For decades, black Americans were often excluded from juries 6 until the U.S. Supreme Court recognized that a jury of only one race is not representative of the community. A jury from which citizens who seek to be well-informed have been systematically excluded is equally unrepresentative.

Such a jury cannot serve the interest of justice. The jurors should 7 represent the full community, not only the segment uninterested in what the media report in newspapers, magazines, radio and television.

Rather than dismiss informed citizens from jury service, thought- 8 ful judges today question them closely about their ability to be impartial. To protect the innocent from being punished, judges already instruct jurors to consider only what they have heard in the courtroom and what the judge has accepted into the record. In almost every case, this means jurors are told to disregard something they have seen or heard in the courtroom. And we trust them to do so.

In the case of Manuel A. Noriega, as with other criminal defen- 9 dants, if the court insists on uninformed jurors, it faces an impossible dilemma: It must either set Noriega free, if an adequately uninformed jury cannot be impaneled, or try him before a jury that is not representative of the community.

Mark Twain's warning in 1871, describing a jury trial in Virginia 10 City, Nev., is even more applicable today:

"A minister, intelligent, esteemed and greatly respected; a mer- 11 chant of high character and known probity; a mining superintendent of intelligence and unblemished reputation . . . were all questioned in the same way and all set aside. Each said the public talk and the newspaper reports had not biased his mind. . . . But of course such men could not be trusted with the case. Ignoramuses alone could mete out unsullied justice."

QUESTIONS AND IDEAS FOR DISCUSSION

1. What is Minow and Cates's thesis? How reasonably and thoroughly do they support it? Evaluate the argument in terms of its logic and persuasiveness.

2. How realistic is it to call for impartial but well-informed jurors? Can it be possible to obtain jurors who are both wholly impartial and entirely capable of reaching a just, well-reasoned verdict? Discuss.

3. What assumption(s) underlies the authors' claim that "if a court excludes potential jurors who follow the news," it is left with "those who are presumably less interested in the civic principles that a jury is expected to uphold" (paragraph 5)?

4. Read the Sixth Amendment to the U.S. Constitution. Does it state or imply, as the authors assert in paragraph 7, that "jurors should represent the full community"? Discuss this issue.

The Threat of Anonymous Juries
WILLIAM M. KUNSTLER

William M. Kunstler is a lawyer and professor of law at New York University Law School; in addition, he is vice president and volunteer staff attorney for the Center for Constitutional Rights. He has written nearly a dozen books, including *The Hall-Mills Murder Case* (1980) and *Trials and Tribulations* (1985), along with numerous articles and book reviews. In this essay, first published in the *Nation* in 1983, Kunstler considers a relatively recent innovation in the jury system, the anonymous jury. Kunstler argues that anonymous juries are more a "prosecutorial weapon" than a means of assuring the welfare of jurors and their freedom to vote their conscience without fear of personal harm.

The recent state and Federal trials of various defendants in what is 1 popularly known as the "Brink's Case" dramatized the use of anonymous juries. Federal Judge Kevin T. Duffy, who presided in the five-month trial of six defendants in a U.S. District Court, promptly granted a motion by the prosecutor to keep the jurors' names secret from counsel and the public and to have them escorted by Federal marshals from the courthouse each day. The government claimed that the move was necessary to insure the jurors' safety and privacy. David S. Ritter, the judge in a state trial, granted a similar request.

The results were somewhat mixed from the prosecution's point of 2
view. The anonymous jury in the state trial in Goshen, New York,
convicted the three defendants of the murder of a Brink's guard and
two police officers; its counterpart in the Federal trial in Manhattan
acquitted two defendants and convicted four others, but threw out the
most serious charges against them. The use of this prosecutorial
weapon in both cases has serious and pernicious constitutional implications for the criminal justice system.

The anonymous jury, which in my view violates every tenet of the 3
Fifth and Sixth Amendments to the Constitution, is of extremely recent vintage. It was first used in the 1977 drug prosecution of Leroy
(Nicky) Barnes in Manhattan's Federal District Court. Ostensibly intended to protect the safety and privacy of jurors and their families, it
is, in reality, a prosecutorial device to increase the likelihood of conviction by giving jurors the impression that a defendant is so beyond the
pale that their very lives would be in danger if their identities were
made public. Small wonder that, following the Federal jury's rejection
of most of the government's case against the six Brink's defendants
because of its unbelievability, Judge Duffy expressed surprise, commenting, "I have never understood juries."

The use of an anonymous jury in the Barnes trial was challenged 4
on appeal. But his counsel did not raise solid constitutional arguments, and the verdict was sustained by a 2-to-1 vote of the U.S. Court
of Appeals. However, the dissenting judge, former Connecticut Governor Thomas J. Meskill, wrote, "I am troubled by the implications of
today's decision and the uses to which it may be put." Quoting Supreme Court Justice William O. Douglas, he said, "Cases of notorious
criminals—like cases of small miserable ones—are apt to make bad
law . . . [T]he harm in the given case may seem excusable. But the
practices generated by the precedent have far-reaching consequences
that are harmful and injurious beyond measurement."

Writing in the *Fordham Law Review*, Prof. Abraham Abramovsky 5
put the case against anonymous juries more sharply:

> In effect, by his instruction with respect to anonymity, the trial
> judge implied that the defendants were so vicious and dangerous
> that anonymity was required to protect the jurors and their families
> from harassment, physical injury or even death. In any prior jury
> service, the jurors would not have been instructed to remain anony-
> mous. Therefore the only reasonable inference that a jury could draw
> . . . was that protection was mandated by the character of the defen-
> dant. It would have been ludicrous for a juror to conclude that he was
> being protected from members of the United States Attorney's office,
> their investigators, or from the judge himself. Thus, before any evi-
> dence was introduced . . . the defendants were depicted, by impli-
> cation, as notorious individuals. This characterization, without any

proof . . . of any conspiracy to tamper with the jury, let alone any actual attempts to do so, eviscerated the presumption of innocence to which these defendants were entitled.

The use of anonymous juries is increasing. In an upcoming Fed- 6 eral drug case in Manhattan in which Barnes will be a government witness, the prosecution requested an anonymous jury and added the stipulation that its members "should be kept together during recesses and taken to lunch each day by the United States Marshal's Service; and . . . at the end of each trial day . . . taken together [by marshals] from the Courthouse to an undisclosed central location from which they can leave for their respective communities." The judge granted the request and further ordered that the jury be sequestered. In a contempt trial of alleged members of the Puerto Rican liberation group F.A.L.N. in Brooklyn's Federal District Court, a similar jury was empaneled. Several months later, in a trial of supposed supporters of the group, the jury was not anonymous. Significantly, the jury in the first trial returned guilty verdicts, while the jury in the second trial was hung.

To my knowledge, during the more than 200 years of this Repub- 7 lic's existence, no juror has ever been harmed by a defendant or his or her supporters, even in prosecutions of alleged members of Murder Inc. and of notorious criminals like Al Capone and Anthony Provenzano, to name but a few cases involving dangerous defendants. As Professor Abramovsky points out, the use of anonymous juries in highly publicized cases deals a "devastating blow to the presumption of innocence before a scintilla of evidence was introduced against the defendant at trial." In addition, it so restricts the voir dire as to render the examination of prospective jurors virtually meaningless, and it makes it difficult for lawyers to challenge them intelligently. For example, lacking names and addresses, lawyers are unable to investigate prospective jurors' backgrounds or even ascertain ethnic affiliations. In the words of Sir Thomas More in Robert Bolt's play *A Man for All Seasons*, juror anonymity means cutting "a great road through the law to get after the Devil."

QUESTIONS AND IDEAS FOR DISCUSSION

1. Kunstler writes here for the (mostly) politically liberal readers of the *Nation*. What changes would you suggest in word choices, examples, organization, or other aspects of the essay were Kunstler to redirect his argument to the typically more conservative readers of the *National Review*? Be specific.

2. Does Kunstler weaken his argument by acknowledging that the results in the Brink's trials, one with an anonymous jury and one with an identified jury, were "somewhat mixed" (paragraph 2)? Comment.

3.   Which of Kunstler's points is argumentatively strongest? Which is most open to challenge? Discuss the reasons on which you base your answers.

Coppolino Revisited
JOHN D. MACDONALD

John D. MacDonald is a mystery writer, the creator of fictional detective Travis McGee, and author of more than sixty mystery novels and several nonfiction works. The latter include *No Deadly Drug* (1968), about the murder of Carmela Coppolino, and *Reading for Survival* (1987). Here, in a selection from *I, Witness* (1978), MacDonald turns his attention to real-life crime and its usual real-life consequence: trial by jury. He argues against the use of technical evidence from "expert" witnesses—scientists, engineers, and the like—before juries of ordinary citizens. According to MacDonald, the practice of subjecting juries to expert testimony on technical matters "is a charade"—and, as a result, the jury system has become little more than a charade itself.

Here is a direct quote from the testimony of Doctor Charles J.   1 Umberger, Toxicologist with the office of Chief Medical Examiner in New York City. He and the late Dr. Milton Helpern had gone to Naples, Florida, in April of 1967 to testify for the Prosecution in the trial of Carl Coppolino, anesthesiologist, at which he was convicted of second-degree murder for killing his wife with an injection of succinylcholine chloride, a paralyzing compound used to stop the patient from breathing on his own during major surgery on the lungs or heart.

With the glazed eyes of the jurors upon him, Umberger said,   2 "Now this case was treated as a general unknown, and when the analysis was started, tissue was set up to cover all categories. For example, one of the first things that was done was to take a piece of kidney. The kidney was ashed and a sample was put on a spectrograph. The purpose of the spectrograph is to determine whether there were any metal compounds. With the spectrographic plate, all but three of the metals can be excluded. Another sample was subjected to what we call a digestion, using an old-fashioned Reinsch Test, plating out the metal on copper. Arsenic, antimony, and mercury, along with silver and bismuth plated out on copper, and from that one can subject the copper plate to an X-ray fluorescent machine and determine whether any of those three metals are there. That is necessary, because in spectrographic analysis there is what is called the volatile metals and these distill out of the crater or the arc and would not produce the spectrum . . ."

As if that wasn't enough, a little further along he got into the 3 procedures by which his lab had isolated and identified the components of the succinylcholine chloride which had killed Carmela Coppolino.

He said, "The one [test] depends upon the formation of what we 4 call ferric hydroxamic imides. That happens to be what we call a generic test for esters, which is another type of organic structure. Succinic acid is an acid and shouldn't react with this reagent. In working with it, what we discovered is if the succinic acid is sublimed at ordinary atmospheric pressure that as a result of that heating it is turned into the anhydride. In other words the two acid groups kind of lock together and water is lost, and then subsequent to that we found that if we put in a little phosphorous pentoxide in that tube and carried out sublimation we could convert the succinic acid without a lot of manipulation over the anhydride."

What sort of people were soaking up all this great information? 5

The jury was composed of twelve men—a retired naval officer, a 6 refrigerator repairman, a construction-crew foreman, two motel owners, a retired clothing salesman, a furniture salesman, a mortgage broker, a maintenance engineer, a fisherman, an air-conditioner serviceman, and a semiretired plumber.

F. Lee Bailey brought on his team of experts to refute the testi- 7 mony of Helpern and Umberger. I quote from the Naples newspaper the following weekend: "One of the most fascinating and immediate impressions received by all was the paradox of conclusions reached by these highly qualified scientists in their efforts to determine what happens to the drug after it is injected into a muscle or vein of the human body."

A Dr. Moya, Chairman of the Department of Anesthesiology at 8 the University of Miami, had testified, in just as much stupifying detail as Umberger, that Umberger's experiments were flawed and his conclusions improper. He said that the compounds found in Carmela Coppolino's body were there in normal amounts and had been released for measurement by the embalming fluid.

The newspaper item ends: "You pays your money and you takes 9 your choice. And a man's life rests on the choice made by the 12 good men and true who listened intently all week from the jury box."

What do we have then, in this and in other trials where contempo- 10 rary expert testimony is given by both sides? Not one of those twelve jurors knew diddly about anesthesiology, toxicology, biochemistry, and pharmacology. They could *not* follow and comprehend the expert testimony. The prosecution lawyers and the defense lawyers knew that the jurors could not follow the expert testimony and evaluate it upon its scientific merits. The experts knew this also.

So it is a charade. 11

Recognizing the fact of charade, one realizes that the jurors will 12 side with that expert who has the best stage presence, who radiates a total confidence in his grasp of the subject at hand, who speaks crisply, with dignity, confidence, and charm, who is neatly and properly dressed and has no distressing mannerisms.

In short, the expert must be precisely the sort of person an adver- 13 tising agency would select to talk about a new deodorant on national television.

The expert who mumbles, slouches, grimaces, stares into space, 14 and keeps ramming his little finger into his ear and inspecting what he dredges up *might* be a far better scientist than the television commercial chap. But there is no real correlation here. The impressive presence is more likely to be the result of a number of appearances as an expert than the result of academic credentials.

In January of 1977 Melvin M. Belli, sometimes known as the King 15 of Torts, published a syndicated defense of the jury system which appeared op-ed in scores of newspapers.

He wrote: 16

> After arguing hundreds of cases, both civil and criminal, I do not believe that I have ever seen a jury that did not give the case under submission its honest judgment and deliberation. Contemporary jurors are not swayed by old-fashioned oratory or legal theatrics; thus jury trials have become a precise, orderly business.
>
> Today, jurors take detailed notes during testimony and ask probing questions about the facts and the law. Frequently they will return from their deliberations and ask the judge to have crucial testimony reread or to repeat his instructions on the applicable statutes. Juries do not want to make mistakes—and seldom do.

The question is obvious. How can jurors make honest judgments 17 about a body of knowledge beyond their capacity to comprehend? Are they going to take notes on the ferric hydroxamic imides, and come back out to ask what a Reinsch Test might be?

Trial by jury, using expert witnesses to clarify the testimony of 18 others and add to the body of the case, worked beautifully in a world which was far simpler in all technologies. In a village culture a scout could be called in to testify as to the origin of the arrow which struck the deceased, showing to the jury those points of difference in fletching and notching which indicated the tribe where it had been made.

In a world more compartmentalized, knowledge becomes increas- 19 ingly impossible to communicate to anyone who has not had a substantial background in the discipline at hand.

A friend of mine has spent most of his life in pure mathematics, in 20 abstractions as subtle as music. He tells me that up until perhaps fifteen years ago it was still possible to explain what he was doing, in rather rough outline, to a bright layman, using analogy, models, little drawings, and so on. But now he tells me that he cannot explain to me where he is and where he is going. He has gone beyond analogy, beyond models and drawings and comprehensible statements. Think of that. What he is doing is out of my reach. And yours. Other disciplines are becoming ever less easy to explain. Computers are playing an ever more active and forceful role in the designing of computers. IBM had a computer exhibit in New York City long ago, a big room full of winking tubes and chuckling sounds. You can hold in one hand a computer that will do everything that one did, and faster.

We have all become that Naples fisherman, wondering at the 21 difference between an ester and an oyster.

Jury trials are becoming ever longer. In notorious trials, the jurors 22 are sequestered for weeks and months. Deadlocked juries are more common. Giving expert testimony has become a profession for scientists who have reason to be disappointed in the rewards from their career alone.

It is possible that the jury system could be saved from its own 23 excesses by a revision of the expert-testimony folkdance.

When it appears that medical or scientific testimony will be a key 24 factor in any case, I would suggest that the prosecution select a single expert to present its side, and the defense do the same. These two gentlemen would then select a third man in their field, satisfactory to both of them. After the third man had listened to the scientific evidence and had a chance to read the documentation and do whatever research might be necessary, there would be a meeting between the experts, the judge, and the attorneys for both sides. The selected expert would give his opinion, and it would be binding on both sides. If, for example, in the Coppolino case, the selected expert backed Umberger's procedures and said that he believed that it had been proven that succinylcholine chloride had been injected into the upper outer quadrant of the left buttock in sufficient quantity to cause death, then the defense would be forced to stipulate that this was indeed so, and it would then be up to the defense to change the plea, or try to show that it would not have been done by the defendant.

If such a procedure were to be instituted in civil and criminal trials 25 we would see trials of less duration. Juries would be more prone to reach agreement on the verdicts. Expenses to both the state and the accused would be dramatically reduced in criminal cases, and reduced for the plaintiff and defendant in civil cases.

I would imagine it would make Mr. Belli's court appearances of far 26 less duration and hence not quite so burdensome to the insurance companies and to the patients of the doctors who must pass along the high malpractice premiums to their patients in the form of higher charges for office visits.

I have taken my samples of expert-witness jargon from the Coppo- 27 lino trial only because I happen to have a complete transcript in my files, and not because I have any feeling that Coppolino was done any disservice by this oppressive conflicting testimony. At this writing he has been a prisoner of the state of Florida for over ten years.

By the time the long days of scientific testimony and the direct and 28 cross and redirect examinations of the seven or eight expert witnesses had gone droning on and on, the twelve jurors had already decided that it was of no moment to them whether or not the succinylcholine chloride was detectable or not.

Here is how the state of mind came about. During the 29 prosecution's direct examination of its leading expert, Dr. Milton Helpern, there came an opportunity to project onto a large white wall behind and to Judge Lynn Silvertooth's right, some very sharp-focus slides taken by the Medical Examiner's office. The courtroom was darkened. There were a dozen of these slides. The very first one brought a sick gasping sound from the spectators and press. It showed, in about a five-by-eight-foot projection, Carmela Coppolino, clothing removed, face down, full length, after three and a half months in a New Jersey cemetery.

Successive slides moved in closer and closer, focusing on the left 30 buttock, then on the upper outer quadrant of the left buttock to show a tiny crater and, near it and below it, the dark stains of five bruise marks. States Attorney Frank Schaub had asked Dr. Helpern, "Could they be the type consistent with the use of human force, the fingers? Could they be caused by a hand pressing down on the body?" In his quiet clinical voice Helpern testified that they could be consistent, and testified as to how he had proven through micro-examination that the bruises had been inflicted shortly before death.

The final slides showed magnified photographs of the incision 31 Helpern had made adjacent to the crater, showing that it was indeed a puncture wound along with a needle track deep into the subcutaneous fat of the buttock.

Now then, because Helpern had testified that he could find no 32 other cause of death, and because the defense offered no plausible alternative reason for the needle track, and because the jurors could readily believe that Coppolino as a nonpracticing anesthesiologist would have access to the substance in question, and because a reasonably satisfactory motive and a provable opportunity had been established by the State, the jurors did not care whether or not the presence of that suck-something could be proven beyond the shadow of a doubt. They had seen the unforgettable pictures, the fingermark bruises, and the needle track, and nobody had stepped up to show she had died of anything else.

And so they drowsed through a lot of it.   33

So let us imagine a similar case where there is no needle track, no 34 pitiful and ghastly slides of the slim dead lady, a case where it really *does* hang on the technical evidence presented.

Want to be a defendant? Want to take your chances in a forum 35 where charm rather than fact is the persuader? Want to pay an additional $50,000 to $150,000 for the transportation, housing, fees, and sustenance of your team of experts, plus the additional legal costs of the preparation and the additional days in court?

Or will you choose arbitration?   36

Final question. *If* it is known that arbitration of conflicting expert 37 testimony *is* available, and the defendant elects to finance a battle of the experts, will it be more difficult to preserve the presumption of innocence?

QUESTIONS AND IDEAS FOR DISCUSSION

1.   *Is* expert testimony a charade? That is, do you find MacDonald's argument convincing? Why, or why not?

2.   This argument additionally connects the use of expert testimony with lengthy trials and deadlocked juries. Is the connection soundly argued? Explain.

3.   MacDonald asks, "How can jurors make honest judgments about a body of knowledge beyond their capacity to comprehend?" (paragraph 17). His answer is that they cannot. Is any other answer possible? Discuss.

4.   MacDonald recommends a solution to the problem of expert testimony: arbitration. Does he make a convincing case for replacing the "battle of the experts" before a jury with arbitration by a third expert party? Discuss. Does he weaken his argument with the last sentence of the essay? Why, or why not?

Grand Juries

ANNA QUINDLEN

Anna Quindlen is a columnist for the *New York Times* ("Life in the 30s" and "Public & Private") and author of several books, including *Living Out Loud* (1988) and *Ethics in America* (1989). Quindlen wrote this defense of the jury system for the *New York Times* in 1990 after juries had acquitted defendants in two widely publicized obscenity trials. In one, the Cincinnati Museum of Art and its director, Dennis Barrie, were acquitted of obscenity for displaying Robert Mapplethorpe's photographs.[1] In the other, the controversial rap music group 2 Live Crew was acquitted on charges that the lyrics to its music were obscene. While Etzioni, Minow and Cate, Kunstler, and MacDonald all find fault—of varying kinds and degree—with the jury system, Quindlen celebrates it as "the only thing in America that still sometimes works." After all the naysayers, does she convince you?

Stupid prosecutor's trick of the month—and the competition is 1 fierce for this one—goes to the assistant state attorney in the 2 Live Crew case who said one of the jurors, a 76-year-old retired professor, was trouble from Day One. "She was a sociologist, and I don't like sociologists," Pedro Dijols said. "They try to reason things out too much."

Now there's an indictment if I ever heard one. You let people go 2 reasoning things out, next thing you know they'll be using logic. And before you know it the place will be overrun with common sense and then where will we be?

In the jury room, that's where.   3

I confess: Like everyone else, I thought the Mapplethorpe jury 4 was going to convict, and that the 2 Live Crew panel would do the same. I pictured them as children, listening to a prosecutor saying: "This is obscene. Why? Because I say so."

I thought one panel would see photographs of things they never 5 imagined took place and didn't want to look at, and respond "guilty." I thought the other would hear nasty, misogynous, violent rap lyrics, and ignore the fact that rock-and-roll mirrors society, and often the dregs of society at that.

Which only goes to show that I had forgotten the blessed jury 6 system, the only thing in America that still sometimes works.

"I wouldn't want my case decided by 12 people too stupid to get 7 out of jury duty," lawyers sometimes say, cracking wise, underes-

---

[1] Two essays in Chapter 11 discuss the Mapplethorpe exhibition in arguments about obscenity and First Amendment rights: Andrew Ferguson, "Mad about Mapplethorpe," and Arthur C. Danto, "Art and Taxpayers." [Ed.]

timating their most important audience. Defense attorneys in the Mapplethorpe case were dismayed that the jury pool consisted largely of people who had no interest in museum-going. The prosecutor was so arrogant in his apparent belief that saying they were dirty pictures made it so that his only real witness was a censorship maven who had written some tunes for Captain Kangaroo.

In Miami, things were little better. The lawyers for 2 Live Crew 8 flavored their case with suggestions that unless you were young, black and male, you might never understand what the group was trying to do in its music. The prosecutors presented a performance tape of the band so badly recorded that it could have been Michael Jackson, "The Mikado," or a transmission from the Times Square subway station.

And then along came the saving graces. A group of strangers 9 come together as a jury, and for some reason that probably has to do with a distillation of civic responsibility, self-importance, and the kind of dedication you can bring to putting together a really difficult jigsaw puzzle in a summer house on a rainy Sunday, they take their mission seriously. Given what lawyers and judges hand them—and that's a big given—they try to do the right thing.

Some people are still angry that the jury didn't slam Marion Barry, 10 the Mayor of Washington.[2] And some people are still upset that jurors were able to find reasonable doubt in the McMartin preschool case.[3] Those cases, and others like them, remind me of looking at photographs of a particularly horrible murder in the offices of the police crime scene unit. "You have no idea who did this?" I said to a sergeant. "Oh we know who did it," he said. "We just don't have a case."

In Miami, the jury foreman was philosophical about the fact that 11 the jurors were less bigoted than the leader of 2 Live Crew, who had written them off as too white, too straight, too old. "He stereotyped us, just as certain people were stereotyping him because of his performance," said the foreman, elevating good sense to an art form.

And in Ohio, a warehouse manager on the Mapplethorpe jury 12 said: "It's like Picasso. Picasso, from what everybody tells me, was an artist. It's not my cup of tea, I don't understand it, but if people say it's art then I have to go along with it." People have used that quote to attack the jurors, but I see it as a commentary on our obscenity stan-

---

[2] In 1990 Washington Mayor Marion Barry was found guilty of cocaine possession. While many people felt that the sentence of six months' imprisonment and a $5,000 fine was unduly harsh, many others felt that the jury's verdict of a misdemeanor rather than a felony was unduly lenient. [Ed.]

[3] The McMartin Preschool case involved widely publicized accusations that teachers at the California school had sexually molested a number of their young students. Charges against most of those accused were eventually dropped, and in 1990 Peggy McMartin Buckey, the school's director, was found innocent after the longest court trial in U.S. history. Her son, Raymond Buckey, received a hung-jury mistrial the same year, after having served five years in prison while awaiting trial. [Ed.]

dards, which are as murky as the bottom of a kid's fish tank. What the juror was saying is what I say every time I see a Wagnerian opera: sometimes artistic merit is hard for the layman to fathom. Or, in plain language, there's no accounting for taste.

They sat and they listened to discussions of composition and 13 parody and prurient interest. Then they went into a little room and looked at the prosecution case, the defense case, the judge's charge and the law, and they went to work. In a country where making a tough decision has receded into the distant mists of our historical past, that is no small accomplishment. "You take away one freedom," one of the 2 Live Crew jurors reportedly said during deliberations, "and pretty soon they're all gone." Put that on a button and I'll wear it.

QUESTIONS AND IDEAS FOR DISCUSSION

1. Identify Anna Quindlen's thesis (if it is implicit, state it). Is this really an essay about the jury system, or could you argue that it is equally or primarily an argument about obscenity? Explain your answer. Evaluate the reasoning in this essay. If it were your essay, what, if anything, would you add to it or change about it to clarify and strengthen its argument further?

2. Does Quindlen consider any of the issues raised by other writers in this chapter? If so, what are her arguments? If not, how would she likely respond, given what she argues here?

3. Do people you know seem to agree with the notion that only those "too stupid to get out of jury duty" (paragraph 7) serve on juries? Are people usually, sometimes, or never right in this belief? Comment. What are the implications, if any, for the jury system?

4. Discuss the following statements made by jurors and quoted by Quindlen. What do you believe the statements mean, and are they right? Can you give reasons or examples of your own that would clarify and support these assertions?

> "I don't understand it, but if people say it's art then I have to go along with it." (12)

> "You take away one freedom, and pretty soon they're all gone." (13)

5. Quindlen is noted for her writing style. Can you suggest why, given this very limited sampling of her prose? Identify phrases and word choices in this essay that strike you as particularly apt, vivid, or unusual. If none does, argue your specific objections (again, based on this one essay) to Quindlen's reputation as a stylist.

SUGGESTIONS FOR WRITING
AND FURTHER DISCUSSION

1. If you have participated in the jury system, consider your experiences and argue either a defense of the system or a particular problem with it. If you defend the jury system, take into account and respond to possible opposing arguments; if you take exception to some aspect of the system, try to recommend a means of correction.

2. Poll students on your campus to determine any misconceptions they may have about the jury system—for example, that juries always have twelve members, that all trials include juries, that a unanimous verdict is always required, that employers must pay you while you serve, that if you don't vote you won't be called for jury duty. Write an essay that summarizes your findings, with your campus community as its intended audience, and argue the extent to which students need to be educated about the legal system and their role in it as citizens.

3. Does the use of psychological evaluation constitute "jury-stacking"? That is, does psychological evaluation tend to create a biased jury rather than one likely to be fair and impartial? Or does such evaluation *counter* "jury-stacking"—on the assumption that jurors are predisposed toward conviction, tending to believe that grand juries do not indict innocent people? Assuming that psychological evaluation *can* determine a juror's probable attitudes, is justice thwarted or served by such evaluations? As a layperson, argue your reasoned opinion.

4. Judge Jerome Frank (1889–1957) was a federal appeals judge in the Second Circuit and an outspoken opponent of the jury system in America. Like Minow and Cate, Frank believed it ill-advised to seat uninformed jurors; unlike Minow and Cate, Frank opposed the jury system entirely. Judge Frank once made the following argument:

> If a surgeon were to call in 12 men untrained in surgery, give them an hour's talk on the instruments used in appendectomies, and let them remove the patient's appendix, we would be appalled. Yet similar operations on men's legal rights are performed every day by juries—*amateurs* entrusted with the use of legal rules which lawyers and judges understand only after long and special training. Yet juries are given the job of ascertaining facts on which depend a man's property, his reputation, his very life![1]

---

[1] Quoted in "The Jury System on Trial," *Senior Scholastic*, 20 Mar. 1964: 10. [Ed.]

How logically convincing is Judge Frank's argument? How emotionally persuasive? With what argument or arguments might you refute his implicit conclusion? Write a short essay that does so.

5. William M. Kunstler asserts that the anonymous jury "violates every tenet of the Fifth and Sixth Amendments to the Constitution" (paragraph 3), but he does not argue the point. Look up the Fifth and Sixth Amendments, and argue the point—or argue against it.

6. John D. MacDonald argues that juries cannot evaluate technical evidence and "expert testimony." Judge Marvin E. Aspen (United States judge for the Northern District of Illinois) asks some similar questions:

> Can we really expect laypersons to comprehend the technical jury instructions that are thrust upon them, when experienced lawyers and judges with adequate time for contemplation still struggle with some of these difficult concepts? Is it possible to draft jury instructions in everyday language and, at the same time, not lose the requisite precision in stating a complex legal principle? Are we satisfied with the all too frequent rationalization of the trial lawyer that the system is fine since the "jury usually gets the right result even though often for the wrong reasons"?[2]

Argue your answers to these questions and those MacDonald raises. If your answers are "no," propose and defend remedies. If your answers are "yes," defend the jury system in regard to the questions Judge Aspen and John D. MacDonald raise. Assume that your readers will be ordinary citizens—past or prospective jurors—not lawyers and judges.

7. Ordinarily, juries render "general verdicts"; that is, they are not required to give any public reason for their decision. Argue for or against this judicial tradition.

8. Despite Melvin Belli's declaration (MacDonald, paragraph 16), jurors are not often allowed to take notes during a trial. Discuss the pros and cons of permitting note-taking by jurors during trials.

9. Decide which of the essays in this chapter argues its claims most effectively—whether or not you like or agree with its conclusions. Argue the reasons for your choice. (You may choose to comment on

---

[2] Rev. of John Guinther, *The Jury in America* (1988), *Judicature* 72.4 (Dec.–Jan. 1989) 255. [Ed.]

the difficulty, if any, of putting aside your own ideas about the issues while you judge the arguments.) Is the most effective argument the best written and the most clearly organized? The most logical? The best documented? Or is it more emotional than logical in its argument? What does the essay show you as a writer about ways to make a point well?

13

THE MORALITY OF ZOOS

So often we take the familiar—and zoos are familiar to most of us—quite for granted. We never think of zoos or circuses or wildlife preserves as presenting moral dilemmas. The following writers do, however, and for a number of different reasons. This chapter begins with a spirited but conventional argument supporting zoos and ends with a radical, Marxist argument opposing them. In between, you will find zoos opposed on the grounds that it is immoral to keep animals in captivity for our amusement, and you will find zoos defended on the grounds that in the face of global warming many species will not be preserved outside the controlled and monitored environments of modern zoos. Are zoos desirable or immoral institutions from the standpoint of animal welfare? Are zoos the best or the worst way to educate and interest people in animal welfare? Do zoos preserve species or distort them genetically and behaviorally? Four writers have four distinct viewpoints on the subject—and you may want to reread the student essay in Chapter 1 for yet another.

The New Zoo: A Modern Ark

NANCY GIBBS

This essay was first published in *Time* in 1989. Its author, Nancy Gibbs, is an associate editor for *Time* magazine who writes here about the form zoos are taking, and the role they are assuming, in the world today. But if you were to read only the first and last sentences, with their talk of natural disasters and great sorrows, you would probably misjudge the content and stance of this essay. In fact, it offers a spirited defense of zoos. With vivid descriptions, good humor, and plenty of specific examples, Gibbs argues that "America's zoos are doing something very right." So is Gibbs doing something very wrong in the way she begins and ends her argument? Probably not, as you will see. As you read, notice throughout the essay how Gibbs uses unexpected phrases, contrasts, and juxtapositions to create energy in her argument.

Call it a natural disaster. The San Diego Zoo spent $3.5 million to 1 build a designer forest that would house five adolescent Malayan sun bears. The zookeepers planted some trees, dug a moat, launched a waterfall, even hooked up a fiber-glass tree with an electric honey dispenser. As company for their wards, they invited lion-tailed macaques, yellow-breasted laughing thrushes, orange-bellied fruit doves and Indian pigmy geese.

When the lush exhibit opened this summer, zoogoers loved it. So 2 did the bears. They shredded the trees, rolled up the sod, plugged the moat—and then one attempted a fast break over the wall. Spectators went scrambling for a zookeeper, who propped up a plywood barrier while another clanged some pots and pans to intimidate the beasts and herd them into a locked enclosure.

Meanwhile at Washington's National Zoo another experiment 3 was under way: scientists wanted to acquaint their rare golden lion tamarins with a facsimile of their natural habitat, a lowland Brazilian forest. But the coddled, zoo-happy monkeys lacked some basic skills—how, for instance, to peel a banana. Instead, they fell out of the trees and got lost in the woods.

At some 150 American zoos in between, the troubles are not very 4 different. The sharks eat the angelfish. The Australian hairy-nosed wombat stays in its cave, and the South American smoky jungle frog hunkers down beneath a leaf, all tantalizingly hidden from the prying eyes of the roughly 110 million Americans who go to zoos every year. Visitors often complain that as a result of all the elaborate landscaping, they cannot find the animals. But this, like almost everything else that goes wrong these days, is a signal that America's zoos are doing something very right.

Just about every aspect of America's zoos has dramatically 5 changed—and improved—from what viewers saw a generation ago. Gone are the sour cages full of frantic cats and the concrete tubs of thawing penguins. Instead the terrain is uncannily authentic, and animals are free to behave like, well, animals, not inmates. Here is a Himalayan highland full of red pandas, there a subtropical jungle where it rains indoors, eleven times a day. The effect is of an entire globe miraculously concentrated, the wild kingdom contained in downtown Chicago or the North Bronx. As American zoos are renovated and redesigned—at a cost of more than a billion dollars since 1980—hosts of once jaded visitors, some even without children, are flooding through the gates. "In the past 15 years," says Cincinnati zoo director Edward Maruska, "we've probably changed more than we've changed in the past hundred."

And all to what end? To entertain, of course, but to do more than 6 that. By junking the cages and building vast biological gardens, the zoos provide a decent, delightful place for animals and people to meet and, with luck, fall in love. Once that bond is made, the visitors discover there is a larger mission at hand, a crusade to join. Between the birth of Christ and the Pilgrims' landing, perhaps several species a year became extinct. By the 1990s the extinction rate may reach several species an hour, around the clock. American zoos are leading the battle to stop that clock and recruit others to the preservationist's cause. "We don't just want you to come here," says David Anderson of the New Orleans Audubon Park. "We're trying to say, 'Do something!' "

The zoos have therefore taken on a role as educators that dwarfs 7 that of any other "recreational" institution. Whole public school systems are redesigning their science curriculums to take advantage of local exhibits, for what better biology classroom could there be than a swamp or a rain forest? The newest facilities, such as the Living World in St. Louis, include state-of-the-art computer technology that turns a simple menagerie into a cross between a laboratory and a video arcade.

Though highly effective at raising consciousness and making con- 8 verts, this is not an easy or a cheap way to run a zoo. At the Tiger River exhibit in San Diego, that lovely gushing waterfall is part of a 72,000-gal. computerized irrigation system. A huge banyan tree has heating coils in its roots to encourage the python to uncoil near the viewing glass. Not far away, an agile cliff-springer mountain goat is contained on the assumption that it will not jump eight feet to a ledge on the moat's far side that is constructed at a precise 30°-angle. "But," admits architect David Rice, "nobody has told the cliff springer that."

Beyond the aesthetic and mechanical challenges, there is the basic 9 issue of what zoogoers should be allowed to see in a naturalistic setting. Zoo directors refer to "the Bambi syndrome," a belief common among visitors that all creatures should be cuddly, or at least not killers. A while back, the Detroit Zoo staff euthanatized a dying goat from the children's zoo and placed it in the African-swamp exhibit, which includes big vultures. Doing what came naturally, the vultures ate the goat. About half the zoogoers who happened upon the scene were fascinated, says director Steve Graham. But the other half averted their children's eyes and scurried away.

For all the increased drama in the exhibits themselves, the real 10 revolution is going on behind the scenes and out in the wild, where a state of emergency exists. To begin with, most zoos no longer take animals from the jungle; they grow their own. About 90% of the mammals and 75% of the birds now in U.S. zoos were bred in captivity, and some are even being carefully reintroduced to their native environs. At the same time, zoo-affiliated organizations like Wildlife Conservation International are working to save whole habitats in 38 countries in Africa, Asia and South America and to reduce the threats to endangered species. Says the Bronx Zoo's visionary director William Conway: "Our objectives are very clear—to save fragments of nature, to preserve biodiversity."

As zoos fight back, they are pulling along the public with some 11 shrewd tactics. Conservationists often select an irresistible, oversize crowd pleaser—pandas are perfect, but snow leopards and black rhinos work fine—and lead a campaign to preserve the creature's habitat. "There is a utility in the concern for the giant panda," says the National Zoo's director Michael Robinson. "Pandas are relatively stupid and uninteresting animals. But they happen to be photogenic and appealing, and they help focus people's attention." Big animals need big swatches of habitat, and so in the process a lot of less sexy species are protected too. To save the African elephant requires saving the Serengeti. That means roughly 5,000 sq. mi. and, as it happens, 400 species of birds, maybe 50 species of mammals and tens of thousands of invertebrates. And the elephants.

Though many of these outlying efforts have been wildly success- 12 ful, the zoos themselves are still the front line. A child who rubs noses, even through the plate glass, with a polar bear or a penguin may be far more likely to mature into an eager conservationist than into one who sees animals as toys or accessories. It is hard to walk around a good zoo without caring, deeply, about whether this miraculous wealth of lovely, peculiar, creepy, unfathomable creatures survives or perishes. And it will be a great sorrow if zoos are ever the last place on earth where the wild things are.

QUESTIONS AND IDEAS FOR DISCUSSION

1. Does the essay convince you of its thesis—that zoos are getting better? Why, or why not? Support your answer with examples from Gibbs's argument.

2. Does Gibbs acknowledge opposing viewpoints? If so, where and how does she do it without weakening her own argument? If not, is her argument's credibility affected by the omission? Comment.

3. How effectively does Gibbs organize her argument? Be specific in your comments.

4. Agree or disagree with this claim: This argument's strong suit is persuasion, not logical reasoning. Give specific examples from the text to support your answer.

Against Zoos

DALE JAMIESON

Dale Jamieson teaches philosophy at the University of Colorado, where he is an associate of the Center for the Study of Values and Social Policy. His particular interests include aesthetics, the philosophy of language, and the ethics of the treatment of animals. This essay was written for inclusion in a British book on animal rights, *In Defence of Animals* (1985, ed. Peter Singer), aimed at a college-educated audience. In reading Jamieson's arguments against zoos, you will notice that, unexpectedly, a large part of the essay focuses on the arguments *for* zoos. Does that strategy work against the author's thesis—or strengthen it? As you read, note the issues that Jamieson raises and the evidence he quotes. Which of his claims would you cite, and which would you challenge, in arguing your own viewpoint about zoos?

Zoos and Their History

We can start with a rough-and-ready definition of zoos: they are 1 public parks which display animals, primarily for the purposes of recreation or education. Although large collections of animals were maintained in antiquity, they were not zoos in this sense. Typically these ancient collections were not exhibited in public parks, or they were maintained for purposes other than recreation or education.

The Romans, for example, kept animals in order to have living 2 fodder for the games. Their enthusiasm for the games was so great that even the first tigers brought to Rome, gifts to Caesar Augustus from an Indian ruler, wound up in the arena. The emperor Trajan staged 123 consecutive days of games in order to celebrate his conquest of Dacia. Eleven thousand animals were slaughtered, including lions, tigers, elephants, rhinoceroses, hippopotami, giraffes, bulls, stags, crocodiles and serpents. The games were popular in all parts of the Empire. Nearly every city had an arena and a collection of animals to stock it. In fifth-century France there were twenty-six such arenas, and they continued to thrive until at least the eighth century.

In antiquity rulers also kept large collections of animals as a sign of 3
their power, which they would demonstrate on occasion by destroying their entire collections. This happened as late as 1719 when
Elector Augustus II of Dresden personally slaughtered his entire menagerie, which include tigers, lions, bulls, bears and boars.

The first modern zoos were founded in Vienna, Madrid and Paris 4
in the eighteenth century and in London and Berlin in the nineteenth.
The first American zoos were established in Philadelphia and Cincinnati in the 1870s. Today in the United States alone there are hundreds
of zoos, and they are visited by millions of people every year. They
range from roadside menageries run by hucksters, to elaborate zoological parks staffed by trained scientists.

The Roman games no longer exist, though bullfights and rodeos 5
follow in their tradition. Nowadays the power of our leaders is amply
demonstrated by their command of nuclear weapons. Yet we still have
zoos. Why?

Animals and Liberty

Before we consider the reasons that are usually given for the 6
survival of zoos, we should see that there is a moral presumption
against keeping wild animals in captivity. What this involves, after all,
is taking animals out of their native habitats, transporting them great
distances and keeping them in alien environments in which their
liberty is severely restricted. It is surely true that in being taken from
the wild and confined in zoos, animals are deprived of a great many
goods. For the most part they are prevented from gathering their own
food, developing their own social orders and generally behaving in
ways that are natural to them. These activities all require significantly
more liberty than most animals are permitted in zoos. If we are justified in keeping animals in zoos, it must be because there are some
important benefits that can be obtained only by doing so.

This conclusion is not the property of some particular moral the- 7
ory; it follows from most reasonable moral theories. Either we have
duties to animals or we do not. If we do have duties to animals, surely
they include respecting those interests which are most important to
them, so long as this does not conflict with other, more stringent
duties that we may have. Since an interest in not being taken from the
wild and kept confined is very important for most animals, it follows
that if everything else is equal, we should respect this interest.

Suppose, on the other hand, that we do not have duties to 8
animals. There are two further possibilities: either we have duties to
people that sometimes concern animals, or what we do to animals is
utterly without moral import. The latter view is quite implausible, and

I shall not consider it further. People who have held the former view, that we have duties to people that concern animals, have sometimes thought that such duties arise because we can "judge the heart of a man by his treatment of animals," as Kant remarked in "Duties to Animals." It is for this reason that he condemns the man who shoots a faithful dog who has become too old to serve. If we accept Kant's premise, it is surely plausible to say that someone who, for no good reason, removes wild animals from their natural habitats and denies them liberty is someone whose heart deserves to be judged harshly. If this is so, then even if we believe that we do not have duties to animals but only duties concerning them, we may still hold that there is a presumption against keeping wild animals in captivity. If this presumption is to be overcome, it must be shown that there are important benefits that can be obtained only by keeping animals in zoos.

Arguments for Zoos

What might some of these important benefits be? Four are commonly cited: amusement, education, opportunities for scientific research, and help in preserving species. 9

Amusement was certainly an important reason for the establishment of the early zoos, and it remains an important function of contemporary zoos as well. Most people visit zoos in order to be entertained, and any zoo that wishes to remain financially sound must cater to this desire. Even highly regarded zoos, like the San Diego Zoo, have their share of dancing bears and trained birds of prey. But although providing amusement for people is viewed by the general public as a very important function of zoos, it is hard to see how providing such amusement could possibly justify keeping wild animals in captivity. 10

Most curators and administrators reject the idea that the primary purpose of zoos is to provide entertainment. Indeed, many agree that the pleasure we take in viewing wild animals is not in itself a good enough reason to keep them in captivity. Some curators see baby elephant walks, for example, as a necessary evil, or defend such amusements because of their role in educating people, especially children, about animals. It is sometimes said that people must be interested in what they are seeing if they are to be educated about it, and entertainments keep people interested, thus making education possible. 11

This brings us to a second reason for having zoos: their role in education. This reason has been cited as long as zoos have existed. For example, in 1898 the New York Zoological Society resolved to take 12 "measures to inform the public of the great decrease in animal life, to stimulate sentiment in favor of better protection, and to cooperate with other scientific bodies . . . [in] efforts calculated to secure the perpetual preservation of our higher vertebrates." Despite the pious platitudes that are often uttered about the educational efforts of zoos, however, there is little evidence that zoos are very successful in educating people about animals. Stephen Kellert's paper "Zoological Parks in American Society," delivered at the annual meeting of the American Association of Zoological Parks and Aquariums in 1979, indicates that zoo-goers are much less knowledgeable about animals than backpackers, hunters, fishermen and others who claim an interest in animals, and only slightly more knowledgeable than those who claim no interest in animals at all. Even more disturbing, zoo-goers express the usual prejudices about animals; 73 percent say they dislike rattlesnakes, 52 percent vultures and only 4 percent elephants. One reason why some zoos have not done a better job in educating people is that many of them make no real effort at education. In the case of others the problem is an apathetic and unappreciative public.

Edward G. Ludwig's study of the zoo in Buffalo, New York, in the   13
International Journal for the Study of Animal Problems for 1981, revealed a surprising amount of dissatisfaction on the part of young, scientifically inclined zoo employees. Much of this dissatisfaction stemmed from the almost complete indifference of the public to the zoo's educational efforts. Ludwig's study indicated that most animals are viewed only briefly as people move quickly past cages. The typical zoo-goer stops only to watch baby animals or those who are begging, feeding or making sounds. Ludwig reported that the most common expressions used to describe animals are "cute," "funny-looking," "lazy," "dirty," "weird" and "strange."

Of course, it is undeniable that some education occurs in some   14
zoos. But this very fact raises other issues. What is it that we want people to learn from visiting zoos? Facts about the physiology and behavior of various animals? Attitudes towards the survival of endangered species? Compassion for the fate of all animals? To what degree does education require keeping wild animals in captivity? Couldn't most of the educational benefits of zoos be obtained by presenting films, slides, lectures and so forth? Indeed, couldn't most of the important educational objectives better be achieved by exhibiting empty cages with explanations of why they are empty?

A third reason for having zoos is that they support scientific   15
research. This, too, is a benefit that was pointed out long ago. Sir Humphrey Davy, one of the founders of the Zoological Society of London, wrote in 1825: "It would become Britain to offer another, and very different series of exhibitions to the population of her metropolis;

namely, animals brought from every part of the globe to be applied either to some useful purpose, or as objects of scientific research—not of vulgar admiration!'' Zoos support scientific research in at least three ways: they fund field research by scientists not affiliated with zoos; they employ other scientists as members of zoo staffs; and they make otherwise inaccessible animals available for study.

The first point we should note is that very few zoos support any 16 real scientific research. Fewer still have staff scientists with full-time research appointments. Among those that do, it is common for their scientists to study animals in the wild rather than those in zoo collections. Much of this research, as well as other field research that is supported by zoos, could just as well be funded in a different way— say, by a government agency. The question of whether there should be zoos does not turn on the funding for field research which zoos currently provide. The significance of the research that is actually conducted in zoos is a more important consideration.

Research that is conducted in zoos can be divided into two catego- 17 ries: studies in behavior and studies in anatomy and pathology.

Behavioral research conducted on zoo animals is very controver- 18 sial. Some have argued that nothing can be learned by studying animals that are kept in the unnatural conditions that obtain in most zoos. Others have argued that captive animals are more interesting research subjects than are wild animals: since captive animals are free from predation, they exhibit a wider range of physical and behavioral traits than animals in the wild, thus permitting researchers to view the full range of their genetic possibilities. Both of these positions are surely extreme. Conditions in some zoos are natural enough to permit some interesting research possibilities. But the claim that captive animals are more interesting research subjects than those in the wild is not very plausible. Environments trigger behaviors. No doubt a predation-free environment triggers behaviors different from those of an animal's natural habitat, but there is no reason to believe that better, fuller or more accurate data can be obtained in predation-free environments than in natural habitats.

Studies in anatomy and pathology are the most common forms of 19 zoo research. Such research has three main purposes: to improve zoo conditions so that captive animals will live longer, be happier and breed more frequently; to contribute to human health by providing animal models for human ailments; and to increase our knowledge of wild animals for its own sake.

The first of these aims is surely laudable, if we concede that there 20 should be zoos in the first place. But the fact that zoo research contributes to improving conditions in zoos is not a reason for having them. If there were no zoos, there would be no need to improve them.

The second aim, to contribute to human health by providing 21 animal models for human ailments, appears to justify zoos to some extent, but in practice this consideration is not as important as one might think. There are very severe constraints on the experiments that may be conducted on zoo animals. In an article entitled "A Search for Animal Models at Zoos," published in *ILAR News* in 1982, Richard Montali and Mitchell Bush drew the following conclusion:

> Despite the great potential of a zoo as a resource for models, there are many limitations and, of necessity, some restrictions for use. There is little opportunity to conduct overly manipulative or invasive research procedures—probably less than would be allowed in clinical research trials involving human beings. Many of the species are difficult to work with or are difficult to breed, so that the numbers of animals available for study are limited. In fact, it is safe to say that over the past years, humans have served more as "animal models" for zoo species than is true of the reverse.

Whether for this reason or others, much of what has been done in using zoo animals as models for humans seems redundant or trivial. For example, the article cited above reports that zoo animals provide good models for studying lead toxicity in humans, since it is common for zoo animals to develop lead poisoning from chewing paint and inhaling polluted city air. There are available for study plenty of humans who suffer from lead poisoning for the same reasons. That zoos make available some additional non-human subjects for this kind of research seems at best unimportant and at worst deplorable.

Finally, there is the goal of obtaining knowledge about animals for 22 its own sake. Knowledge is certainly something which is good and, everything being equal, we should encourage people to seek it for its own sake. For everything is not equal in this case. There is a moral presumption against keeping animals in captivity. This presumption can be overcome only by demonstrating that there are important benefits that must be obtained in this way if they are to be obtained at all. It is clear that this is not the case with knowledge for its own sake. There are other channels for our intellectual curiosity, ones that do not exact such a high moral price. Although our quest for knowledge for its own sake is important, it is not important enough to overcome the moral presumption against keeping animals in captivity.

In assessing the significance of research as a reason for having 23 zoos, it is important to remember that very few zoos do any research at all. Whatever benefits result from zoo research could just as well be obtained by having a few zoos instead of the hundreds which now exist. The most this argument could establish is that we are justified in having a few very good zoos. It does not provide a defense of the vast majority of zoos which now exist.

A fourth reason for having zoos is that they preserve species that 24
would otherwise become extinct. As the destruction of habitat acceler-
ates and as breeding programs become increasingly successful, this
rationale for zoos gains in popularity. There is some reason for questioning the commitment of zoos to preservation: it can be argued that
they continue to remove more animals from the wild than they return.
Still, zoo breeding programs have had some notable successes: without them the Père David Deer, the Mongolian Wild Horse and the
European Bison would all now be extinct. Recently, however, some
problems have begun to be noticed.

A 1979 study by Katherine Ralls, Kristin Brugger and Jonathan 25
Ballou, which was reported in *Science,* convincingly argues that lack of
genetic diversity among captive animals is a serious problem for zoo
breeding programs. In some species the infant mortality rate among
inbred animals is six or seven times that among non-inbred animals. In
other species the infant mortality rate among inbred animals is 100
percent. What is most disturbing is that zoo curators have been largely
unaware of the problems caused by inbreeding because adequate
breeding and health records have not been kept. It is hard to believe
that zoos are serious about their role in preserving endangered species
when all too often they do not take even this minimal step.

In addition to these problems, the lack of genetic diversity among 26
captive animals also means that surviving members of endangered
species have traits very different from their conspecifics in the wild.
This should make us wonder what is really being preserved in zoos.
Are captive Mongolian Wild Horses really Mongolian Wild Horses in
any but the thinnest biological sense?

There is another problem with zoo breeding programs: they create 27
many unwanted animals. In some species (lions, tigers and zebras, for
example) a few males can service an entire herd. Extra males are
unnecessary to the program and are a financial burden. Some of these
animals are sold and wind up in the hands of individuals and institutions which lack proper facilities. Others are shot and killed by Great
White Hunters in private hunting camps. In order to avoid these
problems, some zoos have been considering proposals to "recycle"
excess animals: a euphemism for killing them and feeding their bodies
to other zoo animals. Many people are surprised when they hear of
zoos killing animals. They should not be. Zoos have limited capacities.
They want to maintain diverse collections. This can be done only by
careful management of their "stock."

Even if breeding programs were run in the best possible way, 28
there are limits to what can be done to save endangered species. For
many large mammals a breeding herd of at least a hundred animals,
half of them born in captivity, is required if they are to survive in zoos.

As of 1971 only eight mammal species satisfied these conditions. Paul and Anne Ehrlich estimate in their book *Extinction* that under the best possible conditions American zoos could preserve only about a hundred species of mammals—and only at a very high price: maintaining a breeding herd of herbivores costs between $75,000 and $250,000 per year.

There are further questions one might ask about preserving en- 29 dangered species in zoos. Is it really better to confine a few hapless Mountain Gorillas in a zoo than to permit the species to become extinct? To most environmentalists the answer is obvious: the species must be preserved at all costs. But this smacks of sacrificing the lower-case gorilla for the upper-case Gorilla. In doing this, aren't we using animals as mere vehicles for their genes? Aren't we preserving genetic material at the expense of the animals themselves? If it is true that we are inevitably moving towards a world in which Mountain Gorillas can survive only in zoos, then we must ask whether it is really better for them to live in artificial environments of our design than not to be born at all.

Even if all of these difficulties are overlooked, the importance of 30 preserving endangered species does not provide much support for the existing system of zoos. Most zoos do very little breeding or breed only species which are not endangered. Many of the major breeding programs are run in special facilities which have been established for that purpose. They are often located in remote places, far from the attention of zoo-goers. (For example, the Bronx Zoo operates its Rare Animal Survival Center on St. Catherine's Island off the coast of Georgia, and the National Zoo runs its Conservation and Research Center in the Shenandoah Valley of Virginia.) If our main concern is to do what we can to preserve endangered species, we should support such large-scale breeding centers rather than conventional zoos, most of which have neither the staff nor the facilities to run successful breeding programs.

The four reasons for having zoos which I have surveyed carry 31 some weight. But different reasons provide support for different kinds of zoo. Preservation and perhaps research are better carried out in large-scale animal preserves, but these provide few opportunities for amusement and education. Amusement and perhaps education are better provided in urban zoos, but they offer few opportunities for research and preservation. Moreover, whatever benefits are obtained from any kind of zoo must confront the moral presumption against keeping wild animals in captivity. Which way do the scales tip? There are two further considerations which, in my view, tip the scales against zoos.

First, captivity does not just deny animals liberty but is often 32
detrimental to them in other respects as well. The history of chimpanzees in the zoos of Europe and America is a good example.

Chimpanzees first entered the zoo world in about 1640 when a 33
Dutch prince, Frederick Henry of Nassau, obtained one for his castle
menagerie. The chimpanzee didn't last very long. In 1835 the London
Zoo obtained its first chimpanzee; he died immediately. Another was
obtained in 1845; she lived six months. All through the nineteenth and
early twentieth centuries zoos obtained chimpanzees who promptly
died within nine months. It wasn't until the 1930s that it was discovered that chimpanzees are extremely vulnerable to human respiratory
diseases, and that special steps must be taken to protect them. But for
nearly a century zoos removed them from the wild and subjected them
to almost certain death. Problems remain today. When chimpanzees
are taken from the wild the usual procedure is to shoot the mother and
kidnap the child. The rule of thumb among trappers is that ten chimpanzees die for every one that is delivered alive to the United States or
Europe. On arrival many of these animals are confined under abysmal
conditions.

Chimpanzees are not the only animals to suffer in zoos. In 1974 34
Peter Batten, former director of the San Jose Zoological Gardens,
undertook an exhaustive study of two hundred American zoos. In
his book *Living Trophies* he documented large numbers of neurotic,
overweight animals kept in cramped, cold cells and fed unpalatable
synthetic food. Many had deformed feet and appendages caused by
unsuitable floor surfaces. Almost every zoo studied had excessive
mortality rates, resulting from preventable factors ranging from van-
dalism to inadequate husbandry practices. Batten's conclusion was:
"The majority of American zoos are badly run, their direction incom-
petent, and animal husbandry inept and in some cases nonexistent."

Many of these same conditions and others are documented in 35
Pathology of Zoo Animals, a review of necropsies conducted by Lynn
Griner over the last fourteen years at the San Diego Zoo. This zoo may
well be the best in the country, and its staff is clearly well-trained and
well-intentioned. Yet this study documents widespread malnutrition
among zoo animals; high mortality rates from the use of anaesthetics
and tranquilizers; serious injuries and deaths sustained in transport;
and frequent occurrences of cannibalism, infanticide and fighting almost certainly caused by overcrowded conditions. Although the zoo
has learned from its mistakes, it is still unable to keep many wild
animals in captivity without killing or injuring them, directly or indirectly. If this is true of the San Diego Zoo, it is certainly true, to an even
greater extent, at most other zoos.

The second consideration is more difficult to articulate but is, to 36
my mind, even more important. Zoos teach us a false sense of our
place in the natural order. The means of confinement mark a difference
between humans and animals. They are there at our pleasure, to be
used for our purposes. Morality and perhaps our very survival require
that we learn to live as one species among many rather than as one
species over many. To do this, we must forget what we learn at zoos.
Because what zoos teach us is false and dangerous, both humans and
animals will be better off when they are abolished.

QUESTIONS AND IDEAS FOR DISCUSSION

1.   Jamieson begins with a history of zoos. What are the effects (on
you, the reader) of his doing so? Does his history of zoos strike you as
fair and even-handed, or obviously biased? Give examples.

2.   In paragraphs 6 through 8, Jamieson argues a series of claims.
Does he convince you in this passage that "there is a moral pre-
sumption against keeping animals in captivity" (paragraph 6)?
Comment.

3.   Of the four reasons for having zoos that Jamieson challenges,
which do you find he challenges most successfully? Least successfully? In both cases, why?

4.   This is a long essay. Are you able to follow Jamieson's argument
without difficulty? How does he hold your attention, or at what points
does he lose it?

5.   The last point of this essay (in the final paragraph) is also the
shortest. Could this point, or should it, be developed more fully?
Comment.

The Challenge

JAKE PAGE

Jake Page is a writer who specializes in scientific subjects. From 1970
to 1976, he was science editor of *Smithsonian* magazine, and he was
subsequently founding editor of the Natural History Press, Smithsonian books, and *Smithsonian Air and Space*. He is the author of more
than a dozen books, including *Lords of the Air* and *Songs to Birds*. His
most recent work is *Zoo: The Modern Ark* (1990), a book beautifully
illustrated by the photographs of Franz Maier. In "The Challenge,"

which is the final chapter of *Zoo,* Page argues that "without zoos, there will be no solution" to the loss of species through global warming.

When the Spanish conquistador Coronado reached what is now 1 northern Arizona in the 1500s, he came across a large canyon, at the bottom of which was a stream. Routinely, he sent some men down for water, and they were gone a very long time. He had arrived at the Grand Canyon, and there was nothing in his own experience or in the geological perspective to let him know that the stream was a large river and that it was flowing about a mile below him.

Similarly, there is no way for a child watching what he or she 2 knows is called an elephant on a television set to really see how really huge it is. No amount of film footage can substitute for the awe and delight of seeing and smelling one in the flesh, and for that experience most people have to go to a zoo.

Zoos, along with aquariums and game parks, are one of the great- 3 est potential tools available to society to alter the attitudes of a significant proportion of mankind, to create a deep-seated awareness that we are not rightfully the overlords of this planet but share it with a vast and beautiful array of life-forms, each with intrinsic merit. With a proper attention to a conservation message and ethic in its exhibits, zoos of the world have the opportunity to help create almost a quarter of a billion new conservationists each year, and they are beginning to take on the task.

As long as the gates of zoos are open to the public, however, their 4 most important function will continue to be entertainment, and not just for children. Studies in several U.S. zoos and in Frankfurt have confirmed that, contrary to conventional wisdom, by far more adults and teenagers attend zoos than do small children. Yet, a whole generation of people in Europe and North America has grown up amid a plethora of attractive nature books and wildlife films on television. For this sophisticated audience, it is more necessary than ever to have active animals doing interesting things in a naturalistic setting that reflects the animals' natural habitat. One technique, as at the Toronto Zoo and the San Diego Wildlife Park, is the geographic zoo. At Toronto, lions spend time in a large, well-planted enclosure and can see herds of African gazelle next door. Occasionally a lioness will be seen stalking toward the gazelles. The Dallas Zoo has begun to build a 55-acre (22 ha) "Wilds of Africa," to be the first zoo exhibit anywhere to show every major habitat of the continent. The gorilla habitat takes the visitor along a rain-forest pathway and inside a thatched field research station from which the apes can be observed much as a field biologist would. The Brookfield Zoo in Chicago houses under one roof replicas of three rain forests—Asian, African and South American—accompanied by artificial thunder and rain. Tropical rain-forest replicas have been added to numerous zoos, and more are to come. These are sometimes called "immersion" exhibits. The visitor enters a new environment altogether, feels the humidity, hears the sounds of water, the calls of birds, the growl of a tiger long before catching a glimpse of them.

Such exhibits are not only more entertaining for a more sophisti- 5 cated public but are more educational. This, they say, is pretty much how it is in a rain forest, or at a waterhole on the veld. More and more zoos are cooperating with local natural-history museums, to broaden their own exhibits with museum material and also to liven up museums with live animal displays. The Emen Zoo in north Holland is linked directly to two museums—one that tells the story of evolution by displaying live animals and fossils side by side, and a natural-history museum devoted to changing biological themes such as reproduction or the senses. Another entertainment/education device used by zoos, notably by the St. Louis Zoo, are the "interactive" exhibits employed by many science museums where computerized "games" designed to teach various biological concepts lead one along the path of learning.

In zoo after zoo, the message of these education programs is 6 increasingly focused on conservation—endangered species and the loss of wildlife habitat. In a world of some 5 billion people, and soon to be twice that, it may seem a bit quixotic to educate some 250 million people (mostly already well educated and middle class) each year about the beauty and necessity of wildlife and the need to preserve it and its habitat. Certainly, education is not the only answer, but it can fairly be said that without this kind of understanding, there will be no solution to the problem. And it is precisely such an educated constituency that will help persuade governments, businesses and other funding sources to aid the expensive work that the revolutionary zoo of today is performing on behalf of genetic diversity.

That mankind is going to have to change a lot of expensive habits 7 is rapidly becoming clear—not just from wildlife advocates and other environmentalists but from a complex series of events that we have unwittingly set in motion that may well bring about one of the fastest climatic shifts in the earth's history. This is, of course, the greenhouse effect—the rapid accumulation of gases in the atmosphere (especially carbon dioxide and methane) that let the sun's heat in but keep it from readily escaping. The tendency, thus, is for the earth to heat up, and some scientists say it has already begun. Few dispute that it will occur to some extent. A worst-case estimate has the average global temperature rising as much as five degrees in the next fifty years. Predictions suggest that the warming would be less drastic in the tropics—one or two degrees—and most severe in polar regions—a whopping twelve degrees.

An early effect would be the melting of the ice caps; it is only on [8] polar ice floes that the polar bear, walrus and a variety of seals live. With the floes gone, such animals would have to live in zoos, and probably forever. And, of course, melting ice means higher sea levels. The level of the sea has risen about a foot (30 cm) globally in the past century for reasons that remain obscure, and beaches have been steadily eroding, marshlands filling with standing saltwater. Some greenhouse prognosticators say that a 5 foot (1.5 m) rise in fifty years is possible, far more than is needed to completely drown such places as Florida's subtropical wonderland, the Everglades, as well as virtually every coral reef in the world. (It is more than a natural-history oddity that alligator eggs that hatch at about 80°F [30°C] produce females, while those that hatch at about 93°F [34°C] produce males. The last wild alligators might consist of an entire geriatric generation of males.)

To truly predict the extent and the overall, much less regional, [9] effects of global warming is, so far, beyond the largest computers' capacity, but a few ecologists have developed likely scenarios. Dry areas, such as the American Southwest, could become wetter. An odd result would be that more grass would grow, to densities that would support large brushfires in the dry months that would wipe out most cacti, which are not fire resistant and some of which serve as the exclusive home for certain animal species, for example, owls. In mountain areas, warm-weather zones would move up the slopes, forcing colder zones upward and, because mountains are basically cone-shaped, such zones would inevitably grow smaller, their wildlife diminishing in number and becoming subject to all the dangers inherent in small populations. Reserves set aside for certain species arrays would become unsuitable as their ecological systems changed. Planners have pointed out that wildlife could move away, toward cooler realms, if we were to supply corridors of natural habitat out of the reserves. But most such reserves are virtual islands, surrounded by the implacable barriers of human habitation and activity, and there is little reason to believe that ecosystems, such as forests, are capable of migrating as fast as they would have to. At the end of the Pleistocene, some 10,000 years ago, beech forests in the United States chased the receding ice northward at the rate of 12 miles (20 km) per century. It has been estimated that, if atmospheric carbon dioxide were to double in less than a century, beech forests would have to move 310 miles (500 km) in the same period to be in a suitable climate.

No one is truly expecting the worst-case scenario to come about. [10] Presumably, we will find a way to ameliorate the effects of global warming by changing our habits. And, possibly, some of the measures taken to preserve the climate will also serve to alter some of the human activity that is eliminating wildlife habitat at today's alarming and growing rate. But that there will be a wave of extinctions in any event is certain. The loss of a few acres of tropical rain forest can eradicate untold numbers of insect species. Presently it is estimated that about 2,000 of the approximately 11,000 species of birds and mammals of the world are endangered in the wild. If all the world's zoos were to give themselves over exclusively to captive-breeding programs, they could still handle only some 800 species. Zoos aren't the only answer to this growing problem and no one is more aware of this than the people who work in them. But, it can fairly be said that, without zoos, there will be no solution. Zoos remain among the most crucial garrisons of life in a planetary war of attrition, a war the extent of which cannot be predicted but one for which future generations will hold us utterly responsible.

QUESTIONS AND IDEAS FOR DISCUSSION

1.   What purpose does Page's introduction, with its unusual analogy, serve in his argument? Is the introduction successful—that is, does it engage your interest? Comment.

2.   How strong a case does Jake Page make for global warming as a reason to defend and support the work of zoos? Explain.

3.   Many people who oppose zoos do so in part on the grounds that zoos are frivolous, primarily intended for entertainment. Page concedes early in the essay that zoos' "most important function will continue to be entertainment" (paragraph 4). How (if at all) does the concession affect the strength of Page's argument?

Why Zoos Disappoint

JOHN BERGER

John Berger is a renowned English art critic who has written fiction— from screenplays to novels—as well as art reviews. His art criticism has been gathered into several books, most recently *The Sense of Sight: Writings* (1986). His recent fiction includes *Once in Europe* (1987), a collection of short stories. John Berger's interest in zoos, as expressed in the following excerpt from his book *About Looking* (1980), is related to his interest in art museums: Both are places designed for the public to view things of beauty at firsthand. But Berger's perspective—on both art and animals—is a radical one; moreover, he raises issues that many people have never considered. He raised these issues first for the readers of *New Society* magazine, in which this essay appeared in 1977.

"About 1867," according to the *London Zoo Guide*, "a music hall 1 artist called the Great Vance sang a song called *Walking in the zoo is the OK thing to do,* and the word 'zoo' came into everyday use. London Zoo also brought the word 'Jumbo' into the English language. Jumbo was an African elephant of mammoth size, who lived at the zoo between 1865 and 1882. Queen Victoria took an interest in him and eventually he ended his days as the star of the famous Barnum circus which travelled through America—his name living on to describe things of giant proportions."

Public zoos came into existence at the beginning of the period 2 which was to see the disappearance of animals from daily life. The zoo to which people go to meet animals, to observe them, to see them, is, in fact, a monument to the impossibility of such encounters. Modern zoos are an epitaph to a relationship which was as old as man. They are not seen as such because the wrong questions have been addressed to zoos.

When they were founded—the London Zoo in 1828, the Jardin 3 des Plantes [in Paris] in 1793, the Berlin Zoo in 1844, they brought considerable prestige to the national capitals. The prestige was not so different from that which had accrued to the private royal menageries. These menageries, along with gold plate, architecture, orchestras, players, furnishings, dwarfs, acrobats, uniforms, horses, art and food, had been demonstrations of an emperor's or king's power and wealth. Likewise in the 19th century, public zoos were an endorsement of modern colonial power. The capturing of animals was a symbolic representation of the conquest of all distant and exotic lands. "Explorers" proved their patriotism by sending home a tiger or an elephant. The gift of an exotic animal to the metropolitan zoo became a token in subservient diplomatic relations.

Yet, like every other 19th century public institution, the zoo, 4 however supportive of the ideology of imperialism, had to claim an independent and civic function. The claim was that it was another kind of museum, whose purpose was to further knowledge and public enlightenment. And so the first questions asked of zoos belonged to natural history; it was then thought possible to study the natural life of animals even in such unnatural conditions. A century later, more sophisticated zoologists such as Konrad Lorenz asked behavioristic and ethological questions, the claimed purpose of which was to discover more about the springs of human action through the study of animals under experimental conditions.

Meanwhile, millions visited the zoos each year out of a curiosity 5 which was both so large, so vague and so personal that it is hard to express in a single question. Today in France 22 million people visit the 200 zoos each year. A high proportion of the visitors were and are children.

Children in the industrialized world are surrounded by animal 6 imagery: toys, cartoons, pictures, decorations of every sort. No other source of imagery can begin to compete with that of animals. The apparently spontaneous interest that children have in animals might lead one to suppose that this has always been the case. Certainly some of the earliest toys (when toys were unknown to the vast majority of the population) were animal. Equally, children's games, all over the world, include real or pretended animals. Yet it was not until the 19th century that reproductions of animals became a regular part of the decor of middle class childhoods—and then, in this century, with the advent of vast display and selling systems like Disney's—of all childhoods.

In the preceding centuries, the proportion of toys which were 7 animal, was small. And these did not pretend to realism, but were symbolic. The difference was that between a traditional hobby horse and a rocking horse: the first was merely a stick with a rudimentary head which children rode like a broom handle: the second was an elaborate "reproduction" of a horse, painted realistically, with real reins of leather, a real mane of hair, and designed movement to resemble that of a horse galloping. The rocking horse was a 19th century invention.

This new demand for verisimilitude in animal toys led to different 8 methods of manufacture. The first stuffed animals were produced, and the most expensive were covered with real animal skin—usually the skin of still-born calves. The same period saw the appearance of soft animals—bears, tigers, rabbits—such as children take to bed with them. Thus the manufacture of realistic animal toys coincides, more or less, with the establishment of public zoos.

The family visit to the zoo is often a more sentimental occasion 9 than a visit to a fair or a football match. Adults take children to the zoo to show them the originals of their "reproductions," and also perhaps in the hope of re-finding some of the innocence of that reproduced animal world which they remember from their own childhood.

The animals seldom live up to the adults' memories, whilst to the 10 children they appear, for the most part, unexpectedly lethargic and dull. (As frequent as the calls of animals in a zoo, are the cries of children demanding: Where is he? Why doesn't he move? Is he dead?)

And so one might summarize the felt, but not necessarily expressed, question of most visitors as: Why are these animals less than I believed?

And this unprofessional, unexpressed question is the one worth 11 answering.

A zoo is a place where as many species and varieties of animal as 12 possible are collected in order that they can be seen, observed, studied. In principle, each cage is a frame round the animal inside it. Visitors visit the zoo to look at animals. They proceed from cage to cage, not unlike visitors in an art gallery who stop in front of one painting, and then move on to the next or the one after next. Yet in the zoo the view is always wrong. Like an image out of focus. One is so accustomed to this that one scarcely notices it any more; or, rather, the apology habitually anticipates the disappointment, so that the latter is not felt. And the apology runs like this: What do you expect? It's not a dead object you have come to look at, it's alive. It's leading its own life. Why should this coincide with its being properly visible? Yet the reasoning of this apology is inadequate. The truth is more startling.

However you look at these animals, even if the animal is up 13 against the bars, less than a foot from you, looking outwards in the public direction, *you are looking at something that has been rendered absolutely marginal;* and all the concentration you can muster will never be enough to centralize it. Why is this?

Within limits, the animals are free, but both they themselves, and 14 their spectators, presume on their close confinement. The visibility through the glass, the spaces between the bars, or the empty air above the moat, are not what they seem—if they were, then everything would be changed. Thus, visibility, space, air, have been reduced to tokens.

The decor, accepting these elements as tokens, sometimes repro- 15 duces them to create pure illusion—as in the case of painted prairies or painted rock pools at the back of the boxes for small animals. Sometimes it merely adds further tokens to suggest something of the animal's original landscape—the dead branches of a tree for monkeys, artificial rocks for bears, pebbles and shallow water for crocodiles. These added tokens serve two distinct purposes: for the spectator they are like theater props: for the animal they constitute the bare minimum of an environment in which they can physically exist.

The animals, isolated from each other and without interaction 16 between species, have become utterly dependent upon their keepers. Consequently most of their responses have been changed. What was central to their interest has been replaced by a passive waiting for a series of arbitrary outside interventions. The events they perceive occurring around them have become as illusory in terms of their natural responses, as the painted prairies. At the same time this very isolation (usually) guarantees their longevity as specimens and facilitates their taxonomic arrangement.

All this is what makes them marginal. The space which they 17 inhabit is artificial. Hence their tendency to bundle towards the edge of it. (Beyond its edges there may be real space.) In some cages the light is equally artificial. In all cases the environment is illusory. Nothing surrounds them except their own lethargy or hyperactivity. They have nothing to act upon—except, briefly, supplied food and—very occasionally—a supplied mate. (Hence their perennial actions become marginal actions without an object.) Lastly, their dependence and isolation have so conditioned their responses that they treat any event which takes place around them—usually it is in front of them, where the public is—as marginal. (Hence their assumption of an otherwise exclusively human attitude—indifference.)

Zoos, realistic animal toys and the widespread commercial diffu- 18 sion of animal imagery, all began as animals started to be withdrawn from daily life. One could suppose that such innovations were compensatory. Yet in reality the innovations themselves belonged to the same remorseless movement as was dispersing the animals. The zoos, with their theatrical decor for display, were in fact demonstrations of how animals had been rendered absolutely marginal. The realistic toys increased the demand for the new animal puppet: the urban pet. The reproduction of animals in images—as their biological reproduction in birth becomes a rarer and rarer sight—was competitively forced to make animals ever more exotic and remote.

Everywhere animals disappear. In zoos they constitute the living 19 monument to their own disappearance. And in doing so, they provoked their last metaphor. *The Naked Ape, The Human Zoo,* are titles of world bestsellers. In these books the zoologist, Desmond Morris, proposes that the unnatural behavior of animals in captivity can help us to understand, accept and overcome the stresses involved in living in consumer societies.

All sites of enforced marginalization—ghettos, shanty towns, 20 prisons, madhouses, concentration camps—have something in common with zoos. But it is both too easy and too evasive to use the zoo as a symbol. The zoo is a demonstration of the relations between man and animals; nothing else. The marginalization of animals is today being followed by the marginalization and disposal of the only class who, throughout history, has remained familiar with animals and maintained the wisdom which accompanies that familiarity: the middle and small peasant. The basis of this wisdom is an acceptance of the dualism at the very origin of the relation between man and animal. The rejection of this dualism is probably an important factor in opening the way to modern totalitarianism. But I do not wish to go beyond the limits of that unprofessional, unexpressed but fundamental question asked of the zoo.

The zoo cannot but disappoint. The public purpose of zoos is to 21 offer visitors the opportunity of looking at animals. Yet nowhere in a zoo can a stranger encounter the look of an animal. At the most, the animal's gaze flickers and passes on. They look sideways. They look blindly beyond. They scan mechanically. They have been immunized to encounter, because nothing can any more occupy a *central* place in their attention.

Therein lies the ultimate consequence of their marginalization. 22 That look between animal and man, which may have played a crucial role in the development of human society, and with which, in any case, all men had always lived until less than a century ago, has been extinguished. Looking at each animal, the unaccompanied zoo visitor is alone. As for the crowds, they belong to a species which has at last been isolated.

This historic loss, to which zoos are a monument, is now irre- 23 deemable for the culture of capitalism.

QUESTIONS AND IDEAS FOR DISCUSSION

1. Why, according to Berger's argument, are zoos bound to disappoint? Is the argument sound? Evaluate its logic.

2. Berger compares zoos to museums, the animals in their cages to paintings: How does he use the comparison to argue against zoos? Explain.

3. Paraphrase and explain the last sentence of the essay in terms that another reader, finding it difficult to fully grasp, might readily comprehend. How does this conclusion function in the essay: Does it sum up, for instance, or point beyond the concerns argued?

4. Describe the author's political beliefs insofar as they are revealed through his argument about zoos. Are political ideas central or tangential to this argument? Discuss.

SUGGESTIONS FOR WRITING
AND FURTHER DISCUSSION

1. Go to a nearby zoo and observe the animals, the environment, and the visitors. What conclusions suggest themselves about that particular zoo? Assuming that it will not be dismantled (though you may choose to argue that it should be), how could it be improved? Argue your recommendations in an essay that would be appropriate for an audience consisting of the board of directors overseeing the zoo.

2. In Chapter 1, you read Nan Payne's essay-in-progress about the morality of zoos. In this chapter you have read additional essays on the subject, each advancing a different position. What is your viewpoint on zoos? Defend it in an argument that takes into account the several positions on zoos that you have read.

3. Jake Page argues that pictures are no substitutes for viewing real animals, so we must have zoos. What are the problems with his reasoning? Write an essay that refutes Pages's position (though you may choose not to mention Page or his essay specifically).

4. Does John Berger convincingly argue that zoos are "bound to disappoint"? Write an essay that counters the pessimism of Berger's argument. But be sure to reason at least as carefully as Berger does: Do not allow emotional appeals to substitute for rational ones.

5. Another means of seeing animals at close range is to attend a circus. But many people find circuses even less defensible than zoos. Should circuses be abolished? Write an essay in which you argue your answer to this question, with an audience in mind of college-educated people who attended—and enjoyed—circuses when they were children.

6. Decide which of the essays in this chapter argues its claims most effectively—whether or not you like or agree with its conclusions. Argue the reasons for your choice. (You may choose to comment on the difficulty, if any, of putting aside your own ideas about the issues while you judge the arguments.) Is the most effective argument the best written and the most clearly organized? The most logical? The best documented? Or is it more emotional than logical in its argument? What does the essay show you as a writer about ways to make a point well?

PART THREE

DATA AND DEBATE

In this section, you will find arguments and other supporting material to analyze and evaluate, and to which you can respond with your own arguments. The subjects are broad: the ethics of college sports programs, and the problems and possibilities of affirmative action. You will need to assess the reliability and expertise of the writers, the value of their evidence and arguments, the possibilities they may not have considered. Many issues and viewpoints are represented, but not all. The essays on sports do not take up the important problem of drug abuse among athletes, for example. (You may decide to research and argue a solution.) And the essays on affirmative action and reverse discrimination cover only a few of the multitude of aspects of these issues. (For instance, what about the problem of sex bias in the insurance industry? And is it a real problem, or only an apparent one?) So, despite the quantity of material you find here, plenty still remains to be discovered, considered, and argued about both college sports and affirmative action. You may challenge the following arguments, use the evidence they contain to support your own, or even explore an aspect of the subject they leave untouched. The possibilities are many.

14

COLLEGE SPORTS

Molding the Wrong Kind of Character
GEORGE WILL

Noted for his wit and incisive arguments, George Will is a politically conservative, Pulitzer Prize–winning author and speaker whose syndicated column appears nationwide, along with his biweekly *Newsweek* column. In this essay, published in *Newsweek* in November 1989, Will ventures out of the political arena into the athletic field. How might his arguments be refuted by a reader who disagrees with him? (Avoid the temptation to speculate about whether or not Will was cut from his high school football team.) Can it be argued that the situation has improved since 1989, that the problems Will points to no longer exist?

WASHINGTON—Crisp autumn Saturday morning, second cup 1 of coffee, sports pages full of football news.

Crime wave update from the University of Oklahoma: No more 2 shootings or cocaine busts, but the criminal justice system is booming some more Sooners, this time two convicted of rape. At Notre Dame, coach Lou Holtz is not having fun. His No. 1 ranked Irish are brawling with opponents (before kickoffs, on the field). University officials are delivering a forearm across the windpipe to the idea that Holtz was in any way connected with illegal payments to players at Minnesota, his last coaching stop.

Colorado is challenging Notre Dame for dominance. More than 3 two dozen Colorado players were arrested in a recent three-year period, charges ranging from trespassing, assault and burglary through rape. Hmmm. No news this day from Florida. But in a 22-day period the University of Florida fired its football coach (the one hired five years ago to replace a cheater) for cheating, and its basketball coach and three of his assistants, and lost two quarterbacks this autumn for gambling. It is hard to keep up that pace of scandal.

But the big story this morning is the NFL's permanent suspension 4
of Washington Redskins' defensive end Dexter Manley, for a third
drug offense. He is the second Redskin lost to drugs this month. Team
officials suspected trouble when Dexter missed an appointment with
his reading tutor.

Where did Manley learn that there really are no rules, that drug 5
laws are not serious, that football players can do an end-run around
reality? In school.

Before becoming a Redskin, Manley spent four years making a lot 6
of tackles and money for Oklahoma State University. Restaurateurs
and motel operators in Stillwater thank him. He left school without a
degree (like most NFL players) and still unable to read.

Now Manley has fumbled away millions of dollars. No more of the 7
custom-tailored suits he has been sporting for years. "I'm not gonna
say how I got them. It was my senior year in high school, so you put it
together. I had 37 scholarship offers. So, that's how it works."

Does college football form character? Sure does, by teaching cy- 8
nicism. Nearly one-third of NFL players responding to a survey say
they received illegal payments in college—slipped under dormitory
doors, passed in congratulatory handshakes, left in helmets.

Come for a stroll along the banks of the open sewer that runs 9
through many campuses. Read *The Hundred Yard Lie* by Rick Telander,
formerly lead college football writer for *Sports Illustrated*. Formerly. His
book is his declaration of incurable disgust.

I know, robust reader—yes, you there, looking at your watch, 10
counting the hours until kickoff—you are thinking: Lighten up. At
least the players are being prepared for a profession—football—and
meanwhile are generating pots of money for the math department.

False, twice. About one in 50 players makes it to the NFL, where 11
the average career lasts about three years. And virtually all the money
from the college football bypasses the school's general funds and flows
into the athletic department.

The only solution is to sever universities from this mega-entertain- 12
ment industry. If the NFL wants farm teams, let it do what baseball
does: Pay for them, far from campuses.

Four reforms would help: coaches paid comparably with other 13
faculty and given tenure; no freshman playing or practicing; no spring
practice, and no fall practice before classes start; no special admissions
or curricula for athletes. Some players currently take such courses as
Billiards, Jogging, Advanced Slow-Pitch Softball.

These reforms are utopian. "Student athletes" who attend real 14
classes? Coaches as faculty members rather than entrepreneurs?
Teams as appendages of universities rather than the other way
around? Preposterous. There is too much money and passion on the
other side.

Passion? A juror in a criminal trial swore in an affidavit that he had 15
been pressured by fellow jurors to change his vote from innocent to
guilty so that they could watch the Ohio State-Michigan game.

College football, like most other, smarmy features of American 16
life, prospers by popular demand.

Fair Play for Women?

ALLEN GUTTMANN

Allen Guttmann, a professor of American Studies at Amherst College, has also taught at several European and Japanese universities.
Guttmann's particular interest is the history of sports. Among his
scholarly books on sports are *The Games Must Go On: Avery Brundage
and the Olympic Movement* (1984), which the U. S. Olympic Committee
named its "Olympic Book of the Year," and *Sports Spectators* (1986).
Guttmann reminds us, in this essay excerpted from his *A Whole New
Ball Game: An Interpretation of American Sports* (1988), that one problem
college athletics must confront is long-standing inequities for women
in sports. Guttmann addresses the multiple dimensions of the problem. For example, if a school puts a girl on the boys' tennis team
because it has no girls' team, does it risk damaging her psychologi-
cally because her play is not likely to be as strong as that of her
teammates? "Can those who condemn boxing as brutal and dangerous welcome the entry of women into the ring?" Guttmann's purpose is to demonstrate and argue the complexity of the problem, not
to point to easy solutions.

It is doubtful that sports participation was an important consider- 1
ation in the legislative battles that culminated in the passage of Title IX
of the Education Act of 1972, but the increases in participation in
women's interscholastic and intercollegiate sports have certainly been
abetted by legal changes. Title IX made discrimination on the basis of
gender illegal in all institutions receiving federal support: "No person
. . . shall, on the basis of sex, be excluded from participation in, be
denied the benefits of, or be subjected to discrimination under any
educational programs or activities receiving federal financial assistance." That the inequalities between men's and women's programs
were gross is undeniable. The Syracuse, New York, school board's
1969 budget for extracurricular sports allocated $90,000 to the boys'
teams and $200 to the girls'; when money grew tight, the board elimi-
nated the girls' budget. At the University of New Mexico, the 1970–71
budget for men's sports was $527,000 and for women's sports $9,150.
In comparison to the University of Washington's budget, New Mexico's was wildly feminist: in Seattle in 1973–74, the men received

$2,582,000 and the women $18,000. In response to moral and legal pressure, Washington increased the women's 1974–75 budget to $200,000.

That Title IX has made a difference can also be seen in the before- 2 and-after legal judgments. When Susan Hollander of Hamden, Connecticut, sued her school board for the right to run with the boys' cross-country team because there was no girls' team, John Clark Fitz-Gerald of New Haven Superior Court ruled that

> our younger male population has not become so decadent that boys will experience a thrill in defeating girls in running contests. . . . It could well be that many boys would feel compelled to forgo entering track events if they were required to compete with girls. . . . With boys vying with girls . . . the challenge to win and the glory of achievement, at least for many boys, would lose incentive and become nullified. Athletic competition builds character in our boys. We do not need that kind of character in our girls.[1]

In *Gregorio* v. *Board of Education of Asbury Park* (1971), which was also decided before the passage of Title IX, the Superior Court of New Jersey ruled that girls had no right to join the boys' tennis team merely because there was no girls' team. After the new law came into effect, the U. S. Court of Appeals for the 6th District of Michigan ruled, in *Morris* v. *Michigan Board of Education* (1973), that girls had the right to try out for the boys' tennis team even when there was also a girls' team. The drive toward equality was partially blocked, however, when the Supreme Court decided, in *Grove City College* v. *Bell* (1984), that illegal discrimination within a single department was not grounds for action against an entire college or university. If the geologists refuse to hire women, they are liable to lose their own federal grants, but their colleagues in physical education will continue to be funded.

Although Title IX has forced changes, it has not wrought miracles. 3 Walter Byers of the NCAA lobbied hard against Title IX because it spelled "the possible doom of intercollegiate sports." As the bill approached a final vote, the NCAA fought for Senator John Tower's amendment, which would have exempted the "revenue-producing" sports, most of which turn out to be men's sports. The lobbying failed, but most athletic departments are controlled by men and many continue to resist full implementation of the law.[2]

Debates continue on the meaning of equality. The radical view is 4 that parity must be calculated on the basis of the male/female ratio of

---

[1] John Clark FitzGerald quoted in Bil Gilbert and Nancy Williamson, "Sport Is Unfair to Women," *Sports Illustrated* 38 (May 28, 1973): 95.

[2] Walter Byers quoted in Linda Jean Carpenter, "The Impact of Title IX on Women's Intercollegiate Sports," in *Government and Sport*, ed. Arthur T. Johnson and James H. Frey (Totowa, N.J.: Rowman and Allanheld, 1985), p. 63.

the entire student body; if 52 percent of the *students* are women, female athletes should receive 52 percent of the funding. The more moderate view, accepted by the Department of Education, is that the males and females actually participating in sports form the relevant population: if 30 percent of the *athletes* are female, women's sports should receive 30 percent of the money. Having failed to prevent the enactment of Title IX, the NCAA has been less than Draconian in its enforcement efforts. In the spring of 1984, the organization ruled that a school's failure to equalize the number of male and female teams would be punished by a ban on a national competition—for the women's teams. One suspects that some NCAA members are poor losers.

Debates continue about the opportunity for women to play on 5 men's teams. Many male athletes still feel that their masculinity is undermined by women who outperform them. When Jan Merrill, a middle-distance runner, ran against eight men in a two-mile race in 1979, she came in fifth, which so unnerved Fitchburg College coach Jim Sheehan that he cried out, "I'd die before I would ever be beaten by a woman." Of the Auburn University student whom Becky Birchmore defeated while a member of the University of Georgia men's tennis team, Coach Dan Magill lamented, "It ruined him. I really wish I hadn't done it." Ellen Cornish of Frederick, Maryland, had no chance to ruin the lives of the boys from Thomas Johnson High School; she was dragged from the track before she broke the tape.[3]

Even if one feels that male athletes who are defeated by female 6 athletes will have to live with their fates, other questions remain to be answered. Federal law is currently interpreted to mean that girls whose high school have no girls' tennis team have the right to play on the boys' team, but this may not be the best solution. Most of the girls who play on boys' teams are liable to perform at a level below that of their male teammates. Does this cause the girls psychological damage? And what is the equitable solution to the dilemma of boys who want to join the girls' team because their school has no boys' team in their chosen sport? This may seem like a foolish question, but National Public Radio for August 31, 1986, broadcast a report from Annapolis High School, where two boys have requested to be allowed to join the girls' field hockey team.

On average, men are taller and heavier than women, have faster 7 reaction times, more acute vision, better spatial perception, and greater muscular strength. Women, on the other hand, are more flexible than men and surpass men at very long distance running and

---

[3] Jim Sheehan quoted in Anita Verschoth, "She's His Fair Lady," *Sports Illustrated* 50 (February 26, 1979): 35; Dan Magill quoted in Bil Gilbert and Nancy Williamson, "Programmed to Be Losers," *Sports Illustrated* 38 (June 11, 1973): 62.

swimming. With these physiological facts in mind, Jane English has suggested that we "should develop a variety of sports in which a variety of physical types can expect to excel." If the sports in which women outperform men were as salient in the public's imagination as the sports in which men have the physical advantage, then women would more likely be perceived as men's physical equals. Through their superiority in these "alternative sports" women would have an opportunity to gain in self-respect, which English describes as a "basic benefit" of sports which should be available to all women. Whether such sports can realistically be expected to attain the prestige and popularity of baseball, basketball, football, ice hockey, and other male-dominated sports is, however, questionable.[4]

Some feminists have stressed the cultural factors behind the phys-   8 ical differentials and have concluded that women do not need alternate sports because women have the undeveloped physical potential to equal men's performances in the modern sports now dominated by male athletes. These feminists are correct to assert that socialization, rather than genetic endowment, explains why the average American woman attains her maximum strength at the age of twelve and a half while the strength of the average man continues to increase into his twenties, but it is unlikely that cultural factors can account for *all* the observed gender differences in strength and in sports performance. In official contests (as opposed to recreational situations) a commitment to equality dictates that, as a general rule, men be matched against men and women against women. The ideal legal solution therefore takes into account physical differences when these differences are relevant to athletic performance.[5]

Finally, ethical questions arise for which there are now no satisfac-   9 tory legal answers. Can those who condemn boxing as brutal and dangerous welcome the entry of women into the ring? Should we rejoice that some women now have the chance to suffer the brain damage that is the boxer's occupational hazard? One might respond that boxing should be made illegal for both sexes, but other questions remain. Is the development of female bodybuilding an indication that women are determined to be strong and independent, as proponents say? Or is it a humiliating sign that they merely wish to imitate men? What is the moralist to make of the use of anabolic steroids by women who seek greater muscle mass than can be obtained by Nautilus

---

[4] Jane English, "Sex Equality in Sports," *Philosophy and Public Affairs* 7, no. 3 (Spring 1978): 275, 277.

[5] Jackie Hudson, "Physical Parameters . . . ," in *Women and Sport*, ed. Carole A. Oglesby (Philadelphia: Lea and Febiger, 1978), pp. 19–57; Ann Crittenden Scott, "Closing the Muscle Gap," *Ms.* 3 (September 1974): 49–50, 54, 89; E. A. E. Ferris, "Attitudes to Women in Sport," in *The Female Athlete*, ed. J. Borms, M. Hebbelinck, and A. Venerando (Basel Karger, 1981), pp. 12–29.

workouts alone? Putting the question more generally, *are* there physical and psychological differences between males and females that might allow women to create humane alternatives to some of the distortions and abuses of modern sports?

Back to the Future: Reform with a Woman's Voice

LINDA JEAN CARPENTER AND R. VIVIAN ACOSTA

Linda Jean Carpenter and Vivian Acosta are professors of physical education at Brooklyn College of the City University of New York. This essay was first published in 1991 in *Academe*, the journal of the American Association of University Professors (AAUP). Its original audience was therefore people who, as university officers, members of faculty senates, or otherwise active members of academic institutions, potentially have the chance to effect real changes in college sports programs. Carpenter and Acosta believe that a "female model" of college sports programs, exemplified by the Association of Intercollegiate Athletics for Women of the 1970s, should replace the "male model" exemplified by the history and practices of the NCAA. Do Carpenter and Acosta unfairly stereotype men and women in this essay? Do they fail to consider that many members of their audience will be male—and thereby fail to be fully persuasive? Or do they convincingly argue their point that reform "with a woman's voice" will improve college sports programs for all students, male and female?

The deep and systemic problems of NCAA- and male-dominated 1 college athletics may or may not have solutions. But a growing chorus urging reform is being heard—one to which women need to add their voices. As the brief, ultimately sad history of the Association of Intercollegiate Athletics for Women (AIAW) will show, a model of competitive but humane intercollegiate athletics once existed. Ironically, the NCAA demolished it in the wake of federal legislation intended to provide equity, including equity for women in sports. Those looking for ways to reform the NCAA—as well as reasons the NCAA will never reform itself—need look no further than recent history.

Through the 1960s, women involved in interscholastic and inter- 2 collegiate athletics programs were under the direction of an education-oriented organization made up mostly of women physical educators. Almost universally, athletics programs for females had female coaches and athletic directors. "Ladylike" participation and avoidance of intense competition had historically characterized the program. These characteristics existed to protect females from the perceived ills of men's athletics, and also because most people accepted that females should not, could not, or did not want to compete in sports as intensely as their male counterparts. Of course, times change.

In the early 1970s, two nearly simultaneous events fostered an 3 explosion of interest and participation in women's sports. The AIAW was founded in 1971 by female physical educators who recognized that society's definitions of gender roles were changing. They saw a developing need for the option of more intense competition for the nation's college women as well as its men. Congress enacted Title IX a few months later, in 1972, and gave legislative support to the idea that sex discrimination had no place in education institutions or in their gymnasia and on their playing fields.[1] Only 16,000 women participated in intercollegiate athletics in 1966. A decade later, the number had grown to over 64,000, and now stands at about 158,000. Growth in participation occurred both at the elite level and at the participation-for-its-own-sake level.

Female leaders in American athletics had always hoped to develop 4 a participation model for women that was not necessarily bound by the male model of the NCAA. With the twin advances of the early 1970s, women seemed to have both the desire and the power to move forward in the construction of such a model.

Although colleges and universities did not need to comply with 5 Title IX until 1978, the six years between its enactment and the compliance date saw massive changes. In the name of Title IX, previously separate men's and women's departments of athletics were combined. Almost always, the head of the men's program became head of both the men's and women's programs in the newly combined department, relegating the previous female head administrator to a secondary or tertiary position. Thus, AIAW's and Title IX's anticipated enhancement of the role of women as leaders in athletics programs was not taking place in the 1970s.

During the early and mid-1970s, Title IX was also having an impact 6 on national governance of athletics. Walter Byers, the NCAA executive director at the time, expressed fears held by many male athletic directors when he said that Title IX's call for equity would mean "the possible doom of [men's] intercollegiate sports."[2] These fears were grounded in the notion that establishing equity for women's programs

---

[1] Title IX of the Education Amendments provides that "No person in the United States shall, on the basis of sex, be excluded from participation in, be denied the benefits of, or be subjected to discrimination under any education program or activity receiving Federal financial assistance. . . . " (U. S. Commission on Civil Rights, 180, Section 1681–1686).

[2] Bart Barnes and N. Scannell, "No Sporting Chance: The Girls in the Locker Room," *The Washington Post*, May 12, 1974, A14.

would mean extracting funds and power from the men's programs. Accordingly, soon after the enactment of Title IX, the NCAA tried, through the judicial and legislative systems, to exclude athletics from Title IX.

The NCAA's intense lobbying efforts early in 1974 at the Department of Health, Education and Welfare were the beginning of a series of political strategies that supported very inconsistent and opportunistic points of view. First it lobbied for the exclusion of athletics from Title IX. When that effort failed, the NCAA launched a strong campaign supporting the Tower Amendment, which sought to exclude revenue sports from the jurisdiction of Title IX. The Tower Amendment passed the Senate, but died in committee in June 1974.[3]

The NCAA, however, redoubled its efforts. The intensity and questionable integrity of these efforts were remarkable, even among those who experienced lobbying every day. Title IX was an emotional issue, and feelings ran high. Gwen Gregory, an HEW attorney, said at the time that the NCAA "is determined to sabotage Title IX. . . . They're throwing in red herrings, asking us to be arbitrary. A good deal of the reaction so far to Title IX has been panicky and alarmist, and some of it deliberately distorted."[4] Turning to the courts, the NCAA in *NCAA* v. *Califano* argued the inapplicability of Title IX to athletics on constitutional grounds. It lost again.[5]

Even these losses did not stop the NCAA. Having argued unsuccessfully in Congress and the courts that Title IX should not apply to athletics, it tried a different tactic, portraying the issue as one of athletic governance. To do so, the NCAA had to interpret Title IX as a mandate for NCAA's governing both men's *and* women's athletics under the principle "If you can't beat them, take them over."

What would the NCAA be taking over? According to Charlotte West, AIAW's president in 1978, "The AIAW was serving 100,000 female student-athletes and offering seventeen national championships in twelve different sports . . . the AIAW demonstrated that a progressive, humanistic concept of sport in an education framework is workable and viable."[6] Did the NCAA ploy to take over AIAW make sense? Again in the words of Charlotte West, "Against this background [of AIAW's success], it is difficult to justify the NCAA's repeated attempts to develop a competing program which would undermine this viable organization when women's intercollegiate athletics

---

[3] Alan Chapman, Memorandum to the Chief Executive Officers, Faculty Athletic Representatives and Athletic Directors of NCAA Member Institutions, June 14, 1974, 2.
[4] Barnes and Scannell, A20.
[5] *Memorandum to Presidents of AIAW Member Institutions*, February 21, 1978.
[6] Ibid.

programs are in an emerging state. Neither basic equity nor the legal requirements of equal opportunity call for the NCAA to start programs for women." But to the NCAA, it did make "cents." The takeover of the governance of women's athletics would guarantee the NCAA control of women's programs. It would thus limit the impact that moving toward equity for women would have on men's programs and budgets.

The beginning of the end came in 1980, when the NCAA estab- 11 lished championships for women in some sports. The NCAA's decision, made at its annual convention, entailed little discussion; it was simply announced. A great cry of outrage came from the leaders of the AIAW and from many men who were delegates at the convention. But the AIAW never had a fighting chance. Over the next several years the NCAA offered incentives to institutions to join it rather than the AIAW—offers that the still-young AIAW could not match. These included free trips for women's teams participating in national championships, and free women's memberships for colleges whose men's teams joined the NCAA. Most damaging of all, the NCAA made a deal with TV networks to televise *both* men's and women's basketball finals on the same dates that the AIAW was holding its championship games, depriving the AIAW of its financial base. Although the AIAW filed an antitrust suit against the NCAA and fought an honorable battle, it died and was laid to rest in 1982.

Thus the AIAW, which had a membership roll of 823 colleges and 12 universities and a financial base that included television contracts for national championships, found itself defeated by the much stronger NCAA. Indeed, even before the 1984 *Grove City* v. *Bell*[7] case removed college athletics from Title IX jurisdiction for a time (jurisdiction was totally restored by the Civil Rights Restoration Act of 1988), the AIAW had lost its chance at designing an alternative pattern with a woman's voice for intercollegiate athletics.

The traditionally male-dominated, abuse-ridden NCAA became 13 the governing body for both men's and women's intercollegiate athletics in America. A male model of athletics was all that was left. This model has recognizable characteristics in practice, if not in print. If they *were* written, they might look like this:

- The *athlete* portion of the term *student-athlete* is the more important.
- Student governance of campus programs and student involvement via student athletic associations are extinct phenomena.
- Big is better; winning is everything; the quest for publicity is all-consuming.

---

[7] 104 S.Ct. 1211 (1984).

- The greater the distance from academic control the better.
- The improvement of the student as an athlete is more important than the improvement of the student as a healthy, contributing member of society.
- Selection and fostering of a specific sport are based on the perception of its ability to churn dollars through the system as determined by television—not on participant interest or the sport's ability to provide positive experiences for the student.
- Women, women's sports, and men's minor sports are necessary evils that interfere with the proper development of the "athletic/commercial complex."

It is difficult to say what the female model, had it survived, would 14 look like today, but it might be:

- The *student* portion of the term *student-athlete* is the more important.
- Student governance of campus programs and student involvement via student athletic associations are healthy, viable phenomena.
- Winning is great, but can be compatible with the growth of the individual.
- The greater the cooperation and mutual interest between the academic and athletic aspects of the college experience the better.
- The improvement of the student as an athlete is less important than the improvement of the student as a healthy, contributing member of society.
- Selection and fostering of a specific sport are based on the perception of participant interest and the sport's ability to provide positive experiences for the student.
- Women, women's sports, and men's minor sports are necessary for the proper development of a balanced and responsible athletic/academic complex.

Some might say that it is not fair to label the two divergent models 15 of intercollegiate athletics "male" and "female." However, the "male" model was fashioned by males, adopted by males, retained by males in the face of decades of calls to reform, and with the death of the AIAW, forced upon females who wanted to continue to participate in intercollegiate athletics.[8]

---

[8] For a complementary account of the NCAA takeover of the AIAW, see *Academe*, July–August 1987.

Following the death of the AIAW (which many who witnessed it 16
would describe as "murder at the hands of the NCAA"), women who
wished to be leaders in intercollegiate athletics, particularly in Divisions I and II, had only one viable choice: to adopt the male model
for athletics. If they sought significant institutional support they had
to put *athlete* ahead of *student*. They had to redefine their own self-
worth in terms of win/loss records. They had to consider whether
their value systems allowed them to become as adept as their male
counterparts at circumventing NCAA regulations when those regulations interfered with their attainment of a winning season. They sometimes had to search for athletes who could help the team win even if
the athletes themselves had no chance of winning as students.

Of course, it is possible, even if the AIAW had survived and 17
thrived, that the alternative paradigm it developed would have become more and more like the male model. Perhaps the "male" model
of athletics simply reflects our society as a whole without regard to
gender or pervasive male dominance. If so, the problems facing us as
we call for the reform of intercollegiate athletics are even more overwhelming than we might have realized. For the sake of argument, and
in the interest of maintaining hope for the future, let us assume that
the abuses in athletics today are not symptomatic of a terminally ill
society, but are a separate and distinct illness that might, just might,
be treatable.

The mourning for the sound of a woman's voice in the design of 18
women's athletics continued for some years. Some female leaders left
the field, telling themselves the game was over and they had lost.
Some stayed and tried to maintain their principles and vision within
whatever circle of influence they might have. Some stayed and told
themselves that the future for an alternative to the male model existed
only by "working within the male system." Thus they sought or
accepted positions within the NCAA while convincing themselves
they could be agents for change from within. A price was paid by all.

Those who left athletics did so with unfulfilled dreams and a sense 19
of loss.

Those who stayed and tried to maintain their principles have 20
become more and more isolated.

Those who decided to work from within the NCAA have had less 21
success than they might have wished. At best, they serve as an
acknowledgment by the NCAA that women's athletics is part of the
organization and must be given some degree of recognition and concern. Many of the women who are trying to bring about change from
within the NCAA have struggled valiantly. Unfortunately, they are
playing in a game that uses men's rules on a playing field designed for
men with male referees who have a strong loyalty to the home team.

The men have had decades more practice. Even if the women become more skillful than the men at the men's game, they might win only to find that winning has cost them their souls.

As early as the 1920s, reformers were sounding the call for change 22 in athletics. Rules were made, regulations promulgated, enforcement committees formed, and compliance conferences convened. But changing rules and regulations does not cause reform. That will result only from changing basic principles.

It is unrealistic to believe that reform will come from the NCAA 23 acting without external pressure. A paradigm of financial profit rules the NCAA and the athletic commercial complexes at Division I & II schools. Big-time football and big-time men's basketball do—or at least are perceived to—fit in. In reality, very, *very* few institutions see a profit from either. On most campuses, they churn a great deal of money through the system, but profit is almost always overtaken by production expenses.

Why are women's sports and men's minor sports expected to be 24 financially profitable when the "premier" sports are not? Because those in control of the system structure their programs around the false expectation of financial gain. They say, "Perhaps it won't come this year, but if we spend more money, recruit more effectively, allocate more student time to practice, drop production costs from our accounting—maybe next year will be our year."

But perhaps the lack of profit results from following the wrong 25 principle and therefore looking for the wrong kind of profit. Profit from intercollegiate athletics should be measured not in dollars but in the degree of benefit to the lives of the participants. If the athletic/ commercial complex could change its guiding principles to those more appropriate for an academic/athletic complex, women's teams and men's minor sports would be considered potentially very profitable.

A word about reality: no real reform will occur while individual 26 campuses as well as the NCAA define profit in terms of dollars. As long as big-time football and men's basketball continue to be pampered as potential profit makers, there will be more rules and regulations, but no significant change until or unless such programs collapse under the weight of their abuses. Having made this painful statement, let us hope for a change in principles. Let us consider why now, more than in the past, women's voices have a significant role to play in the call for reform.

The call being heard today differs from that of the past. More 27 voices are calling in unison. The NCAA is highlighting reform, if only because the presidents of its member institutions are pressuring it to cut costs. The presidents are realizing that, no matter why they avoided accounting for their athletics programs, they have stayed away too long. Congress is realizing that it is obliged to be concerned about the education of the nation's youth, including those who are athletically skilled.

Should not women, who have long held the principles of an 28 academic/athletic complex dear, add their voices too? The NCAA has turned a deaf ear to them in the past, but now other ears seem willing to listen. Women must extend their voices beyond the NCAA to those who will and need to hear: faculties, college presidents, and Congress. Staying silent and placing trust in the NCAA to take steps toward the "rewomenization" of athletics will lead to nothing. History is clear:

- In 1972, women coached more than 90 percent of women's teams. Today only 47 percent of the coaches of women's teams are women. More than 99 percent of the coaches of men's teams are men.
- In 1972, women headed more than 90 percent of women's programs. Female administrators now direct only 16 percent.
- Today no women at all are involved in the administration of 30 percent of women's programs.[9]

The glass ceiling in the gymnasium is even lower than in the 29 nation's business offices. Women in today's society have been increasingly encouraged to develop and carve out a future for themselves in all segments of the work force, but in athletics it appears that women are being carved out of the work force.

The current call for reform gives women a special opportunity to 30 be more proactive concerning their future and that of intercollegiate athletics. However, overcoming the pervasiveness of gender discrimination and athlete abuse will require the collective efforts of men and women of courage and goodwill. If your are such a person, you should:

- Define "reform" in athletics to include full gender equity. The devaluation of *student* in *student-athlete* is compounded for women whose athletic participation is also discounted due to discrimination. Abusing student athletes on the basis of gender is at least as bad as abusing them because of their status as athletes.
- Encourage academic accrediting bodies to add a review of the institution's athletics programs for academic *and* equity accountability with respect to the institution's athletes.

---

[9] For a copy of the authors' 1990 thirteen-years summary of the *National Survey on the Status of Women in Intercollegiate Athletics*, from which these data come, send a self-addressed envelope with 52 cents postage to the authors at the Department of Physical Education, Brooklyn College, Brooklyn, N. Y. 11210.

- Call on Congress to require full disclosure of athletic budgets. Where secrecy starts, lying begins.
- Do not let budget constraints caused by cost-cutting "reforms" be used as an excuse for postponing progress on equity issues.
- Look and speak through the glass ceiling. Policies and agendas are influenced by all who share their voices. The presence or absence of female voices in the reformation eventually translates into athletic policies that will affect all who are involved.
- Beware of "reform" merely through the issuing of new rules and regulations. Many of the proposed "reform" changes are cosmetic at best and have a disparate impact on women at worst.
- Complement rules and regulations with principles, philosophy, and commitment.

The female model of sport has a great deal to offer for the future of 31 intercollegiate athletics. Go back to the future and include women's voices for reform.

In "Minor" College Sports, Big Pressure
WILLIAM C. RHODEN

William C. Rhoden writes about sports for the *New York Times*. In this article, the first in a series entitled "Athletes on Campus: A New Reality" that ran in the *Times* in January 1990, Rhoden discusses the campus role of so-called "minor" college sports such as golf and tennis. He quotes students from across the United States on the pros and cons of participating in college sports. Many issues are revealed in this piece: Are the colleges merely taking the place of farm teams or acting as "finishing schools" for not-quite-matured athletes? Are students who must travel and practice long hours able to receive a genuine academic education? Do excessive numbers of athletes in "minor" sports fail to graduate? Are athletes unfairly privileged, with their full scholarships? Do these students "use" colleges? Do the colleges "use" them? Rhoden's article lets students speak for themselves on these questions.

College presidents and athletic directors gathering today in 1 Dallas, for the 84th National Collegiate Athletic Association convention will once again wrestle with the excesses of big-time basketball and football.

But while they focus on those two high-profile sports, profes- 2 sionalization is also growing dramatically in less visible sports, with the potential for the same sort of abuses.

Athletes who once would go straight from high school to the pros 3
are now using college baseball, hockey, tennis and golf programs as
catapults into pro careers. As a result, the campus experience for all
athletes in those sports has changed, becoming so intensive and time-
consuming that even the most conscientious student-athlete finds it
increasingly difficult to balance academics and athletics. Whether a
player is a star or a third-stringer, the new and stringent pro-style
regimen must be followed.

Year-Round Commitment

"Sports have become year-round activities, and in those institu- 4
tions where sports are serious, they are a year-round commitment,"
said Dr. David Goslin, the president of the American Institutes of
Research, an independent, nonprofit research firm specializing in
behavioral and social sciences.

"What we are asking kids to do is hold two full-time jobs: school is 5
one, then they've got sports. It has become a tremendous burden."

Last year the institutes released the results of a five-part study on 6
student-athletes at Division I schools, the NCAA's top level. Among
other things, the report concluded that intensive sports programs had
become by far the greatest consumer of student-athletes' time, and in
many cases had compromised their ability to take full advantage of
their institutions.

The study found that football and basketball players spend an 7
average of 30 hours a week on their sports, and about 13.7 in class. For
other sports, the average given was 24.6 hours a week, but that figure
includes a number of minor sports with minimal time requirements.

In golf, where players practice up to four hours a day and usually 8
miss at least two classes a week during the season, participants spend
more time on their sport than do football and basketball players.
Tennis, hockey and baseball players spend as much time at practice,
and can even spend more time traveling to and from competitions.

"The reason for all this is that the professional sports arena has 9
expanded," Dr. Goslin said. "The professional opportunity is still only
open to a small proportion of athletes in college, and the chances are
small. But there are more teams. The slots have increased. At the same
time, there's fiercer competition for those slots."

College athletic programs at the Division I level have increasingly 10
become like finishing schools for the athletes trying to survive that
competition, offering them year-round training, better coaching, topflight facilities and pro-like schedules.

A Way to Avoid Financial Pressure

Martin Blackman, one of the top tennis players coming out of high 11
school in 1987, had offers from UCLA and USC and accepted a scholarship to Stanford, one of the nation's dominant programs of the 1980's.

Stanford's men's team has won five national championships in 12
this decade; its women's team has won five NCAA national championships since 1982, including consecutive championships from 1986 to
1989.

Blackman, following an increasingly typical pattern, dropped out 13
of Stanford after two seasons and turned professional.

"I thought that I'd be able to improve my game for about at least 14
two years, and I really wanted to experience college," Blackman said.
"The advantage of going to a top college program is that, if you're not
quite ready for the pros, you get the best coaches, you have other guys
on the team you can practice with every day, you have time to work on
your game, and you don't have the pressure of trying to make a living
on the tour."

According to Richard Shultz, the executive director of the National 15
Collegiate Athletic Association, the highest dropout rate among intercollegiate varsity sports is in tennis. He said he could not give the
specific number.

Classes Interfere

College golf, with a season that runs from September to June and 16
tournaments that last three or four days at a time, has become almost a
prerequisite for making a living on the PGA Tour. Turning pro directly
out of high school, which was common until about 15 years ago, has
now become financially and competitively impractical.

"It would have been a lot harder to turn pro without going to 17
college, because you'd have to work on it harder yourself and you
wouldn't get a chance to play against the top people you play against
in college," said Robert Gamez, an all-American golfer at the University
of Arizona last season and the NCAA golfer of the year.

"Sure, you can play the mini-tours and stuff like that," he said, 18
referring to the level below the PGA Tour that is used by those who do
not qualify for the tour right away. "But mini-tours are real expensive;
entry fees are high for the type of money they're playing for."

Gamez said that a drawback of college was that classes interfered 19
with his golf regimen.

"I was kind of tired of the classroom," said Gamez, who dropped 20
out last season after his junior year and earned his PGA Tour card.

"There are a lot of guys on the tour that never finished school. Some guys don't want to go to school, or are not there to graduate, not there to become rocket scientists. They're in there to play golf."

Pro Teams Compete for Baseball Players

The sport with the most dramatic change in status on campus is 21 baseball, where professional teams are now literally recruiting against top college programs for the best high school seniors. Traditionally, talented high school players went straight to the minor leagues and incubated there until the parent club felt they were ready to move up. College was considered a waste of time for a player with pro aspirations and talent.

But the dwindling number of minor league teams, down to a low 22 of 132 in 1973 after reaching a high of 448 in 1949, and the higher caliber of college baseball has made college an attractive option. The better programs offer a 60-to-70-game schedule, often with coaching provided by former pro players and managers.

Last summer, Jeff Hammonds, a talented center fielder from 23 Scotch Plains High School in New Jersey, turned down a $250,000 offer from the Toronto Blue Jays and accepted a baseball scholarship to Stanford. The year before, Alex Fernandez of Pace High School in Miami, one of the nation's top pitching prospects, turned down an offer of $130,000 by the Milwaukee Brewers to attend the University of Miami.

One of Hammond's teammates, Mike Mancini, a pitcher, was 24 drafted by the Baltimore Orioles out of high school but turned down their contract offer to accept Stanford's scholarship.

"The minor leagues just weren't for me," said Mancini, now a 25 sophomore. "Right out of high school, you're 18 years old, you're used to being at home, then all of a sudden, bam! you're on the road. You're in a van or bus every day, traveling four or five or six hours. I didn't see that I was mature enough to handle that at the time."

His counterparts 10 or 15 years ago would have had to handle it, 26 whether they felt mature enough or not, because the level of college competition was so low. But Mancini and the prospects of today have a competitive alternative. Stanford, for example, will play a 61-game schedule that begins Jan. 26 and ends May 20 (later if the Cardinals, who have won two consecutive national championships, participate in post-season play).

Hockey Brings in Some Big Bucks

College hockey, which is the third-largest college revenue-   27
producing sport after basketball and football, now offers advantages
similar to those found in those sports.

As recently as 1980, most high school hockey players with the   28
aspirations of playing professionally went through the Major Junior
Hockey League in Canada, where they began an apprenticeship in one
of three divisions. The better players then joined a professional team
in a minor league or the National Hockey League. It was rare for a
college player to become an NHL success, because college programs
lacked the quality or intensity to prepare a player for the pros.

Today, while 70 percent of drafted players continue to come out of   29
the Canadian Major Junior Hockey League, college is a legitimate
alternative. Increasing numbers of the better high school players, both
Canadian and American, are accepting scholarships to American college hockey programs, for two main reasons.

"I thought I would need an education because I didn't have a   30
clear-cut opportunity for professional hockey," said Warren Sharples,
a goalie at the University of Michigan who was a ninth-round draft
choice of the Calgary Flames out of high school. "Now I know I can
stop at any time. I don't have to play hockey somewhere where I don't
want to play. I can stop if I want to. A lot of players don't have that
option because they didn't get the education."

One of his teammates, Ryan Pardowski, said he decided on col-   31
lege because he was too small physically to survive the rigors of pro
hockey, even at the major-junior level. He wanted time to grow and to
refine his game, and a scholarship gave him the opportunity to do so at
little expense.

So Much Practice, So Little Time

The paradox of the athletic scholarship is that the time demands of   32
today's Division I sports programs, and the athlete's own single-
minded focus on meeting them, often make it impossible for him or
her to exploit fully the academic and extracurricular resources of the
school.

"It's the hours that they put in, but it's also that those are heavy   33
work kinds of hours," said Mary Ann Swain, an assistant dean of
admissions at the University of Michigan. "They work really, really
hard for four, five or six hours a day, and then we expect them to sit

down, focus and concentrate their energies on studying. It's not only that they're running out of hours in the day, they're tired. Just downright physically tired."

A fundamental issue is whether the rigors of balancing education 34 and athletics have become too great for athletes at this level. Those who are less confident in their academic abilities, or more single-minded about athletics, often choose a path of least resistance and take less demanding courses.

"I wanted to be an accountant," said Gamez, the former Arizona 35 golfer. "But it's really hard to take that much time to do your accounting and get good grades."

Some student-athletes have resolved to try to do well in class, but 36 with the understanding that they cannot compete at a championship level athletically and also compete for A's with their more academically-minded peers.

"You have to make some sacrifices in the classroom to be the best 37 you can be in the sport you're doing," said Jennifer Azziz, an all-American basketball guard at Stanford. "I find that people here will put their whole heart into their athletics, at least equal to school work, if not a little before it."

Others find athletics so consuming that it is a struggle simply to 38 stay eligible to play.

"My first semester I got by with just over a 2.0," said Pardowski of 39 Michigan's hockey team, referring to his grade-point average. "Last semester I didn't do well. I went below a 2.0, but my cumulative stayed above it. This semester, if I go below a 2.0, I'm gone."

Too Distracted to Study

Pardowski said that between classes, practice, and getting dinner 40 after practice, he usually doesn't get home until 9 P.M., and is often too distracted to study.

"And you're trying so hard to fit in with hockey, and to make it 41 there," he said, "that you lose your focus that you're here for school. You just kind of go through the motions."

Warde Manuel, who had to stop playing football for Michigan this 42 year because of a degenerative nerve condition, now questions the extent to which high-level competition and academic performance are compatible.

"Athletics takes away some of your ambition for academics," he 43 said. "More now I feel like a student, because I don't have to go to the football building; I don't have to go to practice."

"I never really realized that education could be as fun, that it could 44 be as demanding," he added. "Now I see why people talk about athletics being a challenge in college, because it's so much easier now for me to focus. I'm not as tired, mentally or physically."

"I Feel Cheated"

Another of the frequent complaints among student-athletes at 45 Division I schools, according to the American Institutes of Research surveys, was that athletes had little time to play a role in the student life of their universities.

"I feel cheated in a way," said Tim Williams, a senior linebacker 46 for Michigan, who received the team's scholar-athlete award this season and will graduate next spring with a degree in business. "When I was younger, I felt that college would be full of symposiums, guest speakers, getting involved in groups like Amnesty International. I envisioned letter-writing, being politically active, being wild and crazy, taking more classes and taking advantage of more educational opportunities.

"The reality is that you don't have time for that. I'm upset about it, 47 I guess. But on the other hand I've had an experience that only a handful of people will ever experience."

Another troublesome side effect of more intense college sports 48 programs is the widening social gap between students and student-athletes, and a greater ambivalence in their attitude toward each other.

Some "Sour Grapes" from Classmates

The impression of many students is that scholarship athletes, even 49 those who perform outside the glare of a national spotlight, are not harder workers than students who work at jobs and attend class.

"Some argue that student-athletes get as much as they do because 50 they work so hard," said Paige Oliver, editor of the Auburn student newspaper. "But what about students that have to work full time and put themselves through school? Don't they put in just as many hours working?

"They're not on the field, but they spend just as many hours 51 working at Burger King, or just as many hours working at the mall, or anywhere, pumping gas. They have to live in the dorms or live in an efficiency, and just take what they can get. I feel that's where the students have a problem and that's where the sour grapes come in."

Perhaps the significant difference is that the scholarship athlete 52 holds two full-time jobs and to a greater extent is chained to them both, and is under great pressure to do well in both.

For the tennis player from Sweden, the hockey player from Can-   53
ada or the golfer from Arizona, the stakes in intercollegiate athletics
have intensified across the board.

"You have to have a professional attitude about it," said Sharples,   54
the Michigan goalie. "They treat you as a professional here. The
school puts a lot of money into the athletic programs, and they expect
something in return. It's very intense and you'd be naïve to not believe
that it was a business. It's a professional atmosphere even at the
university level. We have fun, but there is a lot of responsibility.

"The most fun I have playing these days is when I go home at   55
Christmas and I can skate on the outdoor ice out on the lagoon, and
just skate around for the pure joy of it. Here, there is a lot of responsibility and unless you're winning, it's no fun at all."

Punt the Pretense

THE EDITORS OF THE *NEW REPUBLIC*

The following editorial essay appeared in September 1986 in the *New
Republic*, a politically conservative periodical. The essay expresses an
argument that we still hear voiced today: Go ahead and "pay for
play," but openly, not "under the table." The editorial proposes a
three-part reform for college athletics. If this proposal were enacted,
what results would you foresee?

When Len Bias, a star senior on the University of Maryland bas-   1
ketball team, died from a cocaine overdose on June 19 [1986], he was 21
credits short of graduation. In the weeks that followed Bias's death, it
was revealed that other Maryland basketball players routinely flunked
out of school, and then were "re-admitted" to play again. The situation at Maryland was scandalous but typical. For the most part, studying is an incidental pursuit for "student-athletes" at big-time sports
schools.

The athlete's job is to play—that is, to boost ticket sales and TV   2
revenue for his school. Practice and travel make sports a full-time job.
There's little time for anything else. No wonder coaches tell recruits
less about academics than about the glamorous professional career
that will follow college—though they know perfectly well that only a
tiny percentage of even star players ever make it. The rest get no
degree, and no education. That means no career of any kind. Such
exploitation corrodes the academic integrity of America's universities.

Exploitation breeds corruption too, as some players, many of them   3
blacks from poor backgrounds, get "taken care of" with under-the-

table money from alumni, local businessmen, and other "boosters." Others get taken care of by gamblers and drug dealers. Consider the pathetic story of John "Hot Rod" Williams, a former star center on Tulane University's basketball team. Williams is black. He came to mostly white, upper-middle-class Tulane from a broken home after receiving $10,000 from a Tulane booster. He got into the school even though he couldn't read the verbal section of the Scholastic Aptitude Test. As a physical education major, his schedule included "courses" in soccer and volleyball. Tulane's basketball coach helped his impoverished star with as much as $100 a week—a kind gesture, but a gross violation of NCAA rules. Williams figured prominently in a major cocaine and point-shaving scandal at Tulane last year. He was recently acquitted, but as a result of the scandal, Tulane abolished its basketball program. Few schools have responded to sports scandals so forthrightly.

Last January the NCAA adopted Proposition 48 as a "get-tough 4 solution" to the current mess. Yet Prop 48 hardly sets a rigorous new standard. Previously, jocks only needed a 2.0 high school grade average on a 4.0 scale to get into NCAA schools. Prop 48 says the 2.0 average has to be in 11 "core courses," and requires at least a 700 combined score on the SAT. (You get 400 just for signing your name; top score is 1,600.) As Malcolm Gladwell recently pointed out in these pages, such absurdly minimal standards do nothing about the real scandal—the non-education athletes receive once they're admitted to college. . . . More recently, the NCAA showed its true priorities by refusing to shorten the college basketball season. That would have given players more time to study—but would have cost ticket sales and TV dollars.

It's tempting just to scrap the "student-athlete" sham and make 5 college sports openly professional. If some schools are so dependent on basketball and football income to support their academic and athletic programs, why shouldn't they declare their profit-making intentions? The athletic departments at big universities could be independent corporate entities, forking over a share of their revenues in return for the use of school names, and bidding for top high school talent. But this would grossly accentuate one of the worst effects of the current system: that too many kids, especially in ghettos, spend too much time out of school and on the playground, dreaming of pro sports never-never land instead of preparing for a real-world job. The incentives for such fantasies are high enough already.

Between outright professionalism and small-college amateurism, 6 however, there are ways to reduce the current exploitation. Step one is to reduce the emphasis schools now place on athletics. At a minimum, this should mean shorter schedules—one semester each for football and basketball—and repealing the rules that make freshmen eligible for varsity play.

Step two is to tailor educational demands to players' true skills and 7 ambitions. The Bill Bradleys can excel both on the court and in the history department. They should be encouraged to get their degrees in four years. A second group of more modestly talented athletes should have the option of studying one semester, and playing full-time the other. They could finish the final two years of their degrees when their playing days are over, paying for it with scholarship money they didn't use while playing. Michael McPherson of the Brookings Institution has a similar proposal: give athletes four years of athletic eligibility, and six years of financial assistance.

But what about the "Hot Rod" Williamses, who shouldn't be in a 8 four-year college in the first place? As long as colleges are going to admit such students, and as long as they're profiting from the athletes' talents, they owe players a chance to improve academically. That doesn't mean physical education or "general education." It does mean helping them stick to a reasonably demanding academic course load, including remedial work where necessary. Schools could even devise a special degree to award students who complete such a program. Remedial work wouldn't count toward the diploma.

Congressman James Howard of New Jersey has proposed 9 denying tax deductions for gifts to athletic departments that don't graduate at least 75 percent of the athletes they have on scholarship. And any athlete should have to pass all his courses, regular and remedial, with at least a C average. Otherwise, he can't play. A similar rule was just enacted by the Texas public schools for high school sports. It could work for universities, too.

Step three is to grant players a decent share of the wealth they 10 generate for their schools. This is both a matter of basic justice and a means of ensuring that players aren't tempted to accept tainted money. Players should get an annual payment equal to the cash value of their scholarships (at Notre Dame, for example, that's about $11,000). Half of it would be theirs to spend, and half would go into an interest-bearing account, payable only when they complete whatever degree program they chose at the beginning of their careers.

Our proposal may jostle some cherished old notions about ama- 11 teurism. Expect objections from those who profit most from the current "shamateur" system—big NCAA sports powers, TV networks, and local boosters. But an awful lot of people who don't care much for sports do worry about the integrity of the institutions where their children study. Many such people supported Tulane's decision to scrap basketball and the Texas public schools "no pass, no play" rule. The NCAA should be leading the move for academic achievement among athletes, not running away from it. Otherwise it can expect to see more embarrassing headlines about corruption in college sports.

In Defense of College Sports

MICHAEL NOVAK

Michael Novak is a social critic, the resident scholar at the American Enterprise Institute for Public Policy Research (a conservative think tank in Washington, D.C.), and the author of many books. His publications include *The Spirit of Democratic Capitalism* (1982), *Confessions of a Catholic* (1983), and *Taking Glasnost Seriously* (1988). While Novak typically writes about political and religious issues, in *The Joy of Sports* (1976), he argues spiritedly in support of college sports. In this excerpt, he confronts questions such as "Should the universities allow themselves to be used as training grounds for the professionals?" Should the universities "encourage varsity sports in which, at most, 200 or 300 males of the student body can compete"? Most of his answers are resoundingly affirmative; indeed, Novak characterizes academicians who oppose college sports as not truly intellectual and schools without athletic programs as "stuffy" and "arrogant." Read on; there's more!

One of the themes of the new sportswriting concerns abuses in 1 college recruiting. Another is more basic: the use of college teams as a free "farm system" for professional teams. Let me make a proposal outright. Professional teams should pay for the services so provided. A mandatory contribution to a National Collegiate Athletic Association (NCAA) sports fund of, say, $250,000 by each professional team every year would go a long way toward reducing the deficits of college athletic departments. These moneys, fairly distributed, would allow the universities and colleges to direct a portion of their budgets into new programs, especially those for women, without weakening already thinly stretched money-making sports. The colleges provide an invaluable service. Just as great industries in chemistry, metallurgy, aerodynamics, tobacco, agriculture, and other fields contribute to the universities that train their personnel, so should professional sports.

College sports do not need the professionals. Long before profes- 2 sional basketball and football leagues became publicly acceptable, the college game was highly organized, held the allegiance of a fervent public, and reached a high level of excellence.

There were 634 college football teams in 1973, but only 26 profes- 3 sional teams. Not all the players, by far, entertained the ambition of making football their profession. Years ago, Gerald Ford didn't.

But should the universities allow themselves to be used as training 4
grounds for the professionals? Well, there are schools of journalism
and television, political science and agriculture, chemistry and engineering, law and medicine, business and accounting, teaching and
nursing. Is sports the only profession that ought to be excluded? It is
not the least spiritual profession, nor the least mythic, nor the least
central to a culture. The athletic programs of certain schools are likely
to make as great a contribution to the life, vitality, imagination, and
moral unity of a given region as any other school programs. It will pain
professors in other fields to admit it. The president of Kent State tried
to jolt the citizens of Ohio with this declaration in 1973: "The people of
Ohio have a deeper love of football than they do of the classics."
Because of a shortage of funds, he had to fire as many as sixty professors; he could not cut back, he complained, on the commitment to
sports made by the university before he took the job. During the early
days of the energy crisis that same year, a source at the Federal Energy
Office told a reporter: "The surest way to start a revolution in this
country would be to shut down night football, baseball, or basketball
games." To "serious" observers, these are scandalous priorities. I
think them sound.

Colleges and universities exist for intellect, of course. But intellect 5
has many tasks, not the least of which is the creation of narrative and
dramatic forms by which the people live. Most of the faculty and
graduates of universities engage in quite pedestrian and workaday
intellectual tasks. Even those relatively few whose own pre-
occupations came closest to the ideals of "pure intellect" are also remarkably pragmatic, empirical, and highly specialized in their own
working practice. The vast majority of faculty members in a university
are intellectual *workers*, specialists, professionals, whose work is as
grubby as that of other workers in society and just as practical. There
are not many who love ideas for the sake of ideas, whose approach to
their work is, in the ancient and medieval sense, "intellectual." There
are few, in short, who treat ideas as a field of play. Most, indeed, think
their work is more important than that of coaches and players. Economically and socially, however, it would be difficult for them to
prove that their work does have larger public significance. Indeed,
that difficulty is the source of much resentment.

Surprisingly, I have discovered, those intellectuals who are truly 6
intellectuals, who respect the playfulness and freedom of intellect,
who do not regard intellectual exercise as work but rather as play,
passion, and delight, are almost invariably those with the greatest
appreciation for sports. Not all are believers, of course. Some, especially those with more austere European roots, find it difficult to allow
the experience of baseball, football, and basketball entrance through

their rather closely meshed intellectual armor. But a surprising number find joy—usually a secret joy, about which they speak little except to other believers—in the myths, metaphors, and tangible experiences of the great American games.

For they are fascinated by the secrets of the life of the spirit, and 7 they are accustomed to seeking gold in what heavier minds regard as slag. They can scarcely prevent their roving minds from asking: What *is* so gripping about these contests of imagination? How could so many millions be so intensely aroused by them? They themselves absorb secret, forbidden sweetness from sports. As they walk across their campuses, they note that the grandest monuments of the university are built for the liturgies of sport. As they read the paper, they are pleased that the fullest, best-read sections concern sports. They do not need to be clever to separate what's important from what official rhetoricians say is important. They long ago ceased listening to the Serious Persons of our age.

Nevertheless, many university people feel embarrassment about 8 sports. The new president would like to have his university known for its nuclear reactor, its agricultural experimentation, its high-level economics department, its top-ranked law school; he's tired of hearing it called "a football school." The serious students want the university to do relevant things, fight racism, sexism, and maybe capitalism, too (a little ambivalence about that), and disenthrone the fundamentalist pieties of the gods of sport. The faculty, absorbing budgetary cuts, looks sourly at the liquidity of the department of athletics. (The cultural differences between departments of a university may exceed the cultural differences between some nations.) The intellectual onslaught against varsity sports is overwhelming. Except that the people of the state, the alumni, and a rhetorically subdued but intuitively supportive student opinion *want* sports.

Human beings cannot live without rituals. What would faculties 9 be without cocktail parties, committee meetings, and pregnant pauses as they lecture? Where would a city, state, or nation be without the life of the imagination, without a focal point for passions and loyalties and humor and risk? In varsity sports, universities give the nation the most profound and nourishing popular arts accessible to all our citizens. Our other religions are all, despite their universal aims, sectarian; their symbols and liturgies cannot unite as many as sports do. The liturgies and rituals of the democratic state—its Memorial Days, Independence Days, Election Days, State of the Union Messages, presidential press conferences and Dedications, its flags at half-mast, and its parades and appeals—run very thin. You cannot celebrate the state or its leader without running the risk of unbalancing the democracy, as we have already done in the rituals and liturgies so heavily focusing on the

President. There is sex—but sex is, after all, a private rather than a public ritual. Where, then, can a secular society turn, if not to sport, as the chief communal ritual of its citizens? . . .

I said once at the University of Notre Dame—and a young man 10 who heard me reported it next morning to Father Hesburgh, the president, who received the word with (so I am told) a certain horror—that the creation of the myth of Notre Dame football may have been the most brilliant social achievement that university has made, or ever would make, no matter how great or illustrious its contributions in the invention of synthetic rubber, its nuclear experimentation, its civil rights efforts, and so on. Many at Notre Dame, especially among its new and quite brilliant faculty, are somewhat abashed by the attention given Notre Dame football. They minimize football, and try to maximize the university's intellectual stature. Well they should. The point remains that their perspective is far too narrow. The life of imagination, the life of the spirit, needs nourishing if intellect is to flourish. And few phenomena in American life compare with the mythic power of Notre Dame football. . . .

Suppose that an institution wanted to communicate to 40 or 50 11 million persons a certain set of attitudes with respect to the struggles of life, or to teamwork, wit, perseverance, courage, invention, desire. I doubt whether any institution, whatever its resources, could have set out intentionally to fulfill such a goal or accomplished it as deeply, for so many millions, as has Notre Dame. Not all human values are communicated through the liturgy of football, but those that are present are important and quite beautiful enough. It is an enormous accomplishment to have nourished so many on the spirit of Notre Dame.

In the liturgies of schools like Notre Dame—at Ohio State, USC, 12 Texas, Georgia, and others—all can come together: the governor of a state, corporate executives, alumni of every rank, students, and their parents, players, townspeople, citizens from every walk of life. Television carries the images into hospitals and taverns, factory commissaries and police stations, prisons and old folks' homes. Were I the president of a new state university or private college, or a member of the faculty, I would strongly encourage the development of a high-level athletic program within the realistic means of the school. The costs are great, but so are the returns—the rejoicing of the human spirit, the unifying of many.

Some will argue that it is wrong to encourage varsity sports in 13 which, at most, 200 or 300 males of the student body can compete. To be sure, an athletic program should be made to pay a very large share of its own way, more so than other departments; and this is usually the case. A full range of intraschool competition should be encouraged, for women as for men. The development of intercollegiate sports competitions for women should be placed on a realistic, long-term basis. The building of a program that will not become a mockery but will hold the allegiance of many for many years requires planning, time, and money. But a program of maximal participation by all students—even including, perhaps, mandatory athletic requirements for all who matriculate—is properly capped by a first-rate varsity program for the relatively few men and women of highest talent. For every school is a corporation, a persona, and it almost cries out to be personified in mythic conflict with other schools. . . .

Colleges and universities in the United States play a special symbolic role in our society. Although any region that wishes to expand its base for modern industries requires universities to provide trained personnel and to attract research monies from the government, universities are not only organs of research, science, technical innovation, and industrial advancement. They are also symbols of regional character, pride, and assertion. Education itself is a religious institution in this country; its role is considerably more than pragmatic or dryly secular. The professional class of a state—the pharmacists, farmers, lawyers, doctors, engineers, chemists, accountants, teachers, and others—owe their training to local land-grant or other universities. Intercollegiate sports provide a happy and light-serious opportunity for ritual demonstrations of loyalty and rivaly. Arkansas-Texas, Alabama-Auburn, Michigan-Ohio State, California-Stanford, Harvard-Yale, and other sectional contests provide a delicious opportunity for trips, taunts, and happy times. If there were not such ritual occasions in sports, they would have to be invented elsewhere. 14

Universities like Chicago that have turned away from intercollegiate sports seem to suffer from a lack of lightness and fun; a kind of stuffiness and arrogance surround them. The symbolic climate of such schools becomes severe, workmanlike, and internally divisive: department separate from department, school from school, town from town. There are not many activities that can unite janitors, cafeteria workers, sophomores, and Nobel Prize winners in common pleasure. 15

Actual physical participation in sports—in tennis, golf, jogging, swimming, squash, handball, and others—seems everywhere on the rise, among both men and women. Intercollegiate competition should be seen as a felicitous capstone upon this broadening base, an occasion for celebration and delight. 16

The most important contribution of universities and colleges at the present time might be the encouragement of scholars from various disciplines to grasp the genius of our American sports, to study their bearing upon our culture, and to incorporate their cultural reality into the legitimate investigations of their disciplines. In anthropology, eco- 17 nomics, sociology, psychology, literature, history, philosophy, religious studies, and many other fields, there is much to be learned about one of the most impressive realms of experience in our national life. Here stands the stadium and there the basketball arena, competing in visibility with the library and the laboratories. It is not a happy thought that their reality is so often unnoticed, as if the faculty wore blinders. The diminution of academic prejudice in this regard might go far toward bringing the department of athletics into the center of academic discussion, not simply for condescending put-downs but also for praise, admiration, and the enlightenment of all. In this context, the necessary reforms might more easily be carried out in an atmosphere not of *ressentiment* but of mutual high regard.

Corporate Athleticism: A Historical Perspective

NAND HART-NIBBRIG AND CLEMENT COTTINGHAM

Nand Hart-Nibbrig is a professor of public administration and an adjunct professor of political science at West Virginia University. He has written extensively on subjects related to government and education. Clement Cottingham is a professor of political science at Rutgers University who has written on ethnic politics, urban poverty, and comparative politics in developing countries. In 1984, they published a scholarly study, *The Political Economy of College Sports*, in which this essay appears as the third chapter. Here Hart-Nibbrig and Cottingham focus on the history of athletic programs in American colleges as a means of better understanding how "the intensification of athletic emphasis"—and what the authors term "corporate athleticism"—came about. In so doing, they provide fascinating historical data that may be useful as you consider and argue the complex issues that surround college sports today.

Hart-Nibbrig and Cottingham are interested in a historical perspective, but they discuss some questions that remain important—and unresolved—today: Why and how did sports become a primary means of publicizing colleges? What role have sports played in unifying diverse student populations? How did sports become a business? Why did football become the preeminent campus sport? Have black athletes benefited from college sports programs more than they have been exploited by them? As women's sports programs become larger, will they be subject to problems similar to those of men's sports programs? These questions and others are addressed in this essay.

Few would deny that intercollegiate athletics, especially competition 1
between the so-called big powers in football and basketball, has fully

emerged as a significant element in the sports entertainment offered weekly by national television networks, radio, and news media, and increasingly, by cable television networks. The expansion of major college sports events to the point where they have become important contributors to public entertainment is due in part to the development of the media in mass society. But what explains the intensification of athletic emphasis at institutions of higher learning in the first place? What provided the impetus for corporate athleticism?

Our synoptic review of intercollegiate athletics reveals identifiable 2 links as early as the turn of the twentieth century between a growing, aggressive business system—with its free-for-all attitude toward winning at all costs—and the organization of intercollegiate athletics. University and college presidents were quick to see the financial potential of football. They were equally quick to realize the possibilities for recruiting additional students and the opportunities for forging close ties to the most dynamic element in American society, the business community.

Primarily because of brutalities and scandals, regulatory issues 3 emerged surprisingly early in the history of intercollegiate athletics. One realizes in retrospect that rampant commercialism and the scandals associated with big-time athletics are not unique to our time and circumstances.

While there is much that is similar, profound differences do exist 4 in the organization and depth of contemporary links between sports and the business community. In part, these differences stem from the tightly integrated character of the current national economy, typified by large national corporations. But the large corporations are qualitatively different from earlier forms of business in their effect on the emergence of athleticism. This [essay] traces the growth of athleticism, as well as deepens our understanding of those social structures that gave rise to corporate athleticism.

The Early Days of College Sports

Committed largely to the academic life of students, the earliest 5 American colleges cared little about the extracurricular aspects of student life. The earliest days of higher education were characterized by serious classes, studying, and of course religious devotion in chapel. Most students were educated for the ministry at Harvard, Yale, and later Princeton through a curriculum that included Latin, Greek, Hebrew, logic and rhetoric. Harvard's mission, articulated so eloquently in 1937 by Samuel Eliot Morison, was to educate clergy "who would spell the difference between civilization and barbarism."[1] In this statement, Morrison captured both the spirit and the purpose of "higher" education in this country in its early days. He didn't mention college sports.

But this is not to say that sports did not exist at the early American colleges. Puritan goals of "keeping the spirit pure" formed one of the principal justifications for vigorous sports activities. Such activity would fatigue the body and thus enhance "pure living and pure thinking." Students were prompted, however, to train their wills and to become "moral athletes," to eschew those activities generally considered "low and unbecoming of gentlemen and scholars . . ."[2] But that was a bit much to ask, and students began to engage in recreational activities that ushered in the beginnings of intramuralism and led inevitably to intercollegiate competition.

As intramural teams were organized, the desire to test the mettle of teams from neighboring institutions grew. The evolution of campus sports as a club movement promoted and encouraged intercollegiate sports competition, and intercollegiate, rather than intramural, contests gained the greatest amount of student attention.

The historic moment occurred on August 3, 1852, when Harvard challenged and defeated Yale in a crew race on Lake Winnipesaukee in New Hampshire. This event was followed in 1859 by the first baseball game and in 1869 by the first intercollegiate football game in New Brunswick, New Jersey, between Rutgers and Princeton. By 1880 intercollegiate football, with its new rule changes and its first intercollegiate football association, set in motion the beginnings of the American game of football. William Baker, a noted sports historian, suggests that the contest between McGill University of Montreal and Harvard in 1874 was even more important in the development of the American game than was the "first" contest because of the introduction of rugby rules.[3] This change of rules and format not only delighted the spectators, it also provided the newly emergent game with what it needed to surpass in popularity the soccer-like game that was its forerunner. Who would have thought that this pastime invented to satisfy the physical needs of young men of breeding and taste would become the mass-entertainment spectacle it is today?

Even though the watershed of intercollegiate sports occurred with the first football contest, we should not lose sight of the significance of the attraction of crew, or boat races, to those well born. It surely was

---

[1] Samuel Eliot Morison, *Harvard College in the Seventeenth Century* (Cambridge: Harvard University Press, 1937), p. 6.

[2] Ralph Barton Perry, *Puritanism and Democracy* (New York: Vanguard, 1944), 245.

[3] William J. Baker, *Sports in the Modern World* (Totowa, NJ: Rowman and Littlefield, 1982), 128.

not lost to college administrators of the day, who were eager to capitalize on the excitement and the connection with competing schools. The relationship between the publicity generated by the races and increased admissions was something university presidents did not ignore. On this point, Joanna Davenport's speculation may be correct that these races inspired the practice of using sports to publicize a certain institution.[4] The belief that instant institutional fame and prestige accompanied athletic success was reinforced by the growing number of supporters of intercollegiate athletics. It did not take long for administrators to realize that people remembered the prowess of a school's athletic teams and its star performers and not the success of routine academic endeavors.[5]

But in the context of rapid demographic changes and dislocations, 10 football overtook the more patrician sport of racing and emerged as the first of the major sports. Its popularity grew rapidly, and by the turn of the century it was becoming increasingly evident that football was the sport exceeding all others in its capacity to raise revenue. "King football," as it became known, was categorized as a major sport; those generating less money were labeled minor sports. These categories remain with us today, although they are now called, perhaps more accurately, revenue and nonrevenue sports.[6]

By the beginning of the twentieth century, the die had been cast. 11 Football with its increasingly apparent links to commercialism was firmly launched as the principal intercollegiate sport. Frederick Rudolph described the sport thus: "Once the game had enlisted the support of alumni and administration, there was no stopping its growth. For once the *sport* had been accepted, the *games* had to be won.[7] Apparently, the launching of the game brought with it the belief that winning was also necessary.

The earliest years in the development of college football were 12 marked not only by links with the business culture, but also by a heavy infusion of nationalism. In this environment, football actually acted as a stabilizing, unifying, and ultimately democratizing influence.[8] Between 1880 and 1910, new immigrants poured into the cities and

---

[4] Joanna Davenport, "From Crew to Commercialism—The Paradox of Sport in Higher Education" (Paper presented at the Conference on Sports and Higher Education, Skidmore College, March, 1983), 5.

[5] Sanborn Gove Tenney, "Athletics at Williams," *Outing* 17 (1890):142.

[6] Leroy Ervin and Sue McCaffey, "Intercollegiate Football and Higher Education, 1880–1980: A Century of Growth, Commercialization, and Conflict" (Paper presented at the Conference on Sports and Higher Education" Skidmore College, March, 1983), 5.

[7] D. S. Eitzen and G. Sage, *Sociology of American Sport* (Dubuque, Iowa: William C. Brown Co., 1978), 72.

[8] Frederick Rudolph, *The American College and University: A History* (New York: Vintage Books, 1962), 379.

towns of the industrial East and Midwest, creating in the process class and ethnic diversity; established inhabitants expressed considerable concern about the changing character of the urban society. Faced with a decline of ethnic homogeneity on college campuses, university and college administrators were prompted to use the integrative power of a successful athletic program. A winning football team, even in its earliest days, made it much easier for alumni and boosters to generate the funds needed to build additional athletic facilities and to restore a sense of collegiate unity that had been eroded by larger and more ethnically diversified student bodies and by the development of the elective curriculum.[9] Frederick Rudolph stated that "if every man did not take the same courses, at least he had an opportunity to cheer for the same team."[10]

The early twentieth century was a time of great social change, rapid urban and industrial growth, and increasing ethnic diversity. Under such circumstances, finding integrative symbols, especially those capturing the dynamic entrepreneurial spirit of the young nation, was no easy matter. Few articulated this association between sport and nationalism better than Theodore Roosevelt when he declared: "In any republic, courage is a prime necessity. . . . If one is to be a good citizen . . . athletics are good, especially in their rougher form, because they tend to develop such courage."[11]

Sacrifice and loyalty to national ideals were assumed to be part of the active commitment to sport and were highlighted in the work of Luther Gulick, an early twentieth-century leader in the recreation movement and an early contributor to American public administration theory. Gulick asserted that through the loyalty and self-sacrifice developed in team games, "we are laying the foundation for wider loyalty and a more discerning self-devotion to the great national ideals on which democracy rests."[12] So it was on sport generally, and on football specifically, that much of the weight of extending the unifying affective themes of American nationalism rested, a burden and a responsibility dubiously maintained even to this day.

Football's Beginnings

An early indication of the future of intercollegiate sports was the rapidity and ease with which football became a fixture in university

[9] Davenport, "From Crew to Commercialism," 6.

[10] Rudolph, The American College, 381.

[11] Alexander M. Weyand, The Saga of American Football Development (New York: Macmillan, 1955), viii–ix.

[12] Luther Gulick, A Philosophy of Play (New York: Charles Scribner's Sons, 1920), 262.

and campus life. It is instructive to recall how quickly the public seized upon the game (at the beginning more like a combination of soccer and rugby than the game familiar to millions of football fans today) with enthusiasm and exhilaration. Universities and colleges immediately took advantage of this enormous popularity as a vehicle for attracting financial and political support from students, alumni, state legislators, and other prospective contributors. Unlike Cornell's President Andrew D. White, many university presidents were eager to meet opposing colleges on the gridiron in order to "agitate a bag of wind."[13] Apparently, "football as public relations to football as business would not, at some institutions, be much of a distance."[14]

Between 1880 and 1920, college football changed, reflecting more commercial, more "modern" values: secularism, equality of opportunity to compete, specialization and rationalization of roles, bureaucratic organization, quantification, and the quest for records.[15] These new characteristics were evident as early as the 1920s. Modern aspects of college sports can be seen in the changing role of football coaches and the growth of athletic establishments with their increasingly specialized personnel, and no coach exemplifies these changes better than Yale's legendary Walter Camp. It is difficult to imagine a better trailblazer for the newly emergent game of football than this remarkably gifted athlete who in four years as an undergraduate and two as a medical student competed in intercollegiate football, baseball, rowing, swimming, and track and field.[16]

Walter Camp must be regarded as the messenger of modernity to college sports. He carried his gifts as a versatile athlete into coaching to become an innovator in rules and tactics for football, and largely through his organizational genius the rough-and-tumble game of rugby gave birth to the distinctly American game of football. William Baker sees a connection between Camp's work as president of a clock manufacturing company and his imaginative revisions of some of the basic rules of rugby, rules which seemed to Camp disorderly and chaotic. Rugby's scrum, the progenitor of the modern football huddle, Camp thought to be not merely a chaotic mass of interlocked bodies, but an "unreasonable" way to try to move the ball down the field,[17] so he substituted what he thought to be "reasonable," well-planned tactics geared to achieve a well-coordinated momentum in moving the

[13] Kent Sagendorph, *Michigan: The Story of the University* (New York: 1948), 150, cited in Rudolph, *The American College*, 374.

[14] Rudolph, *The American College*, 386.

[15] Allen Guttmann, *From Ritual to Record: The Nature of Modern Sports* (New York: Columbia University Press, 1978), 16.

[16] Baker, *Sports in the Modern World*, 129.

[17] Ibid.

ball. As simple as this change may appear, one can easily imagine the kinds of changes it brought to the emerging game of football; consider for example the many times radio and television sports play-by-play announcers have commented on how a football team had moved with "clock-like precision" down the field in the waning moments of a game.

Through his organizational genius and innovative abilities, Camp [18] created the model for the role of the head coach within a growing and increasingly complex sports system. The development of specific roles, a hallmark of bureaucratic development in any hierarchical organization, can also be traced at the team sports level to Walter Camp. For the first time, the actual training of "specialists" began to occur. Under Camp, the head coach's responsibilities at Yale were extended to include central authority over the administration of specific sporting activities.[18] Camp contributed to the establishment of the formal rules of the game, and he introduced a record-keeping system and bureaucracy for the sport by maintaining extensive records on team formation and training method, a practice that contributed to the standardization of procedures and ensured the continuity of the game. Although college football in Camp's day was different in some respects from its modern counterpart, there is a clear line from Camp's initial methods and procedures to those of the most highly developed and specialized football organization existing today.[19]

Walter Camp's methods caught on, and before long, the introduc- [19] tion of other administrative innovations suggested a growing integration of management values and techniques into college football. As athletic programs continued to expand, university administrators established centrally appointed athletic committees to promote the new values of efficiency and control. Program growth, expanding financial activities, and growing central authority over the administration and management, along with growing alumni insistence on a winning program, established a pattern that remains the model for the modern athletic complex. One result of these changes was that the alumni were integrated into the evolving college sports system.[20]

Football's Growing Pains and Emerging Regulation

Like the game itself, the development of football was full of fits [20] and starts. The game also absorbed its share of public criticism, leveled

---

[18] Ervin and McCaffey, 9.
[19] Ibid.
[20] Rudolph, *The American College*, 382–84; John Savage, *American College Athletics* (New York: The Carnegie Foundation, 1929), 23–24.

especially at its evident brutality. In 1905 alone, 18 athletes died and nearly 150 were injured in collegiate football games. The growing national press, eager for the sensational, seized upon such news, producing a public outcry for the abolishment of football. The outcry was so great that President Theodore Roosevelt himself intervened. In his typical manner of dealing with corruption in public and private life, he called the principals together for lunch at the White House and directed them to clean up the game. The principals in this case were representatives from Harvard, Yale, and Princeton. They responded accordingly by holding a national conference that led to the founding of the first association for the regulation of college athletics: the Intercollegiate Athletic Association (ICAA), later to become the National Collegiate Athletic Association (NCAA).[21] Charged with adopting rules and procedures that would lead to the reduction, if not elimination, of brutality, the formation of the ICAA temporarily muted the criticisms directed at intercollegiate athletics.

By the 1920s there was no returning to a more informal game. 21 College football was fast becoming a "national mania" and its future would be linked with the development of mass entertainment in a growing industrial society. With this growth came "new freedoms, new drives, new searchings for emotional and physical outlets; and sports seemed to provide the one big national denominator."[22] This so-called Golden Era of college sports was a time of stadium building, a time in which universities and colleges engaged in a large-scale construction program of building sport complexes to accommodate growing spectator interest. Yale built a seventy-five-thousand seat stadium, at that time the nation's largest.[23] In 1923 the University of Michigan built a field house large enough to contain a football game.[24] Almost ninety thousand screaming spectators could watch their favorite team parade onto the gridiron at Ann Arbor by 1927, and twenty-one years later a modern $4 million football stadium would be built with the profits from the gate receipts alone, a tradition which continues at Michigan.[25]

On the West Coast, gigantic sports arenas were built in Los 22 Angeles and Pasadena in anticipation of the continued growth of spectator interest. The glitter and glamour of the Roaring Twenties was reflected by the color and imaginative spectacle of big marching bands, majorettes, and that special esprit and reckless abandon captured today by Keith Jackson and other "color" commentators on

---

[21] Guy L. Lewis, "Theodore Roosevelt's Role in the 1905 Football Controversy," *Research Quarterly* 40 (December 1969):717–24.

[22] Rudolph, *The American College*, 382.

[23] Ervin and McCaffey, 15.

[24] Rudolph, *The American College*, 381.

[25] Ibid., 389.

Saturday football games. Truly, as William Baker suggests, the foundations of modern football were laid in the 1920s.[26]

During this time, increasing numbers of football stadia were not [23] the only evidence of growing fan interest. The amount of money being spent by fans on recreational activities was also increasing. The gate receipts of forty-nine major colleges increased from $2,696,345 to over $9,000,000 from 1921 to 1929. Attendance for the same period more than doubled from 1,504,319 to 3,617,421.[27] By 1929, the year the bottom fell out of the stock market, an estimated twenty million people a year were attending college football games.[28]

College athletics was also affected by a little-publicized series of [24] events that amounted to formal recognition that intercollegiate athletics had actually become a part of higher education and that they could hardly be perceived any longer as extracurricular. For example, the 1920s gave birth to athletic dormitories, professional trainers, and full-time athletic coaches, all part of what we have come to recognize as the infrastructure of big-time college athletics. These changes allowed sports programs to grow and opened opportunities for these programs to gain institutional funds. Add to this the continuing growth of alumni associations that increasingly identified themselves with their colleges through sports and the institutionalization of college athletics was all but complete.

Commercialism and College Athletics

Not everyone was impressed by the millions of fans and dollars. [25] Alarmed by the growing commercialism and abuses in recruitment in college athletics, the prestigious Carnegie Foundation issued a report on the situation in 1929. Known as the Carnegie Report on American College Athletics, the study condemned the "paid coach, the gate receipts, the special training," and declared that football was no longer a student's game. Instead, the report called it "a highly organized commercial enterprise," and referred to "professional coaches" and to administrators who "take a slice of the profits for college buildings."[29] The foundation was quite clear regarding responsibility for correcting the situation: "The defense of the intellectual integrity of the college and university lies with the president and faculty."[30]

---

[26] Baker, *Sports in the Modern World*, 217.
[27] Ervin and McCaffey, 15.
[28] W. Freeman, "College Athletics in the Twenties: The Golden Age or Fool's Gold," (Paper presented at History Symposium of the National Association for Sport and Physical Education, Seattle, Wash., April 1977). Cited in Joanna Davenport, "From Crew to Commercialism," 9.
[29] John Savage, *American College Athletics*, viii.
[30] Ibid., xx.

The Carnegie Report was received with a predictable lack of en- 26 thusiasm. Although there was a decline in the recruiting and subsidizing of college athletics following the report's publication, it seems in retrospect to have been due primarily to the effects of the crippling depression and the threat of a major war. Like so many reports gathering dust on library shelves, this one was mostly ignored, except by an occasional scholar and even more occasional reformer.[31] One reason for the Carnegie Report's negligible effect on commercialism in college sports was the existence of a formidable sports clientele—groups that for business and commercial purposes found the promotion of college athletics, especially football, indispensable to their welfare. By the end of the first quarter of the twentieth century, a strong and well-defined sports business network had already emerged and taken on formidable shape.

Perhaps there is a lesson to be learned from history. In spite of 27 repeated efforts to eradicate abuses associated with college sports, it is unlikely that much can be done to correct abuses as long as powerful business connections exist among those who profit from the continuation of college athletics in its present commercial forms. In effect, the basis for greater alumni influence in college sports already existed in the 1920s. In the period up to and including the Savage Report, however, many of the connections were symbolic and not fully realized materially. The alumni in earlier areas could not know the political-economic implications of their intense emotional attachments to their universities' sports programs; contemporary alumni and boosters consciously use their financial resources to lobby not merely for the retention but for the expansion of sports programs. Recent news stories indicating the depth of booster involvement both in the recruiting and retention of topflight college athletes suggest that more is required to rid the system of such abuses than the official ranting and raving we have become so accustomed to hearing.

From Commercialism to Corporate Athleticism— the 1930s to the 1950s

The Great Depression and World War II slowed the rapid growth 28 of college athletics by reducing their budgets. Extracurricular activities were curtailed and athletic contests had to be rescheduled to save travel costs. In retrospect, these adjustments seem merely to have delayed the commercial emphasis in college athletics. For example, the liberaliztion of player substitution rules in the late 1940s actually

---

[31] Ervin and McCaffey, 17.

required an expansion in the size of athlete rosters, and abuses in recruiting, even for reduced athletic machines, continued unabated.[32]

By the early 1950s the NCAA belatedly recognized the problem of commercialism in college sports, so emphatically referred to in the 1929 Carnegie Report, by officially authorizing the use of athletic grants-in-aid. The rationale for doing so was that not only would this policy be realistic, but it would also enable the NCAA to extend its regulatory influence over recruiting practices. In addition, the proponents of this policy extending the NCAA's rule asserted, the Alice-in-Wonderland logic notwithstanding, that granting athletic scholarships and increasing regulatory control would bring about "parity" among the competing institutions and would thereby preserve the amateur status of athletes and the existing system of college athletics.[33] Given the growth of commercialism in college athletics, with all of its associated abuses, one can reasonably question the motivation behind and the intent of these rules. Surely the NCAA's attempt to regulate the recruitment process was not naive; it may well have been motivated by an eagerness to create the appearance of bringing order to a sports system nearly out of control.

Obviously, the NCAA's role in regulating the recruitment of college athletes has been less than a success. One need only look at the growing list of rule violators among the most competitive institutions for evidence of its failure. To give just one example, in 1984 the University of Florida was granted the dubious distinction of being charged with violating more NCAA rules than any university in the NCAA's history. In the more than thirty years since the NCAA adopted its grants-in-aid policy, the business and commercial aspects of college sports, especially in football and basketball at Division I-A institutions, have enhanced neither the return to amateurism nor university control of college sports. . . .

Despite the NCAA's efforts, by the 1950s commercialization had developed to the point that football and basketball players had become commodities in a growing mass entertainment industry, one that now includes the many of the leading universities in the United States. The "scholarship" system was the means by which to procure these players. To obtain scarce athletic talent, universities increased financial "assistance," aided especially by alumni and boosters, who mobilized their efforts to get the best recruits. The circumvention of newly formulated NCAA rules became a business calculation: a felt necessity, worth taking risks for.

---

[32] Ibid.
[33] Ibid., 18.

Minimal as they were, the NCAA limitations on the granting of 32
athletic scholarships did affect the bargaining power of competing
institutions and thus in some ways encouraged the more aggressive
tactics of alumni; some booster groups were tempted to resort to
under-the-table payments and "slush funds" in order to attract athletes who could make the difference between winning and losing. . . .

TV and Corporate Athleticism—the 1960s to the 1970s

The 1960s and 1970s were a period of extraordinary growth for 33
sports entertainment in the United States. Although many expected
professional sports franchises to saturate the country with sports spectacles, few predicted that college and university sports programs
would also join the business of providing "major league" contests.[34]
Crucial to this latest sports explosion was the emergence of television
as the most potent medium of mass communication. If television was
the medium, then mass entertainment was to become the message,
with football and later basketball to become its texts.

The effect of television on the development of commercialism in 34
intercollegiate sport is complex, and certain aspects of that development require closer examination. Television does more than perpetu-
ate the marriage of the mass media to sports spectacles; it has fundamentally changed and reordered the business framework in which
athleticism takes place. It has widened the marketing of the product
and at the same time has begun a restructuring of the sports marketplace itself. Equally important, it has supplanted the sanctions associated with NCAA rules.

Television is the main producer of sports entertainment, and in 35
this capacity, it strengthens the corporate side of big-time, competitive
intercollegiate athletics by defining the terms in which market competition takes place. Only the most naive would assume that efforts to
gain national rankings and television exposure, regardless of the cost
of getting there, are not the prime motivating forces in big-time college
sports. Television has introduced commercialism of a new kind into
college sports. What is different about contemporary commercialism
in intercollegiate sports is the extensive character and organization of
market capitalism as we approach the twenty-first century. We have
moved from the pre-1929, relatively unregulated business system to
the planned organization of corporate institutions and to the more
regulated, integrated arrangement of business systems.

---

[34] Baker, *Sports in the Modern World*, 318.

In some respects, the consequences for universities and colleges 36
able to compete for the "positional goods" of national rank and television revenues are not very different from what we have observed in
the past. The competitors themselves have changed; that is, there are
fewer "private" institutions able to compete in football for national
honors in Division I-A, although this is less true in the case of basketball at the Division I-A level.

The Black Athlete and the Development of
Corporate Athleticism

While great black athletes did play college football as early as the 37
turn of this century, they are notable almost as much for their small
numbers on white campuses as they are for their exceptional talent.
William H. Lewis at Amherst (who played during the years 1890–93),
Fritz Pollard at Brown (1915–19), Paul Robeson at Rutgers (1917–21),
and Fred "Duke" Slater at Iowa (1918–21) come instantly to mind. But
the full emergence of the black athlete on the national scene had to
wait until after World War II for the historic Supreme Court decision
of 1954 outlawing racial segregation in the public schools. During
the 1940s and 1950s, Woody Strode, Kenny Washington, and Jackie
Robinson started a tradition of black athletes at UCLA that continues
in southern California today.

Since 1954 a revolution has been going on. One result has been the 38
emergence of, and in some sports virtual domination by, black athletes; NCAA Division I-A intercollegiate basketball perhaps most dramatically illustrates this black dominance. After years of having almost
no blacks in athletics, the Southwest and Southeast Conferences became well represented by black performers. The University of Texas
added six black football players between 1963 and 1973; the University
of Mississippi, having achieved notoriety for refusing James Meredith
entrance to its classrooms in 1962, added five during these years; and
the University of Alabama, previously best known for Governor
George C. Wallace's personally blocking its doors to prevent the entrance of black students, added thirteen blacks to its athletic teams.[35]
Ironically, the university (probably) had to pay the black athletes to get
them to come. And the University of Pittsburgh, a center for football
talent and the producer of the Dallas Cowboys' All-Pro running back

---

[35] Gregory S. Sojka, "The Education of the Student-Athlete in America: From Divinity to the
Divine" (Paper presented at the Conference on Sports and Higher Education, Skidmore College,
March 1982), 12.

Tony Dorsett, went from two to thirty-one black football players during the same period.[36]

Universities have reaped financial gains from high-visibility, 39 revenue-generating sports of football and basketball, sports in which blacks are disproportionately represented, but they have gained further advantages through their uneven exchange with athletes in other ways as well. Black athletes constitute the lifeblood of major collegiate football and basketball powers. In fact, the dominance of black basketball players is all but total among the strongest teams. Georgetown University is a case in point. In a 1984 game, Georgetown, rated as the nation's best quintet in the early part of the 1984–85 season, played the University of Nevada, Las Vegas, on Georgetown's home court in Washington, D.C. At times all ten players on the court were black, in contrast with the virtually all-white student body of Georgetown cheering their magnificent team on to victory from the stands.

In spite of what they have to offer, black athletes still receive fewer 40 than one in ten of the athletic scholarships given out in the United States. Of those fortunate few who do receive scholarships, approximately 65 percent to 75 percent are not likely to graduate, and of those who do, 75 percent will graduate with degrees in physical education, the acceptable "jock major," which is seldom good preparation for the hard knocks of life after sports.[37]

Harry Edwards, arguably the best authority on the subject of the 41 exploitation of black athletes, has drawn attention to the inadequate compensation often awarded to black athletes. According to Edwards, it is not the athletes who have failed to live up to their part of the bargain; rather, it is higher education which has failed to compensate athletes appropriately for showcasing the universities' high-visibility programs. Universities have benefited directly in the form of huge gate receipts, donors to university programs, television revenues, and national visibility (and what president won't jump at the opportunity to advertise his university during those halftime breaks in the game).[38]

The increasing recruitment of black athletes began as the mass 42 media was transforming much of the financial and economic structure of intercollegiate athletics. With its growing audience appeal, television was increasing the size of the markets for the entertainment products of universities, and thus was directly contributing to the recruitment and exploitation of the paid gladiators hired by institutions to do one thing: perform.

---

[36] Kenneth Denlinger and Leonard Shapiro, *Athletes for Sale* (New York: Thomas Y. Crowell, 1975), 33.

[37] Harry Edwards, "Educating Black Athletes," *The Atlantic Monthly* (August 1983): 31–38.

[38] Ibid.

So blacks fully emerged on the national athletic scene in many of   43
the major colleges and universities at a time when the mass media was
beginning to change profoundly the social character of entertainment
in the United States. Powerful institutional forces, outside and within
black communities, were laying the groundwork for the recruitment
and development of an essential commodity, prime athletic talent.

Women's Athletics and the Development of Corporate Athleticism

Our focus . . . is on those forces that have shaped commercialism   44
and corporatism in the development of intercollegiate athletics, and in
this context, women's sports programs have received little of our
attention because until recently they remained strongholds of amateurism and intramuralism scarcely noticed by nonparticipants and
almost invisible to alumni and boosters.[39] The early mainstays of
women's sports on campus had been croquet, walking, ice skating,
and later tennis, basketball, volleyball, field hockey, track and field,
swimming, and gymnastics. There was little change in the attitude
toward women's sports until the historic passage in 1972 of Title IX,
which required colleges and universities to provide women with opportunities in athletics equal to those extended to men. Title IX was
manifestly clear that there should be no sex discrimination in any
educational institution receiving federal funds. What was not so clear
was how women's programs could be supported without curtailing
the men's programs. Sensing a danger to money-making sports, the
NCAA sued in order to have the revenue-producing sports exempted
from Title IX requirements.[40]

Fearing adverse effects on the ability of major athletic powers to   45
recruit star athletes for their growing programs, the NCAA sought
initially to thwart the effect of Title IX. Having failed to do so, the
NCAA recently took over the championship events for women's athletics from the Association for Intercollegiate Athletics for Women
(AIAW), just at a time when the potential revenue growth and women
athletes themselves may become valuable assets to their institutions as
money-making attractions.[41] More recently, women's athletics suffered a setback when the courts ruled that athletic programs not
receiving federal funds are exempt from Title IX antidiscrimination
provisions.

---

[39] Sojka, "The Education of the Student-Athlete," 15.
[40] Davenport, "From Crew to Commercialism," 21.
[41] Sojka, "The Education of the Student-Athlete," 17.

The full development of corporate athleticism in women's sports 46
teams lies in the future. But already the inevitable signs are appearing
of recruiting "abuses" associated almost exclusively up until now with
highly competitive men's athletics. These abuses are occurring at a
time when television is creating, as it did with the international attraction of Olympic gymnastics, new markets for athleticism of all kinds,
so it seems likely that women's athletics may eventually become the
object of television's exposure and development. Women's athletics
has come a long way from clubhouse intramuralism, and it will go far
as its attractiveness is communicated to larger audiences through the
mass media.

Conclusion

This historical overview of the commercial aspects of intercolle- 47
giate sports reveals several factors that have influenced the present
bureaucratic, and corporate character of college sports. The structure
of intercollegiate athletics was altered by changing socioeconomic
forces that shaped the features of newly commercialized athletics and
defined the recreational needs of students and spectators alike.

At the same time, a new set of values reflecting the growing 48
ascendancy of corporate values and norms was being forged in mass
society. Within this context record keeping took shape as the standard
of excellence and of the "naturalness" of the market model of competition—a model whose cultural corollary is an emphasis on skill acquisition as a condition of fun and personal development.[42]

It is also within this context of changing values that the complex 49
and growing system of corporate athleticism developed, a system that
increasingly demanded both bureaucratic structures and enhanced
specificity of the roles within them. In this context the certified and
thoroughly professional coach became organizer, manager, and entrepreneur. Numerous rule changes making college sports more appealing to wider publics took place. Concomitant with this synthesis of
market and bureaucratic norms was the formidable ability of the market, via television, to penetrate the popular consciousness.

We have noted the popularity of intercollegiate football from its 50
beginnings and the rapidity with which the game was absorbed by
universities and colleges and by the public. The incorporation of a
mass public into the structures of sports-induced market forces is a

---

[42] Richard Grunneau, *Class, Sports, and Social Development* (Amherst, Mass.: The University of
Massachusetts Press, 1983), 143.

pattern that we recognize only too clearly today. In this way, the development of modern sport generally, and intercollegiate football specifically, is at the same time constitutive of and separate from the social context existing at a given time.[43] While we shall not try to explain the entire development of intercollegiate football by a crude Marxist analysis, we believe that market capitalism and its transition to more bureaucratic structures has significantly influenced the historical evolution of college sports from amateurism to corporate athleticism as the dominant organizing mode for big-time college athletics. What the history of commercialism in sports reveals, in short, is the extraordinary reduction of athletics to a limited set of values and beliefs derived primarily from the market system. The emphasis on technique and role differentiation in football, developed initially by Walter Camp, can be seen as an attempt to integrate "scientific" play and "amateurism." As we shall argue in more detail, amateurism is incompatible with the market system, with its subjugation of all organized activity to a rational model of productive efficiency. The attitudes resulting from this productive process were powerful enough that they were able to transform narrow, class-specific responses into the broader, shared cultural experiences that now predominate in mass society.

Do Sports Really Make Money for the University?

BARBARA R. BERGMANN

Barbara Bergmann, a distinguished professor of economics at American University and the president of the American Association of University Professors (AAUP), wrote this essay for the AAUP journal, *Academe*, in 1991. Her argument challenges a claim frequently made by supporters of the present system in college athletics: big sports bring in big money for their institutions. Along the way, Bergmann challenges as well the contentions that sports programs help minority students who might not otherwise get to attend college and that sports programs encourage donations from alumni and the public. Not so, Bergmann asserts, centering her argument on the example of the University of Maryland.

---

[43] Ibid., 140.

It's game time, and from the stands we hear the roar of tens of 1
thousands of adoring fans of our college's team, who have paid a
handsome price for their tickets. Millions more at home are watching
the game on TV, and the network sends our school huge sums for the
privilege of beaming beer commercials to them. Perhaps the alumni,
inspired by our team's valiant effort, will send large checks to our
fund-raisers.

To the naked eye, it certainly looks as though college athletics 2
programs make money. Most writers on the subject firmly believe so.
An article in the *Chronicle of Higher Education* went so far as to say,
" . . . there is no revenue in training doctors and lawyers, [but]
colleges and universities make a substantial, direct and immediate
income from their student athletes."[1]

The pot of gold that successful big-time sports supposedly earn 3
helps to justify the harboring on campus of an entertainment enterprise that has little relation to the university's primary purpose, the
fostering of knowledge. This enterprise gives a lot of spectators—
some students, some faculty, some alumni, some with no campus
connection—a lot of fun. It gives those young people with extraordinary athletic talent a way to develop that talent, and have the consuming experience of rigorous competition.

But big-time sports also give rise to admission and cheating scan- 4
dals, fake curricula for many of the athletes, a boozy kill-'em atmosphere, and the unwholesome sight of the university president
cowering before boosters and booster-trustees. The scandals that ac-
company big-time sports get pretty big at times. But how could any
institution embrace meaningful intercollegiate sports reform, much
less give up trying to compete in the big time, if it means giving up all
that money?

The truth is that "all that money" is nothing but an illusion. The 5
lack of public information about the expenditures that such programs
entail leads to the mistaken assumption that the profits from sports
must be enormous. The revenues are big, but the costs of these programs are as big or bigger. The assumption that institutions derive
financial benefit from sports programs is false in most cases: sports
programs that generate profits used to help finance an institution's
regular programs are exceedingly rare. On the contrary, sports programs can and frequently do drain large sums from the academic
aspects of the budget.

---

[1] Tim Green and Alexander Rosenberg, "Colleges Should Offer Vocational Courses for Athletes," *The Chronicle of Higher Education*, September 25, 1985.

The best way to demystify the financial aspects of big-time college 6
programs is to look at the records of a major public institution that
publishes some information on its athletic budgets. These published
budgets can be misleading, since the cost of providing the athletic
department with telephone service, utilities, and stadium upkeep may
be omitted from the athletic budget and hidden instead in the institution's academic budget. Nevertheless, these athletic department budgets do reveal enough to shatter the illusion of "all that money"
helping the institution.

Looking at a Real Example

The following table shows the published planning budget for the 7
intercollegiate athletic department at the University of Maryland at
College Park for 1986. That was a relatively good period for Maryland
sports. The teams had been doing well. The fallout from the death of
basketball star Len Bias from a drug overdose, the firing of coach Lefty
Driesell, and the money-draining NCAA penalties for the infractions
of his successor were all in the future.

**Planning Budget for Intercollegiate
Athletic Programs, University of
Maryland, College Park, 1986**

Expenses	
Basketball	$ 750,526
Football	1,412,030
Golf Course	474,219
Other Men's Sports	706,109
Women's Sports	542,565
Administrative Personnel	1,345,690
Administrative Operations	1,240,631
Tennis Facility	32,000
Total Expenses	$6,503,770
Receipts	
Basketball Gate	$ 470,000
Football Gate	1,444,000
Golf Course	471,620
Television Distribution	1,750,000
Student Athletic Fee	1,991,384
Other Fees	62,400
Concessions	180,000
Tennis Fees	77,800
Other	56,566
Total Receipts	$6,503,770

Source: University of Maryland, College Park, 1986
Budget.

Intercollegiate athletics programs at Maryland did have hefty 8 revenues coming in during 1986. The university expected receipts that year of $6.5 million. But in what sense did intercollegiate programs "make money"? Maryland's plan called for the intercollegiate athletic program to spend $6.5 million—every dollar it brought in. Not a cent would be left over for any purpose of the university, other than intercollegiate athletics programs.

The University of Maryland's balanced athletic budget was only a 9 plan. State regulations in Maryland require that programs be "self-supporting," so it would have been illegal as well as impolitic to plan to run a deficit. But when the year was over, the athletic department found it had spent more than its income.

The deficit came even though the university athletics program in 10 1986 was a bigger success on the field of battle than expected. The university's teams were invited to make some post-season tournament appearances, and revenues for that year actually climbed to over $8 million. Nevertheless, expenses turned out to be even bigger.

Maryland's athletic department, which loses money even in win- 11 ning seasons, is not an isolated bad-luck case. A survey of institutions with big-time athletics programs carried out by the National College Athletic Association showed that only 1 percent claimed that the financial goal of their athletic program was earning profits to support non-athletic activities of the institution. The rest said they wanted to earn money to expand the athletics program (15 percent), or simply to meet expenses (58 percent) or, more modestly, to keep losses to a minimum (26 percent).[2] In the NCAA survey, 42 percent of big-time athletics programs reported losses in the survey year, with the average annual deficit at $824,000.

Of course, a university whose program avoids losses in one year 12 may easily succumb to them in the next. If the university's teams compile an uninspiring record on the playing field, its attendance and television revenues will slip, and it will lose its chance for post-season appearances for its teams. It is in this sense that the star player or the talented coach brings in a lot of money. Without them, the team is a sure loser, both on the playing field and at the box office.

But at least half the teams have to be losers, and a minuscule 13 number can be big winners. The grinding battle to avoid being one of those losers and to achieve big-winner status tempts institutions to break or shade the rules. Fierce competition is the source of the pressure to recruit talented athletes without regard to whether they meet

---

[2] Mitchell H. Raiborn, Revenues and Expenses of Intercollegiate Athletic Programs: Analysis of Financial Trends and Relationships, 1981–1985, NCAA, P.O. Box 1906, Mission, Kansas 66201 (p. 49).

admission standards, to make them work and travel so they have no chance for a normal academic experience, and to arrange fake courses and passing grades for them.

When on-the-field success brings in revenues that exceed planned 14 expenditures, the spending on sports has a tendency to expand, so there's nothing left over for donations to any academic purpose. When losses occur, the university makes them up from within the university. At Maryland, losses in the athletic program can be covered by draining revenues generated by the summer university and the dining halls. The surpluses these enterprises generate might instead go to academic uses, or might be given back to the students in lower fee levels.

Some athletic programs siphon off regular scholarship monies and 15 give them to athletes to supplement athletic scholarship money derived from boosters. This practice diverts support from academically able students from poor backgrounds who could benefit from a regular education and shifts it to athletes who principally devote their ability, interest, talent, and time to nonacademic pursuits.

To add insult to injury, the athletic program is sometimes por- 16 trayed as a wonderful way for poor members of minority groups to get an education they otherwise could not afford. In fact, these programs may actually reduce opportunities for such people to get a genuine degree. College athletics programs mislead them by fixing their attention on the improbable dream of achieving success in life through professional sports, divert them from efforts to achieve academically, and rob them of the time and financial support for regular study.

Forcing Students to Support the Games

From the Maryland budget, we can see that $2 million—or almost 17 a third of the athletic receipts—was not earned but rather extracted from the undergraduate and graduate students as athletic fees. In return for the fees, a limited number of students could get "free" tickets for the worst seats at some games. Those students on highly restricted budgets and those with little interest in attending sports events would undoubtedly prefer not to have to make such a forced exchange.

It is sometimes claimed that big-time men's football and basketball 18 support the non-revenue intercollegiate sports. A look at the planning budget shows that claim to be false at Maryland. The $3.8 million in revenues in the Maryland planning budget that men's football and basketball were to generate was more than accounted for by the teams' planned expenses and their share of administrative expenses.

Student fees at Maryland cover the expenditures on the non- 19
revenue intercollegiate sports in the planning budget. These compulsory student fees fund intercollegiate competition in baseball,
swimming, soccer, tennis, and women's basketball and field hockey.
These activities should not be confused with programs that would
allow students of less-than-prodigious athletic abilities to get exercise
and have the experience of team play.

The non-revenue intercollegiate sports tend to be as profes- 20
sionalized as men's football and basketball. Many of the athletes involved are zealously recruited, may be admitted despite inability to
qualify under regular standards, may get full scholarships and expenses, and are required to spend more than forty hours a week on the
sport.

Ordinary students get no discernible benefit from the non- 21
revenue intercollegiate sports. They have almost no chance of participating on a walk-in basis. These sports draw few spectators, so the
student body does not even get entertainment from them. The NCAA
requires the big-time sports institutions to support non-revenue
sports at vast expense, but the value of the activity to anybody but the
athletes themselves and their coaches is nil.

Do Sports Encourage Appropriations and Donations?

Some make the claim for athletic programs that, while not bring- 22
ing profits directly, they bring name recognition, increase student
applications, and make it easier to collect money from alumni, state
legislatures, and big donors to academic programs. Successful sports
do bring a university celebrity. But it is doubtful that such celebrity
pays off financially or in other ways for the academic enterprise of the
university. No one has brought forward any evidence of such a payoff.
Several systematic research studies have found no significant correlation between winning teams and appropriations or donations to university academic programs.[3]

At Maryland, the university's fund-raiser told me that he believed 23
the athletic programs actually reduce donations. Those who give generously to the sports program seldom if ever contribute to funds that
can be used for academic purposes. The prominence of athletics on the
campus, even free of scandal, may turn off potential donors who
otherwise might endow a professorship or build a lab or theater.

---

[3] "Do Winning Teams Spur Contributions? Scholars and Fund Raisers Are Skeptical," *The Chronicle of Higher Education*, January 13, 1988, pp. 1, 32–34.

The idea that big-time athletics programs bring millions of dollars   24
to the university is false. They can incur net losses that cost the
university millions that could be used for academic purposes. They do
bring entertainment, drama, and attention, but at a stiff price in
money and integrity.

The First Eligibility Code

NATIONAL COLLEGIATE ATHLETIC ASSOCIATION

This Code was adopted as part of the original NCAA Constitution
(Article VII) in 1906.

The following rules . . . are suggested as a minimum: 1

1. No student shall represent a college or university in any intercollegiate game or contest, who is not taking a full schedule of work as
   prescribed in the catalogue of the institution.

2. No student shall represent a college or university . . . who has at
   any time received, either directly or indirectly, money, or any
   other consideration, to play on any team, or . . . who has competed for a money prize or portion of gate money in any contest, or
   who has competed for any prize against a professional.

3. No student shall represent a college or university . . . who is paid
   or has received, directly or indirectly, any money, or financial concession, or emolument as past or present compensation for, or as
   prior consideration or inducement to play in, or enter any athletic
   contest, whether the said remuneration be received from, or paid
   by, or at the instance of any organization, committee or faculty of
   such college or university, or any individual whatever.

4. No student shall represent a college or university . . . who has
   participated in intercollegiate games or contests during four previous years.

5. No student who has been registered as a member of any other
   college or university shall participate in any intercollegiate game
   or contest until he shall have been a student of the institution
   which he represents at least one college year.

6. Candidates for positions on athletic teams shall be required to fill
   out cards, which shall be placed on file, giving a full statement of
   their previous athletic records.

The Code on Recruiting and Subsidizing of Athletes

NATIONAL COLLEGIATE ATHLETIC ASSOCIATION

This description of NCAA policy is quoted from the annual *Proceedings of the National Collegiate Athletic Association*, 1935. The NCAA has no equivalent formal policy on recruitment and subsidies today.

It is unjustifiable—

1. For a student to receive any subsidy of monetary value, either directly or indirectly, primarily for his athletic services.

2. To employ prospective athletes before they matriculate in an institution, or make advance payment to a prospective student for future services, or to make any guarantee of payment which is not conditioned upon the service being performed in advance of the payment, or to make any payment for services at a rate greater than the current rate for other students in the institution.

3. To permit a boy to participate in intercollegiate contests who has ever received a loan, scholarship aid, remission of fees, or employment, primarily because he is an athlete, through channels not open to non-athletes equally with athletes.

4. For members of athletic or physical education staffs to recruit athletes by initiating correspondence or conversation, or by arranging for interviews with boys who are prospective athletes.

5. To promise prospective athletes employment, loans, scholarships, or remission of fees, except as they may be secured by other students through the regular channels of the institution, and those channels should be outside the athletic or physical education departments.

6. For alumni groups, clubs, fraternities, or other organizations to make promises or direct or indirect subsidies to prospective students, primarily for their athletic ability.

7. To endeavor to persuade a prospective athlete, by offer of a scholarship or job, or by any other means, to transfer from a college where he has made application for admission and has been accepted.

The Principles Governing Financial Aids to Athletes

NATIONAL COLLEGIATE ATHLETIC ASSOCIATION

These rules comprise Section 4 from "The Principles for the Conduct of Intercollegiate Athletics." That code was adopted in 1935 and published in Proceedings of the National Collegiate Athletic Association, *A-II.*

Financial aids in the form of scholarships, fellowships or other- 1 wise, even though originating from sources other than persons on whom the recipient may be naturally or legally dependent for support, shall be permitted without loss of eligibility

a. if approved and awarded on the basis of need by the regular agency established . . . for granting of aid to all students, provided [that aid] shall not exceed the amount of tuition fo instruction and for stated incidental institution fees, or

b. if approved and awarded on the basis of qualifications in which high scholarship on the part of the recipient is the major factor and . . . provided, however, that the existence of such scholarship, fellowship or other aid and its terms are announced in an official publication of such institution, or

c. if awarded on the basis of qualifications of which athletic ability is not one. . . .

In all cases the agency making the award of aid shall give the 2 recipient a written statement of the amount, duration, conditions and terms thereof.

The acceptance of financial aid not permitted by the provisions of 3 this section shall render the recipient ineligible for intercollegiate athletic competition.

d. Any scholarship or other aid to an athlete shall be awarded only through a regular agency approved by the institution for the granting of aid to all students.

e. No athlete shall be deprived of financial aids permitted [in] this section because of failure to participate in intercollegiate athletics.

f. Compensation of an athlete for employment shall be commensurate with the service rendered.

g. No one shall be denied student aid because he is an athlete.

15

AFFIRMATIVE ACTION

Balancing Act

RICHARD STENGEL

Richard Stengel, a Princeton graduate and Rhodes Scholar, is the author of *January Sun: One Day, Three Lives, a South African Town* (1991) and a contributor to *Time* on African-American issues. In the following essay (first published in *Time* in 1987), Stengel summarizes a key affirmative action case, *Johnson v. Transportation Agency, Santa Clara County* (1987). In order to understand more fully the Supreme Court decision on this case and its ramifications, you may need to read Title VII of the 1964 Civil Rights Act (available in the Government Documents section of most large libraries). The salient points are quoted in Antonin Scalia's essay in this chapter. You might also find it useful to learn more about the *Bakke* decision of 1978, in which a white man successfully challenged a medical school admissions procedure on the basis of reverse discrimination. (One good book on the subject is Allen Sindler's *Bakke, DeFunis, and Minority Admissions*, 1978.) Things turned out differently for Paul Johnson.

After four gritty years working on the road for the Santa Clara 1 County transportation agency—patching holes, shoveling asphalt, opening culverts—Diane Joyce applied in 1980 for a less strenuous desk job as a road dispatcher. At the time not one of the California agency's 238 skilled positions was held by a woman. Joyce knew, however, that two years earlier the county had enacted a voluntary affirmative-action policy designed to correct that imbalance.

Paul Johnson, a white male who had worked for the agency for 13 2 years, also applied. He and Joyce were among the seven applicants who scored above 70 on the oral exam and were considered qualified. Joyce scored 73, Johnson 75. The local supervisor picked Johnson, but the county's affirmative-action coordinator recommended Joyce. When she got the job, Johnson got a lawyer. Like Allen Bakke and Brian Weber and countless other white males since the advent of affirmative-action programs some 20 years ago, Johnson claimed he was a victim of reverse discrimination.

In its most significant affirmative-action decision since the murky 3 resolution of Bakke's case against the University of California in 1978, the Supreme Court ruled 6 to 3 that it was permissible for the Santa Clara agency to take sex and race into account in employment decisions. "I'm very proud," said Joyce. "I've waited a long time for this." Said Johnson, who is now retired and lives in Washington State: "I'm shocked and disappointed. A ruling like this will cause prejudice in people who have never been prejudiced before."

After nearly a decade of on-the-one-hand, on-the-other-hand rul- 4 ings, [the] decision provides the clearest declaration yet on the role of affirmative action as a remedy for inequality in the American workplace. For the first time the Supreme Court explicitly ruled that women as well as blacks and other minorities can receive preferential treatment. Even more significantly, the decision endorsed a voluntary affirmative-action plan in a situation where there was no proven history of discrimination; all that was necessary, wrote Justice William Brennan for the majority, was evidence of a "manifest imbalance" in the number of women or minorities holding the positions in question.

The decision affects the most universal of employment situations 5 in America: workplaces where it is hard to prove past discrimination but where there is a statistical shortage of women and minorities in certain positions. It is the strongest link in a chain of decisions suggesting that voluntary affirmative-action programs are a desirable way to right such imbalances.

The ruling, predictably enough, delighted civil rights and wom- 6 en's groups while angering the Reagan Administration and others who have been waging an ardent crusade to roll back affirmative action. Many business groups applauded the decision because it helped clarify the legal status of voluntary programs and is likely to discourage future reverse-discrimination actions.

Johnson's suit was based on Title VII of the 1964 Civil Rights Act, 7 which makes it unlawful for an employer "to deprive any individual of employment opportunities or otherwise adversely affect his status as an employee because of such individual's race, color, religion, sex or national origin." Brennan's opinion was guided by the court's 1979 *Weber* ruling upholding an apprentice program in a Kaiser Aluminum plant in Gramercy, La., that reserved 50% of the slots for blacks. Brennan concluded that the Santa Clara plan was "consistent with Title VII's purpose of eliminating the effects of employment discrimination." He wrote, "Given the obvious imbalance in the skilled craft division and given the agency's commitment to eliminating such imbalances . . . it was appropriate to consider as one fact the sex of Ms. Joyce in making its decision."

The Santa Clara program, which set a temporary "goal" of filling 8 36% of its skilled jobs with women, was an attempt to achieve a "work force that mirrored in its major job classification the percentage of women in the area labor market." Brennan argued that the plan, like that in *Weber*, did not "unnecessarily trammel" the interests of whites by creating an absolute bar to their employment.

In a blistering and forceful dissent, Justice Antonin Scalia wrote 9 that the decision "effectively requires employers, public as well as private, to engage in intentional discrimination on the basis of race or sex." He was particularly critical of the decision to permit statistical imbalances to be criteria for justifying an affirmative-action program rather than requiring there be evidence of past discrimination. "This is an enormous expansion, undertaken without the slightest justification or analysis."

The ruling, Scalia contended, turns Title VII on its head. "The 10 court today completes the process of converting [Title VII] from a guarantee that race or sex will not be the basis for employment determinations, to a guarantee that it often will. Ever so subtly . . . we effectively replace the goal of a discrimination-free society with the quite incompatible goal of proportionate representation by race and by sex in the workplace."

After hearing of the court's decision, President Reagan, who has 11 long maintained that affirmative action is immoral and illegal, said simply, "Obviously, I disagree." From the outset, the Administration has vigorously sought to reverse the course of affirmative action, insisting that hiring goals are the same as illegal quotas. The court has now completely rebuffed that effort. Some observers suggest that the Administration's heavy-handed attempts to dismantle affirmative action may have backfired and pushed the court to assert its position more forcefully.

The difficult and divisive national debate over affirmative action 12 arises from a philosophical tension between two basic American values: the protection of individual rights and the quest for social equality. Opponents of affirmative action argue that each individual has the right to be judged on merit. Setting special standards for blacks or women, they maintain, is demeaning and ultimately destructive, both to society and to those who are the intended beneficiaries. Some prominent blacks and women agree, on the grounds that affirmative action is condescending and leads its beneficiaries to call their own achievements into question.

Proponents of affirmative action contend that equality for all can 13 be achieved only through temporary preferences given to blacks, women and other groups that have historically suffered discrimination. It is perverse, they argue, to use civil rights laws to block the very goals—better opportunities for blacks and women—those laws were intended to further.

Preferential treatment in employment was first mandated by Lyndon Johnson in a 1965 presidential order stating that companies doing business with the Government were required to take "affirmative action" to hire women and minorities. Thousands of private companies followed suit, many of them on the grounds that it was good for business. Since then, affirmative action has helped change the way America does business: the Bureau of Labor Statistics projects that between 1985 and 1995, blacks and women will account for three-fourths of all labor-force growth.   14

The Johnson decision, employers believe, protects their affirmative-action programs from reverse-discrimination suits. "This decision wipes away the last lingering doubts," says James McDaniel, manager of affirmative action at E. I. duPont. "Employers can now statistically correct imbalances without the fear of frivolous challenges." In the past, employers with affirmative-action programs had to worry about disgruntled whites as well as excluded minorities. Notes John Jacob, president of the National Urban League: "I have had companies say to me that they intended to go ahead with affirmative-action programs but were concerned about the mounting litigation brought by white males." While the ruling insulates business from reverse-discrimination suits, it may make them more vulnerable to discrimination claims on the part of women and minorities.   15

Many women judged the decision to be properly tough. "I've always said that affirmative action has to hurt a little," says Stanford Law Professor Barbara Babcock. "This is a decision that hurts." Women's groups saw the ruling as a way of helping them penetrate job markets traditionally sealed off from women. Says Claudia Withers, a staff attorney at the Women's Legal Defense Fund in Washington: "As women see opportunities open, they will apply for jobs where before they felt unwelcome." The decision appears particularly relevant to jobs that require no specialized training—blue-collar employment where most applicants, whether female, black, white or male, are generally on an equal footing.   16

Conservatives regarded the decision as another example of the state's infringing on individual liberties and a retreat from the goal of a truly gender-neutral, color-blind society. Michael McDonald, president of the conservative Washington Legal Foundation, says the plan endorsed by the court "was social engineering on a scale I have yet to see equaled elsewhere. Every special-interest group was awarded the right to a job." Some saw the decision as camouflage for quotas. "It is   17 exactly what civil rights law was designed to free us of," declared Nathan Perlmutter, executive director of the Anti-Defamation League. "I consider performance based on race, color, creed or sex, in the absence of evidence that the person has been discriminated against, to be a form of well-intended but nonetheless mischievous discrimination."

Not all businessmen regarded the ruling as a benison. Many employers feel handcuffed by affirmative action and fret that the latest ruling establishes an even more difficult standard for them to follow. "The Supreme Court has changed the ground rules," says Richard Bradley, vice president of the Merchants and Manufacturers Association, a Los Angeles-based organization with 3,206 members. "Now they're saying unless you lean toward a protected category, you may be committing a discriminatory act." 18

The Johnson case will almost certainly result in more affirmative-action programs on the part of employers. Julius Chambers, director of the NAACP Legal Defense Fund, suggests the ruling will "invite" organizations pushing for affirmative action for women and minorities to persuade employers to enact plans to redress any imbalances in their work force. Says Chambers: "There is less basis for an employer responding that it can't because of the uncertainty of the law." Now, after years of judicial uncertainty on affirmative action, future court decisions are likely to concern the limits on specific plans rather than the validity of the concept. 19

Concurring Opinion in Johnson
JOHN PAUL STEVENS

Supreme Court Justice John Paul Stevens, appointed to the Court by President Richard Nixon in 1975, usually joins the "liberal" voting group in Court decisions. However, his reasoning often differs from his colleagues, and he consistently challenges them: Stevens has written more concurring and dissenting opinions than any other Court member. The following is a "concurring" opinion: a document written by a Court member who joins in the opinion handed down by the court but who wishes to do so from a different perspective or to make additional observations about the case. Stevens makes clear in his first paragraph his reasons for writing. He specifically intends that the decision be interpreted and applied broadly in order that past inequities may be redressed. Accordingly, the history of affirmative action cases is an important part of his opinion. Consider his arguments carefully; you will probably need to read the essay more than once.

While I join the Court's opinion, I write separately to explain my 1
view of this case's position in our evolving antidiscrimination law and
to emphasize that the opinion does not establish the permissible outer
limits of voluntary programs undertaken by employers to benefit disadvantaged groups.

Antidiscrimination measures may benefit protected groups in two 2
distinct ways. As a sword, such measures may confer benefits by
specifying that a person's membership in a disadvantaged group must
be a neutral, irrelevant factor in governmental or private decisionmak-
ing, or alternatively, by compelling decisionmakers to give favorable
consideration to disadvantaged group status. As a shield, an antidiscrimination statute can also help a member of a protected class
by assuring decisionmakers in some instances that, when they elect
for good reasons of their own to grant a preference of some sort to
a minority citizen, they will not violate the law. The Court properly holds that the statutory shield allowed respondent to take Diane
Joyce's sex into account in promoting her to the road dispatcher position.

A New Interpretation

Prior to 1978 the Court construed the Civil Rights Act of 1964 as an 3
absolute blanket prohibition against discrimination which neither required nor permitted discriminatory preferences for any group, minority or majority. The Court unambiguously endorsed the neutral
approach, first in the context of gender discrimination and then in the
context of racial discrimination against a white person. As I explained
in my separate opinion in *University of California Regents* v. *Bakke,*
Congress intended "to eliminate all practices which operate to disadvantage the employment opportunities of any group protected by Title
VII including Caucasians." If the Court had adhered to that construction of the Act, petitioner would unquestionably prevail in this case.
But it has not done so.

In the *Bakke* case in 1978 and again in *Steelworkers* v. *Weber,* (1979), a 4
majority of the Court interpreted the antidiscriminatory strategy of the
statute in a fundamentally different way. The Court held in the *Weber*
case that an employer's program designed to increase the number of
black craftworkers in an aluminum plant did not violate Title VII. It
remains clear that the Act does not *require* any employer to grant
preferential treatment on the basis of race or gender, but since 1978 the
Court has unambiguously interpreted the statute to *permit* the voluntary adoption of special programs to benefit members of the minority
groups for whose protection the statute was enacted. Neither the

"same standards" language used in *McDonald*, nor the "color-blind" rhetoric used by the Senators and Congressmen who enacted the bill, is now controlling. Thus, the only problem for me is whether to adhere to an authoritative construction of the Act that is at odds with my understanding of the actual intent of the authors of the legislation. I conclude without hesitation that I must answer that question in the affirmative.

Bakke and *Weber* have been decided and are now an important part 5 of the fabric of our law. This consideration is sufficiently compelling for me to adhere to the basic construction of this legislation that the Court adopted in *Bakke* and in *Weber*. There is an undoubted public interest in "stability and orderly development of the law."

The logic of antidiscrimination legislation requires that judicial 6 constructions of Title VII leave "breathing room" for employer initiatives to benefit members of minority groups. If Title VII had never been enacted, a private employer would be free to hire members of minority groups for any reason that might seem sensible from a business or a social point of view. The Court's opinion in *Weber* reflects the same approach; the opinion relied heavily on legislative history indicating that Congress intended that traditional management prerogatives be left undisturbed to the greatest extent possible. As we observed Last Term, "[i]t would be ironic indeed if a law triggered by a Nation's concern over centuries of racial injustice and intended to improve the lot of those who had 'been excluded from the American dream for so long' constituted the first legislative prohibition of all voluntary, private, race-conscious efforts to abolish traditional patterns of racial segregation and hierarchy." *Firefighters* v. *Cleveland*, (1986). In *Firefighters*, we again acknowledged Congress' concern in Title VII to avoid "undue federal interference with managerial discretion."

As construed in *Weber* and *Firefighters*, the statute does not abso- 7 lutely prohibit preferential hiring in favor of minorities; it was merely intended to protect historically disadvantaged groups *against* discrimination and not to hamper managerial efforts to benefit members of disadvantaged groups that are consistent with that paramount purpose. The preference granted by respondent in this case does not violate the statute as so construed; the record amply supports the conclusion that the challenged employment decision served the legitimate purpose of creating diversity in a category of employment that had been almost an exclusive province of males in the past. Respondent's voluntary decision is surely not prohibited by Title VII as construed in *Weber*.

Whether a voluntary decision of the kind made by respondent 8 would ever be prohibited by Title VII is a question we need not answer until it is squarely presented. Given the interpretation of the statute the Court adopted in *Weber*, I see no reason why the employer has any duty, prior to granting a preference to a qualified minority employee, to determine whether his past conduct might constitute an arguable violation of Title VII. Indeed, in some instances the employer may find it more helpful to focus on the future. Instead of retroactively scrutinizing his own or society's possible exclusions of minorities in the past to determine the outer limits of a valid affirmative-action program—or indeed, any particular affirmative-action decision—in many cases the employer will find it more appropriate to consider other legitimate reasons to give preferences to members of under-represented groups. Statutes enacted for the benefit of minority groups should not block these forward-looking considerations.

> Public and private employers might choose to implement affirmative action for many reasons other than to purge their own past sins of discrimination. The Jackson school board, for example, said it had done so in part to improve the quality of education in Jackson—whether by improving black students' performance or by dispelling for black and white students alike any idea that white supremacy governs our social institutions. Other employers might advance different forward-looking reasons for affirmative action: improving their services to black constituencies, averting racial tension over the allocation of jobs in a community, or increasing the diversity of a work force, to name but a few examples. Or they might adopt affirmative action simply to eliminate from their operations all de facto embodiment of a system of racial caste. All of these reasons aspire to a racially integrated future, but none reduces to "racial balancing for its own sake." Sullivan, "The Supreme Court—Comment, Sins of Discrimination: Last Term's Affirmative Action Cases," 100 *Harvard Law Review* 78, 96 (1986).

The Court today does not foreclose other voluntary decisions 9 based in part on a qualified employee's membership in a disadvantaged group. Accordingly, I concur.

Dissenting Opinion in Johnson
ANTONIN SCALIA

Supreme Court Justice Antonin Scalia, appointed to the Court by President Ronald Reagan in 1986, is the first jurist of Italian descent to sit on the Court. A conservative advocate of judicial restraint, Scalia believes that judges should leave lawmaking to the legislative bodies. In the *Johnson* case, Scalia not only disagreed with the majority of his colleagues, he disagreed strongly enough to write a dissenting opinion. His thesis is that the Court has turned Title VII of the 1964 Civil Rights Act topsy-turvy, "converting this from a guarantee that race or sex will *not* be the basis for employment determinations, to a guarantee that it often *will.*" Again, read carefully—and several times—in order to fully understand and evaluate Scalia's arguments.

Title VII of the Civil Rights Act of 1964 declares: 1

It shall be an unlawful employment practice for an employer—

(1) to fail or refuse to hire or to discharge any individual, or otherwise to discriminate against any individual with respect to his compensation, terms, conditions, or privileges of employment, because of such individual's race, color, religion, sex, or national origin; or

(2) to limit, segregate, or classify his employees or applicants for employment in any way which would deprive or tend to deprive any individual of employment opportunities or otherwise adversely affect his status as an employee, because of such individual's race, color, religion, sex, or national origin.

The Court today completes the process of converting this from a   2 guarantee that race or sex will *not* be the basis for employment determinations, to a guarantee that it often *will*. Ever so subtly, without even alluding to the last obstacles preserved by earlier opinions that we now push out of our path, we effectively replace the goal of a discrimination-free society with the quite incompatible goal of proportionate representation by race and by sex in the workplace. . . .

On October 16, 1978, the County of Santa Clara adopted an Af-   3 firmative Action Program (County plan) which sought the "attainment of a County work force whose composition . . . includes women, disabled persons and ethnic minorities in a ratio in all job categories that reflects their distribution in the Santa Clara County area work force." In order to comply with the County plan and various requirements imposed by federal and state agencies, the Transportation Agency adopted, effective December 18, 1978, the Equal Employment Opportunity Affirmative Action Plan at issue here. Its stated long-range goal was the same as the County plan's: "to attain a work force whose composition in all job levels and major job classifications approximates the distribution of women, minority and handicapped persons in the Santa Clara County work force." The plan called for the establishment of a procedure by which Division Directors would review the ethnic and sexual composition of their work forces whenever they sought to fill a vacancy, which procedure was expected to include "a requirement that Division Directors indicate why they did *not* select minorities, women and handicapped persons if such persons were on the list of eligibles considered and if the Division had an underrepresentation of such persons in the job classification being filled."

Several salient features of the plan should be noted. Most impor- 4
tantly, the plan's purpose was assuredly not to remedy prior sex
discrimination by the Agency. It could not have been, because there
was no prior sex discrimination to remedy. The majority, in cataloguing
the Agency's alleged misdeeds, neglects to mention the District
Court's findings that the Agency "has not discriminated in the past,
and does not discriminate in the present against women in regard to
employment opportunities in general and promotions in particular."
This finding was not disturbed by the Ninth Circuit.

Not only was the plan not directed at the results of past sex 5
discrimination by the Agency, but its objective was not to achieve the
state of affairs that this Court has dubiously assumed would result
from an absence of discrimination—an overall work force "more or
less representative of the racial and ethnic composition of the population in the community." *Teamsters* v. *United States*, (1977). Rather, the
oft-stated goal was to mirror the racial and sexual composition of the
entire county labor force, not merely in the Agency work force as a
whole, but in each and every individual job category at the Agency. In
a discrimination-free world, it would obviously be a statistical oddity
for every job category to match the racial and sexual composition of
even that portion of the county work force *qualified* for that job; it
would be utterly miraculous, for each of them to match, as the plan
expected, the composition of the *entire* work force. Quite obviously,
the plan did not seek to replicate what a lack of discrimination would
produce, but rather imposed racial and sexual tailoring that would, in
defiance of normal expectations and laws of probability, give each
protected racial and sexual group a governmentally determined
"proper" proportion of each job category. . . .

The one message that the plan unmistakably communicated was 6
that concrete results were expected, and supervisory personnel would
be evaluated on the basis of the affirmative-action numbers they produced. The plan's implementation was expected to "result in a statistically measurable yearly improvement in the hiring, training and promotion of minorities, women and handicapped persons in the major
job classifications utilized by the Agency where these groups are
underrepresented." Its Preface declared that "[t]he degree to which
each Agency Division *attains the Plan's objectives* will provide a direct
measure of that Division Director's personal commitment to the EEO
Policy," and the plan itself repeated that "[t]he degree to which each
Division *attains the Agency Affirmative Action employment goals* will provide a measure of that Director's commitment and effectiveness in
carrying out the Division's EEO Affirmative Action requirements." As
noted earlier, supervisors were reminded of the need to give attention
to affirmative action in every employment decision, and to explain

their reasons for *failing* to hire women and minorities whenever there was an opportunity to do so.

The petitioner in the present case, Paul E. Johnson, had been an 7 employee of the Agency since 1967, coming there from a private company where he had been a road dispatcher for seventeen years. He had first applied for the position of Road Dispatcher at the Agency in 1974, coming in second. Several years later, after a reorganization resulted in a downgrading of his Road Yard Clerk II position, in which Johnson "could see no future," he requested and received a voluntary demotion from Road Yard Clerk II to Road Maintenance Worker, to increase his experience and thus improve his chances for future promotion. When the Road Dispatcher job next became vacant, in 1979, he was the leading candidate—and indeed was assigned to work out of class full-time in the vacancy, from September of 1979 until June of 1980. There is no question why he did not get the job. . . .

The majority emphasizes, as though it is meaningful, that "No 8 persons are automatically excluded from consideration; *all* are able to have their qualifications weighed against those of other applicants." One is reminded of the exchange from Shakespeare's King Henry the Fourth, Part I: "*Glendower*: I can call Spirits from the vasty Deep. *Hotspur*: Why, so can I, or so can any man. But will they come when you do call for them?" Act III, Scene I, lines 53–55. Johnson was indeed entitled to have his qualifications weighed against those of other applicants—but more to the point, he was virtually assured that, after the weighing, if there was any minimally qualified applicant from one of the favored groups, he would be rejected.

Similarly hollow is the Court's assurance that we would strike this 9 plan down if it "failed to take distinctions in qualifications into account," because that "would dictate mere blind hiring by the numbers." For what the Court means by "taking distinctions in qualifications into account" consists of no more than eliminating from the applicant pool those who are not even *minimally qualified* for the job. Once that has been done, once the promoting officer assures himself that all the candidates before him are "M.Q.s" (minimally qualifieds), he can then ignore, as the Agency Director did here, how much better than minimally qualified some of the candidates may be, and can proceed to appoint from the pool solely on the basis of race or sex, until the affirmative action "goals" have been reached. The requirement that the employer "take distinctions in qualifications into account" thus turns out to be an assurance, not that candidates' comparative merits will always be considered, but only that none of the successful candidates selected over the others solely on the basis of their race or sex will be utterly unqualified. That may be of great comfort to those concerned with American productivity; and it is undoubtedly effective in reducing the effect of affirmative-action discrimination upon those in the upper strata of society, who (unlike road maintenance workers, for example) compete for employment in professional and semiprofessional fields, where, for many reasons, including most notably the effects of past discrimination, the numbers of "M.Q." applicants from the favored groups are substantially less. But I fail to see how it has any relevance to whether selecting among final candidates solely on the basis of race or sex is permissible under Title VII, which prohibits discrimination on the basis of race or sex. . . .

It is unlikely that today's result will be displeasing to politically 10 elected officials, to whom it provides the means of quickly accommodating the demands of organized groups to achieve concrete, numerical improvement in the economic status of particular constituencies. Nor will it displease the world of corporate and governmental employers (many of whom have filed briefs as *amici* in the present case, all on the side of Santa Clara) for whom the cost of hiring less qualified workers is often substantially less—and infinitely more predictable—than the cost of litigating Title VII cases and of seeking to convince federal agencies by nonnumerical means that no discrimination exists. In fact, the only losers in the process are the Johnsons of the country, for whom Title VII has been not merely repealed but actually inverted. The irony is that these individuals—predominantly unknown, unaffluent, unorganized—suffer this injustice at the hands of a Court fond of thinking itself the champion of the politically impotent. I dissent.

A Defense of Affirmative Action
THOMAS NAGEL

Thomas Nagel is a professor of philosophy at New York University and the author of several books, including *The Possibility of Altruism* (1970), *Mortal Questions* (1979), and *The View from Nowhere* (1986). Nagel made the following argument in testimony before the Senate Judiciary Subcommittee on the Constitution, June 18, 1981. It was then published in the journal of the Center for Philosophy and Public Policy, QQ, in the fall of 1981. This essay begins, as many do, with careful definitions, for Nagel's argument hinges in part on the distinction he draws between "weak affirmative action" and "strong affirmative action." His thesis is paradoxical: While he regards strong affirmative action as "intrinsically undesirable," Nagel argues that it is justified, particularly for blacks. Moreover, his *defense* of his thesis is on the surface also paradoxical, for he considers the opposition to strong affirmative action carefully and far from dismissively. Read carefully to evaluate how well Nagel resolves his paradoxes.

The term "affirmative action" has changed in meaning since it was 1
first introduced. Originally it referred only to special efforts to ensure
equal opportunity for members of groups that had been subject to
discrimination. These efforts included public advertisement of positions to be filled, active recruitment of qualified applicants from the
formerly excluded groups, and special training programs to help them
meet the standards for admission or appointment. There was also
close attention to procedures of appointment, and sometimes to the
results, with a view to detecting continued discrimination, conscious
or unconscious.

More recently the term has come to refer also to some degree of 2
definite preference for members of these groups in determining access
to positions from which they were formerly excluded. Such preference
might be allowed to influence decisions only between candidates who
are otherwise equally qualified, but usually it involves the selection of
women or minority members over other candidates who are better
qualified for the position.

Let me call the first sort of policy "weak affirmative action" and the 3
second "strong affirmative action." It is important to distinguish
them, because the distinction is sometimes blurred in practice. It is
strong affirmative action—the policy of preference—that arouses controversy. Most people would agree that weak or precautionary affirmative action is a good thing, and worth its cost in time and energy.
But this does not imply that strong affirmative action is also justified.

I shall claim that in the present state of things it is justified, most 4
clearly with respect to blacks. But I also believe that a defender of the
practice must acknowledge that there are serious arguments against it,
and that it is defensible only because the arguments for it have great
weight. Moral opinion in this country is sharply divided over the issue
because significant values are involved on both sides. My own view is
that while strong affirmative action is intrinsically undesirable, it is a
legitimate and perhaps indispensable method of pursuing a goal so
important to the national welfare that it can be justified as a temporary, though not short-term, policy for both public and private institutions. In this respect it is like other policies that impose burdens on
some for the public good.

Three Objections

I shall begin with the argument against. There are three objections 5
to strong affirmative action: that it is inefficient; that it is unfair; and
that it damages self-esteem.

The degree of inefficiency depends on how strong a role racial or 6 sexual preference plays in the process of selection. Among candidates meeting the basic qualifications for a position, those better qualified will on the average perform better, whether they are doctors, policemen, teachers, or electricians. There may be some cases, as in preferential college admissions, where the immediate usefulness of making educational resources available to an individual is thought to be greater because of the use to which the education will be put or because of the internal effects on the institution itself. But by and large, policies of strong affirmative action must reckon with the costs of some lowering in performance level: the stronger the preference, the larger the cost to be justified. Since both the costs and the value of the results will vary from case to case, this suggests that no one policy of affirmative action is likely to be correct in all cases, and that the cost in performance level should be taken into account in the design of a legitimate policy.

The charge of unfairness arouses the deepest disagreements. To 7 be passed over because of membership in a group one was born into, where this has nothing to do with one's individual qualifications for a position, can arouse strong feelings of resentment. It is a departure from the ideal—one of the values finally recognized in our society—that people should be judged so far as possible on the basis of individual characteristics rather than involuntary group membership.

This does not mean that strong affirmative action is morally re- 8 pugnant in the manner of racial or sexual discrimination. It is nothing like those practices, for though like them it employs race and sex as criteria of selection, it does so for entirely different reasons. Racial and sexual discrimination are based on contempt or even loathing for the excluded group, a feeling that certain contacts with them are degrading to members of the dominant group, that they are fit only for subordinate positions or menial work. Strong affirmative action involves none of this: it is simply a means of increasing the social and economic strength of formerly victimized groups, and does not stigmatize others.

There is an element of individual unfairness here, but it is more 9 like the unfairness of conscription in wartime, or of property condemnation under the right of eminent domain. Those who benefit or lose out because of their race or sex cannot be said to deserve their good or bad fortune.

It might be said on the other side that the beneficiaries of affir- 10 mative action deserve it as compensation for past discrimination, and that compensation is rightly exacted from the group that has benefitted from discrimination in the past. But this is a bad argument, because as the practice usually works, no effort is made to give preference to those who have suffered most from discrimination, or to prefer them especially to those who have benefitted most from it, or been guilty of it. Only candidates who in other qualifications fall on one or other side of the margin of decision will directly benefit or lose from the policy, and these are not necessarily, or even probably, the ones who especially deserve it. Women or blacks who don't have the qualifications even to be considered are likely to have been handicapped more by the effects of discrimination than those who receive preference. And the marginal white male candidate who is turned down can evoke our sympathy if he asks, "Why me?" (A policy of explicitly *compensatory* preference, which took into account each individual's background of poverty and discrimination, would escape some of these objections, and it has its defenders, but it is not the policy I want to defend. Whatever its merits, it will not serve the same purpose as direct affirmative action.)

The third objection concerns self-esteem, and is particularly serious. While strong affirmative action is in effect, and generally known to be so, no one in an affirmative action category who gets a desirable job or is admitted to a selective university can be sure that he or she has not benefitted from the policy. Even those who would have made it anyway fall under suspicion, from themselves and from others: it comes to be widely felt that success does not mean the same thing for women and minorities. This painful damage to esteem cannot be avoided. It should make any defender of strong affirmative action want the practice to end as soon as it has achieved its basic purpose. 11

Justifying Affirmative Action

I have examined these three objections and tried to assess their weight, in order to decide how strong a countervailing reason is needed to justify such a policy. In my view, taken together they imply that strong affirmative action involving significant preference should be undertaken only if it will substantially further a social goal of the first importance. While this condition is not met by all programs of affirmative action now in effect, it is met by those which address the most deep-seated, stubborn, and radically unhealthy divisions in the society, divisions whose removal is a condition of basic justice and social cohesion. 12

The situation of black people in our country is unique in this respect. For almost a century after the abolition of slavery we had a rigid racial caste system of the ugliest kind, and it only began to break up twenty-five years ago. In the South it was enforced by law, and in the North, in a somewhat less severe form, by social convention. 13

Whites were thought to be defiled by social or residential proximity to blacks, intermarriage was taboo, blacks were denied the same level of public goods—education and legal protection—as whites, were restricted to the most menial occupations, and were barred from any positions of authority over whites. The visceral feelings of black inferiority and untouchability that this system expressed were deeply ingrained in the members of both races, and they continue, not surprisingly, to have their effect. Blacks still form, to a considerable extent, a hereditary social and economic community characterized by widespread poverty, unemployment, and social alienation.

When this society finally got around to moving against the caste 14 system, it might have done no more than to enforce straight equality of opportunity, perhaps with the help of weak affirmative action, and then wait a few hundred years while things gradually got better. Fortunately it decided instead to accelerate the process by both public and private institutional action, because there was wide recognition of the intractable character of the problem posed by this insular minority and its place in the nation's history and collective consciousness. This has not been going on very long, but the results are already impressive, especially in speeding the advancement of blacks into the middle class. Affirmative action has not done much to improve the position of poor and unskilled blacks. That is the most serious part of the problem, and it requires a more direct economic attack. But increased access to higher education and upper-level jobs is an essential part of what must be achieved to break the structure of drastic separation that was left largely undisturbed by the legal abolition of the caste system.

Changes of this kind require a generation or two. My guess is that 15 strong affirmative action for blacks will continue to be justified into the early decades of the next century, but that by then it will have accomplished what it can and will no longer be worth the costs. One point deserves special emphasis. The goal to be pursued is the reduction of a great social injustice, not proportional representation of the races in all institutions and professions. Proportional racial representation is of no value in itself. It is not a legitimate social goal, and it should certainly not be the aim of strong affirmative action, whose drawbacks make it worth adopting only against a serious and intractable social evil.

This implies that the justification for strong affirmative action is 16 much weaker in the case of other racial and ethnic groups, and in the case of women. At least, the practice will be justified in a narrower range of circumstances and for a shorter span of time than it is for blacks. No other group has been treated quite like this, and no other group is in a comparable status. Hispanic-Americans occupy an intermediate position, but it seems to me frankly absurd to include persons of oriental descent as beneficiaries of affirmative action, strong or weak. They are not a severely deprived and excluded minority, and their eligibility serves only to swell the numbers that can be included on affirmative action reports. It also suggests that there is a drift in the policy toward adopting the goal of racial proportional representation for its own sake. This is a foolish mistake, and should be resisted. The only legitimate goal of the policy is to reduce egregious racial stratification.

With respect to women, I believe that except over the short term, 17 and in professions or institutions from which their absence is particularly marked, strong affirmative action is not warranted and weak affirmative action is enough. This is based simply on the expectation that the social and economic situation of women will improve quite rapidly under conditions of full equality of opportunity. Recent progress provides some evidence for this. Women do not form a separate hereditary community, characteristically poor and uneducated, and their position is not likely to be self-perpetuating in the same way as that of an outcast race. The process requires less artificial acceleration, and any need for strong affirmative action for women can be expected to end sooner than it ends for blacks.

I said at the outset that there was a tendency to blur the distinction 18 between weak and strong affirmative action. This occurs especially in the use of numerical quotas, a topic on which I want to comment briefly.

A quota may be a method of either weak or strong affirmative 19 action, depending on the circumstances. It amounts to weak affirmative action—a safeguard against discrimination—if, and only if, there is independent evidence that average qualifications for the positions being filled are no lower in the group to which a minimum quota is being assigned than in the applicant group as a whole. This can be presumed true of unskilled jobs that most people can do, but it becomes less likely, and harder to establish, the greater the skill and education required for the position. At these levels, a quota proportional to population, or even to representation of the group in the applicant pool, is almost certain to amount to strong affirmative action. Moreover, it is strong affirmative action of a particularly crude and indiscriminate kind, because it permits no variation in the degree of preference on the basis of costs in efficiency, depending on the qualification gap. For this reason I should defend quotas only where they serve the purpose of weak affirmative action. On the whole, strong affirmative action is better implemented by including group preference as one factor in appointment or admission decisions, and letting the results depend on its interaction with other factors.

I have tried to show that the arguments against strong affirmative 20 action are clearly outweighed at present by the need for exceptional measures to remove the stubborn residues of racial caste. But advocates of the policy should acknowledge the reasons against it, which will ensure its termination when it is no longer necessary. Affirmative action is not an end in itself, but a means of dealing with a social situation that should be intolerable to us all.

There's No Gender in Success
PATRICIA L. DOMBRINK

Patricia L. Dombrink, a teacher and freelance writer on issues in education, advocates a point of view that is often lost amid the rush to remedy inequities that have kept women from advancing in their careers and from following traditionally "male" pursuits. She argues that today, the message of the press is that "only those women most unlike their traditional sisters are worthy of being considered successful." But the benefits of affirmative action, Dombrink reasons, should not themselves be permitted to raise psychological barriers to traditionally "female" pursuits. Dombrink's essay, addressed to the educated general public, was first printed in the *Christian Science Monitor* in 1984.

Each year a major magazine for women devotes an entire issue to 1 the topic of success and profiles 10 women who epitomize this concept. After diligently saving these special issues for several years and admiring the role models, I began to notice an ominous pattern. The successful women were those who had careers in heretofore male fields.

Where were the women who were outstanding in teaching, nurs- 2 ing or other career fields regarded as "female"? They were conspicuously absent and remained so in forthcoming issues.

The one time a teacher appeared, she held a Ph.D. in economics 3 and was a professor at a distinguished Ivy League college. The message was clear: only those women most unlike their traditional sisters are worthy of being considered successful.

Where does that leave the very successful women in the so-called 4 service professions? Are they not successful, even when they lead happy, fulfilling lives that make a significant difference in the lives of countless other people?

Have we been defining success in the wrong terms? Does the idea 5 of success—in itself—include the requirement that a woman has broken through that previously solid barrier of prejudice that prevented her from reaching financial heights and power in such fields as engineering, architecture, law or business?

Should women in traditional career fields be ignored, lest their 6 younger sisters do something so *gauche* as choose a "female" career when the 1980s offer latitude unknown to their older sisters?

This new philosophy of success has so permeated the helping 7
professions that many women who would otherwise be drawn to
them eschew them in favor of more "acceptable" fields.

The teaching profession is not drawing the better minds from the 8
ranks of today's college women as it once did as evidenced by test
scores and college grades of those entering the profession.

The bright young women of today are pointed in other directions 9
where they can command high salaries and high visibility, due to the
lesser number of females in these fields.

Many competent women leave the teaching profession annually 10
to take jobs in the private sector, where talent, not merely seniority, is
recognized. Similar circumstances prevail in other female-dominated
professions.

This notion of aping men is likewise found in the dress-for-success 11
look widely depicted in women's magazines. The successful women
are shown wearing 2-piece (if not 3-piece) suits, tailored shirts, and
carrying the obligatory attaché case.

They are schooled in what to say and eat as well, in order that 12
"feminine" characteristics do not intrude in the "male" domain of
business and high finance.

Prof. Henry Higgins of *My Fair Lady* would undoubtedly rejoice to 13
find today's women "more like a man."

The women's movement, which has accomplished so much for so 14
many, must share in the guilt of confusing today's young women.
With the not-so-subtle message that "male" skills are preferable to
"female" skills, it has siphoned off talent and expertise from certain
areas of employment.

Maybe it's time for the news media, particularly the women's 15
media, to proclaim that success is really "self-actualization, being the
best 'me' I can possibly be while continuing to grow and learn," as one
woman has put it.

Maybe it's time to realize that success, after all, has no gender.   16

An Economic Defense of Affirmative Action

BERNARD E. ANDERSON

Bernard E. Anderson, an economist, directs the Social Sciences Division of the Rockefeller Foundation and is president of the National Economic Association. Among his publications are *Negro Employment in Public Utilities* (1970) and *Moving Ahead: Black Managers in American Business* (1978). The following essay was first published in *Black Enter-*

prise magazine in 1982. Its thesis does not focus so much on justifying the practice of affirmative action as on dispelling the idea that affirmative action, as of 1982, is no longer needed. Anderson uses one primary example, that of AT&T, to illustrate his claims.

Is affirmative action still necessary? Many critics argue that atti-   1
tudes toward race relations have improved to a substantial degree and that discrimination is no longer a major factor in explaining employment and earnings disparities among minorities and others. According to these critics, economic growth and the expansion of jobs through unregulated, free market processes is all that is required to improve the economic status of minorities.

However, the available evidence suggests that just the reverse is   2
true. Much of the progress achieved by minorities and women in some occupations and industries was either the direct result of or was substantially influenced by affirmative action remedies to employment discrimination.

Affirmative Action Is Necessary

The position of blacks and other minorities in the economy is like   3
that of the caboose on a train. When the train speeds up, the caboose moves faster; when the train slows down, so does the caboose. No matter how fast the train goes, the caboose will never catch up with the engine unless special arrangements are made to change its position. So it is with minorities and the economy: Even during the best of times, there will be no change in the relative position of minorities unless affirmative action or other special measures are taken.

Policies designed to improve the relative position of minorities are   4
justified by the continuing evidence of racial inequality in American economic life. In 1980, black unemployment was more than twice that of whites (13.2 percent vs. 6.3 percent). Unemployment among black teenagers, now officially reported at close to 50 percent, has been greater than 30 percent throughout the past decade, but has not reached that level among white youths in any year. Further, the employment/population ratio—for some purposes a more instructive measure of labor market participation than the unemployment rate— has steadily declined among black youths while increasing among whites. About 25 out of every 100 black youths had jobs in 1980, compared with 50 of every 100 whites.

Comparative income data also show continuing evidence of eco-   5
nomic disparity between blacks and others. In 1979, the average black family had only $57 for every $100 enjoyed by whites. Even in families

headed by persons fortunate enough to work year round, blacks have failed to achieve parity, earning only 77 percent of the income of comparable white families.

Effects of Past Discrimination

It would be incorrect to say that the continuing presence of such 6 economic inequality is entirely the result of overt or systemic discrimination or that affirmative action alone would improve the economic position of minorities. But there is no question that much of the income and employment disadvantage of blacks and other minorities reflects the accumulated impact of past discrimination. The continuing presence of many seemingly objective policies in the workplace have also had disproportionately unfavorable effects on the hiring, training and upgrading of minority-group workers. Affirmative action has an important role to play in correcting inequities.

In 1969, black workers represented 6.7 percent of the nearly 7 600,000 employees in the Bell System, mostly black women employed as telephone operators. Only 12 percent of Bell's black employees were in management (compared with 24 percent of whites), 7.2 percent were skilled craftsmen (compared with 26 percent of whites), and less than one percent were in professional jobs (compared with 8 percent of whites).

In 1971, the Equal Employment Opportunity Commission (EEOC) 8 charged AT&T and its affiliates with discrimination against minorities and women. In 1975, after prolonged litigation and negotiations, EEOC and AT&T signed a consent decree designed to correct the inequities in the company's employment practices, and to provide back pay to many minority and female employees who had not enjoyed full equal opportunity in the past. In 1979, blacks and other minorities accounted for 14.4 percent of the Bell System's managerial employees, 18.7 percent of the outside craftsmen, 19.1 percent of the inside craftsmen, and 23.3 percent of the sales workers.

The consent decree was the catalyst necessary to spur the com- 9 pany toward many positive changes in personnel policies that top management today lauds as beneficial to the firm. The more efficient and equitable personnel selection and assessment system adopted by AT&T and its Bell operating affiliates puts the telephone company in a much stronger position to compete with other firms in the increasingly difficult and complex information systems markets. The experience of AT&T, and other firms specifically identified as subjects for affirmative action enforcement, is instructive for understanding the potential impact of affirmative action on the occupational status of minorities. For purposes of public policy formulation, such evidence may be more useful than inconclusive studies that attempt to show the relationship between affirmative action and minority employment opportunities.

Women and Minorities in Management in the United States

BUREAU OF LABOR STATISTICS

Occupation	Total employed	1987—Percent of total		
		Women	Black	Hispanic origin
Total, 16 years and over	122,440	44.8	10.1	6.9
Managerial and professional specialty ...	27,742	44.3	6.2	3.7
Executive, administrative and managerial...........................	13,316	37.9	5.6	3.8
Officials and administrators, public administration	474	41.8	9.6	3.9
Financial managers	462	43.8	3.9	3.5
Personnel and labor relations managers	127	53.0	4.0	3.4
Purchasing managers	100	27.8	7.6	3.1
Managers, marketing, advertising, and public relations	444	27.4	3.0	2.3
Administrators, education and related fields	516	48.5	9.9	3.7
Managers, medicine and health	154	59.9	6.9	3.1
Managers, properties and real estate ...	397	43.8	4.6	6.5
Management-related occupations	3,577	48.4	7.4	3.7
Accountants and auditors	1,255	45.7	7.4	3.5
Underwriters, other financial officers	728	49.3	5.8	4.2
Management analysts	178	31.3	7.3	1.3
Personnel, training, and labor relations specialists	381	57.8	10.4	3.7
Buyers, wholesale and retail trade, except farm products	231	49.5	3.3	4.0
Construction inspectors	60	4.0	5.1	5.7
Inspectors and compliance officers, except construction	183	23.6	14.4	4.6
Professional specialty	14,426	50.1	6.7	3.5
Architects	135	12.6	2.2	7.2
Engineers.........................	1,731	6.9	3.5	2.6
Aerospace engineers	104	7.6	5.1	1.5
Chemical engineers	63	10.4	3.7	1.3
Civil engineers	210	4.1	1.9	4.1
Electrical and electronic engineers ...	545	7.2	3.2	2.4
Industrial engineers	221	13.5	3.5	2.6
Mechanical engineers	277	4.2	4.5	2.8
Mathematical and computer scientists .	685	34.1	6.7	2.5
Computer systems analysts and scientists	447	32.1	6.9	2.2

Occupation	Total employed	1987—Percent of total		
		Women	Black	Hispanic origin
Operations and systems researchers and analysts	197	37.7	6.2	3.8
Natural scientists	388	24.1	2.4	2.7
Chemists, except biochemists	120	21.7	2.7	2.5
Biological and life scientists	71	38.4	1.3	2.1
Health diagnosing occupations	793	16.5	3.0	4.5
Physicians	514	19.5	3.7	5.5
Dentists	160	8.9	2.1	3.3
Health assessment and treating occupations	2,148	86.3	7.7	2.9
Registered nurse	1,588	95.1	7.7	2.6
Pharmacists	153	31.1	3.0	1.9
Dieticians	63	90.1	29.5	5.5
Therapists	285	76.3	6.5	3.5
Inhalation therapists	60	63.0	9.0	8.9
Physical therapists	75	74.5	6.1	4.0
Speech therapists	73	90.9	2.8	—
Teachers, college and university	661	37.1	4.6	3.1
Teachers, except college and university	3,587	73.6	9.4	3.9
Prekindergarten and kindergarten ...	389	98.4	13.7	5.1
Elementary school	1,329	85.3	10.0	4.0
Secondary school	1,172	54.3	8.2	3.7
Special education	216	83.5	10.5	1.8
Teachers	480	64.2	7.1	4.1
Counselors, educational and vocational	191	59.5	14.0	5.2
Librarians, archivists, and curators	219	81.8	6.8	2.6
Librarians	196	85.6	7.0	1.9
Social scientists and urban planners ...	316	48.7	5.8	2.7
Economists	113	40.8	1.6	2.3
Psychologists	171	54.6	8.9	2.8
Social, recreation, and religious workers	980	46.6	12.5	5.6
Social workers	507	65.6	18.1	7.0
Recreation workers	81	69.3	13.7	4.5
Clergy	312	6.9	5.7	3.7
Religious workers	82	57.9	2.4	5.7
Lawyers and judges	707	19.7	3.4	2.0
Lawyers	672	19.6	3.0	1.7
Writers, artists, entertainers, and athletes	1,858	45.9	4.7	3.9
Authors	85	50.7	.8	1.7
Technical writers	51	44.4	5.7	1.5
Designers	531	52.0	2.8	4.8
Musicians and composers	169	31.4	8.8	4.3
Actors and directors	88	36.0	3.0	2.6
Painters, sculptors, craft-artists, and artist printmakers	191	53.9	5.8	3.3
Photographers	126	31.1	6.8	3.1
Editors and reporters	267	50.4	4.1	2.6
Public relations specialists	142	56.6	5.9	4.7
Announcers	59	13.3	6.3	5.4
Athletes	69	22.6	8.9	6.4

Numbers in thousands

The Fallacy of Inferred Discrimination

WILLIAM R. BEER

William R. Beer, a professor of sociology at Brooklyn College, has written three books on sociological issues and translated four from French. The following essay appeared in a sociological journal, *Society*, in May/June 1987. It offers an argument akin to Justice Antonin Scalia's, but from a sociologist's viewpoint. In a section of the essay not here reprinted, Beer castigates his fellow sociologists for what he views as their cowardice in ignoring the issues of affirmative action and reverse discrimination. Beer's argument is specific, pointed, and controversial; evaluate it carefully.

Affirmative action, in its original formulation, referred to good- 1 faith efforts to recruit qualified members of designated groups into universities, professions, and other respected and well-paid positions in American society. In the ensuing twenty years, affirmative action, in practice, has come to mean something quite different. In a series of bureaucratic and legal decisions largely unseen or unnoticed by the American public, affirmative action has been translated into a series of quotas (sometimes euphemistically referred to as "goals" and "timetables") that benefit certain groups at the cost of others. (Thomas G. Gee provides a dissection of the false legal dichotomy between quotas and goals in the winter 1986 issue of the *Harvard Journal of Law and Public Policy*.)

The Civil Rights Act explicitly states, "Nothing contained in this 2 Title shall be interpreted to require any employer . . . to grant preferential treatment to any individual or any group because of race, color, religion, sex or national status of any such individual on account of any imbalance which may exist with respect to the total or percentage of persons of any race employed by any employer." Hubert Humphrey, in his impassioned defense of the bill, said that the act "does not require an employer to achieve any kind of racial balance in his work force by giving any kind of preferential treatment to any individual or group." In July of 1986, however, the Supreme Court declared that preferential treatment was constitutional, even when those who benefit have not themselves suffered from discrimination in the past, and when those who are hurt have not themselves been responsible for past discrimination. In March of 1987, the Court added that preference may be shown for less qualified women and minorities over white males. The success of this undemocratic and semiclandestine metamorphosis was symbolized by Supreme Court Justice Powell saying, in the spring of 1986, "In order to remedy the effects of prior discrimination, it may be necessary to take race into account. As part of the nation's dedication to eradicating racial discrimination, innocent persons may be called upon to bear some of the burden of the remedy." This is an echo of Thurgood Marshall's frank statement several years before, "You guys have been practicing discrimination for years. Now it's our turn." Joseph Rauh, the former chairman of Americans for Democratic Action candidly admitted, "You have to have preference for blacks if you really want affirmative action." Although Humphrey promised that affirmative action would never penalize the innocent, it has not only turned out that the policy does so, but that its more candid partisans say that it should. Affirmative action has come to require preferential treatment. Reverse racial and sexual discrimination have come out of the closet.

Fallacy of Inferred Discrimination

There are numerous studies of the "effectiveness" of affirmative 3 action. Most of them simply measure the extent to which "under-representation" of blacks or women or select ethnic groups have been "remedied" as a result of governmental pressure. Affirmative action is deemed effective to the extent that firms or institutions have been coerced into narrowing the gap between the real and a theoretically desirable level of employment or enrollment for designated groups. This line of reasoning is subject to what I call the fallacy of inferred discrimination: the assumption that the extent to which a group is or has been subject to discrimination can be measured by the disparity between its percentage in the population and its percentage in the professions or other prestigious occupations. If a group has relatively few members in elite positions in American society, this is taken as evidence that it was excluded because of systematic past and/or present discrimination. If a group has large numbers in America's prestigious positions, it is presumed not to have suffered seriously debilitating discrimination.

The fallacy derives from a patently false reading of American 4 ethnic history. There is no simple relationship between a group's upward social mobility and the amount of discrimination it suffered in the past. Discrimination can cause low rates of upward mobility, but it does not automatically lead to poor achievement; nor does a lack of discrimination necessarily mean a group will do well. For instance, Jewish Americans suffered pervasive discrimination, but have generally done well, particularly in the professions. The same is true of Japanese Americans and Chinese Americans, whose incomes are better than whites; the median income of Asian Americans in 1980 was $22,713, compared to $19,917 for whites. Conversely, Christopher Jencks, in the July/August 1985 issue of *American Behavioral Scientist*, points out that Irish Protestants who blended easily into the population of Anglo-Saxons, now have markedly lower incomes than Irish Catholics, who suffered comparatively more discrimination. Nicholas Capaldi trenchantly states, in his *Affirmative Action and the Crisis of Doctrinaire Liberalism*, "It has never been shown that discrimination is the sole cause of statistical disparity; it has never been shown that statistical disparity is an acceptable criterion for defining the problem [of discrimination.]"

The influence of the fallacy of inferred discrimination is particu-   5 larly strong among jurists, with some bizarre intellectual consequences. For instance, Robert Fullinwider, in his book *The Reverse Discrimination Controversy: A Moral and Legal Analysis*, provides an erudite discussion of the legal implications of affirmative action and preferential treatment. Nevertheless, in a chapter describing his justification for the second policy, he leaves the realm of juridical discussion and enters a world of sociological fantasy. His argument in favor of reverse discrimination is this:

> What is the role of hiring goals and timetables in this process of affirmative action? They serve as automatic monitors. An employer is supposed to evaluate his recruitment and selection procedures and to appraise the labor pool from which he recruits. His aim is to be nondiscriminatory. What would his selection profile look like assuming nondiscrimination? It is this question that should underlie the establishment of hiring goals. The employer should set his goals at that figure one would expect to be realized under nondiscrimination.

Any honest sociologist could have told Fullinwider that it is im-   6 possible to tell what the occupational distributions of ethnic groups in American society would have been if there had been no discrimination. The cultural and educational backgrounds of immigrant groups, and the differing stages of American social development at which the different groups arrived, are so widely dissimilar that trying to imagine what American society might have looked like if it had not been for discrimination is a sterile intellectual exercise. It is equally impossible to tell what levels of ethnic representation would be like in the future if there were no discrimination. Even a superficial understanding of the past and present processes of racial and ethnic relations in the United States makes clear that it is impossible to assert that if there had been—or were in the future to be—no discrimination, the distribution of these groups in the professions and other occupations would have been what their percentages are in the larger population.

The fallacy of inferred discrimination holds that if there is a dispar-   7 ity between a group's overall percentage in the population and its percentage in a profession, then this is the result of discrimination. It leads to the false inference that if there were no discrimination, then the group would be evenly represented throughout America's occupational hierarchy. The latter is a theoretical assertion we might expect from a legal mind, but a position entirely false to a social scientist. The fallacy has thus far been left unchallenged because this intellectual arena has been abandoned by social scientists and taken over by legal philosophers.

Deaffirmation

MICHAEL ERIC DYSON

Michael Eric Dyson is a professor of ethics and cultural criticism at the Chicago Theological Seminary. In addition, he writes the "Black America" column for *Zeta* magazine. Here, writing for the *Nation* in July 1989, Dyson deplores what he views as an anti-affirmative action movement by the Supreme Court in *Martin v. Wilks* (1989)—just two years after the *Johnson* decision. Dyson argues that the *Martin* decision allows employers to abandon affirmative action altogether. Is he overstating the case? Does the Supreme Court have a clear sense of what should be done about job-related discrimination? Read and decide.

On June 12 a 5-4 majority of the Supreme Court ruled that court- 1 approved affirmative action plans, known as consent decrees, from now on may be challenged by white workers. A week earlier, the Court had overturned by the same margin a longstanding Burger Court interpretation of the law that had placed the burden of justifying discriminatory business practices on employers. And last January a 6-3 majority established debilitating restrictive criteria for minority set-aside programs (see " 'Stigmatic Harm,' " *The Nation*, February 13). All three rulings directly threaten the foundation of equal employment opportunities for women and racial minorities. When it comes to civil rights, it is now clear that Reagan's Court has arrived.

The most recent case, *Martin v. Wilks*, involved white firefighters 2 from Birmingham, Alabama, who claimed they were the victims of reverse discrimination because of a 1981 court-approved plan to hire and promote blacks in equal numbers to whites until the number of black firefighters approached the proportion of blacks in the labor force. The ruling will inevitably cause future consent decrees to be constructed and implemented in a more cautious and tentative way. Because more than 300 new consent decrees are adopted each year by government and private employers, the ruling may precipitate a flurry of aggressive litigation across the country aimed at dismantling the legal employment arrangements that address past discriminatory hiring and promotion practices.

In the wake of this decision, employers (especially in the private 3 sector) may now decide to abandon affirmative action altogether. Chief Justice William Rehnquist's opinion for the majority clearly grants room for employers to maneuver away from implementing all but the most token of affirmative action policies, putatively for fear of violating the rights of those not covered by such plans. Moreover, even though the decision does not directly affect voluntarily adopted affirmative action plans, many such plans were modeled on consent decrees. If court-approved plans are now subject to ligitation, the attack on voluntary programs cannot be far behind.

By allowing white employers to challenge consent decrees years 4 after they have been accepted in court, the decision threatens not only future affirmative action employment policies but past ones as well. Ironically, on the same day, the Court declared in a separate but related ruling that three women who worked for AT&T had waited too long to file suit challenging seniority rules that they claimed discriminated against them.

In one of the cruelest twists suffered by the civil rights movement, 5 white men have successfully appropriated the language of victimization and articulated their own suffering compellingly enough to cancel out the claims of those whose suffering they in large part helped create. What is really on trial in these most recent Supreme Court decisions on employment discrimination, as perhaps it has been all along, is the very idea of affirmative action. The struggle over how best to resolve historic injury inflicted upon racial minorities as a group and on women as a group is forbiddingly complex and perennially frustrating. For the notion and, more acutely, the act of addressing past discrimination through affirmative action entails the denial of certain privileges to others, usually white men, who, though not always individually, at least as a group have benefited from past socioeconomic, educational and employment arrangements that directly and unrelentingly discriminated against women and minorities. Although affirmative action, with its numerical timetables, quotas and goals, is an imperfect means of achieving justice for the wronged, it is the best means currently available, and certainly no more unjust than the racism and sexism that precipitated its development and necessitates its continued existence.

Congress must now move to reassert its original intent in calling 6 on employers to develop equal employment opportunities and affirmative action plans. But in light of the High Court's demonstrated insensitivity to the concerns of minorities and women, we are forced to reassess a strategy that has proved vulnerable to legal rebuff. In particular, those minorities and women who have benefited from past affirmative action policies must take it upon themselves to re-ignite the fight against racism and sexism at a time when social lethargy threatens from within almost as ominously as Supreme Court decisions challenge from without.

The Dangers of Preferential Programs
AN INTERVIEW WITH THOMAS SOWELL

Thomas Sowell has been called "a free-market economist and perhaps the leading black scholar among conservatives" (Fred Barnes, *New York Times Book Review*). Sowell, a senior fellow at Stanford's Hoover Institution, has studied the economic performance of racial and ethnic groups in many countries in an effort to understand what makes them do well or prevents their doing so. His research and conclusions—some surprising, all carefully documented—have been published in such works as *Race and Economics* (1975), *The Economics and Politics of Race: An International Perspective* (1983), and *Civil Rights: Rhetoric or Reality?* (1985).

This interview by an unnamed reporter for the *Public Interest*, a politically conservative journal, took place following Sowell's talk at the Harvard Club of New York on the occasion of the publication of his book *Choosing a College* (1989). These questions and answers were reprinted, along with the speech, in the Spring 1990 issue of the journal. Sowell cites problems and repercussions stemming from affirmative action preferential programs in colleges. He argues, moreover, that preferential programs take on a life of their own— becoming impossible to end even when the inequities they address have ceased to exist.

Question: One of the things that you talk about in your book is the   1
mismatch between the student and the school. There have been so many incidents of overt racism on campus these days; do you think that contributes to it?

Sowell: Absolutely. I am convinced of it for a number of reasons. One   2
is the pattern of these violent outbreaks of racism on campus. The conventional wisdom is that this is all due to the Reagan administration, to the conservative mood in the country. There are institutions that keep track of these things, and their statistics showed that there were more of these outbreaks in Massachusetts alone than in the entire South. You find them at places like Berkeley and the University of Massachusetts and Wellesley much more than you're likely to find them at conservative campuses like Hillsdale, or Whitman, or Davidson.

There is also international evidence. I'm working on a book on 3
preferential policy internationally and wherever those policies are put
in, there is this backlash. The longer the policies have been in place,
the worse the backlash. The worst places are India and Sri Lanka,
which have had these policies for several decades. Sri Lanka is an
especially sad case because they began with what were regarded as
model race relations—far better, let's say, than they've been in the
United States. Within a decade people were burning each other alive
in the streets. The civil war got so bad that some political groups began
to have a vested interest in the polarization, as such, quite aside from
the substantive divisions.

The notion that we seem to have in all our foreign policy—that no 4
matter what the strife is about, you can always come in with some nice
compromise that you've worked out back in the State Department and
give it to both sides and they'll say, "Hey, why didn't we think of
this?"—is naive. No, there are people in Sri Lanka who have a vested
interest in the continuation of the strife because that serves their
power; on both sides, among the Tamils and the Sinhalese, there are
factions who are killing numerous members of their own group because these members want to compromise. This is not one of the
happier examples.

India has gone this route as well. There is a tremendous amount of 5
recurring violence over these preferential policies. In the state of Gu-
jarat alone as many as two hundred people have been killed in riots set
off by medical-school quotas. Ironically, in a recent year, there were
only six places set aside in the quotas—and forty-two people died in
riots over those six places.

Some people have argued that the objection is that one group is 6
losing something to another group and that this is the fundamental
reason for the backlash, but that doesn't stand up to the evidence
either. There are many programs that provide special benefits to many
groups, in India as in other countries. But it is the programs that take
the specific form of preferences and set-asides that cause most of the
violence and most of the litigation.

In the United States as well, there are campuses where the Asian 7
students take far more places than the blacks or the Hispanics, or
sometimes the blacks and Hispanics put together, and yet there is not
the same degree of backlash against them because of the manner in
which they took those places. There's an old song that says, "It ain't
what you do, it's the way that you do it." There are whites who have
no problem with Bill Cosby making tens of millions of dollars a year,
but who would soar through the roof if a black kid is brought in under
a preferential program at a minimum wage to be an assistant apprentice.

Question: Let me propose another possibility—that these preferential 8
programs did have reasons when they were initiated back in the sixties
and that there's a historical gap. The young people today are not
aware of why the programs were established. And black students as
well as white students really have no history of why these things
started. All they see is the present, which is that some students are
getting more than others. Maybe we wouldn't have some of this strife
if the programs were at least put in a historical context for all the
students.

Sowell: That's one possibility. But it seems to me that the pattern of the 9
outbreaks doesn't fit that explanation. Because on campuses that have
all sorts of ethnic-studies programs to explain all of these things to all
sorts of people—those are the campuses where it's worse.

If you look at places where people aren't explaining these sorts of 10
things, there you don't find the outbreaks to the same degree. In any
case, the students do know that live people are being sacrificed because of what dead people did. I don't think that there's any way to
reconcile people to that very easily.

One of the problems with trying to have a right proportion of the 11
people in various places is that there are no "right" proportions. There
is no "right" proportion of Democrats and Republicans in Congress.
That is, there is no proportion that will be mutually acceptable to
Democrats and Republicans. All that can be mutually acceptable is a
process. If you both agree that you will abide by the results of these
processes, then, whatever the results, both can reconcile themselves
to those results. But there are no "right" proportions.

One of the sad things, and again this is an international pattern, is 12
that people talk as if this proportional representation would exist in
the absence of institutional bias. But those who have actually done
studies, sometimes for many years, of countries around the world
have found no such proportional representation anywhere—in sectors of the economy, levels of the economy, institutions, or what have
you.

A woman named Cynthia Enloe at Clark University did a study of 13
military and police forces around the world and their ethnic composition. She could not find a country where either the military or the
police forces were ethnically representative of the society. There were
no such countries. Very often you will find one group overrepresented
in the Navy, and another group overrepresented in the Army. Sometimes it is a majority that's overrepresented, sometimes it is a minority. At one time in Malaysia over half the Air Force pilots were
Chinese. In the Soviet Union a majority of all the sergeants are
Ukrainian.

You could go through the whole list everywhere. Anyone who 14
watches basketball knows that basketball teams are not ethnically
representative of the United States.

It's not even true by position. That is, if you look at baseball, an 15
absolute majority of all outfielders are black. It's hard even to think of a
black third baseman. The last one I can remember was Jackie Robinson. At the end of his career as second baseman they shifted him over
to third.

Question: In the process of researching *Choosing a College*, did you have 16
occasion to look at the effect of any of these quotas or special standards
on the military academies?

Sowell: Only in a minor way. Actually, I looked this up some years 17
ago, or rather it came to me through a leak from the Air Force Academy, which did not cooperate in my research. The Air Force Academy
had an internal memorandum marked "Confidential—for your eyes
only," which came to my eyes; it gave different cut-off scores for
blacks, whites, Asians, and Hispanics for admission to the Air Force
Academy. The Asians had to meet the same standards as the whites,
by the way.

There was also a note at the bottom that those who are athletes 18
may be admitted with scores that did not meet these standards. I don't
remember what the standards were exactly, but they were not impressive standards. You could get in hundreds of points below the average
of the U.S. Air Force Academy if you belonged to the right group.

I never saw any data on how many of each of these different 19
groups had survived the rigors of the academy. Even those data,
which are usually unavailable, are becoming less and less reliable as
you get what someone has called "affirmative grading," which is also
a worldwide phenomenon. In Soviet Central Asia the professors are
under pressure to pass more central Asians. In Israel, at one time at
least, there was a ruling that you could not leave back in the public
schools a disproportionate number of Sephardic Jews as compared to
the Ashkenazi.

One of the many illusions of these policies is that we have such 20
total control over them that we can say that this will be a transitory
policy for this period, and then we'll do this, or we will have it at the
stage of search but not at the stage of admission, or at the stage of
admission but not at the stage of judging and graduating and so forth.
And in country after country this has proved to be an illusion.

I think I'll leave you with the classic example of Pakistan, which 21
back in the 1940s instituted preferential programs for the East Pakistanis because they were greatly underrepresented in all sorts of occupations. But like so many other preferential policies, they began to

spread from the East Pakistanis to other groups, further and further removed from the original rationale. The preferences were supposed to last five or ten years, but they kept on being extended; this all started in the forties and back in 1984 the late president Zia extended them until 1994—even though by 1984 East Pakistan had become a separate country called Bangladesh. The people who were the original beneficiaries of this program were no longer part of Pakistan, but so many other groups had piggy-backed on them that now it became politically impossible to get rid of the preferential programs.

Gender, Race, and Labor Policies

EILEEN BORIS AND MICHAEL HONEY

Eileen Boris, who teaches history at Howard University, and Michael Honey, who taught history at Wesleyan University before joining the Humanities Center in Stanford, California, summarize some of the developments and trends in government labor policies as they concern women and minorities. This essay was first published in 1988 in the seventy-fifth anniversary issue of the *Monthly Labor Review*, a professional journal published by the U.S. Department of Labor. The authors provide useful background information on the history of discrimination and affirmative action in the workplace. Even more, they describe the issues involved in affirmative action now.

When Congress established the Department of Labor in 1913, both 1 women and minority men faced limited employment opportunities. Throughout the Nation, white women in the labor force found themselves in low-paying industrial, clerical, and retail positions. Most Afro-Americans remained in the South where they worked as sharecroppers and agricultural laborers or, if female, domestic servants. But, lured to the North by better-paying industrial work and the labor shortages of the World War I years, blacks would soon begin that mass exodus called the "Great Migration."[1]

While race and gender stood as key determinants of occupation, 2 neither the employment status of women nor that of minority men was among early DOL priorities. The first years of the Department were taken up with other matters, particularly the conciliation of labor

---

[1] For a discussion of labor market segmentation by race and sex, see William Harris, *The Harder We Run: Black Workers Since the Civil War* (New York, Oxford University Press, 1982); and Alice Kessler-Harris, *Out to Work: A History of Wage-Earning Women in the United States* (New York, Oxford University Press, 1982).

disputes. Moreover, the Department took its modern form at the very time that President Woodrow Wilson, under congressional pressure, segregated Federal eating and restroom facilities by race and phased most blacks out of the civil service.[2]

Early departmental programs reflected cultural attitudes towards 3 both white women and Afro-Americans, and thus reinforced the existing division of labor by race and sex. They also suggest how the Department, and the Government as a whole, addressed the needs of women separately from those of minorities, with the problems of minority women often getting lost between the two. The United States Employment Service, an agency of the Labor Department, established a women's and girls' division at the end of 1916 "to guide [women] in desirable industry and avoidance of occupations and places where evil conditions exist." With its emphasis on "suitable" employments and its concern with labor standards such as minimum wages and maximum hours (known as protective labor legislation), this division embodied an attitude that would persist until the late 1960s: [White] women workers required protection on the job because their biology supposedly made them different from men, and thus only certain employments were appropriate for the mothers of the Nation.[3]   4

The social place of Afro-Americans similarly shaped DOL treatment of them. During the early years of the Great Migration, the U.S. Employment Service assisted blacks who sought employment in the North by advising them on available jobs; later, complaints from southern employers, who feared losing their abundant labor supply, led the agency to "withdraw its facilities from group migration."[4]

With the onset of World War I, the Nation hurried to mobilize its 5 labor power while simultaneously increasing productivity. Thus, the Federal Government sought to make the best use of women and minority male laborers for the duration of the emergency. The state would "insure the effective employment of women while conserving their health and welfare" even as their labor was allocated temporarily to men's work; programs for blacks attempted "to increase the efficiency of Negro wage earners by improving their condition" and by

---

[2] See John Hope Franklin and Alfred A. Moss, Jr., *From Slavery to Freedom: A History of Negro Americans*, 5th ed. (New York, Alfred A. Knopf, 1988), pp. 227–318. On the early history of the Department of Labor, see Jonathan Grossman, *The Department of Labor* (New York, Praeger Publishers, 1973), pp. 3–30.

[3] For the history of protective legislation, see Judith Baer, *The Chains of Protection: The Judicial Response to Women's Labor Legislation* (Westport, CT, Greenwood Press, 1978). See also U.S. Department of Labor, *Fourth Annual Report of the Secretary of Labor* (Washington, U.S. Government Printing Office, 1916), pp. 62–64.

[4] *Reports of the Department of Labor, 1917* (Washington, U.S. Government Printing Office, 1918), pp. 79–80.

"promoting cooperation between the races for the harmonizing of their relations."[5] . . .

The New Deal and World War II

The New Deal improved the lives of women and minority male [6] workers, but its programs ultimately reinforced the division of the labor market by gender and race.[6] By the time the Roosevelt administration came to power in 1933, the unemployment and underemployment rates of Afro-Americans were double and triple those of whites in many areas of the Nation. Disproportionately employed in agriculture, Afro-Americans were among the first to lose jobs and the last to obtain relief. The New Deal recovery and reform programs, in combination with the rise of industrial unionism through the Congress of Industrial Organizations, offered hope to the Afro-American community. Many blacks also looked to the Labor Department for economic relief, particularly to Secretary of Labor Frances Perkins—a longtime supporter of racial equality.[7]

Perkins attempted to fulfill these hopes, but the former social [7] worker and her agency lacked the necessary political clout to overcome entrenched opposition to racial equality. Although she influenced the direction of the "alphabet" agencies of the New Deal, Congress removed the Department from direct control over nearly all significant labor programs. Within the Department, however, Secretary Perkins was able to abolish segregated eating facilities and to hire new black employees and promote others. She insisted that the Employment Service find jobs for blacks and whites on an impartial basis, added blacks to the Service's staff, and stopped efforts within the Department to dismiss black elevator operators. . . .

While Afro-Americans and Chicanos in the Southwest faced per- [8] sistent discrimination and were often excluded from New Deal programs, relief agencies assigned women (depending on their race) to traditional female pursuits, like sewing, housekeeping, or typing.

---

[5] For information on women workers during World War I, see Maurine Weiner Greenwald, *Women, War and Work: The Impact of World War I on Women Workers in the United States* (Westport, CT, Greenwood Press, 1980); and *Reports of the Department of Labor, 1918* (Washington, U.S. Government Printing Office, 1919), pp. 114–15, 118–24.

[6] For an extended analysis of this point, see Eileen Boris and Peter Bardaglio, "Gender, Race, and Class: The Impact of the State on the Family and the Economy, 1790–1945," in Naomi Gerstel and Harriet Engel Gross, eds., *Families and Work* (Philadelphia, Temple University Press, 1987), pp. 141–46.

[7] Harris, *The Harder We Run*, p. 95; and Philip S. Foner, *Organized Labor and the Black Worker, 1619–1973* (New York, International Publishers, 1974). For blacks and the New Deal, see Nancy Weiss, *Farewell to the Party of Lincoln* (Princeton, NJ, Princeton University Press, 1983); and Harvard Sitkoff, *A New Deal for Blacks* (New York, Oxford University Press, 1978).

Under Section 213 of the 1932 Economy Act, which called for the dismissal of married persons if their spouse also worked for the Government, Federal agencies tended to discriminate against women, causing the Women's Bureau to protest that, contrary to public opinion, "marital status as a basis for employment or dismissal is not sound."[8] Meanwhile, the industrial codes of the National Recovery Administration incorporated wage differentials by sex and region, which led to lower wages for southern black workers.[9] The Department of Labor protested against these wage inequalities. The Women's Bureau, for example, lodged 465 protests against 182 approved codes, gaining 224 changes in 119 codes, of which nearly three-fourths addressed women's wages. In the end, sex distinctions in wages remained in only slightly more than one-fourth of the approved codes, while over 70 percent of the codes for industries in which industrial home work was prevalent called for its abolition.[10] While NRA prohibition of home work ended with the demise of the codes, the Wage and Hour Division of the Labor Department, which adminstered FLSA, was able to prohibit home work in seven garment-related industries in the early 1940s.[11] . . .

With the shift to war production in 1940 and the entry of women 9 into jobs previously held only by men, the Women's Bureau began to monitor labor standards for war workers, including those relating to lunch and rest periods, nightwork, rotation of shifts, sanitation, and safety. The Bureau specified the labor processes where womanpower could be most efficiently mobilized, providing war plants with detailed analyses of appropriate jobs and working with Employment Service regional labor supply committees. Not content with merely deploying womanpower, the Bureau continued its mission to protect women workers, studying the burdensome double day of homemaker and wage earner and supporting the development of day care and other community services.[12]

---

[8] For the attempt to dismiss married women workers from employment, including jobs in the Federal Government, see Lois Scharf, *To Work and Wed: Female Employment, Feminism, and the Great Depression* (Westport, CT, Greenwood Press, 1980), pp. 43–65. For the Women's Bureau response, see Sealander, *As Minority Becomes Majority*, pp. 58–61. See also Mary Anderson, "Women's Bureau," *Twenty-First Annual Report of the Secretary of Labor* (Washington, U.S. Government Printing Office, 1933), p. 93.

[9] Mary Elizabeth Pidgeon, "Employed Women Under N.R.A. Codes," *Bulletin of the Women's Bureau*, no. 130 (Washington, U.S. Government Printing Office, 1935).

[10] For information on the Women's Bureau and the National Recovery Administration, see the annual reports of the Labor Department for 1933, 1934, and 1935, especially *Twenty-Second Annual Report of the Secretary of Labor* (Washington, U.S. Government Printing Office, 1934), p. 100; and Pidgeon, "Employed Women."

[11] For the history of home work regulation, see Eileen Boris, "Homework in the Past, Its Meaning for the Future," in Kathleen Christensen, ed., *New Era in Homework: Directions and Policy* (Boulder, CO, Westview Press, 1988).

[12] For a summary of activities during the war, see "Women's Bureau," *Thirty-Fourth Annual Report of the Secretary of Labor* (Washington, U.S. Government Printing Office, 1946), pp. 196–208.

Equal pay, or "the rate for the job regardless of the sex of the 10 worker," became a prime goal of the Bureau. Because many women performed processes previously done by men, it appeared particularly important to maintain the rate for the job in order to sustain men's wages after the war. Despite the success of the Women's Bureau in incorporating equal pay into wage scales at Government arsenals and in public contracts, and despite the approval given by the National War Labor Board for the principle that all wage increases should conform to State equal pay laws, employers resisted and few wartime wage orders actually mandated equal pay for equal work.[13]

Although the Women's Bureau probed the conditions of black 11 women workers during the war, it concentrated on discrimination based on sex, not race.[14] The Women's Bureau served as an advocate for women, but no equivalent agency existed in the Department when it came to racial minorities. The Division of Negro Labor did not have the status of a Bureau and its tenure depended on the support of the Secretary of Labor; nor did it provide the sort of clearinghouse for information on civil rights that the Women's Bureau offered the Department for women's issues. Within the Federal Government, racial discrimination came under the purview of the Fair Employment Practices Committee—a product of black demands for full civil rights— and not the Department of Labor.[15]

Thus, the contribution of the Labor Department toward improv- 12 ing the situation of black workers proved singularly disappointing, for reasons similar to those which limited the Department's role during the New Deal. Instead of expanding the Department, as was done during World War I, the President mobilized the labor force for World War II through the War Manpower Commission and other agencies outside its jurisdiction. The most important Departmental division influencing wartime employment was the U.S. Employment Service, which became the "operating arm" of the War Manpower Commission. But, as in the 1930s, local administrators abetted segregation in the South and discrimination in the North. For example, local branches of the Employment Service, along with employers, excluded Afro-Americans from Gulf Coast shipyards, an act which led to intervention by the Fair Employment Practices Committee. The percentage

---

[13] See *Thirty-Fourth Annual Report of the Secretary of Labor*, pp. 204–05. For a perceptive analysis of the struggle for equal pay during the war years, see Ruth Milkman, *Gender At Work: The Dynamics of Job Segregation by Sex during World War II* (Urbana, University of Illinois Press, 1987), pp. 63–83.

[14] "Negro Women War Workers," *Bulletin of the Women's Bureau*, no. 205 (Washington, U.S. Government Printing Office, 1945).

[15] Under Fair Employment Practices Committee scrutiny, the percentage of blacks as war workers increased from about 2.5 percent in 1942 to 8 percent by the end of 1944. See Harris, *The Harder We Run*, pp. 122, 117–18; and Foner, *Organized Labor and the Black Worker*, p. 243.

of blacks placed in war industries by the Employment Service declined during the early mobilization effort, from 5.4 percent of those placed in 1940 to 2.5 percent in early 1941.[16]

Postwar, Cold War: 1945–60

From demobilization in 1945, through the 1950s, advocates of racial and gender equality struggled with limited success for better jobs, wages, and employment levels for women and minority men. In the aftermath of the war, returning veterans regained higher-paying jobs as they replaced female and minority male workers who had been new to the industrial labor force. As disproportionate numbers of minorities and women were laid off, the Labor Department supported legislation to establish a national commission against employment discrimination and to make racial discrimination in hiring unlawful. It also lobbied for legislation that would prohibit discrimination between the sexes in the payment of wages, and called for a commission to study the status of women with the purpose of eliminating discriminatory State and Federal laws. Throughout the postwar period, and especially during the "manpower" crisis of the Korean war, the Department continued to advocate Federal action to end employment discrimination against minorities and to gain equal pay for women. But it persisted in viewing fair employment and equal pay as separate issues, rather than seeing the ways that sexual and racial divisions reflected similar discriminatory labor market mechanisms.[17] . . .

Civil Rights, Women's Rights: 1960–80

The struggle for civil rights and women's rights in the 1960s pushed the Federal Government to take a more active role in ending employment discrimination and improving the economic position of women and minority men. The years of the Kennedy administration set the stage for later affirmative action and manpower programs, with passage of the Manpower Development and Training Act of 1962 and the Equal Pay Act of 1963. The Women's Bureau provided research

---

[16] See Foner, *Organized Labor and the Black Worker*, pp. 238–39, 243.

[17] Milkman, *Gender at Work*, pp. 99–127; Harris, *The Harder We Run*, pp. 125–30; *Thirty-Fifth Annual Report of the Secretary of Labor* (Washington, U.S. Government Printing Office, 1947), pp. 18–19; *Thirty-Sixth Annual Report of the Secretary of Labor* (Washington, U.S. Government Printing Office, 1948), pp. 6–7; and U.S. Department of Labor, "Mobilizing Labor for Defense: A Summary of Significant Labor Developments in Time of Emergency," *Thirty-Ninth Annual Report of the Secretary of Labor* (Washington, U.S. Government Printing Office, 1952), especially pp. 141–43.

assistance to the President's Commission on the Status of Women which, in its 1963 report, recommended equal opportunities in hiring, training, promotion, and pay; improved education and counseling for girls; better labor legislation for women; and "new and expanded services to enable women to meet more effectively their responsibilities as homemakers and workers," especially day care. In later years, the Bureau also supported equal employment opportunities for women, reflecting the changed legal climate generated by Title VII, which overturned protective labor laws for women.[18]

The Presidency of Lyndon Johnson inaugurated a period of un-   15
precedented willingness on the part of the Federal Government to intervene in uprooting structural unemployment, poverty, and employer and union discrimination. Employment opportunity and decent wages and working conditions for women and for black and other minority men were, according to then Secretary of Labor Willard Wirtz, "finally identified and significantly recognized as a matter of right" by the Nation. In large measure, the Nixon, Ford, and Carter administrations continued this committment to reducing economic disparities between whites and blacks and between men and women.[19]

Wirtz most clearly enunciated the philosophy of affirmative ac-   16
tion, the use of government influence to better the status of blacks and other disadvantaged groups within the society. "There are two Americas—one characterized by general affluence and comfort, the other by grim deprivation and daily misery," he reported in 1967, concluding that "further economic growth would not alone rescue prosperity's disadvantaged." The position of minorities resulted from a history of societal prejudice, augmented by social policy and government action or inaction. Thus, only social policy and government action, in tandem with efforts to root out racial prejudice, could reverse this situation.[20] . . .

The Carter administration faced economic "stagflation" during   17
the second half of the 1970s as it sought to redress the economic consequences of racial discrimination. Probably no Secretary of Labor

---

[18] "Women's Bureau," *Fifty-Second Annual Report of the Secretary of Labor for the Fiscal Year Ending June 30, 1964* (Washington, U.S. Government Printing Office, 1964), pp. 217–21; and *Fifty-Fifth Annual Report of the Secretary of Labor for the Fiscal Year Ended June 30, 1967* (Washington, U.S. Government Printing Office, 1967), p. 11. See also Cynthia Harrison, "A 'New Frontier' for Women: The Public Policy of the Kennedy Administration," *Journal of American History*, December 1980, pp. 635–45; and Sealander, *As Minority Becomes Majority*, pp. 133–51.

[19] On the impact of social movements in these years, see William Chafe, *The Unfinished Journey: America Since World War II* (New York, Oxford University Press, 1986). On equal pay, see Nancy E. McGlen and Karen O'Connor, *Women's Rights: The Struggle for Equality in the 19th & 20th Centuries* (New York, Praeger, 1983), pp. 170–75. On manpower, see Grossman, *The Department of Labor*, p. 77.

[20] Secretary of Labor W. Willard Wirtz as quoted in *Annual Report of the Secretary of Labor*, 1967, pp. 1–2. See also *Annual Report of the Secretary of Labor*, 1966, p. 4.

before Ray Marshall had as deep an understanding of the historical nature of the economic disadvantage of black workers.[21] During Marshall's tenure, the Department participated in suits against the steel industry and other large employers for failing to live up to affirmative action agreements in Federal contracts, and helped to win backpay for workers who had been discriminated against. New regulations allowed for accurate documentation of employer discrimination. The Department placed all equal opportunity compliance programs within its Office of Federal Contract Compliance, producing what Marshall called "one-stop administration and enforcement" of equal opportunity laws. This step made it increasingly difficult for employers to evade affirmative action. In a number of cases, those who did so were debarred from Federal contracts. . . .

In the 1980s large cutbacks in Federal spending threatened to gut   18 the Department's efforts to use job training and public employment to help pull disadvantaged communities out of economic depression. Federal job creation programs were particularly hard hit, beginning with the reduction of some 300,000 workers from CETA in 1981. Cutbacks also reduced the Labor Department staff available for implementation of affirmative action and wage and hour regulations. The Office of Federal Contract Compliance adopted a "nonconfrontational" approach, emphasizing technical services for employers. It took steps to eliminate the need for small contractors to adhere to affirmative action guidelines, it urged voluntary compliance, and it rewrote guidelines so as to eliminate the weakest claims for redress at lower administrative levels. By 1984, critics charged that OFCC failed to prosecute antidiscrimination cases. By 1987, it appeared to civil rights and equal rights proponents that vigorous Federal affirmative action programs and public employment programs belonged to the past.[22] . . .

The next quarter-century will require imaginative policies to fulfill   19 the vision of racial and gender justice. If the past is any guide to the future, only persistent Federal action can help win the battle for equal opportunity; the Department of Labor can play a crucial role in this battle.

---

[21] See, for example, Ray Marshall, *The Negro and Apprenticeship* (Baltimore, Johns Hopkins University Press, 1967); *The Negro and Organized Labor* (New York, Wiley, 1965); *The Negro Worker* (New York, Random House, 1967); and, with Virgil L. Christian, Jr., *Employment of Blacks in the South: A Perspective on the 1960s* (Austin, University of Texas Press, 1978).
[22] Annual Reports of the Secretary of Labor, 1981–1985.

Some Key Affirmative Action Cases and Their Outcomes

The following brief identification of key United States Supreme Court decisions concerning affirmative action is drawn from Alan Freeman's essay, "Antidiscrimination Law: The View from 1989" *Tulane Law Review* 64.6 [June 1990] 1407–41), and from Roy L. Brooks's essay, "The Affirmative Action Issue: Law, Policy, and Morality" (*Connecticut Law Review* 22.2 [Winter 1990] 323–56). Freeman is a professor of law at SUNY/Buffalo School of Law; Brooks is a professor of law at the University of Minnesota. These cases are identified below because writers on affirmative action often refer to them and because they offer a summary of trends in Court decisions on the thorny problems of affirmative action and reverse discrimination.

The First Affirmative Action Cases

All three of these cases involved claims of reverse discrimination, [1] all three were resolved—at least partially—in favor of the challenged affirmative action programs.

Regents of the Univ. of Cal. v. Bakke, 1978

Allan Bakke was denied admission to medical school and sued the [2] University of California because it maintained a racial quota, allocating a specific number of places for minority students exclusively. Bakke argued that the plan constituted discrimination against white males, like himself, who were denied admission while minority applicants with somewhat lower qualifications were admitted. The Court ruled 5–4 in Bakke's favor and against racial quotas, but at the same time it held (also 5–4) that "state educational institutions can take race into account in a properly devised admissions program"—that is, "one in which race is only one factor in the admissions process and is used to achieve a 'diverse' student body" (Brooks 326).

United Steelworkers v. Weber, 1979

This case proved to be an important one in the history of affir- [3] mative action. *Weber*

involved a collective bargaining agreement providing for affirmative action efforts to eliminate conspicuous racial imbalances at Kaiser Aluminum plants. The specific controversy arose at a plant in Louisiana where, although the local work force was 39% black, only 1.83% of skilled craftworkers were black. The plan at issue provided for training of production workers to become skilled craftworkers, with 50% of the trainees to be black, regardless of seniority, until the percentage of black craftworkers matched that in the local population. Weber, a white production worker with more seniority than some of the black trainees, charged the union and company with unlawful racial discrimination under Title VII of the 1964 Civil Rights Act. (Freeman 1425)

The Court decided, 5–2, in favor of the challenged affirmative ⁴ action plan. The significance of this case is that it broadened the justification for affirmative action programs. Because of the obvious inequities in the Kaiser hirings, the Court ruled that it was no longer necessary—as had previously been the case—to prove "specific and identifiable victims" of discrimination; "the remedy is a group remedy designed to confer on black workers a fair share of jobs" (Freeman 1426).

Fullilove v. Klutznick, 1980

This case involved a "federal law mandating 10% set aside for ⁵ minority-owned business enterprises" (Freeman 1424). The Court held that the set-aside was appropriate, given the "evidence of a long history of marked disparity in the percentage of public contracts awarded to minority business enterprises . . . [and no] lack of capable and qualified minority businesses" (Justice Blackmun's concurring opinion, qtd. in Brooks 327).

The Move Away from Weber

Beginning in 1984, Supreme Court decisions began to move away ⁶ from the Weber holdings. The Court began to hold that low percentages of minorities in given situations (the workplace, schools, and so on) did not in themselves show illegal discrimination requiring judicial remedy.

Firefighters Local Union No. 1784 v. Stotts, 1984

White workers challenged the protection from layoffs of blacks ⁷ hired under an affirmative action plan. When the Memphis, Tennessee, city government was compelled to lay off some firefighters because of a faltering economy, it released senior white firefighters before releasing blacks hired the previous year. Not to have done so would have been to eradicate the effects of the court-ordered affirmative action plan, but to do so seemed to challenge section 703(h) of

Title VII, "which protects bona fide seniority systems from judicial modifications" (Brooks 329). The Court, ruling in the white workers' favor, "rejected the application of an affirmative action hiring plan (mandated by a consent decree) to a layoff situation" (Freeman 1427).

The Supreme Court ruled in five affirmative action cases in 1986 [8] and 1987. In four of the cases, listed below, "all involving hiring and promotion, the Court upheld affirmative action, often citing *Weber* with approval, yet without any consistent majority voice" (Freeman 1427). In fact, the cases are noteworthy for the large number of separate opinions. (Justices may write separate opinions when they disagree with, agree only in part with, or want to discuss a different aspect of a case from that addressed in the majority ruling.)

Local 28 Sheet Metal Workers v. *EEOC,* 1986

The union had been required under an affirmative action plan to [9] hire a certain percentage of blacks and Hispanics, which for over ten years it had resisted doing. The Court upheld a contempt citation and the affirmative action plan, citing the union's "pervasive and egregious discrimination" (qtd. in Brooks 330). Additionally, the Court ruled, in both this case and the following, that people who had not been specifically and personally victimized by unlawful discrimination in the past could nevertheless benefit from affirmative action plans.

Local No. 93, International Association of Firefighters v. *Cleveland,* 1986

This case is similar to *Sheet Metal Workers.* The Court upheld an [10] affirmative action plan that required an

> even number of minority and nonminority promotions to a certain level and for the promotion of all qualified minorities to certain upper-level positions (there being few of such qualified minorities). Promotional goals, expressed in terms of percentages, were established for different ranks. (Brooks 331)

Johnson v. *Transportation Agency,* 1987

A description of this case and excerpts from two of the opinions [11] written on it appear earlier in this chapter (pp. 553–564).

United States v. *Paradise,* 1987

Ruling 5–4, the Court upheld a promotional quota required of the [12] Alabama Department of Public Safety, ruling that the fifty percent promotional quota for minorities was the only effective remedy available; it was flexible and ephemeral; it was reasonably related to the relevant labor market; it did not impose an unacceptable burden on innocent third parties . . . (Brooks 332)

The fifth case did not affirm *Weber*, even nominally.   13

Wygant v. *Jackson Board of Education*, 1986

In this case, concerning another layoff situation, the Court followed *Stotts* rather than *Weber*, deciding against the application of the affirmative action plan to layoffs.   14

1989: *The Rejection of Weber*

The following three cases "collectively repudiate the implicit principles, if not the actual results, of . . . *Weber*" (Freeman 1429).   15

Wards Cove Packing Co. v. *Atonio*, 1989

In this case, involving an Alaskan cannery, cannery workers and "noncannery" workers were hired through separate channels; almost all of the cannery workers were Asian minorities. Not only were minority workers channeled to the unskilled, "low-status" cannery jobs, but housing and eating facilities were separate for the workers in the two tracks.   16

The Court found that the cannery company practiced no intentional discrimination and returned the burden of proof to plaintiffs, ruling that they   17

had to show how a particular hiring practice specifically caused discriminatory results, being sure to show how many "qualified" non-whites were available for the jobs at issue (as opposed to requiring the employer to justify its practices as ones that selected those who were "qualified"). (Freeman 1431)

The great significance of *Wards Cove* to affirmative action is that it effectively cancels "the assumption, implicit in *Weber*, that serious statistical disparities are presumptive violations of Title VII" (Freeman 1431).

Freeman argues that this decision   18

surely deserves to be called a major civil rights setback. Yet, it is even more dismal than that. There is a Dickensian quality to the opinion, with its excessive solicitude for employer-defendants and its preoccupation with legal technicality (intent, causation, burden of proof), that serves to distance the victims from their own case. (1430)

According to Freeman, "The other two 1989 cases dealt with 're- 19 verse discrimination' challenges to affirmative action programs. . . . Their combined effect is the elevation of reverse discrimination claims to an identical status with claims on behalf of discrimination's historic and traditional victims" (1431–32). These cases are described below.

Martin v. Wilks, 1989

A group of white firefighters successfully challenged the affir- 20 mative action hiring and promotion policies of the fire department in Birmingham, Alabama. The particular significance of the case is that, in order to counter reverse discrimination, it permits whites to challenge affirmative action programs that have been in place for some time and even those established as a result of lawsuits.

City of Richmond v. J. A. Croson Co., 1989

Richmond, Virginia, had set aside 30 percent of total building and 21 repair funds for minority contractors. Previously, only 0.67 percent of contracts had been awarded to minority contractors, despite the fact that half of Richmond's population is black. The Supreme Court upheld (6–3) the reverse discrimination challenge by white contractors, finding insufficient "evidence of racial discrimination [prior to the 30 percent set-aside] to justify the program" (Freeman 1432).

Using and Citing Sources

SUMMARIZING, PARAPHRASING, QUOTING

Once you have finished reading and researching, and you are armed with all sorts of ammunition with which to demolish the opposition in your written argument, two temptations and two difficulties arise. The first temptation is to use every bit of the material you have read with such care, even if some of its evidence is tangential to your thesis, or even if you have so much material that to summarize or quote from all of it will leave you no room or energy to develop your own ideas in response to it. The second temptation occurs when the source material is written so well and so clearly that you cannot imagine expressing the information in any other way. This usually unwarranted humility can result in an unattractive patchwork of a paper largely made up of lengthy quotations seamed together with transitional remarks—or in plagiarism, whether unconscious or deliberate.

Therefore, your first task must be to test your working outline and your evidence against each other. Your reading may have suggested additional points to support your thesis, or it may have exposed flaws in your thesis that require you to modify your stance. Some fascinating material may not fit anywhere in your outlined argument, and you must let that material wait for another day and another essay. On the other hand, what you have learned may suggest a more logical way of ordering the points you propose to make. And inadequacies in the support you have gathered will become apparent as you briefly identify the evidence you have found under each entry in your outline or bare-bones draft (if you use notecards, simply arrange them according to the major points they support). Where support appears inadequate, you must decide whether to modify or eliminate that particular point, or go to the library.

Now, how do you record the supporting material in such a way that you avoid that second temptation? Summarize most of it; paraphrase what is important but difficult to grasp in the original; and quote what is crucial, brief, and clear. If you are using a general or research handbook, these three ways of recording your research are explained in some detail therein. Briefly, to *summarize* is to express another's ideas *in your own words* and to do so in many fewer words than the original. To *paraphrase* is to express another's ideas *in your own words* and to do so in about the same number of words or even more words than the original. To *quote* is to express another's ideas *in that person's own words* and to indicate clearly that you have done so. In each case, you credit the source in your paper.

Even after you have put temptation behind you and have summarized most of your source material and have put aside all of it that is not directly relevant to your argument, the two difficulties remain to be dealt with. The first difficulty is that fitting source material into your own prose may be difficult to manage without ending up with something that reads as if it had been cut and pasted; the second, that the punctuation, pronouns, and verb tenses in the source material may not mesh well with your own writing. When the latter is the case, the quotations seem obtrusive even if they are introduced properly.

In order to overcome or avoid these difficulties, keep in mind a few points:

1. Direct quotations should be few and significant. The paper is to be your essay and your argument, after all. Too many other voices overpower your own. Instead, rely on restatement, summary, and evaluation of much of the source material in your own words.

2. Quotations (and paraphrases and summaries) must be accurate. An inaccurate quotation is careless and can be misleading, and a quotation taken out of context can be distorted.

3. Quotations ordinarily should be preceded or followed by comment or analysis. If a passage does not merit comment or analysis, it usually does not merit direct quotation (in which case, summarize instead).

4. Quotations must be grammatically and logically incorporated into the paragraph in which you use them. They should fit into, not just be appliqued on, your own argument.

5. All sources, whether quoted, paraphrased, or summarized, must be properly cited.

To accomplish these aims, first, take most of your notes in your own words. This bit of advice is timeworn but still valuable. Taking notes in your own words has the initial advantage of requiring that you read closely and truly understand what you are reading, a requirement not exacted by a Xerox machine. In addition, understanding the material will facilitate your use of it in your own argument; and because it will be recounted in your own words, you will avoid the patchwork effect of excessive quotations. (Of course, citations still will be required.) Save direct quotations for brief, brilliant comments, controversial statements, statistics, and personal testimony you feel will strengthen your argument. Always indicate directly quoted material with quotation marks and page references in your notes so that you will avoid confusion later as you write and revise.

INCORPORATING QUOTATIONS

Second, as you write the essay, incorporate quoted material grammatically and logically into your own paragraphs. Quotations should not crop up unannounced, without evident context. Those running longer than three lines of typescript should be indented ten spaces (and instructors may prefer that you also single-space them) and should be introduced by an entire sentence or by a clause and a colon. Shorter quotations also must be given a context that fits them grammatically and logically into your argument and your words. Brief quotations may be incorporated in an almost limitless number of ways as the following examples indicate:

(1)
Mark Antony uses irony in his funeral oration for Caesar. "I come to bury Caesar, not to praise him" (3.2.79–80) asserts just the opposite of Mark Antony's intentions. He uses the oration to praise Caesar backhandedly and to attack Caesar's murderers while pretending to applaud them.

(2)
Mark Antony's funeral oration for Caesar uses irony effectively, for after declaring, "I come to bury Caesar, not to praise him" (3.2.79–80), Mark Antony goes on to attack Caesar's murders through the irony of his repeated reference to "the noble Brutus." As the whole context of his speech makes clear, Caesar's ally means the opposite of what he says here.

(3)

> Never was a funeral oration used to better political effect than that of Mark Antony over the body of the dead Caesar. He begins with a disclaimer: "I come to bury Caesar, not to praise him" (3.2.79–80). Having lulled Caesar's enemies, Mark Antony then turns the crowd against them through the heavy irony of his repeated praise of them, "all honorable men."

In the first example, the quotation serves as the subject of a sentence explaining its meaning. In the second, the same quotation is grammatically embedded within a sentence that gives it a context in the play and in the student writer's argument. The quoted phrase, "the noble Brutus," is incorporated without punctuation because it functions as the object of a preposition. And in the third selection, the quotation is introduced by a clause and a colon as is typical of longer quotations, and the quoted phrase "all honorable men" serves as an appositive describing "them," the murderers.

But suppose that the quotation is written in the past tense, and your paragraph is written in the present; or that the quotation begins with a capital letter, but a capital letter is not needed at the point in your own sentence at which you quote another's words; or that you want to omit words or sentences preceding, following, or in the middle of what you plan to quote—what then? The following pointers should help you resolve most dilemmas of this sort.

Changes

Generally, avoid changes in the quoted material. If you must have them, put brackets around the altered letter or word. Do not alter punctuation except as noted below.

1. If the quoted material begins with a capital letter and its placement in your own sentence requires a lower-case letter, change the initial letter to lower-case. Conservative usage dictates brackets around the altered letter, but brackets can be distracting. Try to re-phrase your own sentence so that the quotation can be incorporated without such changes. (If your typewriter has no bracket keys, you must ink in any brackets required, for parentheses do not indicate added or altered words.) Make the same kind of change if the original quotation begins with a lower-case letter and your grammatical context for it requires a capital.

> *Original Statement:* The one function that TV news performs very well is that when there is no news, we give it to you with the same emphasis as if there were news.
>
> —David Brinkley

As Quoted: David Brinkley has observed that "the one function that TV news performs very well is that when there is no news, [newscasters] give it to you with the same emphasis as if there were news."

2. If the quoted material uses present tense and you would prefer to have it in past tense, avoid making a change in the quoted material by wording your introduction in such a way that the shift in tense is accounted for without changing the original. In brief quotations involving only a single verb, you may change the tense and bracket the altered word, but try to avoid the need to do so by reworking your own sentence or by omitting from the quotation the part containing the troublesome verb.

Original Statement: Those who make peaceful revolution impossible will make violent revolution inevitable.

—John Kennedy

As Quoted: The United States was culpable in the Iranian revolution of 1979 to the extent that it did all in its power to keep the Shah in sole control of the government, despite the widespread opposition to many of the Shah's policies. The U.S. failed to heed John Kennedy's warning made almost two decades earlier: "Those who make peaceful revolution impossible will make violent revolution inevitable."

Original Statement: Boswell is the first of biographers.

—Macauley

As Quoted: In the nineteenth century, Macauley declared Boswell to be "the first of biographers."

3. Commas, semicolons, colons, and periods ending quotations may be changed to the punctuation mark that fits your own grammatical context (usually a period, comma, or no punctuation). Do not end a quotation with double punctuation (the original writer's and then your own).

Original Statement: If the life of a human being is more valuable than the life of, say, a cabbage, this must be because the human being has qualities like consciousness, rationality, autonomy, and self-awareness which distinguish human beings from cabbages. How, then, can we pretend that the life of a human being with all these distinctive qualities is of no greater value than the life of a human being who, tragically, has never had and never will have these qualities?

—Peter Singer and Helga Kuhse, rev. of Robert and Peggy Stinson, *The Long Dying of Baby Andrew* 16

As Quoted: As Singer and Kuhse observe, it is pointless to "pretend that the life of a human being with all these distinctive qualities [such as rationality and self-awareness] is of no greater value than the life of a human being who, tragically, has never had and never will have these qualities"(16).

4. Change double quotation marks (" ") within quotations to single marks (' ') unless the whole passage is set off from the text.

Original Statement: Apparently, now that he knew he was in trouble, his thoughts had turned to his God. "Have mercy!" they heard him shouting indignantly. "I say have mercy, damn it!"

—Clarence Day, *Life With Father* 26

As Quoted: Day's father was a man not to be trifled with, even by Almighty God. On the rare occasion when the senior Day felt the need to call upon his Maker, it was as if he called upon an equal: "'Have mercy!' they heard him shouting indignantly. 'I say have mercy, damn it!'" (26).

Omissions

Whenever you omit parts of a quoted passage, make sure that what you do quote still shows grammatical continuity and logical sense. For example:

Original Statement: Singer and Kuhse (above).

Unclear Abridgment: As Singer and Kuhse cogently argue, " a human being is more valuable than the life of a cabbage . . . because . . . these distinctive qualities are of . . . greater value than the life of a human being who, tragically, has never had and never will have these qualities" (16).

Effective Abridgment: As Singer and Kuhse cogently argue, "the life of a human being is more valuable than the life of a cabbage [primarily because of] . . . qualities like consciousness . . . and self-awareness" (16).

1. If you omit words, phrases, or sentences in the middle of a quoted passage, indicate the omission with ellipses, in this case, three spaced periods (. . .). Use a period followed by three spaced periods if the words on either side of the ellipses are both grammatically complete sentences or if a sentence ends and another begins in the omitted section.

Original Statement: The cult of "reason," so widely applied in the course of the last three centuries, has come to seem to me in a sense a blind alley. Our thoughts and actions may be controlled by but they do not spring from what we call reason.

—Edmund Wilson, *The Dead Sea Scrolls, 1947–1966,* 277

As Quoted: Logic is not the source of ideas, Wilson reminds us: "The cult of 'reason' . . . has come to seem to me in a sense a blind alley. Our thoughts and actions may be controlled by but they do not spring from what we call reason" (*Dead Sea Scrolls* 277).

[An abbreviated form of the title is included, as above, in a reference to one of several works written by the same author(s).]

2. If you omit sentences before the quoted material (as you ordinarily will), do not use ellipses. If you omit words or sentences following the quoted material, and the next words in the sentence are your own, do not use ellipses. But if you end your own sentence with quoted words that do *not* end a sentence in the original, you must use ellipsis dots following the quotation.

> *Original Statement:* Her long, black hair, always drawn and braided in the day, lay upon her shoulders and against her breasts like a shawl. I do not speak Kiowa, and I never understood her prayers, but there was something inherently sad in the sound, some merest hesitation upon the syllables of sorrow.
>
> —N. Scott Momaday, *The Way to Rainy Mountain*

> *As Quoted:* His grandmother's reverence touched him: "I do not speak Kiowa, and I never understood her prayers, but there was something inherently sad" in her quiet chanting.

> *As Quoted:* His grandmother's reverence touched him: "I do not speak Kiowa, and I never understood her prayers, but there was something inherently sad in the sound. . . ." He would never forget it.

Additions

Always make sure that it will be clear to a reader that anything you have added is not in the original quotation. Added words are bracketed. Never confuse brackets with parentheses; if words appear in parentheses, they are assumed to be part of the original quotation.

1. If you insert words of your own into a quoted passage for transition or explanation, put them in brackets.

> *Original Statement:* Wilson's above.

> *As Quoted:* Logic is not the source of ideas, Wilson reminds us: "The cult of 'reason' . . . [is] in a sense a blind alley. Our thoughts and actions may be controlled by but they do not spring from what we call reason" (*Dead Sea Scrolls* 277).

2. If you put some of the quoted words in italics (indicated in a typewritten paper by underlining), follow the quotation with "(emphasis added)."

> *Original Statement:* And love is an impediment to marital happiness. Founded on projection, abetting the quest for indirect self-acceptance, love can contribute neither to candid intimacy nor to self-acceptance.
>
> —Snell Putney and Gail J. Putney,
> *The Adjusted American* 118

As Quoted: Many psychologists have argued that what we call *love* is a destructive emotion: "Founded on projection, abetting the quest for *indirect* self-acceptance, love can contribute neither to candid intimacy nor to self-acceptance (Putney and Putney 118; emphasis added).

3. If the quoted material contains an error, follow the error with "[sic]" so that your readers will know the error is not yours.

Original Statement: In reviewing its provisions, we could not determine how the bill might effect future Supreme Court rulings.

—John Q. Legislator, letter to constituents

As Quoted: Senator Legislator wrote that the committee "could not determine how the bill might effect [sic] future Supreme Court rulings."

CITING SOURCES

Avoiding Plagiarism

As you write your essay, you must cite your sources of evidence whether you are quoting directly, paraphrasing, or summarizing. You must also cite the sources of ideas that are not your own. The only statements that do not require citation are common-knowledge statements, put into your own words, and your original ideas, interpretations, and conclusions. Failure to cite sources, and cite them accurately, constitutes plagiarism—a kind of theft that violates every aim of scholarship and integrity that academic institutions hold dear.

The following thorough definition of plagiarism is quoted from Nancy Hilts Deane, *Teaching with a Purpose*, 5th ed. (New York: Houghton Mifflin, 1972):

> Plagiarism is the presentation of the words, ideas, or opinions of someone else as one's own. A student is guilty of plagiarism if he submits as his own work a part or all of an assignment copied or paraphrased from a source, such as a book, magazine, or pamphlet, without crediting the source; the sequence of ideas, arrangement of material, or pattern of thought of someone else, *even though he has expressed it in his own words* [emphasis added]. Plagiarism occurs when such a sequence of words or ideas is used without having been digested, integrated, and reorganized in the writer's mind, and without acknowledgment in the paper.
>
> Similarly, a student is an accomplice in plagiarism and equally guilty if he allows his paper, in outline or finished form, to be copied and submitted as the work of another; if he prepares a written assignment for another student and allows it to be submitted as that student's work; or if he keeps or contributes to a file of papers or speeches with the clear intent that they be copied and submitted as the work of anyone other than the author.

One difficulty students encounter in avoiding plagiarism is deciding whether some statements are common-knowledge information or the intellectual property of a particular writer. Certainly it is easy to see that you need not cite a source for the dates of wars or of reigns, or the names of presidents, princes, and publishing companies. But what about the formula for making ordinary glass or the fact that *Albion* is a poetic name for England? What about the name of the first black professional baseball player, or his batting average? What about a brief identification of the First Law of Thermodynamics? All these bits of information are, just like the name of the first president of the United States, part of the *body of common knowledge.* Common knowledge is information common to any person informed in a given field. Any textbook on the subject, any specialized (and sometimes general) dictionary or encyclopedia is likely to contain such information.

As you begin your study of a particular field of knowledge, of course, almost everything you learn will be new to you. Initially, then, you may cite sources unnecessarily. You will begin to identify the common knowledge in the field as you read more widely. But when in doubt, cite your source. Better too many citations than too few.

Citing sources accurately and appropriately not only shows you to be an honest scholar but also adds the weight of authoritative testimony to arguments concerning subjects on which you cannot speak personally as an authority. In both ways, proper citation adds to the persuasiveness of your paper. But endless numbers of footnotes do not add to any paper's persuasiveness; they distract readers by continually sending them to the bottom of the page or the end of the paper. Accordingly, the Modern Language Association (MLA)[1] has revised its guidelines for citations in order to eliminate most purely bibliographic notes (notes giving only publication information and page references). The one exception occurs when you want to cite several sources simultaneously, which would require a long and obtrusive parenthetical citation. Discursive notes (notes commenting on, but not strictly part of, the text of the paper) cannot always be eliminated but should be few in number.

As you take notes for your research paper, record all the following information that is applicable for each source. All numbers (except page numbers for prefaces and other front matter in books, which are distinguished from the text proper by the use of lower-case Roman numerals) should be given in Arabic numerals.

---

[1] The MLA citation system is used for papers written in the humanities. Other disciplines have slightly different rules for citations. In the social sciences, the APA citation system briefly summarized on pages 612–613 is the norm. In the natural sciences, the preferred citation system varies. Some references for scientific citations are given on page 613. (This, by the way, is a discursive footnote.)

Books

Author(s)
Editor(s) of anthologies of essays, stories, poems, and the like
Translator (if any)
Title of Chapter or Part of Book (if only part is used; also note page
    numbers of chapter or part used if it constitutes an identifiable
    unit of the book; put title in quotation marks)
Title of Book (including subtitle, if any; both underlined)
Name of Series (if work is part of a series; series name neither
    underlined nor put in quotation marks)
Number of Volumes with This Title (if work is in more than one
    volume; and number of this particular volume)
Place of Publication
Publisher
Year of Publication

Periodicals

Author(s) of Article
Title of Article (in quotation marks)
Name of Periodical (underlined)
Volume Number and Year (for scholarly journals)
Month and Year (for general circulation magazines; include day of
    month for weekly or biweekly magazines and for newspapers)
Page numbers for the entire article (separately record *specific* page
    numbers with passages to be cited within your paper)

Recording all the applicable information on a notecard for each
source will help you avoid return trips to the library when you prepare
your "Works Cited" list.

Citations in the Humanities

In order to meet both the goal of properly citing all source material
and that of eliminating purely bibliographic footnotes, follow one
general principle: *Give the least amount of information needed to send the
reader to the appropriate point in the appropriate text.* Most of the identifying information about each work cited will be given in a list of works
cited at the end of the paper. Citations in the text itself will direct the
reader to a specific page (or line, if the reference is to a poem or play) in
that work; they will not repeat the complete information given in the
list of works cited.

Some additional guidelines follow.

What to Include in Parenthetical Citations

1. Do not repeat in parentheses what you have already said in the text proper.

2. Put as little as possible in parentheses to keep interruptions to a minimum. Author's [2] surname and page number will suffice if you have only one work by that author in your list of works cited. Page number alone will suffice if you mention the author's name in the text proper and you have used no other work by that author.

   If your paper largely concerns works by a single author, you need not repeat the author's name each time you quote or refer to what is obviously one of his or her works.

3. If you have used more than one work by the same person or persons, include an abbreviated form of the title in the citation.

4. If you have used works by different authors with the same surname, give first name or initial as well to distinguish the works from each other.

5. If a work has two authors, include both names in the citation. If it has three authors or more, you may use the first author's name and the Latin abbreviation "et al." (meaning "and others").

6. If you are using an indirect reference—for example, you are referring to a statement by Smith as quoted in a work by Jones—make clear that you are not using the original source by using the abbreviation "qtd. in" (for "quoted in").

7. If your reference is to a poem, indicate line numbers rather than page numbers. Do not use the abbreviations ℓ or $\ell\ell$, which could be confused with numbers. Instead, write out *line* or *lines* until the reference to lines is clearly established; thereafter, just give the numbers.

8. If your reference is to a play, indicate act, scene, and line(s), using Arabic numbers and periods: 3.2.112 would direct a reader to Act 3, scene 2, line 112.

9. The abbreviations *p., pp.,* and *vol.* are no longer used when the reference is clearly to page numbers or volume number.

How to Punctuate Parenthetical Citations

1. Use no punctuation between author's name and page number: (Smith 268)

2. Use no punctuation between title and page number: (*Ideas* 268)

---

[2] References to *author* also apply to *editor* when you are referring to entire anthologies and other compilations.

3. Put a comma between author's name and title (if title is needed): (Smith, *Ideas* 268)
4. Place parenthetical citations after the closing quotation mark and before the period except in the case of long, blocked quotations. Then they follow the period at the end of the quoted passage.

Basic Forms for Lists of Works Cited

Entries in the list of Works Cited are alphabetical. For each, the author's surname is given first, flush against the left margin. Subsequent lines, if any, are indented five spaces from the left margin.

Examples of Basic Forms for Entries in Works Cited List (Alphabetically)

Book

Galbraith, John Kenneth. *The Anatomy of Power*. Boston: Houghton, 1983.

Collection or Anthology

Barthelme, Donald. "Lightening." *Overnight to Many Distant Cities*. New York: Putnam's, 1983.
[reference to component part of book all by one author]
Groutz, Samuel, ed. *Moral Problems in Medicine*. Englewood Cliffs: Prentice, 1976.
[reference to entire book]
Szasz, Thomas. "The Right to Health." *Moral Problems in Medicine*. Ed. Samuel Groutz. Englewood Cliffs: Prentice, 1976.
[reference to component part of book]

Computer Data

"The Decade Ahead: Plan for the Oil Industry." Diskette 14. Marietta, NM: Petroleum Resources, Inc., 1991.

Congressional Document

United States, 101st Cong., 2nd sess. *Cong. Rec.* 14 Apr. 1988: 4315–23. Debate on savings and loan relief.

Film

It's a Wonderful Life. Dir. Frank Capra. RKO, 1946.
[RKO was the film's distributor.]

Interview

Harris, Leon. Telephone interview. 14 Oct. 1990.

Journal Article

Perrine, Laurence. "Donne's 'Confined Love.'" *Explicator* 39 (1980): 35–36.
Brooks, Roy L. "The Affirmative Action Issue: Law, Policy, and Morality. *Connecticut Law Review* 22.2 (1990): 323–357.

Legal Citation

Johnson v. Transportation Agency. 480 U.S. 616 (1987).

Letter

Brady, Judy. Letter to author. 11 March 1991.

Magazine Article

Sachs, Andrea. "Who Should Foot the AIDS Bill? *Time* 16 Oct. 1989: 88.

Newspaper Article

Morgan, Mary Carolyn. "Ease Up, Please, on Single Women . . . ." *New York Times* 15 July 1990, sec. 12: 26.
Dombrink, Patricia. "There's No Gender in Success." *Dallas Morning News* 10 Aug. 1982: 11A.

Review

Aspen, Marvin. Rev. of *The Jury in America*, by John Guinther. *Judicature* 72.4 (1989): 254–55.

Citations in the Social Sciences

The *Publication Manual of the American Psychological Association* explains in detail the most common citation system in the social sciences. The following summary of APA documentation is reprinted with the kind permission of Lynn Quitman Troyka from the *Simon and Schuster Handbook for Writers* (Prentice Hall, 1987), 648–49.

What to Include in Parenthetical Citations

1. If a parenthetical citation comes at the end of your sentence, place the sentence's period after the parentheses.

2. If you are paraphrasing or summarizing material and you do *not* mention the name of the author in your text, do this: (Jones, 1982).

3. If you are quoting, and you do *not* mention the name of the author in your text, do this: (Jones, 1982, p. 65).

4. If you are paraphrasing, summarizing, or quoting material and *do* mention the name of the author in your text, do this: (p. 65).

5. If you use more than one source written in the same year by the same author(s), assign letters (*a*, *b*, etc.) to the works in the References list and do this for a parenthetical reference: (Jones, 1983a).

6. If you refer to a work more than once, give the author's name and year only the first time; then use only the name.

7. If you cite several sources in one place, put them in alphabetical order by authors' last names and separate the sources with a semicolon: (Bassuk, 1984; Fustero, 1984).

Guidelines for the Reference List

1. Arrange the list of sources cited alphabetically by author's last name. For two or more works by an author, arrange the works by date, most recent first.

2. Start with an author's last name, followed by initials for the author's first and middle names. If there is more than one author, name them all (up to six authors)—again starting with the last name and using initials for first and middle names. If there are over six authors, use only the first author and the words *et al.*

3. Put the date of publication in parentheses immediately after the author's name. If you list two works by the same author published in the same year, assign letters (*a*, *b*, etc.) to the year: (1984a), (1984b).

4. Put the title after the year of publication. Capitalize only the first word and any proper names in a title or subtitle. Do not put articles in quotation marks. Underline titles.

5. Put the city of publication and the publisher next. Use short forms for the names of well-known publishers: New York: Harper.

6. Put page numbers next, but use *p.* or *pp.* only for page numbers of articles in newspapers or popular magazines. Do not use *p.* or *pp.* with page numbers of articles in professional journals. In contrast,

parenthetical references to specific pages always include *p.* or *pp.*—no matter what type of source.

7. Start each item at left margin, but if the item has two or more lines, indent all lines after the first line five spaces.

Citations in the Natural Sciences

The following sources will show you the correct documentation methods for various sciences.

Biology

Council of Biology Editors' Style Manual Committee. *CBE Style Manual.* 5th ed. Bethesda, MD: Council of Biology, 1983.

Chemistry

American Chemical Society. *Handbook for Authors of Papers in American Chemical Society Publications.* Washington, DC: American Chemical Society, 1978.

Geology

U.S. Geological Survey. *Suggestions to Authors of Reports of the United States Geological Survey.* 6th ed. Washington, DC: Department of the Interior, 1978.

Physics

American Institute of Physics. *Style Manual for Guidance in Preparation of Papers.* 3rd ed. New York: American Institute of Physics.

Acknowledgments

Advertising Council, "The Problem," public service advertisement. Reprinted with permission.

Bernard E. Anderson, "An Economic Defense of Affirmative Action." From *Black Enterprise,* May 1982. Copyright May 1982 by the Earl Graves Publishing Co., Inc., 130 Fifth Avenue, New York, NY 10011. All rights reserved.

Sheridan Baker, "The Argumentative Edge." Excerpt from *The Complete Stylist* by Sheridan Baker. Copyright © 1984 by Harper & Row, Publishers, Inc. Reprinted by permission of HarperCollins Publishers.

Jacques Barzun, "In Favor of Capital Punishment." Excerpted and reprinted from the *American Scholar,* Volume 31, Number 2, Spring 1962. Copyright © 1962 by the Phi Beta Kappa Society.

Monroe Beardsley, "Emotional Appeals." Excerpt from Monroe C. Beardsley, *Practical Logic,* © 1950, pp. 132–135. Reprinted by permission of Prentice-Hall, Inc., Englewood Cliffs, NJ 07632.

William R. Beer, "The Fallacy of Inferred Discrimination" (section from "Resolute Ignorance"). From *Society,* 1987, published by Transaction, Rutgers–The State University of New Jersey.

John Berger, "Why Zoos Disappoint." Excerpt from *About Looking* by John Berger. Copyright © 1980 by John Berger. Reprinted by permission of Pantheon Books, a division of Random House, Inc.

Barbara R. Bergmann, "Do Sports Really Make Money for the University?" Reprinted by permission of the author from *Academe,* the bulletin of the American Association of University Professors.

Caroline Bird, "The Case Against College." Copyright 1975 by Caroline Bird. Reprinted by permission of the author.

Allan Bloom, "The Education of Openness," (editor's title). From *The Closing of the American Mind,* copyright © 1987 by Allan Bloom. Reprinted by permission of Simon & Schuster, Inc.

Tommy J. Boley, "A Heuristic for Persuasion." From *College Composition and Communication,* 1979. Reprinted by permission of the author.

Eileen Boris and Michael Honey, "Gender, Race, and Labor Policies." From *Monthly Labor Review,* February 1988: 26–36.

Judy Brady, "Why I Want a Wife." From *MS.,* Spring 1972. Copyright by Judy Brady (Syfers). Reprinted by permission of the author.

Roy L. Brooks, passages from "The Affirmative Action Issue: Law, Policy, and Morality." Copyright 1990 by Roy L. Brooks and *Connecticut Law Review.* Quoted by permission of the author and publisher.

Susan Brownmiller, "Let's Put Pornography Back in the Closet." From *Take Back the Night* (Laura Lederer, ed.), 1980. Reprinted by permission of the author.

William F. Buckley, Jr., "Capital Punishment." From *Execution Eve and Other Contemporary Ballads.* Copyright 1972, 1975 by William F. Buckley, Jr. Reprinted by permission of Wallace Literary Agency, Inc.

Thomas Cangelosi, " . . . And Don't Push Single Men, Either." From the *New York Times,* July 15, 1990. Copyright © 1990 by The New York Times Company. Reprinted by permission.

Stuart Carlson, "And the Radon Got Him." From the *Milwaukee Sentinel.* Cartoon by Stuart Carlson, copyright 1988 by Milwaukee Sentinel.

Carnegie Foundation, statistical tables. From *College: The Undergraduate Experience in America."* Reprinted by permission of the Carnegie Foundation for the Advancement of Teaching.

Linda Jean Carpenter and R. Vivian Acosta, "Back to the Future: Reform with a Woman's Voice." Reprinted by permission of the authors from *Academe,* the bulletin of the American Association of University Professors.

Mary Cassatt, *Portrait of the Artist,* self portrait. The Metropolitan Museum of Art, Bequest of Edith H. Proskauer, 1975. (1975.319.1)

Daniel Cohen, "The Death of Napoleon." Copyright © 1988 by Daniel Cohen for *The Encyclopedia of Unsolved Crimes.* Used by permission of the author and his literary agents.

B. D. Colen, "Paying the Price of AIDS." From *Health,* Oct 1988. Copyright 1988 by Family Media, Inc. Reprinted by permission of the author.

Irving Copi, "Deductive and Inductive Reasoning." Reprinted by permission of Macmillan Publishing Company from *Introduction to Logic,* 8th ed., by Irving M. Copi and Carl Cohen. Copyright © 1990 by Macmillan Publishing Co.

Bill Cosby, "The Wife Is in Charge." From *Love & Marriage* by Bill Cosby. Copyright © 1989 by Bill Cosby. Used by permission of Doubleday, a division of Bantam Doubleday Dell Publishing Group, Inc.

Norman Cousins, "The Poet and the Computer." From *Beyond Literacy: the Second Gutenberg Revolution,* R. Patton Howell, ed. Copyright 1989 by the Mentor Society. Reprinted by permission of Saybrook Publishing Co.

Anthony Berkeley Cox, "Dr. Crippen: Was He a Murderer?" From *The Mammoth Book of Murder,* 1989. Reprinted by permission of Carroll & Graf, Publishers.

Freeman Wills Crofts, "The Gorse Hall Mystery." From *Great Unsolved Crimes.*

Arthur C. Danto, "Art and Taxpayers." From the *Nation* magazine/The Nation Co., Inc., 1989.

Edgar Degas, *Seated Portrait of Mary Cassatt*, c. 1884. National Portrait Gallery, Smithsonian Institution, Washington D.C./Art Resource.

Patricia Dombrink, "There's No Gender in Success." From *The Christian Science Monitor*, Aug. 9, 1982.

Michael Eric Dyson, "Deaffirmation." From the *Nation* magazine/The Nation Co., Inc., 1989.

John Elkington, Julia Hailes, and Joel Makower, "Recycling/Precycling." From *The Green Consumer Guide* by John Elkington, Julia Hailes, and Joel Makower. Copyright © 1988 by John Elkington and Julia Hailes. Used by permission of Viking Penguin, a division of Penguin Books USA, Inc.

Amitai Etzioni, "Creating an Imbalance." From *Trial*, Nov.-Dec. 1974. Reprinted by permission of the author.

Andrew Ferguson, "Mad about Mapplethorpe." From the *National Review*. Copyright © 1989 by *National Review*, Inc., 150 East 35th Street, New York, NY 10016. Reprinted by permission.

Alan Freeman, passages from "Antidiscrimination Law: The View from 1989." From *Tulane Law Review*, 1990. Quoted by permission of the author.

Naomi Freundlich, "No, Spending More on AIDS Isn't Unfair." Reprinted from September 17, 1990 issue of *Business Week* by special permission, copyright © 1990 by McGraw-Hill, Inc.

Michael Fumento, "The AIDS Lobby: Are We Giving It Too Much Money?" From *The Myth of Heterosexual AIDS*, by Michael Fumento. Copyright © 1990 by Michael Fumento. Reprinted by permission of Basic Books, a division of HarperCollins Publishers Inc.

Michael Gartner, "Who Is That 'Senior State Department Official' Anyway?" From the *Wall Street Journal*, Jan. 11, 1990. Reprinted with permission of the *Wall Street Journal* © 1990 Dow Jones & Co., Inc.

Nancy Gibbs, "The New Zoo: A Modern Ark." From *Time* (Aug. 21, 1989). Copyright 1989 Time, Inc. Reprinted by permission.

Walker Gibson, "Being Serious Without Being Stuffy." From *Tough, Sweet, and Stuffy*. Copyright 1966 by Indiana University Press. Reprinted by permission of Indiana University Press.

Clement Greenberg, "The Case for Abstract Art." Reprinted by permission of the author.

Germaine Greer, "The Myth of Overpopulation" (editor's title). Excerpt from *Sex and Destiny*, 1984, by Germaine Greer. Copyright © by Germaine Greer. Reprinted by permission of HarperCollins Publishers, Inc.

Allen Guttmann, "Fair Play for Women?" Reprinted from *A Whole New Ball Game: An Interpretation of American Sports*, by Allen Guttmann. © 1988 The University of North Carolina Press. Used by permission of the author and the publisher.

Michael Harrison, "The Duke of Clarence: Prince or Ripper?" (editor's title). From *Clarence: The Life of the Duke of Clarence and Avondale KG, 1864–1892* (first American edition under the title: *Clarence: Was He Jack the Ripper?*) W. & H. Allen & Co., PLC.

Nand Hart-Nibbrig and Clement Cottingham, "Corporate Athleticism: A Historical Perspective," (abridged title). Reprinted by permission of the publisher, from *The Political Economy of College Sports* by Nand Hart-Nibbrig and Clement Cottingham (Lexington, Mass.: Lexington Books, D. C. Heath & Co.). Copyright 1986 D. C. Heath & Co.

David Hitch, "Somewhere Else," editorial cartoon. Copyright 1989 by *Worcester Telegram & Gazette*. Reprinted by permission.

Winslow Homer, *Boys in a Pasture*, 1874. Courtesy, Museum of Fine Arts, Boston. Hayden Collection.

Susan Jacoby, "I Am a First Amendment Junkie." From the *New York Times*, Jan. 26, 1978. Copyright © 1978 by Susan Jacoby.

Dale Jamieson, "Against Zoos." From *In Defence of Animals* (ed. Peter Singer), 1985. Reprinted by permission of Basil Blackwell, Ltd.

Jon Kennedy, "Geriatrics Dilemma," editorial cartoon. Copyright 1989 by *Arkansas Democrat*. Reprinted by permission.

Charles Krauthammer, "AIDS: Getting More Than Its Share?" From *Time*, June 25, 1990. Copyright 1990 Time, Inc. Reprinted by permission.

Charles Krauthammer, "Pornography Through the Looking Glass." From *Time*, March 12, 1984. Copyright 1984 Time, Inc. Reprinted by permission.

William M. Kunstler, "The Threat of Anonymous Juries." From the *Nation* magazine/The Nation Co., Inc., 1983.

Lands' End, "Slow Road to Glory," advertisement #B34. © Lands' End, Inc. Reprinted courtesy of Lands' End catalog.

Flora Lewis, "The People Threat." From the *New York Times*, July 14, 1990. Copyright © 1990 by The New York Times Company. Reprinted by permission.

F. L. Lucas, "On Style" (editor's title). Excerpt from "What Is Style?" *Holiday*, 1960.

John D. MacDonald, "Coppolino Revisited." From *I, Witness: Personal Encounters with Crime*, ed. Brian Garfield. Copyright 1978 by Mystery Writers of America, Inc. Reprinted by permission.

Donald Mann, "Growth Means Doom." From *Science Digest*, April 1983. Reprinted by permission of the author.

Marya Mannes, "How Do You Know It's Good?" From *But Will It Sell?* Copyright 1962 by J. B.

Lippincott Co., Inc. Reprinted by permission of David V. Blow, Executor for the Estate of Marya Mannes.

Doug Marlette, "Front-Runner," editorial cartoon. Copyright 1987 by the *Atlanta Constitution*.

H. L. Mencken, "The Penalty of Death." From *A Mencken Chrestomathy* by H. L. Mencken. Copyright 1926 by Alfred A. Knopf, Inc. and renewed by H. L. Mencken. Reprinted by permission of the publisher.

James Michie, "Dooley Is a Traitor." Copyright 1959 by James Michie.

Newton Minow and Fred H. Cate, "Impartial—Not Ignorant—Juries Needed." From the *Los Angeles Times*, Jan. 26, 1990. Copyright 1990 by Newton Minow and Fred H. Cate. Reprinted by permission of Newton Minow.

Mary Carolyn Morgan, "Ease Up, Please, on Single Women . . ." From the *New York Times Sunday Magazine*, July 15, 1990. Copyright © 1990 by The New York Times Company. Reprinted by permission.

Ronald Munson, "The Example." From *The Way of Words: An Informal Logic*, pp. 329–34. Published by Houghton Mifflin, Inc. Copyright © 1976 by Ronald Munson. Reprinted with permission.

Donald M. Murray, "The Maker's Eye: Revising Your Own Manuscripts." From the *Writer*, Oct. 1973. Copyright 1973 by Donald M. Murray. Reprinted by permission of International Creative Management.

Thomas Nagel, "A Defense of Affirmative Action." Reprinted with the permission of the Institute for Philosophy and Public Policy, School of Public Affairs, University of Maryland, from Thomas Nagel, "A Defense of Affirmative Action," *Report from the Institute for Philosophy and Public Policy*, 1.4 [1981]: 6–9.

The Editors of the *New Republic*, "Punt the Pretense." From the *New Republic*, Sept. 8, 1986. Copyright 1986 by the *New Republic*. Reprinted by permission.

Michael Novak, "In Defense of College Sports." From *The Joy of Sports*. Copyright © 1976 by Michael Novak. Reprinted by permission of Sterling Lord Literistic, Inc.

Douglas E. Olesen, "The Art of Minimizing Waste," speech given on May 10, 1990. From *Vital Speeches of the Day*. Reprinted by permission of Douglas E. Olesen.

John O'Toole, "What Advertising Isn't." From *The Trouble with Advertising*. Copyright 1980, 1985 by John O'Toole. Reprinted by permission of Chelsea House.

Jake Page, "The Challenge." From *Zoo: The Modern Ark* by Key Porter. Text by Jake Page. Copyright © 1990 by Key Porter. Reprinted with permission of Facts on File, Inc., New York.

Michael Parenti, "The Big Sell." Copyright © 1986 from *Inventing Reality: The Politics of the Mass Media*, by Michael Parenti. Reprinted with permission of St. Martin's Press, Inc.

Laurence Perrine, "Donne's 'Confined Love.'" From *The Explicator*, Fall 1980. Reprinted by permission of the author.

William G. Perry, Jr., "Examsmanship and the Liberal Arts." From *Harvard College: A Collection of Essays by Members of the Harvard Faculty (1963)*. Copyright 1962 by the Fellows of Harvard College. Reprinted by permission of Harvard University Press.

Bruce Piasecki, "Beyond Dumping." From the *Washington Monthly*. Reprinted with permission from the *Washington Monthly*. Copyright by The Washington Monthly Company, 1611 Connecticut Avenue, N.W., Washington, D.C. 20009. (202) 462-0128.

Katherine Anne Porter, "Marriage Is Belonging." From *The Collected Essays and Occasional Writings of Katherine Anne Porter*. Copyright 1990 by Houghton Mifflin Co. Reprinted by permission.

Prentice Hall, "Memory Made Easy," advertisement. Reprinted with permission of Prentice Hall Business Information & Publishing Division.

Anna Quindlen, "Grand Juries." From the *New York Times*, Oct. 25, 1990. Copyright © by the New York Times Company. Reprinted by permission.

William L. Rathje, "Rubbish!" From the *Atlantic*, Dec. 1989. Reprinted by permission.

William C. Rhoden, "In 'Minor' College Sports, Big Pressure." From the *New York Times*, Jan. 7, 1990. Copyright © 1990 by The New York Times Company. Reprinted by permission.

Henry Rosovsky, "The Educated Person." From *The University: An Owner's Manual*. Copyright 1990 by W. W. Norton & Co., Inc. Reprinted by permission.

Vermont Royster, "The Death of Socrates." From the *Wall Street Journal*, May 28, 1980. Copyright © 1980 by Dow Jones & Co. Reprinted by permission of the *Wall Street Journal*. All rights reserved.

Vincent Ryan Ruggiero, "Reading Is Reasoning" (editor's title). Excerpt from *The Art of Thinking* by Vincent Ryan Ruggiero. Copyright © 1984 by Harper & Row, Publishers, Inc. Reprinted by permission of HarperCollins Publishers.

Donald Rumbelow, "The Key Documents" (editor's title). Reprinted from *Jack the Ripper: The Complete Casebook* by Donald Rumbelow. Copyright © 1988 by Donald Rumbelow. Used with permission of Contemporary Books, Inc.

Andrea Sachs, "Who Should Foot the AIDS Bill?" From *Time*, Oct. 16, 1989. Copyright 1989 Time, Inc. Reprinted by permission.

Carl Sandburg, "Buttons." From *Chicago Poems*, copyright 1916 by Holt, Rinehart and Winston, Inc., and renewed 1944 by Carl Sandburg. Reprinted by permission of Harcourt Brace Jovanovich, Inc.

John Singer Sargent, *Daughters of Edward D. Boit*, 1882. Courtesy, Museum of Fine Arts, Boston. Marianne Brimmer Fund.

John Singer Sargent, *Two Girls Fishing*, 1912. Cincinnati Art Museum, John J. Emery Fund.

Vernon Scannell, "Making Judgments about Poetry" (editor's title). From *How to Enjoy Poetry*. 1983. Reprinted by permission of Piatkus Books.

Michael Schudson, "An Evaluation of Advertising." From *Advertising, The Uneasy Persuasion: Its Dubious Impact upon American Society*, by Michael Schudson. Copyright © 1984 by Michael Schudson. Reprinted by permission of BasicBooks, a division of HarperCollins Publishers.

Julian Simon, "Growth Means Progress." From *Science Digest*, April 1983. Reprinted by permission of the author.

Laurence Sombke, "Cut the Garbage." From *USA Weekend*, Apr. 21–23, 1989. Copyright 1989 by Laurence Sombke. Reprinted by permission of the author.

Thomas Sowell, "The Dangers of Preferential Programs." Excerpt from "On the Higher Learning in America" by Thomas Sowell. Reprinted with permission of the author from *The Public Interest*, No. 99 (Spring 1990). © 1990 by National Affairs, Inc.

Wayne Stayskal, "No Parole until after 3:00 P.M." Editorial cartoon from *Tampa Tribune*. Copyright 1989 by *Tampa Tribune*.

Richard Stengel, "Balancing Act." From *Time*, April 6, 1987. Copyright 1987 Time, Inc. Reprinted by permission.

James Thurber, "What a Lovely Generalization!" From *My World—And Welcome to It*. 1942. Reprinted by permission of Rosemary Thurber.

Calvin Trillin, "Incompatible, with One L." From his book entitled *Civil Liberties*, published by Ticknor & Fields. Copyright © 1982 by Calvin Trillin.

Mark Twain, "Humor and Honesty" (editor's title). Excerpt from *Mark Twain in Eruption* (Capricorn, 1940). Reprinted by permission of G. P. Putnam's Sons.

U.S. Buyers Network, "These Are Not . . . Sunglasses!" advertisement for Ambervision ® Sunglasses. Used with permission.

U.S. Council For Energy Awareness, "Every Day Is Earth Day with Nuclear Energy," advertisement. Used with permission.

John Updike, "American Children: Two Declarations of Independence for Youth." From *Just Looking* by John Updike. Copyright © 1989 by John Updike. Reprinted by permission of Alfred A. Knopf, Inc.

R. H. Waring, "Logic in Several Flavors" (editor's title). Excerpt from *Logic Made Easy* by R. H. Waring. Copyright 1984 by The Lutterworth Press. Reprinted by permission.

George Will, "Molding the Wrong Kind of Character" (editor's title); "College football programs molding the wrong kind of character" (original title). © 1989, Washington Post Writer's Group. Reprinted with permission.

James Playsted Wood, "The Merits of Advertising" (editor's title); "Advertising and People" (original title). From *This Is Advertising*, pp. 1–11. Published by Crown Publishers. Copyright © 1968 by James Playsted Wood.

Colin Wilson, "The Crimes of Jack the Ripper." From "My Search for Jack the Ripper" in Richard Glyn Jones, ed., *Unsolved! Classic True Murder Cases* (Peter Bedrick, New York, 1987). First published as a series in the *Evening Standard*, London, 1960. Reprinted by permission of the author and David Bolt Associates.

Sylvia Wright, "Quit It, Ompremitywise." From *Get Away from Me with Those Christmas Gifts*. Copyright 1957 by McGraw-Hill, Inc. Reprinted by permission.

George W. Ziegelmueller and Charles Dause, "Testing Data" (editor's title). Excerpt from *Argumentation: Inquiry and Advocacy* by George Ziegelmueller and Charles A. Dause. Copyright © 1975, pages 68–79. Reprinted by permission of Prentice-Hall, Inc., Englewood Cliffs, NJ 07632.

William Zinsser, "The Power of Humor" (editor's title). Excerpt from *On Writing Well*, 3rd ed. Copyright 1976, 1980, 1985 by William K. Zinsser. Reprinted by permission of the author.

Index of
Authors and Titles